Getting and Sp

EUROPEAN AND AMERICAN CONSUMER SOCIETIES IN THE TWENTIETH CENTURY

This collection brings together essays that suggest that the developing history of consumption is not so much a separate field as a prism through which many aspects of social and political life may be viewed. The essays, by many of the historians who have defined contemporary discussion of consumer history, along with younger scholars, represent a variety of approaches to consumption in Europe and America. Yet their commonalities suggest recent directions in the scholarship, raising such themes as consumption and democracy; the development of a global economy; the role of the state; the centrality of consumption to Cold War politics; the importance of the Second World War as a historical divide; the language of consumption; the contexts of locality, race, ethnicity, gender, and class; and the environmental consequences of twentieth-century consumer society. Implicitly, and sometimes explicitly, they explore the role of the historian as social, political, and moral critic.

The essays discuss products – rye bread to garbage disposers to automobiles; corporate strategies, including customer research and chain store development; government policies as different as the American GI Bill and the consumption practices of the former German Democratic Republic; and ideas about consumption, including the language used to express them. Unlike most other studies of twentieth-century consumption, this book provides international comparisons.

Susan Strasser is the author of *Never Done: A History of American Housework, Satisfaction Guaranteed: The Making of the American Mass Market,* and *Waste and Want: Household Trash and American Consumer Culture* (forthcoming). The recipient of many fellowships, including from the Guggenheim Foundation, the Harvard Business School, and the Smithsonian Institution, Strasser has taught at The Evergreen State College, Princeton University, and The George Washington University.

Charles McGovern is curator of American Popular Culture, Division of Cultural History, National Museum of American History. He is the author of *"Sold American": Inventing the Consumer, 1890–1940* (forthcoming).

Matthias Judt is a research fellow at Martin Luther University in Halle/Wittenberg and a former fellow at the German Historical Institute. He is the editor of *DDR-Geschichte in Dokumenten: Beschlüsse, Berichte, interne Materialien und Alltagszeugnisse.*

PUBLICATIONS OF THE GERMAN HISTORICAL INSTITUTE
WASHINGTON, D.C.

Edited by Detlef Junker
with the assistance of Daniel S. Mattern

Getting and Spending

Recent books in the series

R. Po-chia Hsia and Hartmut Lehmann, editors, *In and Out of the Ghet'*
    Jewish–Gentile Relations in Late Medieval and Early Modern Germa

Sibylle Quack, editor, *Between Sorrow and Strength: Women Refugees .*
    Period

Mitchell G. Ash and Alfons Söllner, editors, *Forced Migration ah*
    Emigré German-Speaking Scientists and Scholars after 1933

Manfred Berg and Geoffrey Cocks, editors, *Medicine and Nivil*
    and Medical Care in Nineteenth- and Twentieth-Centur

Stig Förster and Jorg Nagler, editors, *On the Road to T* tals,
    War and the German Wars of Unification, 1861–1' s and

Norbert Finzsch and Robert Jütte, editors, *Institu'*
    Asylums, and Prisons in Western Europe and N

David E. Barclay and Elisabeth Glaser-Schmic'
    Perceptions: Germany and America since 1

UTE

ı
ı

ıS

PUBLISHED BY THE PRESS SYNDICATE OF THE UNIVERSITY OF CAMBRIDGE
The Pitt Building, Trumpington Street, Cambridge CB2 1RP, United Kingdom

CAMBRIDGE UNIVERSITY PRESS
The Edinburgh Building, Cambridge CB2 2RU, UK   http://www.cup.cam.ac.uk
40 West 20th Street, New York, NY 10011-4211, USA   http://www.cup.org
10 Stamford Road, Oakleigh, Melbourne 3166, Australia

© The German Historical Institute, Washington, DC, 1998

First published 1998

Printed in the United States of America

Typeset in Bembo 11/13 pt, in Quark XPress™ [BB]

A catalog record for this book is available from the British Library

Library of Congress Cataloging-in-Publication Data
Getting and spending : European and American consumption in the
twentieth century / edited by Susan Strasser, Charles McGovern,
Matthias Judt.
    p.   cm. – (Publications of the German Historical Institute)
Includes index.
ISBN 0-521-62237-9 (hb). – ISBN 0-521-62694-3 (pb)
1. Consumption (Economics) – United States – History – 20th century.
2. Consumption (Economics) – Europe – History – 20th century.
3. Consumption (Economics) – Germany – History – 20th century.
4. Material culture – United States – History – 20th century.
5. Material culture – Europe – History – 20th century.   6. Material
culture – Germany – History – 20th century.   I. Strasser, Susan, 1948–.
II. McGovern, Charles.   III. Judt, Matthias, 1962–.
IV. Series.
        HC110.C6G48   1998
    339.4'7'09409049 – dc21   98–3707
                                      CIP

ISBN 0 521 62237 9 hardback
ISBN 0 521 62694 3 paperback

In memory of
Roland Marchand
(1933–1997)

Contents

Preface   *page* xi

Contributors   xiii

Introduction   *Susan Strasser, Charles McGovern, and Matthias Judt*   1

PART ONE
POLITICS, MARKETS, AND THE STATE   9

1 The Consumers' White Label Campaign of the National
  Consumers' League, 1898–1918   *Kathryn Kish Sklar*   17

2 Consumption and Citizenship in the United States,
  1900–1940   *Charles McGovern*   37

3 Changing Consumption Regimes in Europe,
  1930–1970: Comparative Perspectives on the Distribution
  Problem   *Victoria de Grazia*   59

4 Customer Research as Public Relations: General Motors
  in the 1930s   *Roland Marchand*   85

5 The New Deal State and the Making of Citizen
  Consumers   *Lizabeth Cohen*   111

6 Consumer Spending as State Project: Yesterday's Solutions
  and Today's Problems   *George Lipsitz*   127

7 The Emigré as Celebrant of American Consumer Culture:
  George Katona and Ernest Dichter   *Daniel Horowitz*   149

8 Dissolution of the "Dictatorship over Needs"?
  Consumer Behavior and Economic Reform in East
  Germany in the 1960s   *André Steiner*   167

PART TWO
EVERYDAY LIFE   187

9   World War I and the Creation of Desire for Automobiles
    in Germany   *Kurt Möser*   195

10 Gender, Generation, and Consumption in the United States:
    Working-Class Families in the Interwar Period   223
    Susan Porter Benson

11 Comparing Apples and Oranges: Housewives and the Politics
    of Consumption in Interwar Germany   *Nancy Reagin*   241

12 "The Convenience Is Out of This World": The Garbage
    Disposer and American Consumer Culture   *Susan Strasser*   263

13 Consumer Culture in the GDR, or How the Struggle for
    Antimodernity Was Lost on the Battleground of Consumer
    Culture   *Ina Merkel*   281

14 Changes in Consumption as Social Practice in West Germany
    During the 1950s   *Michael Wildt*   301

15 Reshaping Shopping Environments: The Competition
    Between the City of Boston and Its Suburbs   *Matthias Judt*   317

16 Toys, Socialization, and the Commodification of Play   339
    Stephen Kline

17 The "Syndrome of the 1950s" in Switzerland: Cheap Energy,
    Mass Consumption, and the Environment   *Christian Pfister*   359

18 Reflecting on Ethnic Imagery in the Landscape of
    Commerce, 1945–1975   *Fath Davis Ruffins*   379

PART THREE
HISTORY AND THEORY   407

19 Modern Subjectivity and Consumer Culture   *James Livingston*   413

20 Consumption and Consumer Society: A Contribution to
    the History of Ideas   *Ulrich Wyrwa*   431

21 Reconsidering Abundance: A Plea for Ambiguity   *Jackson Lears*   449

Index   467

Preface

On October 19–21, 1995, twenty-four scholars from the United States, Canada, Germany (both the former East and the former West), Switzerland, and France met at the German Historical Institute in Washington, D.C., to discuss American and European consumption in the twentieth century. The call for the conference was broad, encouraging participants to think about the relationship between consumption and democracy; the role of consumption in the history of capitalist industry and of the state; the roles of both elites and ordinary people in the shaping of consumption; stratification and variance along lines of class, gender, race, ethnicity, age, and geography; the linkage of identity and consumption; and the environmental consequences of twentieth-century consumer society. Papers were circulated beforehand rather than delivered at the conference, and our time together was spent in stimulating discussions of the intersections and relationships among them rather than on hearing and critiquing individual papers. The chapters in this book are post-conference revisions of most of the original submissions. Besides the authors, thanks are owed to those who participated in the conference and who, for various reasons, are not represented here.

The editors wish to thank the staff of the German Historical Institute for attending to the many details of the conference and the book. Hartmut Lehmann and Hartmut Keil encouraged the conference planning, while Detlef Junker and Martin Geyer kindly provided hospitality for the event, both at the Institute and in their homes. David B. Morris helped to prepare the manuscript for publication. Special thanks go to the series editor, Daniel S. Mattern, who was involved in this book at every stage, from attending the conference to working on the prose of the nonnative speakers to shepherding the manuscript through production.

Washington and Berlin   Susan Strasser
June 1998   Charles McGovern
                                                              Matthias Judt

Contributors

Susan Porter Benson is a professor of history at the University of Connecticut.

Lizabeth Cohen is a professor of history at Harvard University.

Victoria de Grazia is a professor of history at Columbia University.

Daniel Horowitz is a professor of history at Smith College.

Matthias Judt is a research fellow at Martin Luther University in Halle/Wittenberg.

Stephen Kline is a professor of communications at Simon Fraser University, Vancouver.

Jackson Lears is a professor of history at Rutgers, the State University of New Jersey.

George Lipsitz is a professor of ethnic studies at the University of California at San Diego.

James Livingston is a professor of history at Rutgers, the State University of New Jersey.

Roland Marchand was a professor of history at the University of California at Davis.

Charles McGovern is a curator at the National Museum of American History, Smithsonian Institution.

Ina Merkel teaches in the Department of European Ethnology at the Humboldt University, Berlin.

Kurt Möser is a curator at the Landesmuseum für Technik und Arbeit, Mannheim.

Christian Pfister is a professor of history at the University of Bern.

Nancy Reagin is an assistant professor of history at Pace University.

Fath Davis Ruffins is a curator at the National Museum of American History, Smithsonian Institution.

Kathryn Kish Sklar is a professor of history at the State University of New York at Binghamton.

André Steiner teaches in the Department of Economic and Social History at the University of Mannheim.

Susan Strasser is an independent historian living in Takoma Park, Maryland.

Michael Wildt is a research fellow at the Center for the Study of National Socialism, Hamburg.

Ulrich Wyrwa was a research fellow at the now closed Historical Commission, Berlin.

Introduction

SUSAN STRASSER, CHARLES McGOVERN, AND MATTHIAS JUDT

For more than twenty years, American historians of the United States have been exploring the twentieth-century history of shopping, advertising, and marketing as the activities of individuals and as arenas for corporate endeavor. They have studied the meanings of consumer goods as material culture; they have investigated the history of consumer protest and other aspects of politicized consumption and consumerist politics; and they have traced the evolution of commodified leisure, a central feature of consumer society. This interest in the history of consumption is relatively new: For most of the twentieth century, most historians in both Europe and the United States have been preoccupied with the more overt agendas of politics and statecraft. Even the *Annales* school, which attended to the details and mechanisms of daily life in the evolution of economies, showed little interest in the emergence of modern consumer society. Some of the scholars affiliated with the Institute for Social Research in Frankfurt – especially Theodor Adorno, Max Horkheimer, Walter Benjamin, and Siegfried Kracauer – did provide a critical perspective on contemporary consumption and mass leisure in Weimar Germany and interwar Europe. But although that perspective fueled an appreciation of the origins of consumer society, the Frankfurt School never offered any detailed historical account.[1]

Scholarly interest in the history of consumption first emerged during the Cold War, when, as a number of chapters of this book demonstrate, the issue of consumption became a major vehicle in the political and ideological clash of capitalism and communism and consumer goods were described as weapons in the Cold War. With desire for cars, washing machines, and less expensive goods regularly satisfied in the capitalist West but not in the state-socialist East, empty shelves became a sign of the failure of state social-

---

1 See Max Horkheimer and Theodor Adorno, *The Dialectic of Enlightenment* (New York, 1968), and Siegfried Kracauer, *The Mass Ornament: Weimar Essays,* ed. Thomas Levin (Cambridge, 1995). The literature on the Frankfurt School is vast, but the best starting places are Martin Jay, *The Dialectical Imagination: A History of the Frankfurt School and the Institute of Social Research, 1923–1958* (Boston, 1973), and Rolf Wiggershaus, *The Frankfurt School: Its History, Theories and Political Significance,* trans. Michael Robertson (Cambridge, 1994).

ism. Consumerism, some Western leaders proclaimed, would win the battle
against communism. In historical studies, two pioneering works – David
Potter's *People of Plenty* (1954) and Daniel Boorstin's *The Americans* (3 vols.,
1958–73) – located a key to the purported exceptionalism of the United
States in material abundance and consumption. For these authors the plenty
that characterized American life was not only good historical fortune, but a
critical element in American history and a distinctive and determinative
trait of American society.

Such all-embracing statements on national character were characteristic
of consensus history, the postwar strain of American writing that emphasized a fundamentally homogenous and conflict-free past in the United
States. This view began to unravel during the political upheavals of the
1960s and early 1970s. A new American social history, focused on "history
from the bottom up," placed the daily experiences of previously marginalized groups at the center of historical inquiry. Attention to consumption
soon followed. Stuart Ewen's *Captains of Consciousness* (1976) opened the
current round of scholarship with a history of the United States as a consumer culture from a New Left perspective. Over the next two decades,
other historians (many of them represented in this book) have specified and
refined the connections between the development of corporate capitalism
and that of a culture grounded in the consumption of commodities
designed to fulfill, and indeed also to stimulate and redefine, virtually every
human need.[2]

Within a few years, these American historians were joined by colleagues
on the other side of the Atlantic. Some students of European history
pointed out that consumption as a social phenomenon was a central aspect
of the rise of capitalism in the West, and that markets have long been more
active than conventional depictions of societies based on subsistence agriculture suggest. Neil McKendrick, John Brewer, and J. H. Plumb proposed
that the consumer revolution arrived before 1800 in Britain; they described
advertising, commercialized leisure and politics, and innovative production
techniques that brought many new goods into common use. Other European scholars have focused on the seventeenth and even the sixteenth century. Likewise, scholars of early America have established that neither colo-

2 This introduction cannot undertake a full historiography of the origins of consumer studies, but see
   Daniel Miller, *Acknowledging Consumption* (London, 1995); Jean-Christophe Agnew, "Coming Up for
   Air: Consumer Culture in Historical Perspective," in John Brewer and Roy Porter, eds., *Consumption
   and the World of Goods* (London, 1993); Daniel Horowitz, *The Morality of Spending: Attitudes Toward the
   Consumer Society in America, 1875–1940* (Baltimore, 1985), and Charles McGovern, "The Emergence
   of Consumer History," unpublished manuscript, 1988.

nial households nor their localities were entirely self-sufficient, but depended on a well-developed market.[3]

Nonetheless, we can recognize a new kind of consumer society developing during the twentieth century. Throughout the nineteenth century, economic development had brought an ever greater proportion of Americans and Europeans into the money economy, working for others to make money to buy things. More things formerly made at home were produced in factories; more things formerly made by hand were produced by machines. Twentieth-century phenomena were thus the culmination of many decades' worth of development. But the historians who have offered the most comprehensive interpretations of production speak of "revolutions" around the turn of the century, and of differences in kind as well as in scale. Mass-produced goods, available in unprecedented quantities before the Great Depression, constituted the material for mass consumption. So did consumer products like clothing, jewelry, and furniture – products that had many styles and were not always amenable to the requirements and strictures of mass production.[4]

New products and technologies made old ones obsolete as, for example, electric lights replaced oil lamps. Wholly new classes of human activity joined the realm of commodities. Businesses commodified forms of folk culture such as dancing and popular song. Technological innovations spawned new kinds of amusements and new ideas of leisure; experiences became something the masses could buy, while new media altered the nature of representation and the potential of the senses. Changes in transportation and communication revised ideas of distance, space, and time; over the century, firsthand and indirect knowledge of other parts of the world became commonplace among workers and those in the middle classes. In short, consumption patterns, consumer consciousness, and the nature of daily life were significantly transformed, a transformation that corresponded to equally profound changes in production and distribution.

Moreover, over the course of the twentieth century, consumption became central to corporations and government agencies, which attempted to affect household activities in the interests of profit, economic growth,

---

3 See Neil McKendrick, John Brewer, and J. H. Plumb, *The Birth of a Consumer Society: The Commercialization of Eighteenth-Century England* (London, 1982); Carole Shammas, *The Preindustrial Consumer in England and America* (Oxford, 1990); Brewer and Porter, *Consumption and the World of Goods*.
4 On changes in production and distribution, see especially David Hounshell, *From the American System to Mass Production, 1800–1932* (Baltimore, 1984); Alfred D. Chandler Jr., *The Visible Hand: The Managerial Revolution in American Business* (Cambridge, 1977), and Philip Scranton, "Diversity in Diversity: Flexible Production and American Industrialization, 1880–1930," *Business History Review* 65 (spring 1991): 27–90.

and political stability. Marketing concerns grew to dominate corporate decision making about production; consumption has played a key role in some twentieth-century economic theories. Corporate and governmental efforts to influence consumption have brought daily life – people's attitudes, their intimate behavior, and their use of both paid and unpaid time – under the influence of economic institutions, for consumption operates at the intersection of public and private life. Indeed, it has been critical in altering those boundaries: The apparatus of consumption has come to dominate the physical landscape while public policy and political agendas in Western countries have focused on what were once personal concerns.

The innumerable products offered by twentieth-century industry transformed both the work and the diversions of private life, saving household labor and bringing paid entertainment into homes. Shopping and planning for consumption became essential aspects of twentieth-century housework as factory-made goods and commercially provided services supplanted household production and left few alternatives. But the shopping and planning were tasks of a new kind, shaped by the stimulation of consumer desire and the association of buying with pleasure and fantasy manifest in advertising and the design of shopping environments. New commodities and new media for selling them changed people's expectations, desires, and needs, in turn influencing the development of later products.

The recognition that mass consumption is inextricable from daily life and social experience has led to a remarkable outpouring of historical work. Scholars have demonstrated that consumption offers a new focus for some long-standing themes and political concerns. They have also used consumption to blaze some striking new trails and theoretical approaches to previously elusive or unasked questions. Unlike advertisers who use novelty and maturity to tout their wares ("It's New and Improved!" or "It's Old-Fashioned!" or in certain cases, both), the editors of this book offer a more complex contention: Consumption has emerged as a useful focus for historians because it addresses a variety of older questions, at the same time raising other previously submerged but significant issues. The history of consumption is in this sense not a separate field so much as a prism through which many aspects of social and political life may be viewed.

Periodization at this stage is tentative, complicated by uneven patterns of development that were manifested both in individual lives and across societies. As in other "revolutions," new ways coexisted with old; people who bought new products also continued to use things they already had. Wealthier people generally owned new products before poorer ones, and urban life changed more quickly than rural. Some goods and habits found favor quickly while others gained acceptance over generations.

Many scholars agree, however, that World War II represents an important divide, and the chapters of this book reinforce that thesis. Developments during the second half of the twentieth century represent both an expansion and an intensification of changes already under way before the war. Significant new patterns developed in the relationships among people, the things they owned, and the businesses that made and sold those products. A distinctive late twentieth-century way of life emphasized consuming, not producing; the line between advertising and the media used to convey it became blurred; new technologies, and the consumption of experiences as well as of objects, became commonplace; consumption and democratic citizenship became increasingly intertwined in official and popular ideologies. The new consumer society may well be called "postmodern," whatever the ultimate historical fate of that term.[5] In American public discourse and increasingly in European as well, individuals' status as consumers rivaled and even surpassed their identity as workers. In many countries the struggles over that change have defined both the nature of consumer society and that of its historiography, as a number of these essays emphasize.

International comparison sharpens issues of periodization and highlights certain themes. In particular, Germany's very different twentieth-century history – devastation and recovery from both world wars, American and Soviet influence, reunification and the creation of a consumer society in the former German Democratic Republic, and European union – raises intriguing comparative perspectives. The chapters presented in this book raise such themes as the relationship between consumption and democracy; the function of consumption in the development of a global economy; the role of the state in promoting and shaping consumption; the language of consumption (general definitions, metaphors, and usages and the meanings of such specific terms as "scarcity" and "abundance"); and the environmental consequences of twentieth-century consumer society. Many of them emphasize the importance of local contexts and of race, ethnicity, gender, and class, suggesting that there is no one model of consumer society or even of American consumer society. Implicitly and sometimes explicitly, they explore and take positions on the role of the historian as social, political, and moral critic; this stance has accompanied the study of consumer

---

5 The literature on postmodernism is even larger than that on consumption, but some of the definitive connections are made in Frederic Jameson, *Post-Modernism, or the Cultural Logic of Late Capitalism* (Durham, N.C., 1992).

society in both the American tradition and the German one that originated in Marx's commentary on commodity fetishism and continued in the
writings of the Frankfurt School. A number of them remind us that the
twentieth century was the age of communism as well as the age of consumerism, and that each system developed in reaction to the other.

Although they originate in different kinds of research, refer to the histories of half a dozen countries on both sides of the Atlantic and of the
Berlin Wall, and cross the boundaries of a number of intellectual disciplines
and subfields, a number of topics and concepts appear and reappear in these
essays. The intersection of the public and the private, the role of the state
and of political action, the concurrent development of consumer society
and its critique, the relationship between ideas about consumption and
ideas about democracy, the heterogeneity of historical experience, the environmental and cultural consequences of a consumer economy – each of
these may be seen throughout this book. Consumption is discussed from
various standpoints and in different ways: with local and regional as well as
national and international emphases; with particular stress on gender, class,
and race; as a part of domestic and of foreign policies; and in its consequences, again on levels ranging from the private to the global. Above all,
the scholarship collected here reaffirms the importance of twentieth-
century developments to American and European consumer history, and
especially the decisive transformations that followed World War II.

Together, the authors discuss transformations from production-driven to
consumption-driven economies and cultures. In that sense, they contribute
to a contemporary task for intellectuals and politicians worldwide, a reconsideration of common concepts of economic growth. In Western Europe
and the United States, environmental disasters and the formation of Green
parties have increased the influence of environmentalists in political decision making; moreover, the transfer of industrialization to other parts of the
world has begun to threaten the welfare state. Eastern European countries
in the process of transformation from state planning to market economies
face decisions about building up new industries and downsizing or dismantling others, while attempting to bypass the offenses of unchecked capitalism. Rapid industrialization in Asia and South America promotes familiar
problems related to the conditions and the consequences of consumption,
especially an intensification of global pollution. All over the world, the
nature of economic growth and the role of consumption have become
newly problematic, fostering calls for new kinds of thinking.

Although most of the scholars whose work is collected here champion
the role of the historian as critic of consumer culture, they cannot do so as

outsiders, for there is no longer an "outside" in Europe, the United States, or most of the rest of the world. The extension of a global consumer culture has been intensified by the end of the Cold War, the industrialization of countries once considered "third world," and the rapid expansion of new technologies for communications and information transfer. The historical perspectives offered in these essays, embracing the concept of change and rejecting the static, offer a recognition that we can best understand our worlds of goods and ideas if we understand them in process.

PART ONE

Politics, Markets, and the State

The chapters in this book represent a variety of approaches to consumption in Europe and America, yet their common themes suggest recent directions in the scholarship. One of the most striking is the contention that consumption has been critical to the function of state policy across a variety of regimes, despite differing traditions for managing fiscal policy, regulating productive enterprise, and supporting market development. The first part of the book, "Politics, Markets, and the State," highlights work that traces those connections. Its chapters suggest that consumption became critical to economic health and political stability, both as social behavior and as a matter of policy. They establish that in the United States and throughout Europe, the history of consumption was entwined with that of the state; put another way, the history of twentieth-century consumption belies the notion of "markets" as abstract, timeless, independent, or universal.

These chapters reveal a complex relationship among concepts of citizenship, democracy, and consumption. Consumption has become synonymous with citizenship in many contexts during the twentieth century, both expressing individual autonomy and status within society and focusing political ideas about the obligation of the state to individuals. Political citizenship has been recast as consumer behavior, while political activists have extended their concerns to encompass consumption, suggesting that the interests of buyers are proper concerns of the state, and sometimes mobilizing consumers for explicitly political and national purposes. Yet political and economic power are not equal; state policy and social thought that assume otherwise neglect fundamental conditions of daily life and historical change.

The White Label campaign of the National Consumers' League, the earliest American organization to challenge private enterprise under the rubric of consumers, represents, according to Kathryn Kish Sklar, a "revealing intersection of political culture and consumer culture." The League's use of the term "consumer," she suggests, was instrumental in the development of a new understanding of market relations. Led by Florence Kelley, this organization battled exploitative labor conditions and practices by appealing to the power of the consumer's purse, at the same time attempting to mobilize state power through protective labor legislation. Kelley's organization made middle-class women consumers central to a political campaign and encouraged them to act as "social citizens" in the public sphere.

Charles McGovern's essay further explores the conditions under which citizens are consumers and consumers are citizens, examining how consumption came to be the sign of full citizenship in the United States. McGovern argues that the Great Depression turned the government toward state solutions to regulate the consumer economy and enhance purchasing power. Political and cultural support for such a move was accomplished through political language and imagery, twentieth-century adaptations of republicanism and liberalism. Consumer advocates argued for an independent marketplace, free of the corruption of Madison Avenue and rooted in a suspicion of the market and an almost Jeffersonian faith in the buyer's independence, to be achieved through technical expertise and impartial information. Advertisers invoked ideals of liberty and freedom, arguing that consumption itself was the key to individual independence and agency. Both asserted that consumption was a badge of citizenship, the true mark of an American.

Popular accounts of the modernization of European commercial life focus on Americanization, the transfer of this ideology to European soil. Victoria de Grazia's comparative essay argues against such a simplistic analysis, tracing the transformation of European systems of distribution from their nineteenth-century domination by individual bourgeois shopkeepers to a system influenced by chain stores and corporate interests. "Fordism" was met with fierce resistance from local tradespeople in Europe, helping to inspire neomercantilist strategies that varied considerably from nation to nation during the 1930s. Consumer societies developed in accordance with specific economic conditions and political systems, and the evolution of markets depended upon differing cultural traditions, civic ideals, and local customs. Decisively transformed by World War II, European nations could not adopt similar neomercantilist policies afterward, and their commercial paths favored state support of private enterprise based on a model of full consumer sovereignty that was familiar from the United States.

That model was expounded by corporations such as General Motors, the subject of Roland Marchand's case study, which shows how this company used the rubric of democracy to cast its marketing research as the exercise of public will and its questionnaires as a form of voting. Customer research, Marchand asserts, was central to the company's propaganda, which urged Americans to trust business corporations rather than the New Deal to promote the well-being of the nation. Like Sklar, Marchand shows how usage of such terms as "customer," "consumer," and "market" prompted new meanings. He provides a specific example of McGovern's contentions about the identification of consumer preference with democracy, and of corporate interest with that of the citizen.

Lizabeth Cohen provides another perspective on the relationship of citizenship and consumption in the United States during the 1930s, tracing how the New Deal state worked toward a new recognition of consumption as a political interest. She notes that consumers had previously claimed public power and demanded economic regulation on behalf of the public good, but only with the crisis of capitalism in the depression did consumers' interests become explicitly politicized. Cohen shows that the federal government, spurred on by private groups and reformers, took halting steps to embrace consumption as a legitimate facet of citizenship and as a distinct, transcendent political interest with claims to represent a collective public good. But, she notes, political realities and the limits of state activism institutionalized an emphasis on aggregate spending and purchasing power at the expense of individual consumer entitlement or protection.

George Lipsitz argues that the postwar American state broke from New Deal strategies. Heavily influenced by corporate interests, it offered consumption-oriented policies that minimized collective possibilities and encouraged the perception of communities exclusively in terms of market segments. Lipsitz shows that the government adopted tactics that fostered certain *kinds* of consumption, with profound consequences for the nature of American daily life. Major elements of domestic policy, such as federal spending on highways and home loans, created new spatial relations that placed consumer desire at the center of the social world. In wide-ranging observations on both government policy and popular culture, Lipsitz demonstrates that possessive individualism, a hallmark of American liberalism, became identified with consumption; meanwhile consumption was heralded and supported as an individual cure for social ills. Markets were the ultimate replacement for the civic realm, a result decisively fostered by the state. Lipsitz offers a powerful critique of state policies that "since the 1950s [have] favored a vision of consumption practices aimed at eliminating the sites and social relations conducive to the emergence of social movements."

George Katona and Ernest Dichter were two of the first social scientists to study consumer behavior and demonstrate that consumers are not mere abstractions of the marketplace, but very much the products of specific circumstances. Daniel Horowitz traces their careers, emphasizing the attractions that American-style consumption had for some refugees of the Third Reich. Horowitz notes that both Dichter and Katona built careers upon their abilities to procure information about consumers with better acuity than most American analysts. They helped construct the corporate and social-scientific view that consumers make decisions based on a host of subjective but quantifiable factors. The resulting portrait of consumers using goods as psychological instruments for building self-esteem and expressing emotion has dominated advertising and marketing since the 1930s. Dichter's and Katona's conflation of consumption with nationality and civilization functioned particularly well during World War II and the Cold War, when criticism of any aspect of American life might be read as an attack on the nation itself. Their views of their work as a referendum on their adopted nation and on democracy made that work ideally suited to a nation pioneering in the expansion of mass consumption.

André Steiner outlines a vastly different experience of state intervention and regulation of consumption and markets. Tracing broad shifts in consumer policy in the German Democratic Republic during the 1960s, Steiner argues that state policymakers continually confronted the need to facilitate mass consumption at the individual and family levels. This political pressure conflicted with the planners' strategies for controlling the economy, the complexity of which made it inherently difficult to govern. Consumers demanded cheap goods, while state investment required suppressing consumption. Inevitably, Steiner maintains, consumers won their conflicts with the state, not by turning East Germany into a consumers' paradise but by inadvertently thwarting the overall attempt to subject consumer needs, even for the most basic goods, to other concerns. Hindering consumption had too high a political price, despite the costs of subsidizing cheap consumer goods and services without respect to productivity, trade, or other external conditions.

The politics of consumption has been continually contested during the twentieth century, with considerable confusion and conflict over the proper relationship of consumer and state. While the role of the state in promoting and controlling consumption was critical, its role in mediating conflicts proved equally powerful, for consumers' interests were not identical with those of producers, marketers, or vendors. A number of the essays in this part link American conceptions of democracy, corporate interests, and political processes, both hidden and visible. They show that in the United States, citizenship provided a critical justification for public policy in support of consumption, obscuring the ultimate beneficiaries of those processes. Others reveal the limits of state power in controlling and directing markets, suggesting that while governments experienced considerable pressure to dictate or regulate consumer behavior, they were constrained by popular protest and sentiment and by business resistance. If a mandate for government influence on consumption seemed clear, the specifics of that relationship remained a source of controversy in different political and economic regimes.

I

The Consumers' White Label Campaign of the National Consumers' League, 1898–1918

KATHRYN KISH SKLAR

I

In a series of articles that exposed virulent sweatshops in New York City and Los Angeles in 1995, the *New York Times* mentioned no agency capable of mobilizing consumers against sweatshops. One hundred years ago this was not the case. In that era, consumers in a number of eastern and midwestern states combined to create a national league to combat sweatshops and other exploitative labor practices. During the first two decades of the twentieth century the National Consumers' League (NCL) constituted the single most powerful lobbying group for the enactment of labor legislation to protect nonunionized, unskilled workers, particularly women and children, but also including men. How did consumers exercise such power? What can the political mobilization of consumers in the NCL tell us about the relationship between consumer culture and political culture in the first decades of the twentieth century? To address these questions this essay focuses on a revealing intersection of political culture and consumer culture – the Consumers' White Label campaign of the National Consumers' League, which began in 1898 and concluded in 1918.

To achieve its political goals, this NCL campaign constructed an imagined community of consumers and producers. The White Label campaign redefined the communities inhabited by NCL members to include those who produced the goods that they consumed. Beginning at the local level with the actual communities in which NCL members lived, the campaign ranged outward to embrace imagined communities at the state and national levels. This strategy allowed the league to moralize the relationship between

consumers and producers. It also empowered consumers to speak for the
welfare of their communities as a whole. In dozens of major American
cities, women consumers began to exercise the moral and political power
formerly reserved for clergymen, businessmen, or labor leaders. Ultimately,
the campaign contributed to the process of state formation in which state
and national governments assumed responsibility for the welfare of working people.

How were consumers' imagined communities reconstructed? Who benefited from the campaign? Who was excluded? Answers to these questions
carry us into a time quite different from our own, when an emerging van-
guard of upper middle-class consumers exercised significant political power,
and the talents of middle-class women strained against the limitations of
their domestic world. The White Label campaign attributed new meaning
to the economic position of middle-class consumers and urged them to put
their talents to public use.

II

Shaped like a bow tie with a circle in the middle, the Consumers' White
Label announced in its center, "OFFICIAL LABEL: NATIONAL CON-
SUMERS' LEAGUE, REGISTERED NOV. 17, 1899." Its left side stated,
"MADE UNDER CLEAN AND HEALTHFUL CONDITIONS"; the
other side declared, "USE OF LABEL AUTHORIZED AFTER INVES-
TIGATION." To qualify for the label, manufacturers had to submit to an
inspection and meet the following minimum standards, as defined in the
NCL annual reports:

> The State factory law is obeyed;
> All the goods are made on the premises;
> Overtime is not worked;
> Children under sixteen years of age are not employed.[1]

In the first years of the campaign, the NCL's general secretary, Florence
Kelley, performed the inspections herself.

By advocating "clean and healthful conditions," the label revealed its
middle-class origins. Anti-sweatshop campaigns in major American cities in
the 1890s appealed for middle-class support by emphasizing the public
health threat posed by garments produced in disease-ridden tenements.

---

1 National Consumers' League (hereafter NCL) annual reports, 1901–4.

Middle-class consumers were taught to fear that such garments might import smallpox, diphtheria, or other diseases into their homes. The new germ theory of disease transmission lent credence to this view.[2]

Yet middle-class consumers were not alone in their concern for clean and healthful working conditions. Such conditions also mattered to workers. Dank air, filthy floors, and stinking toilets were some of the most objectionable features of sweatshop labor. "The shops are unsanitary – that's the word that is generally used, but there ought to be a worse one used," the strike leader Clara Lemlish said in 1909.[3] Tuberculosis was quite common in the garment industry – induced by the long hours and damp air – and it spread rapidly in unventilated rooms, so the quality of air alone could be a life and death matter to sweatshop workers. Thus health issues forged a common bond between consumers and producers in the garment industry. This was the industry on which the NCL focused its members' attention.

The White Label campaign reached beyond health issues to support other goals that were important to wage earners. Through its "authorized" investigations it sought to enforce state factory laws, to prevent subcontracting (often the means by which sweatshop goods were disguised as factory-made goods), to prohibit overtime (which often required garment workers to work twelve-hour days), and to suppress child labor. How did middle-class women come to advocate such goals? Why did it matter to them whether they bought goods produced under conditions that violated state factory laws, employed subcontractors, required overtime, or used child labor? How did the National Consumers' League make these issues significant to women whose day-to-day existence was not directly affected by them?

The answer to these questions begins with Florence Kelley, who designed the Consumers' White Label and launched the campaign on a national scale. As general secretary of the National Consumers' League, Kelley brought to the White Label campaign a remarkable political background. She was born in 1859 into an elite Philadelphia family with strong allegiances to Quaker and Unitarian reform traditions. Her father, William Darrah Kelley, a Radical Republican congressman, served fifteen consecutive terms between 1860 and 1890. Her mother's aunt, Sarah Pugh, was a

---

2 For the emergence of the germ theory in the 1890s, see James H. Cassedy, "The Flamboyant Colonel Waring: An Anti-Contagionist Holds the American Stage in the Age of Pasteur and Koch," *Bulletin of the History of Medicine* 36 (Mar.–Apr. 1962): 163–76; John Duffy, *The Sanitarians: A History of American Public Health* (Urbana, Ill., 1990), 179–80; and Judith Walzer Leavitt, *The Healthiest City: Milwaukee and the Politics of Health Reform* (Princeton, N.J., 1982), 101–7.

3 Clara Lemlish, "Life in the Shop," *New York Evening Journal*, Nov. 28, 1909, quoted in Leon Stein, ed., *Out of the Sweatshop: The Struggle for Industrial Democracy* (New York, 1977), 66.

leading abolitionist who used her power as a consumer between 1830 and 1865 to boycott goods made by slave labor, especially sugar and cotton.[4]

Kelley began reading government reports at the age of ten (as a way of gaining her father's love) and started using the Library of Congress at the age of twelve (to compensate for her lack of formal schooling). After graduation from Cornell in 1882, she studied law and government at the University of Zurich. There she married Lazare Wischnetetzky, a Russian socialist medical student. Deepening her rebellion against her social and political origins, she gave birth to three children in the first three years of her marriage, experienced a conversion to socialism, and translated writings by Frederick Engels and Karl Marx. Her translation of Engels's *The Condition of the Working Class in England in 1844* is still the preferred scholarly version of that now-classic work.

Ever thereafter Kelley viewed the world through the lens of "scientific materialism," seeing social relations as the outcome of relations to production and tracing a wide range of social problems to the ownership of the means of production by a few. The moral materialism of Engels fit remarkably well with her Quaker-Unitarian background.

After Kelley, Lazare, and the children moved to New York in 1886, she joined the Socialist Labor Party but was promptly expelled for insisting on the importance of the ideas of Marx and Engels. She then became a self-trained expert in labor legislation for women and children, and in the late 1880s she emerged in public culture (backed by her father's high public regard) as one of the fiercest critics of the ineffectiveness of state bureaus of labor statistics. Her life changed in 1891 when Lazare (having never succeeded in establishing a medical practice) began to batter her. She fled with the children to Chicago, where she discovered Hull House and its coterie of college-educated women reformers, with whom she lived for the rest of the decade.

Jane Addams's nephew described Kelley there as "the toughest customer in the reform riot, the finest rough-and-tumble fighter for the good life for others, that Hull House ever knew. Any weapon was a good weapon in her hand – evidence, argument, irony or invective."[5] In Chicago Kelley became the nation's leading authority on the passage and enforcement of labor legislation for women and children. She drafted, lobbied for, and as Illinois's chief factory inspector between 1893 and 1896 (with eleven deputies, five

---

4	For this and other biographical information about Kelley, see Kathryn Kish Sklar, *Florence Kelley and the Nation's Work: The Rise of Women's Political Culture, 1830–1900* (New Haven, Conn., 1995); and Kathryn Kish Sklar, ed., *Notes of Sixty Years: The Autobiography of Florence Kelley* (Chicago, 1986).

5	James Weber Linn, *Jane Addams: A Biography* (New York, 1938), 138–9.

of whom were required by law to be women) enforced trailblazing eight-hour legislation for women and child workers throughout that large industrial state. When in 1896 the innovative governor who had appointed her – John Peter Altgeld – lost the election, her chief financial support during the next three years was reporting on social reform in the United States for German Social Democratic periodicals.[6]

Finally, in one of the more important events in women's public culture in the Progressive era, Kelley was hired in 1899 as general secretary of the newly founded National Consumers' League. In her, the league's executive board got as much leadership as they could handle, and in them Kelley found an institutional setting worthy of her talents.

Although the National Consumers' League did not have the word "women" in its title, it was a women's organization. Like Hull House and other flourishing women's institutions during the Progressive era, it had institutional and fiscal independence that meant that the league could draw on male support on its own terms. Economists and other prominent men served as vice-presidents and the NCL president was always a man. John Brooks of Boston and Newton Baker of Cleveland – two men whom Kelley respected and whose support she appreciated – served lengthy terms as president.

Thomas Bender has defined "public culture" as "a forum where power in its various forms, including meaning and aesthetics, is elaborated and made authoritative." Through the White Label campaign the NCL elaborated and made authoritative the power of middle-class women consumers.[7] In state after state factory laws were strengthened, factory inspections encouraged, hours laws enforced, and child labor discouraged.

Florence Kelley's leadership was crucial to that effort. As early as 1889 she had urged "the formation of a national alliance of women which would furnish its label to all manufacturers of women's clothing" and whose members would "pledge themselves to buy no clothing which is not properly labeled."[8] The next year Josephine Shaw Lowell and others founded the New York City Consumers' League, which in 1891 organized a "White List" of department stores that met the "standard of a fair house" on wages, hours, physical conditions, management–employee relations, and child labor.

---

6 For Kelley's German writings, see Kathryn Kish Sklar, Anja Schüler, and Susan Strasser, eds., *Social Justice Feminists in the United States and Germany: A Dialogue in Documents, 1880–1933* (Ithaca, N.Y., 1998).

7 Thomas Bender, "Wholes and Parts: The Need for Synthesis in American History," *Journal of American History* 73 (June 1986): 126.

8 Unidentified newsclipping [Mar. 1889?], Thomas E. Morgan Collection, University of Illinois, Urbana, vol. 2, reel 6.

Modeled on a list published by British trade unions, the White List avoided the legal challenges that would have defeated the simpler strategy of publishing a black list of firms to boycott.[9] The president of the New York City Consumers' League later wrote that the White List standards were "drafted by the Working Women's Society and modified by us after seeking advice from those firms which had the reputation of treating their employees the most fairly."[10] The White List was periodically revised and printed in newspapers.

The White Label replaced the White List when Florence Kelley took charge of the national league in 1899. Like the list, the label drew a line between acceptable and unacceptable goods. At the same time that it recommended some goods, it excluded others. The White Label imitated the union label, which was first used in San Francisco in 1869 by cigar makers who sought to discourage the purchase of cigars made by Chinese immigrants and to encourage the purchase of union-made cigars. Anti-Chinese sentiment, high in California then, eventually resulted in the passage of the Chinese Exclusion Act by the U.S. Congress in 1882.[11]

Like the union label, the Consumers' White Label tried to promote an "American standard of living," and it thereby created an "other" that it identified as immoral and substandard.[12] Through moral rhetoric that contrasted fair and unfair labor standards, the NCL's label campaign aimed to accomplish for young white women what the union label had gained for white cigar workers in California. Since these young women working in department stores and the garment industry held jobs from which African-American women were excluded, the White Label campaign reinforced racial distinctions at the same time that it improved working conditions for white women and children.

As a symbol, therefore, the White Label was a good example of what Anthony Giddens meant in the *Constitution of Society* when he located the origins of symbolic ideological expressions in specific regions of the social structure. In contrast to Clifford Geertz, who located the power of ideology

---

9 For the avoidance of illegal blacklisting, see Josephine Shaw Lowell, "Report and Testimony Taken Before the Special Committee of the Assembly Appointed to Investigate the Condition of Female Labor in the City of New York," *Documents of the Assembly of the State of New York: One Hundred and Nineteenth Session,* vol. 23, no. 97 (1896): 73. For the illegality of boycotts, see Daniel Robinson Ernst, "The Lawyers and the Labor Trust: A History of the American Anti-Boycott Association, 1902–1919," Ph.D. diss., Princeton University, 1989, 11–46.
10 Maud Nathan, *The Story of an Epoch Making Movement* (New York, 1926), 26.
11 A classic on this topic is Elmer Clarence Sandmeyer, *The Anti-Chinese Movement in California* (Urbana, Ill., 1939).
12 See Larry Glickman, "A Living Wage: Political Economy, Gender, and Consumerism in American Culture, 1880–1925," Ph.D. diss., University of California at Berkeley, 1992.

in symbols themselves, Giddens suggests that symbols are always shaped by the sectors of public life that champion them.[13] The White Label was a white middle-class device. Yet it also evoked the symbolism of white trade unions and their efforts to discourage the patronage of nonunion shops. So the symbol's meanings were unstable and multiple, embracing issues associated with class, race, and gender.

The label was proposed by Florence Kelley in 1898 when she was interviewed for the position of general secretary of the newly formed National Consumers' League, a group that unified flourishing local leagues in New York, New Jersey, Massachusetts, Pennsylvania, Illinois, Minnesota, and Wisconsin. Kelley, who already headed the Illinois Consumers' League, submitted a plan of action for a consumers' label that focused on the conditions under which goods were produced in factories, shifting the leagues' attention to the relationship between consumption and production rather than consumption and distribution. Kelley's proposal identified some factories already worthy of the label, designed the label, created a contract between manufacturers and consumer leagues, and devised "a well considered plan for advertising the label."[14] She was hired. Initially her job description with the league was "inspector and organizer," words that expressed the league's hands-on intentions, but soon her title evolved into the more seemly "general secretary."[15]

Kelley's first goal was to build the league into a strong network of local branches capable of making their power felt in city councils and state legislatures throughout the country. For a group excluded from the franchise and from many other forms of political action, only large numbers could produce effective political action. Therefore, in the first five years of the National League's existence, Kelley devoted herself to building a grass-roots movement. She spent roughly one day on the road for every day at her desk. Her efforts were rewarded by the spectacular expansion of NCL locals, both in numbers and in location. The 1901 annual report mentioned thirty leagues in eleven states; by 1906 there were sixty-three locals in twenty states with about seven thousand members.[16]

13 In *The Interpretation of Cultures* (New York, 1973), Clifford Gertz emphasized the cognitive components of culture – a process that produces meaning and signification. In *The Constitution of Society* (Berkeley, Calif., 1984), 32, Anthony Giddens emphasized that the "relational character of the codes that generate meaning [are] located in the ordering of social practices."
14 Florence Kelley to Katharine Coman, Mar. 20, 1899, Executive Committee of Consumers' League of Massachusetts, minutes, Mar. 30, 1899, Consumers' League of Massachusetts papers, Schlesinger Library.
15 Minutes, Jan. 26, 1899, Consumers' League of Massachusetts papers.
16 "Secretary's Report," NCL, *Second Annual Report, Year Ending March 6, 1901* (New York, 1901), 14; "The Consumers' League of Ann Arbor," *Fourth Annual Report* (New York, 1903), 46–7; NCL, *Seventh Annual Report, Year Ending March 1, 1906* (New York, 1906), 14.

The Massachusetts Consumers' League described the effects of Kelley's leadership in 1903.

[She] can travel from one end of the Continent to the other without losing her hold upon local problems in State Leagues the farthest removed from her bodily presence, stirring our zeal and opening new fields for our activity by *letters*, which are prompt and full as if *letter writing* were the chief occupation of her day. Mrs. Kelley gives us service which it is impossible to overestimate.[17]

Kelley's impressive early gains demonstrated the fertile soil on which her message fell. Local leagues sustained the national's existence, channeling money, ideas, and encouragement into the national office. At the same time locals served as vehicles for the implementation of the NCL's regulatory agenda. The NCL's Consumer Label campaign perfected a double-barreled strategy whereby the young organization built local leagues and at the same time propelled league members into political activism.

The label promised an "investigation" of all manufacturers qualified to use it, and Florence Kelley herself monopolized that responsibility. Having served as the chief factory inspector of the state of Illinois, she was more experienced in factory inspection than any woman in the industrialized world. Yet in her new national capacity working for the league, she faced a strategic decision: She could either limit her inspections and the use of the label geographically to a certain locale (most likely New York City, site of the national's headquarters) or make the campaign a national one and limit it to certain specified goods. She chose the latter and picked goods that most middle-class women purchased frequently – "women's and children's [machine] stitched white cotton underwear." This included "corsets and corset substitutes, skirt and stocking supporters, wrappers, petticoats, and flannelette garments."[18] Fancy, hand-sewn goods were not included because they were not made in factories; therefore, the conditions under which they were produced were less susceptible to inspection and control.

At the height of its success in 1904, the league had licensed sixty factories. The campaign's nationwide success arose from the dynamic whole it created from its three parts: a new understanding of the consumer's economic centrality; the new knowledge it generated about specific working conditions within members' communities; and members' ability to put their new knowledge to political use and implement legislation designed to improve working conditions in their city and state. Undergirded by new

17 "Consumers' League of Massachusetts," NCL, *Fourth Annual Report* (New York, 1903), 37–9.
18 NCL annual reports, 1901–4.

understanding of their own economic position, by new knowledge about their communities, and by new capacity for political action, consumers supporting the White Label campaign became the vehicle whereby the National Consumers' League emerged as the single most politically effective organization of middle-class women in the decades before World War I.

The first step toward political power for NCL members lay in their recognition of their economic significance as consumers. The league's use of the term "consumers" rather than "buyers" emphasized purchasers' dynamic relationship with producers. A consumer used a product – literally consuming it – whereas a buyer merely possessed it. As Raymond Williams has pointed out in *Keywords: A Vocabulary of Culture and Society* (1976), the pairing of production and consumption in the late nineteenth century was a feature of a modern economy in which both producer and consumer were more abstract figures in a more abstract market than was the case in the mideighteenth century, when the term first emerged. But not until the midtwentieth century did the term *consumer* totally replace that of *buyer* or *customer*, both of which are more specific figures. Williams derived his information primarily from the *Oxford English Dictionary*; yet neither he nor the *OED* gave the Consumers' League the credit it deserves for promoting the term, which, as the league began to use it around 1890, quickly acquired a resonance it had heretofore lacked.

This new view of the centrality of consumers caught on immediately with academics as soon as it was expressed by the New York City league after 1890. T. H. Marshall, dean of British economists and professor at Cambridge University, wrote in the *Harvard Journal of Economics* in 1897, "We need to turn consumption into paths that strengthen the consumer and call forth the best qualities of those who provide for consumption." Amasa Walker declared in the *Annals of the American Academy* in 1894 that "it is only in the consumption of wealth that we find the reasons for the rise of some (nations) and the fall of others." Carroll Wright referred favorably to the Consumers' League in his *Outline of Practical Sociology* in the late 1890s. At the same time, Arthur Hadley, president of Yale University and professor of economics, wrote:

As years go on, I am more and more impressed with the idea that economic reform is likely to come through the agency of the consumer rather than from any other source. I think the Consumers' League is taking a very important step in the direction of such reform.[19]

19 Quoted in John Brooks, "The National Consumers' League," NCL pamphlet, 1899.

Responding to the Consumers' League vision, Professor Simon N. Patten of the University of Pennsylvania, wrote, "The producer is merely an agent of the consumer and if the latter is persistent in demanding better things and conditions society will be at length remodeled and transformed."[20] Summarizing this recognition, an NCL publication in 1902 declared, "Everywhere in the college world teachers of economics are finding in the League a field for the exercise of applied economics."[21] The league was becoming a laboratory for the study of consumer culture.

The NCL emerged just at the moment when economists were seeking new ways to characterize market relationships. Relations between capital and labor were only part of the puzzle; the consumer was also crucially important. The league was a leader rather than a follower in this theoretical shift. After 1907, particularly with the publication of Patten's *New Basis of Civilization* that year, the economic centrality of the consumer became for economists a new gospel. Like women consumers in the NCL, economists were responding to the ripening of consumer culture. Yet their ideas about the power of consumers seem to have been significantly shaped by the social and political power displayed by the National Consumers' League.

Of course, neither the league nor economists were the first to discern the importance of mass-based consumers in the late nineteenth and early twentieth centuries. That prescience belonged to those within the labor movement who advocated the eight-hour day as a vehicle whereby wage earners could become consumers as well as producers. Most prominent among these was George Gunton, whose 1889 pamphlet, "The Economic and Social Importance of the Eight-Hour Movement," argued that the eight-hour day would lead to the employment of more workers and thus "enlarge the market for commodities to that extent."[22] Daniel Horowitz has analyzed how Gunton's writings changed when he came under the influence of middle-class and elite groups. Yet Florence Kelley and the NCL were influenced by a flow of ideas in the other direction – from working class proponents of the eight-hour day to middle-class advocates of eight-hour legislation. The Consumers' White Label campaign was an important example of that flow. For them the center of the economic drama was occupied by the middle-class consumer, not the working-class consumer.

20 Simon Patten correspondence with John Brooks, quoted in John Brooks, "The National Consumers' League," NCL pamphlet, 1899.
21 Brooks, "The National Consumers' League."
22 George Gunton, "The Economic and Social Importance of the Eight-Hour Movement," pamphlet publication of the American Federation of Labor, Eight-Hour Series, no. 2 (New York, 1889), 13.

In a torrent of speeches and writings during the first decade of the twentieth century, Florence Kelley carried this gospel of consumers as the shapers of their community's future to groups of middle-class women in large and small cities throughout the nation. For her and for the league, knowledge of the centrality of consumers to the economic marketplace was valuable for one reason and one reason only: as a spur to moral action. As she put it, the league sought to cultivate

the spirit which changes passive approval, appreciation, and sympathy into that dynamic conscience which constrains its owner to look into a subject and *act* upon the convictions gained in looking. This will be our never ending task so long as there remains one careless purchaser or one unlabeled garment. When there are no more indifferent purchasers, the work of the League will be a perfect work.[23]

This millennialist rhetoric linked the White Label campaign with nineteenth-century reform traditions that emphasized the relationship between personal conscience and social salvation. In city after city the White Label campaign fostered that relationship.

The White Label emphasized the choice that knowledge entailed. Choice was a key ingredient of the new cornucopia of consumer goods available in department stores, and choice was the essence of the White Label campaign. Kelley exaggerated that choice when she wrote in an NCL publication in 1901: "We can have cheap underwear righteously made and clean; or we can have cheap underwear degradingly made and unclean. Henceforth, we are responsible for our choice." By connecting the home and the marketplace in new ways, the campaign purveyed knowledge that directly challenged the power of anonymous market forces – especially those competitive practices that drove down the price of goods with cheaply paid labor. The league did not object to cheapness gained through technological change, but it did oppose cheapness "attained by making children run foot-power machines in tenement kitchens."[24] The responsibility for child labor rested with the consumer. As Kelley declared in 1905, "No one except the direct employer is so responsible for the fate of these children as the purchasers who buy the product of their toil."[25]

Kelley believed her campaign of informed morality was superior to earlier anti-sweatshop crusades based on pity and fear. As she put it, "Since mid-century appeals have been made to the pity of the purchaser on behalf

23 NCL, *Second Annual Report.*
24 Florence Kelley, "Aims and Principles of the Consumers' League," *American Journal of Sociology* 5 (Nov. 1899): 290.
25 NCL, *Sixth Annual Report* (New York, 1905).

of the unhappy employees in the garment trades," and recently "physicians, inspectors, and volunteer investigators" have "appealed to the fears of the community" about disease emanating from sweatshops, but "little benefit has been reaped from all the stirring of the emotions."[26] Fear and pity were less effective and less sustained mobilizers of collective action than knowledge and morality.

As the conveyor of trustworthy knowledge and the synthesizer of community accomplishments, the Consumers' League was just as crucial to the consumer as the consumer was to the economy. As one of Kelley's annual reports stated,

This is the function of the Consumers' League to strive unweariedly to educate the public, by providing trustworthy information as to what is actually happening in the work of industry, and by making known all methods used in the country, for improving conditions, so that each community may profit by the experience of all.[27]

As part of their emphasis on trustworthy knowledge, consumers' leagues in Massachusetts and New York obtained from state regulatory agencies the names of tailors who subcontracted work to sweatshops, then passed on these names to their members.

On the basis of NCL knowledge, purchasing could therefore become a moral act. As Kelley wrote in 1902, "The women of every community have read of the horrors of the needle trades and are ready to give the preference in their shopping to the righteous manufacturers when they can do so without much exertion"; that is, when they could readily obtain information from an organization like the league.[28] Thus, the responsibility of the consumer was threefold: to recognize her direct relationship with the producer, to learn about producer's working conditions, and to limit her purchases to goods made under moral conditions.

Most of the dozens of new NCL locals formed between 1900 and 1905 promoted the label as their first project. In this regard the launching of the Consumers' League of Kentucky was typical. It was organized in 1901 following a meeting of the General Federation of Women's Clubs in Milwaukee where the delegates from the Woman's Club of Louisville heard Maud Nathan and Florence Kelley discuss the New York and National Consumers' leagues. The minutes reported that "the first work was to urge the purchase of muslin underwear bearing the Consumers' League label. Efforts were

26 Ibid.   27 Ibid.   28 NCL, *Third Annual Report* (New York, 1902).

made to get Consumers' League label goods in all the leading department stores. An exhibition of these goods was held."

In Louisville, as elsewhere, the label campaign ineluctably carried consumers' league members into new realms of knowledge about their communities that they otherwise would not have encountered. It did so by raising detailed questions about working conditions that were new to this middle-class constituency as they searched for manufacturers who qualified for the label. The White Label campaign encouraged middle-class women to seek new forms of knowledge and to question the conditions under which consumer goods were made. It also reorganized their understanding of how those conditions related to their own lives.

Did the manufacturer subcontract to home workers in tenements? Were children employed? Was overtime required? Were state factory laws violated? Were working conditions safe and sanitary? How far below the standard set by the Consumers' Label were their own state laws?[29] Should the state issue licenses for home workers? What was the relationship between illiteracy in child workers and the enforcement of effective child labor laws? Was their own state high or low on the NCL's ranked list showing the numbers of illiterate child workers in each state? Should laws prohibit the labor of children at age fourteen or age sixteen? Should exceptions be made for the children of widows? Could workers live on their wages or were they forced to augment their pay with relief or charitable donations? How energetically were state factory laws enforced? How could local factory standards be improved? Such questions, which were quite alien to middle-class women in 1890, by 1905 had acquired personal meaning and moral significance for thousands of politically active women. This was no small accomplishment.

Just as the label prompted these questions, answers to the questions led league members to take new forms of action. For example, the Louisville League in 1902, according to its minutes, "assisted in passing the Child Labor Law and the Compulsory Education Law and amending them at many sessions of the Legislature. Cooperated in enforcing both, by working with the truant officers, visiting the homes of truants, and supplying shoes and clothing necessary to return them to school." Later the league boasted that it "secured the passage of the ten hour law for women, which is the only labor law for women in Kentucky." Expressing the league's commitment to translating knowledge into power, the minutes continued, "This

---

29 See, e.g., the questions posed in Mary I. Wood, *The History of the General Federation of Women's Clubs* (New York, 1912), 147.

law is poor but it has served as the basis on which the League has gained the
ear of employers and employees to discuss hours, wages, and working conditions."

State leagues differed in the degree to which they worked with state
officials, but wherever leagues existed they created new civic space in which
women used their new knowledge to expand state responsibility. For example, this dynamic can be seen in the close relationship that leagues forged
with state factory inspectors. In 1901 the Wisconsin League worked closely
with the state's only woman factory inspector. The Michigan League
secured two women on the State Board of Factory Inspectors and
the secretary of the New Jersey League made factory inspection part of
her duties.

The NCL drew on an even larger constituency by carrying its vision to
the General Federation of Women's Clubs (GFWC). By 1900 the GFWC
had grown to thirty-six state federations of more than 2,600 clubs with a
membership of more than 155,000.[30] At the federation's Biennial Meeting
that year, Kelley and others introduced delegates to the work of the Consumers' League, and federation officers "asked the delegates to report favorably to their respective clubs and federations upon the work of the
League."[31] The results, Kelley said in 1901, "are still perceptible at our office
in the form of invitations for speakers, requests for literature, and a vast
increase in correspondence and in the demand for labeled goods in many
diverse parts of the country."[32]

State federations of women's clubs responded by appointing "standing
committees to promote the work of the Consumers' League." Addresses by
NCL officers became a regular event at annual meetings in such far-flung
areas as South Carolina, Utah, and Washington. Where statewide consumers'
leagues existed, they worked closely with state federations of women's clubs.
"For a time at least," the official historian of the General Federation of
Women's Clubs wrote in 1912, "the quickened conscience made the average woman . . . a more intelligent purchaser."[33]

By 1903 both the National Congress of Mothers and the National American Woman Suffrage Association had created Child Labor Committees,
and Florence Kelley headed both. In these capacities, she said, "it has been
possible to secure a hearing for the truth." Although rooted in local communities, the campaign ultimately embraced a national community.

30 Wood, *History of the General Federation of Women's Clubs,* 131–2.
31 NCL, *Second Annual Report,* 15.
32 Ibid.   33 Wood, *History of the General Federation of Women's Clubs,* 178.

III

But "truth" had other dimensions in addition to the moral ones elaborated by the league. Economically, the White Label campaign aided large producers who could achieve economies of scale in the pricing of their goods and who profited from the more stable work force attracted by better working conditions. These economic facts of life became dramatically apparent in the partnership that John Wanamaker and his department stores forged with the White Label campaign. One of the league's largest approved manufacturers, Wanamaker originated what became a staple of the campaign – exhibits of garments bearing the label, augmented by pictures of sweatshop labor juxtaposed to pictures of workers producing Wanamaker garments. Wanamaker carried the exhibit to state and international fairs throughout the United States in the decade before World War I. For him the White Label campaign offered a perfect opportunity to give his commercial leadership a moral aura and at the same time consolidate his economic power.

In its alliance with Wanamaker, the campaign affiliated with one of the most prominent features of consumer culture: the trend toward large retail stores. However, in other respects the campaign opposed powerful economic currents – currents that ultimately overwhelmed its effort to carry nineteenth-century moral notions of individual conscience into the twentieth-century marketplace. The strongest of these was advertising.

As early as 1899, Kelley recognized advertisements as the moral consumer's enemy, deeming them "distinctly not meant to educate or instruct, but to stimulate, persuade, incite, entice, and induce the *indifferent* to purchase."[34] In Kelley's moral universe, the verbs "educate or instruct" conveyed positive values associated with individual enlightenment, but "stimulate, persuade, incite, entice, and induce" highlighted the loss of individual control that the NCL associated with the unenlightened consumer. Yet apart from their moral rhetoric, Kelley and the NCL developed no effective means of opposing the lures of advertising among their middle-class constituency.

The NCL's vulnerability before the growing power of contemporary advertising was captured in its efforts to compete with the "style and finish" of garments more fashionable than their white-listed ones. By asking members to purchase what we today would call "intimate" garments from certain designated manufacturers, the White Label campaign used aspects of

---

34 Kelley, "Aims and Principles of the Consumers' League," 294–5.

women's gender identity to reconstruct their politics. This strategy could
backfire. In 1902 Kelley's annual report complained that "purchasers have
cared for style and finish more than for the assurance of the league that less
attractive garments were made under more righteous conditions." Rank
and file members apparently won this struggle, for in the same report Kelley referred to the "charming garments" offered by John Wanamaker.[35]
Wanamaker's exhibit, itself a form of advertising, showed that moral
garments need not be totally devoid of style. His exhibits could overcome consumer doubts about the "charming" quality of labeled goods at
the same time that they instructed observers in good and bad working conditions.

After 1906 the National Consumers' League moved away from the White
Label campaign and put its public power to new uses. That year, working
with its local league in Oregon, it sponsored a pathbreaking case before the
U.S. Supreme Court, in which the court for the first time recognized the
validity of sociological evidence. The so-called Brandeis Brief was actually
written by Brandeis's sister-in-law, Josephine Goldmark, who was Florence
Kelley's chief assistant. In 1917 the league again worked with its Oregon
local to establish the constitutionality of hours regulations for men in non-
hazardous occupations. Between 1910 and 1923 the league conducted a
successful campaign for the passage of minimum wage legislation, which in
1938 became the basis for the adoption of minimum wage provisions in the
Fair Labor Standards Act. In this way the NCL's White Label campaign
became an opening wedge for more general protections for American wage
earners.[36]

The NCL officially ended the campaign during World War I. Kelley later
explained:

We announced to the trade unions that we had no intention of competing with any
label that they might desire to establish, but would withdraw from the field whenever they could afford convincing evidence of organization in the needle trades
capable of bearing a trustworthy label. This condition arose during the war and we
abandoned our label.[37]

---

35 NCL, *Third Annual Report*.
36 For more on this strategy, see Kathryn Kish Sklar, "Two Political Cultures in the Progressive Era: The
   National Consumers' League and the American Association for Labor Legislation," in Linda Kerber,
   Alice Kessler-Harris, and Kathryn Kish Sklar, eds., *U.S. History as Women's History: New Feminist
   Essays* (Chapel Hill, N.C., 1995), 36–62.
37 Florence Kelley to Seward Simons, Mar. 20, 1926, NCL papers, box C-4, "Consumers Label and
   Labeling, Prosanis Label." However, no label was established in the women's garment industry until
   after 1930. In the late 1920s the "Prosanis label" was organized in the women's garment industry in
   New York by a combination of unionists and reformers, but it disappeared by 1929.

Kelley had always realized that the league's label might undercut efforts to establish a union label within the garment industry. This possibility was realized in 1918, when

[t]he Consumers' League was denounced in the press of New York City by an officer of the United Garment Workers' Union, who is also a national officer of the American Federation of Labor, as an organization whose label has been used by employers hostile to organized labor.

Believing the consumers' label had outlived its usefulness, Kelley recommended at the annual meeting of her board that it be ended.

However, even before the NCL conceded the use of the label strategy to trade unions in the garment industry, the league's success with the tactic had run its course. In a "final test" of whether to continue the label campaign in 1918, the NCL hired an agent to travel to local leagues and investigate the extent of their cooperation with the national's Label Committee. The results supported Kelley's belief that the league should cease its label work, since the tour among locals found "no valuable, new, local cooperation with the Label Committee, or with the League."[38]

In the mid-1920s, however, when the political climate grew hostile to labor generally and to the NCL's goals of labor legislation in particular, the league revived its White Label strategy, applying it to the candy industry, in which, as in the garment industry twenty years earlier, young women were employed for scandalously low wages. Responding to the 1923 U.S. Supreme Court decision in *Atkins v. Children's Hospital,* which ruled the Washington, D.C., minimum wage for women unconstitutional, the league tried "to keep the light turned upon the appalling effect of the . . . Decision by means of the Candy White List."[39]

Fundamentally the label campaigns of the National Consumers' League were a form of advertising. They carried messages about working conditions to consumers who otherwise might not know about the work processes governing the goods they bought. At the height of its success during the decade before 1910, however, the campaign amounted to more than advertising. Then, riding the crest of the wave of Progressive reform, the NCL used the Consumers' White Label to orchestrate citizen involvement in legislative action. As such the campaign deserves a place alongside school suffrage (extension of suffrage to school board elections) as one of

---

38 Florence Kelley to Miss Wiggin, Jan. 25, 1918, NCL papers, box C-3, "Consumers Label and Labeling General File."
39 Florence Kelley to Ruth M. Kellogg, Sept. 11, 1929, NCL papers, box C-4, "Consumers Label and Labeling, Prosanis Label."

the most extensive expressions of women's political activism before the passage of the Nineteenth Amendment in 1920.

IV

What conclusions can we draw about this campaign, which demanded a personal commitment strong enough to resist the attractions of the bargain counter, advertisements, fashion, and even personal comfort? Four seem especially important.

First, the campaign drew women into public life in ways that validated what might be called their "social citizenship" almost twenty years before the passage of the women's suffrage amendment to the Constitution.[40] The campaign stretched women's gender-specific activism to achieve class-specific objectives.[41] By confronting large social questions that grew out of but reached beyond issues related to women and children, women demonstrated their value as equals to men in public life.

Second, women's voices "elaborated and made authoritative" new forms of power in public life. The campaign created a new "supply" of women's power. The "demand" for that power came from the need within newly evolving liberalism for an ethical buttress to support state intervention in the economic marketplace. Moral materialism, or the belief in the morality of materially based relationships, provided such a buttress. The step from concern about women and children to concern about class relations and the advocacy of state intervention was an easy one for many women to take.

Third, NCL members provided innovative answers to "the social question." In its component parts, that question included the largest issues then being debated in public life, namely, What do the social classes owe one another? How could civil society affect the marketplace economy? Where should middle-class people stand in relationship to the changes precipitated

---

40 On women's "social citizenship," see Wendy Sarvasy, "From Man and Philanthropic Service to Feminist Social Citizenship," *Social Politics: International Studies in Gender, State, and Society* 1 (fall 1994): 306–25.

41 For more on the use of gender to achieve class goals, see Kathryn Kish Sklar, "The Historical Foundations of Women's Power in the Creation of the American Welfare State, 1830–1930," in Seth Koven and Sonya Michel, eds., *Mothers of a New World: Maternalist Politics and the Origins of Welfare States* (New York, 1993). This interpretation emphasizes the remarkable prominence of women's public culture in this time and place as a result of the voluntarist basis of American politics. Women's public power and public culture generally were not only a good *match* in the United States, they came from the same roots, which if we had to characterize them in one word would be "voluntarist." That voluntarist tradition made it difficult for public culture generally to validate state interference in market-based relations, but that tradition made it easier for women's voluntary organizations to take initiatives that validated such interference.

by massive industrialization, urbanization, and immigration? Where should middle-class people stand in relationship to the often violent struggle between capital and labor, and how might that conflict be mediated by the state?

Fourth, in our own time liberalism has been defined as a set of principles whereby practitioners of divergent conceptions of the good can peacefully coexist. But liberalism requires what today's public culture calls a "level playing field." Florence Kelley and her women colleagues in the National Consumers' League helped create that fictive field.

2

Consumption and Citizenship in the United States, 1900–1940

CHARLES MCGOVERN

During the Great Depression and New Deal consumption, citizenship, and democracy came to public light in an urgent way. The crisis and apparent near collapse of capitalism generated upheavals in politics that the election of Franklin Roosevelt in 1932 went only partway toward resolving. Such issues as the cost of living, prices, shortages of goods, substitutions, quality of foods, conditions under which goods were made or sold, and safety had for many years lent a political cast to aspects of consumption. Yet only during the New Deal's long-term groping toward political and economic solutions to the depression did the concerns of consumption and consumers become established as a permanent part of public discourse. With protracted battling over policy and with cultural conflicts fostered by economic and social realities, American people fitfully but firmly came to equate the consumer with the citizen, a consumer standard of living with democracy, and the full participation in such an economy of spending and accumulation with being an American.

The association of consumption and citizenship certainly was not new to political thought or even to the United States, but the advent of a consumer society in American in the half century before the depression laid the foundations for this acceptance.[1] By 1930, the vast majority of Americans participated in the industrial economy for getting and spending their

---

1 There is no overall account of the transformation of the United States into a consumer economy and culture, but see, for some of the most synoptic suggestions, Warren Susman, *Culture as History: The Transformation of American Society in the Twentieth Century* (New York, 1984); T. J. Jackson Lears, *Fables of Abundance: A Cultural History of Advertising in America* (New York, 1994); William Leach, *Land of Desire: Merchants, Power, and the Rise of a New American Culture* (New York, 1993); James Livingston, *Pragmatism and the Political Economy of Cultural Revolution, 1850–1940* (Chapel Hill, N.C., 1994); and Martha L. Olney, *Buy Now Pay Later: Advertising, Credit and Consumer Durables in the 1920s* (Chapel Hill, N.C., 1991).

daily living, although the implications of that fact for government, culture, or social life were not fully clear. Numerous commentators had marveled at the remarkable and prolonged post–World War I prosperity, which apparently reached deep into the middle and working classes, prompting some to argue that mass consumption of industrial goods had wrought a kind of permanent revolution in social life as well as in business. Yet only a few pundits such as Simon N. Patten, Walter Lippmann, and Walter Weyl had connected the new basis of consumption – a broad mass access to goods – with American politics, culture, or nationality.[2] Those who did comment on this for the most part were either from the world of business or from the professions – most notably advertising, home economics, and consumer product testing, itself derived from engineering, physics, and home economics.[3]

The two professions I examine here – advertising and product testing – articulated strong and opposing visions for consumption as American citizenship in the years before 1930, outlooks that would clash openly and with increasing bitterness throughout the depression.[4] Their partial resolution was foregrounded in the New Deal adoption of consumerist policies and Keynesian economics in 1938, which today still serve as touchstones for government economic policy, even as they today meet serious challenges.[5] George Lipsitz has traced the consequences of the camouflaged

2 See, e.g., parts of Walter Lippmann, *Drift and Mastery* (New York, 1914); Walter Weyl, *The New Democracy* (New York, 1913); see also such statements as James P. Warbasse, *Cooperative Democracy* (New York, 1920). Of course, Simon N. Patten's *New Basis of Civilization* (1907) has been regularly cited and noted as one of the first American articulations of the benefits of a consumerist orientation. See discussions in Daniel Horowitz, *The Morality of Spending: Attitudes Toward the Consumer Society in America, 1875–1940* (Baltimore, 1985), 30–7; Livingston, *Pragmatism and the Political Economy,* 67–77; Lears, *Fables of Abundance,* 111–17; Donald Fleming, "Social Darwinism," in Arthur Schlesinger Jr. and Morton White, eds., *Paths of American Thought* (Boston, 1960), and, in greater depth, Daniel M. Fox, *The Discovery of Abundance: Simon N. Patten and the Transformation of Social Theory* (Ithaca, N.Y., 1967).
3 Such business commentaries include Paul Mazur, *American Prosperity: Its Causes and Consequences* (New York, 1928); George H. Phelps, *Our Biggest Customer* (New York, 1928); Edward A. Filene, *The Way Out: A Forecast of Coming Changes in Business and Industry* (Garden City, N.Y., 1925); Earnest Elmo Calkins, *Business the Civilizer* (Boston, 1928); Calkins was head of a major New York ad agency, although this book was less an apology for advertising than a celebration of the business transformation of American life through mass circulation goods and media.
4 By advertisers, I mean those professionals who created, deployed, and placed advertising for products, services, and companies primarily in national media, along with those businesses who employed them. Customary usage by 1900 had designated the business client as the *advertiser* and the creator of advertising the *advertising agent.* See Daniel Pope, *The Making of Modern Advertising* (New York, 1983). Although a great deal of advertising was carried on in local media, especially newspapers, this period witnessed the ascendancy of national agencies: They wielded the greatest influence within the field; their clients in the aggregate spent the most money on advertising.
5 Alan Brinkley, *The End of Reform: New Deal Liberalism in Recession and War* (New York, 1995), 65–137, 168–9, offers a thorough and convincing account of the steps taken by the Roosevelt administration toward economic policies that center on individual consumer interest, most notably with the goal of increasing purchasing power through regulation of production, distribution, and pricing along with

manner in which government underwrote certain aspects of consumer spending after World War II. He argues that the federal preference for consumption along individualist and private lines at the expense of communal and public projects has extracted a definite cost from cities and local communities, despite the claims of proponents.[6] Yet such a policy shift began before World War II during the intense struggles over defining citizenship through consumption.

Why is it necessary or appropriate to trace the discourse of professional groups for an understanding of the broader histories of consumption? First, these professional groups themselves occupied a close proximity to consumers; their own professional legitimacy was based on claimed expertise about consumers' behavior, predilections, and desires. In effect they functioned as mediators between industrial producers and distributors, on the one hand, and the buying public, on the other.[7] Those claims of expert knowledge of consumers derived (in the advertisers' case) from market surveys, canvassing, and detailed investigations of retailers and media. Most tellingly, advertisers' anecdotal perceptions and experiences with consumers often wielded the most influence in constructing their ideas of consumers. Product testing advocates based their knowledge on the case files of the federal government's Bureau of Standards and Bureau of Home Economics, and after 1927, on direct contact with interested consumers. In that year the first private and nonpartisan consumer product testing organization, Consumers' Research, began providing information on a wide variety of products to prospective consumers.[8] Second, these professionals addressed

deficit spending to stimulate the economy. See also Ellis W. Hawley, *The New Deal and the Problem of Monopoly* (Princeton, N.J., 1965); Dean May, *From New Deal to New Economics: The American Liberal Response to the Recession of 1937* (New York, 1982); and Robert Collins, *The Business Response to Keynes in America* (New York, 1982).

6   See George Lipsitz's chapter in this book.

7   This was not a disinterested position, to be sure; advertisers were clearly in the pay of manufacturers and marketers interested in selling goods, and advertisers' own success would be judged primarily in terms of sales. Similarly, product testers and home economists were subject to different pressures and market forces seeking their expertise on the consumer. Indeed, such pressures caused a major rift in home economics during the depression, and the only reason it did not challenge product testing in the same way was that product testers rigidly attempted to avoid such temptation by redefining the scope of their goals to escape the claims of business. See Charles F. McGovern, "Sold American: Inventing the Consumer, 1890–1940," Ph.D diss., Harvard University, 1993, chaps. 6 and 7; see also Carolyn Goldstein, "Mediating Consumption: Home Economists, Consumers and Corporations," Ph.D diss., University of Delaware, 1994. Roland Marchand, *Advertising the American Dream: Making Way for Modernity, 1920–1940* (Berkeley, Calif., 1985), and Lears, *Fables of Abundance,* are the best explications of the position advertisers occupied in both the distribution system and the larger bureaucratic social order.

8   These claims, of course, were self-serving, but they were bound up with some of the most important and earliest attempts to interact directly with consumers to determine their preferences, their usages, and the problems they confronted. For advertising, see Peggy Jean Kreshell, "Toward a Cultural His-

consumers repeatedly and continually. Advertisers of course enjoyed a huge advantage in this regard; the vehicles of commercial advertising – most of the press and mass circulation magazines, billboards, outdoor signage, and, from the 1920s on, radio – reached hundreds of millions every day.[9] Product testers had much less access to large audiences, but even so, their cause and points of view found champions in influential liberal journals as well as best-selling books that garnered national notoriety. When New Dealers began examining questions of consumer policy, Consumers' Research was supplying information, expertise, and ideas to Washington, D.C., and its consultants.[10]

This close proximity did not imply that professionals identified wholly with consumers. Highly educated, much more affluent than the consumers they represented, these professionals did not eagerly embrace all aspects of the consumer society. Even the most enthusiastic admen were ambivalent about consumption and the mass access to goods that seemingly was transforming American life. Indeed, they looked disdainfully on the desires, tastes, habits, and social origins of the vast majority of Americans. I have argued elsewhere that they viewed consumers and their goods ambivalently, intrigued by the vast array of products, amusements, pastimes, and fashions, yet firmly rejecting the tastes and habits of the masses. Whereas admen and consumer advocates were fiercely opposed on the questions of the consumer's best interest or the important characteristics of buyers, these two professions shared remarkably similar views about consumers.[11] They placed themselves squarely in a cultural elite, whose tastes paralleled and

tory of Advertising Research: A Case Study of J. Walter Thompson, 1908–1925," Ph.D diss., University of Illinois at Urbana-Champaign, 1989, 322–64; Ralph M. Hower, *The History of an Advertising Agency: N. W. Ayer & Son at Work, 1865–1939* (Cambridge, Mass., 1939), 88–94, 261–5; Paul Cherrington, *The Consumer Looks at Advertising* (New York, 1928); Susan Strasser, *Satisfaction Guaranteed: The Making of the American Mass Market* (New York, 1989), 124–63; Marchand, *Advertising the American Dream;* and the chapters by Roland Marchand and Daniel Horowitz in this book. For the history of product testing, see McGovern, "Sold American," chaps. 5 and 6; Norman Isaac Silber, *Test and Protest: A History of Consumers' Union* (New York, 1982).

 9 In *Making of Modern Advertising,* Pope claims that the structure of advertising and modern market segmentation was in place by 1920. Moreover, advertising expenditures by 1929 had reached nearly $3 billion annually, although this would then fall off 40 percent through the first half of the depression (26) and in general (18–61). For the advertising stake in radio, see Susan Smulyan, *Selling Radio: The Commercialization of American Broadcasting, 1920–1934* (Washington, D.C., 1993), and Robert McChesney, *Telecommunications, Mass Media, and Democracy: The Battle for the Control of U.S. Broadcasting, 1928–1935* (New York, 1993). By 1930 there were some 12 million homes with radios; the number would become 40 million a decade later, with average listening times about four hours daily.

10 See McGovern, "Sold American," chap. 6; Otis Pease, *Responsibilities of American Advertisers, 1920–1940* (New Haven, Conn., 1958); Charles O. Jackson, *Food and Drug Legislation in the New Deal* (Princeton, N.J., 1970).

11 McGovern, "Sold American," chaps. 2 and 6: Lears, *Fables of Abundance;* Lawrence Levine, *Highbrow/Lowbrow* (Cambridge, Mass., 1988).

reinforced their own social position. They embraced the language of authenticity to discredit mass consumption and elevate their own tastes. By investing their own preferences with the authority of the "real" in a culture long suspicious of artifice, they made those tastes the yardstick of reality. Advertisers in particular were acutely aware of the differences between themselves and "the Public." A copywriter at J. Walter Thompson, the toniest and most socially sensitive of the big Madison Avenue agencies, laid out the facts for his colleagues:

> None of our New York writers belongs to a lodge or a civic club; only one in twenty-five ever attends a political meeting; not one ever goes to a public picnic. Only one out of five goes to church except on rare occasions. Half never go to Coney Island or to a similar resort; the other half go once in one or two years. This – in a nation that can almost be described by such experiences. Considerably *over* half our writers have never had the experience of living within the average national income of $1580 per family per year, and half can't even remember any *relatives* or *friends* who live on that figure! While 5% of all homes have servants, 66% of our writers are blessed with domestics. Only one in eight does his or her grocery shopping; half buy their own drug supplies and 60% shop in department stores. The men writers are virtually unanimous in their agreement that shopping is something to be avoided entirely. All this in an agency that depends on the retail sale of staple consumer goods to the masses for its principal income![12]

Such language and attitudes showed that admen viewed consumers as irrational, dangerous, and inferior, and that material abundance only reinforced their benighted condition.[13] Yet such scorn coexisted with the compelling utopian and sensual attractions of consumer culture and goods – attractions that proved hard for such professionals to dismiss or resist. That ambivalence would be only partially resolved during the depression.

The two views of consumption's political and civic aspects developed in part as a result of professionalization. JoAnne Brown has argued that professions adopt specific strategic metaphors to explain and to protect their expertise. Those metaphors offer important insights, not only into the ways professions perform but also the ways in which their fields are embraced or

---

12 Wallace Boren, "Good Taste in Advertising Copy," *JWT Forum* (Jan. 7, 1936): 6, record group 2, box 7, f. 1, J. Walter Thompson Archives, Duke University. For discussions of the implications of that perception, see Marchand, *Advertising the American Dream*, 25–116, and Lears, *Fables of Abundance*, 154–61, 229–33.

13 For a compelling statement of this phenomenon, see Andreas Huyssen, "Mass Culture as Modernism's Other," in Andreas Huyssen, ed., *After the Great Divide: Essays in Cultural Criticism* (Bloomington, Ind., 1987). Marchand, *Advertising the American Dream*, 52–87, and Horowitz, *The Morality of Spending*, capture some of the other complementary ambivalences of other observers of consumption.

reshaped in public discourse. It is important to pay attention to the metaphors themselves, since they help determine the meanings we place on our lives. As social and cultural constructs, metaphors are tested and preserved in ritual, through repeated patterns of behavior that societies evolve to create coherence and meaning from experience. Thus not only do metaphors arise from social experience, but by their preservation in the social systems of language and ritual they also help structure and define experience, by limiting the number of ways for relating that experience. This in turn suggests that we pay attention to metaphors of economic and political matters, including consumption. The capacity of metaphor to structure meaning thus in a very real sense shapes the material conditions of our lives. Only when people's experience and desires lead them to question the reality those metaphors routinely describe do they then have the opportunity to change the material conditions of their lives. The metaphors offered to explain political and economic experience, including representations of consumption, wealth, and goods, help determine ways in which those resources are allocated. As Murray Edelman notes, "It is language that evokes most of the 'political' realities people experience."[14]

Consumer professionals used the language, imagery, and concepts of politics not only to legitimize themselves but to describe consumption, goods, their own services, and ultimately consumers themselves. Their consistent use of political language linked consumption and citizenship in several key fields. Although the associations of consumption, citizenship, and capitalism might seem farfetched today, the specific arguments about consumption as the key to American citizenship were in fact very attractive in this period. Even as advertisers and consumerists clashed over the best interests of consumers, their shared notions of consumption as citizenship gained power because they described a social world in which consumers lived that very few other concepts from public discourse actually addressed. Whereas the abstractions of political thought held little attraction for the majority of consumers, the equating of citizenship with goods and consumer pastimes was for many the tangible expression of the promise of American life.

THE POLITICAL LANGUAGE OF ADVERTISING

Advertising became a profession to sell goods. Working at the service of corporate manufacturers and clients intent on reaching mass publics through

---

14 JoAnne Brown, *The Definition of a Profession: The Authority of Metaphor in the History of a Profession, 1890–1930* (Princeton, N.J., 1992), and "Professional Language: Words that Succeed," *Radical History Review* 13 (May 1986). See George Lakoff and Mark Johnson, *Metaphors We Live By* (Chicago, 1981); Murray Edelman, *Political Language: Words That Succeed and Policies That Fail* (New York, 1974), 3.

national as well as local media, advertisers utilized a set of political metaphors to describe consumption, goods, and consumers. In metaphors equating consumers with citizens and purchasing with voting, admen portrayed consumption as the true exercise of the individual's civic role and public identity; consumption was the ritual means of affirming one's nationality as an American. They identified their own work of persuasion as politics – the promulgation of ideas and programs for the common good to be affirmed or rejected through a public, communal, and voluntary process. George Frederick compared advertisers' claims to public leadership with politicians:

To call one a writer and the other an advertiser; one a statesman and the other a seller of merchandise, is, after all, a very faint distinction without a fundamental difference. . . . The measure of all public men, as well as of business concerns, is the extent to which they can carry public opinion and responsive action with them for their ideas, and the extent to which these ideas increase the wealth and happiness of society. The advertiser need be no more afraid of this test than the statesman.[15]

Bruce Barton, a popular writer and head of one of the most prestigious ad agencies, was even more direct. "Without public opinion, nothing can be done in a world of democracies. We advertising people work with the tools by which public opinion is formed and directed."[16] The advertiser had to be, of necessity, a statesman, a leader in the guise of a servant.[17] For him, public opinion was measured in popular preference for things.

If advertisers portrayed themselves as politicians, then they saw consumers as citizens. The central political comparison in advertising was the electoral metaphor. Advertisers equated the consumer's dollars with the franchised citizen's vote. Purchasing was like voting, an expression of free and individual choice, a form of social and (usually) public activity. According to advertisers, consumer-citizens wielded the sovereign power of the state by choosing among brand-name advertised goods in the manner of voters at the polls, who selected those candidates they felt would serve them best. Admen constantly reminded consumers that their purchases "elected" certain products to public service and elevated the businesses that produced them to positions of national leadership. The home economist and business

15 J. George Frederick, ed., *Masters of Advertising Copy* (New York, 1925), 29. The argument in the next several paragraphs is taken from McGovern, "Sold American," chaps. 2 and 3.
16 Bruce Barton, "I Believe," *The Wedge* 20, no. 13 (1930): n.p., BBDO Archives [Batten, Barton, Durstine, and Osborne], New York City. I am grateful to Paula Brown of BBDO for allowing me access to these files.
17 Barton was one of the few advertising men who followed that dictum to the limit: He served one term in Congress beginning in 1938 as a Republican representative from Manhattan, making a national mark as one of a trio of FDR's most unswerving Republican opponents.

consultant Christine Frederick proclaimed that consumers "vote in broad democratic fashion at great popular elections, the polls being open every-day at a million or more retail stores."[18] The elections were constant and unremitting, and the voting public could always shift their votes to other candidates.

There were several direct implications of this association of political sovereignty with economic activity, itself a staple of liberal thought. If consumers were voters, then sales meant leadership, authority, and legitimacy for those who offered the products. Advertisers regularly interpreted widespread sales or popularity as an indication of corporate legitimacy. In advertisers' terms, consumers elevated to national public "leadership" the major corporations that were already transforming American life through legal, economic, and social revolutions. This is not to imply that advertisers were the only ones who thought this way, nor that they were original. By making these associations a staple element of both their communications with consumers and their relationships with clients, critics, and the state, advertisers made central to their work assumptions that consumption was a critical part of American national destiny. The liberal ideal of private individuals seeking their interests through civil society and government, of course, has a long history.[19] Advertisers made that relationship a staple of their appeals, and their association was persuasive enough that such ad claims were often considered as much a portrayal of the United States as mere sales talk.

By voting for goods, consumers also voted for the corporations that provided them. Thus the electoral metaphor claimed that consumers were sovereign, despite the corporate restructuring of business, law, and society in which they had little overall influence and which was in fact a loss of power.[20] Edward Filene, department store magnate and the Johnny Appleseed of credit financing, summed up the sentiment: "The masses of America have elected Henry Ford. They have elected General Motors. They have elected the General Electric Company, and Woolworth's and all the other

---

18 Christine M. Frederick, *Selling Mrs. Consumer* (New York, 1929), 322ff.; see also "Overlooking the Consumer," *Printers' Ink* 92, no. 9 (Sept. 2, 1915): 86. Bruce Barton captured this dilemma in one of his characteristic business sermons, which he repeated on the dinner and convention circuit for years, "Which Knew Not Joseph," Barton File, BBDO Archives.

19 C. B. Macpherson, *The Political Theory of Possessive Individualism* (Oxford, 1962), is the classic account of its immediate origins. For the American context, see Joyce O. Appleby, *Liberalism and Republicanism in the Historical Imagination* (Cambridge, Mass., 1992).

20 See Alfred D. Chandler Jr., *The Visible Hand: The Managerial Revolution in American Business* (Cambridge, Mass., 1977); Martin Sklar, *The Corporate Reconstruction of American Capitalism, 1890–1916: The Market, Law and Politics* (New York, 1988); and Livingston, *Pragmatism and the Political Economy.*

great industrial and business leaders of the day."[21] The ascendance of the great producers, advertisers implied, gave them a mandate not only to serve but to govern. Roland Marchand has shown how General Motors (GM) used the rhetoric of democracy to cast its "Customer Research" as the public interest; GM claimed to base its product designs on customer preferences, and thus its autos truly were "Of the People, By the People, and For the People."[22] Such strategies disguised the private interests of the corporation with public service and the common will. Linking ideas of leadership and authority with products located the symbols of corporate authority in the everyday lives of millions. The pervasiveness of the electoral metaphor suggested that consumption might prove a powerful counterforce should it challenge politics directly for popular favor. The assumption that corporate stewards and interests were most fit for governing would be highlighted during the Great Depression, when alternative politics challenged business dominance of public discourse and policy.

If consumption was like voting, then consumer suffrage could easily be construed as a right of all Americans. Clearly advertisers emphasized that connection especially in its construction of women as consumers. Advertisers spent most of their energies and efforts in reaching women consumers. One of the most durable tropes of American business was that "the consumer" in fact meant *women*, and that women spent 85 percent of all consumer dollars. James Collins in 1901 summed up the industry wisdom: "The advertiser talks vaguely of a creature which he calls, variously, 'he,' 'it,' 'clientele,' and 'the public'; yet that creature is woman, pure and simple."[23] Although this notion ceded patriarchal authority over money matters too hastily, its remarkable durability among marketers, businessmen, and commentators gave women a very visible role in this activity, which was discussed in private terms but which in fact was very much public and communal.

Whereas certain political issues might be framed as matters for the family or the male breadwinner, the assumed referent for consumers of most

---

21 Edward A. Filene, with Charles Wood, *Successful Living in This Machine Age* (New York, 1932), 98–9.
22 See Roland Marchand's chapter in this book.
23 James H. Collins, "The Eternal Feminine," *Printers' Ink* 35, no. 13 (June 26, 1901): 3. For other expressions of the same sentiment, see Nellie Ballard, "Advertising as a Woman Sees It," *Judicious Advertising* 4, no. 6 (Apr. 1906): 51; G. Albert Strauss, "Women's Magazines and Their Power," *Printers' Ink* 67, no. 10 (June 9, 1909): 40, and "'I Spend Half My Life in the Kitchen,'" *J. Walter Thompson News Bulletin,* no. 1121 (Jan. 1925): 9–14. See also Hazel Kyrk, *A Theory of Consumption* (New York, 1923); Benjamin R. Andrews, *Economics of the Household* (New York, 1923); Wesley Clair Mitchell, "The Backward Art of Spending Money," *American Economic Review* 2, no. 2 (June 1912): 269–81; all echoed from the academy the assertion that the vast majority of consumer dollars were spent by women.

goods most of the time was to women, especially homemakers.[24] Advertisers linked ideas of freedom, sovereignty, and rights with consumption, portrayed as women's work. During the era when women fought for and achieved suffrage and organized a public and political agenda around concerns that had been relegated to the supposed domestic sphere, advertisers borrowed from (and arguably trivialized) women's demands for full participation in public life by portraying consumption as the best (and only) means to that end.[25]

Advertisers encouraged women to hold fast to brand loyalty and refuse substitutes as a matter of their rights and the exercise of their sovereign freedoms.[26] Consumption became the means to women's independence by offering convenience and by saving household labor. Such appeals were the foundation of advertising for cleansing powders, kitchen and laundry equipment, soap, vacuum cleaners, and even Shredded Wheat. The New York Vacuum Cleaner Company pursued this line of thinking to its logical extreme, showing its product lifting women "Up from Slavery."[27] But by this reckoning, freedom became simply freedom of choice; what were women to gain? As presented in advertising, proper consumption not only lessened onerous household tasks but offered liberty for activity within or, more likely, outside the home. Advertisers frequently portrayed women's self-determination as consumption itself. Freedom arose from and gave birth to more opportunities to consume.[28]

Another major thread of the political language of advertising was its equation of democracy and social equality. Consumption was a symbol of American social democracy and the engine of social equality. In the fifty

---

24 There were, of course, cases of appeal to others – automobiles, sporting goods, certain campaigns for food or clothing, insurance and financial securities, where the assumed target was male, and increasingly in the 1920s and 1930s (through the medium of radio) children. See Strasser, *Satisfaction Guaranteed,* and Steven Kline, *Out of the Garden: Toys, TV, and Children's Culture in the Age of Marketing* (London, 1993).

25 For only a short list of the scholarship documenting this change, see Mary P. Ryan, *Women in Public: Between Banners and Ballots, 1825–1880* (Baltimore, 1990); Kathryn Kish Sklar, *Florence Kelley and the Nation's Work* (New Haven, Conn., 1995); Robin Muncy, *Creating a Female Dominion in American Reform, 1840–1935* (New York, 1991); Paula Baker, *The Moral Frameworks of Public Life: Gender, Politics, and the State in Rural New York, 1870–1930* (New York, 1990); Nancy Cott, *The Grounding of Modern Feminism* (New Haven, Conn., 1987); and Edith Mayo, "From Parlor to Politics," exhibition at National Museum of American History, Washington, D.C., 1989 to the present.

26 See, e.g., ads for Kellogg's cornflakes, in *Good Housekeeping* 46, no. 4 (Apr. 1908): n.p.; *Printers' Ink* 93, no. 1 (Oct. 7, 1915); for Tetley's *Good Housekeeping* 44, no. 3 (Mar. 1907): n.p; "Our Own Page," *Women's Home Companion* 39, no. 9 (Sept. 1912): 3; and the series "Scientific Shopping" by Walter S. Hine in *Good Housekeeping* 49 (Mar.–Apr. 1909).

27 See McGovern, "Sold American," 106–8; the advertisement is in the "Housekeepers Directory," *Good Housekeeping* 49, no. 6 (Dec. 1909).

28 *Ladies' Home Journal* 37, no. 3 (Mar. 1920): 57; *Saturday Evening Post* 184, no. 34 (Feb. 17, 1912): 28, and 193, no. 28 (Jan. 6, 1923): 103.

years after 1880, observers praised as revolutionary the mass market's ability to distribute large quantities of goods throughout much of American society; certainly the low prices and wide distribution of many national brands allowed admen to claim that consumers had equal access to their wares.[29] Although admen were aware that most goods were consumed predominantly by the upper and the prosperous middle classes – no more than one-third of American society – still the idea of inclusive democracy in and through products was central to advertising's political language.[30] Roland Marchand has termed this theme the parable of the "democracy of goods": Consumers enjoyed the best goods in the world at the lowest prices. Neither kings nor millionaires had access to finer things than the common people. Cheap prices made the best automobile tires, oatmeal, motor oil, vacuum cleaners, and so forth, available to all. As the makers of Jell-O noted, "The Butler Serves and the Housewife Too."[31]

Again several corollaries follow from this idea. The democracy of goods strengthened American political democracy, as advertisers argued that mass social acceptance of products united consumers in other respects. Because advertisements tended to invoke only one product at a time, they leveled social differences only in a fragmentary way; few advertisements were as preposterous as the copywriter Claude Hopkins's social Darwinist claims that Quaker Oats was the staple dish, the brain food of the ruling classes, and that the poor and downtrodden need not and should not be resentful or deprived of their ticket out of poverty: "Quaker Oats costs only one-half cent per dish." A class system had no place in the democracy of goods. In fact classes were virtually absent. Although advertisers were acutely aware of social differences (and certainly by the 1920s they knew that they were selling most goods to a relatively constricted market), their portrayals, language, and economics invoked an organic classless society. King Gillette editorialized in 1910, "There are no idle rich in this country today – no leisure class. It is asked of every man – what is he doing? . . . The Gillette Safety Razor is the symbol of the age – it is the most democratic thing in the world. The rich man is not shaved in bed by his valet as he was a generation ago. He uses a Gillette and shaves himself – in three minutes."[32] Such

29 William Black, *The Family Income* (New York, 1907), 6–7; Edwin Balmer, *The Science of Advertising* (New York, 1907), 32–5; [True Story Magazine], *The American Economic Evolution* (New York, 1930), 7; Phelps, *Our Biggest Customer;* Harold Eldredge, *Making Advertisements Pay* (Columbia, S.C., 1917), 31.

30 Marchand, *Advertising the American Dream;* Black, *Family Income;* and Walter B. Pitkin, *The Consumer* (New York, 1932), are among the most frank discussions of the limits of markets in general.

31 Marchand, *Advertising the American Dream,* 217–22, 290–5. For Jell-O, see *Pictorial Review* (Dec. 1918): 66.

32 *Saturday Evening Post,* Sept. 17, 1910, 56, and Apr. 16, 1910, 56.

claims certainly resonated with other business thought, but only when the depression convincingly belied them were advertisers forced to shift their position.

A final set of political ideas in consumer advertising was that consumption and goods were characteristic activities and symbols of American nationality – being a good American meant being a good consumer. These were not arguments grounded in economic nationalism (most businessmen and their advertising henchmen rejected those arguments, at least over the first half of the twentieth century) but rather in cultural nationalism. Since the early nineteenth century, advertisers had routinely and even systematically invoked American symbols and political and historical figures to sell products. Before there was any kind of sustained national market, political and national imagery was used to sell products and, arguably, nationalism itself to American peoples.[33] Through constant assertions that their products were part of a specifically American mode of living, advertisers forged powerful links among consumption, nationality, and culture; with frequent reminders that their wares served explicitly "American" needs and ideals, advertising cast goods as the material expression of American identity and consumption as the means to become American. They presented consumption as the distinct heritage and privilege of living in the United States. Consumption was in effect the national folkways.

By the corporate era, advertisers were also calling a host of products "national" as a designation to imply both widespread acceptance and some sort of official sanction. The second aspect of consumption as national culture was advertisers' persistent depiction of consumption as the characteristic folkway of true Americans, and goods as the true symbols of American nationality. Being an active avid consumer was the hallmark of American life: Admen designated everything from fountain pens to grape juice to laundry machines as "American" and in countless ads showed products and consumers partaking in rituals that confirmed their nationality and that, in effect, naturalized them as citizens of the United States.

This notion of naturalization was not simply rhetorical. In the early twentieth century, the widespread visibility and distribution of many products spawned a second aspect of language and imagery, that of Americanization and immigration. Fath Davis Ruffins has traced the long history of ethnic and racial imagery throughout American advertising and commer-

33 John William Ward, *Andrew Jackson: Symbol for an Age* (New York, 1955); Keith E. Melder, *Hail to the Candidate: Presidential Campaigns from Banners to Broadcasts* (Washington, D.C., 1992); Karal Ann Marling, *George Washington Slept Here: Colonial Revivals and American Culture, 1876–1986* (Cambridge, Mass., 1988); Robert Jay, *The Trade Card in Nineteenth-Century America* (Columbia, Mo., 1987).

cial products. She argues that the use of largely stereotypical imagery not only commodified the exoticism of Africans, aboriginals, and Asians, but strongly grounded consuming products as an exercise in becoming American. For whites consumption was a means to losing the alien and threatening aspects of ethnicity, whereas for African Americans, Asian Americans, and Native Americans, such imagery served as a reminder of the unbridgeable gap of race.[34] This process was most pronounced after the turn-of-the-century migrations from Europe. Although they never considered their primary task to be the unification of American culture, advertisers through their own fears and fascinations regarding the diversity of ethnic and racial culture confirmed their desire to encourage cultural conformity through mass consumption.

Advertisers, who were often privately fearful or disdainful of the consuming masses, recognized in consumption the quickest path to Americanism and to a coherent and uniform civilization. In "teaching the immigrant not to fetch and carry," but to go to the store, advertisers were not only creating markets but helping create a much more stable and cohesive American culture, one that would not be frayed by social divisions.[35] In the agency executive Frank Presbrey's words, advertising was behind

most of the growth of a national homogeneity of our people, a uniformity of ideas which, despite the mixture of races, is to be found greater here than in European countries. . . . Constant acquisition of ideas from the same sources has caused Americans living thousands of miles apart to be alike in their living habits and thoughts, in their desires and in their methods of satisfying them [36]

A General Foods executive, Ralph Starr Barton, noted with satisfaction that "[i]n a country made up of many diverse races, it may well be that one of the strongest national ties is the common use and possession of the same kinds of foods, the same kinds of clothing, the same kinds of automobiles, and the same kinds of countless other things that advertising has helped make national necessities."[37]

For advertisers, consumer goods were the hallmarks of a new culture, truly united and integral, despite its multiple ethnic and racial components.

---

34 See Fath Ruffins's chapter in this book.
35 Andrew B. Heinze, *Adapting to Abundance: Jewish Immigrants, Mass Consumption, and the Search for American Identity* (New York, 1989); Elizabeth Ewen, *Immigrant Women in the Land of Dollars* (New York, 1985); Kathy Peiss, *Cheap Amusements* (Philadelphia, 1986); Lizabeth Cohen, *Making a New Deal* (New York, 1990).
36 Frank Presbrey, *The History and Development of Advertising* (New York, 1929), 613. This sentiment is expressed throughout much of the advertising writing on the profession in the 1920s.
37 Ralph Starr Barton, "What the Modern Advertiser Owes the Public," in William A. Vawter Foundation on Business Ethics, ed., *Ethical Problems of Modern Advertising* (New York, 1931), 27.

Although they often based their campaigns on specific social associations and tropes, their general strategy presumed that the broader the markets for most goods, the more uniform and stable American culture would be. While they privately held to a social hierarchy based on class, taste, and cultivation, they publicly celebrated a vast and unified culture based on the common acceptance of consumer goods and the common pursuit of consumption in which all were equal.

Finally, national advertisers constructed a vision of nationality and a common civilization based on consumption. While privately aware of vast differences in class, income, education, and cultural backgrounds that separated the majority of Americans from the ideal types portrayed in ads, in their advertising and in their descriptions to employers admen stressed the social inclusiveness of consumption. They claimed that American culture had been built on the civic and cultural values embodied in consumption, invoking historical figures, myths, and settings to show that consumption was the American heritage and folkway: "[P]erhaps this is a nation of money grubbers as we have often been called. . . .[But] Americans are the greatest spenders as well as the greatest earners in all economic history." The reasons were ingrained in American history: "[T]hrough three hundred years of pioneering . . . of pushing back frontiers of so vast a land . . . three traditions have become established traits of the American people. *The necessity for labor . . . the necessity for education . . . and the need for mechanical power to free workers for other pursuits.*"[38] The desire for labor-saving devices, the desire for a better life as expressed in more and better things, the restless search for material improvement in daily life, all were the traits of a people that undergirded "a new independence, a new democracy built on the permanent foundation of economic freedom."[39] Consumption was the foundation of a distinctly American way of life; this was the new order of the ages.

CONSUMER REPUBLICANISM

The enterprise of private consumer product testing and consumer advocacy in the United States had roots in different professional disciplines, principally home economics, engineering, physics, and the social sciences. Starting in 1927, but building on research and ideas that dated back to Thorstein Veblen and beyond, Consumers' Research became the first private organization to provide independently generated scientific information

38 N. W. Ayer & Son, *In Behalf of Advertising* (Philadelphia, 1927), 226, 228. Elisions and emphasis in original.
39 Ibid., 229–30.

on a variety of name-brand goods to individual consumers.[40] Product testing, and its grounding in science, became a principal agent in the ideology
of consumerism that drew on very different American political traditions
than those of advertising and commerce.[41] Although the ranks of consumer
advocates were comparatively thin, their popularity among liberal reformers
and activists ensured that their ideas gained support in areas far beyond the
reach of their numbers. Those ideas were in some measure a response to
national advertising, but they were grounded in long-standing popular suspicion of artifice, hostility to corporations, and a strong bias for the utilitarian and instrumental. As first assembled and set forth by the economist and
pundit Stuart Chase in *The Tragedy of Waste* (1925) and then *Your Money's
Worth* (1927) with F. J. Schlink, the cluster of political metaphors and ideas
we may call "consumer republicanism" resonated with and followed from
earlier American traditions and language. They became the core of an oppositional vision of consumption that just as adamantly claimed consumption
as a badge of American citizenship and a right of American life.[42]

At the center of consumer republicanism was a form of ideal Jeffersonian independence not only in the marketplace but also in society at
large – each individual consumer required and deserved independent and
scientifically valid information about goods and purchasing. If dollars were
votes, and spending money was the act of voting, then consumers had a
right as well as an obligation to know exactly what and whom they were
electing. Consumer republicans argued that the marketplace under new era
capitalism undermined that independence by keeping them ignorant of
goods. Consumerists argued that people lacked technical knowledge or
necessary experience in the wide variety of goods required in "getting and
spending" a living, at nearly any income level.[43] In Robert S. Lynd's phrase,
the vast majority of American consumers were "illiterate," lacking in basic
knowledge about goods and unable to assess their qualities.[44] Consumer

40 Other groups, most notably the National Consumers' League, had organized consumers, but their
    principal concern focused on the conditions under which goods were made or sold; there was little
    residual concern over quality or performance of goods themselves unrelated to the social conditions
    of their origin. See Kathryn Kish Sklar's chapter in this book.
41 There is no book-length study of Consumers' Research, but its ideas are treated extensively in
    McGovern, "Sold American," and Kathleen Donahue, "Toward the Good Society: The Consumer in
    American Political Thought," Ph.D. diss., University of Virginia, 1993. The organization is also men-
    tioned in Persia Campbell, *Consumer Representation in the New Deal* (New York, 1940); Helen Soren-
    son, *The Consumer Movement* (New York, 1941); and Robert Mayer, *The Consumer Movement:
    Guardians of the Marketplace* (Boston, 1989).
42 This and the next several paragraphs condense arguments in McGovern, "Sold American," chaps. 5
    and 6.
43 See Mitchell, "The Backward Art of Spending Money," 269–76; Henry Harap, *The Education of the
    Consumer* (New York, 1924); Kyrk, *Theory of Consumption,* 123.
44 See Robert S. Lynd, with Alice Hanson, "The People as Consumers," in United States, President's
    Research Committee on Social Trends, ed., *Recent Social Trends in the United States: Report of the Pres-*

republicans located this ignorance in the rise of mass society and the revolutions in production and distribution, which made available a stunning and bewildering variety of goods. In most cases, their origins, manufacture, and makers were completely unknown to consumers. Consumer society's second foundation existed on the mass migration from country and village to the city, with the consequent loss of ties to the land, to crafts and home production, to the physical origins of goods. In the trek from peasant hut to city apartment, consumerists charged, people had lost their historic firsthand contact with their communities and with things. Mass production shrouded the origins and contents of goods; the lack of self-sufficiency in a complex society made consumers unfit to judge their qualities. Without that past experience, or any other knowledge, consumers were utterly dependent on corporations, advertisers, retailers, and salesmen, all of whom stood to gain from that dependence.[45] As Chase and Schlink wrote in 1927, "In the face of the new competition, utterly disorganized, with no defense except a waning quality of common sense, the ultimate consumer makes his blundering way, a moth about a candle. To talk of his bargaining power is to talk about a nonalcoholic America. There is no such thing."[46]

Advertising only made such ignorance worse in attacking whatever knowledge consumers might have retained from experience. To compound their ignorance, advertising corrupted people's desires by emphasizing the irrelevant, the illusory, and the impossible.

We buy not for the value of the product to meet our specific needs but because the story told on every billboard, every newspaper and newspaper page, every shop window, every sky sign, every other letter we receive – is a pleasing stimulating and romantic story. It bears a Message Straight to Our Hearts. But whether or not it is a fairy story we do not know save through the bitter and wasteful process of trial and error.[47]

Advertising was not disinterested truthful information about products but just the opposite. Consumerists argued that Madison Avenue regularly and systematically offered irrelevant, untrustworthy, and harmful information

   ident's Research Committee on Social Trends, 2 vols. (New York, 1933), 2:881; the idea is also at the core of Harap, *Education of the Consumer.*

45 Stuart Chase and Frederick Schlink, *Your Money's Worth: A Study in the Wastes of the Consumer's Dollar* (New York, 1927), 27–8; Stuart Chase, *The Tragedy of Waste* (New York, 1925), chaps. 3–7. This sketchy history was echoed not only by consumer republicans, but by business spokesmen and apologists. See Ayer, *In Behalf of Advertising;* Calkins, *Business the Civilizer,* 13–14, for two examples.

46 Chase and Schlink, *Your Money's Worth,* 34–5. Writing some years later, Robert S. Lynd, a sociologist and member of the New Deal's Consumer Advisory Board, called this book "the *Uncle Tom's Cabin* of the abuses of the consumer." Robert S. Lynd, "Democracy's Third Estate: The Consumer," *Political Science Quarterly* 51, no. 4 (Dec. 1936): 497. See also Kyrk, *Theory of Consumption,* 103–11.

47 Chase and Schlink, *Your Money's Worth,* 26.

about goods, often coupled with trivial and degrading ideas about the relationship of people and things. Consumerists generally insisted that the primary purpose and essence of most goods were instrumental: They were tools rather than totems. That meant that most goods could be reducible to scientifically derived standards and specifications, a neutrality that itself stood independent of marketplace discourse and served to ensure the consumer's own autonomy. Consumer republicans acknowledged that people also used goods to subjective ends, for self-definition and self-transformation. But they drew a line. "Man does not live by bread alone. Mystery and wonder are implicit in his makeup. But do we want it in soup, plaster, wall board, soap, fertilizers and bug killers?"[48] Ultimately, advertising attacked and undermined the consumer's independence, not only through deceit, but more perniciously by continual assault at every turn. Amid an incessant barrage of sales arguments, the consumer could not hope to maintain a steady independence.

Consumer republicans adopted an antimarket sentiment that in effect argued that people had the right to live their lives as free of the marketplace as they wanted. Since the autonomous individual was the fundamental unit of society, consumerists argued that desire should flow only from the individual to the market; the market existed simply to meet human needs. Consumerists in effect argued for the right to be free of the intrusions of modern commerce. Advertising represented unwanted invasion and consumption itself was a presumption on the individual's time and person. As a *Consumers' Research* editorial put it:

[I]n refusing to purchase things which they do not need and do not want, consumers will be providing the best foundation for the lasting prosperity of the greatest number. The fact that so many consumers have become sick of being continually sold new gadgets and have painfully acquired a wish to conduct their affairs without a continual stream of calls from super-salesmen or a daily orgy of aimless and needless shopping, is the price which business enterprise has paid for applying an ever increasing and ever more unscrupulous pressure on the masses of our population – to spend without any regard for their needs or resources.[49]

The marketplace also eroded the individual's identity. By assessing everyone's individual character through the person's possessions, the marketplace obscured the self behind a veil of mass-produced baubles. Heirs to a Puritan tradition of plain speaking and suspicion of artifice, consumerists viewed the market's seductive symbolism and copious abundance as threats to both self-knowledge and social relations. Since the marketplace spuriously made

48 Ibid., 164.   49 *Consumers' Research General Bulletin* 1, no. 3 (Sept. 1932): 2.

things the democratic measure of people, the only recourse for consumers was to reject marketplace logic that implied that an individual's character was defined by or mutable in things. Consumerists did not deny the symbolic, aesthetic, or subjective, but they sought to limit the sway of those criteria by enabling individuals to have the means to make such choices for themselves. The marketplace did not foster self-cultivation, it hindered it.

At bottom this was an argument for limiting the scope and sovereignty of the market; consumerists adamantly contended that it was synonymous with neither society nor the civic realm. The market was subservient to both; whereas such grass roots groups as Consumers' Research saw the pursuit of happiness through consumption as important, they also insisted that the marketplace could only address a part of human experience, and that both society and nation were superior to the realm of getting and spending.

Consumer republicans also contended that consumption was an expression of American culture and history, although with considerably less enthusiasm than advertisers. First, they acknowledged that consumption guided and defined the process of getting a living. The abundance of consumer life was inescapable and as American as Abraham Lincoln: Every American was a consumer. As such American civilization was increasingly defined by consumption.[50] Invoking an idealized nineteenth-century village as the exemplar of a simple harmonious society of sovereign producers and consumers, Chase and Schlink called forth traditional American suspicions of cities. They also called on opposition to luxury and tapped a long-standing belief, given new force in the 1920s and 1930s, that the earlier agrarian-based life was more truly "American" than the urban life and manufactured culture of mass society.[51] The values they prized most highly in goods – simplicity, durability, frugality, efficiency, functionality – they linked to long-standing American traditions, especially of old stock Yankee and New England descent.

The ideal of the consumer republican vision was that self-sufficient individuals could choose for themselves, without dependence on a corrupt marketplace. Goods were merely tools for the work of living and individual self-cultivation. Spending money was like voting, but the elections were a perversion of democracy unless consumers could make independent

50 Chase and Schlink, *Your Money's Worth,* 5; see also Robert S. Lynd and Helen Merrell Lynd, *Middletown: A Study in American Culture* (New York, 1929).
51 Such literary expressions as the collection by Twelve Southerners, *I'll Take My Stand: The South and the Agrarian Tradition* (Baton Rouge, La., 1931); critical essays such as Ralph Borsodi, *This Ugly Civilization* (New York, 1929); and the book by Stuart Chase, *Mexico: A Study of Two Americas* (New York, 1931), all captured some of this same spirit.

choices.[52] But since consumers were citizens, the state had some obligation to ensure that they did have "free and fair elections." It was the consumerists' turn to the state in the early depression that brought them squarely into conflict with private enterprise, even as the consumer was brought into public discourse.[53] The political and economic changes of the depression, on the one hand, and the cultural realignments of the era, on the other, affirmed consumption as the badge of citizenship and American nationality.

CONSUMPTION, CULTURE, AND CITIZENSHIP IN THE
DEPRESSION: A BRIEF SUMMARY

These threads of conflicting views came into open conflict with the advent of the depression and the New Deal. Lizabeth Cohen has outlined the ways in which this period saw the transition to consumer-oriented policies in response to public demands grounded in the recognition that to be a fully enfranchised citizen meant being a consumer and participating fully in the consumer economy.[54] As noted, the depression revealed the extent to which the entire society depended on its ability to consume for the necessities of daily living. In the abortive National Recovery Administration (NRA) and the AAA (Agricultural Adjustment Administration), the New Deal hosted fitful and largely ineffective attempts to include consumers' interests in national planning of production and prices. That they were run by businessmen and others who did not put the consumer first was not lost on consumer advocates, nor on such New Dealers as Rexford Tugwell, Leon Henderson, and Mariiner Eccles, who themselves became influential voices for consumer interests within the administration.[55] After the second New Deal seemingly ground to a halt in the wake of the failed Supreme Court packing attempt and the 1937 recession, President Roosevelt finally adopted a Keynesian policy of spending to increase purchasing power. The government also adopted consumer protections with antitrust activity, the regulation of prices, packaging, and other devices. Such government commitments were bolstered by the demands of numerous political groups for protective legislation and regulation. For better or worse, the United States was on a road that identified the consumer as citizen and that made enhancing purchasing power the focus of federal intervention in the economy.

52 See Kyrk, *A Theory of Consumption*, 25–128.
53 See Robert S. Lynd, "The Consumer Becomes a Problem," *Annals of the American Academy of Political and Social Science* 173 (May 1934): 1–6.
54 See Lizabeth Cohen's chapter in this book. My interpretation is largely in agreement with Cohen's.
55 Hawley, *New Deal and the Problem of Monopoly*.

That process was informed and highlighted by the open warfare that developed among and between consumer advocates, business, media, and advertising; social organizations from labor unions to the General Federation of Womens' Clubs; and the government. Consumer advocates turned to the government for relief in the early 1930s; after the promising beginnings of the NRA, radical groups like Consumers' Research concluded that neither the government nor liberals would go far enough to protect consumers.[56] More moderate groups such as the NRA Consumers' Advisory Board, cooperative groups, and liberal businessmen sought to mediate between the demands of consumers for protection and satisfaction and the demands of business to operate free of regulation of pricing, production, labor practices, packaging, or promotion. Large corporations, feeling the pinch of hard times and the loss of cultural leadership enjoyed during the 1920s, fought bitterly against any regulation to protect consumers, even as they fretted privately about their own failures.[57] National advertising appropriations declined by 40 percent between 1930 and 1935, even as the number of radios (by then the most lucrative advertising medium) throughout the country nearly doubled.

Facing an embattled future against a popular leader and a hostile and restive public, businessmen grasped for a new way to regain popular favor. In a major speech before the conservative National Association of Manufacturers in 1935, Bruce Barton sounded the call:

Industry and politics, at the moment, are competitors for the same confidence and favor of the same patron, the public. Politics knows it; industry, for three years has acted as if it did not. . . . Why should we bother with the servants of the people when we can talk to the people themselves? Why indeed bother with Anybody when there is Everybody? We have a story to tell but we do not tell it. We have great benefits to confer upon the people if they will give us the opportunity, but we must persuade them that we are more reliable than the politicians; that we will work for them more cheaply and with more satisfaction. . . . Industry in the long run, can and will do more for the people and their children than politics can ever do. But first it must beat politics with its own weapon; it must speak not only to the mind but to the heart.[58]

---

56 McGovern, "Sold American," 346–62; Campbell, *Consumer Representation in the New Deal;* and Robert Lynd, "Democracy's Third Estate: The Consumer."

57 Pease, *Responsibilities of American Advertisers;* McGovern, "Sold American," 319–45; Lears, *Fables of Abundance,* 235–58.

58 Bruce Barton, "The Public," speech delivered to the Congress of American Industry, in conjunction with the annual convention of the National Association of Manufacturers, Dec. 4, 1935, n.p., Barton File, BBDO Archives. The speech appeared in edited form as "Business Can Win Public from Politician," *Printers' Ink* 173, no. 11 (Dec. 12, 1935): 17–24.

Barton's speech set the tone for an aggressive counter–New Deal effort, a broad program of public relations, advertising, entertainment, parades, and pageants, all of which promoted the message that consumption was the paramount end in life, that private enterprise was more in tune with public needs than activist government, and that the fruits of corporate enterprise – consumer goods and consumption – defined and served "the American Way of Life."[59] That effort infused much of corporate advertising throughout the late 1930s and even during World War II, in what one historian has termed the "private war of American advertising."[60] The basic promotional tools and messages were a cornerstone of a continual effort to counter and undermine the welfare state and labor unionism throughout the postwar era.[61]

What did the public do? It turned to the government and to various alliances with labor, consumer groups, local clubs, extension agents, to organize, boycott, or otherwise get greater satisfaction from goods and purchasing. But it turned to corporate enterprise continually for its goods; by World War II, consumption had begun to approach pre-depression levels. While Barton and his peers worried about the loss of legitimacy, corporations recovered most of their markets if not their hallowed status, in the long run. Consumers made clear that they accepted aspects of both the corporate and republican visions of consumer-citizenship: the corporate emphasis on liberal individualism and the republican emphasis on virtue, community, and morality, at least in some instances.[62] Those differing visions continue to inform public discourse to the present day, especially in relationship to questions of economic growth and equity.[63]

Finally, consumption was not simply measured out in goods, services, and exchange. As James Livingston suggests, what might be the deepest source of consumption's staying power is that for many people, consumption offered the means to agency and self-determination that was eroded or bitterly contested in other areas.[64] The reinvention of political citizenship in consumption is not surprising if self-determination remains at the core

---

59 For contemporary accounts, see S. H. Walker and Paul Sklar, *Business Finds Its Voice: Management's Effort to Sell the Business Idea to the Public* (New York, 1937), and Milton Wright, *Public Relations in Business* (New York, 1938).

60 Frank Fox, *Madison Avenue Goes to War: The Strange Military Career of American Advertising, 1941–45* (Provo, Utah, 1975).

61 Elizabeth Fones-Wolf, *Selling Free Enterprise: The Business Assault on Labor and Liberalism, 1945–60* (Urbana, Ill., 1994).

62 See, e.g., Mark H. Leff, "The Politics of Sacrifice on the American Home Front in World War II," *Journal of American History* 77, no. 4 (1989): 1296–1318.

63 See Jackson Lears's and Susan Strasser's chapters in this book.

64 See James Livingston's chapter in this book, along with his *Pragmatism and the Political Economy*.

of American politics. This chapter does not suggest that consumption
became the sole or most powerful means to self-determination or agency
in American life, nor that the vast social inequities of American capitalism
that were challenged during the New Deal and after could simply be
addressed by more things for more people. The idea, however, that individuals and communities could find in consumption the ready means to self-
cultivation and agency should not be readily dismissed. It was the consistent
and utopian use of popular culture, individual and collective desire, by the
great majority of Americans – the same forms of mass entertainment that
both fascinated and repelled consumer professionals – that perhaps held the
major key to the ways in which consumption and citizenship merged.
Movies, radio, popular music, dancing, comics, fairs, and expositions, all
addressed the public and civic aspects of American life by couching them in
private, consumerist terms. It was in the visions of consumption and desire
offered by these forms, and in their relationship with consumers, that perhaps we may get a sense of the cultural significance of consumption as a
new basis of American civilization, a new mode of citizenship. Although
this helped foster the illusion of complete commonality that gave rise to a
consensual view of American life after World War II, the convergence of
many Americans on popular culture as a means of expressing and achieving
their own self-determination argues forcefully that we look to the pleasur-
able for the political, to the subjective for the civic, and to goods for the
place where citizens define for themselves, the good.[65]

65 See the essays in George Lipsitz, *Time Passages: Collective Memory and American Popular Culture* (Minneapolis, 1990), for examples of the many ways this played out in the postwar era.

3

Changing Consumption Regimes in Europe, 1930–1970

Comparative Perspectives on the Distribution Problem

VICTORIA DE GRAZIA

The evolution of modern systems of distribution is astonishingly understudied, considering that goods load up with meaning as they are moved from producers to purchasers. Here, I want to characterize this evolution from a particular perspective, namely, the changeover in continental Western Europe from what might be called a bourgeois to a Fordist mode of consumption. This transformation started to gather impetus in the 1920s and then met enormous resistance during the mid-1930s. Starting up again on wholly new economic, political, and social premises in the early 1950s, the evolution of mass distribution systems accelerated in the second half of the 1960s. By the early 1970s, Germany and France, as well as several smaller states including Belgium, Holland, Switzerland, and the Scandinavian countries, together with areas of north-central Italy, were at home with mass marketing, the supermarket, chain retailing, and the many other techniques and institutions that historians of the subject have characterized as the hallmarks of modern commerce.[1] At least until recently: For the history of modern commerce now has a new endpoint, the so-called post-Fordist dis-

---

1 There are, of course, significant studies of distribution by specialists and there are important sociohistorical studies of particular institutions, notably the department store. For the former, see in particular James B. Jefferys and Derek Knee, *Retailing in Europe: Present Structure and Future Trends* (London, 1962); see also James B. Jefferys, *Retailing Trading in Britain, 1850–1950: A Study of Trends in Retailing with Special Reference to the Development of Cooperatives, Multiple Shop, and Department Store Methods of Trading* (Cambridge, 1965); Richard S. Tedlow, *New and Improved: The Story of Mass Marketing in America* (New York, 1990); Robert Bartels, ed., *Comparative Marketing: Wholesaling in Fifteen Countries* (Homewood, Ill., 1963); John Benson and Gareth Shaw, eds., *The Evolution of Retail Systems, c. 1800–1914* (Leicester, 1992). For a specific institution, see a recent synthesis, William Lancaster, *The Department Store: A Social History* (London, 1995), in addition to the venerable study of H. Pasdermadjian, *The Department Store: Its Origins, Evolution, and Economics* (New York, 1949). On the

tribution systems using computerized communications systems to link segmented markets and vastly more intricate and dense global commodity
chains.[2]

Far from offering a seamless narrative about the progressive modernization of European commerce, in which the modern sector prevails over the
traditional, and innovative, usually U.S. marketing methods prevail over
archaic, time-worn European commercial techniques, this analysis considers the transformation of distribution systems with an eye to varying legacies of social stratification and competing strategies of economic development, highlighting the different charges these lend to changes in practices
and level of consumption.[3] Because the influence of American models of
mass consumption was so pervasive during the changeover to mass consumption in Europe, this history inevitably entails a transatlantic and comparative dimension. During the interwar years, more so in the depressed
1930s than in the relatively buoyant 1920s, anybody with an eye to updat-
ing local distribution systems, much less building mass consumer markets,
referred to the United States's experience as the premier mass consumer
society. Although "Americanization" may be a too-chewed-over and conceptually cumbersome term to characterize the changes we want to discuss

European department store, there is nothing comparable to William Leach, *Land of Desire: Merchants,
Power and the Rise of a New American Culture* (New York, 1993).

   What is missing is the study of distribution as "a social power structure" (Bartels, *Comparative Marketing,* 187). One fruitful approach is exemplified by Geoffrey Crossick and Hans-Gerhard Haupt,
The Petite Bourgeoisie in Europe, 1870–1914 (London, 1995), its focus the persistence of the petty
bourgeois way of life, embedded in the institutions of local manufacture, retailing, and distribution of
nineteenth-century Europe. Ben Fine and Ellen Leopold in *The World of Consumption* (London,
1993) lay out conceptual and empirical bases for the analysis of systems of provisioning in food and
clothing.

2 See Richard S. Tedlow, "The Fourth Phase of Marketing: Marketing History and the Business World
Today," in Richard S. Tedlow and Geoffrey Jones, eds., *The Rise and Fall of Mass Marketing* (New York,
1993), 8–35. On the 1980s marketing revolution in Europe, see Carl Gardner and Julie Sheppard,
Consuming Passion: The Rise of Retail Culture (London, 1989); see also the data presented in a marketing manual by Patrick Molle, *Le Commerce et la distribution en Europe* (Paris, 1992), and Brenda Sern-
quist and Madhav Kacker, *European Retailing's Vanishing Borders* (Westport, Conn., 1994). Some key
social and cultural ramifications are examined in Frank Mort, *Cultures of Consumption: Masculinities
and Social Space in Late Twentieth Century Britain* (London, 1996).

3 This is a sketch of a section of a larger study, "America in Europe, 1930–1970," other parts of
which have been published or presented as papers. See "Americanism for Export," *Wedge* 7–8
(1985): 74–81; "The Exception Proves the Rule: The American Example in the Recasting of Social-
ist Strategies in Interwar Europe," in *Pourquoi n'y a t-il pas de socialisme aux Etats-Unis?* (Why Is There
No Socialism in the United States?) (Paris, 1987), 167–92; "Mass Culture and Sovereignty: The
American Challenge to European Cinemas," *Journal of Modern History* 61, no. 1 (Mar. 1989): 53–87;
"The Arts of Purchase: How U.S. Advertising Subverted the European Poster," in Phil Mariani and
Barbara Kruger, eds., *Remaking History,* Discussions in Contemporary Culture, no. 4 (Seattle, 1989),
221–57; "The Challenge of American Advertising Arts in 1920s Europe," in *L'age des metropoles, les
années 20s* (catalogue) (Montreal, 1991); "Changing Consumption Regimes: 1930s–1960s, Time,
Money, and Work in the New European Household," paper presented at the conference La con-
struction historique du temps du travail, European University Institute, European Forum, 1994–5,
Oct. 28–29, 1994.

here, the analysis needs to account for the references to the United States's prior, if not avowedly superior accomplishments that crop up in every discussion over transforming distribution – from debating the relationship between manufacturers and wholesalers to dissecting consumer tastes. Eventually, American machinery, institutional models, techniques, and capital would prove very influential from the late 1940s in carrying out the changeover to mass distribution. But over the whole period from the 1920s to the 1970s, European societies were doubly challenged: on one level to respond to pressures emanating from the United States to widen and deepen markets both domestically and internationally; on another, to recognize the concept of social citizenship, in the terms in which it came to be defined in the United States, namely, as entitlement to a decent standard of living. This was to be achieved not by redistributive politics under the aegis of the Left, but in an avowedly apolitical way: by extending throughout society by means of high levels of individual consumption the huge accumulations of goods and higher profits obtained from enhanced productivity.[4]

That said, my concern here is to emphasize not the convergence of paths around a single hegemonic American model of consumer modernity as much as the diversity of trajectories. Ultimately, developments in each area were embedded in very different relationships between state and market, varying modalities of class stratification, and different notions of the rights and duties of citizens. In the 1930s and the 1960s, this variation determined notably different politics toward the modernization of distribution systems, in particular, the practices that affected consumers most directly, namely, local retailing.

DEFINING THE "PROBLEM" OF MODERN DISTRIBUTION

The problem of distribution was brought into focus in 1930s Europe as the intense emphasis on mass producing goods typical of the 1920s gave way to worries about finding markets in the face of depressed export trade and

---

4 Applying the term "social citizenship" to the American context and highlighting increased levels of consumption clearly constitute a broadening, some might say a corruption, of its original meaning, as advanced by the British reformer and political philosopher T. H. Marshall, *Citizenship and Social Class and Other Essays* (Cambridge, 1950; reprint, London, 1992). In Marshall's view, social citizenship, meaning effective equality, was acquired through welfare state reforms and other kinds of redistributive politics in the wake of World War II. Thereby, subjects who had been marginalized by market forces and thence deprived of economic and political equalities acquired through the recognition of individual rights and the acquisition of political suffrage reacquired social rights. The use of the term "social citizenship" here naturally risks that it be conflated with another neologism, "consumer citizenship." To speak of an American notion of social citizenship is to emphasize the difference between that social well-being acquired through individualist consumption and that acquired by means of collective provisions of welfare in terms of entitlement, power, and the definition of the good society.

shrinking domestic outlets. These worries, manifest in the surge of specialized studies, conferences, and institutions devoted to the study of distribution (which included advertising and marketing as well as wholesaling and
retailing), derived from several concerns.[5] The first concern, a long-
standing one, was the squeeze on small retailers as a result of competition.
The second was the Malthusian bias of businessmen, who were accused of
either ignoring the problem of outlets on the grounds that supply would
create its own demand or obstructing markets with cartels, tariffs, and other
market-constraining arrangements. A third concern were the rising costs of
distribution as a percentage of the total cost of goods to consumers. This
trend became clearly visible in the wake of the stabilization of European
currencies in the mid-1920s. In spite of government efforts to deflate prices
by cutting wages, retailing costs stayed stickily high. Finally, there was the
concern, dear to modernizing movements of the 1920s, to "rationalize"
society. The European scientific management movements were especially
prone to conceive of rationalization in a totalizing sense. If production was
to be revamped, managerial techniques had to be applied to all of the
anachronistic institutions on which production depended. Distribution
stood first and foremost, its operations, although visibly crucial to economic
efficiency, having hitherto eluded precise calculations of costs and benefits.[6]

A study of each European country would surely offer evidence of indigenous pressures to revamp the circuits of distribution. However, U.S. business
interests drove the effort to transcend national borders and conceptualize
distribution as an issue of global significance. The main way in which they
exercised this influence, leaving aside the actions of multinational enterprise, was through international nongovernmental agencies, the International Chamber of Commerce, or ICC, in the lead. Reorganized in the
wake of the war at the initiative of U.S. businessmen, the venerable ICC
proudly pioneered its new role as "international partner of the national
capitalist," supporting the "unspectacular but constructive everyday work of
experts" in a new "diplomacy of technics."[7] That "the problem of distribu-

5 For a contemporary bibliography, spanning the United States and Europe, see *Distribution in the
   United States: Selected References 1932–1942, with Supplement on Distribution in Foreign Countries and
   Particularly in Great Britain* (Washington, D.C., 1943); see also the published catalogue of the Kiel
   Library for World Economic History, Bibliothek, Institut für Weltwirtschaft, Kiel, Germany.
6 The following offer the most complete overviews of the interwar problematic: G. De Leener, *Les
   problèmes de la distribution* (Brussels, 1934); Roger Picard, *Formes et methodes nouvelles des entreprises com-
   merciales* (Paris, 1936); Jacques Dansette, *Les formes evoluées de la distribution: Problème économique-
   problème psychologique* (Brussels-Pauli, 1944). For studies on specific retailing institutions also address-
   ing larger issues of distribution, see in particular Werner Gabler, *Probleme der amerikanishen
   Warenhausen* (Zurich, 1934); Richard Mutz, *La vente à prix unique considerée comme nouvelle méthode
   d'organisation du commerce de détail,* rev. ed., trans. René Stolle (Paris, 1934).
7 George L. Ridgeway, *Merchants of Peace: Twenty Years of Business Diplomacy Through the International
   Chamber of Commerce, 1919–1938* (New York, 1938), 263–75.

tion" was central to this optimistic Hooverist diplomacy is suggested by the fact that the very act of sustained cooperation, ratified at the Washington Conference in 1931, took the form of the International Bureau of Distribution.

On that occasion, the ICC officials presented a magnificent multivolume study of business trends in Europe and the United States, volume 5 of which was called *Europe–United States of America: Trends in the Organization and Methods of Distribution in the Two Areas.* In it, the rapporteurs, in their own words, deployed a "method of attack that was objective and analytical," aggressively using numbers to create a surface – the market – that by minimizing historical differences allowed for comparability.[8] In fact, there was a remarkable disparity between the skimpiness of statistical data available to study Europe and the plethoric amounts available for the United States, where distribution had been the object of overweening business and governmental scrutiny since the turn of the century. Aside from suggesting that the problem occupied a very different position in the two areas, the sheer quantity of the U.S. data (and the prospect of prodigiously more with the compilation of the first national Census on Distribution in 1930) assured that American developments offered the basis for future comparisons and that U.S. practices defined the goals and means of distribution.

Hence, to predict from U.S. experience, the up-to-date term "distribution" should soon replace the anachronistic "commerce" still commonly used in Europe. Now the word "commerce" in common English usage since the seventeenth century, connoted reciprocal benefits of exchange and buying and selling together. In French (*commerce*) and Italian too (*commercio*), as well as in German (*Werbung*), it conjured up merchants and middlemen, as well as the corner grocer. Commerce implied that distribution was the main business of merchandising, but not the only one. By contrast, to use the term "distribution" was to treat commerce as only one of "the various activities and processes between the production of goods in final form for use and their delivery to and acceptance by the consumer." Others would include advertising and marketing. At the same time as the semantic deployment of "distribution" ousted the old middlemen of the commercial nexus, it championed a new human agent, the consumer. Indeed, the distinguishing feature of the "modern" distribution system was to "satisfy consumer wants by the most direct routes and at the lowest costs." To

---

8 *Europe–United States of America*, vol. 5: *Trends in the Organization and Methods of Distribution in the Two Areas* (Geneva, 1931). The preface was drawn up by F. P. Valentine, president of the Committee on Distribution of the American Section of the International Chamber of Commerce (ICC) and for the European side by L. Urwick, president of the International Management of Geneva, who was responsible for the comparative dimension of the volume.

conceptualize the terrain of distribution, the report likewise jettisoned the older notion of market as the sphere of exchange, abstracted from the physical sites in which exchange had once occurred, to speak of not one, but three markets: the "general market," which was an entity measured by assessments of territorial size, ethnic divisions, income, wealth, and so forth, and the actual "consumer" and "industrial" markets, both constituted by means of effective marketing techniques.[9]

In the process of acquainting experts with the techniques to measure the productivity of distribution networks, the report mapped out the panoply of institutions and procedures that in the United States were commonly referred to as the "channels of distribution."[10] At the same time, the report highlighted the anachronisms and social biases in European statistical gathering: In France, true to long-standing mercantilist outlooks, state offices assiduously gathered figures on grain prices and exports; German statistical inquiries focused on retailers in the interest of protecting the old *Mittelstand* of craftsmen and shopkeepers. Generally speaking, investigators of consumer expenditure practically exempted the bourgeoisie from scrutiny in the name of privacy, whereas they rummaged about in working-class households on the grounds that the data they accumulated from family budgets were necessary to calculate fair wages, organize social work, and provide relief. Finally, the report gave short shrift to the idea that the market occupied a distinct physical place or should be circumscribed by national boundaries. This study was proudly described as the first ever to regard the whole European area (excluding European Turkey and Soviet Russia) as a regional market, comparable as such to that of the United States. Indeed, the rapporteurs emphasized the commonalities of tastes and needs among Europeans within a wide inner circle extending from Edinburgh to Bilbao to Milan, Berlin, and Stockholm. Without overestimating the influence of this single report, it is safe to say that from 1931 until the early 1950s when the European Productivity Agency of the Organization for European Economic Cooperation launched Europe-wide surveys under the auspices of the United States–backed European Recovery Program (Marshall Plan), the ICC was the major reference point for European projects to modernize distribution.[11]

9 Ibid., preface, 10ff.
10 Margaret G. Reid, *Consumers and the Market,* 2d ed. (New York, 1939), 88ff.
11 ICC publications include various brochures and documents published by the International Distribution Committee on the occasion of ICC congresses, e.g.: *Practical Guide to the Most Important Publications in Several Countries Bearing on Consumption and Market Study,* doc. 6902 (Paris, 1939); Dudley A. Clark, comp., *Distribution Censuses: An International Study* (Paris, 1951); *Terms Commonly Used in Distribution and Advertising* (Basel, 1940), and various subsequent editions; International Chamber of Commerce, ed., *Distribution in 15 Countries: Statistical Survey,* no. 17 (Paris, 1953).

THE BOURGEOIS VERSUS THE FORDIST MODE
OF CONSUMPTION

Working off American notions about the essential facelessness of markets, ICC literature rarely dwelled on regional or national differences that were structural and cultural rather than income driven, accumulated over time, and the result of the different legacies of earlier commercial-capitalist development. Yet these legacies clearly stood behind the significant differences that in the 1931 report leaped out from the statistical charts yet the text glossed over as mere differences of degree in the interests of conceptualizing a common modernizing project and fostering transatlantic commerce.

Accordingly, U.S. circuits of distribution could be said to reflect a society in which the strategies of mass production industries to widen and deepen markets had early coalesced with the interests of the state, large distributive trades, and consumers to recast distributive chains in order to lower costs, regulate retail demand, and satisfy (and shape) mass consumer tastes. By the turn of the century, what we might call the mass or Fordist model of distribution - at the risk of anachronism since its development antedated by at least two decades that of the Ford factory system – involved the retooling of the whole circuitry of commercial mechanisms, from corporate design and production management to the floor displays of local shops. Eventually, the United States's distribution revolution gave rise to new systems of wholesaling and retailing – their pillars, the department store, chain-management operations, and mail-order houses. It also generated whole new industries such as advertising, as well as a new administrative science, namely, marketing. The circuitry was completed with the establishment of scores of governmental and private institutions to coordinate and study distributive processes, from the several specialized bureaus of the Department of Commerce and the National Industrial Conference Board to the National Bureau of Economic Research, the U.S. Chamber of Commerce, the National Department Store Association, a half-dozen major business schools, and numerous corporate marketing departments.

The long-term conditions favoring this circuity's establishment surely date to before the onset of large-scale corporations. The United States's relatively slight dependence on foreign trade pushed business back on developing protected home markets. In that sense, the United States's development contrasted with that of Great Britain, where food imports in the face of declining agriculture sped innovations in distributive systems.[12] Unlike Great Britain's free trading elites, though, the dominant political coalitions

12 Jefferys, *Retailing Trading in Britain*, 38ff.

in the United States were committed to protectionism. Nonetheless, they were generally unsympathetic to mercantilist attitudes toward intrastate and local commerce. Hence the United States was virtually without the structures of monopoly and privilege of old regime Europe, taking the form of guilds, internal trade barriers, and tariffs, or artificial burdens such as tax stamps on postings, newspapers, and other media. Since American cities had never been legally privileged sites of commerce, unlike the bourgeois towns of Europe emerging from feudalism, they lacked the periodic fairs and markets typical of European urban centers. In the absence of a true aristocracy or of a bourgeois culture that aped aristocratic mores, Republican ideology treated merchants less disdainfully than elsewhere. The growing belief that distribution could be organized as rationally and efficiently as production was a striking innovation with respect to views that treated the distributive trades, wholesaling in particular, as parasitical excrescences on productive enterprises, beset by monopolies and privileges, tainted by carnival humbug, and in the hands of peddlers, hucksters, speculators, and the other unsavory denizens of "Jewish" capitalism. Moreover, American business interests quickly acquired the confidence that rationality on the production side could go hand in hand with irrationality on the consumption side; impulse buying, product obsolescence, and ludic subcultures were all to be encouraged – in the interest of a more intense, rapid, and predictable circulation of goods.[13]

In the United States, by contrast to continental Europe, major innovations in distribution began in the late nineteenth century as large corporations responded to relatively higher wages and urbanization with standardized production lines. Their efforts to secure outlets in turn revolutionized wholesaling practices at the same time as the intensifying competition locally recast the retail trade. Meanwhile, national advertising changed the whole conception of the *market*, which now came to be identified with *marketing*. Accordingly, the market embraced a potentially infinite number of consumers, meaning all of those who might be reached with information about the manufacturers' products, their entity being estimated through statistically based marketing "sciences."[14]

13 For the nineteenth century, see George Burton Hotchkiss, *Milestones of Marketing: A Brief History of the Evolution of Market Distribution* (New York, 1938); see also Harold Barger, *Distribution's Place in the American Economy Since 1869* (Princeton, N.J., 1955); on the institutions of mass marketing, see Susan Strasser, *Satisfaction Guaranteed: The Making of the American Mass Market* (New York, 1989), and Richard S. Tedlow, *New and Improved: The Story of Mass Marketing in America* (New York, 1990). The effort to dominate the "irrational" and ludic elements of consumer culture was a constant goal of corporate elites, according to T. J. Jackson Lears, *Fables of Abundance: A Cultural History of Advertising in America* (New York, 1994).
14 On early development of marketing sciences, see the foreword of a special issue on marketing of the *Annals of the American Academy of Political and Social Science* 209 (May 1940): xii. Howard T. Hovde

This redefinition of the scale and significance of the market was given enormous impetus not only by the sustained rise in incomes from the turn of the century through the 1920s, but also by mammoth increases in consumer demand propelled by immigration and the neediness of a rapidly urbanizing population. In response to this demand, as early as the Progressive era, we can identify the emergence of a modernizing coalition, formed of larger-scale industrialists, wholesalers, and retailers; consumer organizations; government; and labor, all of whom were more or less interested in unrestricted domestic trade, economies of scale, standardized manufacture, and lower retail prices.

In this context, we can appreciate the huge growth and professionalization of advertising, which, together with novel pricing and display, offered a depersonalized mediation between manufacturers and consumers, at the same time as it appropriated the functions of the traditional intermediaries – local retailers with respect to both. In other words, oligopolistic firms under pressure to preserve their market shares linked their fortunes to the development of specialized agencies and modern communications technologies to replace the trust and information afforded by local knowledge.[15]

In continental Europe, by contrast, distribution remained deeply embedded in the bourgeois mode of consumption. With that term, I want to call attention to the consumption dimension of the pyramidal class constellation typical of European societies down through the 1950s. That different classes consume differently is a truism. Unlike in the United States, however, in which the huge and rapid influx of new goods, the social and physical mobility of the population, and rising incomes quickly generated a large middle stratum of consumers, drastically eroding the previous linking of consumption to class, in continental Europe the carefully demarcated systems of "barriers and levels" in consumption persisted down to World War II.[16] That the continental European hierarchy of taste and expenditure

---

proposed the discontinuation of the word "distribution" insofar as it was synonymous with marketing and confused with the specialized use of the term in economic theory.

15 Histories of advertising commonly imply that modern marketing provided information about new goods such as could not have been provided by older forms of retailing. However, there is no inherent reason that local retailers could not supply information. In Europe they continued to offer that service well into the 1970s.

16 This aspect of the European social stratification system has only been investigated at all systematically in France, by sociologists and anthropologists working under the influence, broadly speaking, of Emile Durkheim, starting with Charles Gide. The tradition of investigating consumer habits, focusing on family budget studies, continues in the twentieth century, starting with the absolutely central, but untranslated works of Maurice Halbwachs, *La classe ouvrière et les niveaux de vie: Recherches sur la hierarchie des besoins dans les sociétés industrielles contemporaines* (Paris, 1912); *L'evolution des besoins dans les classes ouvrières* (Paris, 1933). The brilliant work of Edmond Goblot focuses on the "barriers and levels" at work, including fashion, education, and household mores, *La barrière et le niveau: Etude sociologique sur la bourgeoisie française moderne* (Paris, 1925; reprint, Paris, 1967). For the same period, see Marcel Mauss's insights into the development of a commercially driven "national habitus," in "Notion

lasted so long was surely the result of low wages.[17] However, the consummate refinement of bourgeois taste and careful codification of cultural power around it were also inherited from old regime classifications of social distinction based on consumption. These were persistently incorporated into business strategies that very early, in view of narrow domestic markets, oriented manufacture to craft production on behalf of quality-conscious elites.[18] Even when income differences could be observed to diminish in the interwar years, patterns of household expenditure continued to differ notably, coding rank within the upper and middle classes, segregating the households of craft and small retailers and employees from workers, and setting off urban consumers from the vast semiautarkic peasant world in the countryside.[19] Indeed, the persistence of such consumption hierarchies during the interwar period in spite of the growing mass market, some increases in working-class incomes, and the declining fortunes of many bourgeois families suggested that differential consumption habits remained as significant to marking class boundaries as in the pre–World War I era.

The absence of a middle market was strikingly visible in the dualistic structure of the distribution system. The contrast was stunning between, on

de technique du corps" (1934), first published in *Journal de Psychologie* 32, nos. 3–4 (Mar.–Apr. 1936), and reprinted in Marcel Mauss, *Sociologie et Anthropologie,* 4th ed. (Paris, 1968), 365–8. From that body of work, it is a short leap to the studies of Pierre Bourdieu and his notion of cultural capital, e.g., Pierre Bourdieu, *Distinction: A Social Critique of the Judgement of Taste,* trans. R. Nice (Cambridge, Mass., 1984).

17 To compare wages and income is perhaps easier than to compare the effects of rising wages on standards of living and the nature of class stratification. In general, see Peter Scholliers, ed., *Real Wages in 19th- and 20th-Century Europe: Historical and Comparative Perspectives* (Oxford, 1989). On the United States compared to Great Britain, see Peter R. Shergold, *Working-Class Life: The "American Standard" in Comparative Perspective, 1899–1913* (Pittsburgh, 1982); on Germany compared to the United States and Great Britain, see Gerhard Bry, *Wages in Germany, 1871–1945* (Princeton, N.J., 1960); on Italy, see Mario Saibante, "Il tenore di vita del popolo italiano, prima dell'ultima guerra in confronto con quello degli altri popoli," in Centro di studi e piani tecnico-economici, Comitato interministeriale per la Ricostruzione, ed., *Piano per le importazioni e le esportazioni,* Pubblicazioni, no. 5 (Rome, 1947), app. C. The perception of the significant differences bound up with consumption, together with reflections on the difficulties of establishing comparisons, is signaled in Pierre Abelin, *Essai sur la comparaison internationale des niveaux de vie ouvrièrs* (Paris, 1938).

18 This argument is developed by Whitney Walton, *France at the Crystal Palace* (Berkeley, Calif., 1998); and with even greater precision and a more sweeping scope of analysis by Leora Auslander, *Taste and Power: Furnishing Modern France* (Berkeley, Calif., 1996).

19 Class differentiation in household expenditures is, of course, the subject of long traditions of study, dating back to midnineteenth-century pioneers, E. Ducpetiaux, F. Le Play, and E. Engel. For our period, in additional to Halbwachs, see Henry Delpech, *Recherches sur le niveau de vie et les habitudes de consommation (Toulouse, 1936–1938)* (Paris, 1938). On the rural household in France, see Antoine de Cambiaire, who estimated that 20 percent of the total national output of goods and services was consumed within the households in which it was produced and did not pass through the market. Antoine de Cambiaire, *L'autoconsommation agricole en France* (Rennes, 1952). In Italy, which was somewhat more rural than France and where household autarky was pushed by the fascist regime, autoconsumption was estimated at one-third the total national product. Vera Zamagni, "Dinamica e problemi della distribuzione commerciale al minuto tra il 1880 e la II guerra mondiale," in *Mercati e consumi: Organizzazione e qualificzione del commercio in Italia dal XII al XX secolo,* Archivo Storico del'Industria Italiana, Studi del commercio (Bologna, 1986), 598.

the one hand, the modernity of the grand department stores and the specialized luxury shops of the major towns and provincial capitals that catered to shoppers in search of the novel and exotic unnecessary and, on the other hand, the traditionalism of the myriad drab retail outlets that provided staples to customers who spent as much as half their income on food. By contrast with the United States, where department stores accounted for about 10 percent and small independent shops for 57 percent of the annual turnover in retailing (the remainder being accounted for by chains), on the Continent, even in the best of times, the former accounted for perhaps 5 percent whereas small retailers contributed from 79 percent (Germany) to 91 percent (Italy).[20] The bourgeois mode of consumption was also visible in outlooks toward innovation. Laissez-faire ideologies notwithstanding, the regnant outlooks favored both sheltering national markets from outside competition and protecting acquired positions within domestic markets whether by vulnerable retailers in battle against left-wing cooperatives and national chains or by overbearing big manufacturers manipulating cartel arrangements.

The tensions engendered by the bourgeois mode of consumption were visible in class conflict around distribution. This conflict was manifest in the formation of vigorous left-wing cooperative movements, not to mention the huge hostility to them. It was also evident in the animus against the spread of mass consumption, not just because mass consumption implied redistributive policies, but also because it upset consumption-reaffirming class hierarchies. That struggles over the politics of distribution would figure so prominently in the push to the Right in interwar politics acknowledged the swing position of middle classes whose fortunes seemed so bound up with traditional retailing practices; in France, shopkeepers were still regarded as the pillar of the republic; in Germany, the backbone of the nation.[21]

THE CENTRALITY OF THE SMALL RETAILER

If we focus here not on the most innovative players, but on the most traditional, namely, small retailers, it is because they played such a pivotal, if fun-

---

20 See Vera Zamagni, *La distribuzione commerciale in Italia fra le due guerre* (Milan, 1980), 23; see also "Le conseguenze della crisi del '29 sul commercio al dettaglio in Europa," *Commercio* 9 (1981): 10.
21 A wide-ranging overview is found in Rudy Koshar, ed., *Politics and the Lower Middle Classes in Interwar Europe* (New York and London, 1990). Contemporary analyses highlight the abiding resonance of the shopkeepers' cries of "wolf," notwithstanding their diminishing numbers among middle class occupational categories. Ernst Maheim, "Les consommateurs, les classes moyennes et les formes modernes du commerce de detail," *Revue Economique Internationale* 29, no. 1 (Jan. 1937): 228–56; see also Fernand Simonet, *Le petit commerce du detail: Sa lutte avec le grand commerce du detail* (Paris, 1937), 70ff.

damentally ambiguous role in shoring up the bourgeois mode of consumption. On the one hand, they were fated to be losers. Or at least so it appeared from the high mortality rates of single firms and the repeated dire predictions about their imminent demise by liberal and Marxian political economists. On the other hand, small retailers laid claim to being the mainstay of the bourgeois social system, by virtue of their venerable lineage, their proprietorship, and their performance as cultural-economic mediators in the hierarchy of consumption. Although many individual firms were fated to live and die like mayflies (*Eintagsfliege*), to recall Werner Sombart's disparaging description, the category as a whole displayed a Darwinian tenacity, being constantly replenished by struggling rural immigrants and the urban underemployed.[22]

That small retailers could claim – or it could be claimed on their behalf – that they were central to the mechanism of bourgeois social-cultural reproduction could resonate as truth if we imagine for a moment the operations of the typical European food retailing establishment of the 1930s. This would have been an unincorporated one family business, owned and operated with help from relatives or from one or two paid workers. Store hours would have been as long as ten to twelve hours daily, but the shopkeeper might reopen well after closing if the customers or their custom were sufficiently important. Clients were mainly from the neighborhood, and they would have known both the shopkeeper and each other. They shopped daily, often using credit, buying necessities almost exclusively. They were indifferent to packaging and, being little exposed to advertising, rarely bought with an eye to brand names. The shopkeepers or their assistants took their order, fetched the articles from behind the counter, measured them out, wrapped them, touted up the prices, and either took cash or debited the sum to the account book. If there were any eccentricity in the orders, on the side either of excess or of privation, it would have been noted by one and all.

All else being equal, the shopkeeper too was a traditionalist. Because his customers were bound to him by ties of community and credit, he had little reason to innovate. Many of his business calculations were intuitive, mistakes in his own favor offsetting errors in respect to his creditors and customers. He would have set prices "irrationally," which is to say that he did not compare them to the "market," namely, to the prices set by his competitors in other localities nor even his own original outlays or the costs of

---

22 Simonet, *Le petit commerce du detail,* passim; Dansette, *Les formes evoluées de la distribution,* 70ff.; Dietrich Denecke and Gareth Shaw, "Traditional Retail Systems in Germany," in Benson and Shaw, eds., *Evolution of Retail Systems.*

restocking, as turnover was slow and record keeping negligent. In a pricing system with much haggling and discounting, in which owners and clients pretty much agreed on the relationship between price and value, the price system was infinitely and often casually customized.[23] In practice, this might mean that the shopkeeper sweetened prices for madame's captivating servant girl, musing about her charms and deferring to madame herself, who kept an eagle eye on the household ledger books. But he extended no favors to the aged and half-deaf widow, and he trifled with the sums charged to the slatternly housewife who entrusted a dim-witted neighbor lad to haul home her groceries.

It is notorious that this solidaristic form of commerce had long been under pressure, and that from the 1880s, if not earlier, the retailing trades had developed an elaborate ideology of defense, in the course of which they clarified their role in the preservation of the class order, craft traditions, and national consumer culture. In Germany, this defense was especially vociferous and organized, the context being disquiet over the precarious status of the *Mittelstand*, pervasive outlooks that saw society as a fixed natural social hierarchy, and real doubt about whether modern commercial civilization was not wholly antithetical to Germany's status as a *Kulturnation*, in which the courage of stalwart *Helden* (heroes) of Prussia's aristocrat past checked the chicanery of parvenu *Handler* (merchants).[24] Over time, it was claimed on behalf of small retailers, they were the part that represented the whole of the middle class. Their preservation was indispensable to the sanctity of the bourgeois order itself.

THE CRISIS OF THE BOURGEOIS MODE: NEOMERCANTILISM VERSUS REFORM COALITIONS

The Great Depression of the 1930s set the stage for the last struggle around the bourgeois mode of consumption. In the course of this crisis all defenses would be pulled out, most radically and violently in Germany. The ultimate outcome was the elimination of small-scale retailing as the mainstay and signifier of the bourgeois mode of consumption. Thereafter the distribution

---

23 See comments on actual and ideal practices by Otto D. Schaefer, director of the Reichskuratorium für Wirtschaftlichkeit, International Chamber of Commerce, *Helping Retailers to Better Profits: The Comparison of Retail Operating Costs,* no. 86 (Paris, 1934), passim; see also Jefferys, *Retailing Trading in Britain,* 48ff.

24 The contrast was incorporated into the title of Werner Sombart's notorious *Helden and Händler* (1916), a wartime tract counterpoising heroic Germany with merchant Britain. On the nineteenth-century petty bourgeois defense more generally, see Geoffrey Crossick and Hans-Gerhard Haupt, eds., *Shopkeepers and Master Artisans in Nineteenth-Century Europe* (New York, 1984); for the best known terrain of struggle, see Philip Nord, *Paris Shopkeepers and the Politics of Resentment* (Princeton, N.J., 1986). For Germany, see Robert Gellately, *The Politics of Economic Despair* (London, 1975).

system would slowly be reshaped around a new middle-class social formation. Its innovators would be an amalgam of modernizers from old firms
and entrepreneurs in new endeavors such as marketing and advertising.The
circuitry would move from the local and personal to the national and impersonal. More and more, business culture would change its emphasis from the
efficiency of the producer to the rationality of the consumer. Distribution,
which had once been an appendage of the producer, a central ally of a mercantilist conception of political economy, would move to be the dynamic
factor of economic growth and an ally of the consumer.

   In this respect, the 1930s were truly crisis years for the old arrangements
of distribution and the myriad interests invested in them. With the compression of industrial prices, commercial costs started to show up hugely,
inducing experts to investigate prices and costs while agitating consumers
with a new awareness of their collective interests. With demand so unpre-
dictable and consumer purchasing power, although apparently rising overall, fluctuating erratically, more and more resources were devoted to service
competition. This trend put great pressure on small retailers, who in turn
loudly protested the unfair competition of multiple-shop firms and variety
chain stores. Increasingly, state policy was uncertain as to whether to support wages and workers by backing more efficient distribution or to support retailers with price maintenance and other protections. Both choices
had wide political ramifications, the former being especially risky since the
modernization of retailing implied association with left-wing cooperativism, unfettered big business, and the cosmopolitan outlooks identified
with the United States and international "Jewish influence."To support the
rationalization of retailing also risked losing influence over consumers to
unbridled consumption and impersonal market forces.

   The powerful coalitions of interest that shaped up around the defense of
traditional retailing practices in the mid-1930s thus cannot be dismissed as
the last gasp of desperate petty bourgeois shopkeepers, now under the wing
of conservative and fascist politicians. The most conspicuous results were
laws that directly or indirectly sought to restrict and limit the development
of the multiple-shop, variety chain store, and other forms of large-scale
retailing. These were introduced in most of the states of western continental Europe, Austria and Germany in the lead. The major exceptions were
Italy, where new laws seemed unwarranted because of prior legislation and
the slow introduction of new retailing practices, and Sweden, whose evolution was closer to that of Great Britain and the United States.[25]

25 Walter Froelich,"European Experiments in Protecting Small Competitors," *Harvard Business Review*
    17, no. 4 (summer 1939): 442–52; see also Walter Froelich, "Changes in the Central European Retail

Behind this legislation lay the struggle between two outlooks on the modern market: One, the Americanized or Fordist vision, foresaw a whole new nexus of institutions revolving around the rationalized distribution networks of major corporations. This outlook emphasized low unit costs, standardized goods, high turnover, and consumer choice. In the United States it was supported by the New Deal, organized labor, and big business, and consumers were its beneficiaries. The other outlook can be described as neomercantilist. This advocated protected markets within which government and the corporatist organizations of wholesalers and retailers would revamp distribution. This outlook claimed to reconnect craft and customers by improving the quality and range of goods and of the services established to sell them. The coalition behind it included those sectors of big business operating through cartelized distribution systems. It had the widespread support of small retailers and gained backing from the state. It operated at the expense of the consumer.

The latter coalition exploited the idea that European distribution had to be treated as a "social question," the solution to which would be found both in legal protections and a more organized and scientific approach to defending middle-class interests. Arguing against those who highlighted the statistical insignificance of the small retailer to the middle classes and reproached them for their monopolistic pricing practices, supporters spoke of "social utility" and "economies of locality," intangibles such as community goodwill and services such as store credit, repair work, and advice, which were especially important to neophyte consumers and to operation of new consumer durables such as radios and household electric appliances.[26]

In national policy considerations, arguments in support of the small retailer were secondary to broader arguments that to defend the small retailer was also to safeguard the social order and national identity. Ultimately, autarkic economic policies designed to protect national industries and balance of trade affected consumption as well as production. Late 1930s autarkic regimes, notably in Germany and Italy, contemplated all kinds of restraints on domestic consumption, including curbs on alien institutions like the

---

Trade," *Journal of Marketing* 4, no. 3 (Jan. 1940): 259–63; David R. Craig, "Recent Retailing Trends in Europe," *Dun's Review* 47 (Dec. 1939), 5–9.

26 Simonet, *Le petit commerce du detail*, 70ff.; see also Hermann Levy, *The Shops of Britain: A Study of Retail Distribution* (London, 1947). In an important study from the late 1930s, not published until after the war, Hermann Levy took the British case to argue that there was a social utility, if not economic logic, behind the persistence of small shopkeeping in a retailing economy that was in many respects as modern as the American, but where small retailers accounted for 60 percent of total retail turnover and 80 percent of the total establishments.

chain store and bans on luxury imports such as coffee, advertising and shop window signs in foreign languages, and cultural commodities like film and fashion. All of these goods and innovations challenged conventional notions of value, craft, and appropriate consumer behavior.

THE CHAIN STORE: PRICE, QUALITY, AND CONSUMER SOVEREIGNTY

In the eyes of the neomercantilist coalition, the variety or unit price store was the archdevil. Chain retailing was by no means new in Europe. The older multiple shops, as they were also called, had usually specialized in particular trades, such as food, women's wear, or shoes. In other words, they delivered familiar assortments of goods at familiar prices, only with greater efficiency. By contrast, the unit price store grouped together all variety of expensive merchandise, from processed foods and feather dusters to windup clocks, selling the whole range at one or two fixed prices. As in the five and dime stores in the United States, the prices might range: in Germany from 10 pfennigs to 1 mark, then from 10, 25, 50, 75, to 100 marks; in France, from 1 to 50 centimes up to 3, 25, and 50 francs. In sheer quantity, stores of this type were not especially numerous in the mid-1930s: There were perhaps twelve thousand in all of Europe, including Great Britain. Whereas they accounted for as much as 7 percent of the retail turnover in England, they yielded only 1.3 percent in France, 1.5 percent in Germany, and 0.3 percent in Italy, compared to 23 percent in the United States.[27] Few of these enterprises were actually promoted by U.S. firms. With its 759 European subsidiaries, Woolworth's was the conspicuous exception.[28] In spite of its relatively small numbers the chain store became the object of wide-ranging regulation in all European countries except Britain and Sweden, where the protectionist coalitions proved unsuccessful.[29]

27 Figures derived from Giuseppe Lucrezio, *I magazzini a prezzo unico in Europa e in America* (Città di Castell, 1943), 5. On the one-price store in Europe, see Marguerite Ensèlme, "Les Magasins à prix uniques: leur fonction dans le commerce du detail," J.D. diss., University of Bordeaux, 1936, in addition to Mutz, *La vente à prix unique considerée*, and especially Simonet's nuanced study, *Le petit commerce du detail*.

28 There is no study of Woolworth's in Europe; information can be culled from Mutz, who was a consultant to the firm, *La vente à prix unique considerée*; see also *Transatlantic Trade* (June 1937), which has Woolworth operating eighty-two stores in Germany, fourteen in Berlin alone.

29 On the contentious politics around American chain stores in the 1930s, see Joseph Cornwall Palamountain Jr., *The Politics of Distribution* (Cambridge, Mass., 1955); on the legal significance of the 1936 Robinson-Patman Act, see Ewald T. Greter, "Marketing Legislation," *Annals of the American Academy of Arts and Sciences*, special issue no. 209: *Marketing in Our American Economy*, ed. Howard T. Hovde (May 1940): 165–75.

Since the one-price store was not unlike the department store or other retailing innovations that similarly offered new variety, high turnover, and low prices as a function of economies of bulk buying and low operating costs, one might appropriately ask, Why no such resistance? Like chain stores, of which they were an offshoot, the one-price stores were accused of various unfair practices: cornering manufacturers, cutting wages for employees, selling brand names discounted as bargain bait, and depriving the communities in which they were situated of their rightful share of the market profits. In turn, regulations against them took the form of price maintenance, discriminatory taxes, restrictions on services, and outright curbs on new establishments.

The resistance was motivated by fear of losing the values and identity embedded in earlier forms of commerce. Thus, the most troubling issue for observers was the success, evidenced by the chains' incursions, of modern retailing's strategy of moving downward and outward in terms of class and locality. One-price marketing responded to two major gaps in the distribution cycle that the department store, with its tendency to remain in the major commercial cities and to move to an upscale clientele, had not addressed: One gap was the outlying urban areas and towns under 100,000 people; the other was the gap between quality and price that was satisfied by offering a range of nonbranded convenience goods at low fixed price.[30] Previously the institutions of retailing had cleaved to the division between luxury and subsistence, between the "palace of consumption" and the lowly food provisioner. Now, in search of new profits, with capital and know-how from the department stores themselves, large-scale operators appropriated the successful ploys of the department store in the display, assortment, turnover, and pricing of goods. In so doing, the one-price store damaged small businesses by undercutting their position with respect to suppliers and their influence over consumers.

Indeed, small businesses desperately complained about their loss of control over pricing goods. Unable to lower costs or improve services, they responded by seeking regulations to maintain prices. But price maintenance was a hard policy to sustain unless the elasticity of demand was small as it was for staples or in the absence of rival outlets. Moreover, prosecuting violators was difficult. Sometimes efforts backfired; in Catholic, corporatist, and heavily regulated Austria, it was reported that the special tribunals set up to prosecute independent retailers for underselling their competitors

---

30 Mutz, *La vente à prix unique considerée*, 2–3.

only enhanced the defendants' popularity. Not surprisingly, customers bitterly resented that store owners should be sentenced for selling too cheaply.[31]

The protest against the one-price variety store was directed not just against lower prices but the use of price to establish quality. The changeover from individualized pricing to fixed, clearly marked prices is a momentous one since it demands that consumers and retailers adopt a new understanding of value. In the typical small store stocked with a familiar set range of items, price policy permitted some bargaining, precisely because both merchant and client agreed on estimates of the item's quality, its craftsmanship, and its use. As the quantity of new goods proliferated and new items were offered for sale, customers could not easily determine the relationship between quality and price.[32] To orient customers, the one-price store grouped goods according to price categories, the marked price thereby fixing the "objective valuation" of the good. In turn, the housewife, having satisfied the need for staples, was offered a clutter of new goods. She could use her pin money, say ten pfennigs, fifty centimes, or five lire, to choose among them. Lacking other product information, she relied on the posted price to estimate the worth of the object's characteristics. The upshot of this system, it was protested, was to gull ignorant customers into buying "useless" and "bad quality" articles. Its real fault was to undercut the shopkeeper's mastery and to challenge the tenets of a moral economy based on fixed needs for fixed social groups.[33]

Behind the protest over the shift in power from the personalized shopkeeper to impersonal large-scale retailing, we can discern protests against

31 Froelich, "European Experiments," 449.
32 We must emphasize the various significance attributed to money, as Viviana Zelizer suggests in "The Social Meaning of Money: Special Monies," *American Journal of Sociology* 95, no. 2 (Sept. 1989): 342–77. The relationship of price consciousness to purchasing power is explored briefly but suggestively in Hugo E. Pipping, *The Standard of Living: Its Conceptualization and Place in Economics,* Societas Scientarum Fennica, no. 17 (Helsingfors, 1953), 178, which also underscores the ambiguous attitudes toward money in societies in which currency fluctuations confuse money values. "People use money as a yardstick, but do not trust it when they have become index-minded in time of war and inflation, nor do they trust it when status and standards are devalued." As soon as customers can avail themselves of self-service, Philippe Perrot remarks with some overstatement, "le savoir d'achat" can become as important as "le pouvoir d'achat"; that is, "purchasing knowledge becomes as important as purchasing power" (Philippe Perrot, *Les dessus et les dessous de la bourgeoisie: Une histoire du vetement au XIXe siècle* (Paris, 1981), 155).
33 In effect, the new pricing system is a preliminary response, pending a far broader and more intense initiation, to the problem of initiating to new products consumers who previously had been habituated to define the appropriate categories for the interpretation of their needs under the influence of highly structured socialization patterns. When the characteristics of goods change quickly and continuously, so much so that the goods become rapidly changing constellations of qualities and previous categories of need dissolve, individuals' capacity to judge becomes disoriented. On this, see William Leiss, *The Limits to Satisfaction: An Essay on the Problem of Needs and Commodities* (Toronto, 1976), 88ff.

the disruptive implications of "consumer sovereignty." The term, as originally conceived in American usage, implied recognition of the formal freedom of choice of consumers, made operational by higher income and the
intense competition of market agents.[34] In Europe, social reformers had
advanced ideas of consumer agency akin to this concept since the turn of
the century. For example, the leading theorist of French cooperativism,
Charles Gide, had long advocated that the consumer be king. In a charming word play on Descartes's motto, French cooperativists stressed the centrality of consumption to personhood by placing the slogan *Je depense, donc
je suis,* on the masthead of their journal.[35]

However, consumer citizenship in the European context emphasized
social participation rather than individual freedom, equality of rights
acquired through economic redistribution and political organization rather
than by means of consumer choices exercised in the marketplace. In any
case, the possibility of enhancing citizenship rights by means of increased
consumption, according to European views, presumed that consumers
shared a common understanding of taste and quality. If this was not an
innate characteristic or the result of a shared standard of living, it was readily acquired through the camaraderie of consumer cooperatives and political associations. Consequently, it was with real dismay that reformers discovered that when offered wider choice, consumers who were assumed to
satisfy their wants with "the purchase of objects that were unique and individual" showed a "distinct preference for uniformity in necessities but also
in taste in general."[36] Unguided by any standard but price, modern consumers threatened to forsake not just an economic institution, local retailing, but also a social and cultural legacy that was indispensable to the class
order and to community solidarity.

The spread locally of an out-of-control American style of consumer sovereignty, together with the growing internationalization of markets for consumer goods in the wake of World War I, raised the scary uncertainty that
the growing taste for everyday commodities wouldn't be satisfied within

---

34 On the origin of and multiple and ambiguous meanings of the term "consumer sovereignty," see
   Jerome Rothenberg, "Consumer Sovereignty," *International Encyclopedia of the Social Sciences* (New
   York, 1968), 3:326–35. Rothenberg argues that the term, although implied in Adam Smith's work
   and in that of the neoclassical economists, is first used only in 1936 by W. H. Hutt in *Economists and
   the Public* (London, 1936).
35 The Cartesian bon mot is, of course, "Je pense donc je suis." On cooperativism and the fertile thinking about consumption at the turn of the century, see Rosalind L. Williams, *Dream Worlds: Mass Consumption in Late Nineteenth-Century France* (Berkeley, Calif., 1982). On French cooperativism generally, see Ellen Furlough, *Consumer Cooperation in France: The Politics of Consumption, 1834–1930*
   (Ithaca, N.Y., 1991).
36 Pierre Arlet, *La consommation, l'education du consommateur* (Sarlat, 1939), 143ff.

the confines of the national market. This dread fueled protectionist campaigns to "buy national" as early as the mid-1920s. From the middle of the
next decade, Europe's so-called command economies took up the issue of
regulating consumer behavior in the interest of economic planning and
national security.[37] In that context, observers referred to the American
experience, not to condemn the idea of consumer sovereignty (as admirers
of American free-trade capitalism might expect), but to extol the protectionist impulses that in the United States during the late nineteenth century had inspired the world's first "buy national" campaigns. European consumers had to develop "a national economic consciousness," a French
observer recalled. In support, he fulsomely acknowledged the economist
Simon N. Patten's insistence on engendering "national habits of consumption" consistent with the U.S. resources and production skills. Most French
consumer theorists limited themselves to advocating consumer education,
to teach consumers to request the "quality" of "artisan" products in the face
of "taste for the standardized, ersatz, product line."[38] Some were becoming
sharply aware that drives to nationalize consumption standards could degen-
erate into political outrages. The same French expert who approved of Patten's protectionism cringed at the sight of the placards at the 1934 Nuremberg rallies of the Nazi Party that read, "Tell me where you buy, and I'll tell
you who you are. If you can't pass up a Jewish or foreign merchant, you
aren't German."[39]

POSTWAR STOCKTAKING

The neomercantilist strategies that shored up the bourgeois model of consumption were so deeply implicated in the new order from 1940 to 1945
that Nazi Germany established on the European continent that its final
defeat in April 1945 reverberated in every practice with which it was associated – including protected and traditionalist distribution systems.[40] In the
event, the problem of distribution emerged from the war with a new profile: the sheer destruction of commerce in bombed out urban neighbor-

---

37 On command economies and consumption, see the important studies of Gaston Defossé, *La place du
    consommateur dans l'economie dirigée,* 2d ed. (Paris, 1941), and Henry Laufenburger, with M. David and
    P. Benaerts, *L'organisation du commerce dans l'economie dirigée* (Paris, 1944), together with his earlier "La
    consommation dirigée en Allegmagne," *X Crise,* no. 36 (Mar. 1937): 23–31.
38 Arlet, *La consommation,* 143ff.; see also Georges Blanc, *Le consommateur dans l'organisation de l'economie:
    Consommation libre ou consommation dirigée?* (Bar-Le-Duc, 1943).
39 Arlet, *La consommation,* 149.
40 Already during the war, the Americans, not to mention their allies, foresaw the central role of distri-
    bution (and consumption more widely) in reconstruction. Dansette's study, completed just miles
    away from the passage of the war front in Belgium in 1944, testifies to this optimism.

hoods and wrecked transport and communication systems. The black market and currency fluctuations wreaked havoc with traditional delivery systems as did years of rationing. On top of this, there was pressure to supply occupying armies, destitute civilians, and swelling refugee populations.

The biggest challenge of all sprang from U.S. political and ideological hegemony, which pressed home the intellectual bankruptcy of mercantilist outlooks. In postwar reconstruction debates, protectionism was linked not just to Nazi control, but also to the USSR's closed economy. At the same time, Americanizers advanced a notion of democracy that put consumer choices and satisfaction at the center of reconstruction. Leading European experts visited U.S. retailing organizations and firms in the context of the European Recovery Program (ERP) "productivity missions" and as the American supermarket began to appear to be a feasible model with the development of the Common Market and Europe's "auto-frigo" revolution of the early 1960s. American brands flooded onto the European distribution networks, and in the 1960s, and perhaps sooner, U.S. capital was invested in European retailing operations.[41]

Nevertheless, although Europeans interested in modernizing distribution networks had become well acquainted with the latest in U.S. techniques and methods, often under programs sponsored by the ERP, significant transformations did not occur until the second half of the 1950s. The huge increase in self-services in 1950s Europe is symptomatic: rising from 1,200 in 1950 to 45,500 in 1960, including 600 supermarkets.[42] This rise was especially notable in the land of small shops, Germany, where labor shortages and the rising pay in industry sucked away family and paid employees from the traditional retailers. In 1951 there were still only 39 self-service stores in West Germany. By 1955 there were 203; by 1960, only five years later, their number had shot up to 17,132. By 1965 West Germany had more than 53,000 self-service shops.[43]

---

41 K. H. Henksmeier, "The Economic Performance of Self-Service in Europe," OEEC, EPA, 1960; the French journal *Libre-Service Actualité*, which was in close contact with fraternal institutions in Belgium, West Germany, and the United States, provides a limpid picture of development from within the movement. See also Michael Wildt's important *Am Beginn der "Konsumgesellschaft": Mangeler-fahrung, Lebenshaltung, Wohlstandshoffnung in Westdeutschland in den fünfziger Jahre* (Hamburg, 1994), especially the pages highlighting American assistance to independent chains in the interest of solving the "small shopkeeper problem" and establishing a bulwark against communism.

42 Jefferys and Knee, *Retailing in Europe,* 106. More generally on the new trajectory of mass consumption see Howard P. Whidden, "Birth of a Mass Market: Western Europe," *Harvard Business Review* 33, no. 3 (May–June 1955): 101–7; François Gardès, "L'evolution de la consommation marchande en Europe et aux U.S.A. depuis 1960," *Consommation: Revue de socio-economie* 30, no. 2 (Apr.–June 1983): 3–32; see also Louis Levy-Garboua, "Les modes de consommation de quelques pays occidentaux: Comparaisons et lois d'évolution (1960–1980)," *Consommation: Revue de socio-economie* 30, no. 1 (Jan.–Mar. 1983): 4–52.

43 Wolfgang Disch, *Der Gross- und Einzelhandel in der Bundesrepublik* (Cologne, 1966), 60.

These changes, which have been characterized as amounting to a "commercial revolution," have to be seen in the context of broader changes in the European market, society, and values. The most obvious change was rising income, which must in turn be traced to the enhanced productivity that resulted from technological innovations and economies of scale and scope that would have been unthinkable without the widening and deepening of European markets under the pressure of U.S. free-trade doctrines. In effect, the formation of the Common Market after 1957 caused Europe to look more like the inner circle of the two Europes identified in the ICC's 1931 distribution study.[44]

State policy was obviously significant to this change, although different legislation seems to have produced not dissimilar results, other factors being equal. Thus the French laws of December 31, 1945, and May 24, 1951, and the emphasis in the Second Plan on promoting consumption carried a strong message on the need to modernize distributive networks. By contrast, West Germany's restrictive *Ladenschlussgesetz,* the Shop Closing Act of 1956, reflected the fear of *Verdrangungswettbewerb,* or "displacing competition," that the "social market" of West Germany's Christian Democratic government was supposed to prevent. Overriding the opposition of the self-styled "consumer democrat," Ludwig Erhard, the architect of West Germany's economic miracle, the law was passed with the support of unions, retailers' associations, and conservative Catholics. Whether this legislation testified to a persistent reverence for the small retailer, social Catholic distaste for mass consumption, or the tight labor market of the German economic miracle bears study. Although it was bothersome to consumers, nothing suggests the law curbed the modernization of distribution or the competitiveness of big German retailers. In Italy, retailing continued to be governed by the late 1920s regulations. It is doubtful that this alone appreciably slowed the modernization of retailing. Other factors such as high unemployment and the Italian Republic's casual attitude toward collecting taxes from small entrepreneurs were far more significant in preserving small retailers.[45]

More generally, we have to look at the vast social and cultural transformations behind the remarkably accelerated spread of mass consumption

---

44 J. Frederic Dewhurst et al., *Europe's Needs and Resources: Trends and Prospects in Eighteen Countries* (New York, 1961), chap. 5.

45 On postwar retailing generally, two period documents, see Jefferys and Knee, *Retailing in Europe,* passim; on France, see René Peron, "Les commerçants dans la modernisation de la distribution," *Revue française de sociologie* 32, no. 2 (Apr.–June 1991): 179–208; on Germany, see Bruno Tietz, *Konsument und Einzelhandel: Strukturwandlungen in der Bundesrepublik Deutschland von 1950 bis 1975* (Frankfurt am Main, 1966).

from the mid-1950s through the 1960s: the extraordinarily rapid rates of population growth composed of high postwar birth rates and immigration; the huge urbanization with its proliferation of new households, the result of rural exodus and "decohabitation"; the new needs and values that were the result of higher incomes, exposure to new products, access to credit, and new gender roles, all of which responded to and reinforced changing class stratification.

When we speak of the transformation of the pyramidal structure of class relations under bourgeois society, what Henri Mendras calls the "middle-class constellation," we need to remember that this entailed a triple change: The first involved the reclassifying of differences within the bourgeoisie proper, as a rentier class was transformed into a professional elite, with a life-style publicized as akin to that of the middle class of cadres. The second change involved the redefining of the relations between the working class and a lower middle class, formed less and less of craftsmen and shopkeepers and more of salaried employees in service occupations. Finally, change entailed the elimination of the peasantry.[46] Urbanization was obviously crucial to all of this; it promoted new consumer mores and needs and gave impetus to the new entrepreneurship in distribution, flourishing around the edges of the old town centers and in the provinces away from the capital cities. In France, some of the leading innovators came from the western agricultural regions of Normandy and Brittany, the latter a real backwater until its remarkable modernization in the 1960s. The transformation of the Norman wholesaler Promodès from a regional company focusing mainly on wholesaling into a large diversified international group focusing on retailing was emblematic. The new company joined two rivalrous old family grocery firms, the venerable Duval-Lemonniers of Carentan and the Halleys of Cherbourg, who merged their forces in the early 1960s to go national. In 1962, they opened the first supermarket; in 1964, the first large cash-and-carry self-service; in 1970, the first hypermarket; in 1976, their first stores abroad; in 1979, they went public on the Paris Stock Exchange; and in 1980, they opened their first store in the United States. The scope of this development, the company history aptly records, suggests, "More than a change of size, it is a change of culture" (Plus qu'un changement de taille, c'est un changement de culture).[47]

With fuller study on, say, changes in family decision making processes, income distribution, and household organization, we shall better capture

---

46 Henri Mendras and Alistair Cole, *Social Change in Modern France* (Cambridge, 1991); Luc Boltanski, *The Making of a Class: Cadres in French Society*, trans. Arthur Goldhammer (Cambridge, 1987), has notably important observations about the formation of a middle-class life-style.
47 *Promodès: Du cabas au caddie: Histoire d'un pionnier de la distribution* (Paris, 1987), 11.

the cultural dimension of this consumer revolution. Edouard Leclerc, the onetime Jesuit seminarian from Landerneau in Brittany turned apostle on behalf of discount food selling, gives us some insight into the pattern of acceptance and resistance that accompanied his giant success.[48] The first customers for his no-frills food discount centers were distinctly upper class, namely, functionaries, cadres, and bourgeois; all were people capable, as he tells it, of calculating how to improve their standard of living. They had no qualms about shopping around for the best price to cut costs on food in order to save for car payments, keep up mortgages on apartments, and make the down payments on second homes. Evidently, they also had the necessary equipment in the form of modern kitchens (with refrigerators) and automobiles, flexibility to schedule shopping, and ample shopping skills. As for the decor? "They couldn't give a hoot. They don't go into a store to dream, to be blown away. They have what they need at home. The neon lights, music, chrome, mirrors of variety stores (*bazars populaires*) might still dazzle people who live in slums." Leclerc was confident that the lower classes too would soon follow the upper classes. If we give their initial obstinacy a more sympathetic reading, it appears not at all illogical: Abiding economic insecurity, the physical immobility of those lacking transportation, the traditionalism of female roles, and the conservatism of self-protective subcultures all would have deterred experimentation. If Leclerc simplified the issue, he captured the logic impelling change: "As soon as unskilled workers and agricultural laborers have to pay car installments at the start of the month, they too would learn that 'a sou is a sou,' that it's far better to shop at the discount center, ugly though it is, than to pay for the smiles and shop windows at the corner grocer."[49]

CONVERGENCES AND DIFFERENTIATION IN THE
PERSPECTIVE OF POST-FORDISM

By the late 1960s, the new institutions of distribution appeared to be a major force shaping a "one-class market" in Europe.[50] Even optimists were excited by the swooping upward curves in the diffusion of consumer durables; observers highlighted that these curves tended to overlap, indicating that basic appliances were spreading across classes whose consumption habits had not previously touched and across regions that had hitherto appeared utterly distant from each other in development. As new national

48 Etienne Thil, *Combat pour la distribution: D'Edouard Leclerc aux supermarchés* (Paris, 1964).
49 Ibid., 79.   50 The expression is Whidden's in ibid., 102.

standards of consumer well-being were established and rising income blunted some of the sharp differences in the patterns of provisioning and purchase of household durables, it seemed that Western Europe had converged with the United States around a common model of consumer modernity.[51]

Yet examined from the vantage point of the 1990s, this development retained many hallmarks of Europeanness. The commercial revolution saw the persistence of small retailers alongside the big, the reworking of old types of cooperation such as retail buying groups, and the establishment of voluntary wholesale chains whereby the small-scale retailers combined with each other and with wholesalers to obtain economies of scale and specialization. Through the 1970s, it was common to characterize the persistence of older forms as backwardness or resistance to modernity. Yet in a new global context, the persistence of old styles of segmented, localized retailing and the linkages between the traditional and the new made sense. In the quest after outlets and suppliers in a highly competitive and ever-more globalized marketplace, these well-articulated local networks presented advantages when supported by local government and in quick reach of distant suppliers and outlets through computerized communications.

From the vantage point of the 1990s a European narrative of the rise of mass consumer society could doubtless be told such as to diminish, if not exclude the influence of the United States. Whether that is useful heuristically or is only an ideological exercise to redress the United States's preponderance in the recent European past is to be debated. What can be said for now is that American experience of 1920 to 1970 should not be identified with modernity in itself. The very interactions of European enterprise with American models demonstrate that there was more than one path of transition from a regime of scarcity and constraint to one of consumer abundance. In continental Europe, this transition was especially travailed, and the structures, social dynamics, and habits of mind accumulated in the process are unlikely utterly to disappear.

---

51 The catching up by class and region is carefully documented in the regional study by a Breton sociologist, Dominique Badault, working with American sampling and statistical techniques. *Equipment du logement et demande de biens durables en Bretagne, 1962–1968,* Resultats d'enquetes effectuées en 1962 et 1968 avec le concours de la DGRST, Centre Regional d'Etudes et de Formations economiques (Rennes, 1971); see also André Piatier, *Structure et perspective de la consummation européenne: Marché commun et Gran-Brétagne* (Paris, 1967).

4

Customer Research as Public Relations

General Motors in the 1930s

ROLAND MARCHAND

In the summer of 1926, members of the General Sales Committee of the General Motors Corporation (GM) discussed a tantalizing "specialized" sales strategy. A direct-mail booklet "featuring all GM products," it appeared, might tap a "particularly fertile field." That market, identified for a targeted campaign, consisted of "Ford owners of two years standing."[1] The conception of this group as worthy of special sales promotions from General Motors did not stem from some capricious whim or from some motive of vengeance induced by intense corporate rivalry. Every aspect of the underlying logic of the proposed campaign drew its credibility from an exercise in what would come to be called "customer research."

The architect of this aggressive strategy was Henry ("Buck") Weaver, later characterized by the public relations counselor Edward Bernays as "a brilliant enthusiast" and "a loose wheel" within GM management.[2] In 1926, Weaver served as "assistant to the director" within the Sales Section at the corporation's Detroit headquarters. Through questionnaires in the form of a "postcard analysis of consumer preferences" of thousands of car owners, Weaver had determined that they were buying new cars at an average fre-

I am indebted to the participants in the conference, The Development of Consumer Society in the Twentieth Century, hosted by the German Historical Institute, Washington, D.C., and the Smithsonian Institution, Oct. 1995, for provocative and helpful comments on an earlier version of this chapter. I also owe particular thanks to Daniel Robinson of York University for his discerning comments and suggestions on an early draft and to Sally Clarke of the University of Texas, Austin, both for her very careful reading and critique of an earlier draft of the essay and for the opportunity to read her work-in-progress on the marketing significance of customer research at General Motors.

1 "Notes on Minutes of General Sales Committee," June 18, 1926, folder 1 of typed summaries of General Sales Committee Minutes, carton 2, General Motors Collection, Baker Library, Harvard School of Business Management (hereafter GMC, Baker).
2 Edward L. Bernays, *Biography of an Idea: Memoirs of Public Relations Counsel Edward L. Bernays* (New York, 1965), 552.

quency of two and one-half years. He also noted that a slightly decreasing percentage of owners of Ford cars were expressing the intention of buying a Ford the next time. Therefore, some seven thousand owners of 1924 Ford cars could be expected to be prime candidates for a new GM car in 1927. Not only would a direct-mail campaign to all owners of two-year-old Fords be likely to recruit those seven thousand for GM, Weaver speculated, but such a strategy might "bring about dissatisfaction on the part of still further Ford owners."[3]

Only the year before, as GM production and profits were advancing at a gratifying rate, Buck Weaver had developed another survey, of quite a different sort. Seeking to determine the prime areas of the nation in which to locate "virgin buyers" (those who had not previously owned an automobile), he had compiled an extensive analysis, "The Development of a Basic Purchasing Power Index by Counties." Originally intended to guide the company as to where to put its greatest sales and advertising effort and where to authorize dealerships in order to avoid destructive competition,[4] the study examined statistics from government records on such elements as population figures, bank deposits, numbers of retail outlets, and income tax amounts. The result, as Weaver announced, was "an index so basic in its nature that it may be readily used for practically all kinds of consumer merchandise." Weaver's study gained prestige from its selection for the 1925 Harvard Award for Scientific Research in Advertising and was published the next year in the *Harvard Business Review*. Weaver made a point of contrasting his "scientific analysis" with the "arbitrary opinion" on which sales quotas had typically been based in the past.[5]

Weaver's study of purchasing power by country fell clearly within the sphere of market research as it had developed over the previous decade in the United States. The Curtis Publishing Company had embarked on the first widely publicized series of marketing surveys in 1911 when it commissioned Charles Coolidge Parlin to make studies first of the agricultural implement industry and then of the operations of department stores.[6] By 1923, a business journalist was able to point to dozens of current market

---

3 "Minutes of General Sales Committee," folder 1, carton 2, GMC, Baker.
4 On GM's greater attention to dealers than Ford's and its efforts to curtail competition among dealers through rationalized, bureaucratic control, see Sally Clarke, "Consumers, Information and Marketing Efficiency at GM, 1921–1940," *Business and Economic History* 25 (fall 1996): 189–90, and Richard S. Tedlow, *New and Improved: The Story of Mass Marketing in America* (New York, 1990), 162–4, 173–5.
5 Henry G. Weaver, "The Development of a Basic Purchasing Power Index by Counties," *Harvard Business Review* 4 (Apr. 1926): 275–6; Jean M. Converse, *Survey Research in the United States: Roots and Emergence, 1890–1960* (Berkeley, Calif., 1987), 444 n. 29.
6 Robert Bartels, *The Development of Marketing Thought* (Homewood, Ill., 1962), 108–9.

surveys in a *Saturday Evening Post* article, "The Producer Goes Exploring to Find the Consumer." By the end of the 1920s, ten texts on marketing research had appeared. Within this burgeoning field, broad indexes of buying power by locality complemented the more numerous studies of sales turnover for specific products in selected retail outlets.[7] General Motors would continue occasionally to conduct such surveys; certainly it paid attention to the results of similar studies made by others. But it was "customer research" through questionnaires to car owners, the basis on which GM plotted its audacious direct mail strategy in 1926, that within a decade would become one of the corporation's most publicized activities.

What distinguished "customer research" within the broader field of marketing studies? Although General Motors, and Buck Weaver himself, seemed to use the words "consumer" and "customer" almost interchangeably in describing their research, the term "customer" (eventually employed in the official title of Weaver's expanding operations, the GM "Customer Research Staff") carried particular resonances that distinguished customer research from market surveys. The latter produced only statistics about anonymous consumers, whereas customer research more often elicited feedback from specific customers, often yielding individual remarks that were powerful in their frankness and specificity. The term "customer" also implied an individual who could, at least ideally, be personally known and who, in implied contrast to the image of the muddled or frivolous generic consumer, had purposely sought out and purchased a specific brand. To pay attention to customers, in contrast to "markets" or "consumers," was to seem to value individuals and to pay attention to their personal preferences.[8]

In the late 1920s, however, an explicit theory of customer research had yet to emerge. Buck Weaver explored a variety of survey methodologies; his studies ranged over a vast spectrum of topics – from optimal advertising media to "The Junker Problem" (the accumulating competition from used cars).[9] Although Weaver stressed the connections of each of his studies to

---

7 Converse, *Survey Research*, 88–90; Peggy J. Kreshel, "The 'Culture' of J. Walter Thompson, 1915–1925," *Public Relations Review* 16 (fall 1990): 85.
8 The term "customer" also resonated most clearly with Weaver's penchant to envision his operations as restoring "something akin to the close personal contact and human relations that existed between the product and the consumer before the days of large-scale operations." Henry G. Weaver, "Consumer Questionnaire Technique," *American Marketing Journal* 1 (July 1934): 117. On the less abstract aura of the word "consumer" as contrasted with "customer," see also Kathryn Kish Sklar's chapter in this book.
9 H. G. Weaver, "Personal Interviews vs. Direct Mail Questionnaires," typescript, May 18, 1933, 2, box 18, Edward R. Stettinius Jr. papers, Alderman Library, University of Virginia (hereafter Stettinius papers); H. G. Weaver, "An Analysis of Advertising Media with Particular Reference to National Magazines," typescript, June 1928, attachment to Weaver to C. F. Kettering, Aug. 24, 1928; H. G. Weaver, "The Manufacturer, the Dealer and the Used Car," typescript, Apr. 1927, attachment to B. G.

sales policies, as appropriate for a member of the staff of the GM Sales Section, his speculative forays recurrently touched upon such larger policy
issues as the desirability of frequent design changes, the actual and desirable
rates of automobile obsolescence, and customer preferences in styling.
Weaver took considerable pride in infusing "drama and interest into the
printed word . . . personalizing and individualizing a mass technique." He
sought to create an intimate, conversational ambiance in his questionnaire
booklets with phrases such as "[b]y the way" and through what *Fortune*
characterized as "deliberately careless typography." Respondents could complete many sections of the surveys simply by checking a box next to one of
several choices of pictographs (see Figures 4.1 and 4.2).[10]

In 1932 and 1933, Weaver's operations suddenly acquired a larger dimension, an enhanced stature, and a wider role within the corporation. Now the
impact of the Great Depression and its challenge to the public stature of big
business spurred GM's leaders to reappraise their strategies in both marketing and public relations. In mid-1931, General Motors appointed Paul Garrett, formerly a financial editor for the New York *Evening Post,* as its first
full-fledged public relations director. It soon underlined its new level of
commitment to this corporate function by allotting an unprecedented paragraph of testimony to the importance of public relations in its annual report.

Although General Motors never failed to earn a profit, even in the worst
years of the Great Depression, the size of that profit had plunged from $248
million in 1929 to only $165,000, in 1932.[11] That latter year, the company
contracted with J. David Houser, a leading independent in survey research,
to carry out investigations of the competitive positions of each of its cars,
the relative importance of various consumer attitudes on car buying, and
GM's need for corporate image advertising. Houser's findings accented the
importance of corporate prestige and corporate communications with the
public. From surveys of some twenty-five thousand people, Houser con-

Koether to Kettering, June 17, 1927; General Motors Sales Section and New York Office Statistical
Staff, "The Domestic Automobile Market: Its Past and Future," typescript, Nov. 1928; and H. G.
Weaver, "The Junker Problem," enclosure to Weaver to C. F. Kettering, July 21, 1928; all in
Unprocessed Reports and Surveys, Charles F. Kettering papers, GMI Institute Alumni Foundation
Collection of Industrial History, Flint, Michigan (hereafter GMI). On the emergence of the used car
as a threat to new car sales and dealer profits, see Tedlow, *New and Improved,* 155–7.

10 General Motors Corporation Sales Section – Consumer Research, "Questionnaire Technique,"
typescript, with revisions in pen, May 31, 1933, 1–2, box 18, Stettinius papers; Converse, *Survey
Research,* 98; *General Motors World* 11 (Oct. 1933): 4; *Fortune* 19 (Mar. 1939): 51. It is instructive to
compare Weaver's early sensitivity to developing an attractive, user-friendly mode of communication
with consumers to the starkly austere mode of address that a rival for their attention and allegiance,
Consumers' Research, would adopt. See Charles F. McGovern, "Sold American: Inventing the Consumer, 1880–1940," Ph.D. diss., Harvard University, 1993, 309.

11 Alfred P. Sloan Jr., *My Years with General Motors,* ed. John McDonald with Catharine Stevens (New
York, 1964), 176.

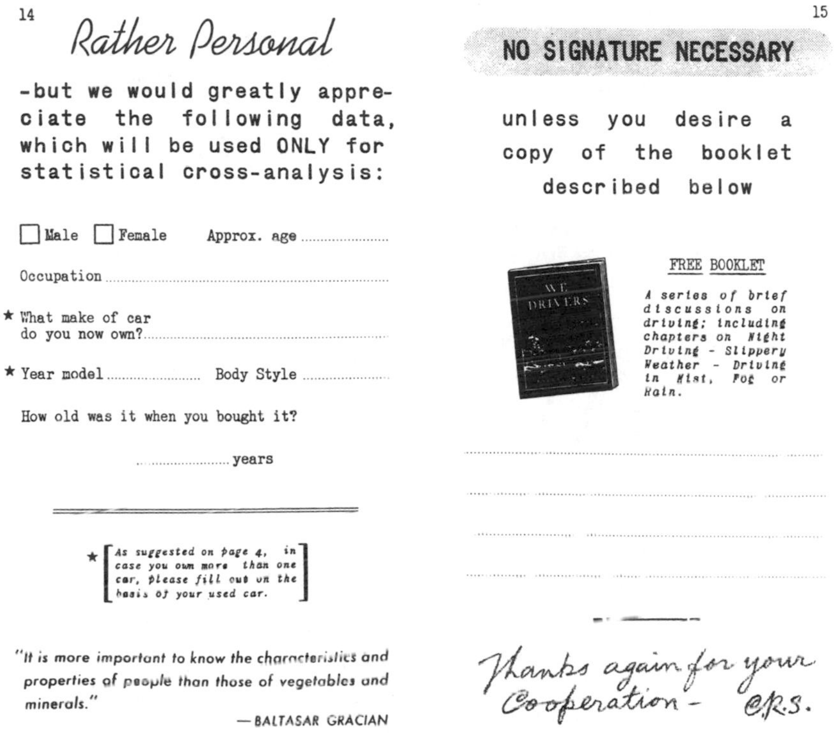

14

Rather Personal

-but we would greatly appreciate the following data,
which will be used ONLY for
statistical cross-analysis:

☐ Male ☐ Female   Approx. age ....

Occupation ....

★ What make of car
do you now own?...

★ Year model .... Body Style ....

How old was it when you bought it?

.... years

★ ⎡ *As suggested on page 4, in* ⎤
  ⎢ *case you own more than one* ⎥
  ⎢ *car, please fill out on the* ⎥
  ⎣ *basis of your used car.* ⎦

"It is more important to know the characteristics and
properties of people than those of vegetables and
minerals."
                                    — BALTASAR GRACIAN

15

NO SIGNATURE NECESSARY

unless you desire a
copy of the booklet
described below

FREE BOOKLET

*A series of brief
discussions on
driving; including
chapters on Night
Driving - Slippery
Weather - Driving
in Mist, Fog or
Rain.*

*Thanks again for your
Cooperation - C.R.S.*

Figure 4.1. General Motors Corporation, "Did You Ever Buy a Used Car?" (1935), 14–15,
Special Collections, Edward R. Stettinius Jr. papers, University of Virginia, Charlottesville.
Copyright 1978 GM Corp. Used with permission GM Media Archives.

cluded that attitudes toward the corporation as a whole significantly influenced people's car-buying decisions. Such attitudes, he observed, often
reflected "the amount of interest shown in giving the public what it wants."
Although GM trailed Ford badly in car owners' views of which company
had "done the most for the country," it led Ford by a substantial margin in
public perceptions of its sensitivity to consumer desires.[12] Perhaps more
emphasis on its little-publicized work in customer research could widen
that gap.

Suddenly in 1933, "out of a clear blue sky" in the reckoning of the public relations pioneer Edward Bernays, GM's president, Alfred Sloan, commissioned Weaver to develop "a comprehensive proposal on consumer

12 Neil H. Borden and Martin V. Marshall, *Advertising Management: Text and Cases*, rev. ed. (Homewood,
    Ill., 1959), 393, 396–7; Houser Associates, "The Public, The Automobile, and the General Motors
    Corporation, sect. 2, Institutional: A Nation-Wide Survey," typescript, 1932, 21–2, box 19, Stettinius
    papers; J. David Houser, *What People Want from Business* (New York, 1938), 127, 144.

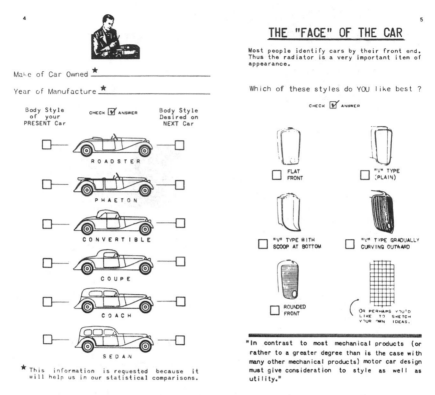

Figure 4.2. General Motors Corporation, "The Proving Ground of Public Opinion" (1933), 4–5, Charles F. Kettering papers, GMI Alumni Historical Collection, Flint, Mich. Copyright 1978 GM Corp. Used with permission GM Media Archives.

research."[13] Within a few months, this proposal had resulted in a new independent unit within the corporation – the GM Customer Research Staff – with a status "on a par . . . with the famous Research Laboratories and Proving Ground."[14] General Motors now went public with a press release on Customer Research and a special message to GM stockholders. Customer Research, President Sloan announced, was now an *"operating philosophy"* within General Motors that "must extend through all phases" of the business.[15]

13 Bernays, *Biography,* 552.
14 General Motors Corporation, "Press Release for 'The Advertiser,'" Press Releases folder, 1934, General Motors Public Relations Library, Detroit (hereafter GMPRL).
15 Weaver, "Personal Interviews," 1, 4, 6; "Notes on Executive Committee Minutes," Aug. 11, 1932, carton 2, GMC, Baker; "Press Release," Oct. 14, 1933, GMPRL; Alfred P Sloan Jr., "The Proving Ground of Public Opinion," *Printers' Ink* (Sept. 21, 1933): 92–3; *24th Annual Report of the General Motors Corporation for Year Ended December 31, 1932,* Historical Corporate Reports Collection, Baker Library.

The amplification and consecration of customer research at GM had certainly transpired quickly. But Bernays was quite myopic in ignoring the context from which this corporate stratagem had emerged. Paul Garrett, very soon after assuming leadership of the new GM Public Relations (PR), had urged company executives to recognize that "no big corporation in the world must rise or fall so completely on its reputation with Mr. and Mrs. Jones, their small boy and the daughter at school, as General Motors."[16] Garrett began in PR by working "from the inside out," initiating a program to solicit the views of stockholders who had recently sold part or all of their GM stock. Many small stockholders expressed delight and amazement that the giant corporation had taken a personal interest in their views. Garrett mimeographed extensive selections from the flood of stockholder responses and distributed them widely to other GM executives. GM, he argued, should recognize the value of such solicitations of the advice and opinions of individuals as had prompted letters to GM that announced proudly, "I am really still in the [General Motors] family," or acknowledged, "It flatters me that your great company noticed my name as a stockholder."[17]

The capacity of the customer research questionnaires to convey a similar impression of personal attention to the public now magnified Weaver's role. He had become increasingly aware of the "human understanding" that his deliberately cordial and user-friendly questionnaires seemed to evoke. And a trade journal had recently observed that GM was reaping public goodwill by "taking the public into the firm's confidence and asking for its advice . . . inferring that General Motors is actually interested in what the individual thinks and is anxious to accept his advice."[18] Here, certainly, was one way to advance Paul Garrett's objective of reaching out to the "Joneses." Customer Research emerged as one answer to converging corporate concerns about internal morale, the political environment, customer dissatisfaction, and the development of a long-range strategy.[19]

Thus, in addition to their role in garnering marketing data, Weaver's Customer Research surveys had acquired a major public relations mission by 1933. Significantly, GM now authorized Weaver to make one critical change in his operations. Instead of sending out questionnaires with no GM identification, as had been Weaver's practice in the past, they would

16 Paul Garrett, "A Bigger and Better General Motors," typescript, Oct. 3, 1931, 2, GMPRL; Bernays, *Biography*, 547.
17 Paul Garrett to Charles Kettering, Aug. 5, 1931, Sept. 18, 1931, GM, New York, 1931 folder, and Garrett to Kettering, Nov. 28, 1933, GM, New York, 1933 folder, Kettering papers, GMI.
18 "General Motors Ask the Buyer for Opinions," *Canadian Advertising Data* (Nov. 1932): 14, 25. I am indebted to Daniel Robinson for calling this article to my attention.
19 On the range and depth of such concerns within GM in 1932, see the correspondence of GM executives in the "10 Point Program" folder, carton 1, GMC, Baker.

now go out "in the name of the General Motors Corporation." Weaver's previous surveys had made it clear, he reported, that "[p]eople like to have their advice sought." But only by putting its name on the questionnaires could GM fully "capitalize on the tremendous by-product of goodwill and sales influence" of the surveys, of the flattering effects on the individual of having his views solicited by a giant corporation. With its name specifically attached to the survey, GM would glean that goodwill that would likely result from the "touch of judicious flattery" of the questionnaire booklet.[20]

For both Weaver and the corporation as a whole, customer research now took on elevated significance. Bernays notes that Weaver wrote to him in July 1933, "I am now convinced that the approach of running of a business from the customer viewpoint is perhaps bigger than any of us really realize." And Weaver predicted that the corporation would realize "an even greater and more secure prosperity" by "recognizing the ultimate consumer as the hub about which all our activities revolve and cementing all of our public relations with a more liberal measure of human understanding." Customer research, Weaver concluded, "establishes GM as a democratic institution by playing up the importance of the consumer instead of playing up the importance of the producer." President Sloan, returning to Paul Garrett's theme of a lost relationship between big business and the individual citizen (a theme that Weaver had also stressed in explaining the need for customer research), observed that the operations of General Motors were "too big . . . too far flung" for the company to rely any longer on "casual contacts and personal impressions" of public attitudes. By pooling the "practical experience" of thousands of motorists "with the technical skills of General Motors engineers and production experts," however, the "gulf between the customer and those responsible for guiding the destiny of the institution" could be bridged.[21]

Surely here was a conception of the operations of a large business corporation that was worthy of being termed a "philosophy." Conducted "on a highly scientific basis," customer research would provide the corporation with a "correct interpretation of what the public actually thinks." Here, in consummate form, was an operating model of free enterprise performing perfectly its role within a business system conceived on what Charles McGovern calls an "electoral model."[22] That the corporation, like an elected

20 "Notes on Executive Committee Minutes," Aug. 11, 1932, GMC, Baker; Weaver, "Personal Interviews," 1, 4, 6; [Henry G. Weaver], "False Teeth and Chewing Gum: Thought Starter No. 80," n.d., p. 5, box 592, Stettinius papers; Sloan, "Proving Ground," 92–3; "General Motors Ask," 25.
21 Bernays, *Biography,* 552; Weaver, "Consumer Questionnaire Technique," 118; Weaver, "False Teeth," 5; Sloan, "Proving Ground," 92–3; H. G. Weaver, "The Proving Ground of Public Opinion," *General Motors Magazine* (1933): 15, 43, box 19, Stettinius papers.
22 See Charles McGovern's chapter in this book; and McGovern, "Sold American," 377.

political representative, operated entirely in the service of consumers was made apparent in its active solicitation of their ideas and choices. Weaver, with his penchant for dramatic visual explications, placed customer research as the crucial feedback component within a chain that linked the company's Engineering Department with Production and then with Sales, the dealer, the consumer, and – via customer research – back with Engineering again (see Figure 4.3).[23] Envisioning something like what has recently come to be labeled "mass customization," yet assuming that consumer desires were sufficiently similar that they could be satisfied with a few models and designs, the industrial producer would respond sensitively to the needs and desires of the mass of customers.[24] Obviously, no interventions in the form of government regulations could improve upon such a "democratic" relationship.

In his own writings, Weaver stipulated the evident exceptions to such a model that the practicalities of sophisticated modern industry required. The company, with its "obligation to contribute to scientific progress and advances in design," would have to rely on its own experts for good engineering practice and an adequate vision of the future. After all, the layman could "hardly be expected to project himself very far beyond that which he sees and experiences in his daily life." But just as a layman might work with an architect and contractor in planning his new house, relying on their expertise and knowledge of the practical, he might also play a role in helping the manufacturer understand "social desires for style, appearance, comfort, appointments, which . . . *do not lend themselves to laboratory research.*" Since this kind of psychological information was as crucial as the technical information GM was learning through tests at its Proving Ground, a facility long publicized in company advertising, the process of customer research warranted the accolade "The Proving Ground of Public Opinion."[25]

As GM's Customer Research Staff expanded its activities after 1933 it devised further refinements to improve the quality of the information it derived. The user-friendly, fetchingly illustrated questionnaire booklets worked well to engage prospective respondents and ensure a good rate of returns. Weaver made sure to include some open-ended questions and emphasized that "side remarks" by the respondents *should be encouraged in every way as constituting one of the most valuable aspects of consumer research.* In

23 Attachment to H. G. Weaver to O. E. Hunt, Oct. 8, 1932, GM Detroit, 1932 folder, Kettering papers, GMI; General Motors Corporation, "The Philosophy of Customer Research," pamphlet [1933], New York Public Library, 2. Weaver's diagram later gained recognition in a major textbook on business psychology. See Edward K. Strong Jr., *Psychological Aspects of Business* (New York, 1938), 175.
24 See B. Joseph Pine II, *Mass Customization: The New Frontier in Business Competition* (Boston, 1993).
25 General Motors Corporation, "Philosophy of Customer Research," 12–13.

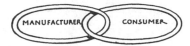
Under the conditions of the one man shop, with the head of the business serving as designer, manufacturer, purchasing agent, salesman and service expert,- an intimate understanding of customer tastes and desires was automatically assured.

MODERN INDUSTRY

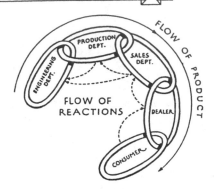

By the very nature of things, the bigger an institution grows, the wider becomes the breach between the customer and those responsible for guiding the destiny of the institution.

With producer and consumer so widely separated it becomes increasingly difficult to keep the business sensitively attuned to the requirements of the customer.

GENERAL MOTORS

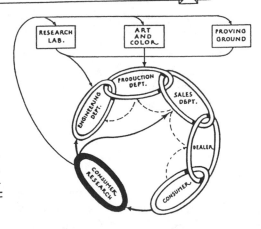

There is a need for some kind of a liaison which would serve as a substitute for the close personal contact which existed automatically in the days of the small shop.

CONSUMER RESEARCH
- aims to fill this need by providing an auxiliary and more direct line of communication between producer and consumer.

H. G. W. — SALES SECTION — GENERAL MOTORS — DETROIT, MICHIGAN.

Figure 4.3. Henry G. Weaver, Diagram of Consumer Research, Weaver to O. E. Hunt, Detroit, 1932 folder, Charles F. Kettering papers, GMI Alumni Historical Collection, Flint, Mich. Copyright 1978 GM Corp. Used with permission GM Media Archives.

an analogy to the use of guinea pigs in medical research, he also contended that since "[t]he important things that we have learned about guinea pigs have come – not so much from studying guinea pigs in the mass, but through conducting exhaustive experiments on a few prime specimens," GM should select out a group of "prime specimens" of its own. Such "special correspondents" or "Motor Enthusiasts," those who took a special interest in automobiles, could provide information of special value about technical issues and possible future trends. By isolating an "elite group" for special questionnaires, according to Jean Converse, GM made a notable contribution to the advance of survey research.[26]

Weaver exhibited his ingenuity, and perhaps also his audaciousness, when he circulated a memorandum within the corporation in mid-1933 on "The Toy Industry as an Influence in Style Trends." Noting that his customer research questionnaires in 1932 had revealed that the public was attracted to the elements of "aero-dynamic design" in the more "rakish" lines of the new Graham, Packard, and Chrysler models, he speculated that "a general acceptance of real streamlining" might occur much sooner than expected because of the fascination of children with toy airplanes. Remarking on the large number of airplanes and other toys of streamline design being sold at "the 10 cent stores and toy shops of America" and the prevalence of streamline images in the movies, in popular science magazines, and in the "Buck Rogers" comic strip, Weaver drove home his point visually by attaching copies of a poster advertising a streamlined coaster wagon for children. The majority of toy cars being sold were now "of the ultramodern streamline design," he reported. American families were seeing "some manifestation of streamlining at every turn of the way." This familiarity, along with the influence of youth in family decisions, should alert GM not to allow itself to fall behind the curve of change.[27]

Weaver's interest in style issues, and his inclusion of questions on design and streamlining in questionnaires distributed during 1932 and 1933, contributed to another "refinement" in GM's survey research – one that contributed to the company's competitive advertising strategies rather than to the advancement of survey research techniques. Since at least 1932, Weaver had paid close attention to audience reactions at the annual auto shows. After he had "escorted twenty non-automobile people" through the exhibits

26 Weaver, "Personal Interviews," 2, 6–7; T. J. LeBlanc to Customer Research Staff, Oct. 31, 1933, GM Detroit, 1933 folder, Kettering papers, GMI; Converse, *Survey Research,* 91.
27 H. G. Weaver, "The Toy Industry as an Influence on Style Trends," typescript memorandum, July 5, 1933, GM Detroit, 1933 folder, Kettering papers. See also "The Proving Ground of Public Opinion," typescript newsletter, Sales Section, GM, Dec. 1, 1932, GM Detroit, 1932 folder, Kettering papers, GMI.

at the 1932 show in Chicago, he reported that people spoke of General
Motors as being conservative stylistically. Young people, he observed, were
"almost without exception in favor of the more radical designs. They seem
to like the pointed nose radiator better than the rounded front." GM, he
warned, would "encounter sales resistance during the coming year" because
some competitors were less conservative stylistically. As an antidote, he suggested several arguments that might "'unsell' the prospect who is leaning
toward a freakish design."[28]

The phrase and concept of "freakish design" proved to be of particular
strategic value by 1934. In both 1933 and 1934, Weaver put a deliberate
"spin" on the questionnaires, in these instances not identified as GM literature, that he distributed at the auto shows. While probing the respondents'
views on tendencies toward streamlining, the illustrated booklets asked,
"Do any of the new models impress you as being too RADICAL or
'FREAKISH'?" (see Figure 4.4). And, in an account of the operations of his
new Customer Research Staff, Weaver observed that the "typical buyer
seems to be able to unconsciously draw a dividing line between freakish art
and sound art." When Chrysler introduced the radically new "airflow"
design in 1934, GM worried about the loss of market share and the costs of
retooling it would incur if Chrysler's design won great popular approval.
The Customer Research Staff, through the very wording of its questionnaires, labored to assist potential buyers in drawing the right dividing line
on "sound art" and in applying GM's epithet "freakish" to the new Chrysler.
Consulting the survey results (with whatever effects the GM spin had
achieved), Weaver reported that people disliked the radical styling of the
Airflow by a substantial margin, although most remained "undecided."[29]

GM decided to exploit this marginal advantage by making its systematic
inquiry into customer tastes the focus of its 1934 national advertising campaign. Its prominent slogan "An Eye to the Future, an Ear to the Ground"
emphasized that GM "did not make rash changes, without consulting the
people's desires." Insisting that GM's very modest steps toward streamlining
had "hit the very centerpoint of public favor" and had perfectly embodied
"the public's notion of the fashionable 1934 motor car," the General Motors
ads attributed this success to the fact that "[m]onths before production, in

<hr>

28 H. G. Weaver, "Consumer Reactions at 1932 Chicago Show," typescript memo, Feb. 12, 1932, 1–3,
6–7, GM Detroit, 1932 folder, Kettering papers, GMI; Jim Ellis, *From Billboards to Buicks* (New York,
1968), 101–3.

29 Weaver, "Proving Ground," 43; Customer Research Staff, "The Proving Ground of Public Opinion," questionnaire booklet, 1933, Kettering papers, GMI; Arthur J. Kuhn, *GM Passes Ford,
1918–1938: Designing the General Motors Performance-Control System* (University Park, Pa., 1986),
221–2; Ellis, *From Billboards*, 101–3.

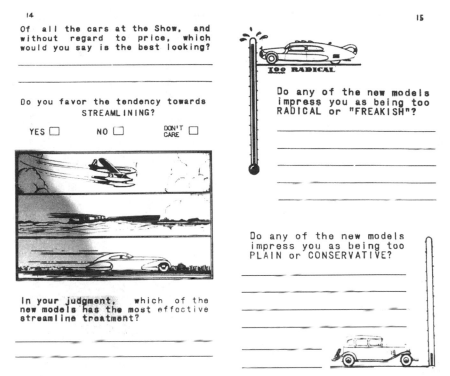

Figure 4.4. General Motors Corporation, "Questionnaire," National Automobile Show (1933), Charles F. Kettering papers, GMI Alumni Historical Collection, Flint, Mich. Copyright 1978 GM Corp. Used with permission GM Media Archives.

more than a million letters sent to car owners," GM had "checked our designs against *what the public wanted.*" In an unsubtle slap at Chrysler, each ad also boasted that GM's attention to public sentiments had helped it protect the public "against ill-timed or dubious experiments."[30]

General Motors did not confine its reproaches to Chrysler. It also rebuked the New Deal by suggesting that corporations far surpassed any federal agencies in paying meaningful attention to consumer interests. Casting its questionnaires as a form of popular vote, and claiming that it derived its ideas and designs from "the common sense of the common people" (see Figure 4.5), GM proclaimed itself a democratic, representative, "public-

---

30 *Saturday Evening Post,* Apr. 14, 1934, 42–3; Apr. 28, 1934, 38–9; July 14, 1934, 38–9; June 9, 1934, 34–5; *General Motors World* 13 (Apr. 1934): 4; Paul Garrett to Charles Kettering, Apr. 17, 1934, GM, New York, 1934 folder, Kettering papers, GMI.

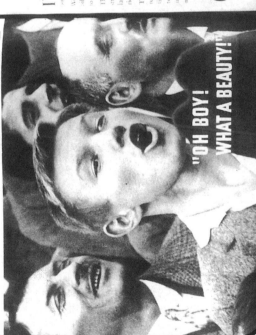

Figure 4.5. *Saturday Evening Post*, Apr. 28, 1934, 38–9.

minded" institution, worthy of the characterization "*OF* THE PEOPLE, *FOR* THE PEOPLE, *BY* THE PEOPLE."[31] Customer research, thus, gained a central place in GM's anti–New Deal propaganda. Increasingly alarmed by the government's inroads into the autonomy of business executives, Sloan (who would later refer to his "tirades against the New Deal")[32] and other GM leaders emphasized the "democratic" aspects of customer research in their efforts to advance the economic education of the American people. In 1936, for instance, the customer research operation was enlisted as a feature story in the most critically timed advertisement in an election season campaign to persuade Americans to look to the business corporation, rather than to perpetuation of the New Deal, for the nation's well-being.[33]

This advertising campaign, originating in mid-1936, adopted the slogan "Who Serves Progress Serves America." All of the ads in this series, according to a Harvard Business School analysis, "sought to teach fundamental economic truths in terms of specific examples chosen from General Motors experience." Although Roosevelt's New Deal might claim to serve the people, the argument in the ads implied, it was the manufacturing companies that responded to the people's wants and needs by enabling them to choose the products they wished and by raising their standard of living through production efficiencies.[34] It was corporations such as General Motors that, by sending out "more than a million letters to car owners," had made themselves the representatives of the people, assessing their "tastes and desires." In a culminating ad in the series, which appeared only two weeks before the November 1936 election, General Motors juxtaposed an historical vignette of an election scene with a photograph of members of the GM Customer Research Staff reviewing the questionnaire responses. This operation, the

---

31 *Saturday Evening Post,* Apr. 28, 1934, 38–9; July 14, 1934, 38–9. This vision of the corporation as democratically responsive to the wishes of all the people did not, obviously, recognize any of the limits on the freedom of the consumer that Ulrich Wyrwa attributes to "unequal distribution of prosperity," nor does it acknowledge that immense role that images of class standing had played in GM's own advertising in the 1920s or the "class related car cultures" and "the consumption dimension of the pyramidal class constellation" that Kurt Möser and Victoria de Grazia identify within European consumer markets during this era. See the chapters by Wyrwa, Möser, and de Grazia in this book.

32 Sloan is quoted in Ed Cray, *Chrome Colossus: General Motors and Its Times* (New York, 1980), 321.

33 Thus, GM claimed to do far more directly and practically what Lizabeth Cohen describes as government gestures under the New Deal to give "a real voice to consumers" and to take their interests "better into account." See Cohen's chapter in this book.

34 Here, quite unambiguously, GM set forth what Jackson Lears has described as "advertising's one-dimensional vision of mass-produced plenty" and what Daniel Horowitz describes in George Katona's vision as a kind of republican (with a small "r") vision of "consumer sovereignty." See the chapters by Jackson Lears and Daniel Horowitz in this book.

caption pointed out, constituted "the 'ballot box' of a great business." In what amounted to an election editorial, General Motors asked – in light of this visual demonstration of the exercise of public choice through corporate customer research – whether the nation should proceed toward "restriction and regimentation" or whether it should allow the true creators of wealth to serve their constituencies (see Figure 4.6).[35]

General Motors reaped much praise from within the business community for both the advertising series and its ongoing work in customer research.[36] In its November 14, 1938, issue, *Time* magazine made Weaver's Customer Research its cover story. By 1939, *Fortune* magazine was prepared to credit Weaver and his operation for greatly enhancing mutual understanding between this immense corporation and the "small consumer." The mass mailings, with their "ingratiating, arresting, and informal tone," made it sound, *Fortune* observed, "as though GM thought its customers were individually as well as collectively important." As a "small-town Democrat and individualist at heart," *Fortune* concluded, Weaver was leading a GM crusade "to preserve the right of the individual to be heard and serviced in an increasingly collectivized society."[37] Had customer research, then, successfully connected the feedback loop and ensured the presence of the consumer voice, even that of the "small" consumer, within the counsels of big business?

In considering this issue, it is pertinent to observe that Weaver had quite consistently recognized an educational, as well as information-gathering, role for the customer survey. It was a virtue of the folksy questionnaire booklet that it not only amassed quantifiable responses but "talks with folks." Although Weaver was eager to establish his credentials as a professional in the design of survey instruments, he never spurned opportunities to achieve multiple purposes through them. Originating as the tools of the Sales Division, the questionnaires always sought to create or retain customers for GM cars as well as to solicit their views. Moreover, Weaver observed in 1934, the greatest significance of the activity was not to accumulate "big figures" but rather to "restore something akin to the close personal contact and the human relations that existed between the producer and the consumer before

---

35 *Saturday Evening Post,* Oct. 24, 1936, 48–9; Borden, *Advertising Management,* 398–9.
36 *Fortune* even used GM's customer research as the model and justification for its own public opinion surveys, instituted in 1935. *Fortune* 12 (July 1935): 65–6.
37 *Fortune* 19 (Mar. 1939): 51, 141; *Saturday Evening Post,* June 23, 1934, 30–1; Oct. 24, 1936, 48–9. Thus, GM saw customer research as repealing the apparent law noted by Louis Pinto: "Markets are not concerned with individuals." See Louis Pinto's paper presented at the conference, The Development of the Consumer Society in the Twentieth Century, German Historical Institute, Washington, D.C., Oct. 1995.

Figure 4.6. *Saturday Evening Post*, Oct. 24, 1936, 48–9.

the days of large-scale operations."[38] The statistical results obtained through the fact-finding function of his surveys, Weaver cautioned, would never adequately reflect their larger "human interest and goodwill" results.[39] And, although Weaver sought facts from consumers about their attitudes and preferences, he also undertook to "educate" them in various ways through the process. "We have the problem of influencing the customer's mind," Weaver pointed out, and "[t]he more we know about the customer's mind the better we are fitted to process it."[40]

The possibilities of putting spin on the survey, of devising it to sell even as it researched, stirred Weaver's ingenuity from the beginning. By 1933 he was making explicit distinctions between those of his surveys that constituted "simon-pure research" and those the company distributed "for reasons of propaganda." The large survey at the end of 1933 he characterized as "primarily a piece of sales propaganda."[41] Weaver believed that he had built a subtle sales stimulus into the questionnaire. It would not only induce the recipient to "spend from 30 minutes to a full evening thinking about automobiles in general and General Motors products in particular" but also "incidentally emphasiz[e] . . . the obsolescence of his present car."[42] The direct mail questionnaire, Weaver observed, was actually superior to the personal interview as "a channel for imparting information" to the consumer. The research questionnaire was proving to be "a potent tool for bringing the dormant prospect up-to-date, dissatisfying him with his old car, making him more intelligent on questions of design." All of this "pave[d] the way for a more effective sales effort."[43]

Weaver's ideas for elaborating the uses of customer research were nothing if not prolific. In mid-1935, in a twenty-page memorandum, he proposed that GM undertake an auxiliary program, which would "involve a finesse, a strategy, and an indirection which is practically unknown in the auto industry." General Motors should subtly "tie in" with an emerging nationwide network of local junior auto clubs, supplying GM literature and arranging to use the clubs as "a channel" for circulating and collecting

38 Weaver, "Customer Questionnaire Technique," 117.
39 H. G. Weaver, "A Bad Feature of Customer Research," memo, Sept. 6, 1933, box 550, Stettinius papers; Customer Research Staff, "Final Report of 1933 Study," typescript, 1933, GM Detroit, 1933 folder, Kettering papers, GMI.
40 Henry G. Weaver, "Consumer Research and Consumer Education," *Annals of the American Academy of Political and Social Science* 182 (Nov. 1935): 93, 96–8; Henry G. Weaver, "Tuning in with the Customer," *Market Research* 7 (July 1937): 16–17.
41 Customer Research Staff, "Final Report," 1. Some of the purists, by 1936, were decrying "the use of research to propagandize" as "a cankerous spot on commercial research." *Market Research* 4 (Jan. 1936): 21.
42 Weaver, "Bad Feature."
43 Weaver, "Personal Interviews," 5; Customer Research Staff, "Final Report," 1.

the customer research questionnaires. The boys would gain access to homes more easily than any professional interviewers, would give a "neighborhood" character to these GM contacts with the public, and would prove, in the process, that GM was not an "old-time, cold-blooded corporation," but rather an institution that could "be big and still be human."[44]

Of course, even without the added finesse and intimate elements of this personalized distribution system, subtlety in the construction of customer surveys was the "keynote." Because "[a]sking advice is a subtle form of flattery," Weaver explained, the survey questionnaire booklet, itself, worked to get "under the skin" of the potential buyer, "preselling" him on General Motors as a friendly, solicitous company and catching him "off his guard" by asking his advice. Customer Research, Weaver argued later, was "a powerful catalytic agent," working in a "subtle manner . . . without danger of offending" to "dissatisfy" the respondent with his old car.[45] Desirable as such spin might be from a sales standpoint, the customer research questionnaire, burdened with such objectives, could hardly maintain its purity as an instrument of information about consumer desires.

What, then, of the feedback chain in which customer research facilitated the injection of consumer voice into automobile design? Such a participatory role had certainly been promised in the title established for the 1934 version of the survey booklet – "Your Car as YOU would build it."[46] GM ads in 1934 had gone so far as to suggest that "more than a million car owners" had "'sat in' on our conferences, so to speak," and that GM's engineering and design changes had hit the "bull's eye" of popularity by unequivocally representing "*what people want*" (see Figure 4.7).[47] Weaver clearly aspired to play the role of spokesman for the public, and *Time* magazine obligingly reported in 1938 that 185 of the public suggestions had "found their way into . . . GM cars."[48]

But Weaver had long recognized the inherent restraints on the power of his findings to shape corporate decisions. Of course he did not confess this publicly. Internally, he preferred to attribute his lack of influence to difficulties in gaining attention for his findings in GM's dispersed management. He also privately accepted stringent discounts on the value of his customers'

44 H. G. Weaver, "Customer Research Proposal," typescript, July 1935, 2–4, 16–17; GM Detroit, 1935 folder, Kettering papers, GMI.
45 Weaver, "Customer Research Proposal," 3; Weaver, "False Teeth," 2, 4–5, 7.
46 Customer Research Staff, Press Release, July 1934, GMPRL. The General Motors ad in the *Saturday Evening Post,* Mar. 16, 1935, 38–9, displayed the new questionnaire booklet and noted that "more than a million copies" had gone out to car owners.
47 *Saturday Evening Post,* May 12, 1934, 40–1, and May 26, 1934, 40–1, and June 23, 1934, 30–1.
48 *Time,* Nov. 14, 1938, 66, 68.

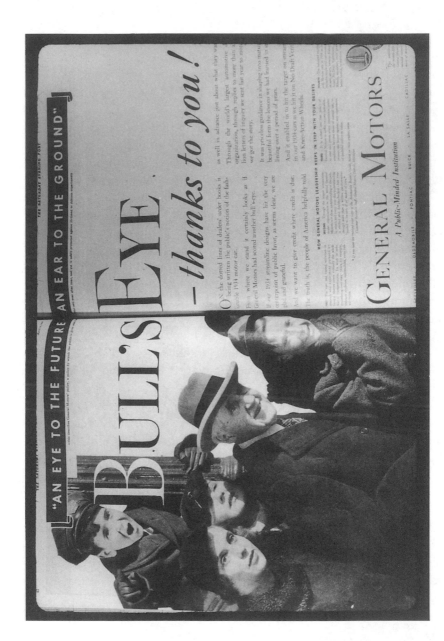

Figure 4.7. *Saturday Evening Post*, Apr. 14, 1934, 42–3.

input. Since his program of customer research depended on matter-of-fact-ness and subtlety in "reaching the public consciousness," he lamented, there was "nothing sufficiently spectacular to force its attention upon our own people." Contrasted with Broadway signs or even advertising campaigns, the survey was "an under-cover activity." He would attempt to keep the results of his work before the other company executives, including crucial car division leaders, he avowed, by passing along mimeographed excerpts from his daily return mail.[49]

Even more to be feared than the inattention of the technical and design men was their contempt. In 1932 Weaver had sought to face this problem directly by quoting the criticisms of one GM engineer: "*The general tone of the questionnaire reflects a respect for the engineering knowledge of the consumer which is out of line with the facts of the case.*" Although he readily explained publicly that the company did not expect expert technical proposals from the mass public, but simply testimonies to their psychological and aesthetic reactions to style and mechanical features, Weaver privately went further to reassure the corporation experts. He fully accepted the proposition that the layman was incompetent "as a technical adviser to the automotive engineer," Weaver explained, but GM's technical experts should realize that "from a psychological standpoint" he had found it necessary "to inject [a] harmless note of flattery in order to offset the resistance [of the customer] toward answering the ordinary type of questionnaire." All the company could expect from the layman was insight into "his reactions to engineering developments" as they affected "his physique, his nerves, his temperament, and . . . his pocket book."[50]

Such insights, however lacking in technical expertise, were still invaluable to the manufacturer, Weaver insisted. Producers of automobiles could ill afford to rely only on informational feedback from the market itself. Through a historical comparison, Weaver explained how serious imperfections in market-generated information had accompanied the increasing size and complexity of mass production and mass distribution. Once, he reminisced, "when industry was characterized by small shops making simple products for local consumption," the producer had enjoyed "intimate personal contact" with the customer. He had been "able to arrange his purchasing, plan his production, meet changes in the style trend, direct his sales, and render a personal service with a finesse not easily paralleled by the modern manufacturer, with all his highly specialized organization facili-

49 Weaver, "Bad Feature."
50 H. G. Weaver to O. H. Hunt, Oct. 8, 1932, GM Detroit, 1932 folder, Kettering papers, GMI. Emphasis in original.

ties." But in modern industry, with "producer and consumer ... more widely separated," keeping a business "in tune with the requirements of its customers" had become increasingly important and increasingly problematic.[51] In some sense, the "chain" that had once linked producer and consumer through a face-to-face market relationship now had to be reforged through processes that recognized the inability of the market to supply the kind of timely and sophisticated information that mass producers required.

But were the leaders of General Motors entirely convinced that they needed the feedback from customer research to make crucial decisions? Did they need the customer to "sit in" at the design conference? GM executives had seemed to prove their inherent shrewdness in assessing public tastes during the 1920s as they triumphed in the competition with Henry Ford.[52] Although it may be doubted that GM's executives and engineers viewed input from Weaver's research with such contempt as Edward Bernays later suggested ("Company officials ... thought they knew what the public wanted and considered the survey Weaver's play toy"),[53] still they had reason, especially given the extensive lead time required in the design and retooling process, to rely mainly on what they considered their own well-attuned instincts. Moreover, as Alfred Sloan later pointed out, survey research encompassed a serious flaw. Consumers often did not know what they wanted, and statements made in advance of the decisive act of purchase, such as those that might be elicited by research questionnaires, might actually foster false expectations.[54]

I have chosen to explore some of the dimensions of early customer research in the United States through the single case study of the operations at General Motors during the 1920s and 1930s. Certainly GM was far from being either the pioneer in such research or its sole major practitioner. Utility companies and a variety of other businesses had carried out house-to-house surveys of customers early in the century, and such other big businesses as Norge Refrigerators and General Foods conducted significant surveys of customers in the 1930s.[55] Hundreds of other companies and their advertising agencies carried out or sponsored one of the many other forms of market research – from "pantry inventories" to measures of over-

51 Weaver, "Consumer Research," *Annals,* 93–4.
52 On this competition, see Tedlow, *New and Improved,* 112–81, and Kuhn, *GM Passes Ford.*
53 Bernays, *Biography,* 552.
54 Sloan, *My Years,* 239–40. See also "Notes on Mr. Sloan's Recorded Session of June 2, 1955," in "Memorandum, Mr. McDonald to Himself," June 2, 1955, carton 3, GMC, Baker.
55 David B. Sicilia, "Selling Power: Marketing and Monopoly at Boston Edison, 1886–1929," Ph.D. diss., Brandeis University, 1991, 472, 499, 512–13, 525–6, 586; *Market Research,* 4 (Jan. 1936): 3; 4 (Feb. 1936): 3–4; *Tide,* 9 (Dec. 1934): 12; *Printers' Ink* (Dec. 19, 1935): 92.

the-counter influences on sales by brands.[56] But General Motors, which could claim by 1939 to carry out the largest customer research operation in the world, with a staff of thirty-seven and expenditures of $300,000 a year, surely ranked first among the surveyors of consumers.[57] That level of financial commitment demonstrated GM's sensitivity to the need for information about consumers to ensure "efficient" marketing;[58] it also reflected that corporation's particular zeal in advancing its public relations, a task that other large corporations would increasingly undertake.

Because the leaders of General Motors, in their fervent opposition to the New Deal, recognized so great a responsibility for the proper "economic education" of the public during this era, the tendency of the "two-way street" of its linkage with consumers to become more of a unidirectional path for propaganda and manipulation was somewhat atypical. In its predominant application, by the mid-1930s, GM's customer research can only be characterized as exemplifying to a striking degree what William Graebner defines as "democratic social engineering."[59] Just as such social engineering was "explicitly participatory," with those whose ideas or actions were to be shaped deliberately made "part of the process" and induced "to *feel* that they had participated," so the paramount goal in many of Weaver's 1930s surveys came to be "to contrive the impression" that GM's customers "were individually as well as collectively important."[60]

More specifically, striking parallels link GM's mode of customer research with the kind of employee attitude testing that Sanford Jacoby describes at Sears, Roebuck between 1938 and 1960. Devised as "a tool for avoiding unionization or for mitigating the impact of recently organized unions," such attitude tests were, like GM's questionnaires, only "nominally scientific" and sometimes used as a deliberate "instrument of propaganda."[61] It was simply too tempting, for executives highly cognizant that the company was paying the entire cost to construct such vehicles of communication, not to apply top-down spin on their content.

We can still imagine the pristine purity and confidently assumed exacti-

56 R. B. Alspaugh, "Present Status and Future Outlook of Consumer Research in Commercial Firms," *American Marketing Journal* 2 (Jan. 1935): 80; Howard D. Hovde, "Recent Trends in the Development of Market Research," *American Marketing Journal* 3 (Jan. 1936): 10.

57 *Fortune* 19 (Mar. 1939): 138.

58 See Clarke, "Consumers, Information and Marketing Efficiency," 186–7, 192–3.

59 William Graebner, *The Engineering of Consent: Democracy and Authority in Twentieth-Century America* (Madison, Wis., 1987), 3–5.

60 Ibid., 4; *Fortune* 19 (Mar. 1939): 141.

61 Sanford M. Jacoby, "Employee Attitude Testing at Sears, Roebuck and Company, 1938–1960," *Business History Review* 60 (winter 1986): 613, 627, 630–1; Sanford M. Jacoby, "Employee Attitude Surveys in Historical Perspective," *Industrial Relations* 27 (winter 1988): 75–81.

Figure 4.8. *Saturday Evening Post*, June 23, 1934, 30–1.

tude of customer research in the way that *Fortune* conceived it in 1939 when it praised Weaver for questionnaires that disclosed "what people really want in a car." But it is difficult to exclude the blunt reality of scale. At their very best as diagnostic tools for "anticipating human reactions" and obtaining "side lights on psychology," Weaver acknowledged, the questionnaires succeeded most fully when they evoked individual remarks in response to open-ended questions.[62] In that sense, they served mainly to secure – albeit with a larger reach – the same kinds of anecdotal responses that dealers and salesmen had previously provided. The use of consumer surveys to obtain aggregate information about public tastes and preferences would continue to expand as part of increasingly sophisticated marketing operations – but these would also, increasingly, be administered by independent agencies and research organizations. Manufacturers would always find it difficult to avoid the temptation to put a sales or public relations spin on their communications with the customer.

Although the "idealist" in Buck Weaver might have wished to view customer research as an instrument in perfecting and legitimizing big businesses as "democratic" servants who responded sensitively to people's wants and needs, a more realist voice, within Weaver's consciousness and within corporate management as a whole, was willing to see it "capitalized from a goodwill standpoint." In that sense, GM had found its best spokesman in the enthralled youngster who shared with the nation's audience of readers his thrill at seeing his father recognized by a great corporation. "Look dad," he shouted excitedly, "a letter from General Motors!" (see Figure 4.8).[63]

62 *Fortune* 19 (Mar. 1939): 51; Weaver, "Consumer Questionnaire Technique," 115.
63 Weaver, "Consumer Questionnaire Technique," 14; General Motors, "Press Release," Aug. 10, 1934, GMPRI.; *Saturday Evening Post,* June 23, 1934, 30–1.

5

The New Deal State and the Making of Citizen Consumers

LIZABETH COHEN

When historians trace the expansion of a mass consumer economy and society in twentieth-century America, they inevitably focus on eras of economic prosperity, such as the 1920s and 1950s, when consumer markets expanded and merchandisers innovated in advertising, retailing, and credit. This focus on the dynamic moments of producer and consumer interaction in the private economic sphere, however, misses the crucial role that state policy-making played in creating a postwar world where mass consumption not only shaped the economy, but also altered the political realm, becoming a new vehicle for delivering the traditional American promises of democracy and egalitarianism. As a mass consumption–driven economy made possible a more adequate standard of living for more people than ever before in the decades after World War II, the consumer in the economic realm became increasingly identified with the citizen in the political realm. Full participation in American postwar society came to mean a complicated intermeshing of the economic and political rights of "citizen consumers." The larger study I have undertaken will examine in depth what I call the "Consumer's Republic" that emerged after World War II.[1] Related to that study, this essay challenges a periodization for the growth of mass consumer society that stresses eras of economic prosperity and argues instead that the Great Depression of the 1930s – as a crucial period of modern American state building – established the groundwork for the centrality of consumption and consumers in the postwar era. In the process of constructing the New Deal state during the 1930s, a wide range of people – from ordinary citizens to policymakers – began to recognize for the

The John Simon Guggenheim Memorial Foundation and New York University supported the research for this chapter.
1 Lizabeth Cohen, *A Consumer's Republic: The Politics of Consumption in Postwar America* (forthcoming).

first time that consumer interests and behavior had central economic and political consequences for American society.[2]

To assert the importance of the 1930s is not to deny the legacy of the previous three decades. By 1930, several prerequisites were in place. First, all Americans, regardless of how much money they had to spend, by now recognized that mass consumption – the production, distribution, and purchase of standardized, brand-name goods aimed at as broad a buying public as possible – characterized a significant, and growing, share of consumer activity. Americans varied tremendously in the extent to which they participated in mass consumer markets as a result of their wealth, personal preference, and place of residence (whether rural or urban, and even according to their city neighborhood). Yet the expansion of a middle class with more time and money to spend, the extension of consumer credit and installment buying, and the burgeoning of advertising all under way during the decade ensured that by its end, more and more people considered themselves mass consumers.[3]

Second, although governments acted only minimally to regulate consumption and thereby protect consumers from unfair prices, substandard and sometimes dangerous products, and misleading advertising during the business-dominated era of the 1920s, some precedents had been set during the Progressive era of reform earlier in the century. That drive to discipline industrialists had led to a two-pronged attack that benefited the consumer, along with other groups: antitrust legislation culminating in the Federal Trade Commission Act (FTC, 1914) to restore fair competition and thereby protect the consumer from unfairly jacked-up prices and passage of the Pure Food and Drug Act and the Meat Inspection Act (1906) to set some minimal standards for the safety and quality of goods increasingly being produced for national markets. By the 1920s, however, hardly anyone was worrying anymore about legislation to protect consumers, and in fact the general acceptance of a doctrine of "voluntary compliance" further weakened the already limited authority of the Food and Drug Administration

2 Readers should also see the chapter by George Lipsitz in this book for further discussion of how state policy during the New Deal and the postwar period stimulated consumption. Charles McGovern's chapter analyzes how advertisers and those whom he calls "consumerists" began to link consumption and citizenship before World War II.

3 Lynn Dumenil, *Modern Temper: American Culture and Society in the 1920s* (New York, 1995), 76–97; Lizabeth Cohen, *Making a New Deal: Industrial Workers in Chicago, 1919–1939* (New York, 1990), 100–58; Robert S. Lynd and Helen Merrell Lynd, *Middletown: A Study in American Culture* (New York, 1929); President's Research Committee on Social Trends, *Social Trends in the United States,* 2 vols. (1933; reprint, Westport, Conn., 1970); Martha Olney, *Buy Now, Pay Later: Advertising, Credit, and Consumer Durables in the 1920s* (Chapel Hill, N.C., 1991).

(FDA) and the FTC. Rather, a Republican-dominated Washington felt that the consumers' and manufacturers' joint interests were best served by allowing business to pursue unfettered technological innovations and economic efficiencies; the free market would do the rest to deliver to consumers the best quality goods at the cheapest price. During the 1920s, Americans engaged in mass consuming more intensively than ever before, in a national marketplace where manufacturers, distributors, and advertisers essentially enjoyed free rein. But so long as exciting new products like automobiles, radios, and household appliances kept coming onto the market, and affluence seemed to be growing – at least for the middle and upper classes, who could afford these consumer durables – few challenged the status quo by calling for stronger regulation.[4]

Finally, although consumer consciousness was not high in the production-driven prosperity of the 1920s, consumers had set some precedents earlier in organizing themselves to assert influence in the marketplace. Occasionally over the previous two decades, housewives at the local level had successfully boycotted butchers and other merchants to bring down prices when they climbed too high. For example, in kosher meat boycotts of 1902, rent strikes in 1904 and 1907–8, and cost-of-living protests of 1917, New York's immigrant Jewish housewives appealed to women within their own communities to use their collective strength as consumers to bring down prices.[5] More visible nationally had been the effort of middle-class women's reform organizations such as the National Consumers' League (NCL) and its state chapters to organize mostly female consumers to use their purchasing power to improve the wages and working conditions of employed women and children. From 1908 through the early 1920s, NCL members used an appeal to "ethical consumption" to lobby impressively for protective labor legislation, child labor laws, and other improvements in the retail and industrial workplace. Only on rare occasions, however, did the

---

4 On consumer-oriented legislation during the Progressive era and the dearth of consumer activity during the 1920s, see Robert N. Mayer, *The Consumer Movement: Guardians of the Marketplace* (Boston, 1989), 10–19; Helen Sorenson, *The Consumer Movement: What It Is and What It Means* (New York, 1941), 6–9; Mark V. Nadel, *The Politics of Consumer Protection* (Indianapolis, Ind., 1971), 3–16; Lucy Black Creighton, *Pretenders to the Throne* (Lexington, Mass., 1976), 7–18.

5 Paula E. Hyman, "Immigrant Women and Consumer Protest: The New York City Kosher Meat Boycott of 1902," *American Jewish History* 70, no. 1 (Sept. 1980): 91–105; Dana Frank, "Housewives, Socialists, and the Politics of Good: The 1917 New York Cost-of-Living Protests," *Feminist Studies* 11, no. 2 (summer 1985): 255–85; Annelise Orleck, *Common Sense and a Little Fire: Women and Working-Class Politics in the United States, 1900–1965* (Chapel Hill, N.C., 1995), 27–30. See Sorenson, *Consumer Movement,* 7, on more middle-class women's protests through Housewives Leagues against the price of eggs and apples in Chicago and Philadelphia around 1912 and Gary R. Mormino and George E. Pozzetta, *The Immigrant World of Ybor City: Italians and Their Latin Neighbors in Tampa, 1885–1985* (Urbana, Ill., 1990), 157, on consumer boycotts in Tampa during World War I.

NCL concern itself with the exploitation of the consumer.[6] The Seattle labor movement similarly used consumer boycotts to punish employers during its impressive organizing drives after World War I.[7] In short, organized consumers and workers – although strongly committed to improving the quality of working-class life – shared the assumption of government policymakers and businessmen that bettering the conditions of production held the key to building a healthier American economy and society. Consumers benefited from the fruits of mass consumption and might even try to improve the conditions under which these goods were produced, but few people before the 1930s considered consumers a self-conscious, identifiable interest group on a par with labor and business whose well-being required attention for American capitalism and democracy to work.

The Great Depression changed many aspects of the American political economy. A national welfare state emerged, industrial relations were restructured around state-sanctioned collective bargaining, and the federal government assumed a more active role in the economy. Less often mentioned but equally noteworthy was a growing recognition by those in and out of government of the importance of the consumer interest. By the end of the depression decade, invoking "the consumer" had become an acceptable way of promoting the public good, of defending the economic rights and needs of ordinary citizens. As the economist John Kenneth Galbraith argued in his *American Capitalism* of 1956 and the historian Ellis Hawley elaborated a decade later, the New Deal's lasting impact, even if haphazardly improvised like so many of Roosevelt's policies, lay in institutionalizing the concept of "countervailing power" or "counterorganization." By this Galbraith and Hawley meant the New Deal government's efforts to promote the organization of economically weak groups and then to balance the interests of one power concentrate against another, thereby restoring the economic equilibrium upset by the Great Depression without having to confront more directly existing bastions of power such as American business.[8]

6 Allis Rosenberg Wolfe, "Women, Consumerism, and the National Consumers' League in the Progressive Era, 1900–1923," *Labor History* 16, no. 3 (summer 1975): 378–92; Kathryn Kish Sklar, "Two Political Cultures in the Progressive Era: The National Consumers' League and the American Association for Labor Legislation," in Linda K. Kerber, Alice Kessler-Harris, and Kathryn Kish Sklar, eds., *U.S. History as Women's History: New Feminist Essays* (Chapel Hill, N.C., 1995), 36–62; Landon R.Y. Storrs, "Civilizing Capitalism: The National Consumers' League and the Politics of 'Fair' Labor Standards in the New Deal Era," Ph.D. diss., University of Wisconsin, 1994, chap. 1; "National Consumers' League: Memorandum for National Social Work Council," n.d. but c. 1924, Erma Angevine papers, Rutgers University Special Collections (Rutgers), box 5, folder B-1 "Florence Kelley"; "History of Consumers League of New Jersey (1900–1950)," Consumers' League of New Jersey papers (CLNJ), Rutgers, inventory file. See Kathryn Kish Sklar's chapter in this book.
7 Dana Frank, *Purchasing Power: Consumer Organizing, Gender, and the Seattle Labor Movement, 1919–1929* (New York, 1994).
8 John Kenneth Galbraith, *American Capitalism: The Concept of Countervailing Power* (Boston, 1956); Ellis Hawley, *The New Deal and the Problem of Monopoly: A Study in Economic Ambivalence* (Princeton,

In developing this argument, Hawley stressed the New Deal's empowerment of the farmer, laborer, and small businessman, but its growing attentiveness to consumers as a way of institutionalizing and protecting the public interest fits as well. As the federal government vastly expanded in authority, it became imperative politically that the general good somehow be represented; making the "consumer" a residual category and charging the state with protecting that interest became ways of mitigating against the excessive power of other political blocs, including the state itself. Attending to the consumer also conformed to another prevailing tendency of the New Deal, the commitment to ameliorate a severely damaged economy without jettisoning the basic tenets of capitalism. Empowering the consumer seemed to many New Dealers a way of enhancing the public's stake in society and the economy while still preserving the free enterprise system.

Historians of the consumer movement often consider its concrete achievements during the 1930s meager.[9] What those assessments miss, however, is that the Great Depression spawned a larger reconceptualization of the role of the consumer among state policymakers and in civil society that World War II and the postwar period would extend. "I believe we are at the threshold of a fundamental change in our popular economic thought, that in the future we are going to think less about the producer and more about the consumer," the Democratic presidential contender Franklin Delano Roosevelt forecast in his last campaign address before being nominated in 1932.[10] Although FDR's administration would only gradually break with the classical economic thinking that had dominated during the 1920s and early depression, by the end of his presidency in 1945 he had presided over a recalibrating of the balance between consumer and producer interests thought necessary to keep a democratic society and capitalist economy healthy.

Roosevelt's perception that the consumer was becoming more central likely grew out of a rumbling of consumer discontent that had begun in the mid-1920s and intensified as the depression worsened in the early 1930s. In best-selling books such as Stuart Chase's *The Tragedy of Waste* (1925), Chase and Frederick J. Schlink's *Your Money's Worth* (1927), and Schlink and Arthur Kallet's *100,000,000 Guinea Pigs: Dangers in Everyday Foods, Drugs, and Cosmetics* (1933), economists, engineers, and social activists began

N.J., 1966), 187–90. See also Alan Brinkley, "Prosperity, Depression, and War, 1920–1945," in Eric Foner, ed., *The New American History* (Philadelphia, 1990), 132–3 for helpful treatment of what he terms a "broker state."
9 Creighton, *Pretenders to the Throne*, 25–7; Hawley, *New Deal and Problem of Monopoly*, 198–204, 275.
10 Quoted in Persia Campbell, *Consumer Representation in the New Deal* (New York, 1940), 17.

to call for impartial product testing and enforced commodity standards to protect consumers from the deceptions of merchandisers. Consumers, they argued, were paying too high a price for the success of mass production. Soon after *Your Money's Worth* appeared, Schlink transformed his small local consumer club and testing lab in White Plains, New York, into a more substantial national organization, Consumers' Research, with its own monthly publication, *Consumers' Research Bulletin*. Other independent product testing organizations – Intermountain Consumers' Service and Consumers Union – followed. Although highly critical of the abuse of consumers, particularly by advertisers, these consumer advocates did not call for any major structural changes in the economy or government. Rather, they hoped that scientific research into product quality would allow the free market to work better, by creating more knowledgeable consumers to counterbalance exploitative merchandisers. As Americans faced steadily declining incomes with the deterioration of the economy in the 1930s, they increasingly looked to the burgeoning consumer movement's books and publications for help in stretching their dollars.[11]

FDR's interest in the consumer was also undoubtedly provoked by liberal reformers both within and outside his circle of advisers as they grappled with ways to pull the United States out of the Great Depression. Rexford Tugwell, Gardiner Means, Raymond Mohl, and Adolph Berle Jr. were all Columbia University professors (three economists and a lawyer) who advised Roosevelt's campaign and on his election became part of his so-called brain trust. In advocating a more planned economy to balance the narrow self-interest of business, these economic advisers considered consumers a crucial part of the larger community whose interests needed to be taken better into account.[12] Furthermore, a political challenge to the Democratic Party and Roosevelt from the Left put the consumer at the center of a critique of the mainstream political parties. In the fall of 1929, the Democratic and educational theorist John Dewey and the progressive economist Paul Douglas founded a new third party, the League for Independent Political Action, around the interests of consumers, because "the needs and troubles of the people are connected with problems of consumption, with problems of the maintenance of a reasonably decent and secure standard of living." The existing parties, they argued, grew out of "that stage of American life when the American people as a whole felt that society was to

---

11 Mayer, *Consumer Movement,* 20–2; Creighton, *Pretenders to the Throne,* 19–22; Sorenson, *Consumer Movement,* 31–55.

12 Alan Brinkley, *The End of Reform: New Deal Liberalism in Recession and War* (New York, 1995), 37–40, 67–72; Arthur M. Schlesinger Jr., *The Age of Roosevelt: The Crisis of the Old Order* (Boston, 1957), 398–403.

advance by means of industrial inventions and their application," and Americans still clung to protecting the interests of producers – at the expense of consumers – even when that era had long passed.

Although the league was loosely based on the British Labour Party, it saw its primary political base not in the working class but in the middle class – teachers, small merchants, and white-collar workers – which in Dewey's words "represents most adequately the interests of the consumer." The league never gained much popular political support and in targeting the middle classes even managed to alienate otherwise sympathetic socialists. But Dewey and Douglas's prominence in Progressive circles and their writings, such as Dewey's three-part series "The Need for a New Party" in the *New Republic* (March–April 1931) and Douglas's *The Coming of a New Party* (1932), drew attention to the converging interests of consumers in the economy and voting citizens in a democracy.[13] Even before the New Deal had come into being, the consumer was being clothed in the mantle of the public interest. Over the course of the 1930s, New Deal policymakers would experiment with different ways of recognizing consumers, and consumers themselves would increasingly mobilize around that identity to make economic and political demands of those in power.

The New Deal acknowledged consumers in two ways that were often intertwined. First, several key New Deal agencies had consumer offices within them to give official representation to that perspective. Second, economic understanding of why the United States was suffering from such a severe depression and what was necessary to pull it out increasingly focused on consumer behavior.

The National Recovery Administration (NRA) was the keystone of the first New Deal program for economic recovery, and its inconsistent treatment of consumers reflects the Roosevelt administration's initial ambivalence about supporting consumers alongside producers. Without undertaking a full-fledged analysis of the strengths and weaknesses of the NRA, it can be said that the NRA both established the importance of the consumer in economic recovery and failed to empower consumers sufficiently to shape the program in their interest. The basic premise of the NRA endorsed the centrality of the consumer in the economy: government policies to increase purchasing power would draw the nation out of depression. In theory, "codes of fair competition" allowed industrialists from particular

---

13 John Dewey, "The Need for a New Party," *The New Republic*, Mar. 18, 1931, 115–17; Mar. 25, 1931, 150–2; Apr. 1, 1931, 177–9; Paul H. Douglas, *The Coming of a New Party* (New York, 1932); Robert B. Westbrook, *John Dewey and American Democracy* (Ithaca, N.Y., 1991), 443–50; Schlesinger, *Crisis of Old Order*, 142, 198, 436.

sectors to agree without fear of antitrust prosecution on common policies, particularly setting minimum prices and hourly wages and maximum working hours. With prices and wages raised and jobs spread around, consumer demand would be increased. As better-off, employed consumers bought more goods at high prices, producers ranging from farmers to manufacturers would prosper, in turn creating more consumer demand. In recognition of their key role in recovery, the NRA administrative structure called for consumers to be represented along with labor and business on the NRA code authorities, as well as through a Consumer Advisory Board and later a specially appointed consumer representative.

But although the NRA in principle represented an important break from Hooverite Republican strategies for dealing with the depression, which were based on an assumption of overproduction rather than underconsumption, the way the NRA was implemented ultimately perpetuated Republican tendencies such as the cartelization of major industries and denigrated Democratic innovations such as giving a real voice to consumers. Much of the backpedaling was due to the leadership of General Hugh Johnson, the NRA's first director, who thwarted efforts to empower consumers at every turn. He preferred invoking the mutuality of interests between business and the consumer through patriotic campaigns, such as those featuring display cards with the NRA's blue eagle that urged, "When you buy cigars you help provide incomes for farmers, labor, salesmen, dealers and yourself. Buy now."[14] Most basically, however, New Dealers may have articulated different commitments than their Republican predecessors, but in Roosevelt's first administration they still functioned within a classical economic paradigm where attention focused on achieving recovery through more efficient production, with the assumption that increased consumption would automatically follow. Underconsumption may have been a root cause of depression, according to the Democrats, but the route to improving consumer fortunes – and hence the economy – still lay with assisting business, not its customers.[15]

The NRA's Consumer Advisory Board (CAB) was caught in this contradiction. Staffed with liberal, consumer-minded economists, sociologists, and reformers, it battled the code authorities and NRA administrators to protect consumers when prices seemed fixed too high, to seek quality stan-

14 Sorenson, *Consumer Movement*, 163.
15 On the economic thinking of the Republicans and the creators of the NRA, see Brinkley, *End of Reform*, 36–9, 69–82; John Kenneth Galbraith, *The Affluent Society* (Boston, 1958), 16–18; Alan Sweezy, "The Keynesians and Government Policy, 1933–1939," *American Economic Review* 62, no. 2 (May 1972): 116–17; Hawley, *New Deal and the Problem of Monopoly*, 188–90.

dards and labeling of goods, and to sponsor consumer councils on a coun-
tywide basis "to make consumers' wants known" through an experimental
program headed by Paul Douglas. When the NRA became defunct in 1935,
the CAB was considered weak and a failure, along with the rest of the
NRA. But it nonetheless made a mark, at least on national consciousness.
As the sociologist Robert Lynd, who served on the CAB, noted, "It was no
secret around Washington as the NRA episode wore on that the consumer
representatives in Washington embodied this 'public interest' in their proposals day in and day out far more nearly than did either of the far bigger
and better supported advisory boards representing industry and labor."
Whereas once business was assumed by definition to serve the general welfare as it prospered, by the end of the NRA it was generally understood
among policymakers that the public interest needed independent representation to balance producers and, to a lesser extent, labor; acknowledging
"consumers" as a distinct constituency seemed to offer a viable approach.[16]

The story was much the same in the other New Deal agencies that recognized the consumer interest: The consumer viewpoint became institutionalized even though concrete achievements toward protecting consumers' rights and needs were often limited. The Office of the Consumer
Counsel in the Agricultural Adjustment Administration (AAA) was among
the most effective, because of both its official status within the agency and
the strong leadership exercised by the liberal reformers Frederick C. Howe
and Donald E. Montgomery as counsels. Whereas the AAA devoted itself to
increasing farm prices by controlling supply to restore the livelihoods – and
purchasing power – of farmers, the counsel's office watched out for the
consumer, lobbying to ensure that farm produce was plentiful enough and
price increases fair. Although the Counsel did not always succeed in protecting consumers' best interest, he and his department managed to keep
the public informed about how agricultural policy affected them through
press conferences, radio broadcasts, and the regular publication of the *Consumers Guide,* which by the mid-1930s had become almost a service organ
of the consumer movement.[17]

16 Robert S. Lynd, "Foreword," in Campbell, *Consumer Representation in the New Deal,* 11. On the
   NRA and specifically the CAB, see Campbell, *Consumer Representation in the New Deal,* 27–88; Persia Campbell, *Bringing the Consumer Point of View into Government* (Greeley, Colo., 1958), 14–17;
   Sorenson, *Consumer Movement,* 14–20; Hawley, *New Deal and the Problem of Monopoly,* 75–146; "The
   Consumer Movement," *Business Week,* Apr. 22, 1939, 45; Dexter M. Keezer, "The Consumer Under
   the National Recovery Administration," *Annals of the American Academy of Political and Social Science*
   172 (Mar. 1934): 88–97; Paul H. Douglas, "The Role of the Consumer in the New Deal," *Annals of
   the American Academy of Political and Social Science,* 98–106.
17 For a detailed discussion of the Consumer Counsel of the AAA, see Campbell, *Consumer Representation in the New Deal,* 194–261; Campbell, *Bringing the Consumer Point of View into Government,* 17–18;

Another effective effort at involving consumers in New Deal programs revolved around delivering reasonably priced electricity to American farmers. The Tennessee Valley Authority (TVA, established 1933) and particularly the Rural Electrification Administration (REA, established 1935) organized and financed cooperative associations to bring electricity to rural America, so poorly served by private power companies that, as late as 1935, nine of ten rural homes were not electrified. In mobilizing people at the grass roots, these government-sanctioned and -supported cooperatives became long-lasting strongholds of consumer activism.[18] Furthermore, a number of other successful New Deal agencies not commonly associated with consumer advocacy in fact aimed at protecting consumers while also propping up the institutional foundations of capitalism: The Federal Housing Administration (FHA) and Home Loan Corporation (HOLC) offered consumers dependable, low-cost home financing, the Federal Deposit Insurance Corporation (FDIC) guaranteed bank deposits, and the Securities and Exchange Commission (SEC) regulated public offerings of corporate securities.[19]

Less successful was the Consumers Council of the National Bituminous Coal Commission. Although empowered by Congress to represent the consumer point of view on a commission established to revitalize the bituminous coal industry, the council faced tremendous hostility from the commission during its short existence from 1937 to 1940.[20] Nor did anything come of the concerted effort of New Dealers like Leon Henderson, Jacob Baker, and Thomas Blaisdell to establish a Department of the Consumer to balance the Departments of Commerce, Labor, and Agriculture and coordinate government activities related to consumers.[21] But even though the New Deal frequently fell short in delivering on its commitment to the consumer – often because traditionally powerful constituencies like business were favored – New Dealers from FDR on down persisted in trumpeting the consumer interest as a way of making more palatable the state expansion in which they were engaged. Roosevelt justified the new consumer offices in his New Deal agencies as representing "a new principle in

Erma Angevine and Dr. Caroline F. Ware, *Effective Consumer Participation: Consumer Participation in Federal Decision Making* (Washington, D.C., 1981), 7–8, Erma Angevine papers, Rutgers, box 6, folder E-4.

18 Mayer, *Consumer Movement,* 23–4; Angevine and Ware, *Effective Consumer Participation,* 9.

19 Pearce C. Kelley, *Consumer Economics* (Homewood, Ill., 1953), 145; Warren C. Waite and Ralph Cassady Jr., *The Consumer and the Economic Order* (New York, 1949), 124–5.

20 Nadel, *Politics of Consumer Protection,* 21; Campbell, *Bringing the Consumer Point of View into Government,* 18–19; Sorenson, *Consumer Movement,* 19–20.

21 Sorenson, *Consumer Movement,* 19; Creighton, *Pretenders to the Throne,* 27, 39; Douglas, "Role of the Consumer in the New Deal," 104.

government" that consumers have the right "to have their interests represented in the formulation of government policy. . . . Never before had the particular problems of consumers been so thoroughly and unequivocally accepted as the direct responsibility of government. The willingness to fulfill that responsibility was, in essence, an extension and amplification of the meaning and content of democratic government." Gardiner Means, on leave from Columbia to serve on the NRA's CAB and as economic adviser on finance to the secretary of agriculture, elaborated that consumer representation in government "may well be the key that will open the way to a truly American solution of the problem which is leading other countries in the direction of either fascism or communism." By empowering consumers, these state builders seemed to be reassuring themselves as well as others, a strong federal government could become a vehicle for greater democracy rather than an agent of totalitarianism, as many skeptics feared.[22]

The New Deal's recognition of consumers went beyond giving their representatives seats at agency negotiating tables. In 1938 the first substantial regulatory legislation since the Progressive era passed Congress: the Food, Drug, and Cosmetic Act and the Wheeler–Lea Amendment to the Clayton Anti-Trust Act of 1914. These were not easy laws to push through. Five years of debate, delays, and revisions plagued the visionary consumer protection legislation originally proposed by Assistant Secretary of Agriculture Tugwell in 1933, and the results reflected compromises with food, drug, cosmetics, and advertising industries determined to stave off further state regulation. But although consumer advocates then and after rightfully despaired of the difficulties encountered in strengthening basic consumer protections, particularly in getting the government to set standards for commodities, it is important not to lose sight of the fact that here, too, the events of the 1930s reversed trends under way during the 1920s to minimize the state's role in mediating between producers and consumers. Rather, by the end of the decade, as a result of these two new laws, the FDA's jurisdiction was extended to include cosmetics and medical devices, its ability to require new labeling and prevent adulteration and misbranding was expanded, drug manufacturers needed to prove to the FDA that products were safe before they could put them on the market, and enforcement procedures against hazardous substances were strengthened. Furthermore, although consumer advocates lost the battle to give control over advertising to the more stringent FDA rather than to the FTC, in the end the FTC

22 *The Public Papers and Addresses of Franklin D. Roosevelt with a Special Introduction and Explanatory Notes by President Roosevelt*, vol. 3: *The Advance of Recovery and Reform, 1934* (New York, 1938), 57; Gardiner C. Means, "The Consumer and the New Deal," *Annals of the American Academy of Political and Social Science* 173 (May 1934): 7.

gained new powers over harmful business practices, including the right to take action against advertising that threatened the public interest, whether or not competition was jeopardized. These 1938 laws were far from models of consumer protection legislation, yet they marked another way that consumer interests had become a renewed concern of the state by the end of the 1930s.[23]

Most of this discussion has focused on the official recognition that the New Deal gave consumers through institutionalizing consumer representatives in federal agencies and sponsoring legislation to protect their interests. Overall, it was a mixed record, with greater evidence of ideological commitment than concrete achievement. The other way that the Roosevelt administration gave new importance to consumers – by considering consumer behavior the key to economic recovery – proved more acceptable. The growing conviction that consumers held the present and future health of the American capitalist economy in their hands made the consumer interest of pressing economic – not just political – significance. As I have already argued, enhancing consumer purchasing power was the goal of New Deal recovery programs beginning with the NRA and AAA. But as government policymakers increasingly accepted Keynesian economic theory, particularly after the economic nose dive brought on by the "Roosevelt depression of 1937–38," pump priming moved to an entirely new level, with government spending to expand mass consumption becoming the assumed route out of depression toward renewed economic growth.[24]

The Keynesian paradigm was most explicitly developed in John Maynard Keynes's *The General Theory of Employment, Interest, and Money* of 1936, although it was already popular in reform circles. It became widely accepted by government economists by the late 1930s, was reinforced by the wartime economy, and then had its heyday with the unprecedented capitalist prosperity of postwar America. Keynesianism shared the New Deal's earlier conviction that underconsumption was the root cause of the depression and that increasing purchasing power was the key to recovery. What dif-

23 Mayer, *Consumer Movement,* 24–5; Sorenson, *Consumer Movement,* 12–14; Nadel, *Politics of Consumer Protection,* 16–18; "Business Reports to Executives on the Consumer Movement," *Business Week,* Apr. 22, 1939, 44–5.
24 My discussion of Keynesianism has benefited from the following works: the masterful intellectual history in Brinkley, *End of Reform,* 65–85, 116–17, 231–5; Alan Sweezy, "The Keynesian Revolution and Its Pioneers: The Keynesians and Government Policy, 1933–1939," *American Economic Review* 62, no. 2 (May 1972): 116–24; George Soule, "This Recovery: What Brought It? And Will It Last?" *Harper's* 174 (Mar. 1937): 337–45; Galbraith, *Affluent Society,* 16–18, 188–93; Daniel Bell, *The End of Ideology* (Cambridge, Mass., 1988), 75–80; Martyn J. Lee, *Consumer Culture Reborn: The Cultural Politics of Consumption* (London, 1993), 80–1.

fered, however, was that under Keynes's influence economists now argued that in a mature economy like America's private investment and self-regulating markets alone could not support sufficient growth. Rather, the government would have to play a major role in fueling aggregate demand – through such strategies as jobs programs, public works, or tax policies – and thereby raise the level of production and employment. Whereas proponents of classical economics, including FDR in his first term, had worried about balancing the budget, Keynesians argued that deficit spending by government was often necessary to fuel aggregate consumer demand and did not endanger the overall health of the economy. With the Keynesian revolution, then, consumers became responsible for high productivity and full employment whereas a decade earlier that role had belonged to producers.

As New Dealers pursued a Keynesian policy of boosting demand in the late 1930s, they felt they were enhancing American democracy much as they did when they institutionalized the consumer perspective in a growing state bureaucracy. Keynes and his followers felt that the fate of democracy in the world as an alternative to communism and fascism rested on America's success in reviving capitalism. Within the United States, moreover, Keynesianism was thought to encourage greater economic egalitarianism because dynamic consumer demand depended on a wide distribution of purchasing power; concentration of wealth in a few hands, in contrast, led to excessive saving and only minimal spending. Mass consuming was thereby becoming an integral part of American democratic life. As Ernest Erber, a regional planner, reminded a younger colleague years later, "The prosperity of this nation is built upon spending, not saving. You might be too young to recall the campaign waged by Chambers of Commerce against money hoarding during the 1930s. During those grim days, the man who spent freely was extolled as a national hero and the one who saved his money as a public enemy."[25] "Mass consumption" – the participation of the mass of Americans in purchasing goods not only became the ideal route to capitalist prosperity for the nation, but also seemed to promise a citizenry of economic equals, without necessitating a direct attack on inequality. John Kenneth Galbraith in fact would lament in the midst of the supposedly prosperous 1950s that as a result of Keynesian thinking, conservatives and liberals alike had become invested in an expanding economy as the best way to improve all Americans' standard of living, allowing them to ignore

25 Ernest Erber to John P. Wiet, July 28, 1964, Ernest Erber papers, New Jersey Room, Newark Public Library (hereafter NPL), box B, folder 2.

the need to redistribute wealth or reduce economic inequality, which persisted nonetheless.[26]

As Roosevelt accepted the renomination for president in Philadelphia in 1936, he assured Americans, "Today we stand committed to the proposition that freedom is no half-and-half affair. If the average citizen is guaranteed equal opportunity in the polling place, he must have equal opportunity in the market place."[27] With these words on June 27 and through his administration's actions before and after that day, FDR linked the consumer with the citizen in a democracy. Consumers needed representation in government to give voice to the general good; consumers needed protection through legislation to avoid exploitation by manufacturers and advertisers; consumers, by actively participating in a mass consumption economy, kept alive the nation's traditional commitments to democracy and equality. By the end of the decade, consumers had become a distinctive interest group whose well-being had major consequences for the survival of American capitalism and democracy.

Yet despite the growing importance of the consumer during the 1930s in all of the ways mentioned, it was the least politically threatening conception of the consumer – consumers in the aggregate as engine of economic growth – that public officials embraced. That consumers by the end of the decade were valued more for the money they spent than the way they championed the public good would have a bearing on how the "Consumer's Republic" developed in the postwar era. Mass consumption would prove central to American society after the war, but consumer purchasing power in the aggregate aimed at delivering economic prosperity and democratic egalitarianism would prevail over the rights and protections of individual consumers.

In focusing on the way policymakers and economists in Washington conceptualized the consumer interest during the 1930s, this essay has told only half the story. Many consumers themselves also became much more conscious of their identities and interests as consumers. Examination of Washington's increased concern with consumers is incomplete if not put in the context of a grass roots upsurge of consumer activism over the decade, often overlooked as a result of scholars' tendency to stress the revival of

26 Christopher Lasch, *The True and Only Heaven: Progress and Its Critics* (New York, 1991), 72–4; Galbraith, *Affluent Society,* 96–7.

27 "'We Are Fighting to Save a Great and Precious Form of Government for Ourselves and the World' – Acceptance of the Renomination for the Presidency, Philadelphia, Pa., June 27, 1936," *Public Papers and Addresses of Franklin D. Roosevelt, with a Special Introduction and Explanatory Notes by President Roosevelt,* vol. 4: *1936* (New York, 1938), 234.

producer activism through the labor movement of the 1930s. In some cases, as with the consumer movement's lobbying for protective legislation, the link between grass roots organizing and government response is easily discernible. In other cases, the impact of consumer assertiveness on policy is harder to track. Regardless, the New Deal's sudden attention to consumers as a residual category of the public interest offered otherwise underrepresented groups an opportunity to become another "countervailing power" worthy of official recognition. Farmers had found that their difficulties making agriculture profitable were of central concern to the New Deal "broker state." Industrialists' struggles to revive their mills and factories had become the project of the NRA. Workingmen had gained a voice through both the revived – and increasingly male-oriented – labor movement of the 1930s and New Deal policies that recognized workers' right to organize and bargain collectively, such as Section 7A of the NRA and the National Labor Relations Act. Ethnic groups had seized the opportunity offered through the building of a national, broad-based Democratic Party to institutionalize themselves as the Polish Democratic Club or the Italian-American Democratic League.[28] Although farmers, male workers, and ethnic Americans were among those who participated in the new movement of organized consumers, the strongest voices were those of groups not otherwise well represented – women and African Americans. For these groups, identification and activism as consumers offered a new opportunity to make claims on those wielding public and private power in American society.

But an analysis of the social and political pressures for state action on behalf of consumers is beyond the scope of this essay. Rather, I have focused here on the way that statemakers from President Roosevelt on down assigned new importance to the consumer in the midst of severe depression and not prosperity, and how they made mass consumption and mass consumers more central to political and economic policy. Citizen consumers were made from the top down as well as the bottom up.

28 Hawley, *New Deal and the Problem of Monopoly;* Elizabeth Faue, *Community of Suffering and Struggle: Women, Men, and the Labor Movement in Minneapolis, 1915–1945* (Chapel Hill, N.C., 1991); Cohen, *Making a New Deal.*

6

Consumer Spending as State Project

Yesterday's Solutions and Today's Problems

GEORGE LIPSITZ

As we approach the end of the twentieth century, "socialist" states have disappeared and been replaced by governments based on market capitalism. Formerly antiimperialist and anticolonialist leaders in Asia, Africa, and Latin America compete with each other to make concessions to the International Monetary Fund and the World Bank in order to secure outside investment. The active oppositional movements of the 1960s no longer exist; mass protest and grass roots organizing no longer threaten the immediate interests of the powerful in any meaningful way. Trade unions in advanced capitalist countries have suffered sharp declines in membership and have systematically surrendered the gains they had made by midcentury.

Neoconservatives have secured control of state policy everywhere.[1] They have cut state spending on education, health, and welfare; privatized public enterprises; liberalized trade; devalued currency; restricted credit; lowered wages; and eliminated significant areas of business regulation. For years, we have been told that all of these measures were necessary to bring about economic growth, social stability, and cultural unity. But what has actually taken place instead?

Lower wages and reduced public spending have led to less buying power, increased unemployment, unendurable debt, and economic austerity. During the social democratic era from 1948 to 1973, global gross national product (GNP) grew by almost 5 percent every year. But with the emergence of neoconservative policies between 1974 and 1989, it grew at only half the rate of the previous period. Since 1989, growth has been even slower.[2] In

---

1 I use the term "neoconservative" to distinguish the active, authoritarian, interventionist, probusiness conservatism of Thatcher, Reagan, and Gingrich from the limited, libertarian, laissez-faire conservatism of previous eras.
2 Dan Gallin, "Inside the New World Order," *New Politics* 9 (summer 1994): 114.

Asia, Africa, and Latin America, the income gap between the rich and the poor doubled during the 1980s. In Brazil alone, the top fifth of income earners secure 26 times more than the bottom fifth.[3] Globally, the wealthiest fifth of the world population, living mostly in Europe and North America, maintains an income 150 times greater than that of the poorest fifth, living mostly in the southern hemisphere.[4] Seventy-seven percent of the world's population earns 15 percent of global income.[5]

Thirty percent of the world's work force, more than 820 million people, either are without jobs or are working for less than subsistence wages.[6] The number of refugees in the world in 1992 grew by about 10,000 per day, with about 19 million forced outside their national borders and another 24 million "internally displaced." Never have so many people been forced to seek refuge and asylum.[7] Although the low wage labor of refugees fattens the profits of transnational corporations and helps lower prices and hide the stagnation of real wages for workers in advanced industrialized countries, it also registers the verdict on neoconservative structural adjustment policies in Asia, Africa, and Latin America by residents of those continents. As Walden Bello argues:

> Perhaps it is the migrants who most clearly perceive the truth about structural adjustment; it was intended not as a transition to prosperity but as a permanent condition of economic suffering to ensure that the South would never rise again to challenge the North. If that is the case, flight is a rational solution. Migrants are not obsessed nomads seeking the emerald cities . . . ; they are refugees fleeing the wasteland that has been created by the economic equivalent of a scorched earth strategy.[8]

In the United States the figures are less stark, but decline and stagnation are no less real. Thirty-eight million workers in the United States lost their jobs in the 1970s as a result of plant shutdowns, cutbacks in municipal and state spending, and computer generated automation. Between 1979 and 1984 more than one-fifth of new full-time jobs paid less than seven thousand dollars per year (in 1984 dollars). For the entire 1980s, 85 percent of new jobs were in the lowest paying categories. Forty percent of the U.S. work force had no pension plans and 20 percent had no health insurance.

---

3 Walden Bello, *Dark Victory: The United States, Structural Adjustment and Global Poverty* (London, 1994), 52.
4 Davidson Budhoo, "IMF-World Bank Wreak Havoc on the Third World," in Kevin Danaher, ed., *50 Years Is Enough: The Case Against the World Bank and the International Monetary Fund* (Boston, 1994), 22.
5 Bello, *Dark Victory,* 52.
6 Robin Wright, "A Revolution at Work," *Los Angeles Times,* Mar. 7, 1995, H1.
7 Gallin, "Inside the New World Order," 121.
8 Walden Bello, "Global Economic Counterrevolution: How Northern Economic Warfare Devastates the South," in Danaher, ed., *50 Years Is Enough,* 19.

The real income of the richest 1 percent of the population increased by close to 20 percent, while the real income of the poorest 40 percent of the population suffered a 10 percent decline. In a period when housing costs doubled and the prices of basic necessities increased by 100 percent, real discretionary income fell 18 percent between 1973 and 1989.[9]

The rise of transnational corporations and the seeming inability of the nation-state to trap the newly mobile capital by regulating, taxing, or directing it toward socially useful ends have something to do with the rise of new technologies, with the ways in which satellite, computer chip, and fiber-optic technologies have increased the mobility of capital, separated management from production, and encouraged the kinds of post-Fordist flexible accumulation relying on the exploitation of low wage labor. But neoconservative ideology to the contrary, almost all of the advantages enjoyed by capital in the post-Fordist era have been the products of state action, not private initiative. Business mobilizations in the 1970s and 1980s poured new money into politics, securing a base for probusiness policies and raising the costs of entry into the political sphere for groups with fewer resources. Business influence encouraged massive expenditures on "defense" that provided a steady flow of capital into the coffers of large corporations. Business interests shaped changes in the tax code that made investment income more valuable than wage income, that encouraged investment in automation to increase the use of low wage labor, investment for corporate acquisitions and real estate, and discouraged investment in enterprises likely to produce large numbers of high paying jobs.

Government research and development spending shaped the development of key technologies like containerization and computerization so that they would serve the interests of business and promote "downsizing," "restructuring," and "reengineering" in ways that strengthened capital against labor. The Department of the Navy drew up the first plans for containerization in shipping, which made it possible to export heavy industrial production to low wage countries. The Department of Defense drew up the first plans for computer communication networks like the Internet. These research and development efforts on new technologies by the military not only socialized the risk of developing technologies whose profits could then be expropriated privately but also directed technology itself along lines conducive to business needs. Thus, the contemporary eclipse of the state by the power of private capital and transnational corporations

9 Katherine S. Newman, "Uncertain Seas: Cultural Turmoil and the Domestic Economy," in Alan Wolfe, ed., *America at Century's End* (Berkeley, Calif., 1991), 116–17, 121; William Chafe, *The Unfinished Journey: America Since World War II* (New York, 1988), 449.

hides the crucial role of the state in promoting, protecting, and preserving the technologies, social relations, and economic interests of corporate capital and finance. The ever growing inequality and maldistribution of wealth in the United States and around the world in an era of enormous economic growth and record corporate profits are no accident or anomaly; they are the intended consequence of deliberate policies enacted by the state in the interests of business.

Since concerted and consistent action by the state has been responsible for such serious declines in resources, life chances, and quality of life for most people, one might expect oppositional social movements to arise. Popular pressure could still coerce the state into fiscal policies that subsidized economic infrastructure rather than capital flight, that equalized rather than stratified economic opportunity, that enforced fair wages and hours laws as a means of raising rather than lowering global working conditions. The state is still quite capable of setting up institutions aimed at equalizing power relations between capital and labor or between capital and consumers.[10] Why have social movements fighting for these changes been so slow to emerge? Again, state policies hold some of the answers. The neoconservative politicians and ideologues who have worked assiduously to diminish the capacity of the state to serve as a source of social justice have devoted enormous energies toward strengthening the state as an instrument of repression and incarceration to protect the interests of capital. At the same time, neoconservative political mobilizations have succeeded in enabling capital to evade responsibility for the policies that it has profited from by blaming the ensuing social crises they cause on their main victims. Ever since the Nixon presidency, neoconservative politics have relied on "moral panics" about crime, welfare, and "drugs, sex, and rock 'n' roll" to blame the social disintegration and economic decline caused by their own policies on their primary victims – working women, low wage laborers, racialized minorities, the unemployed, and the homeless.

Yet as important as it has been for neoconservatives to mobilize state resources and to demonize the primary victims of their policies, they have also benefited from the success of previous state policies promoting the primacy of consumer spending as the center of the social world. Their expressly political activities have hidden and obscured the workings of politics, rendering largely individual and personal grievances that are actually collective and social. We see evidence of this history all around us, even if we are unaware of its origins. In advanced capitalist countries at the close of

10 Simon Head, "The New, Ruthless Economy," *New York Review of Books* 43, no. 4 (Feb. 19, 1996): 51.

the twentieth century, activities associated with consumer spending occupy the center of the social world. Government fiscal policies privilege the confidence of consumers and the avarice of investors over the interests of ordinary citizens and workers. Developers destroy viable neighborhoods and demolish ecologically sustainable areas in order to secure maximal profits from luxury commercial and residential projects. Television programming divides families into market segments, colonizes intimate moments and personal spaces for advertising purposes, and promotes infantile narcissism and grandiose desires. Political campaigns revolve around manipulative media messages that project entertaining identities while demonizing opponents. The "information superhighway" thus looks more like a shopping mall than a public thoroughfare. Educators and artists find themselves forced to deliver immediate gratifications and evoke familiar pleasures to sustain the attention of audiences in search of nothing more than amusement. Most important, the love of gain that lies at the center of contemporary culture and politics elevates the desire for personal advantage over the collective civic responsibility necessary for solving serious social problems.

The origins of today's problems lie in yesterday's solutions, especially the response by U.S. business and government to the mass mobilizations and egalitarian movements of the 1930s. Elsewhere in this book, Lizabeth Cohen and Charles McGovern offer important and original insights into the complicated links of consumer identities to citizenship during the Great Depression. My purpose here is somewhat different: to show how the exercise of state power since the 1950s has favored a vision of consumption practices aimed at eliminating the sites and social relations conducive to the emergence of social movements.

The Great Depression harmed the political reputation of capitalism and enabled the Left to position itself as a credible force for improving the material conditions of ordinary people. As the cult of the common person replaced that of the heroic rugged individual of the 1920s, general strikes, trade union organizing, and populist politicians like Huey Long demanded action from the state to address economic and social crisis. Under the leadership of Franklin Delano Roosevelt, representatives of government, business, and labor created institutions of countervailing power like the National Labor Relations Board, the Works Progress Administration, and rural cooperatives. The New Deal also used government expenditures to stimulate consumption and promote asset accumulation. The National Housing Act of 1934 created the Federal Housing Administration (FHA) and put the credit of the federal government behind home lending in order to encourage construction and real estate development. Provisions of FHA home lending policies allowing lower down payments and self-amortizing loans were aimed at limiting excessive savings and encouraging immediate spending. The Social Security Act of 1935 addressed parallel issues; by assuring workers that they would have money available in their old age, social security made it possible for them to engage in less saving and more spending in the present. In addition, many of the expenditures for public works during the New Deal created reservoirs, telephone and electric power lines, and paved roads aimed at stimulating suburban growth.[11] Low wages and high unemployment during the 1930s undercut these measures, but when defense spending for World War II generated full employment and full production, and when postwar mobilization by workers won significant wage increases, a consumption based policy of economic growth became possible.[12]

At the end of World War II, workers sought to reap the rewards of the prosperity that their labor had helped to create. They waged the largest strike wave in American history between 1944 and 1949. In the summer of 1945, United Auto Workers local union representatives called for conversion of defense plants into government run factories geared to meeting consumer needs for housing and transportation. During the 1945–6 General Motors strike, one popular demand from the rank and file was to make the company pay wage increases out of profits intended for stockholders rather than out of price increases that would be paid by workers and consumers. Business and government officials worked hard to contain working-class demands for a role in shaping decisions about the postwar economy and for a greater share of the national wealth. They made concessions, but only in ways that guaranteed expanded opportunities for private profit – highway construction rather than rapid transit, loans for single-family detached suburban houses rather than federally funded public housing or loans for renovating existing units, private pension plans and government loans for veterans rather than universal plans securing housing, medical care, pensions, and education like those adopted in other industrialized countries. Most important, they tried to divide unionized from unorganized workers, to encourage workers to think of themselves as atomized consumers rather than part of a collective body of workers or citizens.[13]

---

11 Kenneth Jackson, *Crabgrass Frontier: The Suburbanization of the United States* (New York, 1985); Jill Quadagno, "Welfare Capitalism and the Social Security Act of 1935," *American Sociological Review* 49 (1984): 632–47; M. Patricia Fernandez-Kelly, "Migration, Race, and Ethnicity in the Design of the American City," *Urban Revisions* (Los Angeles, 1994), 17.

12 George Lipsitz, *Rainbow at Midnight: Labor and Culture in the 1940s* (Urbana, Ill., 1994).

13 Ibid., 253–7.

Some economic theorists had identified underconsumption as a serious problem for the U.S. economy as early as the 1880s, and sophisticated corporate liberals devised diverse schemes based on welfare capitalism throughout the twentieth century. But only the confluence of successful social movements in the 1930s and 1940s, the crisis of capitalism during depression and war, and concerns about reverting to depression after the war could have generated the levels of government spending, the increased wages, and the business–government–labor agreements required for implementation of the earlier visions. Government spending during World War II doubled the size of the economy and gave especially impressive gains to big business. As they looked to government for direct defense spending as well as help in securing raw materials and markets overseas after the war, big business leaders accepted labor–management agreements and government programs aimed at stimulating consumption as necessary legitimation for the capital accumulation they secured from the state.

Between 1947 and 1953, federal spending on highways, home loans, and infrastructure enabled 9 million people to move to suburbs, a 43 percent growth that expanded the suburban population to nearly 30 million people. Three-quarters of suburban units were owner occupied, and advertisers noted with relish the higher spending patterns among young families in the newer suburbs.[14] Federal home loan policies that restricted down payments to 5 or 10 percent and the home owner's mortgage tax deduction gave these families increased disposable income, while easy credit and installment buying made a wide range of commodities more affordable. Builders created 30 million new housing units in the two decades following World War II; federal subsidies helped increase the percentage of home owners in the population from below 40 percent in 1940 to more than 60 percent in 1960. Spending on automobiles averaged $7.5 billion per year in the 1930s and 1940s but approached $30 billion by 1955.[15] Residential mortgage debt accounted for less than 20 percent of disposable income in 1946 but climbed to 55 percent by 1965.[16]

As Nixon's "kitchen debates" with Khrushchev demonstrated, the Cold War also shaped the strategy of mass consumption. During World War II, government officials and private advertisements had emphasized postwar prosperity as a crucial aim of the war, presenting images of full refrigera-

---

14 "The Lush New Suburban Market," *Fortune,* Nov. 1953, 128.

15 Susan Hartmann, *The Home Front and Beyond* (Boston, 1982), 165–8; John Mollenkopf, *The Contested City* (Princeton, N.J., 1983), 111.

16 Michael Stone, "Housing: The Economic Crisis," in Chester Hartman, ed., *America's Housing Crisis: What Is to Be Done?* (London, 1983), 122.

tors, powerful automobiles, and new homes even more often than appeals based on the ostensible aims of the war – victory over fascism and the triumph of the Four Freedoms.[17] In the postwar period, material abundance in the United States presented an alternative to communism; democratic access to consumer goods implied a broader democracy of life chances. Increased consumption served as a barrier against radicalism at home, but also as an image that might keep other nations out of the Soviet orbit. State Department policymakers urged European allies to adopt policies of mass consumption and mass production as both an alternative to the kinds of authoritarian rule that raised memories of prewar fascism as well as a convenient way of preparing European markets for the goods that U.S. corporations wished to sell to them.[18]

During the 1950s real wages increased by 20 percent, and by 1966 half of all workers and three-fourths of those under the age of forty had moved to suburban areas.[19] Workers secured regular vacations with pay, pensions that freed up more money for current spending, and expectations of intergenerational upward mobility. But these state subsidized improvements in material wealth also helped reconstruct the political and social world of the worker. Government-financed urban renewal destroyed urban ethnic neighborhoods that had been sources of support and solidarity for striking workers during the 1930s and 1940s, while strict contract provisions and the Taft–Hartley law mobilized trade unions as disciplinary agents guaranteeing shop floor peace to management in return for higher wages. These measures deployed the power of the state to eclipse the trade union or the ethnic inner city neighborhood with participation in a commodity driven way of life in which identities as consumers would become more important than competing identities as workers, citizens, or ethnic subjects. While relying on the power of the state, they also hid the state, privileging private acts of consumption over collective behavior and presenting the carefully constructed world of commodity relations as if it were the product of democratic choices.

Urban renewal and suburban growth played a particularly important role in transforming identities in the postwar era by creating new spatial rela-

---

17 Robert Westbrook, "'I Want a Girl Just Like the Girl That Married Harry James': American Women and the Problem of Political Obligation in World War II," *American Quarterly* 42, no. 4 (Dec. 1990): 587–614.

18 D.W. Ellwood, "The Impact of the Marshall Plan on Italy; The Impact of Italy on the Marshall Plan," in Rob Kroes, R.W. Rydell, and D. J. F. Bosscher, eds., *Cultural Transmissions and Receptions: American Mass Culture in Europe* (Amsterdam, 1993), 100–24.

19 David Brody, *Workers in Industrial America: Essays on the Twentieth Century Struggle* (New York, 1980), 192.

tions among communities and families that encouraged the internalization of consumer desires as the center of the social world. Similar to the processes in Germany described by Michael Wildt, new configurations of public and private space emerged as part of a project of creating new patterns and expectations within consumer practices.[20] Nowhere was this new configuration of domestic and public space more evident than in the combination of commercial network television and Disneyland, two seemingly private enterprises that benefited from enormous subsidies from the state.

Throughout its history, commercial television has offered relentless and unremitting messages elevating the purchase of consumer goods over every other endeavor, but television too was made possible only through action by the state. State expenditures on research and development during World War II helped perfect the technology of home television, while federal tax policies allowing corporations to deduct the costs of advertising from their income solidified the medium's economic base. Government antitrust action against Hollywood studios broke up a monopoly in the motion picture industry at the same time that a Federal Communications Commission ruling sanctioned the network system for television. Government action restricted stations to the narrow VHF band, granted networks ownership and operating rights to key franchises in major cities, and insulated early broadcasters against competition by putting a freeze on the development of new stations between 1948 and 1952. The private investors who secured enormous profits from television and the media managers who exerted enormous influence on the country because of it owed their wealth, influence, and power to a state that they then sought to undermine at every turn.[21]

In her exemplary scholarship on consumer society and the introduction of commercial network television to U.S. homes, Lynn Spigel details an extraordinary movement of cultural performances from city streets to suburban living rooms. Attendance at motion pictures, sporting events, concerts, and other public performances plummeted between 1947 and 1955. Despite an unprecedented rise in disposable income for middle-class families, total recreational spending suffered a 2 percent decline during those years. Migration to the suburbs pulled customers away from traditional sites of public entertainment and encouraged the growth of home-based entertainments including television viewing and listening to high-fidelity phonographs. Department stores in suburban malls lured customers away from

20 See Michael Wildt's chapter in this book.
21 George Lipsitz, *Time Passages: Collective Memory and American Popular Culture* (Minneapolis, 1990), 45.

crowded downtown shopping by offering free parking, while suburbanization undermined mass transit, exacerbated traffic jams, and contributed to an increase in commuting and a corresponding shortage of parking spaces in the inner city.[22]

Spigel identifies "a profound preoccupation with space" as an important characteristic of the postwar period. Realtors and home builders proclaimed the advantages of detached single-family homes with spacious backyards over the bungalows, duplexes, and apartments of central cities, while urban renewal, highway construction, and FHA home loan policies all contributed to provide drastic penalties for urban life and lavish subsidies for suburban dwelling. The modernist goal of "merging spaces" found powerful expression in suburban homes, argues Spigel, in picture windows, glass walls, landscape paintings, scenic wallpaper, and continuous dining–living areas. Television became an important part of the new suburban space. Manufacturers marketed television sets as a form of "going places," as a way of maintaining connections with a wider world while inhabiting the secure spaces of suburbia. Interior settings used in early television programs emphasized depictions of outside spaces as they might appear through windows displaying city skylines or suburban hillsides, and popular authors echoed advertising rhetoric when they saluted the new medium for "bringing the world to people's doorsteps."[23]

Television advertisers boasted that their medium offered "not just a view, but a perfect view." Unlike the cinema or other spectator amusements that entailed the risk of bad seats, unruly neighbors, and irreversible commitments to what might turn out to be disappointing spectacles, television claimed to place the spectator at the scene of the action with a perfect view and freedom from outside distractions. In that way, television echoed the appeal of suburbia itself just as it echoed the spatial logic of a place that soon came to stand as the symbolic center of the new social world – Disneyland. In 1952 Walt Disney purchased land for his theme park for forty-five hundred dollars per acre; as a result of his own enterprise and the appreciation of land values in California it was worth eighty thousand dollars per acre by 1965.[24] Located at the confluence of major freeways in a suburban area certain to grow because of FHA home loan policies and federal government defense spending, like suburbia and television, Disneyland guaranteed satisfaction through predictably perfect views and regimented experi-

22 Lynn Spigel, "Installing the Television Set: Popular Discourses on Television and Domestic Space, 1948–1955," *Camera Obscura,* no. 16 (1988): 20.
23 Ibid., 14–15, 17–18.
24 Leo Litwak, "A Fantasy That Paid Off," *New York Times Magazine,* June 27, 1965, 25.

ences. If television was an indoor medium aspiring to the complexity of the world outside, Disneyland emerged as an outdoor place emulating the predictability and security of the safe suburban home.

Walt Disney raised the capital for Disneyland by selling a Sunday night series to the American Broadcasting Company, but television provided him with the amusement park's guiding aesthetic as well as its start-up capital and advertising. Nearly every decision about Disneyland grew from a concern about vision. Disney engineers regraded the terrain so that visitors would not see the outside world once inside the park, and they made sure that each "theme" land would be self-contained and not visible from the others. Disney insisted on one central entrance to the park because he believed that people would become "disoriented" if they entered by different gates. He wanted the spectacle of Sleeping Beauty's Castle to pull visitors down through the Main Street shops into the rest of the park. Underground tunnels hid power lines from view and enabled costumed "characters" from each theme land to travel to their destinations without being seen in "inappropriate" locations.[25]

The biographer Bob Thomas underscores the desire to control vision as the dominant aesthetic behind Disney's amusement park. "He wanted everyone to be channeled in the same way, to have their visit to Disneyland structured as part of a total experience," and "he saw the need for Disneyland to flow, as did a movie, from scene to scene."[26] To secure that controlled flow, Disney decided on mechanical animals rather than real ones for the jungle boat ride, "so that every boatload of people will see the same thing."[27] For the Main Street section of the park, he ordered buildings scaled full-size on the ground floor, but reduced to five-eighths scale on the second story to make them seem larger and deeper, to give an illusion of intimacy and an aura of play."[28]

The managed gaze of the Disneyland experience had commercial as well as aesthetic purposes. As visitors entered the park, they passed through Main Street on their way to Sleeping Beauty's Castle. This corridor led them (visually and physically) into the inviting shops along the street. The turn-of-the-century decor and charming scale of the buildings disguised their commercial purpose with a veneer of wholesome fantasy. Indoor passages

25 Paul Goldberger, "Mickey Mouse Teaches the Architects," *New York Times,* Oct. 22, 1972, 40, 92. Margaret I. King, "Disneyland and Disney World: Traditional Values in Futurist Form," *Journal of Popular Culture* 15, no. 1 (Sept. 1981): 120.
26 Bob Thomas, *Walt Disney: An American Original* (New York, 1976), 251–2.
27 Ibid., 251.
28 Sonja K. Forbes and Ann Gill, "Michel Foucault's Theory of Rhetoric as Epistemic," *Western Journal of Speech Communication* 51, no. 4 (fall 1987): 393.

made it easier to move from shop to shop than to travel back out to the
street, inscribing shopping as the recommended first activity of a day at Disneyland. Purchases of Disneyland artifacts further advertised the films, comic
books, and television projects of the host corporation, while food and drink
purchases directly and indirectly enriched concessionaires who paid Disney
large sums to give their products monopoly status on Main Street, not only
securing a captive clientele, but also advertising their importance by associating their brand names with the "family fun" for sale at the park.

Retailers everywhere copied Disney's successful style. One developer
and department store magnate concluded, "Main Street's purpose (in Disneyland) is exactly the same as Korvette's [department store] in the Bronx,
but it manages to make shopping wonderful and pleasant at the same time.
I'm sure people buy more when they're happy."[29] Promotional literature
for Disney tried to distance itself from television viewing, but appealed to
its aesthetic contours at the same time, claiming, "Up until now, audience
participation in entertainment was almost nonexistent. In live theater,
motion pictures and television, the audience is always separate and apart
from the actual show environment. . . . Walt Disney took the audience out
of their seats and placed them right in the middle of the action, for a total,
themed, controlled experience."[30]

The "total, themed, controlled" experiences of Disneyland and of television fit perfectly with the spatial relations of the suburban communities that
they both reflected and shaped. Suburbs also offered "a perfect view" for a
price – an exclusive lawn and backyard for each household. Backers of Disneyland, television, and the suburbs all stressed their benefits to the "family,"
but all three entities helped bring into being a new kind of family unit.
Children needed their parents' money to gain access to the wonders of Disneyland, television, or suburbia. Disneyland and television hailed young
viewers as consumers, presenting them with advertising messages disguised
as play. Suburban communities characterized by sprawling distances and
private residential spaces left little room for children to design or appropriate play sites of their own. The formally organized recreational center
replaced the spontaneity of the street, just as the station wagon came into
use as an antidote to suburban distances and the dearth of public transportation.

The preoccupation with controlling social and physical spaces at Disneyland corresponded to the aura of exclusivity sought in the suburbs. Local

29 Paul Goldberger, "Mickey Mouse Teaches the Architects," *New York Times,* Oct. 22, 1972, 94.
30 Quoted in Mark Gottdiener, "Disneyland: A Utopian Urban Space," *Urban Life* 11, no. 2 (July 1982):
    161.

zoning and deed restrictions guaranteed suburban homeowners control over space, and not so coincidentally over the racial and class composition of their neighborhoods. Homogeneous visual stimuli underscored this homogeneity of race and class, as suburban landscapes sought to control the contradictions displayed freely in urban areas. The designer John Hench explained Disneyland's "language of vision" in much the same way. "Most urban environments are basically chaotic places," Hench complained, "as architectural and graphic information screams at the citizen for attention. This competition results in disharmonies and contradictions that serve to cancel each other. A journey down almost any urban street will quickly place the visitor into visual overload of all the competing messages into a kind of information gridlock."[31] By contrast, Hench described Disneyland as a locus of harmony, as a site that aspired to linear precision. He boasted of the park's "orderly progression," which he described as "similar to scenes in a motion picture."

Yet the motion picture analogy is not quite right. Disneyland's four- and five-minute rides interspersed among innumerable concession stands bear less resemblance to the closed and complete narratives of film than they do to the spasms of storytelling that serve to capture television audiences for commercials. Just as television programs serve to naturalize the world of consumer goods by turning even domestic dramas into de facto fashion shows and shopping catalogues, the entertainment at Disneyland is itself a commercial, a simulation of stories sold by Disney in other media.[32] The Disney organization creates narratives that place shopping at the center of human activity. For example, Disney World's publicist Charles Ridgway describes that park's Cinderella castle by asking readers to "imagine a full-size fairy-tale castle rivaling Europe's finest and all the dream castles of literary history in space-age America. A castle without age-crusted floors and drafty hallways – a palace with air-conditioning, automatic elevators and electric kitchens. A royal home grander than anything Cinderella could have imagined."[33] From this perspective, the story of Cinderella is no longer about class barriers, sibling rivalry, oedipal conflicts, or even romance. The "dream castles of literary history" lose their connection to political history, but instead, fairy tales and literary history function as deficient precursors of the present. This vision connects the past with dirt and bodily discomfort, celebrating the present most of all for its air-conditioning and electric kitchens.

31 Quoted in Randy Bright, *Disneyland: The Inside Story* (New York, 1987), 48.
32 See Michael Sorkin, "See You in Disneyland," in Michael Sorkin, ed., *Variations on a Theme Park: The New American City and the End of Public Space* (New York, 1992), 205–32.
33 Goldberger, "Mickey Mouse," 40.

Disneyland quickly established itself as an extraordinarily successful commercial space. Three years after the park's opening, Disneyland attracted more visitors every year than the Grand Canyon, Yosemite, and Yellowstone national parks combined. In its first decade of operation, an estimated 25 percent of the U.S. population had visited the park. But Disneyland helped restructure citizenship as well as spectatorship. It provided narratives about the American past carefully designed to erase politics, depicting a turn-of-the-century town with no workers and no immigrants, Abraham Lincoln but no slavery, Aunt Jemima but no Nat Turner. More important, architects and urban planners turned to Disneyland and Disney World as models for turning ceremonial public space and historic buildings into themed and controlled shopping malls as anchors for urban redevelopment.

The design aesthetic pioneered at Disneyland thrives in the shopping malls developed by James W. Rouse and his imitators, first in the suburbs, but now in the center of many of the nation's largest cities. Like Disneyland and Disney World, Rouse shopping centers display a modernist faith in besting nature via artificial landscapes and climate control. They reframe public space as shopping space, and they pursue exclusivity and segregation through active security patrols and through their preference for high priced specialty shops maximizing sales per square foot over merchandisers selling staples. They build upon the managed gaze developed in Disneyland, on television, and in suburbs by presenting "perfect" views of local landmarks like the harbors in Boston, Philadelphia, New York, and Baltimore as stimuli for shoppers.

Publicity by the Rouse Corporation and its admirers in magazines including *Fortune* and *Business Week* touted Rouse's success as proof of the superior ability of the private sector to solve social problems. Yet Rouse relied on extensive state subsidies for his projects. Urban Development Action Grants provided him with more than $110 million in federal aid, and records of the Department of Housing and Urban Development show another $168 million in public money funneled into twelve of Rouse's projects.[34] In Toledo, local investors and city officials provided Rouse $13 million for improvements, dedicated payback receipts from a $10 million federal grant, and secured a $9.5 million loan from a local bank for Rouse's Portside project. But when half of the tenants left the development in two years and the project failed, Rouse walked away unaffected, having invested none of his own money.[35] A profile in *People* in 1981 presented Rouse as a

34 Robert Guskind and Neal Pierce, "Faltering Festivals," *National Journal,* Sept. 17, 1988, 2310.
35 Ibid.

businessman capable of "saving cities" by building low cost housing for minorities, quoting his prediction that "by the end of the '80s a black family will be able to live comfortably wherever it wants in almost every American city."[36] But the foundation that Rouse expected to provide $10 million a year for low cost housing by 1990 (and eventually $20 million per year) lost more than $1.5 million in 1985, nearly $2.6 million in 1986, and more than $5 million in 1987.[37]

In New York's South Street Seaport, the Rouse Corporation angered local residents and community groups by leaving the public only a six-foot-wide walkway along the harbor, reserving the rest for private businesses. The architecture critic Craig Whitaker notes that the imperatives behind this usurpation of public resources arise from the demands of commerce: "In order to create a market, the developer often needed to control (architecturally and financially) some of the public domain, and in order to keep the developer interested, the politician needed to give up some of that same domain."[38] Consequently, a development celebrated for attracting citizens back to the harbor actually restricts their access to it. The harbor becomes a marketing lure, and the shopping mall near it offers privileged views of public resources only to those with the money to pay for fancy condominiums and restaurants.

These festival malls present what J. B. Jackson terms "other-directed architecture" – self-conscious spaces directed to tourists. They turn everyone into a spectator and offer sociability only under terms conducive to maximizing profits. They presume permanent divisions among places for work, residence, and shopping. They demand huge subsidies from taxpayers in the form of land clearance, tax abatement, and tourist promotion but undercut local merchants with ties to the community, and drain public resources for police, fire protection, and basic services. They refashion local history and hopes for community into the practice of shopping for new commodities under climate-controlled conditions, much as television and Disneyland do. They sell back to people in diluted form an image of the social life that they helped destroy. They turn urban sites into urban sights and encourage a public life based on private insulation from fearful contradictions.

Not every Rouse mall is the same; the company's projects in Boston and Baltimore have been economically viable and much used facilities. Yet the failure of many of Rouse's festival malls, the enormous subsidies they receive

---

36 Andrea Pawlyna, "James Rouse, A Pioneer of the Suburban Shopping Center, Now Sets His Sights on Saving Cities," *People,* July 6, 1981, 71.

37 Guskind and Pierce, "Faltering Festivals," 2309.

38 Craig Whitaker, "Rouse-ing Up the Waterfront," *Architectural Record* 174, no. 4 (Apr. 1986): 67.

from the state, their negative effects on neighborhood businesses and local tax burdens, and their inability to generate any funds to deal with urban problems have not led to any serious rethinking of the relationship between consumer spending and the public interest. When Community Employment Training Act projects lose money or fail to produce jobs, they appear again and again in public discourse as "proof" of the failure of the state to solve social problems. But when massive subsidies to private developers and individuals produce real debacles, the reputation of the private sector remains untarnished. In part, this is because contributors to political campaigns and media conglomerates benefit personally from even failed projects using public money, but also because the privatized welfare measures of the postwar period and the reorganization of social space in the suburbs have established consumer desire as the central unifying narrative of our nation, a narrative tapped most fully by Ronald Reagan in his years as president.

As co-host of the televised opening ceremonies at Disneyland, as a performer in commercials for General Electric, and as president of the United States, Reagan sacralized consumer desire with extraordinary skill. At the 1988 Republican National Convention he read a letter from a small boy who announced that he loved America because it had just about every flavor of ice cream you could want. As president, Reagan offered more for less, enacting tax cuts but promising no decline in government revenues, increasing defense spending but declaring no need for deficit spending, and ending regulation of the savings and loan industry by promising that market-based love of gain could solve the nation's problems more successfully than government expenditures. Reagan encouraged Americans to think they could have it all, as in his 1986 State of the Union speech, in which he announced, "In this land of dreams fulfilled where greater dreams may be imagined, nothing is impossible, no victory is beyond our reach, no glory is too great."[39] When hubris enabled the government to accumulate a larger national debt during Reagan's terms in office than had accumulated in the entire previous history of the nation and produced massive unemployment, homelessness, unchecked health hazards, and substantial sums wasted on bailing out the speculators in the savings and loan industry, Reagan concluded that his policies were working.

Ronald Reagan's performance in what he called "the role of a lifetime" depended upon the strength of the neoconservative political mobilization that brought him to power. For almost fifty years memories of the Great Depression and conservative complicity with fascism hindered the Right in

---

39 Kathleen Hall Jamieson, *Eloquence in an Electronic Age* (New York, 1988), 161.

the United States. But along with the fiscal crisis of the state in the 1970s and the emergence of global capital, conservative political mobilization successfully portrayed private capital as the engine of economic growth while depicting social welfare spending as a drain on productive resources. The failure of conservative economics to deliver the prosperity it has promised or to confront the consequences of the economic inequality it has engendered places an even greater emphasis on consuming commodities as distraction from serious structural problems and as reparations for failing to resolve them. In this context, the extent to which commercial popular culture places consuming commodities at the center of the social world has enormous import for whether oppositional social movements are possible. If commercial culture makes us think that politics is impossible, that state support of capital is productive but social welfare spending is wasteful, then we may well have become the people that those interested in unlimited freedom for capital want us to be. On the other hand, if commercial culture contains contradictions that may yet connect us to a broader social world, then consumer culture is only one of many terrains where political struggle may yet take place.

Commercial popular culture affects the forms of cultural expression that we see as well as the terms by which they come to us. It is not just that every piece of entertainment is accompanied by advertising messages or must win the approval of advertisers or investors in order to appear, but that the commercial and industrial matrices in which popular culture is located go a long way toward shaping the identity of its products. In consumer society, cultural expression emerges directly from the search for market segments, the psychology of market sites, the exigencies of market practices, and the experiences of market pleasures. To the extent that we accept the definition of ourselves encouraged by market segmentation, that we accept the social relations mandated by the sites of commercial reception and production, that we attune our intellects and moral standards to the dictates of market practices, and that we succumb simply to market pleasures as the ultimate horizon of cultural and social experience, the chances for oppositional social movements will certainly be slim.

The search for market segments in consumer society gives rise to specific cultural creations that hail us as part of target populations desired by advertisers. For example, the television program "Sixty Minutes" came into being because of the Columbia Broadcasting System's desire to fuse their Sunday afternoon football watching audience with their Sunday night viewers of mystery stories. They created a program that combined the confrontation (and time clock) of competitive sports with the processes of investigation, induction, and deduction common to murder mystery and drama. Previously programmers had viewed the late afternoon and early evening on Sundays as a kind of sacred family time, addressed through children's programming or "wholesome" family entertainment. But the search to fuse distinct market segments led the network to create a new social group whose visible demographics made them more attractive to advertisers and more lucrative to the networks than a mere family audience could be. Similarly, "made for television movies" in the 1970s began to draw their determinate shape from similar demographic considerations. When the American Broadcasting Company's "Monday Night Football" games attracted overwhelming numbers of male viewers, rival networks began counterprogramming movies with women's themes (and often protofeminist viewpoints) in order to deliver effectively to advertisers the potential market segment completely unaddressed by advertisers on "Monday Night Football." In the 1980s, advertisers found a way to cater to two previously distinct demographic groups at once by programming shows that parents and children would both be interested in, but for different reasons. "Family Ties" depicted an adult couple in the 1980s whose youthful experiences in the 1960s shaped their values. By contrast, their children, and especially their son, reflected the "values" of the 1980s, in this case ardent conservatism and reverence for Ronald Reagan. In similar fashion, "The Wonder Years" centered on the experiences of a child, but positioned him in the present looking back at adolescence in the 1960s. This kind of fused marketing appeared in motion pictures as well, in the film *Dirty Dancing,* set in the 1960s, and previously in *Grease,* a 1970s musical evoking nostalgia for the 1950s but starring contemporary stars John Travolta and Olivia Newton John singing pop songs destined for album sales and the pop charts in the present.

Market sites also help determine the forms that commercial culture takes. Janice Radway explains that romance novels appear in small paperback form because they can be held with one hand by mothers with young children or by busy housewives who might need one hand free to attend to household responsibilities while they read.[40] Tania Modleski's studies of televised daytime game shows reveal a similar connection between text and context. Familiar theme songs, loud bells and buzzers that signal correct and incorrect answers, and audience applause signal the fate of contestants to women whose work in the home draws them away from continuous visual contact with the screen.[41] Radway and Modleski focus on the physical sites of reception, but the social site that a cultural expression occupies can also shape its content. Horace Newcomb points out that the serial narrative

40 Janice Radway, *Reading the Romance* (Chapel Hill, N.C., 1984).
41 Tania Modleski, "Rhythms of Reception," in E. Ann Kaplan, ed., *Regarding Television: Critical Approaches, an Anthology* (Frederick, Md., 1983).

form of television soap operas, nighttime dramas, and even situation come-
dies stems from commercial rather than aesthetic considerations. Advertisers interested in associating their product with popular performers prefer
serial narratives because they enable audiences to build consistent identification with stars and situations that make it easier to predict the number
and nature of a program's viewers.[42]

Market practices also help determine the content of commercial culture.
In his innovative work on "hooks" in popular music, Gary Burns shows
how producers try to make a strong impression at the beginning of a record-
ing because they know that many radio programmers test hundreds of songs
at a time and will continue listening only if something strikes them strongly
at the start. The programmers claim the same interest in relation to their listeners; they fear that music that starts inconsequentially will lead listeners to
switch to another station. As a result, devices like the electric sitar beginning
on B. J. Thomas's "Hooked on a Feeling" or the "misleading" orchestral
introductions to 1970s disco songs result from the market practice of the
niche of the industry in which they are located rather than from the inspi-
ration or intuition of composers. In other cases, advertising messages become
products themselves - sometimes intentionally as products plugging other
products such as baseball cards or music videos, sometimes unintentionally
as commercials whose production values make them desirable on their own
merits such as Irma Thomas's singing commercials for Gulf Coast Loan
Corporation in New Orleans or the White Port lemon juice commercial
that became a rhythm and blues hit under the title "WPLJ." Sometimes this
occurs in completely calculated fashion like the professional ice hockey
team in Anaheim owned by the Disney Corporation and named after that
firm's motion picture hit *The Mighty Ducks.*

Market pleasures also provide their own kinds of cultural expression
when consumers become producers as in the case of hip hop artists who
turn their memories of past hits into current musical productions. The
Bomb Squad producing samples for Public Enemy try to "work in the red
zone," that is, program samples that will break the speakers on which they
are played. Hank Shocklee of the Bomb Squad prefers recorded samples to
drum machines, because the machines are too good and do not capture the
way real drummers slide drumsticks along the skins, play slightly late, or
make other mistakes that make the music interesting to Shocklee. He even
likes the audio hiss that sampling puts underneath hip hop music, because
he thinks "the hiss acts as glue and holds everything together."

---

42 Horace Newcomb, oral presentation, University of Southern California, Dec. 1, 1989, author's notes.

The search for market segments, the significance of market sites, the function of market practices, and the creative fusions made from market pleasures all encode commercial culture with the imperatives of commerce. They teach us to take pleasure in our own inscription into market segments. They naturalize materialism and artifice, while encouraging us to aspire to the identities that fit the categories most convenient for marketers. Most important, they give us identities as consumers that cut us off from the responsibilities and opportunities of citizenship by dividing us into market segments, by elevating consumer time over historical time, and by colonizing our imaginations to make us more malleable as consumers.

Yet the very need for novelty and the global appetites of consumer culture also make other fused identities and practices possible. Especially in the post-Fordist era, capital creates contradictory identities, stoking consumer desire and grandiose hopes for autonomy, fulfillment, and pleasure while delivering austerity, social decay, and fragmentation. In the short run, even these frustrations can work to promote yet another round of consumer identities and choices, but in the long run, they may open up the very wounds that they claim to heal.[43] If the current moment in world history offers us precious few examples of what scholars call the "old social movements" – that is, movements with a common ideology, rooted in struggles over places like factories, cities, and states, and seeking political power for themselves – it nonetheless offers us ample opportunity to observe "new social movements" characterized by immediate interests, coalition politics, shared cultural concerns, and a perceived necessity to work through the contradictions of existing institutions rather than an effort to seize old ones or create new ones.

The Lavalas movement in Haiti, for example, made use of popular music that combined traditional *rara* rhythms, voodoo practices, and commercial recordings to bring people into the streets in support of agrarian reform and against the nation's military dictatorship and its complicity with transnational capital. In Chiapas, Mexico, the Zapatista Liberation Front emerged out of ten years of liberation theology discussion groups on January 1, 1994, in armed struggle in rural Mexico that they augmented with the use of the Internet, English-language graffiti in Los Angeles and Mexico City, and fax machines. U.S. rhythm and blues records broadcast on Radio Bantu by the South African government as a means of attracting listeners to racist government propaganda inadvertently helped made the English language the lingua franca capable of uniting tribal groups speaking different languages

43 Fredric Jameson, "Reification and Utopia in Mass Culture," *Social Text* 1, no. 1 (1979).

and providing the opportunity for expressly politicized readings of songs whose lyrics seemed to contain no overt political message.[44] The same shared expectations and market identities that make displaced Andean Indians in South American cities consumers of new cultural commodities like *chicha* music also have given rise to thousands of neighborhood associations and political campaigns to secure social services.

For all their reach and scope, market segments, market sites, market practices, and market pleasures do not yet determine our social being totally. Commercial culture provides an inescapable terrain for social connection and identity formation, but contradictions among members of the same market segment, the differential access to power revealed in the style and prestige hierarchies of the mass media, the creative subversion and inversion of market practices by consumers, and the utopian aspects embedded within market pleasures all provide potential sources of contradiction and conflict. The disintegration of the social fabric under neoconservatism and the increasingly apparent inability of market oriented solutions to meet individual and collective needs increase conservatism's stake in cultural issues, mandating countersubversive witch hunts against the very popular music and films that a consumer oriented economy relies on, as well as hysterical and counterproductive crusades against imagined foreign enemies and demonized domestic villains. Unlike the Reagan years, when conservatives pretended that reforms in their own self-interest would trickle down to the rest of the population, the current "Contract with America" era assumes a zero-sum game with declining rather than expanding opportunity; it defensively guards existing privileges and threatens that conditions might get even worse. Under these conditions, oppositional movements demanding state action to restrain rather than unleash capital become possible.

To be sure, any oppositional social movement would have to move beyond the present hegemony of consumer identities to challenge the enduring significance of the state as an instrument of repression and capital accumulation, to identify the human and economic costs of the transnational economy, and to struggle for employment, education, health care, and political rights for the increasingly disenfranchised and disinherited population of the world. There is no reason for ungrounded optimism on any of these issues, but as Stuart Hall argues, just because the game is not going very well, there is no reason to concede that it is over.

44 Charles Hamm, *Putting Popular Music in Its Place* (Cambridge, Mass., 1995), 210–48.

7

The Emigré as Celebrant of American Consumer Culture

George Katona and Ernest Dichter

DANIEL HOROWITZ

With its adaptation of Marxism and its emphasis on the role of the mass media, the Frankfurt School has provided the most widely recognized analysis of consumer culture to come out of Europe in the 1930s and influence Americans in subsequent decades. Beginning in the 1940s, George Katona and Ernest Dichter celebrated what many leading émigré intellectuals were critiquing: the impact of consumer culture on American life. Katona (1901–81) relied on his surveys of consumer expectations carried out at the University of Michigan from 1946 to 1972 to assert that the optimistic and sensible American consumer would heroically prevent the nation from experiencing the inflation and instability that ravaged Europe in the years between the two world wars. Dichter (1907–91) made a handsome living in the United States helping corporations understand the psyche of consumers. In the process, he linked democracy with purchasing, redefined the roles of middle-class women, and promoted a distinctly antipuritanical vision.

Although the pictures drawn by Katona and Dichter of the American consumer differed in many respects, they shared a belief, shaped by their experiences in Europe and the United States, that American consumers were critical to the promotion of growth, democracy, and stability. They both gave a special importance in their analysis to the new middle class of salaried and professional employees and to the leadership of educated experts, social and behavioral scientists especially, as forces that would prevent fascism from coming to America. They believed the action of consumers and experts would make state intervention less necessary. Their careers remind us of the transatlantic nature of intellectual life in the middle of the twentieth century, how dreams and fears born in Central Europe in the 1920s and 1930s made their way into American life beginning in the late 1930s. In the end both the interwar economic turmoil in Europe and the postwar abundance in America blunted the critical edge of their take on consumer culture. James Livingston's chapter in this book provides a suggestive background for the relationships between subjectivity and consumer culture that Katona and Dichter explored. Moreover, as George Lipsitz demonstrates in his chapter, the kinds of work that Katona and Dichter did – supported by corporations, foundations, universities, and the state – were critical in legitimizing a role for the consumer and consumer spending that had powerful implications for public and private life.

GEORGE KATONA AND THE HEROIC AMERICAN CONSUMER

Born in Budapest on November 6, 1901, Katona grew up in a prosperous Jewish household.[1] A 1919 Communist takeover of Hungary prompted him to move to Germany, where he earned a Ph.D. in experimental psychology in 1921. The hyperinflation that shook Germany in the early 1920s provided the impetus for him to study the ways psychology and economics might shed light on the dynamics of rapid price increases. In 1926 he settled in Berlin. There from Max Wertheimer (1880–1943), one of the founders of gestalt psychology, Katona learned about the psychological analysis of perception. In Berlin, Gustav Stolper (1888–1947) provided much of Katona's training in economics and, at *The German Economist,* a forum for his ideas. Stolper fostered in Katona an interest in inflation, business cycles, emotional moods, and the consumer as well as a belief in a public role for the scholar, an appreciation of capitalism's powers, a dislike of excessive state expansion.

During the late 1920s and early 1930s Katona became fascinated with America as a consumer society. He appreciated the efficiency, modernity, and flexibility of its businessmen and exaggerated the spread of prosperity across social classes. In particular what compelled his attention were the inventiveness and extent of American consumer credit, the power of marketing, the importance of brand reputation, and the tendency toward conformity. "Minor changes can be deceiving," he wrote right after the stock

---

1 The best introduction to Katona's career, which contains a bibliography of his writings, is Richard Curtin, "Curtin on Katona," in Henry W. Spiegel and Warren J. Samuels, eds., *Contemporary Economists in Perspective* (Greenwich, Conn., 1984): 2:495–522. See also *New York Times,* June 19, 1981, sec. B, 6; George Katona, *Psychological Economics* (New York, 1975), viii–ix; Burkhard Strumpel, James N. Morgan, and Ernest Zahn, eds., *Human Behavior in Economic Affairs: Essays in Honor of George Katona* (San Francisco, 1972); Toni Stolper, *Ein Leben in Brennpunkten unserer Zeit: Wien, Berlin, New York: Gustav Stolper, 1888–1947* (Tübingen, 1960). The Bentley Historical Library, University of Michigan, Ann Arbor, Michigan, has Katona's papers.

market crash of 1929 with an optimism that would characterize his postwar views; "the line of American prosperity is going upward without interruption."[2]

Shortly after Hitler came to power in 1933 and banned *The German Economist,* Katona immigrated to the United States. He worked in Stolper's investment office on Wall Street until illness cut short his business career. By the time he had recovered fully in 1939, the year in which he became a United States citizen, Katona returned to his long-standing academic interests in psychology, economics, and inflation. Books he published in the five years beginning in 1940 launched his career. In *Organizing and Memorizing* (1940) he made clear his debt to Wertheimer at the same time that he laid the groundwork for his own later work on psychological understanding.[3] *War Without Inflation* (1942) was Katona's first extended exploration of the connections among psychology, economics, and inflation. Assuming the reasonableness of the consumer and putting aside whatever reluctance he had to sanction government power, he argued that of prime importance in fighting the war without inflation was the role of the state in the creation of a gestalt, a comprehensive set of cultural expectations that would influence group psychology and work against price increases.[4] In *Price Control and Business* (1945), Katona, relying on the work of Paul Lazarsfeld, first used survey methods based on "free-answer interviewing" to obtain information that would explain the impact of household behavior on the economy.[5]

Katona did not agree with those who believed that the war's end would cause a return to depressed prewar conditions. Rising levels of aspiration, he argued, would emerge from the sense people had of their contribution to the war effort, encouraging them to aspire "to a higher social and economic status." Moreover, wartime shortages would "create an emotional halo round the goods and activities of which one is deprived."[6] He remained confident that "public and private agencies" could ensure an appropriate atmosphere that would in turn keep inflation in check.[7] Like other profes-

---

2 George Katona, "Konsumfinanzierung: Die amerikanische und die deutsche Praxis," *Der Deutsche Volkswirt* 1 (Nov. 19, 1926): 241 (hereafter Katona's name is abbreviated as GK); GK, "Das 'Verkaufen': Ein Grundproblem der amerikanischen Wirtschaft," *Der Deutsche Volkswirt* 1 (Oct. 29, 1926): 149–51; GK, "Der New Yorker Börsenkrach," *Der Deutsche Volkswirt* 4 (Nov. 1, 1929): 139, 142.
3 GK, *Organizing and Memorizing: Studies in the Psychology of Learning and Teaching* (New York, 1940).
4 GK, *War Without Inflation: The Psychological Approach to Problems of War Economy* (New York, 1942), 14, 18–19, 20, 23, 57–8, 61, 81, 147, 204.
5 GK, *Price Control and Business: Field Studies Among Producers and Distributors of Consumer Goods in the Chicago Area, 1942–44* (Bloomington, Ind., 1945), 153–5.
6 GK, *War Without Inflation,* 186–8, 196.   7 GK, *Price Control,* 223.

sionals confident they could guide democracy, Katona gave the expert the task of helping the public develop "frames of reference for new experiences."[8]

By 1945 Katona was on the way to more than a third of a century of writing on the impact of consumer expectations on the national economy. As the war was ending, he worked on a government project that focused on whether people's spending habits after the war would produce excessive inflation.[9] In 1946, those involved in this project moved to the University of Michigan, where they helped establish the Survey Research Center.[10] From 1946 to 1972, Katona directed path-breaking surveys of consumer finances and expectations. At the same time he served as a professor of both economics and psychology and earned a reputation as the dean of behavioral or psychological economics. The surveys of consumer expectations made it possible for him to explore the relationship between psychology and economics, to grapple with problems of inflation, and to realize how postwar America differed from interwar Germany.

The surveys provided a wealth of information on the economic resources and psychological expectations at the household level. Interviews focused on questions about reasons why people saved, the household's liquid assets, plans for spending (especially for consumer durables and vacations), and the willingness to rely on consumer debt.[11] Katona asserted that his surveys sustained a record for prescience and reliability in explaining the relationship between consumers' attitudes and economic activity.[12] Many decision makers in government and business closely followed the reports. Over time the European Common Market, the federal government, the Conference Board, the Gallup Organization, and several other private polling groups developed surveys of consumer expectations.

Beginning in 1946 and continuing until the early 1970s, Katona offered his vision of America as a middle-class consumer society, revealing his special sense of appreciation for his new homeland. For Katona, consumer attitudes played a critical role in predicting and controlling the overall direction of the American economy. Relatively small changes in willingness to

8 GK, "The Role of the Frame of Reference in War and Post-War Economy," *American Journal of Sociology* 49 (Jan. 1944): 340, 346–7.
9 Rensis Likert, "Courageous Pioneer: Creating a New Field of Knowledge," in Strumpel, Morgan, and Zahn, eds., *Human Behavior,* 4–6.
10 James N. Morgan, "A Quarter Century of Behavioral Research in Economics: Persistent Programs and Diversions," in Strumpel, Morgan, and Zahn, eds., *Human Behavior,* 15.
11 "Surveys of Liquid Asset Holdings," *Federal Reserve Bulletin* 31 (Sept. 1945): 865; Lewis Mandell et al., *Surveys of Consumers, 1971–72* (Ann Arbor, Mich., 1973), 303–26.
12 GK, *The Powerful Consumer: Psychological Studies of the American Economy* (New York, 1960), 33–50, 215–19.

spend made the difference between inflation and deflation, prosperity and recession.[13] Katona argued that the 40 percent of American families in the "upper middle" or "discretionary-income group" with incomes in the early 1960s between six thousand and fifteen thousand dollars provided the "backbone of the mass consumption economy," controlling more than half of all personal income. He asserted that it was this group's spending on automobiles, appliances, and leisure that made a crucial difference in the nation's economic activity.[14]

Drawing on his pre-1945 experiences as well as on what the surveys revealed, Katona described a society in which the reasonable, aspiring consumer had a heroic role.[15] When people made important purchases under new circumstances, he asserted, they were problem solvers.[16] "People resist speculative fever as well as despondency," he wrote in 1958, perhaps with the German inflation of the 1920s in mind, "unless their sanity is crushed by a series of repeated shocks." By regulating themselves, consumers provided economic stability "either by serving as a brake to inflationary trends or by stepping up their demand when the economy needed new incentives."[17]

Above all, the rising aspirations of American consumers, Katona argued, were a critical factor in the health of the postwar economy. Countering those who believed that prosperity was "its own gravedigger," Katona argued instead that the ability to satisfy wants "makes life easier but does not necessarily result in soft living and waste."[18] The "ideal of higher living standards and consumer comforts" was expansive, "penetrating into Europe, Asia, and Africa. Even communist countries," Katona noted, "are not immune to the sweet poisoning emanating from America."[19] Yet if Abraham S. Maslow emphasized the emergence of nonmaterialistic needs, at least until the early 1970s Katona tended to focus on new but not necessarily higher ones. Although he acknowledged that more public monies had to

13 Katona gave glimpses of this overall interpretation in his 1946 and 1947 surveys, spelled them out more fully in GK, "Financial Surveys Among Consumers," *Human Relations* 2 (1949): 3–11, and offered the first complete statement in GK, *Psychological Analysis of Economic Behavior* (New York, 1951).
14 GK, *The Mass Consumption Society* (New York, 1964), 9–10, 12–14.
15 GK, *Powerful Consumer*, 238.
16 GK, "A Study of Purchase Decisions," in Lincoln H. Clark, ed., *Consumer Behavior*, 4 vols. (New York, 1955), 1:31–2.
17 GK, "Attitude Change: Instability of Response and Acquisition of Experience" *Psychological Monographs: General and Applied* 72: 10, whole no. 463 (1958): 29, 32–5.
18 GK, "The Predictive Value of Data on Consumer Attitudes," in Clark, ed., *Consumer Behavior*, 2:72; GK, *Mass Consumption Society*, 6.
19 Ibid., 6, 67–8; GK, *Powerful Consumer*, 137, 173, 191; GK, Burkhard Strumpel and Ernest Zahn, *Aspirations and Affluence: Comparative Studies in the United States and Western Europe* (New York, 1971), 171.

154 *Daniel Horowitz*

be spent on education and health care, he nonetheless emphasized that the development of more positive attitudes toward spending on social needs would be possible "only if more immediate wants are satisfied." Echoing a widely shared notion of the period, Katona said that the mass consumption society had taught "that the solution to mass poverty is not cutting the pie into different-size slices," but increasing its size.[20]

Katona questioned the puritanical and antimaterialistic streak in American social thought, envisioning a society based on expanding wants. To those like John Kenneth Galbraith who deplored preoccupation with material goods and wastefulness, Katona argued in 1964 against opposing "cultural aspirations with material interests." For millions, affluence meant not "abundance and indulgence," but "a new concept of what are necessities and needs." Although Katona concentrated primarily on purchasable pleasures, on occasion he argued that "higher standards . . . appear to set the stage for, rather than to impede, cultural aspirations."[21]

An examination of what Katona neglected or minimized makes it possible to begin to understand the implications of his perspective. Until changes in public policy and funding directed attention to households for whom the American dream was out of reach, the surveys concentrated on those with incomes large enough to buy a range of consumer durables.[22] As he wrote in 1964 only shortly after others were rediscovering poverty, "ours is a middle-class society with middle-class comforts."[23] This focus not only kept his attention off the consuming styles of the wealthy but also postponed his consideration of issues of poverty and unemployment.[24] Moreover, the surveys reflected the bias of social sciences in the 1940s and 1950s when they interviewed the male "head of spending unit" even though advertisers and social critics had long recognized the importance of women in consumption.[25]

Nor could Katona develop a theory as encompassing as that of others such as Galbraith. Despite Katona's emphasis on the power of social groups and media, the household appeared isolated from mediating institutions. The surveys also failed to consider the influence of gender, ethnicity, and political orientation. Moreover, dichotomies of optimism/pessimism and good times/bad times made the interviews incapable of giving a full sense of how people felt about what and how they consumed. Katona tended to

20 Ibid., 53, 64–7, 131.   21 GK, *Mass Consumption Society,* 4, 62–3, 66–7, 283.
22 GK et al., *1966 Survey of Consumer Finances* (Ann Arbor, Mich., 1967), 268; GK, *1967 Survey of Consumer Finances* (Ann Arbor, Mich., 1968), 7.
23 GK, *Mass Consumption Society,* 12, 66.
24 The word "poverty" did not appear in the index of GK's 1960 *Powerful Consumer* but did four years later in *Mass Consumption Society.*
25 "A National Survey of Liquid Assets," *Federal Reserve Bulletin* 32 (June 1946): 579.

separate work and consumption and to a considerable extent neglected the contributions of workers and entrepreneurs.[26] He minimized the power of corporate capitalism to shape patterns of spending. In important ways his celebration of the consumer as the critical element in an economy was a counter to government intervention.[27] In postwar America, he wrote, "it would be consistent with the American preference for voluntary and private action in maintaining our system if we give increasing thought to the reinforcement of the stabilizing role that may be played by consumers."[28]

Implicitly Katona was answering those who had once thought totalitarianism might come to America. He believed the consumer heroically prevented inflation, totalitarianism, and economic instability. Bent on self-improvement, aspiring to a higher standard of living, embracing the benefits of materialism, embodying bourgeois values, Katona's consumer provided both the engine and the balance wheel of the postwar economy. His picture of the middle-class consumer as a sensible social learner became a defense of what he saw as the essential elements of the American way of life – democracy, prosperity, the middle class, and individual economic effort. A liberal democrat without a Marxist or social democratic past, Katona paid little attention to issues of equity, celebrated America's uniqueness, and was cautious about state economic intervention.

Throughout the postwar period, serious inflation remained for Katona the greatest threat to prosperity and social order because it fostered "mutual mistrust and conflict" among social groups. For more than a quarter of a century after 1945, he was confident that the government and consumer united in keeping price rises in check. Yet at times, he saw danger. During the Korean War he worried about the costs of excessive inflation. In 1960 he said, "Runaway inflation is one of the greatest possible evils." Serious inflation, he believed, occurred when war, military defeat, or governmental change prompted people to "break with the past" and "grope for a new understanding of the situation." Despite these concerns, from 1945 until the early 1970s Katona was usually confident that inflation would remain low because consumers would save the day.[29]

Events in the early 1970s undermined Katona's optimism. In 1972, just as he began an active retirement, the investigations he had developed

---

26 For a summary of his later views of business behavior, see GK, *Psychological Economics,* 287–333.
27 Ibid., 361; see also 286, 295, 297 for some favorable views of government activity.
28 GK, *Mass Consumption Society,* 307, 314.
29 GK, *The People Versus the United States: An Education Resource Unit* (Washington, D.C., 1952), 1–2; GK, *Powerful Consumer,* 28, 208; GK, *Psychological Analysis of Economic Behavior,* 260; GK, "Psychology and Consumer Economics," *Journal of Consumer Research* 1 (1974): 2.

revealed the increasing pessimism of American consumers.[30] As the OPEC oil embargo, stagflation, the war in Vietnam, environmental problems, and Watergate shook the confidence of the American people, history seemed to conspire to bring about just such a situation as he had long hoped the nation would avoid. Americans lost confidence in experts who themselves seemed unable to right wrongs. Attitudes became more volatile as consumers no longer understood what was going on about them. Uncertain and confused, they seemed to have lost their optimism.[31] Consequently, in the 1970s, consumers stepped up their purchases in anticipation of rising prices, thus adding fuel to inflation, something they had not done since 1950.[32]

These events prompted Katona to define progress in nonmaterialistic terms. In the process, he drew on what Kurt Lewin and Maslow had written about the importance of self-fulfillment and higher aspirations.[33] Predicting "dire consequences for the American economy" should Americans come to expect "an end to the era of personal progress," Katona looked forward to a new kind of future, one in which people would "develop desires for higher-order social and cultural attainments." He pointed to signs of a "transformation of the 'I' into a broader 'We,' which implies an identification with one's neighbors, one's community, and one's environment."[34] The new, humane economy, he wrote, would have "to better accommodate the human needs for security, continuity, equity, and self-actualization."[35] Ironically, Katona and his respondents thus came somewhat late to what others had begun to realize earlier – that, once a certain income level was reached, friendship, work, environmental quality, peace, and family were more important than additional income.

As he had sixty years earlier in the Germany to which he returned in 1981, Katona still saw rapidly rising prices as the most serious threat to economic well-being.[36] The last article he wrote, prepared for delivery in Berlin, was largely pessimistic. Katona died there on June 18, 1981, the day after he received an honorary doctorate in economics from the Free University. He had come a long way and yet in some sense he had stayed in the

30 Richard T. Curtin, "Indicators of Consumer Behavior: The University of Michigan Survey of Consumers," *Public Opinion Quarterly* 46 (fall 1982): 347.
31 GK and Burkhard Strumpel, *A New Economic Era* (New York, 1978), 2, 6, 115.
32 GK, *Essays on Behavioral Economics* (Ann Arbor, Mich., 1980), 12.
33 GK, "Psychology and Consumer Economics," 7.
34 GK, "Persistence of Belief in Personal Financial Progress," in Burkhard Strumpel, ed., *Economic Means for Human Needs: Social Indicators of Well-Being and Discontent* (Ann Arbor, Mich., 1976), 102, 104.
35 GK and Strumpel, *New Economic Era*, 132; Katona, *Essays*, 18, 81, 87.
36 GK, "Interdisciplinary Research," in *Ehrenpromotion von Prof. Dr. George Katona, Ann Arbor, Michigan am 15. Juni 1981* (Berlin, 1982), 42–3.

same place. It was interwar Germany that had made him focus on social cognition, inflation, and the consumer – and that made him worry about the danger of American inflation in the last decade of his life.

BIRTH OF A SALESMAN: ERNEST DICHTER AND OBJECTS OF DESIRE

Born in Vienna on August 14, 1907, Dichter attained maturity under inauspicious conditions.[37] His father was a traveling salesman whom his son considered "spectacularly unsuccessful." Young Dichter faced poverty and at times starvation, at least well into his teens. Dichter left school at fourteen to help support his family, working first in his uncle's department store in Vienna. There he developed a fascination with new ideas about merchandising and with new consumer items, some of which his uncle brought back from the United States. It was also in the department store that his uncle had unintentionally, Dichter later wrote, provided "objects" for his nephew's "sexual training course." He and a female employee had to be "very inventive," Dichter recalled of a time when he was about seventeen, as they "stood up behind rows of kitchen utensils and sundry china ware, glasses, and, around Christmas time, behind dolls and electric trains."

This and other experiences helped shape the characteristic features of Dichter's ideology, which emphasized creative discontent, the pleasure of goods, and the desire for security. From his father's failure as a salesman emerged his own success as one. In his uncle's department store Dichter learned about selling, the presentation of merchandise, and the connection between sexuality and consumer goods. His hunger helped engender in him a drive for success and a love of consumer goods. The tragedies of World War I and the sweep of fascism across Europe prompted him to mold a vision of an America where democracy and consumer culture were inseparable.[38]

By 1925 Dichter resumed his formal education, eventually earning a Ph.D. in psychology at the University of Vienna. His mentor, Charlotte Bühler, opposed the theories of Sigmund Freud and emphasized self-realization in her pioneering work in humanistic psychology. Doctorate in

---

37 Among the best sources of biographical information are "Ernest Dichter," *Contemporary Authors,* 44 vols. (Detroit, 1976), 44:190, and *Who's Who in America;* obituary, *New York Times,* Nov. 21, 1991, 12; Ernest Dichter, *Getting Motivated by Ernest Dichter: The Secret Behind Individual Motivations by the Man Who Was Not Afraid to Ask "Why"* (New York, 1979) (hereafter Dichter's name is abbreviated as ED). Daniel Horowitz, interview with ED, Apr. 8, 1986, Peekskill, N.Y. There are two sets of ED's papers: one at the Dichter residence in Peekskill and the other at the University of Vienna.
38 This paragraph and the previous one rely on ED, *Motivated,* xi, 1–5, 8, 48, 55–7, 91, 137–8, 145, 147–8, 162, 168.

hand, Dichter hustled to earn a living by the practical application of psychology, including the development of an adult education course on advertising in 1935–6. From 1934 to 1937, after studying with a member of Freud's original circle and being analyzed by an American living in Vienna, Dichter opened a private psychoanalytic practice at Berggasse 20, across the street from the home of the aging Freud. As much as any other experience, Dichter's work at the Psychoeconomic Institute in Vienna in 1936 shaped his future. There Lazarsfeld was doing commercial market research for which he used in-depth interviews. Then one day, Dichter was arrested and interrogated, because, unbeknown to him, the institute had been used during fascist rule in Austria as a place for what the authorities considered illegal activities. Soon after his release, he found out that the official Nazi newspaper in Germany had included his name on a list of subversives. He quickly realized that as a Jew and as someone suspected of disloyalty, he would have difficulty securing decent employment in Vienna.

In early 1937, Dichter went to Paris, where he worked as a salesman. He realized that his success depended less on a product's quality and price than on his ability to project the power and conviction of his own beliefs. In the spring of 1938, when the vice-consul in Paris pressed him about why the United States should permit his entry, Dichter "made the best sales pitch of my whole life." He argued he could contribute to America an ability to motivate people to solve problems by using depth psychology, based on psychoanalysis, to understand the real reasons they made the choices they did, especially as consumers. With only one hundred dollars to his name, Dichter arrived in New York in September of 1938. Shortly afterward, an American professor of phonetics asked him whether he wanted to learn how to lose his Viennese accent. Dichter decided on "an all-American" accent. "That way," he said, people "would not be suspicious of my foreign background."[39]

Dichter's success in the United States was quick. With Lazarsfeld's help, he was employed three days after his arrival. Soon Dichter took a position with *Esquire,* where he carried out research for an advertising agency in 1939, with a study of Ivory soap that relied on extensive nondirective interviews. Dichter's conversations revealed an erotic element in bathing, "one of the few occasions when the puritanical American was allowed to caress himself or herself." The interviews confirmed Dichter's vision of the gestalt of a product. A bar of soap, he asserted, had a personality that advertisements could evoke.[40]

39 Ibid., 41–2.   40 ED, *Strategy of Desire* (Garden City, N.Y., 1960), 33–4; ED, *Motivated,* 34–5.

Later in 1939 Dichter began a study that brought him fame across the nation and beyond. He accompanied his boss at *Esquire* to Detroit to help Chrysler promote the Plymouth. Chrysler's agency hired Dichter (but not his boss), and he quit his job at the magazine, going to work on Plymouth's marketing problem by interviewing consumers. In the process, he discovered the importance of convertibles in selling a wider range of cars. Associating a convertible with the excitement they believed a mistress would give them, once at the dealership middle-age men nonetheless bought a sedan, which they associated with their wives. Trade magazines picked up the story of the car as wife or mistress and *Time* followed, complete with a picture of Dichter, who had been in the United States for only eighteen months. In March 1940, the newsmagazine accepted Dichter's self-promotion and described him as "the first to apply to advertising the really scientific psychology," one that tapped "hidden desires and urges."[41] Notoriety yielded a well-rewarded job as a director of psychological research with Plymouth's advertising agency. Dichter and his wife, who had married in Vienna in 1935, were now secure enough to start a family. They gave both children what their father acknowledged as "unmistakeably American names."[42]

When Dichter left the advertising agency, he spent five years in the research division at CBS, where he worked under Lazarsfeld. Then in 1946 he went out on his own, establishing the Institute for Motivational Research, a company that applied his brand of market research for major corporations. Eventually the firm, which operated out of a mansion in Croton-on-Hudson, had sixty-five employees, several thousand part-time interviewers, and more than a dozen franchises in the United States and abroad. Dichter offered himself as the nation's leading practitioner of motivational research (MR) who relied on Freudian insights. He packaged himself by using controversial, speculative, and Freudian remarks to capture the attention of image-hungry clients and audiences. He relied on intensive, open-ended in-depth interviews that often lasted several hours and that employed free association and projective techniques. In order to understand the underlying meaning consumer goods and experiences had for a person, Dichter focused on hidden, irrational, and often sexualized reasons for consumers' behavior, especially those that could be explained by formative (but not necessarily during childhood) experiences.

Although in some senses not strictly a Freudian, as much as anyone else Dichter conflated consumption and therapy. He projected the image of himself as a scientist who diagnosed problems and promoted health in indi-

41 *Time*, Mar. 25, 1940, 46–7.   42 ED, *Motivated*, 14. Misspelling in original.

viduals and society, to say nothing of what he did for the balance sheets of his firm and those of his clients. His interviews, he claimed, helped not only advertisers in their quest to sell merchandise but consumers in their search for self-understanding. Easily shifting from market researcher to therapist, he asserted that properly marketed consumer goods could help people grow in self-awareness and self-esteem. Thus in 1947, he spoke of how cosmetics helped women "get rid of an awareness of personal inferiority, real or imagined," by providing "a form of psychological therapy."[43] Beyond this, as early as 1946, reacting to what he saw as the sickness that produced Nazism and also fearing threats to American democracy, Dichter saw himself as someone who offered mass therapy to a sick nation.[44]

The notion of the market researcher as therapist to a troubled society was at the core of Dichter's 1947 *The Psychology of Everyday Living.* His interviews revealed that underneath the patina of postwar confidence, Americans were driven by feelings of "impotence, chaos, and futility." So Dichter called for "'selling' techniques" as a part of a larger strategy of "social engineering" that would "impel people to live democratically." To foster democratic, cooperative, and tolerant behavior, specialists in mass communication could devise "very specific concrete tasks which each individual can accomplish" and would enable the person to overcome "illogical thought processes that cause group antagonisms." This use of mass culture for democratic purposes, far from undermining profitability, would increase "the entertainment values" of the media.[45] As he articulated a role for himself as social engineer and therapist, Dichter continually conflated consumer culture and therapeutic well-being, mass communications and democratic culture, market research and social criticism. More interested in reducing frustration by solving specific problems than in chasing after what he felt were abstract and unachievable goals, he celebrated a democracy that was tough-minded and realistic.

Seeking to enhance his business and to realize his desire to become accepted as a social philosopher who would counter Vance Packard and Galbraith, in *Strategy of Desire* (1960) Dichter provided his most ambitious, if still unsystematized, synthesis. He sought to prevent the United States from suffering the consequences of the Nazism that he had escaped, at the

43 ED, *Everyday Living* (New York, 1947), 142–5.
44 ED, "Radio and Television Audience Research," in Paul Lazarsfeld and Frank Stanton, eds., *Radio Research* (New York, 1946), 380.
45 ED, *Everyday Living,* 233–9.

same time that he helped his adopted nation fight Soviet Communism. To social scientists, including motivational researchers, fell the task of devising the means of preventing the public from oversimplifying issues "in a socially dangerous way," in the process fostering individual independence and helping people overcome their fear of reality. To do this he emphasized the satisfaction of realistic goals in the realm of consumer culture. The front line "defenders of a positive outlook on life, the real salesmen of prosperity, and therefore of democracy, are the individuals who defend the right to buy." Consequently, buying was proof "that we are not living in a world controlled by dialectical materialism but in a world built on individual initiative."[46]

In this epic struggle, the social scientist as social engineer could best support democracy by devising marketing strategies that would "assure the development of a positive attitude on which prosperity is based." At its core, this strategy involved inducing people to associate buying with personal creativity. At moments, Dichter was positively lyrical about the way people grew psychologically as they gained an increasing intimacy with objects. He absorbed what Marxists called the fetishism of objects. "We want to know," he wrote, "how we can read into, understand, and interpret the human quality that exists in a piece of furniture."[47] Dichter differed from Marxists, in that for him the fetishism of an object was laudable, something that MR could enhance.

This link between the material and spiritual components of goods enabled him to launch an attack on moralistic skeptics of consumer culture. As early as 1939, in a study of breakfast cereals, Dichter lamented the hold of puritanism on America. Drawing on interviews the institute conducted, he later concluded that Americans worried too much about the burdens of the good life, in large measure because of the puritanical tradition that equated consumption with sin. The solution, Dichter argued, was to become less guilty and to enjoy life more. He called on Americans to develop a "morality concept" based on "the ability to achieve self-realization through leisure and control of technical difficulties of the world which surrounds us." In the fight with the USSR, the real test of the America's success was whether it provided a "feeling of growth, self-realization and achievement." In this and other contexts, the MR practitioner's role was to liberate people's desires, diminish their guilt, and show them how to achieve spiritual

46 ED, *Strategy*, 169, 204.   47 Ibid., 93, 170–2.

ends through material means. "If the desire for freedom and discovery can be expressed through the glamour of a new convertible," he remarked, "I willingly accept responsibility for combining two strong human desires" to aid advertisers, the economy, and individuals.[48]

Although in Vienna Dichter had learned from his mentor the importance of self-realization, not until he had to defend himself and MR against Packard's attack in *The Hidden Persuaders* (1957) did he begin to link the spiritual and the material. In the process, from the early 1960s on Dichter came increasingly to emphasize the importance of self-fulfillment and creative discontent, almost always in connection with the consumption of new goods and services. Here he fully discharged the émigré's gratitude to his adopted land. Dichter was not just earning a living by promoting both his services and specific products. He was also participating in the reconstruction of American society in the postwar world. In the process of making specific recommendations, he was also celebrating the broadening of the middle class in a way that minimized the importance of those beyond the pale, defining the American dream in opposition to what he saw as the Soviet nightmare, and linking the consumption of goods with psychological well-being. From the beginning of World War II, he argued, the middle class had grown with additions from above and below but especially from the inclusion of workers. His job was to offer to people new to the middle class products that symbolized "achievement" rather than "a static way of life."[49]

If Packard had attacked Dichter for the way his work promoted commercialism and undermined autonomy, Betty Friedan in *The Feminine Mystique* (1963) accused him of playing a key role in linking consumer culture with the way housewives achieved identity, creativity, and sexual pleasure. If Dichter's relationship with those who hired him necessitated that he pay minimal attention to African Americans and those outside the middle class, the opposite was the case with gender. Women purchased a very high percentage of the kinds of goods Dichter worked to promote and were a similarly high proportion of the people he interviewed. Moreover, men in the advertising business had traditionally seen women consumers as easily swayed by emotional appeals, a tendency that Dichter's emphasis on the irrational reinforced.

---

48 [ED], "The Psychology of Breakfast Cereals," memorandum prepared by Research Department at J. Stirling Getchell, Inc. [1939 or 1940], ED papers, Peekskill (hereafter EDP), 4–5; ED, *Strategy,* 16, 19, 255, 258, 173.
49 "Does Your Prestige Stop Sales?" *Motivations* 1 (Feb. 1957): 1–2.

Dichter's discussion of the relationship between his work and women's roles was inseparable from his larger vision. Central to his response to women's situation were his emphasis on consumption as therapy, his insistence on the centrality of the creative discontent of the consumer, his stress on realistic solutions to relieve frustration, and his belief that his job was to show corporations how to link pleasure with purchases in order to overcome puritanical self-restraint. Yet as Friedan recognized, the net effect of Dichter's work was the containment of women. In a report done for a household products company in 1940, he argued that since housework was "*filled* with gratifications," women's dislike of it had to be due "to some *outside influence* because it *cannot possibly* be as unpleasant as most women claim." Because such work lacked "*social approval* and *appreciation,*" especially in contrast with professional work, the solution to the problem was obvious. Use advertisements "to give housework *Dignity* and *Social Approval,*" he advised, by emphasizing the efficiency, responsibility, and creativity involved. Friedan well understood how Dichter worked to squelch women's independence and how he set out to manipulate women's desires in order to increase sales. She realized that he used the language of science and professionalism to give women the illusion of achievement, that he promoted labor-saving methods that did little to relieve drudgery, and that he played on women's guilt over not being more perfect housekeepers.[50]

Ironically, Betty Friedan discovered Dichter when the importance of MR was waning. Although Dichter remained active until the end of his life, he shifted the emphasis of the services he offered. Then, in 1970, he suffered a heart attack in a setting fraught with significance, appearing on a platform with a black nationalist who called for $150 billion in reparations to compensate for centuries of slavery and racism. Throughout his career as a market researcher, Dichter had paid minimal attention to African Americans, focusing instead on the groups his clients targeted: white, mostly suburban, middle-class Americans. Reacting against the notion of separatism that he associated with Nazism, he used a cosmopolitanism to minimize racial and ethnic differences. Now in 1970, Dichter rejected the notion of compensation for past ills. In reply, his adversary called him a racist. Shortly thereafter, Dichter suffered a coronary. He sustained a hectic schedule as a

50 [ED], "The Psychology of Household Tavern Products," report prepared by the Research Department of J. Stirling Getchell, Inc., Aug. 1940, 9, 11, EDP; Betty Friedan, *The Feminine Mystique* (New York, 1963), 206–32; ED, *Everyday Life,* 18, 227, 230–1; "The Psychology of House Cleaning Products," *Motivations* 2 (May 1957): 10–13; ED, *Handbook of Consumer Motivations: The Psychology of the World of Objects* (New York, 1964), 126–7.

lecturer, consultant, and author well into the 1980s; he died of heart failure on November 21, 1991.[51]

Although in many ways Dichter's professional life peaked in the 1960s, in the last thirty years of his life he dealt with two issues central to the way American writers have grappled with affluence: the critique of materialism and the onset of the energy crisis. In the late 1950s, Dichter noticed among those he interviewed the emergence of what he called the Inner Joneses, people who turned away from status striving and desired to achieve greater individual self-expression. As a man who made his living by helping clients take advantage of social changes, Dichter demonstrated how corporations could benefit from the turn to what he called the new hedonism, the search for pleasure and the rejection of puritanism. Speaking the language the counterculture would increasingly discover in the 1960s but offering solutions different from theirs, by 1964 Dichter was talking about how Americans could free themselves from the "tyranny of things," as he envisioned, for example, Americans forging "social links" by sending commercial greeting cards.[52]

In the following years, what persisted was the tension between his critique of consumer culture and his suggestions of ways that purchases in the marketplace enabled Americans to achieve self-realization. Although he spoke in the language of self-fulfillment, unlike Maslow, Dichter linked a series of higher and higher desires with the consumption of goods and experiences. Yet at moments in the last two decades of his life, he seemed to be moving to a position that severed the connection between happiness and consumption. In his 1979 autobiography Dichter acknowledged that his childhood experiences meant that he had difficulty enjoying money. Self-realization also triumphed over consumer culture in the quotation he selected to accompany his entry in *Who's Who:* "I believe," wrote this man who had spent a lifetime promoting happiness achieved through goods but whose teacher had described a less materialistic road to self-realization, "that the definition of happiness is constructive discontent. . . . the goal itself is much less important than growth, striving, and self-fulfillment."[53]

However, if his early experiences and his formal education taught Dichter that affluence did not inevitably yield happiness, the energy crisis of the 1970s caused him to reaffirm his commitment to an antipuritanical vision. Throughout the 1970s, he attacked the reemergence of "the old

51 ED, *Motivated,* 4, 118–19; *New York Times,* Nov. 23, 1991.   52 ED, *Handbook,* viii.
53 Ibid., 238; ED, "Inner Jones," *Harvard Business Review;* ED, *Motivating Human Behavior* (New York, 1971), 98; ED, *Total Self-Knowledge* (New York, 1976), 266; ED, *Motivated,* 142, 145; *Who's Who.*

puritanical, Calvinistic American philosophy" that was now causing what he called "an orgasm of masochism." What underlay Dichter's optimism was the confidence born of what his interviews revealed and of his experience as successful émigré. "The typical American," he concluded, will not want "to wallow too long in a passive role of a suffering victim." Though he felt logic made clear that people should tighten their belts, he argued that as they responded to the threat of scarcity induced by the energy crisis, Americans would seek "solid, lasting values" in luxury goods such as diamonds, pursue additional enjoyments of gourmet foods, use color to cover up or escape from "the greyness of economic gloom," and opt for natural materials as they rediscovered nature. Once again, Dichter was doing what he did best: conflating marketing advice and social philosophy as he argued that consumption would "permit us to devote more time to self-discovery, continuous education, culture in all its various forms."[54]

To the end, Dichter remained optimistic. He hoped the energy crisis would not tempt Americans to "switch over to a rigid, timid, and planned economy, to such a degree that we shall lose what has always pulled America out of previous difficulties; our verve, ingenuity, and daredevil philosophy." And then Dichter ended his 1974 talk on the energy crisis with a phrase he wanted on his grave, one that drew together his European education and his faith in America: "Why Not?"[55]

CONCLUSION

As much as anyone else in the postwar world, George Katona was responsible for surveying the changing mood of the American consumer and Ernest Dichter for teaching Americans how to consume. A number of factors explain why their take on consumer culture lacked a critical edge. In Berlin and Vienna of the 1920s and 1930s, two European cities in the forefront of the experience of mass culture, they had already encountered societies fascinated by innovations in consumption even as they looked to America to see what the future held in store. Before they emigrated, they had developed an appreciation of American consumer culture because the United States offered what Germany and Austria lacked: what they saw as the links among new products, economic freedom, and political democracy.

54 ED, "Let Your Money Liberate You," *Vital,* Sept.–Oct. 1978, 90–2; ED, "Consumer Goods – Boom or Doom?" published article, c. 1974, source unknown, EDP; ED, "Energy Crisis – Boom or Doom," unpublished speech, c. 1974, EDP; ED, "Conquering the Future Through New Thinking," unpublished speech, 1975, 10, EDP.
55 ED, "Energy Crisis"; for Dichter's wish that it be on his grave, see ED, *Motivated,* 65.

Looking at the world from Berlin and Vienna in the 1930s, they understood their own emigration as a way of enjoying the fruits of affluence and of a world safe from the threat of Nazism.

For Katona and Dichter, as well as for members of the Frankfurt School, issues surrounding consumer culture provided a test case for the question of whether it was possible to reconcile modernization, democracy, and mass society. If Katona and Dichter resembled their Marxist peers in some ways, they differed in others. They eschewed a sense of European superiority as they readily appreciated American values and institutions. As people who achieved considerable success in and adaptation to their new homeland, they used their skills more to appreciate than to criticize what they found. Determined to make the best of adverse situations, they took to America a flexibility and optimism that stood them in good stead professionally but often made their observations shallow.

Katona and Dichter believed that professional experts played critical roles in helping Americans come to terms with consumer culture in what they saw as positive ways. They attacked puritanical restraint and celebrated the middle-class consumer. They linked consumer culture to a series of larger personal and social goals. They believed that affluence underwrote democracy. They saw America as a white middle-class society whose strengths would prevent the emergence of totalitarianism in their adopted land and would underwrite restraint of state intervention into the economy. They bought the American ideology of consumption as an essential component of one's aspirations. Their adopted country inspired in them the passion of converts and helped give their lives a particular cast. Their careers present the paradox of sophisticated Europeans who, drawing on their experiences before their arrival in the United States, became so captivated with America that they identified with their audience, celebrating, at times excessively, America as a society of middle-class consumers.

8

Dissolution of the "Dictatorship over Needs"?

Consumer Behavior and Economic Reform in East Germany in the 1960s

ANDRÉ STEINER

In the socialist countries of Eastern Europe, political prerogatives largely established the boundaries of individual consumption, much as they directed the economy as a whole. From an economic standpoint, consumer behavior was determined, above all, by personal income and the availability, diversity, quality, and price of goods.[1] The central economic decision-making body, that is, the government or the leading figures in the Communist Party, exerted extensive control over these factors, although their control was never total. The state set wages and prices and administered the supply of goods with the aim of eliminating the interaction between supply and demand. This is what the Hungarian sociologist Ferenc Fehér and others mean by the phrase "dictatorship over needs."[2] Yet this formulation, in a pure form, was more theoretical than actual. By (incompletely) fixing these factors, the state could only limit and constrain consumer behavior; it never succeeded in eliminating the freedoms inherent in economic matters.

In the German Democratic Republic, or GDR, a growing economic crisis prompted the ruling political party, the Socialist Unity Party (Sozialistische Einheitspartei Deutschlands, or SED), to carry out comprehensive economic reform in 1963. The reform was called the New Economic System (*Neues Ökonomisches System*). Its purpose was to liberate the economy from its political guardians and to introduce over time profitability as an

---

1 Other aspects, such as psychological, social, and cultural issues, are treated only peripherally. Other economic factors, such as advertising, product image, and sales culture, need also not be treated in depth, since as a result of the widespread shortages in these countries they could only play a minor role in the issue in question. On this point, see Ina Merkel's chapter in this book.
2 Ferenc Fehér, Agnes Heller, and György Márkus, *Dictatorship over Needs* (Oxford, 1983), 88–90.

evaluative yardstick. This chapter looks at whether politics continued to shape consumer behavior, even in this context. I focus primarily on retail prices because they provide an illustrative example of the contemporary political doctrine.

As it functioned in Eastern Europe, state socialism claimed to be able to coordinate the economy ex ante at the macro level. In contrast to the Western economic system, whereby balance is maintained ex post through the market and prices,[3] the idea was to create a balance transparently and deliberately in advance by means of a plan. To this end, it was necessary for the market and the pricing system, which acted as independent sources of information and decentralized regulatory instruments, to disappear. As a possible source of economic uncertainty, prices had to be excluded. Yet they were still needed as a basis for calculating value. They were also necessary as a means of producing incentives to achieve the economic results that were desired by central planners. The demands made on prices resulted from these two functions. First, they had to be consistent on a rational basis, while remaining constant for as long as possible. However, given the dynamism of economic processes, this principle constituted a contradiction. Those responsible only recognized this fact in due course and assumed that it could be overcome. Second, the effects envisaged by the central economic body were not the same for all sectors, and as a consequence there had to be different incentives in the form of prices. This resulted in a relatively complicated system of different, administratively fixed prices for the same goods, depending on the sector in which they were bought or sold. Here, it is important to note that the prices used within industry were different from the retail prices paid by consumers. The link between the two pricing systems – indispensable as it was from an economic viewpoint – was guaranteed by the national budget in the form of extensive duties and subsidies.[4]

Under state socialism the overall extent of consumption was centrally controlled – in the case of the GDR, by the SED leadership – and competed directly with investment. There was always a built-in tendency in the system to increase investment at the expense of consumption, one of the main reasons these countries did not develop into consumer societies. Since the ruling party also aimed to create a more just society that would provide a sense of security for all, however, it had to ensure a certain minimum stan-

3 On the practical results for consumption in the Western system in the case of West Germany, comparable with that of the GDR, see Michael Wildt's chapter in this book.
4 For the structure and characterization of the system, see János Kornai, *The Socialist System: The Political Economy of Communism* (Oxford, 1992).

dard. In East Germany, moreover, the direct comparison with standards in West Germany greatly influenced the goods made available for consumption and the population's assessment of its own standard of living. For the SED leadership, it was a balancing act between securing long-term economic growth and meeting the needs of consumers. In addition, the party leaders had to accept that the people held them directly responsible for its daily welfare. This resentment culminated in the uprising of June 17, 1953, which continued to exert a traumatic influence over these leaders until 1989. This uprising and the fact that the border to West Germany remained open until 1961 dictated that all attempts to create stronger ties between wages and individual productivity would remain halfhearted. Industrial workers, in particular, also undermined such attempts As a result, they were able to increase their incomes much faster than originally planned.[5]

Nevertheless, according to internal government sources, by 1959 real incomes in East Germany had only reached 124.8 percent of the 1938 level, whereas the figure stood at 153.1 percent for West Germany.[6] Assuming that prewar incomes were the same in both parts of Germany, real incomes in the GDR were 18.5 percent below those in the Federal Republic. This can be attributed, above all, to the fact that prices in East Germany were higher. After food rationing had been lifted in 1958, retail goods and services cost an average of 20 percent more than in West Germany. The prices for butter, meat, rye bread, baked goods, fish, and other foodstuffs as well as for rents, electricity, and public transportation were far below actual costs. And they were far cheaper than in the West. In contrast, the prices for industrial goods, such as gas, cars, television sets, washing powder, refrigerators, and textiles were very often much higher than the original costs. Textiles, clothing, coffee, tea, alcohol, and tobacco, for example, were much more expensive for consumers in the GDR. When rationing was lifted for political reasons in 1958, prices for foodstuffs were fixed at the lowest possible level. The result was an increase in government subsidies that favored the relatively high consumption of certain of these foodstuffs. Low rents and duties on services caused an increase in the demand for foods and industrial goods.

The reason for high consumer prices for technical consumer goods and textiles was that in these areas product changes had been more marked.

5 Peter Hübner, *Konsens, Konflikt und Kompromiss: Soziale Arbeiterinteressen und Sozialpolitik in der SBZ/DDR 1945–1970* (Berlin, 1995).
6 Präsidium des Bundesvorstandes des FDGB, Komitee für Arbeit und Löhne, Politbürovorlage: Konzeption für die Erhöhung der Wirksamkeit des Arbeitslohnes . . . 15.3.60, Stiftung Archiv der Parteien und Massenorganisationen der DDR im Bundesarchiv, Zentrales Parteiarchiv der SED (hereafter SAPMO-BArch, DY30) IV 2/608/40.

Prices for new products were largely calculated on the basis of the actual costs, with the lack of state control and the "seller's market" opening up an enormous opportunity for price manipulation. In addition, the state imposed high duties on these goods, which were intended to cover the subsidies for foodstuffs, rents, and public transportation. Even within the domain of industrial goods, however, prices for individual categories differed in relation to cost. For some industrial goods, especially children's wear, prices were pegged low for social reasons. The prices of a large number of goods were no longer related to the costs of production, as originally envisaged by the system, a fact that resulted in a diversity of subsidies.[7] Especially in Berlin in the 1950s, consumers had the opportunity to compare Western and Eastern prices directly, after a short ride on the subway. Understandably, the majority of the population connected this economic regime to the political legitimization of a separate East German state.

Prompted by this pressure, the SED in 1958 announced publicly that the "main economic task" should be to overtake West Germany by 1961 in per capita consumption of all important foodstuffs and consumer goods.[8] Consequently, consumption assumed a greater importance in the SED's social policy. However, for this objective to be achieved, there had to be an enormous boost in investment. In the industrial sector alone it increased by 10.5 percent in 1958, 29.8 percent in 1959, and again by 13.1 percent in 1960.[9] These exaggerated investment programs and the failure of the Soviet Union to deliver goods and materials as anticipated, coupled with the collectivization of agriculture, which went forward at the same time, provoked an acute economic crisis. Major supply shortages appeared that affected the whole population. Meat, sausages, butter, cheese, shoes, underwear, and washing powder, in particular, became scarce commodities. The deterioration in the supply of goods during the economic crisis of 1960–1 became a major factor in people's life choices. In many cases, it tipped the scale in favor of fleeing the GDR. The departure of thousands of skilled employees further aggravated the shortages because under the current economic situation neither central authorities nor factory managers could link individual incomes to individual productivity. Moreover, the exodus to the

---

7 Preisvergleich DDR – Westzone (Stand 31.12.58), Bundesarchiv Berlin(-Lichterfelde) (hereafter BArch Berlin) DE1/9891; Büro der Regierungskommission für Preise, Dr. Dost an Abt. Planung und Finanzen, Pfütze, 11.10.62, SAPMO-BArch, DY30 IV 2/608/72.
8 *Protokoll des V. Parteitages der SED* (Berlin, 1959), 68–70.
9 Calculated according to Statistisches Bundesamt, Aussenstelle Berlin, Bestand Staatliche Zentralverwaltung für Statistik, no. 7829.

West had assumed such proportions that production was suffering simply because of the lack of labor.[10] To solve these problems, the political leadership and the central economic agencies of the country turned to bolstering the supply of goods. Limiting demand was deemed politically inexpedient. Regarding basic foodstuffs, a potentially serious political issue, the government's intent was to continue centralized production and distribution. With other goods, price regulation via the mechanism of supply and demand was considered. Yet East German political leaders had no specific proposals on how to translate these ideas into actual practice within the existing political and economic order. But even broaching the very idea must have been regarded as sensational, given the prevailing political dogma.[11] These and other considerations nevertheless remained fragmentary and were considered impracticable in the current political situation since they would have inevitably entailed price increases. Thus, the crisis affecting the economy and the supply of goods required first a political solution and only then an economic one. On the basis of this insight, and after consultation with the Soviet Union, the SED decided to erect the Berlin Wall, dividing the city physically and cutting off West Berlin from its hinterland.[12]

With the Wall offering protection and a respite for the regime, the SED deemed it possible to restrict incomes and to increase retail prices. For this purpose, it initiated a campaign calling on workers to produce more in the same period for the same wages. Obviously, this policy caused resentment and even passive resistance among workers. It also explains the campaign's limited success.[13] In addition, prices were raised for shoes, notions, and textiles, especially fashionable garments. Even cars, washing machines, and radio and TV sets became more expensive, although the official reason given was technical improvement. The prices for fruit, vegetables, and potatoes also rose. In the case of meat, fish, and coffee, the range of goods shifted to more costly grades. Even prices for certain services were increased. The consequences of the price increases implemented between fall 1961 and mid-1962 accounted for at least 15 percent of the growth in retail sales in

10 Cf. Auszug aus der stenographischen Niederschrift der Beratung über die Durchführung des Planes 1961 . . . am 21.6.61, SAPMO-BArch, DY30 IV 2/2029/198.
11 Information für die Mitglieder und Kandidaten des ZK über Massnahmen . . . , 15.3.61, SAPMO-BArch, DY30 IV 2/608/51.
12 Cf. André Steiner, "Politische Vorstellungen und ökonomische Probleme im Vorfeld der Errichtung der Berliner Mauer: Briefe Walter Ulbrichts an Nikita Chruschtschow," in Hartmut Mehringer, ed., *Von der SBZ zur DDR: Studien zum Herrschaftssystem in der Sowjetischen Besatzungszone und in der Deutschen Demokratischen Republik* (Munich, 1995), 233–68.
13 Einige Probleme der Entwicklung des Produktionsaufgebotes, 6.10.61, SAPMO-BArch, DY30 IV 2/2029/205; Probleme der Lohnentwicklung, Sept. 1962, SAPMO-BArch, DY30 IV 2/608/40.

1961 over the previous year.[14] The explosive nature of these price hikes resulted from the fact that for years the party leadership had promised that consumer prices would be kept stable or even reduced. On the whole, however, the variety of industrial consumer goods decreased. Retail sales of industrial goods dropped by 3 percent in 1962 compared to 1961, and despite price increases.[15] As a result, there was a higher demand for foodstuffs, although supplies had decreased as a result of a crop failure in 1961. By introducing customer cards, meat and butter rationing was for all intents and purposes reintroduced.[16] In total, income restrictions and price increases caused real incomes to drop by approximately 2.5 percent within a year after the building of the Berlin Wall.[17]

The fact that the SED Politburo had to sanction each individual price increase shows clearly the political importance attached to these measures. The Politburo also noted that the workers were complaining about having to perform better while paying more for their daily shopping. The oft-repeated mantra of stable prices in the GDR was called into question, and some panic buying resulted.[18] The head of the central planning authority believed that this was the most difficult stage in East German history and that "socialism would now have to prove its stability."[19] The public realized that the "long lines" forming in front of shops and the increase in prices were related to the closing of the border. Moreover, their yardstick for judging the standard of living remained West Germany.[20] Such comparisons did little to bridge the gap that had opened up between the people and the social system as a result of economic inadequacies.

The SED leadership also came to realize that the only way to bring about improved economic performance was to reform the current system. After lengthy discussion and some experimentation, summer 1963 saw the adoption of an overarching concept for economic reform.[21] The purpose of this

---

14 Abt. Planung und Finanzen, Bericht über die Wirkung der Preismassnahmen . . . , 11.8.62, SAPMO-BArch, DY30 IV 2/608/72; *Statistisches Jahrbuch der DDR 1976* (Berlin, 1976), 249.
15 *Statistisches Jahrbuch der DDR 1976* (Berlin, 1976), 249.
16 Probleme der Versorgung der Bevölkerung, SAPMO-BArch, DY30 IV A2/2021/96.
17 SPK, Übersicht über die Kaufkraftentwicklung . . . , 22.9.62, SAPMO-BArch, DY30 IV A2/2021/247.
18 Abt. Handel, Versorgung und Aussenhandel an Honecker, 13.10.61, SAPMO-BArch, DY30 IV 2/608/71.
19 Information über die Stellvertreterberatung der SPK vom 14.3.62, 15.3.62, SAPMO-BArch, DY30 IV A2/2021/247.
20 Abt. Organisation und Kader, Kurzinformation über Stimmungen und Meinungen . . . , 7.6.62, SAPMO-BArch, NV4182/968.
21 *Richtlinie für das neue ökonomische System der Planung und Leitung der Volkswirtschaft* (Berlin, 1963). Cf. Gert Leptin and Manfred Melzer, *Economic Reform in East German Industry* (Oxford, 1978); Jörg

New Economic System was to promote a sense of responsibility and autonomy within the various branches of industry and within individual companies. At its core was the idea that branches should be guided by economic
incentive and that plans should only establish a general framework. As centers of "socialist concerns," the management of individual industrial
branches, which previously had been allocated funds from the national budget, were now expected to produce their own financing on the basis of a
limited number of central regulations. Planning was to be decentralized as
well. Another decisive factor was that the gross output ratio was no longer
to be used to assess the performance of branches of the economy and sin-
gular companies. In the past, this had led to a situation whereby companies
were rewarded for consuming as much material as possible. Now, the sole
criterion for the measurement of performance was profit. The level of profit
largely determined the bonuses for both workers and management. But for
profits to play that role at all, it was necessary to create the basis for undis-
torted cost accounting. Until that time, the evaluation of industrial prices
had been carried out according to different principles, which meant that a
unified approach was necessary. However, the retail prices the public paid
were not to be affected by the reorganization of the industrial pricing system. This requirement in turn caused new problems that were quickly identified by the pricing authority.[22] That these warnings were ignored indicates that political expediency still prevailed. To maintain retail prices at the
same level, new subsidies had to be granted because, in the wake of the
industrial price reform, the prices had to increase for basic commodities
and, subsequently, for all industrial goods. Yet companies tended to stop
production of state-subsidized goods, presumably out of fear of stepped-up
cost monitoring and the need to reduce subsidies. Since the SED suspected
that this effect might adversely affect the supply of industrial goods, it
decided that consumer prices should remain stable and that production
should continue during the reform of industrial prices.[23] The effectiveness
of such administrative measures, however, was questioned even by the
responsible department within party headquarters.[24]

Roesler, *Zwischen Plan und Markt: Die Wirtschaftsreform 1963–1970 in der DDR* (Berlin, 1990). Subsequently, the author presents a detailed analysis of this reform, based on the corresponding files in
the archives of the former GDR.

22 Büro der Regierungskommission für Preise an Abt. Planung und finanzen, 11.10.62, SAPMO-
BArch DY30 IV 2/608/72.
23 SPK, Niederschrift über Diskussion . . . des Politbüros zur 1. Etappe der Industriepreisreform am
14.1.64, SAPMO-BArch, DY30 IV A2/2021/250.
24 Abteilung Planung und Finanzen, Stellungnahme zur Vorlage . . . , 13.1.64, SAPMO-BArch, DY30
J IV 2/2A/1011.

Although questions of consumption played a secondary role in the reform, they had a direct bearing on it in two ways. In the future, wages and bonuses were to be tied more strongly to job performance and qualifications. In addition, the aim of the reform was to tailor the supply system to the needs of the people. Since resources were finite, one had to create economic incentives and to invent efficient methods. In principle, retail prices were to be maintained at the same level throughout the industrial price reform; in practice, the relations among prices, sales, costs, and profit were to be optimized by flexible pricing. This was supposed to increase the supply of many consumer items in the long run. Moreover, the party leadership intended to streamline subsidies for rents with the aid of regulations. Rents were to reflect whether the number of tenants was above or below average.[25] Initially, however, these proposals were not integrated either into the reform concept or into policy because of potential political fallout. Indeed, East German citizens had not failed to notice that pronouncements about overtaking West Germany in terms of per capita consumption had ceased.[26] Whereas East German leaders trumpeted the introduction of lower prices, especially for basic foodstuffs, rents, or energy, in actual fact the SED leadership was very realistic about how standards of living in the GDR compared to those in the West. They also understood how far it could go in public, as can be seen from the following excerpt from a statement sent to Soviet leaders in Moscow:

In addition, our propaganda must not focus one-sidedly on those factors that are favorable for the GDR, while tacitly ignoring the higher prices for many consumer goods. We also must not boast about our economic development using percentage figures of development when the situation for the population of the GDR is still unfavorable with regard to many products. On the whole, the people in the GDR have a realistic idea of the standards of living in the two German nations.[27]

For the public, however, the situation remained tense. Company managers used the reform in part to raise work norms for pay regulation, thus establishing a closer link between the development of incomes and individual performance. The decisive factor, however, was that the changes in the pay structure had to be implemented without causing loss of income for the work force. This in turn provided new possibilities for wage increases;

---

25 Niederschrift über die Ausführungen Ulbrichts 17.11.62, SAPMO-BArch, DY30 J IV 2/202/50; Walter Ulbricht, *Zum neuen ökonomischen System der Planung und Leitung* (Berlin, 1966), 184–8.
26 Abt. Parteiorgane, Kurzinformation über die ersten Stellungnahmen . . . , SAPMO-BArch, DY30 IV A2/2021/80.
27 SPK, Stellungnahme zur Ausarbeitung "Der Lebensstandard der Bevölkerung der DDR," 1.10.63, SAPMO-BArch, DY30 IV A2/2021/249; Ulbricht an Abrassimow, 16.10.63, SAPMO-BArch, DY30 J IV 2/202/33.

for that reason many employees initially supported the reform concept.[28] As a result, 84 percent of the increase in the net national product was accounted for by private incomes during the first two years, that is, in 1964–5.[29] Because of the pay raises, however, companies felt the need to increase prices in order to maintain profit levels. At the same time, because loopholes existed in the still incomplete price regulations, continuous price hikes that had not been approved from above occurred. Besides, the government was not interested in reducing prices generally since it was a seller's market.[30] Although there was substantial improvement in the overall supply situation in the first years, the supply of status-related consumer goods, such as cars, refrigerators, and washing machines, clearly fell short of demand.[31] Even the reformers eventually realized that "price rigidity had to be overcome"[32] and that, in the future, retail prices also had to be coupled with the development of supply and incomes. In short, this meant that party leaders wanted prices to be mediated by supply and demand.[33] The general situation forced them to consider such heretical measures; these considerations, however, were never realized in the GDR economy.

The industrial price reform was carried out in stages. When the setting of industrial prices for consumer goods began, the question arose as to whether it would be realistic to insist on the maintenance of retail prices. Companies had found ways to pass along to the consumer some of the higher prices for basic commodities, materials, and fuel that had already come into effect. In addition, when the new industrial prices for consumer goods were fixed, it became apparent that the gap between them and retail prices was growing. Therefore, the number of goods for which state subsidies were required rose. In the discussion of these issues, top government officials felt politically constrained since they had repeatedly promised that industrial price reform would not affect the public.[34] Yet they had to concede that economic reasoning dictated that they not provide subsidies. Willi Stoph, the head of government at the time, argued that companies would

---

28 Hübner, *Konsens,* 84, 87.
29 Abt. Planung und Finanzen, Thesen zur Entwicklung der Konsumgüterpreise, 18.3.66, SAPMO-BArch, DY30 IV A2/2021/676.
30 Abt. Planung und Finanzen: Schlussfolgerungen für die politische Führungstätigkeit . . . , 8.7.64, SAPMO-BArch, DY30 IV A2/601/70.
31 VWR, Analyse über die Versorgung der Bevölkerung . . . , 1.4.65, BArch Berlin DE4-S/14-4-65.
32 Büro für Industrie und Bauwesen beim Politbüro, Grundorientierung für die weitere Arbeit . . . , 29.8.63, SAPMO-BArch, DY30 IV A2/2021/671.
33 Beirat für ökonomische Forschung, Thesen zu weiteren Gestaltung der Industriepreise . . . , 10.9.64, BArch Berlin DE1/VA-42591.
34 Niederschrift über den TOP 1 der Sitzung des Präsidiums des Ministerrats vom 22.4.65, BArch Berlin DC20-I/4-2913.

stop the production of subsidized goods as they had in the past, that this would seriously hamper economically important relationships between producers and traders, and that it would be impossible to control the multitude of administrative measures as well as the large number of subsidies required. For political reasons, however, he wanted to postpone any solution until the industrial price reform had been completed.[35]

The more persistent reformers within the central planning authority demanded that these problems be solved, together with the reorganization of industrial prices. They believed that otherwise it would not be possible to arrive at an economically consistent price structure, given the plethora of administrative regulations. They proposed a compromise between the political goals and the economic requirements. With a view to limiting the consequences for the public, they suggested that the average price of classes of products should remain constant, not the price of every individual item. In addition, they held the view that a certain number of products should become more expensive, and prices for others should be reduced. They wanted to minimize the gap between the new industrial prices and current retail prices.

The planning authority simultaneously raised a number of fundamental questions that had never before been addressed, that had to be solved in the long run, and that were revisited at a later stage. At issue was the apparent discrepancy between the consumer prices for foodstuffs and industrial goods, as well as textiles and technical consumer goods.[36] Per capita consumption of basic foodstuffs meanwhile far exceeded prewar levels and even West German levels in some cases. The high consumption of butter prompted the SED party chief, Walter Ulbricht, to voice public concern about the people's health.[37] However, this was simply a reflection of the excess purchasing power resulting from the fact that industrial goods were either unavailable or too expensive. In 1965, a television set cost 2,050 marks; a refrigerator, 1,350 marks; a washing machine, 1,350 marks; whereas the average gross monthly income was 633 marks.[38] In the case of TV sets, the state tax accounted for 42 percent of the price that wholesalers had to pay to manufacturers, to which was added a trade margin of around 8 percent. For refrigerators, 40 percent of the retail price was accounted for by

35 Stoph, Information über gegenwärtige Probleme der Durchführung der Industriepreisreform, 20.5.65, BArch Berlin DE1/VA-45339.
36 SPK, Vermerk zur Information des Genossen Stoph über gegenwärtige Probleme . . . , 31.5.62, BArch Berlin DE1/VA-45339.
37 *Protokoll der Verhandlungen des VI. Parteitages der SED. 15. bis 21. Januar 1963* (Berlin, 1963), 1:153.
38 *Statistisches Jahrbuch der DDR 1968* (Berlin, 1968), 81, 433.

the profit margin, which was largely shifted to the national budget.[39] As a result, party leaders considered the possibility of using the comprehensive subsidies to support low-income groups. The hefty subsidies for children's clothes were also called into question because no one could guarantee that the savings would actually reach the intended beneficiaries. Instead, the intention was to increase direct child benefits. Meanwhile, SED politicians emphasized that changes "in such a sensitive area" could only be implemented gradually. In any case, the solution of the problems relating to the price structure required, above all, a sufficient supply of goods.[40]

In summer 1965 the pricing authority proposed adjusting industrial and retail prices, especially for products used by both industry and consumers, such as nails, screws, or tools. This was necessary because companies were turning to the retail market, where prices were lower, to satisfy their demands, for example, for tin. Of the products regarded as purely consumer goods, only "luxury goods and collector's items," such as sailboats, trailers, and Dresden china, were to become more expensive. In all other cases where industrial prices were higher than retail prices, as a result of preproduction costs, subsidies were to be maintained.[41] These ideas were approved on the condition that they help prevent a dip in real incomes.[42] Nevertheless, leading government officials revisited the question of totally abolishing subsidies in the framework of an overall concept for raising living standards. Such a thoroughgoing solution, however, would have required exact calculations about the necessary resources and possible benefits. Since these were unavailable, the plan could not be discussed.[43] Moreover, in fall 1965 there were disputes within the East German leadership over future levels of economic growth, its preconditions, and further reform measures. Against this background, it was quite understandable that in November 1965 the head of government banned internal and public discussions of consumer prices.[44]

39 Untergruppe Konsumgüterpreise, Zum Problem: "Konsumgüterpreise im neuen ökonomischen System," 6.1.67, SAPMO-BArch, DY30 J IV 2/202/414; Ministerium der Finanzen, Standpunkt und Vorstellungen über die Konzeption . . . , 28.1.69, SAPMO-BArch, DY30 IV A2/2021/428.

40 Abt. Planung und Finanzen, Thesen zur Entwicklung der Konsumgüterpreise, 18.3.66, SAPMO-BArch, DY30 IV A2/2021/676; Abt. Planung und Finanzen, Stellungnahme zu einigen Problemen der Entwicklung der Einzelhandelsverkaufspreise . . . , 17.1.69, SAPMO-BArch, DY30 IV A2/2021/684.

41 Regierungskommission für Preise, Behandlung von Einzelproblemen . . . , 28.6.65, SAPMO-BArch, DY30 IV A2/2021/235.

42 Sektor Finanzen, Stellungnahme . . . , 1.7.65, SAPMO-BArch, DY30 IV A2/2021/235.

43 Aktenvermerk über die Sitzung bei der SPK . . . , 21.9.65, SAPMO-BArch, DY30 IV A2/2021/740; Niederschrift über den Tagesordnungspunkt II . . . der Sitzung des Präsidiums des Ministerrats vom 28.10.65, BArch Berlin DC20-I/4-2913.

44 Niederschrift über den TOP 4 . . . der Sitzung des Präsidiums des Ministerrats vom 25.11.65, BArch Berlin DC20-I/4-2913.

In early July 1966 *Neues Deutschland* (New Germany), the official party newspaper, carried an inconspicuous government statement on page 2 that as of July 11 the prices for nylon stockings (the East German brand name was Dederon) would be lowered an average of 35 percent. With respect to goods used by both industry and consumers, the article announced both price cuts and price increases. Subsidies on consumer goods that had been labeled "luxury goods and collector's items" the previous year were abolished. These measures were intended to cut prices.[45] Their adoption meant that the price changes discussed a year earlier were for the most part put into effect. Because it was regarded as a precondition for the conclusion of the industrial price reform, it was done prematurely and with great haste. Those responsible for the price changes apparently were not cognizant of the economic repercussions;[46] the party apparatus had early on criticized their lack of political sensitivity.[47]

Given the repeated promises to maintain stable prices, these changes, although quite rational from an economic standpoint, did not sit well with the public. In heated discussions in shops, at work, or in private, people expressed their disapproval because they feared further price increases. The price cuts contained in the package were not appreciated because, as with stockings, the public had been demanding them for quite some time and hence regarded them as overdue. Moreover, the public made a direct connection between the changes and the industrial price reform, which was exactly what the party leadership had hoped to prevent. The public also compared their situation directly with that of West Germany.[48] The fact that these comparisons were rather indiscriminate illustrates the rather fuzzy East German reception of developments in West Germany. Yet one need only look at the situation in the Federal Republic, where a steep rise in the number of automobiles symbolized rising prosperity, to understand why the most angry arguments concerned expensive auto parts. Household automobile ownership was 9.4 percent in the GDR in 1966, compared to 27 percent and 47 percent in West Germany in 1962 and 1969, respectively.[49]

45 *Neues Deutschland,* July 10, 1966.
46 Niederschrift über den TOP 3 . . . der Sitzung vom 3.11.66, Niederschrift über die Ausführungen des Ministers für Handel und Versorgung . . . am 17.11.66, BArch Berlin DC20-I/4-2913.
47 Abt. Handel, Versorgung und Aussenhandel, Stellungnahme zur Vorlage . . . , 6.6.66, SAPMO-BArch, DY30 IV A2/2021/68.
48 Abt. Konsumgüter und Preiskontrolle, Information, 23.8.66, SAPMO-BArch, DY30 IV A2/2021/676.
49 Ralf Rytlewski and Manfred Opp de Hipt, *Die Bundesrepublik Deutschland in Zahlen 1945/49-1980: Ein sozialgeschichtliches Arbeitsbuch* (Munich, 1987), 140; *Statistisches Jahrbuch der DDR 1976* (Berlin, 1976), 312.

Apparently, the SED leadership and the government were stunned by this reaction, coming as it did during a vacation period. They believed that the root of the problem was that the public had not been sufficiently educated. But they failed to realize that they were trapped in a policy of their own making. The current head of government confirmed that the people "were thinking about these things, sometimes not even maliciously or in opposition," but that there were "certain things [the people] did not understand." In addition, he pointed out that all economic processes operate within a political context and that it is precisely the lack of such information that is seized on by the "enemy" in the West.[50] The fact that the price changes were not carried out all at once – as was originally intended – but rather as a correction of individual prices over a longer period, when the government had already expressed harsh criticism, casts a revealing light on the central management's ability to control developments. At the end of September 1966 the government ordered a general price freeze. By then, however, around twenty-six thousand prices had already been changed.[51]

Within the party, the trauma and fears caused by these events were so strong that it decided not to allow any more changes in retail prices during and after the final stage of the industrial price reform, effective January 1, 1967. This also spelled the end of the compromise between economic needs and the political imperative to keep retail prices level, although a year's work had already been invested in keeping average prices for certain classes of products constant while adjusting the prices of individual goods to the level dictated by the industrial price reform. This method should have nearly eliminated the differences between industrial and consumer prices for individual consumer goods.[52] During the last stage of the industrial price reform, the central administrative agencies went to great lengths to ensure that consumer prices would not change nor would there be a decline in the production of consumer goods.[53]

By the late 1960s, however, prices of many individual goods had remained largely constant but the average prices of a large number of product classes had increased. Between 1962 and 1967 average prices for industrial goods rose by 2.5 percent. In 1968 alone they increased by 3.3 percent. This

50 Ausführungen des Genossen Minister Rumpf und Diskussion . . . in der Sitzung des Ministerrats am 21.7.66, BArch Berlin DC20-I/4-2913.
51 Niederschrift über den TOP 3 . . . der Sitzung vom 3.11.66, BArch Berlin DC20-I/4-2913.
52 Niederschrift über den TOP 2 . . . der Sitzung des Präsidiums des Ministerrats vom 8.9.66, BArch Berlin DC20-I/4-2913; Sektor Finanzen, Information zur Sicherung der Konsumgüterpreise, 12.9.66, SAPMO-BArch, DY30 IV A2/2021/676.
53 Information über den gegenwärtigen Stand und die Probleme . . . , 1.12.66, SAPMO-BArch, DY30 IV A2/2021/225.

increase was attributed, above all, to the average price of textiles, which rose by 4.6 percent during the first five years and by 10.6 percent in 1968. This year also saw an increase in the use of synthetic fibers in this product class. The increase in average prices continued until 1970 and affected almost all types of industrial goods and even some foods. By the beginning of 1970, the prices for men's coats had gone up by 65 percent and the cost of refrigerators by 10 percent compared to 1967. Yet the average price remained constant or even dropped for many goods.

The main reason for the increases was the availability of an ever larger number of high-end consumer goods – for a higher price, of course. The prices for new products were practically all fixed at a higher level than those of old goods, plus a higher state duty. Since companies were not interested in producing the cheaper range of goods, these disappeared from the shelves and average prices rose. Behind the scenes, however, some of the companies manipulated these processes. The quality of new products had been improved only apparently or negligibly, fueling ongoing public discussion of price hikes.[54] Even a commission created by the party leadership to look into price problems stated that "although individual prices remained stable, there can be no question of an overall stability in price levels." [55] Normally, this should have pleased those responsible for running the economy because it was a way of dampening excess purchasing power. What annoyed the SED leadership, however, was that the public construed it as price creep and hence as yet another broken promise. In addition, high prices curbed the consumption of such goods, deluded the central economic agencies into believing that the market was saturated, and preserved the existing pattern of consumption. Consequently, this commission believed that supply should exert primary influence over the relationship between demand and supply. Nevertheless, it also felt that consumer prices should be more flexible and that compensation should be offered to low-income groups. Regarding distribution, the SED believed that those segments of the population in which incomes were growing faster than average prices benefited most from the improvement in living standards.[56] It was chagrined to learn that these groups included the remaining independent entrepreneurs, owners of seminationalized companies, and self-employed tradesmen. Since they were

---

54 Abt. Planung und Finanzen, Stellungnahme zu einigen Problemen . . . , 17.1.69, SAPMO-BArch, DY30 IV A2/2021/684; Abt. Planung und Finanzen, Information über die Entwicklung . . . , 23.6.69, SAPMO-BArch, DY30 IV A2/2021/678; Analyse der Entwicklung . . . , BArch Berlin DC20-I/3-807.

55 Untergruppe Konsumgüterpreise, Zum Problem: "Konsumgüterpreise im neuen ökonomischen System," 6.1.67, SAPMO-BArch, DY30 J IV 2/202/414.

56 Ibid.

not the target of the SED's social policy, the party felt compelled to enact new countermeasures.

During the period of economic reform, all ideas relating to the development of consumption were based on investments' receiving a high priority. But when the plan called for dramatically increased production in 1969–70, the party tried to find new ways to save resources, especially in the area of consumer goods. The first concept envisioned, among other things, higher tax rates for private entrepreneurs, self-employed tradesmen, and freelancers. The main thrust of this package, however, was aimed at a drastic decrease in subsidies for rents, services, and retail prices, as well as a substantial increase in the prices consumers paid for new high-end products. The new principles for fixing the prices of consumer goods should "trickle down" without major pronouncements. In addition, a social component was included that gave preferential treatment to industrial workers.[57] In early April 1970, the Politburo approved this program and suggested only a few amendments.[58] Stoph insisted on the gradual abolition of state subsidies. In contrast, Erich Honecker, then a Politburo member, wanted to exempt interest rates, energy prices, and rents from these increases. Ulbricht pointed out that the majority in the party was not politically prepared to react to questions of that kind. From an ideological viewpoint, socialism had been synonymous with a low level of prices and price stability. Although he suggested that this "propaganda [was] primitive," he admitted that he himself was basically trapped by his own propaganda and ideology.[59] In the following months, the responsible economic agencies formulated the general concepts more precisely and looked more closely into the economic repercussions. The government discussed the results in early July 1970. For the remaining self-employed individuals, taxes and other duties would be increased; subsidies for children's wear and children's shoes would be abolished, and child benefits would be raised. Subsidies for certain goods, especially high-quality goods, would also be terminated. Moreover, the range of high-end goods would be expanded. To compensate low wage earners, their incomes would be raised. In general, the main purpose was to demonstrate a higher degree of flexibility when setting consumer prices. Thus, attempts to plan consumer prices were supposed to balance supply and demand.[60]

---

57 Halbritter an Mittag, 21.1.70: Konzeption zur Ausarbeitung von Massnahmen . . . , 13.1.70, SAPMO-BArch, DY30 IV A2/2021/434.

58 Protokoll der Politbürositzung am 9.4.70: Halbritter, Massnahmen und Vorschläge . . . , 25.3.70, SAPMO-BArch, DY30 J IV 2/2A/1433.

59 Cf. Handschriftliche Notizen von Gerhard Schürer, BArch Berlin DE1/VA-56078.

60 Präsidium des Ministerrats, Beschluss zur Durchführung von Massnahmen und Vorschlägen . . . vom 3.6.70, BArch Berlin DC20-I/4-2226.

This notion contained a novel approach to the control of consumption by economic means, but at first it raised more questions than it was able to answer, and it could not be implemented overnight.

Originally, these measures had been initiated as part of an effort to liberate funds for an ambitious investment program to modernize East German industry. But when the SED admitted in summer 1970 that it had taken on too much, these funds were used to cope with the acute economic difficulties caused by this program. These difficulties manifested themselves in shortages of smaller consumer items, such as toothbrushes and toilet paper, whereas supplies of industrial goods, such as television sets and washing machines, were for the most part adequate.[61] In September 1970 the Politburo decided that the lowest income brackets should be raised, that steps should be taken to reduce the incomes of owners of private companies and the self-employed, that the range of high-quality and expensive products should be expanded, and that subsidies for certain industrial goods should be abolished.[62] Since these measures turned out to be insufficient, however, in November 1970 party leaders considered for the first time raising prices of basic foodstuffs, such as meat, sausages, and butter, as well as that of electric energy. At the same time, financial compensation was offered to lower-income groups. The prices for readily available industrial products (for example, refrigerators and washing machines) were to be cut with a view to striking a balance between supply and demand. For the time being, rents and the prices for services and public transportation were exempted because it was impossible "to keep them under control in social and economic terms."[63] At the end of November, however, the Politburo reversed its decision to raise the prices of basic foodstuffs and retreated from this taboo subject. Instead, it was resolved that, in addition to the measures adopted in September, employee social welfare contributions should be increased, the price of spirits should be raised 20 percent, and the range of more expensive foodstuffs enlarged. In exchange, it was decided to raise some wages and extra benefits and to roll back prices for textiles.[64] These changes were to be introduced gradually during the first quarter of 1971, with the party well aware of the fact that they would not solve fundamental problems, such as the discrepancy in consumer prices between industrial goods and foodstuffs. Once again, the SED leadership had disregarded economic needs for fear of suffering the political consequences of its own policy.

61 Cf. Tisch an Ulbricht: Information, 2.11.70, SAPMO-BArch, DY30 J IV 2/2A/1479.
62 Protokoll der Politbürositzung am 15.9.70, SAPMO-BArch, DY30 J IV 2/2A/1464; Stoph, Maßnahmen zur besseren Ausnutzung . . . , SAPMO-BArch, DY30 J IV 2/2A/1465.
63 Schürer, Begründung zur Vorlage "Probleme des Volkswirtschaftsplanes 1971," SPK, Persönliche Notizen über die Beratung . . . im Politbüro am 3.11.70, BArch Berlin DE1/VA-56118.
64 Protokoll der Politbürositzung am 30.11.70, SAPMO-BArch, DY30 J IV 2/2A/1481.

At the fourteenth meeting of the SED Central Committee in December 1970, this package of measures was presented to a wider audience, if not exactly to the public. At the meeting, the head of the Dresden SED came out against increases in the social welfare contributions scheduled for the first of the year because nobody had been prepared for such a step and it would be unwise to announce it shortly before Christmas. The Politburo withdrew this planned increase without objection.[65] Two passages delivered by Stoph at the meeting were subsequently published; one referred to the proposed increase in lower incomes, the other to the decision not to raise prices for butter, meat, and other basic foodstuffs.[66] Apparently, this information was intended to encourage workers to earn this "advance" by increasing performance the following year.[67] However, since the passage from Stoph's speech that explained what lay behind such an assumption was not published, the public concluded that only the prices for butter, meat, and other basic foodstuffs would not be raised. This belief in turn resulted in numerous rumors, discussions, and expressions of disapproval.[68]

As of mid-December 1970, discontent inside the GDR was underscored by demonstrations, strikes, and the general political unrest in Poland, which had resulted from price increases.[69] This may explain why the party leaders and the government abandoned a number of planned price hikes in January 1971 The decision to retreat was inconsequential, since the planned increases affected "a multitude of individual products with major political implications but only negligible economic effects."[70] The biggest economic consequence was anticipated from the pending increases in the price of some alcoholic beverages. Taking into account future price cuts, these proposed increases were to account for an additional 79 million marks per annum. When balancing out all measures aimed at increasing or reducing purchasing power, however, the end result would have been a boost in consumer purchasing power of 1.3 billion marks.[71] Clearly, the original plan had backfired. Demand was strengthened and subsidies expanded. It is no surprise, therefore, that the general public by and large welcomed these measures; they had not expected such large price cuts. On the contrary,

65 Stenographische Niederschrift der 14. Tagung des Zentralkomitees 9.-11.12.70: Zweiter Beratungstag, SAPMO-BArch, DY30 IV 2/1/414.
66 Willi Stoph, *Zum Entwurf des Volkswirtschaftsplans 1971: Aus der Rede auf der 14. Tagung des ZK der SED 9.-11.12.70* (Berlin, 1970), 31–4.
67 Stenographische Niederschrift der 14.Tagung des Zentralkomitees 9.-11.12.70: Erster Beratungstag, SAPMO-BArch, DY30 IV 2/1/413.
68 Zentraler Operativstab, Information . . . , 16.12.70, SAPMO-BArch, DY30 IV A2/2021/428.
69 *Archiv der Gegenwart* 40 (1970): 15951–3.
70 Halbritter an Mittag, 21.1.71: Gemeinsamer Vorschlag des Politbüro und des Präsidium des Ministerrates . . . , SAPMO-BArch, DY30 IV A2/2021/680.
71 Ibid.

they had reckoned with even greater price hikes for alcohol and industrial goods.[72]

In addition to the unrest in Poland, the government's flip-flop was presumably sparked by power struggles within the SED. Erich Honecker, who had already been designated unofficially as the new party leader, had set new directions of a policy that later was to characterize his era. His efforts to oust Ulbricht would have been in vain had they not been supported by the Soviet Union. This explains why, in contrast to Ulbricht, he tried to take his cue from the superpower to the east. In February 1971, following Soviet thinking, the Politburo formulated a new "main task," which was designed to improve further the people's standard of living on the basis of high economic growth.[73] Unlike Ulbricht, who went to great lengths to increase efficiency and subsequently the standard of living, Honecker pursued the opposite path. By raising living standards and offering comprehensive social benefits, he intended to provide an incentive to improve economic output. His goal was to make the system more attractive to the people by deliberately situating their needs more at the center of state interest and thus pacifying them in this way. At a Politburo meeting in March 1971, Honecker demanded a policy that rejected future increases in retail prices. He believed this policy would create popular confidence in the party and the state: "You can never govern against [the will of] the workers!"[74] As a logical consequence, the SED formally decided in August 1971 to keep consumer prices stable.[75]

At the beginning of the Honecker era, the supply of consumer goods improved and incomes increased directly and indirectly via extensive social measures. Consumers were in a much better position to satisfy their needs, and the social climate became more favorable for consumption generally. The party leaders' expectations that an improvement in economic performance would follow, however, were never realized. The anticipated long-term economic expansion did not take place because endogenous incentives in the economic system remained limited. Furthermore, economic incentives on the individual level were not directly connected to better possibilities for consumption. On the contrary, improvements in social secu-

---

72 Halbritter, Sieber an die Mitglieder und Kandidaten des Politbüro, 1.2.71: Information . . . , SAPMO-BArch, DY30 IV A2/2021/680.
73 Protokoll der Politbürositzung am 16.2.71, SAPMO-BArch, DY30 J IV 2/2A/1499.
74 Protokoll der Politbürositzung am 23.3.71, SAPMO-BArch, DY30 J IV 2/2A/1505; Niederschrift über die Beratung . . . am 23.3.71 im Politbüro, 24.3.71, BArch Berlin DE1/VA-56131.
75 Protokoll der Politbürositzung am 3.8.71, SAPMO-BArch, DY30 J IV 2/2A/1529; Beschluss über Massnahmen zur Sicherung der Stabilität der Verbraucherpreise, SAPMO-BArch, DY30 J IV 2/2A/1530.

rity, which were not linked to individual performance, negatively influenced individual incentives in the long run. As a result, during the 1970s more was consumed than produced in East Germany, ultimately leading to a substantial increase in the country's foreign debt. A greater supply of consumer goods and the expansion of the social welfare system were largely financed through foreign credits. This consumption "on credit" was one of the causes of the subsequent failure of the system.

In sum, the emphasis on economic profitability during the period of economic reform prompted thinking about how to shape the structure of retail prices on the basis of economic reason. However, these considerations never went beyond the framework established by the system. For the central economic agencies, prices and incomes remained to a large extent a means of channeling consumer behavior. Private households did not determine prices by making autonomous purchasing decisions. Accordingly, a minimalist attempt to dissolve the "dictatorship over needs" was not undertaken. The main concern was to keep retail prices constant. Changes were seriously considered only when economic constraints or emergency situations left no alternative. The implementation of such policies, however, was determined first and foremost by political expediency. Price hikes were limited to those groups unable to defend themselves in the same way as workers could; the latter had repeatedly demonstrated their strength by organizing local walkouts. Hence, the products that became more expensive were usually the so-called luxury goods and collector's items. The SED cunningly used this ploy to create envy. Since East Germans were already envious of the West German living standard, they thought it only fair that those in their own country who were better off sacrifice accordingly. The egalitarianism typical of SED ideology, which contradicted the demands for coupling individual performance and income, also left its traces. It contravened, however, reformers' efforts to offer higher performance incentives. The benefits of advantages, such as price cuts, were to be reaped by the general public. A policy aimed at mass loyalty is hardly suited to bringing about economic profitability. Because of the incalculable risks, the leadership repeatedly shied away from abolishing most of the state subsidies and reallocating the available resources to lower-income groups. As a result, the structure of retail prices continued to produce waste and frustration. Thus, for consumers, the structure of East German society also remained highly political, despite its purported freedoms, something that should not surprise given the general characteristics of the system and the limited range of the 1963–70 reforms.

PART TWO

Everyday Life

The second part of this book, "Everyday Life," gathers together essays that trace patterns of consumption, investigate the meanings of particular consumer goods, and describe how individual people have responded to developments in the consumer economy. They emphasize familiar technologies – cars, toys, and kitchen utensils – and family tensions, and they place quotidian detail in broader contexts. A number of these pieces demonstrate that new consumer habits often involved profound shifts in values, represented by clashes of generations and of interests. Many of them focus on gender, suggesting that it has shaped people's understanding and experience of consumption in daily life. On closer inspection, the path to a consumer utopia that most economists and a number of historians imagine as painless and enthusiastic actually entailed hesitancy, conflict, and difficult choices. Even as people have embraced new goods and their possibilities, those decisions have often been accompanied by seismic cultural changes and by struggle at the mundane but significant level of everyday life. Complexity is a common thread of these essays, which remind us that there was no single path to a global consumer culture.

The state's role in valorizing particular types of markets has depended on specific political and cultural conditions. Kurt Möser's chapter describes how the German people's experience of World War I fostered an awareness and demand for cars and, more universally, motorcycles; here, experiences that apparently were private again had state origins. Möser points also to an ensuing recognition by Third Reich leadership of the utility of a mobile society trained to use automobiles, and of the possibilities for the car as a symbol of state power and modernity.

Susan Porter Benson's work in the records of the Women's Bureau offers individual stories that draw a connection between wage earning and consumption. Establishing that the United States was hardly a consumer paradise for the working class even during the prosperity of the 1920s, Benson explicitly challenges "the focus on middle-class abundance of most of what has been written about the history of consumption." For the people she studies, limited budgets demanded a level of self-denial that conflicted with new attitudes about consumption. Consumer culture came to working families only with conflicts over attitudes toward thrift and luxury that were often generational and that operated as screens for issues of control and authority within the family. Moreover, gender differences shaped both the discourses and the experiences of consumption, contributing to the portrayal of women – even those who earned wages – as consumers.

Consumer goods themselves, as symbols and as material culture, are central in the making of cultural values and of conflicts over consumption practices. Nancy Reagin's study of German housewives' organizations in the interwar period focuses on the work of the household, linking consumer goods to the political issues discussed in the first part of the book. These organizations embraced modern ideas about the "rational" household, held exhibitions that gave thousands of housewives the opportunity to examine new products, and promoted product testing. At the same time, they resisted the "American" model and fostered nationalism through menu planning: Apples and rye bread, staples particularly abundant in Germany, became symbols of the German nation itself. These organizations were Nazified as part of the general transformation of Weimar women's organizations; their Nazi successors for the most part carried on their consumer policies and approaches to housekeeping. As Germany entered the postwar era, the fundamental popular attitudes toward consumption fostered by these groups laid the foundation for adaptation to the modern Western consumer world.

Susan Strasser's chapter focuses on a single postwar American commodity, the electric garbage disposer, to demonstrate how consumer goods both foster and symbolize shifts in cultural values. For Strasser, the popular adoption of the disposer represents new assumptions about waste and reuse. Proponents of the disposer touted its convenience, its labor-saving qualities, and the previously unattainable level of kitchen hygiene it fostered. Labor saving and a new attitude that devalued food waste were joined in the "particular vision of an abundant life represented in the new kitchens of postwar American housing." Strasser argues that the disposer symbolized the consumerist utopia of postwar America, a world in which new goods eliminated, camouflaged, or rerouted centuries-old tasks, and where the consequences of such changes remained invisible for a long time. Only with the environmental movement, Strasser concludes, was the disposer challenged as a mixed blessing; by then this product had taken root in daily life. At that moment the society that believed itself to be a consumer's paradise saw those dreams challenged by the hidden consequences of unchecked growth, accumulation, and waste.

Ina Merkel's chapter on the particular form of mass consumption prevalent in East Germany during the 1960s reveals cultural tensions and values at the heart of popular practice. She emphasizes that the consumer culture of the German Democratic Republic was not isolated; many East Germans were involved in a continual East–West discourse, exposed to Western television and radio and to the experiences of relatives across the border. Nor was it homogeneous; like capitalist consumer culture, it was marked by distinctions of class, social standing, gender, and generation. Merkel perceives distinct historical phases in the development of GDR consumer culture, suggesting a periodization based on generational change. Outlining characteristic shopping routines and responses to particular products, she argues that East Germans developed complex strategies for satisfaction in an economic system that seemed to offer only limited response to consumer demand. At the heart of such strategies were a mix of long-held attitudes toward luxury and functionality, and new beliefs about abundance. Merkel shows that East German consumer culture and behavior combined individual determination to realize individual desires with a strong sense of the government's obligation to ensure plenitude for all.

For West German consumers, the postwar "economic miracle" proved exciting, chaotic, and taxing. Michael Wildt shows that the "multiplication of options and [the] diversification of practices" represented by new and unfamiliar consumer goods engendered profound cultural changes. Here, as in East Germany and the United States, historical change had a significant generational element. New products designed to reduce labor in homemaking revived the tension that Nancy Reagin describes in the context of the 1920s between acknowledging the housewife's desire for convenience and reaffirming her competence and importance as measured in time and effort. Self-service retailing made consumers more independent and weakened the relationship between consumers and retailers. At the same time, it encouraged manufacturers to offer advice, service, and corporate image along with material goods, a shift that Wildt calls a "transfer of influence from the personal to the semiotic." Consumption became a more private undertaking, with each family dependent upon its own wisdom and devices. This change represented a shift away from communal and intergenerational traditions that had shaped German consumption and housekeeping for years, a new phase of consumption that Wildt links with West Germany's postwar accommodation to democracy.

Matthias Judt's chapter explores the experience of place, offering a German perspective on the conjunction of retail developments, suburbanization, demographic change, and increased reliance on the automobile in the postwar Boston metropolitan area. Maintaining that retailing characterizes the region's development and redevelopment, Judt sketches the spatial dimensions of postwar consumption and of the state policies that encouraged and supported its growth. He closes with a comparison with eastern Germany after unification, where new investment has favored American-style suburban shopping centers over downtown department stores.

Steven Kline traces the impact of consumer culture on children. The study of toys, for Kline, illustrates "a fundamental restructuring of the economy in which the legitimation and promotion of leisure has itself become a significant aspect of global economic expansion." He argues that the growth of the commodity system merged with changing American child-rearing theory and practices, strengthening the emphasis on toys and play as necessary for development. He describes two shifts: to a notion of toys as tools for children's work early in the century, then to an understanding of toys as part of a growing entertainment industry after World War II. The new emphasis on commercial items for play resulted in a virtual commodification of childhood, as manufacturers targeted children, the most captive and susceptible market of all. Using television and licensing arrangements, marketers created symbolic worlds to sell products that addressed essentially every aspect of children's lives and every stage of their growth. The very processes of play were modified, as toy makers learned to market to the changing practices, family patterns, and vulnerabilities of children's lives, taking advantage of children and socializing them to the commercial marketplace at a very early age.

Christian Pfister examines the limits of universal eternal material abundance and the long-term consequences of consumer society, using physical parameters such as energy output, natural resources, and labor. With the experience of Switzerland as his example, he describes the four decades since the 1950s as a period of significant transformation, not simply rapid modernization: A society and a culture based on environmentally sustainable behavior gave way to the contemporary global consumer culture. Pfister's economic and environmental analysis provides a frame for many of the issues and topics raised by other essays in the volume – chain retailers and shopping malls, highway construction, and government sponsorship of consumption both at home and abroad. He argues that confronting the limits of consumption requires public policies that emphasize restraints on purchasing and on growth; at the same time, he suggests that consumers themselves must integrate older values of thrift and economic rationality, as well as the human obligation to live as citizens in a world not fully under their control.

Fath Davis Ruffins's chapter explores the intersections between the postwar development of American consumer culture and the concurrent emergence of conflicts about and consciousness of race and ethnicity. Ruffins examines imagery about African Americans, Latinos, and other minorities as it appeared in American commercial life in general and advertising in particular. She describes such stereotyped commercial characters as Aunt Jemima and the Frito Bandito but moves beyond the concept of stereotype to demonstrate the complexity of the processes by which images operate, and the important relationships between commercial imagery and social realities. She identifies three crucial postwar developments: the emergence of middle-class minority market segments, the politicized protest of stereotyped imagery, and the creation of a new imagery of ethnic diversity. A growing rhetoric of freedom that permeated American culture forced Madison Avenue to pay attention to previously ignored or stereotyped groups; at the same time, the actions of minority business people and political activists created new constraints and opportunities. Ruffins's essay reminds us both of the role of imagery in the ideological developments described in other chapters, and of the analytic importance of heterogeneity in understanding the experience of American consumer culture.

9

World War I and the Creation of Desire for Automobiles in Germany

KURT MÖSER

War is the greatest of all agents of change. It speeds up all processes, wipes out minor distinctions, brings realities to the surface.

– George Orwell, *The Lion and the Unicorn*

THE 1920S: DESIRE FOR AUTOMOBILES IN ADVERSE CONDITIONS

Following World War I, several factors adversely affected the popularization of car ownership in Germany, which lagged behind that of other Western countries. In the mid-1920s, there was one car for every 250 Germans. In France and Britain, in contrast, the figure was half of that.[1] The reason for Germany's lower rate of car ownership was primarily economic. Quite unlike in the United States, the cost of purchasing and operating automobiles in Germany was simply far too expensive. The portion of the population able to afford personal motorized transportation was comparatively small, increasing significantly, if only gradually, in the second half of the decade. The inflation crisis of 1922–3, reparations, and the precarious situation of the German economy were among the factors that negatively influenced car ownership. The disposable income of most families was not high enough to operate even a modestly priced motor vehicle.

Government policies, moreover, impeded individualized road transportation. Taxes on privately owned automobiles and, to a lesser extent,

---

1 Hans-Carl Graf von Seherr-Thoss, *Die deutsche Automobilindustrie: Eine Dokumentation von 1886 bis 1979*, 2d ed. (Stuttgart, 1979), 634.

motorcycles were quite heavy. Private motor vehicles were declared to be "luxury goods" and therefore nonessential. Comparatively high maintenance costs also added to the financial burden. Without having to examine government regulations very closely, it is easy to conclude that neither the economic nor the legislative climate was positively disposed toward automobiles.

Apart from restrictions on privately owned automobiles, commercial motorized vehicles also suffered from the lack of state protection. Under the political and economic conditions of interwar Germany, utility vehicles were frowned upon. Bureaucrats in the state-owned railway, the Reichsbahn, were aware that a conflict among different systems of transportation was emerging. Through several measures, they attempted to curb the competition from road transportation, for example, by restricting private truck licenses or regulating road fees. All this discouraged shopowners, small transport companies, contractors, or moving companies from buying trucks and/or switching over to motorized road transportation.

The conversion to motorized road transportation was particularly problematic in the early postwar years. Prohibitions against driving motor vehicles, a limited fuel supply, and the lack of spare parts or rubber tires all served to hamper the operation of motor vehicles. For years to come, bureaucratic licensing regulations presented obstacles for individual and company owners.[2] Finally, the turbulent political events of the postwar era restricted general mobility, witnessed government requisitioning of vehicles, and occasioned the frequent setting up of roadblocks.

The post–World War I era also found the motor vehicle industry in disarray. The availability of former military vehicles lowered the demand for new vehicles, and the dire economic situation discouraged the introduction of new makes and improved models. In addition, manufacturers had not implemented new and more efficient production methods during the war because the military authorities bought vehicles regardless of the cost.

In 1920 the German correspondent of the American journal *Automotive Industries,* W. F. Bradley, summarized the sorry state of road traffic after the war and its main causes:

In the big provincial cities, such as Munich or Leipzig, it can be declared that the use of private automobiles is practically unknown. . . . The high initial cost of automobiles, the 15 percent luxury tax on their purchase price, the heavy state

2 An example: "Die Regierungs- resp. Polizei-Präsidenten erteilen den Zulassungsschein erst nach Anhörung des Reichsverwertungsamtes, das seinerseits die Gesuche vom Standpunkte des rechtmässigen Erwerbes aus prüft," *Allgemeine Automobil Zeitung,* 1919, 18.

taxes, the scarcity and the cost of gasoline and tires are in themselves sufficient to restrict automobile movement without any government decree.[3]

Despite these odds there was a surprisingly keen interest in automobiles after the war; they had a "high profile" in postwar society. Judging by the number of articles about and illustrations of automobiles in mass circulation publications, and their appearance in literature, film, and the arts, they attracted and captivated the public's attention. Automobiles were now seen much more positively than they had been in previous decades. In 1928 the *Allgemeine Automobil Zeitung* stated "that the extraordinarily strong hate for automobiles that was common in Germany has vanished, even in the smallest village. . . . The conviction that it is necessary to drive has been taken for granted by the German people."[4]

Not only was the desire for automobiles on the rise, but a "boom" of sorts was also in the making. Of course, the demand for automobiles far outstripped the ability of the market to supply it. Any answer to the question of why this *Nachfragereserve,* or surplus demand, was difficult to satisfy must take into account the influence of several factors, such as official discouragement. Nevertheless, the nominal number of people for every car dropped from 510 in 1921 to 100 in 1932.[5] This large drop in the number of people per automobile is quite astonishing when one considers contemporary conditions. There was indeed an embryonic "equipping the masses with automobiles," but it was not based on automobiles, as in the United States, rather on two-wheelers. This situation was rather specific to Germany. In fact, Germany had the largest number of motorcycles of any European country, both absolutely and relatively in relation to the population. The typical German motorized vehicle was a light motorcycle, not because it was desired but because it was comparatively affordable – a "substitute car" that lacked protection against the elements and the capacity to transport a larger family but a typical "first-time buyer's vehicle" that fueled the desire for a proper automobile.

How did the demand for motor vehicles overcome the previously mentioned odds? In addition, how was the market for automobiles able to succeed against adverse economic conditions? Indeed, the forces of attraction

---

3 Quoted by Heidrun Edelmann, *Vom Luxusgegenstand zum Gebrauchsgut: Die Geschichte der Verbreitung von Personenkraftwagen in Deutschland* (Frankfurt am Main, 1989), 32.

4 Original: "dass aus dem Volksbewusstsein der ehemals in Deutschland so ausserordentlich starke Autohass bis ins kleinste Dorf hinein verschwunden ist. . . . Die Überzeugung, dass man Auto fahren muss, ist auch fast ebenso selbstverständliches Gemeingut des gesamten deutschen Volkes geworden" *Allgemeine Automobil Zeitung,* 1928, 8.

5 Seherr-Thoss, *Die deutsche Automobilindustrie,* 634.

would have to be rather strong to overcome all of these negative tendencies. Why did the mass desire for automobiles and the buying of motorized transport, which seemed to go against all relevant economic and political factors, nevertheless prevail?

Different academic fields have given different reasons for the success of specific technologies – in this case, a transportation system – in a specific environment and in the face of various competitors. The most common view purports technological causes: A technology succeeds simply because it is better than what came before or the competition. This is hardly the case with motor vehicles in the 1920s; they were still uncomfortable, unreliable, and not very easy to drive for the less technologically minded. Others have advanced economic or legislative reasons – a technology is financially more efficient either for owners or for the national economy, or it is favored or even sponsored by the government. As we have seen, this does not appear to be true in our case. In fact, pressure "from below" was exerted on official decision makers to change their skeptical position vis-à-vis automobiles. Official statements tried to play down the relevance of privately owned vehicles – although recognizing the national importance of trucks – thus drawing a sharp contrast to public desire.[6]

The theory that a technology is accepted and widely adopted because its advantages and attractions are better publicized or advertised may partly explain the desire for motorized vehicles. But as an answer to the aforementioned questions, it is not entirely satisfactory. Nor is the notion of a conspiracy of oil companies tenable, since oil trusts were weaker than the "coal barons" (*Kohlebarone*) who supported the railroads.[7] Moreover, in the 1920s the majority of politicians and technocrats in a position to influence the debate were opposed to individual motor vehicles.

In short, the reasons most commonly used to explain the success of a particular technology are quite unsatisfactory. Some historians tend to stress causes related to their own special interests. But instead of isolating single causes, I am interested in assessing the influence of factors that are difficult, if not impossible, to quantify, but that may contribute to an answer to the following question: Why were so many Germans willing to devote large portions of their personal income to privately owned mobility? The answer, I believe, lies at the juncture of values, images, and the positive or negative evaluation of material objects. Heidrun Edelmann lists in her recent book some of the conditions needed to explain the transformation of automo-

---

6 See Edelmann, *Vom Luxusgegenstand zum Gebrauchsgut,* 29.
7 See the controversy about the theories of David Beasley, quoted in Clay McShane, *Down the Asphalt Path: The Automobile and the American City* (New York, 1994), 98.

biles into consumer products in post–World War I Germany.[8] Some of these conditions are rooted in decisions that were political (tax policies) or economic (introduction of the purchase-for-hire system). But some of them concern questions of economic optimism or pessimism, or of individual purchasing decisions. These questions can be answered only if we take into account the peculiar structure of society during the Weimar Republic, a society characterized by the process of coming to terms with the experience of World War I. The desire for automobiles in the 1920s was a social phenomenon deeply rooted in the specific circumstances of postwar German society. In this chapter, I argue that car culture was closely linked to the war experience, the changes caused by the war, and the establishment or change of social values that increasingly favored automobiles. World War I altered the structure of consumer wishes: Interest in convenience and fascination with technology enabled a large part of society to view automobiles as a highly desirable means of transportation, as a valuable investment, and as a potential individual possession.

Who, if anyone, was behind the popularization and integration of automobiles in German society? Did particular individuals or social groups actively promote the automobile? Was a particular social "agent" involved? In this chapter, I investigate the actual situation and some of the intended and unintended consequences related to these questions.

THE RELEVANCE OF AUTOMOBILES

What is most important, and not at all obvious, is the fact nearly every class and social group in Germany at the time viewed automobiles as highly significant. From the very start, automobiles were not regarded neutrally, that is, simply as machines. They were instruments of distinction: the favored vehicles of flaneurs and dandies in turn-of-the-century Paris; the prestigious and powerful movable grandstands used by the Kaiser and his family to exhibit themselves to the public; the dangerous epitome of modernity and velocity in races; symbols of an emphatically new age to avant-garde artists and poets. But they were by no means mass products; they were definitely upper class and elitist.

All of this changed after the war. Several parallel car cultures were evolving in Germany and each reflected the divided and increasingly antagonistic social structure of the Weimar Republic. The war and its violent aftermath convinced nearly every group of the particular relevance of motorized

8 See Edelmann, *Vom Luxusgegenstand zum Gebrauchsgut*, 15–16.

road transportation. Automobiles were thought to be relevant to nearly everybody, although for different reasons. Different types of vehicles were, of course, given different images and invested with different meanings. To list only a few:

(1) *Surplus war trucks* were employed to carry revolutionaries to remote areas in order to "agitate" rural folk, thus becoming vehicles for transporting the impending revolution, symbolizing revolutionary speed (see Figure 9.1);

(2) "Middle-class" *sedan cars* were the vehicles of choice for the self-assured bourgeoisie;

(3) *Sports cars,* or open touring cars, linked mental images with new cultural media; in the prewar era, this had been the image of the "adventure car";

(4) High-powered *luxury cars* became the transportation means of the dashing upwardly mobile class and of high-society women;

(5) Heavy *gentleman's motorcycles* were vehicles to show off masculine, motor-related values;

(6) *Trucks* and delivery vehicles were used in growing numbers even by smaller companies;

(7) The petit bourgeois *utility car* became the mainstay of the large class of crafts-men and small-business owners;

(8) *Light motorcycles* became the practical vehicles of extended range (both phys-ically and socially) of working-class people, enabling them to travel greater distances to work and leisure destinations;

(9) Motor vehicles of all kinds were the symbolic transportation of the spirit of mechanization by which conservative revolutionaries intended to overthrow the bourgeois society.

I suggest calling this system of highly varied types and makes of motor vehicles, conveying different images and status for different groups, *class-specific car cultures.* Longing for these vehicles, owning them, driving them were therefore located in a complex political and social structure. Gender and partisan politics were reflected in automobiles. Discussing automobiles, despising or adoring them, adapting them to new types of cultural activities – such as beauty contests (*Schönheitskonkurrenzen*) for automobiles and women alike – loaded them with very different types of meaning. A car culture in the 1920s became a "symbolic field" wherein wider issues were discussed. Historians have not yet properly explained this cultural focus on automobiles, that is, their symbolic significance in the Weimar Republic.

In this chapter, I propose an additional reason for people's readiness, or even their longing, to accept this new device, to indulge in it, to use it, to own it, or to spend a considerable part of their income on it, even if it was expensive or beyond their modest means. What promotes the transforma-tion of a technological object into a consumer good? Here, I suggest that this transformation was strongly connected to the events and outcome of

Figure 9.1. Revolutionaries and motor vehicles: German soldiers on a truck in Berlin, Nov. 9, 1918. © Bundesarchiv, Koblenz. Used with permission.

World War I. Did the image of the car change during the war, and, if so, did this change influence subsequent desire for car ownership? To answer these questions, we need to look more closely at this watershed event in modern German history.

WORLD WAR I AND ROAD TRANSPORT

In the words of the British prime minister, David Lloyd George, World War I was an "engineer's war."[9] It was the first war in history in which motorized road transportation played a major role. To link the car culture of the 1920s to the developments of the war, we need to look briefly at the "syndrome" of World War I, which has been called the "original catastrophe of the twentieth century" (*Urkatastrophe des 20. Jahrhunderts*).[10]

Two archetypes found in many pictorial histories of the war help document the changing role of motorized vehicles. The first shows a road with rows of marching soldiers and a speeding staff car in the foreground (see Figure 9.1). This picture is typical for the early phase of the war, whereas a

---

9 Karl-Heinz Ludwig, *Technik und Ingenieure im Dritten Reich* (Königstein/Taunus, 1979), 32.
10 Wolfgang Michalka, ed., *Der Erste Weltkrieg: Wirkung, Wahrnehmung, Analyse* (Munich, 1994), 3.

Figure 9.2. Public transport during World War I: German troops moving up the line in Romania, 1916. © Bundesarchiv, Koblenz. Used with permission.

second type of photograph is widely found later on: a supply road with a column of crowded trucks traveling to the front (see Figure 9.2), or several motor ambulances, perhaps even with woman drivers, often artillery pieces drawn by motorized tractors.

These pictures illustrate the evolution of the use of automobiles during the war, from vehicles for transporting individual members of the army staff to multipurpose vehicles for conveying the masses and moving heavy equipment. The speeding staff car became the symbol for the arrogance and superiority of high officers, replacing the image of superiority of the horse-mounted officer riding above the marching privates.[11] The truck transporting troops in cramped conditions, however, acquired the image of "equality" war transport, symbolizing German "war socialism" (*Kriegssozialismus*).

The earlier contrast between the officer's automobile and the marching foot soldiers was also evident in the German organization of transport. In the beginning of the war, no staff vehicles were integrated into the organization of the army. In August 1914 members of the Imperial Automobile

11 Paul Fussell, "The Enemy in the Rear," in *The Great War and Modern Memory* (New York, 1975; reprint, New York, 1981–2).

Corps Volunteers (Kaiserliche Freiwillige Automobilkorps) –together with their vehicles and, more often than not, paid drivers – were given a temporary officer's commission. They were only formally enrolled in the officer's list and therefore officially made part of the army in May 1915.[12]

Whereas the mostly upper-class staff car drivers/owners retained some of their gentleman driver's image during the war, army trucks were much more workmanlike. Even before the outbreak of hostilities, each army was equipped with an army truck unit (*Armee-Kraftwagen-Kolonne*, or *AKK*).[13] In September 1914, 9,739 trucks were assigned to the army, together with 4,000 staff cars, ambulances, and motorcycles.[14] The increase in the number of trucks precipitated efforts to reorganize motorized units, leading, on the one hand, to a more centralized structure headed by a *Feldkraftfahrchef* (head of field motorized transport), and, on the other, to the assignment of truck units to ever smaller military structures as corps or divisions.[15] The result was the creation of 236 *Divisions-Kraftfahr-Kolonnen* (divisional truck units). In November 1917 the German High Command assembled a number of these units at their disposal for the purpose of more effective troop transport and munitions supply for the coming western offensives.[16] At the war's end, the German army had 25,000 trucks, 12,000 staff cars, 3,200 motor ambulances, and 5,400 courier motorcycles.[17]

Even before the war, the military established a program to support the purchase and maintenance of private trucks in times of war. This program, supporting a special type of *Subventionslastkraftwagen* (subsidized truck), had been initiated in 1908. It gave 4,000 marks each to individuals or companies who bought trucks that fulfilled certain requirements, and it contributed 1,000 marks annually for five years to their operating costs.[18] A total of 800,000 marks was allocated to this program; a year later the figure topped 1 million marks.[19]

Quite often a soldier's first acquaintance with the convenience of motorized transport was when he became wounded. By 1916 motorized ambu-

12 Militärgeschichtliches Forschungsamt, ed., *Deutsche Militärgeschichte in sechs Bänden, 1648–1939* (Herrsching, 1983), 5:262.
13 For its organizational structure, see ibid.   14 Seherr-Thoss, *Die deutsche Automobilindustrie,* 71.
15 For the organizational history, see Militärgeschichtliches Forschungsamt, ed., *Deutsche Militärgeschichte,* 5:263.
16 Ibid.   17 Seherr-Thoss, *Die deutsche Automobilindustrie,* 72.
18 E.g., the capacity to carry 4,000 kilograms, a minimum speed of 16 kilometers per hour (or 12 kilometers per hour when fitted with iron tires), minimum power output 30 horsepower, climbing ability 1:8. See Hans-Otto Neubauer and Michael Wessel, *Die Automobile der Benzstadt Gaggenau* (Hamburg, 1987), 76. For dimensions, see also Seherr-Thoss, *Die deutsche Automobilindustrie,* 38.
19 Ibid., 69.

lances were in service on the Western Front and had become the regular means of transporting casualties from the first-aid posts to the casualty clearing stations. Ambulance trains took over after that, moving wounded soldiers farther to the rear. Other opportunities for the common German infantryman to come into contact with vehicles powered by the internal combustion engine included chapel trucks, mobile dental surgical units, delousing trucks, and even motorized pigeon carriers. Apart from the ubiquitous four-ton *Subventionslastwagen,* many specialized vehicles were built, among them, trucks mounted with antiaircraft guns and winch and gas trucks for carrying observation balloons or drinking water. In 1914 *Armee-Fleisch-Kraftwagen-Kolonnen* (army meat automobile units) were brought into service. One of the most important developments was the mechanization of field artillery, that is, the employment of prime movers (called *Kraftzug*). When the fighting in 1918 demanded greater mobility, as a result of rapidly shifting fronts, motorized artillery finally came into its own.

In sum, motorized transport became much more prominent during the course of World War I. Soldiers of the mass armies became increasingly exposed to motorized vehicles of all kinds. The image of automobiles changed from that of a sports and upper-class leisure vehicle to one of true utility. A contemporary German technology textbook praised motorized transport and stated that "to the end of the war, the number of motorized units continually increased. They were made available for every large operation. During all operations, in big offenses and in defensive battles, they did extraordinarily well wherever used."[20]

In hindsight this optimistic, semiofficial view has to be put into a broader perspective. Germany certainly lacked the early successes of British and French engineers to improve the ability of vehicles to travel cross-country and to produce motorized vehicles on a mass scale. German manufacturers never built more than a handful of tracked supply vehicles. By 1918 the German army had a tank designed by a consortium – the A7V vehicle – but only twenty-three of them were ever built. German armored units of the last few months of the war primarily used captured British tanks. Armored cars had been developed by Germany, but they, too, were built only in small numbers.

Might not the relatively small numbers of automobiles (cars and trucks)

---

20 Original: "Unausgesetzt bis Kriegsschluss wurden die Kraftfahrverbände vermehrt; zu allen grossen Operationen wurden sie planmässig bereitgestellt. Bei allen Operationen und bei den Grossangriffen und den Abwehrschlachten haben sie überall vorzügliches geleistet." Max Schwarte, ed., *Die Technik im Weltkriege, unter Mitwirkung von 45 technischen und militärischen fachwissenschaftlichen Mitarbeitern* (Berlin, 1920), 223.

actually used by the German army in World War I disprove the thesis of this chapter, namely, that the use of motorized transport was important? The number of vehicles is only part of the story. Not only soldiers but also civilians were exposed, actively and passively, to modern motorized transportation. A great number learned to drive trucks, staff cars, and courier motorcycles. This was an important factor in the stress German military authorities put on road transport. Relevant, too, was the "public" image that motorized vehicles acquired: Because they were used by the military authorities, they became linked with government or official efforts.

To date, historians have placed undue importance on the idea that Germany relied to a much greater extent than its enemies on narrow-gauge railway networks to supply its trenches. This is only partially true. Although it was still a war of soldier's boots, horse's hooves, and iron rails, automobiles were omnipresent, particularly at the focal points of fighting and action. Accordingly, they had a greater impact on those who came into contact with them during the *Grosskämpfe* (great battles) than their actual numbers might otherwise suggest. It is generally true that the soldiers marched into battle and were supplied by railways and horse-drawn wagons. But the internal combustion engine had a very high profile, on the battlefield and behind the lines: It was at the center of the action, either as transport or as a fighting vehicle. Many of the specifically new features of warfare in World War I were connected with mechanized transport. Thus, a link was formed between the image of the *Materialschlacht* and the motor.

Even on the home front, motorized transport acquired a higher profile. Since civilians had been exposed to motor vehicles far more during the war than they had been before it, many looked at them in a new way. This also affected women. Seen superficially, there is no obvious reason why women's attitudes toward automobiles should have changed because of the war, but they did. Women also took an active part in the revolution in road transport, as total mobilization for the war progressed. They participated in cultivating both images of the automobile, the "utilitarian" and the "prestigious." The latter was represented by the female driver of staff cars or ambulances of prestigious volunteer services, whose "adoption of a uniform became the sign of sought-after professional status."[21] On the other end of the scale were women bus drivers or drivers of agricultural machinery, doing less glamorous but highly useful work. In factories or in the public transportation system, many women replaced the men who had been called to arms. In some cases, in fact, factory managers even preferred

21 Diana Condell and Jean Liddiard, *Working for Victory? Images of Women in the First World War, 1914–1918* (London, 1987), 26; see also illustrations 48–9.

women since they would never be drafted. All too often men who had been taught to drive were called to serve in the military as soon as they had completed their driver's course. The loss of newly trained employees cost companies money; women who had been trained and who continued to work thereby repaid the initial investment. The first woman to receive a truck driver's license in the South German state of Baden was Maria Oberle, a country girl employed by the Rheinische Gummiwaren-Fabrik in Mannheim. She had been hired to raise pigs for the worker's meat supply but was persuaded to attend a driving school in 1916 so that she might replace drafted drivers.

In addition, the symbolic value of the internal combustion engine must not be underrated, despite the fact that German soldiers and civilians never made a direct connection between national feelings and road transport. The French were able to do so in two cases – the Paris taxis helped win the Battle of the Marne in 1914 and supplied the line during the defense of Verdun two years later, the *voie sacrée* (holy road). The British had their sentimental ties to motorized transport as well, traveling in requisitioned London double-decker buses, some of which continued to display their original destination signs.[22] A similar symbolic enhancement of the status of cars and trucks was not present in postwar Germany. There was, however, a brief "car madness" at the beginning of the war as the German public became excited by the news that French automobiles were using German roads to transport gold to Russia. The public was eager to set up "patriotic" roadblocks and "[s]oon every single house, every small village felt they had to erect traffic obstacles."[23]

But not just society's attitudes toward motorized transport changed; during the war the organization of road transport was also transformed. The growing number of vehicles on German roads required efficient organization, traffic regulation, and an infrastructure of repair facilities. To cope with the dense traffic on most of the supply roads, new ways of organizing it had to be found. Indeed, after 1916 the components of an elaborate road traffic system were established behind the Western Front; for example, road signs, organized traffic police, repair facilities, and gas stations were broadly introduced, although actions of the French army were even more radical. Nevertheless, postwar road traffic was largely modeled on the pattern estab-

---

22 See Chris Ellis, *Military Transport of World War I, Including Vintage Vehicles and Postwar Models* (London, 1970), illustration no. 26.
23 Original: "Schon fühlte sich jedes einsam stehende Haus, jedes Dörfchen . . . veranlasst, auf ihren Strassen Verkehrshindernisse zu errichten." *Allgemeine Deutsche Automobilzeitung*, no. 8 (Feb. 1916): 9.

lished during the war. The basic elements of this system existed, of course, already before 1914 (for example, road signs), but these had been organized only locally. Yet during the war, the system was streamlined and centralized. Together with production and engineering developments, much was undertaken to transform motor vehicles into an efficient means of mass transportation.

Finally, during the war German society as a whole became familiar with motorized road transportation on a scale as yet unseen. The war popularized a product that had heretofore been viewed as elitist. The link between war and technological developments crystallized in the combination of road transport and the internal combustion engine. Automobiles were transformed from niche vehicles to a main component of the system of road transportation, as they were integrated into the effort of the whole society to win the war. These were the technical, social, and ideological prerequisites for the altered image of motor vehicles in the postwar society and thus created the conditions for a potentially limitless vehicle market.

CONSEQUENCES OF THE WAR: TECHNOLOGY AND SYSTEM

Military transports were a conspicuous part of the landscape in post–World War I Germany. Many military cars and trucks were pressed into civilian use; as a result, there was a devaluation of automobiles and especially trucks in the immediate postwar period. Army surplus vehicles were abundant and were being sold off by a state-owned company. Some were not quite legally demobilized, finding their way into unlikely places, such as remote rural areas. The reason was that they were left or sold cheaply on the black market when the German army retreated and discipline broke down. Erwin Blumenfeld, a conscripted *Krafter* (slang for "driver") in the war, recalled such an episode after crossing the Rhine at Cologne: "My old crate was limping along miserably on two cylinders through the icy German regions until the fuel ran out on the outskirts of Kassel, where I was able to sell it to a farmer for one hundred and fifty marks."[24]

German industry, its engineers and its products, were all influenced by the war. Many engineers, who toiled for military establishments during the war and who looked for civilian applications for their skills after 1918,

---

24 Original: "Meine Karre hinkte kläglich auf zwei Zylindern durch die vereisten deutschen Gaue, bis das Benzol aufgebraucht war und ich sie kurz vor Kassel für hundertfünfzig Mark an einen Bauern verpatzte." Erwin Blumenfeld, *Durch tausendjährige Zeit: Erinnerungen* (Munich, 1976), 209.

found work in the automobile industry. Likewise, manufacturers desperately tried to stay in business by turning to the civilian market. It is conspicuous that companies that had played a major role in the German war effort, such as Mauser or Krupp, and engineers who had worked in the defense field threw themselves into building motorized vehicles for the general population. The tiny Krupp scooter and the Mauser *Einspurauto* (a large motorcycle with an enclosed body) tried to establish themselves in the market with "affordable" two-wheeled road vehicles. The Mannheim airship manufacturing company Schütte-Lanz launched a line of light wooden car bodies that fit the chassis of small cars put out by different manufacturers. The civilian car market was seen as the obvious substitute for the previously unlimited military demand.

In the immediate postwar era, some of the attempts to create an automobile for the average consumer approached the technical problems of affordability in innovative ways. A considerable amount of the military's know-how was invested, and a military engineer's "can-do" attitude prevailed. Moreover, the war accelerated the process of standardizing and simplifying parts as well as cutting down the number of vehicle types. Thus, the new products that emerged, and the new markets that were created for them, were equally influenced by the war.

But this situation did not last. A number of factors stalled the effort to market popular postwar road vehicles. As previously mentioned, there were a number of factors adversely affecting the popularization of automobiles in post-1918 Germany. Probably the most significant one was the purchase price, which had also been linked to the war. Pampered by the military authorities, who had paid nearly any price, manufacturers failed to introduce more efficient production methods. Only in the late 1920s were new products and new construction techniques introduced. The assembly line, a symbol of the new method of mass production, was introduced in Germany only in the second half of the 1920s. This was true for the production not only of passenger cars but also of agricultural tractors, notably by the Lanz company in 1926.

In addition, the authorities were not consistent in digesting the war experience. Immediately after the armistice, official German statements clearly trumpeted the future importance of the motor vehicle. Considering that "the circumstances of the times absolutely demanded the use of motor power,"[25] the Prussian War Ministry drew up plans for the efficient organi-

25 Original: "die Zeitumstände gebieterisch auf die Verwendung motorischer Kräfte wiesen." *VDI-Zeitschrift*, 1919, quoted in Edelmann, *Vom Luxusgegenstand zum Gebrauchsgut*, 29.

zation of traffic in the future. In a memorandum, it was suggested that an imperial office (*Reichsamt*) be established to centralize and improve the organization of road traffic.[26] Thus, an attempt was made to apply the war experience of regulating car and truck traffic behind the front and within the country. The system of motorized traffic that had developed during the war was seen as a model for a centralized and efficient civilian system. Despite the fact that most of these proposals were rejected, or were implemented only much later, there was keen awareness of the need to streamline the transportation system born of the necessities of war.

The structure of the market was also influenced by the war experience. The numerous specialized types and uses of road vehicles paved the way for widespread civilian applications. During the war, motor vehicles had demonstrated their multiple uses. This versatility was exploited and extended after the war.

The *Kleinauto,* or compact car, for example, was developed and used during the war in growing numbers, as a result of its frugal use of Germany's dwindling resources.[27] Experiences with the small car prepared engineers (and potential users) for the manufacture of a small popular car in the 1920s. There was little doubt that a "people's car" had to be simple and cheap. Its shape, technology, and construction were worked out during the war. But it was by no means clear which solution would be best – sizing down an ordinary car, introducing cheaper production methods or materials, or applying new technologies such as the *Einspurauto.*

The improved reliability of automobiles and motorcycles was another important factor in their increased popularity. In wartime, they had achieved a much higher degree of practicality, were easier to operate, and were much less prone to breakdown. Self-starters, automatic ignition, timing advances, and other devices enabled even less mechanically minded drivers to use them. This was – at least in Germany – to some extent counterbalanced by a decrease in the quality of certain components, such as tires, and by the increase in the use of substitute materials and low-grade petrol. To cope with these limitations, German engineers had to rely on solutions that gave them – up to a point – a technological advantage. In general, however, the war transformed automobiles from "adventure vehicles" to a practical and increasingly reliable means of all-around transportation, yielding a certain "user-friendliness" that was indispensable for ordinary people.

26 Ibid., 28–9.   27 This was pointed out by Schwarte, *Die Technik im Weltkriege,* 237.

THE CONSEQUENCES OF THE WAR:
MENTALITIES AND MARKETS

The two antagonistic images of road transport identified during the early war years – the "elitist" and the "utility" vehicle – continued to prevail in the first half of the 1920s. But these images were highly fractured, thus forming the class-specific car cultures of the Weimar period already discussed. There were, of course, many social factors that contributed to the rise of a car culture. Wolfgang Sachs has pointed out, for example, that the acceptance of automobiles by women played a major role.[28] But many of the social developments that favored motor vehicles can be traced directly back to the modernization brought about by World War I.

One example of this is the appearance of the drivers. A glimpse at the figure of the *Herrenfahrer* (gentleman driver) or even at the first-time motorcycle owner of the 1920s reveals another type of link with the war. The typical driver looked like a fighter pilot. (This is a qualitative argument: a question of style, images, even physiognomy.) In photographs from the 1920s, even dignified family men riding low-powered light motorcycles could look (and perhaps even feel) like famous fighter pilots. They were clad in jackets, helmets, and boots that resembled pilot's garb known from photographs widely publicized during the war to create public heroes.[29] There were, of course, practical reasons for such dress: the availability of clothing, boots, helmets, and goggles from wartime surplus. These items were sold off cheaply in huge quantities after the war. But one cannot doubt that a large number of motorcycle owners clearly styled themselves after the powerful images of pilots. In marked contrast, older photographs often show wives and children in the passenger saddle, dressed in ordinary street clothes.

This highlights an important dimension of men's desire for motorized transport. By buying and driving even an inexpensive motor vehicle, it was possible to participate in a strong and powerful social image that had gained salience during the war. This pattern is only too familiar today. By shopping for a prestigious, if sometimes not entirely practical product, the potential buyer invests in and becomes part of an attractive image – in this case, an image featured prominently in contemporary German society, as numerous editions of books on or by fighter aces readily illustrate. Automobile com-

28 Wolfgang Sachs, *Die Liebe zum Automobil: Ein Rückblick in die Geschichte unserer Wünsche* (Reinbek/Hamburg, 1984), 51–5.
29 This is especially true in Germany, where cheap editions of biographies or autobiographies of fighter pilots sold extraordinarily well. For instance, 526,000 copies of Manfred von Richthofens, *Der rote Kampfflieger* (Berlin, 1917), were sold before 1920.

panies reacted to this pattern by styling their automobiles to resemble airplane fuselages and designing gas tanks to look like the fuel tanks of biplanes.

Another powerful image of motorized transport in the 1920s was linked with agitation and collective aggression, an image that had already been projected before the war, for example, by the futurists, notably by Filippo Tommaso Marinetti. To the aggressive image of speed in postwar Germany was added the notion of collectivity. A typical sight in the difficult years when Germany was on the brink of civil war was a troupe of soldiers, revolutionaries, or militiamen, crowded on a speeding truck, flags waving.[30] This image of a type of "public" transport was not limited to the political Left, since it was also appropriated by Reichswehr troops and by the revolutionary Right. Because it linked revolution, aggression, collectivity, and the internal combustion engine, this image was broadly influential and formed a typical 1920s mental picture of "modernity." This type of agitation, wherein road vehicles supported novel forms of mass political mobilization, foreshadowed their use later in the 1930s.

This connection between people's cars and social conflict, aggression, and the clash of the technological and pastoral worlds was also reflected in art and literature. A striking example is the hunt for automobiles in Hermann Hesse's *Steppenwolf* (1927). In this episode, the car culture and war are brought into close proximity. Automobiles become an allegory for the conflict between man and technology more generally: "The battle between people and machines, long prepared, long expected, long feared, was now starting."[31] The conversation between one of the car hunters and a victim thus links an enforced speed limit with the destruction of automobiles as symbols of aggressive machinery: "'Why did you shoot at us?' 'Because you were driving too fast.' 'We drove at a normal speed.' 'What was normal yesterday is not normal today, Mr. District Attorney. Today, we think any speed at which a car is driving is too fast. We are now destroying all automobiles, all of them, and the other machines, too.'"[32]

This literary treatment of an old and important German cultural debate, that is, the debate over the value of technology and machinery in modern

---

30 A typical event of a "revolutionary truck corps" agitating villages in 1919 is narrated by Erich Knauf in his *Ça ira: Reportagen-Roman* (Berlin, 1930).
31 Original: "es war der Kampf zwischen Menschen und Maschinen, lang vorbereitet, lang erwartet, lang gefürchtet, nun endlich zum Ausbruch gekommen." Hermann Hesse, *Der Steppenwolf* (Frankfurt am Main, 1971), 196.
32 Original: "'Warum haben Sie denn auf uns geschossen?' 'Wegen zu schnellen Fahrens.' 'Wir sind mit normaler Geschwindigkeit gefahren.' 'Was gestern normal war, ist es heute nicht mehr, Herr Oberstaatsanwalt. Wir sind heute der Meinung, es sei jegliche Geschwindigkeit, mit welcher ein Auto fahren möge, zu gross. Wir machen die Autos jetzt kaputt, alle, und die anderen Maschinen auch.'" Ibid., 201.

society, gave voice to a moment in time when (civil) war and automobiles held attraction for many. This combination is rather typical for the 1920s. Motorized traffic became the new symbolic field wherein this old debate was now played out – in an environment in which World War I had pulled down the barriers to open expressions of violence.

In acquiring and driving a motor vehicle, the owner made an affirmative statement about his position in the social debate on the role of technology. The growing desire and the growing market for automobiles thus reflected a change in a society that increasingly tried to reconcile technology and culture, creating a vague modernism.

Dominated by war and aggression, these images of two-wheelers and trucks contrasted other, albeit similar, images that were more peaceful: the car as a democratic vehicle, the epitome of equality and the participation of everyone in a modern and mechanically oriented culture. Of course, this image was acquired from the mass car culture in the United States, the con-temporary utopia of mass automobile ownership.

In the mid-1920s, the alleged classlessness of automobiles in the United States, exemplified by the Model T Ford, was widely discussed in Germany in the context of the debate over *Fordismus* (Fordism) and *Amerikanismus* (Americanism). This image appealed especially to technocrats, who also hoped to enter into a circle of production-consumption like the one that was thought to exist in the United States: high productivity leading to high wages, thus expanding spending power and the buying of products, and thereby increasing demand that would trigger investment in better produc-tion methods. The crucial role of automobiles in this "spiral of wealth" was easily identified and lent itself to imitation. The Left was also attracted to the idea of the automobile as an agent of social change – "the revolution-ary car will serve the revolutionary worker's class."[33]

The German public, however, was not entirely enthusiastic about an American-type mass consumerism fueled by automobiles. In particular, the idea of a basic, "classless" automobile was not all that attractive. Despite the collapse of the monarchy and the creation of a democratic republic, Ger-man society after the war remained a society of classes. Class divisions were also projected onto modes of transportation. Thus, the automobile market was highly segmented. In fact, German automobile manufacturers proudly emphasized the elitist and "tooled" character of their automobiles, denounc-ing American mass production and the system of spare-parts distribution.[34]

33 Original: "das revolutionäre Automobil wird der Sache der revolutionären Arbeiterklasse dienen." *Metallarbeiter-Zeitung,* 1930, quoted in Sachs, *Die Liebe zum Automobil,* 58.
34 Carl Benz, *Lebensfahrt eines deutschen Erfinders* (Leipzig, 1936), 113–14.

German manufacturers' adoption of Fordist methods and the tentative use of assembly lines in the 1920s did not immediately lead to cheaper automobiles. Despite intense discussion, Fordism did not catch on in Germany overnight. Even mass-produced automobiles never had the classless image of the Model T. To produce automobiles or motorcycles for "the masses" in Germany did not mean to create standardized products with a "basic model" image and a unitary style and color.

The war had only altered the process, already begun, of promoting the motor vehicle as an accepted, highly acclaimed cultural object. The prewar years had seen automobiles elevated from parvenu vehicles, from the means of transporting the chic counterculture flaneur, to the heights of acclaim. The Kaiser, and notably his son, Prince Heinrich, promoted automobiles as acceptable, even patriotic. In the 1920s, automobiles became symbols of distinction for the upper classes, perhaps the most prestigious object to own and to exhibit. But this process was slowly supplemented by the more "democratic" image of mass ownership.

After World War I, new values emerged in German society: a more hedonistic approach to life, greater mobility among broader strata of the population, an inclination to take vacations to more distant places. These changes were also linked to the influence of the war.[35] The new type of tourism had a strong connection to motor vehicles, which provided not only a convenient means of transportation but a mobile "home away from home" as well.[36] As means for increasing mobility, motor vehicles were perfectly suited to satisfy the new desire for leisure, travel, and vacations. It can be said that during the war a large part of the German population developed a taste for mobility and for the mechanized means to achieve it. There were, of course, antecedents: Individual mobility had already been possible with the bicycle. It has been observed that many qualities attributed to the motor vehicle, such as individual mobility, an element of fun beyond the basic transport function, and increased range for trips and holidays, had been attributed to bicycles for at least a few decades.

Accordingly, it was not so much increased mobility as such that was desired, but rather an increased readiness to spend money on individual mobility. Conspicuous consumption of automobiles became a value in and of itself. To buy a motor vehicle was a decision often made without regard to rational arguments or financial advantages. Longing for an automobile is one thing; it is quite another to buy one if it is expensive and beyond your

---

35 Paul Fussell, *Abroad: British Literary Traveling Between the Wars* (New York, 1980).
36 See, e.g., the article "Wochenende des Kraftfahrers," *Motor,* May 1927.

means. It may well have been that for a judge's family, for example, the railway was the more obvious, and certainly the cheaper, way to meet its mobility needs. The primary function of automobiles and motorcycles may not have been to compete with other means of transport. Yet motor vehicles had some distinct advantages. Besides being more convenient, they ranked much higher as status symbols. Automobiles provided their owners not only with a more individualized, if more expensive, means of transport but also with an object to demonstrate their actual or claimed social position.

This "bonus" should not be underestimated in a social climate where status still mattered, no less than in decades past. The class-specific car cultures of the Weimar era were fast becoming a means to distinguish one social group from another. It was no longer merely an upper-class phenomenon. Along with the intense discussion about the need for a vehicle for the masses, which was primarily thought of as an affordable means of transportation, the increased significance of the secondary functions of motor vehicles also became visible. Thus, with the transformation of the automobile into a consumer object, the modern pattern of consumerism began to emerge.

Since the desire for automobiles filtered down, owning one became a way for the German middle classes to manifest their upward mobility, to take part in an accepted game of distinction, to assess one's role in society, and to find an acceptable means for demonstrating status. This happened in a society where such values were becoming increasingly important and where societal dynamics were increasingly reflected in transportation modes. Motor vehicle ownership became a suitable symbolic field for the society, a task automobiles had not been able to fulfill in the prewar era because ownership and the desire to acquire an automobile were considerably more limited.

Advertisements and public relations are often regarded as the main reason for the sales of automobiles. But advertisements, which themselves play with images and cultural values, are only partly responsible for the increase in automobile ownership. The more important question is how social values – which in the twentieth century increasingly have largely been economic values, which again translate as spending power – are implemented and how the balance between them is altered. To spend a smaller proportion of the family income for housing and a greater proportion for motorized mobility tells us a great deal about changing values.

In summary, the popularization of automobiles in Germany in the 1920s involved the following aspects: Motor vehicles were transformed from sport into multipurpose and utility vehicles; their sheer quantity increased manifold; forms of organization developed during the war were introduced; the public demanded a "people's car" and the industry reacted with new war-related types and production methods. The new, diversified markets after the war reflected a diversified society.

The popularization of automobiles and the growth of the vehicle market also played a role in the vigorous postwar debate about the causes of Germany's defeat. Discussions were held on the relationship of traditional soldierly values to technology. In this debate about the role of technology in the lost war, a minority claimed that an excessive dependence on "material" – that is, artillery, weapons technology, and mechanized transport – would necessarily cause the qualities of the soldier to deteriorate. In contrast, another group maintained that one of the reasons for Germany's defeat was precisely the technology deficit, or the insufficient "wartime labor mobilization" of society. The degree of "total mobilization" – a term coined by Ernst Jünger – in Germany was estimated to have been too low. Influential books such as Max Schwarte's *Die Technik im Weltkriege* (1920) pointed out that German authorities severely underestimated the role of technology in modern warfare, while praising the achievements of German engineers. It is no wonder that road transportation played an important role in these debates. Not only the overwhelming force of the Entente's industrialized weapons, but also its superior development and production of motorized vehicles were to blame for Germany's defeat.

A theory widely discussed in the early 1920s was that the lack of trucks hampered the German advance in the spring offensives of 1918. Some military authorities blamed the failure of what was expected to be a forerunner to the blitzkrieg on the absence of adequate numbers of motor vehicles. To correct this problem, a group of younger German officers tried to exploit the potentialities of the automobile. The ideas of Heinz Guderian, who later led tank armies in the actual blitzkrieg period from 1939 to 1941, were directed especially toward the creation of a mobile force, using the motorized transport for supply duties to develop a fully mechanized army (see Figure 9.3). He agreed with British military writers who emphasized motorized warfare, praising them for having put the tank "in the middle of the emerging motorization of our age, therefore becoming the pathfinders of a new type of grand warfare."[37] In his 1927 article "Bewegliche Truppenkörper" (Mobile troop units), Guderian directly linked the necessity of

---

37 Original: "mitten in die entstehende Motorisierung unserer Epoche hinein und wurden so die Bahnbrecher einer neuartigen Kriegführung grossen Stils," quoted in Militärgeschichtliches Forschungsamt, ed., *Deutsche Militärgeschichte*, 9:575.

Figure 9.3. The road of aggression: German motorized unit in Poland, Sept. 1939. © Bundes-archiv, Koblenz. Used with permission.

a motorized army with the general trend of mechanization and spread of automobiles in his society: "Never in living memory have the prospects of mobility been so good as they are today in the age of the motor and the radio; the achievements of technology are practically forcing themselves on the soldier." Guderian demanded a "full use of the rich technological resources of our time."[38] In this statement, he made plain the military relevance of mass motor-vehicle ownership. Hence, in the early 1920s, the discussion about a potential mass market for mechanized vehicles began to acquire a military edge in Germany.

These forward-looking German officers also recognized the importance of roads built to military specifications. In a 1925 article that described "Die Lebensader Verduns" (The main artery of Verdun), Guderian observed that to increase its capacity this *voie sacrée* (sacred way) had two separate roadbeds. The conclusion he drew from studying this archetypal supply

---

38 Originals: "Noch nie seit Menschengedenken hat aber die Beweglichkeit solche Aussichten gehabt, wie jetzt im Zeitalter des Motors und des Radio; die Errungenschaften der Technik zwingen sich gradezu dem Soldaten auf" and "voll(e) Ausnutzung der reichen technischen Hilfsquellen unserer Zeit," quoted in Militärgeschichtliches Forschungsamt, ed., *Deutsche Militärgeschichte,* 9:578.

road from World War I and the lesson for German road-building in the interwar period were clear: The next generation of highway, the *Autobahn*, also had to have a divided roadway for each direction of traffic.[39]

In a broader sense, influential postwar concepts included the attempt to reconcile traditional soldierly values with technology. Jünger proposed resolving the conflict and stated that the tentative use of technology in the world war was a mistake and that, in the next war, technology would play a critical role. Thus, a new concept of the German soldier slowly began to emerge that included a rigorous adoption of modern technology. Jünger decreed that the modern type of mechanized warrior – in his case a fighter pilot – would have to have a "cool head on top of a hot heart," and that in the heat of battle attentiveness to dial gauges and control instruments would be essential for the mechanized elite soldier.[40] This thinking combined mechanization and the "motor" with the desirable qualities of the modern warrior, reflecting the general tendency of society in the 1920s to bring technology and culture into line.

This way of processing the war experience fit into another tendency that had started before the war: to view mechanization – and especially motor vehicles – not as a threat to traditional values of "Germanness" but as a means to enhance them and to project them even more successfully in times of crisis. Yet the radical Right developed the concept of the motorized German fighter, which later proved to be fatal, quite early. Although the Nazis did not originate this concept, it fit very well with their rearmament program, which was in full swing by 1935. Exploiting a broad social trend, the Nazi regime reversed the official policy of discouraging road transportation, which had more or less prevailed during the Weimar Republic.

To a number of younger officers in the Reichswehr, the ongoing debate over mechanization and war clearly meant that the German people would have to be "conditioned" for using technological weapons and for driving and maintaining motor vehicles. Familiarity with communication technology, planes, and, especially with automobiles and motorcycles became intrinsic to Germany's attempt to be better prepared for the next war; the military was convinced that combining these systemic factors would contribute to a successful future effort. The militarization and popularization of automobiles within German society thus became synonymous.

Within this framework, it is clear that not only a "motor-minded" population, but also a strong and self-reliant automotive industry would be

39 Friedrich Kittler, "Auto Bahnen," in Wolfgang Emmerich and Carl Wege, eds., *Der Technikdiskurs in der Hitler-Stalin-Ära* (Stuttgart, 1995), 119.
40 Ernst Jünger, *Werke,* vol. 1: *Tagebücher 1* (Stuttgart, n.d.), 369.

necessary. Accordingly, a strong capacity to export automobiles and to fulfill the mechanized transportation requirements of the army in a future war were considered essential. This contrasted with the realities of the German automobile market in the 1920s, where imported automobiles had a strong market share as a result of lower customs duties (after 1926) and of better values and designs. The "Buy German" campaign and the numerous articles on this topic in automotive magazines had in mind the desired autarky that was characteristic of national economic policies. The desired outcome was not only a mass market for automobiles but also the domination of that market by German manufacturers.

But we have to proceed cautiously: It is difficult to assess the influence of these ideas on the actual attitudes toward automobiles and the automobile market. We can gauge only indirectly military reasons for supporting the consumption of automobiles. It remains, for example, a matter of historical debate whether or not Nazi promotion of automobiles was primarily driven by the needs of the military. Without settling the matter, it seems to echo the opinion voiced earlier by innovative German officers that a "mass mechanization of the military" was the prerequisite for any preparation for the next war. In the 1920s, Adolf Hühnlein, who later led National Socialist motorized units, claimed that equipping the German people with automobiles was a major factor in the modernization of the German army.[41] The crucial role of a technological solution was stressed in the journal *Die Reichsautobahn*: "Large-scale motorization, as attempted by the government, is only feasible if the industry manages to produce automobiles with price tags and operating costs that also match the wages of the lower income groups."[42] Thus, for Nazi leaders the support of consumerism in the field of vehicles also had a very real military context – the lessons of the last war.

But a theory that equated the drive to increase automobile popularity with the goal of creating an identification between the masses and the Nazi regime – with the help of an attractive and desired mass consumer object – was not without its problems. In the 1930s, Hitler was able to play off public interest in automobiles that had developed in the post–World War I era. The exploitation of existing desire for car ownership for political purposes was significant, however; this was a process that could be described

---

41 Ludwig, *Technik und Ingenieure im Dritten Reich,* 315.
42 Original: "Motorisierung in grossem Umfange, wie sie von der Regierung angestrebt wird, ist nur möglich, wenn es der Industrie gelingt, Fahrzeuge herzustellen, deren Anschaffungspreis und Unterhaltskosten den Einkommensverhältnissen auch der breiteren Volksschichten entsprechen," quoted in "Die Reichsautobahnen fördern das deutsche Volksautomobil," *Die Reichsautobahn* 2 (1934): 21.

as the formatting of consumer desire. Symbolic modernization, the genuine fascination of leading Nazi politicians for automobiles, and the economic and productive technology boost to Germany's industry all have to be taken into account.

Hitler himself set a personal example – he was very often seen riding in a large black Mercedes – through his appearance and a substantive speech at the International Car Exhibition in 1933, in which he outlined his program for stimulating car ownership. Tax-exemption policies, abandoning of general speed limits, and a subsequent highway construction program generated a systemic approach to the all-out promotion of road transportation. Among these components, scholars have devoted most of their attention to the building of the *Autobahn* network. The debate about its widely differing aims – aesthetic, military, political, or economic – continues to this day.[43] The National Socialist Automobile Corps (Nationalsozialistische Kraftfahrkorps, or NSKK) was a motorized Nazi Party organization that combined driver education with military training. It was joined in 1934 by the project to develop and construct a mass "people's car" or *Volkswagen*.

The decision to go ahead with the Volkswagen has to be seen in the larger context. Apart from the superhighway building program, the idea of a truly affordable people's car was broached soon after the Nazis came to power. Consumers could purchase the Volkswagen, designed by Ferdinand Porsche, through an organized savings program: "If you want to drive your own car, you have to save 5 marks a week" (Fünf Mark die Woche musst du sparen, willst du den eignen Wagen fahren). This plan involved collecting trading stamps in savings booklets, closely resembling the familiar discount system of consumer cooperatives. A huge plant was built near Fallersleben (today, Wolfsburg) for the sole purpose of manufacturing this automobile. A name bandied about quite often in the 1920s, the Volkswagen – the full copyrighted name was *Deutscher Volkswagen* – encountered the typical ambivalence and numerous additional functions automobiles always seem to have.[44]

However, we should carefully assess the military purpose of the Volkswagen project, perhaps the largest single state-planned project promoting consumerism in Germany. It would be wrong to describe it as being developed solely for war, as Ernst Niekisch has: "The Volkswagen had to form a reserve

43 See Rainer Stommer, ed., *Reichsautobahn: Pyramiden des Dritten Reiches: Analysen zur Ästhetik eines unbewältigten Mythos* (Marburg/Lahn, 1982).
44 See, e.g., "Die Bestrebungen, einen billigen, preiswerten Wagen, einen sogenannten 'Volkswagen'. . . zu schaffen," *Der Motorwagen*, no. 27 (1921): 591.

of motorized vehicles that the army could fall back on."[45] The symbolic power of the project is also quite important: A mass-produced automobile for the *Volksgemeinschaft* (national community) dovetailed nicely with the Nazi modernization drive, even if such a car was irrational in light of an economy that was constricted by the lack of capital and raw materials. The popular car was not so much the platform for an eventual military vehicle, but rather for a "nation of drivers" – of technically minded soldiers who would avoid the mistakes of the last war in the coming one.

Despite the government's intention that the Volkswagen would be privately owned, a link to the image of automobiles as public property that had been cultivated in the era of World War I remained. Thus, in addition to the Volkswagen Porsche also designed a people's tractor (*Volksschlepper*) to motorize German agriculture. Like the Volkswagen, the *Volksschlepper* was built in large numbers only after World War II. It proved a mainstay for West German farmers until the mid-1960s. An attempt to build a wooden jet-powered people's fighter (*Volksjäger*) to be flown by the Hitler Youth, who had been trained in gliders, proved highly unsuccessful. But the concept of the *Volk* product clearly indicates how much Germans relied on the centralized introduction of motorized transportation – and not on the market.

With the Volkswagen project, however, the class-specific car cultures fell under the influence of the totalitarian state and its attempt to close down and centralize the market. During the 1930s, however, the people's car remained in the developmental stage – throughout the decade many different models were built and publicly discussed. Yet none of the tens of thousands of stamp savers ever received a Volkswagen. Nevertheless, the project illustrates the tendency of the German state to take matters into its own hands in an attempt to organize or coordinate the market.

Some manufacturers opposed the state-run project for a people's car. Opel, the General Motors-owned subsidiary, was at the forefront of this campaign. Attempts to resist state intervention were partly motivated by the fear that their own mass-production automobile, the Opel Kadett, would be threatened with unfair competition. Opel also fought the Volkswagen project because it believed that a car with the required equipment and features could not be produced for less than one thousand reichsmarks.

Naturally, the military authorities' direct and pragmatic interest in the Volkswagen project was great. The potential for requisitioning of privately owned automobiles for military service must not be overlooked. The con-

---

45 Original: "Der Volkswagen sollte eine Reserve motorischer Fahrzeuge schaffen, auf welche das Heer zurückgreifen konnte," quoted in Ernst Niekisch, *Das Reich der niederen Dämonen* (Hamburg, 1953).

cept of the *Subventionslastwagen* still hovered in the minds of the military authorities. The special situation of the German army, with the restrictions placed on it by the Treaty of Versailles, played a certain role. Under these restrictions, the Germans had to rely on a strong force of privately owned vehicles if war, which was then considered inevitable, broke out. After 1930, in the event of mobilization, the Reichswehr planned to seize 100,000 automobiles in order to transport 300,000 troops and their gear from the eastern to the western Reich borders in approximately two days.[46]

Military transport vehicles of the blitzkrieg era could be cynically described as "people's cars of the 1940s," and, as is widely known, the Volkswagen itself had strong ties to World War II. Although the stamp savers never got their cars, it was the model on which Porsche based a new construction called the *Kübelwagen*, a versatile scout car that used various Volkswagen technologies and the same engine. This military version of the Volkswagen saw service on all fronts from 1940 to the end of the war.

The new highways were also put into military use. As Bertolt Brecht stated in his well-known poem from 1940, "On a Milepost of the Motorways": "We who built these roads/ Will drive on them only/ In tanks and trucks."[47]

POSTSCRIPT: THE POSTWAR SITUATION

Many components of the unsuccessful Nazi policy to promote automobiles for the German masses became, in a completely different political context, the basis for the postwar popularization of automobiles in West Germany. Many of the promises made by the aggressive Nazi campaign for automobiles in the 1930s were fulfilled two decades later, under very different political circumstances. By 1960, West Germans were driving hundreds of thousands of Volkswagens on superhighways built or planned by the National Socialists in the 1930s. At least in the guise of the Federal Republic, Germany had become a nation of drivers. At first glance, the differences from the 1930s are obvious. In West Germany, the construction of highways and the operation of the automobile market were less aesthetically, militarily, and politically charged than before.

And yet scholars have recently challenged the notion of a "depoliticized" German postwar car culture. Dietmar Klenke interprets the "Ger-

---

46 Ludwig, *Technik und Ingenieure im Dritten Reich*, 307.
47 Original: "Auf einem Meilenstein der Autostrassen: / Wir, die diese Strasse gebaut haben / Werden auf ihr fahren nur / In Tanks und Lastwagen," Bertold Brecht, *Gesammelte Werke in 20 Bänden*, vol. 9: *Gedichte 2* (Zurich, 1976), 736.

man national cult object and the specific aggressive and individualistic style
of driving in the 1950s and 1960s as a form of processing the 'national catastrophe' of 1945." He suggests that the potential of militarism joined forces
with the new postwar liberalism to produce a novel way of increasing the
number of automobiles.[48] This also explains how automobiles could become
so significant for West German identity. The high social importance of automobiles after World War II seems to be quite different from their importance during the Third Reich – but also clearly related to it.

48 Dietmar Klenke, *"Freier Stau für freie Bürger": Die Geschichte der bundesdeutschen Verkehrspolitik,
   1949–1994* (Darmstadt, 1995).

10

Gender, Generation, and Consumption in the United States

Working-Class Families in the Interwar Period

SUSAN PORTER BENSON

When I began my current project on working-class consumption in the interwar period, I believed that the glass was half full – that I would find working-class cultures permeated by mass consumption and working-class material life transformed by automobiles, household appliances, and ever more fashionable ready-made clothes. The vaunted post–World War II prosperity that stands between us and the interwar period colored my view of the earlier period, as did the focus on middle-class abundance of most of what has been written about the history of consumption. I should have known better. I had evidence from my work on department stores, which showed their preoccupation with the middle-class minority that commanded significant discretionary income as well as my memories of a 1950s working-class community in which scarcity edged out abundance despite Congress of Industrial Organizations (CIO) union wages.[1]

After digesting a great deal of evidence about working-class families' lives between 1919 and 1940, I have concluded that in fact the glass was

Thanks to Edward Benson, Susan Strasser, and Sharon Strom for helpful comments. The research on which this chapter is based was supported by the National Endowment for the Humanities, the National Humanities Center, the University of Missouri Research Council, and the Weldon Spring Fund.

1 For the present purposes, I define as working-class those families whose income was derived from nonsupervisory wages and salaries, whether earned at blue-collar or white-collar jobs. Such a category covers a broad range, from the deeply destitute to the comfortable, but what all shared was a degree of insecurity of employment and a degree of irregularity of income. This is, of course, a crudely descriptive category, but my reading of the available evidence convinces me that such families were at opposite ends of the same spectrum, their differences were those of degree rather than of kind and were distinct from those of families whose higher income allowed not only a higher standard of living in the present but the accumulation of capital for long-term security. See Susan Porter Benson, *Counter Cultures: Saleswomen, Managers, and Customers in American Department Stores, 1890–1940* (Urbana, Ill., 1986).

half empty. I emphasize the constraints placed on working-class demand and the ways in which working-class people negotiated them, rather than the possibilities offered by the marketplace. The material aspects of working-class people's lives did, of course, improve in certain ways, but the improvements seem to me to be less striking than the continuing budget strictures under which families operated. The payments on an overworked housewife's electric washing machine might necessitate dire scrimping on all other expenditures, and the luxury of a car might mean forgoing any leisure spending and even such incidentals as a daily newspaper. Both working-class and middle-class people had choices in the marketplace, but those choices had a different content and meaning. Middle-class families could enjoy a variety of consumption delights without forgoing basic comforts. Working-class families' choices demanded close calculation; the impulse for consumer gratification constantly warred with the need for self-denial, all in a context in which the satisfaction of basic needs was by no means guaranteed.

The difference between the half-full glass and the half-empty glass is not superficial, but one that results from changing the whole framework in order to understand consumption from the point of view of the working class. Whereas much of what has been written about middle-class consumption adopts a supply-side perspective, emphasizing factors such as advertising, market research, new and more elaborate products, and an expanding retail and service sector, I have found a demand-side perspective to be far more revealing about working-class consumption. Despite the rich consumer choices, the seductive blandishments to buy, and the compelling material dreams on offer, for working-class families the major concern was not what the marketplace brought to them but what they brought to the marketplace. The connection between wage earning and consumption was especially close for these families, and the study of the second cannot be as distinct from the first as it can be in studying the middle class. The historian also needs to look inside the working-class family in order to understand the dynamics of allocating scarce resources; the more vexed the choices, the more complex and intriguing the processes by which they are made.

This is not the only way the story can be told, but – given my sources and the questions I ask of them – it is the way that now seems the most compelling to me.[2] I draw here primarily on two types of sources: first, the

2 Because the families who appear in these sources in no way constitute a representative sample – such was not the intent of any of those who created the documents – and because the information on these families is far from standardized, it is inappropriate to subject these data to close statistical analysis. I have at some points made some quantitative statements, but they should be taken as rough indi-

raw data of the Women's Bureau of the United States Department of Labor, and second, case studies of families experiencing unemployment or suffering from the Great Depression. The Women's Bureau raw data consist mostly of reports on home visits with woman workers around the country during the 1920s. The women were selected unsystematically from employers' rosters or because of the agents' chance encounters; African-American and immigrant women are well represented, mirroring their high rates of labor-force participation. The case studies of families affected by unemployment or the depression were conducted by social service agencies and social science researchers and selected families according to various criteria, most frequently requiring that they include a married couple and some minor children. They begin in the winter of 1928–9 – before the depression – and continue into the mid-1930s. Both types of sources focus on the more hard-pressed end of the economic spectrum – the Women's Bureau data because families in which women turned to wage earning tended to be poorer than those in which women did not, and the unemployment/depression studies for obvious reasons.

A recurrent theme in both types of data, however, is that of the pervasive economic insecurity of working-class life during the interwar period. Short hours, technological unemployment, and seasonality of work plagued workers during the 1920s; when the depression came, it intensified familiar patterns and mobilized familiar strategies rather than presenting the working class with entirely new circumstances. For those who partook more lavishly of the consumption delights of the 1920s, the break between the two decades seems sharper, but for these working-class families the depression looks more like a deeper and longer version of the uncertain employment patterns of the 1920s. I therefore consider the interwar period as more continuous than do conventional accounts, which see it as opposing periods of prosperity and want.

My sources provide, on the whole, fuller information on the place of women than of men in the family economy. The Women's Bureau data provide only occasional information on sons and brothers, the unemployment studies discuss whole families more even-handedly, and most of the sources that fall outside these two main categories also focus on women. Many of the researchers who generated these data (all, for example, of the Women's Bureau investigators) were female. These sources are, therefore, one of the few areas of historical documentation where the sources are biased toward

cations and not exact measures. More significant is the fact that the patterns and responses I discuss tend to occur in all racial/ethnic groups.

the role and experience of women and filtered primarily through the eyes of women researchers.

Beyond the female bias in these particular sources, they partook of more general gendered discourses and practices. They show how powerfully the gendering of labor-force participation and rewards shaped gendered discourses of consumption. They tend to problematize women's wage earning and to regard men's wage earning as natural, perpetuating the gendering of "production" as male and "consumption" as female. One of the most intriguing aspects of these documents is the disjuncture between the received ideas about gender and the accounts of the day-to-day operations of family economies, revealing the slippage between discourse and practice in a highly contested moment.

Relations between generations in working-class families provide a revealing window on the ways in which consumption was affecting the family economy, tempting individuals with expenditures that might not serve the family interest but still not entirely dissolving ties of mutual obligation and shared goals. During the 1920s and 1930s, the family wage remained an elusive ideal for most working-class families and the husband/father's wage earning efforts required supplements by other family members. I have dealt elsewhere with some of the implications of wives' or mothers' wage earning for consumption and the family economy, and here I shall concentrate on children's impact in these areas.[3]

Children's wage earning was, of course, not new, and it continued to be regarded as a family obligation; during the interwar period, however, it took place in a context different from that of its early industrial origins. Child-labor and compulsory-education laws took away some of parents' control and delayed the age at which children could begin to make cash contributions to the family fund. This legislation, often subverted by parents and children alike, varied in provisions, year of enactment, and severity of enforcement in different states and was certainly not new to the 1920s. What was novel was its intersection with at least three other factors that were more historically specific to that decade and the following one: First, employers increasingly obsessed with efficiency and productivity went

3 "Living on the Margin: Working-Class Marriage and Family Survival Strategies in the United States, 1919–1941," in Victoria de Grazia, ed., with Ellen Furlough, *The Sex of Things: Gender and Consumption in Historical Perspective* (Berkeley, Calif., 1996). In the current essay, I include in the category of children those living with their parent(s), either unmarried or fairly recently married. By doing so, I do not mean to suggest that children's economic connections with their parents necessarily end when they leave the parental home or marry, but that the nature of relationships between coresident unmarried children and their parents is in general qualitatively different from that between married children living independently and their parents.

against the era's infatuation with youth and preferred experienced workers to inexperienced children just out of school, even when they were in their middle or late teens. Second, as advertising, expanded mass production, and the commercialization of leisure inundated the marketplace with ever more inducements to spend money, material dreams and aspirations expanded. Nonearning children became more expensive to maintain. Wage-earning children, even when they dutifully turned over their pay envelopes to their families, might still be a net drain on the family budget, and in any case they made increasing demands for money of their own to spend. Third, the expansion of consumer credit, especially installment credit, during the 1920s further eroded family control over children who contracted independently for continuing expenditures. All in all, children – even as they remained vital contributors to the family economy – became an increasingly mixed economic blessing. The result was a pervasive confusion about generational roles that frequently erupted in conflict over the family's claims on children's wages.

The tension between traditional expectations and new patterns of behavior is reflected eloquently in the language used to describe children's contributions to the family fund. The most frequent and, at first glance, transparent single description of the disposition of a daughter's wages in the Women's Bureau raw data is "All to mother," meaning that the mother received all the child's earnings. Depression-era studies used this trope as well. Irvin Child, writing of families headed by southern Italian immigrants during the late 1930s, noted, "Most families require that as long as a child is still living at home, regardless of his age, he must turn over all his wages to his parents."[4] Such practices were by no means observed only in immigrant families; Ruth Shonle Cavan and Katherine Howland Ranck, in a study of Chicago families of whom two-fifths were native born, noted, "It is customary among many families in the lower middle class [their term for working class] for the adolescent children to turn all money earned over to their mother, at least during the first few years of their employment."[5] The vision of the obedient child turning her back on the temptations of the marketplace and subordinating personal interest to family welfare clearly held a peculiar power over the imagination of social scientists, government investigators, and working-class informants alike.

---

4 Irvin Child, *Italian or American: The Second Generation Conflict* (New Haven, Conn., 1943), 106.
5 Ruth Shonle Cavan and Katherine Howland Ranck, *The Family and the Depression: A Study of One Hundred Chicago Families* (Chicago, 1938), 92. At least two thirds of the families in this study were working class.

When "all to mother" did not apply, however, the language became less clear in its import. About as many women paid board as turned over their entire pay envelopes, and about half as many were described as contributors to family support to one degree or another. The material distinctions between these categories remained murky. Daughters described as paying board and contributing to family support frequently paid similar amounts into the family fund, and the two labels appear to be randomly scattered through the interview forms. The difference in inflection, though small, seems to mark a crucial difference in a family's, or a daughter's, self-perception. A board-paying daughter presumably was positioned in a fee-for-service relationship to her family, whereas a daughter contributing to family support was cast as part of the family's collective effort. Unfortunately, the sources are virtually mute about the roots and consequences of that distinction.

Those who gave all to mother, paid board, or contributed to family support nonetheless had one thing in common: All were characterized as substantial contributors to the family fund. In comparison, those described as providing only for their own support were a distinct minority – only about 7 percent of the total. The interwar period was, clearly, a time in which the economic obligations of daughters to their families were varied and in the process of continuing negotiation, but it is notable that these negotiations resulted in apparent economic autonomy for only a small fraction of wage-earning daughters.

Partly because my sources discuss far fewer sons than daughters and partly because sons' contributions to the family economy were more clearly defined and understood, a similar set of conventions for describing sons' economic relationships to the family does not emerge. Sons were more likely than daughters to discharge their obligations with a specific sum of money. Even during the depression, only a handful of sons were described as turning over their entire wages to the family. In families with employed sons and daughters both, there was in fact an asymmetry in contributions; Cavan and Ranck cite numerous such examples from the depression, as do the Women's Bureau interviews from the 1920s.[6] In only two cases – that of Kansas City meat-packer siblings and that of two sisters and a brother in a Waterloo, Iowa, family – did daughters and sons contribute equal amounts. Given men's generally higher wages, however, the daughters almost certainly contributed a higher proportion of their income than their brothers

6 Ibid., 92.

and were left with a smaller sum to use at their own discretion.[7] More typically, a worker in a Rhode Island light-bulb factory turned her entire sixteen-dollar paycheck over to her mother, while her machinist brother contributed only twelve dollars of his thirty-dollar earnings to the family fund.[8] An Omaha packinghouse worker gave her mother eight dollars per week, but her clerical-worker brother, who almost certainly earned considerably more than she did, contributed five dollars. Their mother told the Women's Bureau investigator, "He needs so much himself."[9]

This may well have been true; an office worker had to be more elegantly fitted out for work than a bacon packer. But in most cases what stands out are the more censorious terms applied to sons than to daughters, and the fact that these terms target the sons' character flaws rather than sketching them in relational terms as was the case with daughters. The improvident son appears repeatedly in the Women's Bureau raw data, perhaps because the stories are told from the perspective of mothers or sisters, who may have resented male claims to autonomy in the marketplace as well as other arenas. A Richmond factory worker who turned over her whole paycheck to her mother told a Women's Bureau investigator that her brother "waste[d]" his substantial earnings, giving small and irregular amounts to the family.[10] A Providence rubber-factory worker gave her mother "practically all she makes" to compensate for two brothers who didn't "pay enough even to cover their board" and a father who was, in his wife's words, "none too good."[11]

The lazy son who would or could not contribute significantly to the family also finds his place in the sources. Winnie Pankau, a meat packer in St. Joseph, Missouri, complained that her son took after his deserting father: He was "shiftless and [didn't] keep any job long" even though she was hard put to support him and his two school-age siblings.[12] An Atlanta hat maker reported that her brother worked irregularly and did little to help her sup-

---

7 National Archives, Washington, Records of the Women's Bureau, Record Group 86, Raw Data for Published Bulletins, bulletin no. 88, *The Employment of Women in Slaughtering and Meat Packing* (1932), box 122, 31–25; bulletin no. 19, *Iowa Women in Industry* (1922), box 7, Hall. After the first reference to each bulletin, I refer to data from this source in these forms: "NA, RG 86, PB [bulletin number], [box number], [schedule number or name]." Schedules for bulletin nos. 60 and 88 can easily be located by the schedule number; folder names are not necessary. For other bulletins, the schedule forms cited are in the home-visit folder unless otherwise noted. I include a folder name only in the few cases where it is necessary for easy location of the cited schedule.

8 NA, RG 86, PB no. 21, *Women in Rhode Island Industries: A Study of Hours, Wages, and Working Conditions* (1922), box 8, 25–7.

9 Ibid., PB no. 88, box 123, 46–5.

10 Ibid., PB no. 10, *Hours and Conditions of Work for Women in Industry in Virginia* (1920), box 3, Falls.

11 Ibid., PB no. 21, box 8, 31–2.   12 Ibid., PB no. 88, box 123, 51-Pankau.

port their widowed mother and invalid sister.[13] Mirra Komarovsky, in
her study of families affected by unemployment, characterized the idle
twenty-two-year-old son of a former railroad engineer as "easygoing, pleasant, but lazy." He scorned a low-paying job, saying, "Hell, working all week
for $7.00! There's no percentage in that."[14] Cavan and Ranck, in a similar
study, encountered an even choosier young Chicagoan who turned down
an eighteen-dollar-a-week job in 1934.[15] Roger Angell, in a third depression study, noted of one son, "His chief interest seemed to be to have a good
time."[16]

To be sure, we do meet noble and hard-working sons. A Nashville shirt-
factory employee had worked to supplement her husband's earnings while
her high-school-student son did the housework. When he graduated, he
went to work and contributed his wages to the family so that his mother
could keep house. A twenty-three-year-old man willingly supported his
invalid mother and unemployed stepfather, even though his three siblings
refused to chip in and the stepfather labeled his stepson's only pleasure –
playing the guitar – a "waste of time" and forbade him to practice at home.[17]
The son of a widow disabled in an industrial accident held a steady job, did
all the housework, and even cut the cabbage and peeled the potatoes for
soup before he went to work in the morning.[18] The point is not that all
sons resisted contributing to their families, but that substantial numbers of
sons – and virtually no daughters – were portrayed as shirkers. Sons, as a
group, seemed less able to balance their own consumer desires and their
own interests in controlling their time and effort with their families'
demands for support in a way that convinced other family members that
they were doing their best for the family.

Although the sources portray daughters as generally more willing to
contribute to their families, a closer look reveals that they did not always
represent a "profit" for the family. When a family was relatively well off, as
was an Iowa family in which the father and two brothers were coopers, it
might count daughters' earnings a dead loss to the family fund. The Iowa
cooper told a Women's Bureau agent that he was happy to have his laid-off
daughter at home: she "just spent the money when she did work."[19] But a

13 Ibid., PB no. 22, *Women in Georgia Industries: A Study of Hours, Wages, and Working Conditions* (1922), box 9, folder "Home visit schedules – Atlanta," Crowley.
14 Mirra Komarovsky, *The Unemployed Man and His Family* (New York, 1940), 99.
15 Cavan and Ranck, *The Family and the Depression,* 142.
16 Roger Angell, *The Family Encounters the Depression* (New York, 1936), 108.
17 Social Welfare History Archives, Minneapolis, Helen Hall Papers, box 44, folder 1, profile of John.
18 NA, RG 86, PB no. 60, *Industrial Accidents to Women in New Jersey, Ohio, and Wisconsin* (1927), box 33, 3185.
19 Ibid., PB no. 88, box 122, Sioux City A-4.

dutiful young woman who turned over her pay envelope to her mother or willingly paid board might not have been much more help to the family's budget than this free-spending daughter or a selfish son. Mothers receiving unopened pay packets repeatedly noted that their daughters' entire wages did not fully pay the cost of their support; those collecting board payments similarly reported that they received less than the market rate and even less than the actual cost of their daughters' support. Low wages were not just a mark of women's – especially young women's – subordinate status in the work force, but they also marked them as disappointing contributors to the family fund and as second-class consumers.

Behind the trope "All to mother" unfolded a drama that revolved as much around consumption as around duty. In only one instance was it pre - sented purely as a matter of family discipline; parents who had immigrated from Bohemia to Iowa asserted that they "still [had] control over" their daughter and therefore over her pay envelope.[20] In cases where the family was in dire straits, the arrangement appeared to benefit the family fund; Vera Dorn, a South Carolina drug company worker, normally paid her family five dollars per week board, but when her father lost his job in 1922 she began to turn over her whole paycheck.[21] Such was increasingly the case when unemployment spiraled during the depression.

More often during the 1920s, however, "All to mother" was less a matter of parental control or familial desperation than one of mutual benefit. Mothers and daughters in, among other places, St. Louis, Omaha, Kansas City, Chicago, Providence, and Newport, Rhode Island, acknowledged that a young woman's paycheck didn't necessarily cover her cost of living, even at home. Katherine Sawbol, a Kansas City meat packer, noted that her mother had paid the substantial bills for her recent appendectomy and that "she gets more than she gives" to the family fund.[22] Even without the economic disaster of a serious medical problem, a St. Louis candy maker described her situation in almost identical terms: "She gets back more than she gives in."[23] A Providence laundry worker told a Women's Bureau agent that she "probably pays for self," but, noted the agent, "Mother thinks not" because her daughter's "shoe[s] and coat[s] cost so much[:] $12 for shoes that wear away."[24]

20 Ibid., PB no. 9, box 7, Uherka.
21 Ibid., PB no. 32, *Women in South Carolina Industries: A Study of Hours, Wages, and Working Conditions* (1923), box 16, Dorn.
22 Ibid., PB no. 88, box 122, 32–9.
23 Ibid., PB no. 25, *Women in the Candy Industry in Chicago and St. Louis: A Study of Hours, Wages, and Working Conditions in 1920–1921* (1923), box 12, St. Louis – Seeger.
24 Ibid., PB no. 21, box 8, 14–4.

Similarly, many families noted how little working daughters could afford to pay for board. The mother of a Chicago candy-factory worker said that she was "not making her carfare and board."[25] An Enid, Oklahoma, Woolworth employee earned only enough for clothes and spending money, leaving nothing for board; she told a Women's Bureau agent, "If I had to pay board I guess I'd have to find a job that paid more."[26] A worker in an overall factory in Petersburg, Virginia, made an almost identical comment.[27]

The fact that daughters' board payments did not fully offset their cost to their families could not help but elide the distinction between paying board and contributing to family support. A mid-1929 Cincinnati Consumers' League study argued that, far from benefiting from low-cost family board, wage-earning women were actually "skimping on expenditures for other budget items to contribute toward the family's support."[28] Working-class voices are absent from the Cincinnati study, but an Omaha mother's description of her selfless daughter – "No go to show. Nothing." – suggests how much daughters might deprive themselves to contribute to family support.[29]

Clothing absorbed a large proportion of wage-earning daughters' salaries and consequently became a major item of concern in discussions of family economies. Kathy Peiss has argued eloquently that clothing was for young woman wage earners both a medium of self-expression and an entry ticket to the world of commercialized heterosociality, but in the sources I use clothing appears as much as a cause of worry as a source of satisfaction.[30] Mary Lou Corley, the only steady earner in her household of five, fretted that her "family need[ed] her help" but that it took "most of what she earn[ed] to buy her clothes."[31] Presumably, in her small mill village, the standards for dress were not extravagant. After a year in the work force, a young Rhode Island woman could not "earn enough to pay for even her own clothes & [was] running into debt."[32] Some mothers were resigned to continuing expenditures for clothing: the mother of a Kansas City meatpacking worker, Rose Pestock, reported ruefully of her daughter that it

25 Ibid., PB no. 25, box 12, Chicago – Rychlechi.
26 Ibid., PB no. 48, *Women in Oklahoma Industries: A Study of Hours, Wages, and Working Conditions* (1926), box 25, 12.
27 Ibid., PB no. 10, box 3, 51.
28 Frances R. Whitney, *What Girls Live On – and How: A Study of the Expenditures of a Sample Group of Girls Employed in Cincinnati in 1929* (Cincinnati, 1930), 13; see also 19.
29 NA, RG 86, PB no. 88, box 123, 42–123.
30 Kathy Peiss, *Cheap Amusements: Working Women and Leisure in Turn-of-the-Century New York* (Philadelphia, 1986), 62–72.
31 NA, RG 86, PB no. 22, box 9, folder "Home visit schedules – Georgia," 61–1.
32 Ibid., PB no. 21, box 8, 59–14.

took "all she makes to dress – there is something every Saturday to be bought in way of [her] clothes."[33] Some mothers were less sympathetic. When an Ohio woman lost a finger in an industrial accident, her mother commandeered over half her compensation payment on the grounds that "she would only spend it for clothes."[34]

My sources do not describe the wardrobes these daughters bought, but, given that they could probably afford only relatively cheap low-quality clothing that needed to be frequently replaced, it is unlikely that they were lavishly dressed. Even when they paid outlandish sums – the Providence laundry worker's twelve-dollar shoes, for example – they shopped in a context where high prices did not necessarily mean high quality. Two comments by daughters injured in industrial accidents support this interpretation. A Wisconsin woman, after only two months of disability, reported that she "needed shoes and clothes at once" when she received her compensation payment.[35] An Ohio woman went to stay with an aunt in the country a month after her accident because she needed clothes and she "thought it wouldn't matter if [she] had none in the country."[36] If these women's experiences were typical, working daughters had few enough clothes that they suffered if their wardrobes were not replenished for a month or two.

To note the importance of dress in daughters' expenditures is not to argue that sons were immune to the lure of clothing; one Atlanta man, for example, spent all his earnings on clothes, even in the face of his family's utter destitution.[37] For both women and men, clothing exerted a strong attraction, as it had since young working-class people's early nineteenth-century promenades on New York's Bowery.[38] But three factors appeared to charge daughters' clothing expenses with greater energy in family discussions. First, because of wage-earning daughters' closer economic ties to their families and (as we shall see) their greater willingness to yield control over their wages to their mother, their expenditures were more closely monitored. Second, women's clothes were by and large more fragile than men's and required frequent replacements, so that they were more of a continuing nuisance than men's often more expensive but also more durable clothes.[39] Third, long-standing ideas about women's vanity and their use of earnings as "pin money" had marked their desires for clothing as a sign of

---

33 Ibid., PB no. 88, box 122, 31–22; see also box 123, 42–53.   34 Ibid., PB no. 60, box 33, 2336.
35 Ibid., PB no. 60, Box 33, 1776.   36 Ibid., PB no. 60, box 33, 2535.
37 Marion Elderton, ed., *Case Studies in Unemployment Compiled by the Unemployment Committee of the National Federation of Settlements* (Philadelphia, 1931), 22–3.
38 Christine Stansell, *City of Women: Sex and Class in New York, 1789–1860* (Urbana, Ill., 1987), 89–100.
39 Thanks to Sharon Strom for suggesting this point to me.

234

self-indulgence. All in all, the spotlight on women's clothing made their bodies a contested site of consumption in a way that it did not for men.

Daughters' meager wages reflected employers' views of them as dependents and in turn intensified their dependency in their families. In general, giving wages "all to mother" meant consigning oneself to a dependent status as a consumer. Rather than autonomously dispensing her income, the daughter had to submit to maternal scrutiny of whatever spending money she requested. But in some cases, daughters actually chose or willingly acquiesced in this dependent relationship because it gained them access to their mother's superior consumer acumen. The same skills of close calculation and canny bargaining that working-class women honed in the management of the family budget could be mobilized to manage their daughters' wages as well. The mother of Alice Hennings, a phonograph-factory worker in Dubuque, boasted that she could "make the money go farther than Alice can."[40] An African-American laundry worker in Atlanta, about to enter Spelman Seminary, gave her check to her mother, who purchased on her behalf.[41] And Mattie Burnett, a South Carolina spinner, told a Women's Bureau agent that she preferred to let her mother buy "for her what she needs and wants – likes to do that rather than pay board and buy her own things." Burnett may have chosen this arrangement because her family was doing fairly well at the time of the interview, with two brothers in the labor force; she might have calculated that her mother would see to it that she got more than her share since she, as the first child to enter the labor force, had for some time borne the primary responsibility for the family's support.[42]

Dependent these women might be, but it was in part a calculated dependence. "All to mother" could be a consumer strategy rather than a sign of filial duty, a way to gain access to a larger share of the family fund or to tap their mother's skills to get more for their scarce dollars. Not surprisingly, this strategy appealed most to those who earned the least. The Cincinnati Consumers' League study showed a marked tendency for women with lower earnings to give "all to mother;" three out of five who earned the least (between ten and fifteen dollars per week) did so, but only one out of ten earning the most (from fifteen to twenty-five dollars).[43]

When parents were censorious of wage-earning daughters, they blamed consumption desires rather than, as they did with sons, character flaws or an unwillingness to work. A Russian-born immigrant to Iowa whose husband

40 NA, RG 86, PB no. 19, box 7, Hennings.
41 Ibid., PB no. 22, box 9, folder "Home visit schedules – Atlanta," Helen Howard.
42 Ibid., PB no. 32, box 16, 61-G.   43 Whitney, *What Girls Live On,* 11–12.

and a daughter were unemployed complained to the Women's Bureau agent, "My girls want clothes, clothes," and parodied their demands: "It's Mamma pay everything."[44] Daughters' drains on the family budget often loomed larger than sons' deficiencies. A Kansas City meatpacker reserved her harsh words for her eighteen- and nineteen-year-old daughters because they "don't make much and they want everything," while taking no notice of the role of a twenty-one-year-old son who, according to the Women's Bureau agent, "won't work."[45] A cultural lens sharply focused parents' attention on daughters as consumers and evoked especially intense responses.

Despite the strongly gendered tone of the discourse of family economies, in some respects wage-earning daughters and sons were in quite similar situations. Although unwillingness to work was almost exclusively laid at the feet of sons, inability to find work plagued both sons and daughters, who faced serious difficulties in establishing themselves as steady workers. They fell short as supplementary breadwinners because of the difficulties they faced in the labor market as entry-level workers. A young Atlantan had secured a prized job with the post office, and his mother had bought him the necessary bicycle on the installment plan. When the bicycle was stolen, he lost his job and was unable to find another.[46] A nineteen-year-old woman in the same city lost job after job because of "failure to adjust."[47] An eighteen-year-old Des Moines, Iowa, man had never learned a trade and could secure only irregular work.[48] A number of mothers decided to remain in meat-packing plants and keep their daughters home to do the housework because they could, as more experienced workers, earn more.[49] Untrained and inexperienced workers certainly fared badly in the job market, but vocational education did not necessarily better a young worker's chances for success. Four midwestern families, three in Kansas City, Kansas, and one in St. Joseph, Missouri, had invested in job training for their children, but neither the two sons and a daughter who were business school graduates nor the daughter trained as a beauty operator were able to find positions commensurate with their skills.[50] After three years at Boston's Mechanics Arts High School, Martin O'Connor found only odd jobs for two years, and no jobs at all for two years after that.[51]

44 NA, RG 86, PB no. 88, box 122, Sioux City – A-3.   45 Ibid., 32–3.
46 NA, RG 86, PB no. 22, box 9, folder "Home visit schedules – Atlanta," Poss.
47 Elderton, *Case Studies of Unemployment,* 166.   48 NA, RG 86, PB no. 19, box 7, Osborn.
49 Ibid., PB no. 88, box 122, 31–4; box 123, 42–21 and 56–15.
50 NA, RG 86, PB no. 88, box 122, 36–10; box 123, 51–37; box 122, 36–20 and 32–46.
51 Elderton, *Case Studies,* 326.

All of the foregoing examples are from the 1920s, but young workers faced even greater problems getting started during the depression, although again the difference between the two periods is one more of degree than of kind. A Salt Lake City boy eagerly quit school but found no easy berth in the labor force, bouncing around between short-term jobs in a bakery, in a garage, or as a common laborer before work dried up completely.[52] Only one of three sons of a Polish immigrant to Chicago found steady work; the other two turned to petty crime and gave the family nothing but grief.[53] Even the relatively favorable labor market of Washington, D.C., offered little to either African-American or European-American daughters.[54] And, of course, when children lost their jobs, their families had to assume the burden of their support. In the light of these examples, we need to qualify assumptions about youth's advantage in the labor market with a perception of young people's difficulties in finding a secure berth in a labor market that increasingly prized efficiency, productivity, and low turnover. It is also worth remarking that when it was a case of inability rather unwillingness to earn, the problem was linked to both sons and daughters.

Children's contributions to the family coffers waxed and waned according to a variety of circumstances that were not always gendered. Some families voluntarily lowered their claims to their children's wages, but in only one case does this appear to be linked to gender. The mother of an Iowa pharmaceutical employee feared the temptations of prostitution; she told the Women's Bureau agent that she never asked for her daughter's whole pay packet because "that was the cause very often of girls getting money and clothes in other ways."[55] At the time of the interview, the daughter was not paying even her customary five dollars per week board because she was purchasing a Victrola on the installment plan. More often parents expressed a growing generalized sense of children's entitlement to their wage. Other parents were simply not comfortable taking all that their children earned: A worker in a small Georgia cotton mill worried that she was unable to save anything out of her pay, but still "wanted her daughter to be able to keep some" of her own wages.[56] Depression pay cuts and unemployment gave many families no choice but to take less of a contribution from their children. A District of Columbia father reported that his daughters were earn-

52 Elderton, *Case Studies,* 322.   53 Cavan and Ranck, *Family and the Depression,* 142.

54 National Archives, Records of the Women's Bureau, Washington, Record Group 86, Division of Research, Unpublished Studies and Materials, box 14, folder "Housing Survey 1933 District of Columbia – Schedules," 5 and 104.

55 NA, RG 86, PB no. 19, box 7, Kernahan.

56 Ibid., PB no. 22, box 9, folder "Home visit schedules – Georgia," 46–3.

ing only twelve dollars per week apiece and "they can't pay board on that"; his son, too, took a pay cut and stopped paying board.[57] Conversely, the unemployment of other family members often led children to give their parents more of their wages. A South Carolina woman gave all that she earned when her father was out of work, but only five dollars per week when he had a job.[58]

Other factors being equal, in the long run children gave less of their income, either absolutely or proportionately, to the family fund. One major cause of decreased contributions was an impending marriage. Helen Griger, an Omaha packinghouse worker, contributed enough to her family to pay for her own support for the first three years she worked, but then she became engaged and her mother cut her board to three dollars per week – well below the cost of her maintenance – in order to allow her to save for her marriage. Griger remarked that she felt "very fortunate in this unusual arrangement,"[59] but it hardly seems to be unique. At least two other Omaha families and a Chicago family renounced their claims to board from a daughter who was about to be married,[60] and one St. Louis son received the same consideration from his family.[61]

Even when a marriage was not in the near future, both sons and daughters tended to retain more spending money as time passed and they developed more sense of entitlement to their own wages.[62] One young Chicago woman dutifully turned all of her wages over to her mother during five long years of the depression but finally began to demand some for her own use. Cavan and Ranck nicely captured both her parents' ambivalence about this development and their understanding that her contribution was something to be negotiated and not demanded: "The mother thought her daughter wanted too many clothes, but both parents agreed that she was a 'good girl' who did what they wanted her to do."[63]

Consumer credit was increasingly a factor in children's economic roles in the family and attracted sons and daughters alike. Children learned early lessons about credit from the widespread working-class tradition of buying groceries "on the book" at neighborhood stores. Sadie Tanner Mossell noted that two-earner African-American families in Philadelphia

57 Ibid., Unpublished Studies and Materials, box 14, folder "Housing Survey 1933 District of Columbia – Schedules," 84; see also 101.
58 NA, RG 86, PB no. 32, box 16, Dorn.   59 Ibid., PB no. 88, box 123, 41–53.
60 Ibid., 42–135 and 42–36; box 120, 17–83.
61 NA, RG 86, PB no. 25, box 12, St. Louis – Rose Miller and Elizabeth Miller.
62 See, e.g., E. Wight Bakke, *Citizens Without Work: A Study of the Effects of Unemployment upon the Workers' Social Relations and Practices* (New Haven, Conn., 1940), 125–6.
63 Cavan and Ranck, *Family and the Depression,* 163–4; quotation from 164; see also 92–4.

relied on this custom so that their children could buy food while their parents were off at work.[64] Mossell does not comment on children's perceptions of their experience of buying "on the book," but other sources indicate that they found the experience to be charged with shame. An eleven-year-old girl in a Pittsburgh family struggling with unemployment asked a settlement worker: "Miss Moore, do you like to ask people for trust? I used to be ashamed, but my mother would say, 'Go down to the store, Mary, and tell them we'll pay when your father's working.' I hated to go, but I couldn't not, could I, for then we wouldn't have had anything to eat."[65]

As they matured and began to earn their own wages, daughters and sons experimented with the installment credit that proliferated during the 1920s and 1930s. None of the studies reported systematically on consumer credit, but the very limited evidence indicates that women most often went into debt for clothes, and men for radios. Installment credit was of course a bad bet economically, taking the most from those who had the least. The Cincinnati Consumers' League study noted that one-third of the lowest-paid women had resorted to installment buying (virtually all of them for clothing), but only three of the fifty medium-level earners and none in the highest-paid group had done so. All of the installment purchases cost more than the median expenditure for the particular item by all women in the study.[66]

Installment credit could be a source of family pleasure and recreation. The radios bought by the sons surely held this potential, although the sources do not speak directly to this issue. More often, possibly because of the middle-class bias of the investigators, consumer credit was linked to family resentment or even conflict. Two St. Joseph, Missouri, sisters bought home furnishings on the installment plan; one made payments on an over-stuffed parlor set, the other on a player piano. The latter commented, "My father never made more than $15 a week so if we want anything nice we have to get [it] ourselves."[67] An Indianapolis woman desperately trying to stay out of debt while her husband was in prison was deeply upset when her nineteen-year-old daughter and eighteen-year-old son, the oldest of her nine children, freely made installment purchases.[68] An East St. Louis brother and sister had teamed up to buy a car. Their Czech-born mother

---

64 Sadie Tanner Mossell, *The Standard of Living Among One Hundred Negro Migrant Families in Philadelphia,* app. to *Annals of the American Academy of Political and Social Sciences* 98 (Nov. 1921): 186.
65 Elderton, *Case Studies,* 97.   66 Whitney, *What Girls Live On,* 22.
67 NA, RG 86, PB no. 88, box 123, 56–11 and 56–12.   68 Elderton, *Case Studies,* 335–6.

was "so out of patience – she can't talk about it," although she did remark to the Women's Bureau investigator, "Children so queer in America."[69]

The worst conflicts occurred when family members found themselves burdened with debts contracted by a relative. An East St. Louis meat packer bought herself a "nice coat," but then was laid off and unable to meet the payments. Apparently because the coat, however nice, was a necessity, her stepfather had to take over the payments. The resulting bad feelings "almost caused a rupture in the family."[70] The conflict was not, however, only inter-generational. An unscrupulous Chicago man bought himself a seventy-five-dollar suit in his sister's name, giving the address of the factory where she worked. Hounded on the job by the ruthless merchant, the young woman was desperately paying off the debt at two dollars per week.[71] In the insecure economy of the working-class family, installment debt was not a good bet. Although it promised immediate consumer gratification, it did so at the cost of higher prices than for cash purchases and – if payments could not be maintained – at the risk of the loss of both the item purchased and all money paid in up to that point. In family economies based on close calculation and careful economizing, it was no wonder that installment debt was a source of family conflict for both sons and daughters.

The days in which children's earnings were indisputably and completely the property and gain of their families – if ever indeed there had been such a day – were clearly gone by the interwar period. Wage-earning sons and daughters were impelled both by a sense of family duty and by the desire for consumer gratification. Families dealt with the resulting conflicts in a wide variety of ways, but the emphasis was on negotiation, on giving in a little to children's individual aspirations in order not to lose their contributions entirely.

Age, class, and gender shaped working-class daughters' and sons' experiences in the labor market, the marketplace, and the family. Age, in the picture painted by my sources, is the most powerful shaper of labor-force experience. Despite the ever-higher cultural value placed on youth during the 1920s and afterward, these young people were at pains to establish themselves as steady workers. Class doubtless shaped their work lives in other respects, but what we see most clearly here are its effects on their lives and identities as consumers. The pressures to consume assaulted all Americans

69 NA, RG 86, PB no. 88, box 123, 24–50.   70 Ibid., 21–3.
71 NA, RG 86, PB no. 25, box 12, Chicago – Annuzzio.

more relentlessly beginning in the 1920s; for working-class families, though, self-denial rather than self-fulfillment through consumption was the rule.

Most notably of all, these documents show how gender shaped different discourses and experiences of consumption. The family discourse around wage earning and consumption cast men as individuals, attributing good or bad performance as earners and family members to strengths or defects in their character. It placed women relationally, embedding them in the family as dependents rather than showing them as autonomous persons. Men were assessed for their qualities as workers, and their faults were expressed as failures of the work ethic. Women were portrayed as consumers, with their limited ability to contribute to the family fund taken for granted because of their disadvantaged position in the work force and their lapses couched in terms of their desires for consumer goods, especially clothing. The discourse sounds remarkably like that Jeanne Boydston has found surrounding housework in the early republic: Men's work was work, and women's was a matter of duty.[72]

The experience of consumption was as gendered as the discourse, although in a strikingly different direction. Sons simply held on to more of their higher earnings and disbursed them as they liked. Women's consumption was more closely tied to the family because of the "all to mother" pattern and their lower wages. Their consumption was more directly and specifically contested, particularly around clothing, and the joys of shopping and buying recede into the background. Ironically, then, daughters' and sons' experience in the marketplace belied the terms of the discourse. Men were in fact the more autonomous consumers, and women were the more reliable workers and the more dependable – if limited – contributors to the family fund. Understanding both the discourse and experience of working-class consumption in the United States in the interwar period teaches us many lessons about the limits of abundance and the persisting connections between production and consumption, but perhaps it shows us most of all how intensely gender shaped this world of consumption.

Daughters and sons were subject to similar disadvantages in the labor market and to similar temptations in the marketplace, but both they and their families responded to them in gendered ways. Sons were seen primarily as producers, daughters primarily as consumers. The discourse of working-class family consumption, although saying many of the same things about daughters and sons, nonetheless emphasized women's dependency and connections to the family and men's individualism.

---

72 Jeanne Boydston, *Home and Work: Housework, Wages, and the Ideology of Labor in the Early Republic* (New York, 1991), chap. 7.

Comparing Apples and Oranges

Housewives and the Politics of Consumption in Interwar Germany

NANCY REAGIN

Even in autumn, the fruit of our homeland, the apple, is unrea
sonably neglected [by housewives] and in its place many sorts
of oranges are consumed in astonishing quantities.

> – *The German Housewife*, 1927

[Under the Four Year Plan] we attempted [to guide house-
wives] to return to the healthier foods of our ancestors, and
above all to reduce the excessive demand for meat, which was
common in all highly civilized societies . . . we especially
advocated the use of whole grains . . . and whole grain bread
(*Vollkornbrot*).

> – Else Vorwerck, 1948[1]

This chapter examines how the politics of consumption during the interwar period were framed and pursued by German housewives' organizations. It is part of a larger project that analyzes the ways in which the *Hausfrau* and housewifery were redefined under successive political regimes and
links the competing images of the *Hausfrau* that bourgeois housewives'

Research for this article was made possible by grants from the German Academic Exchange Service
and by Pace University. It benefited greatly from careful readings and criticisms by the members of the
German Women's History Group, and especially by Renate Bridenthal, who shared her own research
with me. I am also indebted to Kirsten Schlegel-Matthies, who generously shared copies of her own
sources.
1 Taken from her memoir; Vorwerck led the Political Economy-Home Economy division of the
  National Socialist Women's Bureau.

organizations advanced during this period to their politics of consumption. Within this framework, I will focus on three areas: the ambivalent values assigned to categories of products (especially foods) in these discussions, the trade-off between wasting labor and wasting resources in consumption and housework, and the balance of power or authority between the housewife–consumer and small retailers or artisans. There were strong continuities in all of these areas between 1914 and 1939, which still resonated in the post-1945 period.

The politics of consumption, like the housewives' organizations themselves, had its roots in World War I. The Allied naval blockade on the Central Powers had devastating consequences for German civilians, as the state pursued an unsuccessful policy of autarky, resulting in food shortages, widespread malnutrition, and increased mortality rates in every age category. The results were politically explosive; as "butter riots" and food-related protests undermined the Wilhelmine state, a heated discussion developed within and outside government circles about what constituted an equitable distribution of foodstuffs. Civilians' wartime experiences, along with debates about food distribution, helped crystallize the persona of the "consumer" (implicitly feminine) and popularized the idea of a reciprocal relationship between state and consumer.[2]

The bourgeois women's movement (in its wartime form, the National Women's Service) became the main vehicle through which the government tried to mold housewives' shopping and cooking habits to meet the needs of autarky. The Women's Service distributed recipe booklets and the model menus (*Speisezettel*) published in newspapers to adjust civilians' diets to match available ingredients. These menus stressed foods that would be featured in discussions throughout the next twenty-five years: potatoes, dark bread, and substitutes for fat in cooking. The Service also helped found housewives' associations in most German cities; these groups developed a variety of services to help housewives cope with shortages of every type of product. Housewives' associations offered courses on cooking and on ways to create substitutes for scarce commodities; in some localities, they established consumer cooperatives in conjunction with rural housewives' organizations.[3] The urban housewives' associations created a national organiza-

2 For an intriguing analysis of the politics of food consumption in World War I, see Belinda Davis, "Food Scarcity and the Empowerment of the Female Consumer in World War I Germany," in Victoria de Grazia and Ellen Furlough, ed., *The Sex of Things: Gender and Consumption in Historical Perspective* (Berkeley, Calif., 1996), and "Home Fires Burning: Politics, Identity, and Food in World War I Berlin," Ph.D. diss., University of Michigan, 1992, 277–327, 521–36; see also Anne Roerkohl, *Hungerblockade und Heimatfront* (Stuttgart, 1991).
3 See Roerkohl, *Hungerblockade,* 205–10. For a description of housewives' associations in one locality,

tion, which changed its name after the war to the National League of German Housewives' Associations. Its main competitor in organizing urban housewives during the Weimar period was the Housewives' Union of the Catholic Women's League; the two organizations pursued almost identical policies with regard to consumer issues.[4]

On the spectrum of Weimar partisan politics, both organizations were centrist to right wing: Their overall politics thus contrasted sharply with that of their American counterparts, such as the women's consumer group led by Florence Kelley.[5] The Catholic Housewives' Union was closely affiliated with the Center Party. The larger National League was politically "neutral" in theory, but many of its leaders belonged to the far-Right German National People's Party.[6] Their consumer politics would reflect this broader conservatism, as both groups attempted to fuse the rationalization of housework (a self-consciously "modern" stance) with economic nationalism, which stressed an antimodern protectionist approach to consumer issues.

The consumer politics of these Weimar housewives' organizations was strongly influenced by the "rational" model of housewifery and consumption offered by American home economists such as Christine Frederick. Frederick (whose work was translated into German) and her German disciples, especially Dr. Erna Meyer (author of the best-selling advice manual *The New Household*), attempted to apply Taylorism to the household by teaching "scientific management" to housewives.[7] Advice literature (in mag-

see Nancy Reagin, *A German Women's Movement: Class and Gender in Hanover, 1880–1933* (Chapel Hill, N.C., 1995), 187–202. Renate Bridenthal gives a politically sophisticated analysis of rural housewives' organizations in "Organized Rural Women in the Conservative Mobilization of the German Countryside in the Weimar Republic," in Larry E. Jones and James N. Retallack, eds., *Between Reform, Reaction, and Resistance: Studies in the History of German Conservatism from 1789 to 1945* (New York, 1993), 375–405.

4 The National League was largely Protestant and almost entirely bourgeois. For an analysis of the League during the Weimar period, see Renate Bridenthal, "'Professional Housewives': Stepsisters of the Women's Movement," in Renate Bridenthal, Atina Grossmann, and Marion Kaplan, eds., *When Biology Became Destiny: Women in Weimar and Nazi Germany* (New York, 1984), 153–73. See also Kirsten Schlegel-Matthies, "*Im Haus und am Herd*": *Der Wandel des Hausfrauenbildes und der Hausarbeit 1880–1930* (Stuttgart, 1995), 191–228. Working-class housewives' organizations were established in only two cities, since the Social Democrats rejected the idea of creating a separate housewives' organization within the labor movement.

5 See the article by Kathryn Kish Sklar on Kelley's National Consumers' League in this book.

6 See Bridenthal, "'Professional Housewives,'" and "Class Struggle Around the Hearth: Women and Domestic Service in the Weimar Republic," in Michael Dobkowski and Isidor Walliman, *Towards the Holocaust: Anti-Semitism and Fascism in the Weimar Republic* (Westport, Conn., 1983), 243–64; for a study of the National League's work and politics at the local level, see Reagin, *German Women's Movement*, 221–48.

7 For an excellent study of the ways that Germans perceived America during the 1920s, and how the American model influenced German rationalization, see Mary Nolan, *Visions of Modernity: American Business and the Modernization of Germany* (New York, 1994). Nolan's work includes an insightful dis-

azines, books, and government publications) and the emerging discipline of
home economics thus publicized the American model of housework and
consumption within Germany. Members of German housewives' organizations also traveled to America during the 1920s to observe U.S. households
firsthand and published accounts of their experiences; these first-person
reports indeed became something of a genre in publications of housewives'
groups during the 1920s.[8] Their reaction to "rationalized" American housework was overwhelmingly positive, but (as discussed later) they were sometimes made uneasy by consumption patterns that they perceived among
American housewives.

To German home economists, government officials, and housewives' organizations, "rationalization" was defined primarily as the rearrangement of
the workplace and reform of work methods according to time-and-motion
studies. The housewife's "workplace" was above all her kitchen, the production site for meals. Housewives' associations and home economists urged
that German kitchens be reduced in size and reorganized, to save the housewife unnecessary steps and motions and to make cleaning easier. Examples of
the new, smaller kitchen were depicted and propagated repeatedly in housewives' magazines, in special exhibits (discussed later), and in home economics journals. Much of the new government-sponsored housing built during
the 1920s included such kitchens.[9] Experts also studied housewives' work
methods (in dusting, mopping, and so on), and the government's National
Productivity Board published booklets and posters that showed easier, simpler, and more efficient ways for women to accomplish these tasks.[10]

cussion of how the supporters of rationalization targeted working-class housewives, but she has little
to say about the impact of the American model on bourgeois housewives and their organizations.
For the movement to rationalize German housekeeping in general during this period, see Schlegel-
Matthies, *"Im Haus und am Herd,"* 153–90; Hiltraud Schmidt-Waldherr, "Rationalisierung der
Hausarbeit in den zwanziger Jahren," in Gerda Tornieporth, ed., *Arbeitsplatz Haushalt: Zur Theorie
und Ökologie der Hausarbeit* (Berlin, 1988), 32–54; Barbara Orland, "Emanzipation durch Rationalisierung? Der 'rationelle Haushalt' als Konzept institutionalisierter Frauenpolitik in der Weimarer
Republik," in Dagmar Reese et al., eds., *Rationale Beziehungen? Geschlechterverhältnisse im Rationali-
sierungsprozess* (Frankfurt am Main, 1993), 222–50.

8 Housewives' organizations published numerous accounts by these observers in their yearbooks and
magazines, as did professional home economists. Some examples include the article by Lissy
Sysemihl-Gliedemeister, "Über amerikanische Frauentätigkeit," *Jahrbuch des Reichsverbandes Deutscher
Hausfrauenvereine* (1929): 141–55; articles in *Die Deutsche Hausfrau* 12 (1927): 74, and 13 (1928): 17,
52, 88, 122; articles in *Hauswirtschaftliche Jahrbücher* 2 (1929): 23, and 3 (1920): 65, and 4 (1931): 104.

9 See the article on the Frankfurt kitchen exhibition in *Die Deutsche Hausfrau* 12 (1927): 68; Schlegel-
Matthies, *"Im Haus und am Herd",* 155–73; Nancy Reagin, "Die Werkstatt der Hausfrau: Bürgerliche
Frauenbewegung und Wohnungspolitik im Hannover der Zwanziger Jahre," in Adelheid von Saldern
and Sid Auffahrt, eds., *Altes und neues Wohnen: Linden und Hannover im frühen 20. Jahrhundert* (Seelze-
Velber, 1992), 156–64.

10 These time-and-motion studies were sponsored and publicized by the Home Economics Group of
the National Productivity Board.

Most supporters of rationalization agreed that the new homes and kitchen–workplaces would not include the consumer durables (washing machines, vacuum cleaners, electric or gas stoves, refrigerators) that were allegedly ubiquitous in American households as a core component of American domestic rationalization. German industrialists and government officials argued that Germany was simply too poor to copy the comparatively high wages and widespread ownership of durable goods that characterized American society.[11] The majority of households (that is, working-class families) simply could not afford these appliances, although many bourgeois housewives could. A 1928 study of Berlin found only 45 percent of all households had electricity; of these, 56 percent had electric irons (by far the most popular of the "new appliances" nationally), 28 percent had vacuum cleaners, and only 0.5 percent had washing machines. In America, by contrast, 76 percent of homes with electricity had irons, 30 percent had vacuum cleaners, and 26 percent had washing machines.[12] The German version of domestic rationalization, with its reorganized kitchens and dearth of labor-saving appliances, has been called an "austere vision of modernity," certainly a fitting characterization of working-class households.[13]

Housewives' associations advocated these consumer durables for their (bourgeois) members, while endorsing a variety of smaller "rationalized" products for all households. These included the standardized products that were promoted by the National Productivity Board and the German Standards Committee, ranging from pots and utensils to mattresses, which were designed to be more efficient, easier to clean, or more durable. Housewives' groups also helped popularize products with "modern" design or materials, such as the new Jena glass cookware, along with the sleek, simplified furniture and interior design developed by the Bauhaus movement and others during the 1920s.[14]

The Americanized vision of household modernity – both austere and expansive versions – assumed tangible form for consumers in hundreds of exhibits, large and small, mounted by housewives' associations during the late 1920s. The largest, such as the massive 1928 show "Home and Technol-

11 Nolan, *Visions of Modernity*, 216; Schlegel-Matthies, *"Im Haus und am Herd,"* 171–3.

12 The results of the entire study are given in Schlegel-Matthies, *"Im Haus und am Herd,"* 173. For the popularity of irons in particular, see Herrad U. Bussemer, Sibylle Meyer, Barbara Orland, and Eva Schulze, "Zur technischen Entwicklung von Haushaltsgeräten," in Tornieporth, *Arbeitsplatz Haushalt,* 122. The spread of ownership of appliances was hindered not only by their cost, but by the high price of electricity, which was beyond the budgets of most working-class families.

13 Nolan, *Visions of Modernity*, 207.

14 See, e.g., Klara Neundörfer, *Haushalten* (Königstein im Taunus, 1929); Ludwig Neundörfer, *Wie Wohnen?* (Königstein im Taunus, 1928); "Gute und schlechte Formen im Haushalt," *Frauenland* 20 (1927): 78. For the work of National Productivity Board, see Nolan, *Visions of Modernity*, 214–15.

ogy" (Munich) and "Nutrition" (Berlin), were created in conjunction with
government, business, and industry, and were reviewed and publicized in
newspapers and magazines nationwide. Parts of both exhibits were subsequently combined to create a "traveling exhibit" that visited a series of German cities. Even a midsized exhibit, such as the "Blue Apron" show created
by Düsseldorf women's associations in 1930, could attract fifteen thousand
visitors in a month. In smaller cities and towns, local housewives' associations created their own shows or contracted with firms that specialized in
producing these exhibits. In return for the housewives' endorsement, promotion, and donated materials, these firms organized the shows using their
own exhibits (along with material from local businesses) and gave the local
housewives' association a share of the proceeds.[15]

These exhibits showcased every aspect of household rationalization,
including model kitchens, living rooms, bedrooms, and bathrooms; the
largest would provide several models for every room, for households with
different income levels. Visitors could see demonstrations of the new household appliances that used electricity or gas, along with information on the
cost of using these products. In some shows, entire kitchens or laundry
rooms from the United States stood alongside German models. Bedrooms
and living rooms reflected the new style of interior decoration. In many
shows, visitors could also purchase the appliances and furniture on display.
Most shows also stressed "rational" nutrition, which urged the consumption
of more fruits and vegetables, and included cooking demonstrations offering visitors a taste of these healthier dishes and distributing recipe booklets.
Other rooms might include materials on rationalized methods of housework or shopping.[16]

Exhibits on the "new household" were usually organized by housewives'
groups, but other women's associations (such as confessional or teachers'
organizations) would hold annual conventions in conjunction with such
exhibits, in order to offer their members special tours of the shows. In many
cities, pupils from domestic science classes toured the exhibitions. City
dwellers came by the thousands, attracted by free food samples, discount
coupons, and opportunities to buy the latest gadgets. One critic remarked

15 See *Der Haushalt als Wirtschaftsfaktor: Ergebnisse der Ausstellung Heim und Technik* (Munich, 1928);
   *Frauenwirken in Haus und Familie: Die Ausstellung der Düsseldorfer Frauenverbände: Rückblick und Aus-
   blick* (Düsseldorf, 1930). *Die Deutsche Hausfrau* also regularly carried reports on these shows, large and
   small, from all over Germany. See the correspondence between housewives' associations and firms
   specializing in these shows in Niedersächsisches Hauptstaatsarchiv (hereafter NH) Hann 320 I, no.
   47, and in the archive of the Katholischer Deutscher Frauenbund (hereafter AKDFB), files 1–74–4
   and 1–74–5.
16 See *Frauenwirken in Haus und Familie* and *Der Haushalt als Wirtschaftsfaktor.*

that the atmosphere of the exhibits often resembled that of annual fairs.[17] These shows ensured that many (if not most) housewives would have been exposed to the vision of the modern household, even if their daily reality did not include its technology.

The "rational" shopping habits that housewives' organizations advocated, however, reflected the ambivalence that these associations felt toward mass production and the American model of the consumer society. Housewives' associations had class investments that led them to defend small retailers and artisans (the backbone of the *Mittelstand* or middle class) from the threat posed by department stores, one-price stores, consumer cooperatives (affiliated with the socialist labor movement), and chains of larger retailers. Many members of housewives' associations in fact were married to small businessmen or craftsmen. Housewives' associations therefore often denounced the "cheap" quality of mass-produced goods (*Dutzendwaren*), and reminded their members that small retailers could give better advice and more personalized service. Articles that their magazines published on consumer issues also showed strong distrust and dislike of the advertising and promotion that accompanied mass production. Like home economists, housewives' associations stressed repeatedly that "the most expensive product is still the cheapest" over the long run because it lasts longer and advised readers to buy the best quality they could possibly afford (which implicitly meant buying from craftsmen).[18]

Although they rejected department stores and mass production, housewives' groups still sought to empower the housewife–consumer in her dealings with retailers and artisans through increased consumer education about products (*Warenkunde*). The housewife's *Warenkunde,* the result of detailed education about the qualities and attributes of products, would help equalize the relationship between merchants and consumers, and housewives' organizations tried to educate their members in meetings and publications. Since housewives did not always have the time to acquire this knowledge, however, the associations went further. The National League of German Housewives' Associations created a center to test consumer products in 1925. Manufacturers could submit their products, which were tested for durability, cost of operation, and ease of use; those that the center judged worthy could carry the league's symbol (a sun stamp) on their products and advertising. Home economists and housewives' magazines advised women

---

17 See the critical article in *Deutsche Hauswirtschaft* 21 (1936): 114.

18 The saying "the best is still the cheapest," apparently predated World War I, and was picked up by housewives' organizations; the strong preference for "quality" in consumer goods is of course still very much evident in German discussions today.

to "look for the sun symbol" when shopping.[19] In many larger cities, housewives' organizations established advice centers with permanent exhibitions
on the "new household," where consumers could obtain information about
new products. The largest and most elaborate was the so-called Heibaudi,
which advised over fifty thousand consumers in 1932.[20] Housewives' organizations and home economists also emphatically and consistently warned
housewives against the use of credit or buying on time; paying cash, they
argued, put the housewife–consumer in a stronger position vis-à-vis merchants. All of these policies were attempts to strengthen the position of
housewives, since small retailers and artisans derived much of their authority from their specialized knowledge about products and their control over
access to credit.

However, the consumer education of housewives' organizations included
much more than just the promotion or evaluation of new technology and
household rationalization. Much of their work in this area, perhaps even the
bulk of it, was concerned with the more fundamental consumption issue of
food. After all, housewives' associations had been created to deal with issues
relating to foodstuffs, and food politics was among these organizations' chief
preoccupations. Leaders of housewives' groups acknowledged that not all
households could afford durable goods, but all had to purchase food: Foodstuffs were therefore the area in which they hoped to have the most impact
on consumers' purchasing decisions. These organizations' exhibitions thus
always devoted considerable space to cooking demonstrations and recipe
distribution in the model kitchens. Their advice centers included rotating
exhibitions on nutrition and cooking, and their publications devoted as
much space to food choices as they did to rationalized housework. But
although they paid as much attention (or more) to apples as they did to
vacuum cleaners, their discussions of food still expressed the full range of
anxieties and aspirations that the new consumer society evoked.

The most important fears and hopes of housewives' discussions about
food centered around the promotion of "German" foods and the rejection
of imported foodstuffs. This was part of the general support for protectionism predominant during the 1920s, and it reflected the anxiety that "unre-
strained" consumption would undermine traditional social hierarchies. Buy-

19 The testing center was publicized in almost all advice literature, housewives' magazines, and often
   had a booth at the larger household exhibitions. See, e.g., Erna Meyer, *Der neue Haushalt* (Stuttgart,
   1926), 152. For the background and operating procedures of the testing center, see Schlegel-Matthies,
   "Im Haus und am Herd," 194–6. The center was modeled on the American Good Housekeeping
   Institute, and was the first of its kind in Europe.
20 Heibaudi stood for *Hauswirtschaftlicher Einkaufs- Beratungs- Auskunftsdienst;* see the article on it in the
   Jahrbuch des Reichsverbandes Deutscher Hausfrauenvereine from 1928.

ing German foods would help protect German farmers above all, but house-wives' associations also linked German foodstuffs to more traditional diets and life-styles. Further, they associated buying foreign foods with the same lack of "social responsibility" that led many housewives to desert local busi-nesses and artisans for department stores or chains. Housewives' economic nationalism also reflected their close alliance with farm women's organiza-tions, whose members demanded protective tariffs especially for "women's sphere of agriculture – milk products, poultry, eggs, fruit, and vegetables."[21] Throughout the 1920s, urban housewives' associations worked with Ger-man food producers to try to influence housewives' choice of products. In the process, they helped further develop categorizations of food begun dur-ing World War I, in which products were assigned ambivalent and conflict-ing attributes. They continued to promote rationalization, which stressed abundance in some areas (the acquisition of durable goods, for example). Protectionism, however – conceptualized as "socially responsible" consump-tion – was an even higher priority.

Some of the foodstuffs that housewives' organizations tried to promote were the same products they had stressed during World War I, because wartime autarky had relied on the same products that protectionism singled out in peacetime: potatoes and dark bread. Large sections of Germany's arable land supported rye or barley crops better than wheat. To be "self-sufficient" in grain, therefore, and support local farmers, German consumers would have to eat breads made with rye flour and utilize the wheat that Germany had to the fullest by eating whole wheat bread. German con-sumers, however, shared the almost universal Western preference for lighter (or white) wheat breads, with their connotations of luxury.[22] Housewives' organizations thus joined agrarian interests in promoting rye as the "patri-otic" grain, distributing booklets and presenting slide shows that explained that rye bread had more fiber, was more nutritious, and helped German farmers. Wheat bread, especially the light rolls (*Brötchen*), was to be seen as a luxury and reserved for occasional use. Housewives' associations promoted "rye days," and when a delegation from the housewives' National League met with President Paul von Hindenburg in 1928 (in conjunction with the opening of a large exhibition), the league's magazine later noted that the president singled out the league's promotion of rye for praise. Hindenburg stressed that he himself ate only rye bread, proclaiming, "A patriot eats rye

21 Bridenthal, "Organized Rural Women," 401.
22 The preference for white bread was widespread, and widely bemoaned by social reformers, who simply could not understand why workers preferred the (less nutritious) white bread, and rejected the cheaper foods associated with poverty.

bread," a point that housewives' groups stressed repeatedly in their consumer education.[23]

Housewives' organizations went beyond the products promoted during World War I, however, in their consumer education. Some of their most passionate rhetoric attacked the so-called southern fruits (*Südfrüchte*): imported tropical fruits, especially bananas and oranges. Housewives' publications repeatedly denounced mothers who bought oranges and bananas for their children, arguing that these imports hurt German farmers and Germany's balance of trade; tropical fruits were labeled unnecessary luxuries. Housewives' organizations recognized that Germany's climate did not supply local fruit year round but argued that a conscientious housewife would buy German fruits in season and put them up or store them in her cellar over the winter. Housewives who chose instead to buy imported fruits during the winter were simply lazy and socially irresponsible. Apples were particularly praised as "the German fruit" and frequently juxtaposed against bananas or oranges. One 1927 article in *Die Deutsche Hausfrau* criticized lazy housewives who "shy away from the small efforts that are necessary when apples are stored in the cellar": checking stored apples daily, turning them regularly, and using up those that were going bad. "That is why many housewives prefer oranges," the author concluded angrily; "it is simply easier for them to buy as many as they need at the moment."[24] Other writers combined the rejection of tropical fruits with the recurrent distrust of advertising, blaming the promotion of tropical fruits by the advertising industry. " 'Eat bananas' scream hundreds of alluring advertisements at us," wrote one author in the Catholic Housewives' Union magazine; "is it any wonder, then, when we fall victim to this unscrupulous advertising?"[25]

Housewives' organizations also championed butter, although the politics of butter consumption was more complex and problematic than that of other foodstuffs. Butter had been much coveted during World War I; its distribution had been one of the most hotly debated issues during the war,

---

23 Promotion of rye bread was a regular theme in housewives' publications. For the meeting with Hindenburg, see *Die Deutsche Hausfrau* 13 (1928): 92–3. For an example of a "rye day," see *Die Deutsche Hausfrau* 15 (1930): 56. For correspondence with agricultural interests and examples of the propaganda distributed by housewives, see AKDFB, file 1–70–2. The promotion and government protection of rye had a long history, stretching back into the Wilhelmine period, when the Emperor, too, had endorsed rye as the "patriotic" grain.

24 "Hausfrauen, kellert Äpfel ein!" *Die Deutsche Hausfrau* 12 (1927): 168–9.

25 "Eine Lücke in der Front! Betrachtungen zum Auslandskonsum," *Frauenland* 23 (1930): 188. Articles and other material that denounced purchasing imports, including tropical fruits, were ubiquitous in housewives' publications. See, e.g., the articles in *Die Deutsche Hausfrau* 11 (1926): 177, 12 (1927): 116, 13 (1928): 179; in *Frauenland* 23 (1930): 185, 242, and 24 (1931): 130, 194. For the discussions within housewives' organizations about tropical fruits, see AKDFB, file 1–73–3 and NH Hann 320 I, no. 79, vol. 1.

while margarine had been one of the substitute foodstuffs promoted in its place.[26] Butter, once again widely available, was thus a symbol of peacetime and normalcy. It was also produced in Germany and was seen as a "natural" product. By contrast, many housewife–consumers viewed margarine with suspicion, because of its "unnatural" and dubious ingredients. Its national provenance was also questionable, since even if it was manufactured in Germany, it was made of imported raw materials (including whale blubber and coconut oil); some of the best known brands (such as Sanella), moreover, were owned by foreign corporations.[27] However, housewives' organizations could not simply promote the use of butter over margarine – as they did apples over oranges – because Germany imported much butter as well: Danish butter in particular was widely preferred. And leaders of housewives' associations were aware that many households could not afford butter, which cost about twice as much as margarine.

Housewives' groups could and did appeal to their members to buy German butter rather than Danish butter. To substitute for margarine and to aid German dairy farmers, organizations also began to promote a dairy product called *Quark*, which could be made from the milk left over from butter production. Unknown to many German consumers during the 1920s, and unavailable in many areas, *Quark* was used as a bread spread (in place of butter or margarine) or in making desserts. Both of the larger housewives' organizations, working with the German Dairy Board, pushed it enthusiastically. Housewives' groups distributed samples of *Quark* to their members, to familiarize them with its taste, along with recipes that used it; they also lobbied local retailers to carry it.[28] These promotional campaigns, which the National Socialists carried forward after 1933, apparently established *Quark* as a product. To this day it remains a staple foodstuff in Germany.

Finally, housewives' organizations worked with the fishing industry to promote the consumption of fish, especially herring. Fish was not promoted in competition to any foreign foodstuff but rather advocated in order to protect the jobs of fishermen and the German fishing industry.

26 For an interesting discussion of the psychological significance of butter to German consumers, and an account of the "butter riots" that took place during the war, see Davis, "Food Scarcity."
27 See the correspondence of the Catholic Housewives' Union regarding margarine in AKDFB, file 1–74–5.
28 For the promotion of *Quark* by the Catholic Housewives' Union, see the correspondence in AKDFB, file 1–70–2. For an example of one of the articles that housewives' magazines ran to publicize its use, see *Frauenland* 24 (1931): 131. The correspondence in housewives' organization files indicates that many of their members were unfamiliar with *Quark*, hence the need to distribute *Kostproben* (samples for tasting). Complaints that it was not well known or widely carried in stores persisted into the 1930s; see Bundesarchiv Berlin-Zehlendorf, NS 44–35, minutes of the schooling course for nutritional advisors, Sept. 20, 1937.

Housewives' organizations distributed recipes and flyers promoting fish consumption and sent some of their members to courses sponsored by the industry to be trained in cooking unfamiliar varieties. Graduates of the courses returned home to teach fellow housewives.[29]

Fish, *Quark*, rye bread, apples, and German butter were promoted specifically and vehemently, while white bread, oranges, and bananas were stigmatized. Above and beyond these particular foodstuffs, German housewives' organizations also argued in their publications and exhibits that housewives had a patriotic duty to buy German; writers frequently criticized the German consumer for being partial to foreign goods and asserted that other nations' consumers were far more loyal to native products. A typical 1928 article in *Die Deutsche Hausfrau* bemoaned the fact:

Doubtless the German consumer still has the belief that a foreign product is more interesting and elegant . . . she who buys perfume from the firm of Coty puts money in French hands . . . foreign carpets are also unnecessary, since the German carpet industry has been producing the most wonderful carpets for decades; their patterns are easy for us to understand, while the figures on a Smyrna or Persian rug require a degree in philosophy . . . [Paris fashions] are also superfluous. In Germany there is also a fashion industry; its products may be somewhat different, but they perhaps are more suited to the essence of German womanhood.[30]

Housewives' organizations and home economists consistently linked the individual woman's purchasing habits to the national economy, making explicit the link between personal consumption and political life. They argued that if the German housewife would only buy German, then unemployment would be reduced, Germany's balance of trade would be improved, and Germany would be better able to pay the "tribute" of reparation payments imposed by the Treaty of Versailles. In her housekeeping manual *The New Household,* Erna Meyer even blamed the hyperinflation of the early 1920s on Germans' purchase of unneeded foreign luxuries. During the early 1920s and after 1929, many writers indeed came close to arguing that German housewives could single-handedly rescue Germany's economy.[31]

---

29 See the correspondence regarding fish consumption in AKDFB, file 1–74–2. See also the articles promoting fish consumption as an act of solidarity with German fishermen, in *Die Deutsche Hausfrau* 11 (1926): 160, 14 (1929): 44, and 16 (1931): 51.
30 From "Volkswirtschaftliche Verantwortung der Frau bei Einkäufen," *Die Deutsche Hausfrau* 13 (1928): 179–80.
31 See Meyer, *Der neue Haushalt,* 135. For other examples of writers who linked the average household's consumption habits to the national economy, see Cilli van Aubel, "Bedeutung und Aufgabe der Frau als Verbraucherin in der Wirtschaft," in Katholischer Deutscher Frauenbund, ed., *Frau und Wirtschaft: Vorträge der 11. Generalversammlung des KDF in Breslau* (Cologne, 1931); "Hausfrau-

After the onset of the depression, the "Buy German" campaigns mounted by both urban and rural housewives' associations became insistent and almost incessant, as housewives' groups (allied with German industrialists) hosted "German weeks" in most areas, with displays in store windows, public skits, musical performances and plays, or parades. Perhaps assuming that the depression ruled out the purchase of foreign rugs and fashions for most consumers, the German weeks focused primarily on food products. One play, *Buy German Products!,* produced by housewives' groups in many cities, was set in a marketplace; the farm women who sold German produce there banded together with female shoppers to drive out a woman who sold bananas and oranges.[32]

The American model of consumption and housework, along with rationalization in general, was thus attractive for German housewives' organizations, but not when it conflicted with protectionism. The argument that housewives should preserve apples rather than buying oranges year round was rooted in more than simple protectionism, however: It reflected specific notions regarding the trade-off between wasting labor and wasting resources when planning housework. When it came to foreign fruits and mass-produced imports, housewives' associations fell back on an older, more labor-intensive vision of housework and consumption and demanded that housewives put up or recycle foodstuffs and clothing (which took more effort, but saved resources and cash) rather than buying cheap mass-produced replacements (which was "wasteful" in terms of materials, but also labor-saving). This strategy made sense within the budgets of lower-income households, but housewives' organizations were clearly advocating this approach for all families, no matter how well off, since the approach was seen as virtuous per se. Even for the well-to-do, "socially responsible" consumption meant choosing more labor-intensive forms of housework in some areas, in order to support economic nationalism.

In this respect, the American model – otherwise viewed in generally positive terms – made observers from German housewives' groups uneasy, as they perceived a link between the "wastefulness" of American households and rationalization. The most extreme example of this critique was a 1928 article in *Die Deutsche Hausfrau* that argued that rationalization had taught American housewives to assign a market value to their own labor, which they then included in calculations as to whether tasks were "worth"

Einkauf-Volkswirtschaft," *Die Deutsche Hausfrau* 11 (1926): 177–9; "Was-wie-wo kauft die Hausfrau?" *Die Deutsche Hausfrau* 14 (1929): 163.

32 See the copy of the play in NH Hann 320 I, no. 50; material on "German weeks," in AKDFB, file 1–73–3.

doing. When it came to washing underwear, for example, American women concluded that it was cheaper to buy new underwear rather than washing it themselves or having it washed, and that attitude supposedly led to the custom of disposable underwear. The article concluded that in America "there are no homes in our sense of the word. People simply buy cheap underwear and throw it away after they have worn it. . . . Heaven preserve us from this Americanization of the household."[33]

The preference for labor-intensive approaches to some areas of housework was linked to an alternative vision of housewifery that competed with the American model of scientific management during the Weimar period and ultimately eclipsed that model after 1933: the master housewife. Throughout the 1920s, the Catholic Housewives' Union and one faction of the housewives' National League promoted the concept. They borrowed the language and hierarchy of German guilds and artisans (along with other symbols derived from traditional customs) to envision the ideal housewife, a woman who had taken special training courses and passed tests (as did artisans) that certified her as knowledgeable and skilled in every aspect of homemaking. Once she had achieved this certification, she could take on "apprentices," girls who had finished their schooling and would now be trained for careers as servants. Ultimately, the servants would rise (marry) and become housewives themselves.[34] As depicted in Weimar discussions, the proposed master housewife was an expert at saving resources (and wasting labor): she could "make new things out of worn-out objects." She put up, canned, or stored foods of every kind when they were in season; sewed clothes for all family members; repaired and altered worn clothes; ensured thriftiness through meticulous bookkeeping; and wasted not.

The master housewife became the dominant model after the National Socialists came to power in 1933. The women's movement as a whole was *gleichgeschaltet* ("brought into line" or Nazified): Feminist organizations within the movement were dissolved, and more conservative associations (including the housewives' National League) joined Nazi-led umbrella groups, primarily the National Socialist Women's Bureau. The Catholic Housewives' Union became moribund, as the Catholic Women's League

---

33 See "Erwerbstätigkeit und Hausfrauengeist," *Die Deutsche Hausfrau* 13 (1928): 50–2. One can imagine what the writer would have thought of disposable diapers.

34 See Bridenthal, "Professional Housewives," and "Organized Rural Women," 395–6; Schlegel-Matthies, *"Im Haus und am Herd,"* 222. The "apprenticeship" proposal, which some supporters wanted to make mandatory for all female *Volksschule* graduates, was in part an attempt to obtain domestic servants without pay. The "master housewife" proposal was however a real bid for professional status and state certification.

was forced to restrict itself to religious activities.[35] By the end of 1935, the National League was dissolved outright into the Women's Bureau Division of Political Economy–Home Economy. After its dissolution, the League's members were encouraged to join the Home Economics Division, which the National Socialists intended as a mass organization for all German housewives that would transcend the class boundaries of the Weimar housewives' organizations.[36]

Between 1933 and 1935, the Women's Bureau (and its subordinate component, the housewives' National League) continued to support the protectionism of the new regime. It also supported the Nazis' attempts to bankrupt Jewish businesses through consumer boycotts, blurring the distinction between foreign and German–Jewish producers and retailers. One example was the publicity that housewives' publications gave to a new label for all "Aryan" clothing, which they urged consumers to buy to drive the "influence of Jewish taste" out of German fashions.[37] Beginning in 1936, however, the main task assigned to the Home Economics Division was to organize German housewives to support the Nazis' Four Year Plan, which aimed to rearm Germany, promote German autarky, and prepare for war. Imports of consumer goods were restricted in order to subsidize the flow of imported raw materials required by German armaments industries. This forced the regime to strive for autarky particularly in the area of food production; the National Socialists defined this as "nutritional freedom" and urged German housewife-consumers to support German farmers in the "battle for production."[38]

As Tim Mason has noted, the regime in fact wanted to have its cake and eat it, too: Its goal was to rearm as quickly as possible while encouraging a tolerable level of consumption. The results of the restriction of imported

35 For the fate of different wings of the women's movement after 1933, see Reagin, *German Women's Movement*, 246–7.
36 See Claudia Koonz, *Mothers in the Fatherland* (New York, 1987), 160–4. I was unable to find figures for how many women from the National League joined the Home Economics division, but surviving records from the Northern Westphalian district claimed that the overwhelming majority of league members in its region joined voluntarily. See the Nordrhein-Westfälisches Staatsarchiv Münster (hereafter NWSM), NS-Frauenschaft Westfalen-Nord, no. 340, report from Bielefeld, Jan.-Feb. 1936.
37 See the articles in the National Socialist *Frauen-Warte* 1 (1932–33): 471, and 2 (1933–34): 90. NWSM, NS-Frauenschaft Westfalen-Nord, no. 326, "Boykottanordnungen." See also the article on "Aryan" clothing in *Die Deutsche Hausfrau* 20 (1935): 103.
38 For National Socialist economic policies, see Burton Klein, *Germany's Economic Preparations for War* (Cambridge, Mass., 1959); Alan Milward, *The German Economy at War* (London, 1965); R. Overy, *The Nazi Economic Recovery 1932–1938* (London, 1982). Nazi goals for housewife–consumers were summarized by Else Vorwerck (head of the Home Economics Division) in "Die volkswirtschaftliche Aufgabe der Frau," *NS Frauen-Warte* 5 (1936–7): 449. See also "Nährungssicherheit, Devisenfrage, Hausfrau," *Die Deutsche Hauswirtschaft* 21 (1936): 75.

foodstuffs were fewer bananas and oranges on the German market and chronic (but not acute) shortages of meat (particularly pork, since much of the nation's fodder was imported) and fats of all kinds. The Home Economics Division attempted to compensate for these restrictions in the framework of its "Kampf dem Verderb" (Fight against waste or spoilage) program by publicizing approaches to housework that stressed recycling, preventing waste of resources, promoting "German" foods.

The products that were *not* available for consumption were determined by the regime. Within this framework, however, the Home Economics Division picked up and carried forward the same kinds of foodstuff promotions that Weimar housewives' organizations had mounted; as noted, a policy of autarky stressed roughly the same products protectionism did. The Home Economics Division thus continued to stress the consumption of *Quark,* fish (to replace meat), and darker types of bread. Tropical fruits were no longer an issue, and in their place the division advocated that housewives put up every fruit and vegetable that the German climate could grow and collect wild fruits, herbs, and edible plants. The Home Economics Division differed from the Weimar housewives' groups, however, in the amount of resources at its disposal and thus also in the scale of its programs: The division was able to mount massive campaigns to reach every German housewife and shopper. It issued suggested weekly and monthly menus and shopping lists (modified to include regional tastes) that reflected the current availability of staple foodstuffs. These menus and lists were then printed in newspapers and magazines, publicized on radio programs, posted in factory floors and marketplaces, and inserted in female workers' pay envelopes. As they had in their previous incarnations as Weimar housewives' associations, local division chapters continued to offer cooking courses that taught housewives how to cook fish, use *Quark,* and put up a variety of produce. Free cooking courses had always been popular draws during the Weimar period, and they continued to enroll thousands of women in each district annually. The Home Economics Division strove for a *Gleichschaltung* (Nazification) of housewives' menus. Its aim, said one Nazi woman leader, was that housewives should even boil fish in a National Socialist fashion.[39]

39 Quoted in Adelheid von Saldern, "Victims or Perpetrators? Controversies About the Role of Women in the Nazi State," in David Crew, ed., *Nazism and German Society, 1933–1945* (New York, 1994), 148. For the Home Economics Division's campaigns, see the correspondence and publicity materials in NWSM, NS-Frauenschaft Westfalen-Nord, no. 122 and no. 378; Bundesarchiv Berlin-Zehlendorf NS 44/44 and NS 44/46. See also Margarete Adelung, "Der 'Kampf dem Verderb' im Haushalt mit sparsamen Mitteln," Ph.D. diss., Ludwig-Maximillians-Universität, Munich, 1940; Else Vorwerck, "Hauswirtschaft in Selbstverwaltung. Ein erster grosser Versuch 1934–1945," typed manuscript, 1948.

The Home Economics Division elaborated on Weimar organizations' arguments about the virtues of "German" foodstuffs. Weimar housewives' groups had claimed that rye and other darker breads were healthier than wheat bread, but the Home Economics Division expanded this assertion to cover the "Germanized" diet in general. Its publications repeatedly stressed that a diet with more whole grains and less meat and fats was patriotic, healthier, and more natural. Linking up their proposed diet to the broader Nazi ideology of blood and soil, one annual report for the Northern Westphalian Division claimed that

the boundless imports of the postwar period seduced our housewives into making demands on the German market no longer connected to the soil, as in earlier times. City women had actually come to ignore the growth and cycles of the natural environment that surrounded them. Fresh strawberries in winter were now simply seen as a delicacy . . . [we must] bring the city woman back to a way of thinking that is bound to German soil and nature.[40]

Some writers went further, arguing that local grains and foodstuffs even suited the digestive system of the German "race" better. Division nutritional advisers were taught that "all [ancient] Aryans, possessing the surer instincts of primitive man, chose whole grains as the main source of nutrition dictated to us by Nature . . . [mass production] led us onto a false [dietary] path. But now modern nutrition again recognizes the vitamin content and value of whole grain bread [*Vollkornbrot*]."[41]

Of course, the "German" diet and measures against waste entailed a more labor-intensive style of housewifery, which was compatible with both the quality of the cuisine promoted by the National Socialists and with the ideal of the master housewife. The Home Economics Division continued and expanded the "master courses" and "apprenticeship" programs created by Weimar housewives' organizations, and in 1939 the training and testing program for master housewives was granted state certification.[42] The style of housewifery pursued by the master housewives featured in the division's chief magazine, *Deutsche Hauswirtschaft,* was at times astonishingly labor-intensive; one example among dozens will be given here. Potatoes were of course heavily advocated by the division (and heavily eaten by consumers),

40 From the 1936 annual report in NWSM, NS-Frauenschaft Westfalen-Nord, no. 378.
41 From the minutes of a schooling course for nutritional advisors, held on April 24, 1939. Bundesarchiv Berlin-Zehlendorf, NS 44–7; see also "Über die deutsche Volksernährung," *Deutsche Hauswirtschaft* 21 (1936): 129; Vorwerck, "Hauswirtschaft in Selbstverwaltung," 30–1.
42 For certification, see July 1940 report on the work of the NS Frauenschaft in wartime in NWSM, NS-Frauenschaft Westfalen-Nord, no. 122.

and the division was concerned that no scrap of potato should be wasted. Housewives were admonished to peel potatoes after they had been boiled rather than before, to achieve thinner peelings and thus less waste (although fingers might sting from peeling glowing potatoes). Still, there might be leftover potatoes, which must not be wasted, and families might well rebel against the awfulness of recurring leftover potatoes. The Home Economics Division therefore distributed dozens of recipes involving leftover boiled potatoes. One suggested mashing the potatoes, mixing them with flour and milk to make dough that could then be rolled into noodles. The potato noodles should then be formed into "snail" shapes, which were to be coated in a bread crumb mixture, and finally sauteed until crisp.[43] The entire process, designed to use up leftover potatoes for a side dish, might well take forty-five minutes.

The master housewife was also supposed to make up daily, weekly, and annual work plans; *Deutsche Hauswirtschaft* published models. This idea carried forward the idea of rational management of housework, but the proposed plans included a staggering amount of labor in order to conserve resources. The format and language of "scientific management" were thus preserved, although the real goal of household rationalization – saving time and effort – was vitiated. The work plans were also somewhat abstract and unreal, since they made no allowances for interruptions by children and hardly allowed time for child care at all. One daily plan included two small time slots for feeding a toddler but assumed that the child would not require any attention otherwise and included the thorough cleaning of the entire house, plus the preparation of a full hot meal, in one morning.[44]

As a master artisan herself, the housewife portrayed by the Home Economics Division respected and relied upon the authority of other artisans, as well as small retailers; in other words, she did not pursue the methods that Weimar housewives' groups had used to acquire authority vis-à-vis craftsmen and merchants. The Home Economics Division did not advocate *Warenkunde*; instead, it promoted *Käufererziehung,* "training" customers to respect the needs and demands of artisans and merchants. The division ordered all local chapters to hold evenings on the "Craftsman and Housewife," which were to educate housewives to prefer artisans' work to mass-produced goods and to respect the customs and authority of artisans and

---

43 See the recipe in *Deutsche Hauswirtschaft* 20 (1935): 123.
44 See the work plans given in *Deutsche Hauswirtschaft* 23 (1938): 6–9. In general, children were largely absent from housewives' advice literature in both the Weimar and Nazi period, at least compared to modern literature.

shopkeepers.[45] This campaign was part of the larger National Socialist *Mittelstandspolitik,* which paid at least lip service to the preservation of traditional social stratification and middle-stratum groups.

The Home Economics Division's intentions regarding the trade-off between wasting labor or resources, as well as the relationship between housewives and small businessmen, were clear; housewives' reception of these campaigns, and the degree of success that the division achieved, are more difficult to gauge. Fish consumption in fact rose almost 50 percent between 1934 and 1938, but in other areas, consumers altered their diets only slightly in response to the division's campaigns, or not at all. Rye bread consumption increased about 12 percent during the same period, but wheat bread consumption also increased by 10 percent. The consumption of vegetables rose over 20 percent in 1936 but sank thereafter; fruit and fat consumption fluctuated within narrow ranges during the same period. The Women's Bureau claimed that as a result of its efforts *Quark* consumption rose by 60 percent, a figure that could not be confirmed independently.[46]

One of the few sources that convey housewives' reception of the division's programs are the monthly reports submitted by local chapters, which must be used with caution. Most reported that their cooking courses were popular, a claim supported by enrollment figures, and that fish consumption had increased through their efforts, but allowed that other aspects of the "Kampf dem Verderb" program were less popular. One report admitted that a film shown to all chapters on how to prevent waste or spoilage met with mixed success: "[while the film was being shown] voices were raised in the auditorium that asked 'What! Are we in elementary school here? Any child knows that!' etc. These were not pampered ladies who said this; completely ordinary women enthusiastically joined in criticizing the film."[47] Ordinary housewives might well have found the Home Economics Division programs patronizing since in many respects its campaigns stressed approaches to housework and consumption that working-class housewives already pursued. Limited incomes had long forced many housewives to adopt labor-intensive but thrifty methods of housekeeping. Another response mentioned in several local chapters' monthly reports was the fear of consumers that the regime would revive wartime conditions for foodstuffs. Shortages

---

45 See the materials and correspondence on housewives vis-à-vis merchants and artisans in NWSM, NS-Frauenschaft Westfalen-Nord, nos. 133, 309, 90, and 313. See also the articles on relationships with retailers in *Deutsche Hausfrau* 20 (1935): 86, and *Deutsche Hauswirtschaft* 21 (1936): 245.
46 See Walther G. Hoffmann, *Das Wachstum der deutschen Wirtschaft seit der Mitte des 19. Jahrhunderts* (Berlin, 1965), 624 and 632. For *Quark,* see Adelung, "Kampf dem Verderb," 48.
47 See the Oct. 1936 monthly report in NWSM, NS-Frauenschaft Westfalen-Nord, no. 378.

of fat and meat, promotion of darker breads, and campaigns to collect wild plants for food were reminiscent of the privations of World War I, and some housewives apparently became apprehensive as a result of the similarities between the Four Year Plan and government policies during World War I.[48]

The women of the Home Economics Division were working within a set of constraints imposed from above, but in many ways, they were also carrying forward consumer policies and approaches to housekeeping that Weimar organizations had developed. Attempts to pursue autarky between 1914–1918 and again after 1933, combined with the protectionism of the Weimar period, meant that housewife-consumers were exposed to a consistent set of consumer foodstuff politics for over twenty-five years. During the Weimar period in particular, bourgeois housewives had been able to contribute to and articulate these policies for themselves.

For bourgeois housewives in particular, this continuity in food politics must have helped to assign many foodstuffs to one of two categories, each of which acquired ambivalent sets of attributes. After years of such propaganda, butter, tropical fruits, and imported foodstuffs overall had probably acquired conflicting connotations: They could be seen as tempting, hard-to-obtain symbols of peace and prosperity (literally, forbidden fruit) or alternatively stigmatized as unpatriotic, unnecessary luxuries that wasted resources and displaced local products. These discussions also constructed a second category of products – whole grain bread, *Quark,* and fish – that were labeled patriotic, more "natural," healthier, and abundantly available because they were indigenous to Germany. This second group was also associated, however, with privation, war, and a state-run economy.

These categorizations and assigned attributes persisted for years, and perhaps still resonate today: Of all possible Western consumer products they could have chosen, East Germans who came through the Berlin Wall in 1989 stereotypically rushed to purchase tropical fruits. And other Germans, from a political background diametrically opposed to National Socialism, still celebrate the healthfulness of *Vollkornbrot* and occasionally criticize the imports of tropical fruits in winter as a waste of energy and resources.[49] The tendency of West German housewives to waste labor rather than resources

48 See NWSM NS-Frauenschaft Westfalen-Nord, monthly reports in nos. 60 and 309. After the beginning of World War II, the ideal of the master housewife and labor-intensive housework increasingly conflicted with the regime's need to mobilize married women for work outside the home in order to support the war effort. The National Socialists were ultimately unable to resolve this conflict: Since wartime employment of women outside the home would undercut the ideals promoted throughout the 1930s, the regime's leadership pursued the mobilization of married women only half-heartedly and inconsistently. See Tim W. Mason, *Nazism, Fascism, and the Working Class* (New York, 1995), 178–88.

49 East German consumers' reactions to the Western "cornucopia" were certainly also a response to the consumer policies of the state and the difficulties of obtaining good bananas at that time.

(compared to American housewives) has also characterized the post-1945 period, along with the comparative strength of small retailers and craftsmen. The consumer politics of interwar housewives' organizations did not produce these results, but they are part of the historical background of modern consumption habits and helped shape the culturally specific meanings of terms such as "waste," "abundance," and "good housewife" that have characterized German discourse since 1945.

12

"The Convenience Is Out of This World"

The Garbage Disposer and American Consumer Culture

SUSAN STRASSER

I

"Our disposer came with the house, and I thought it was just a gimmick to increase its cost," a California housewife told the interviewer for a nation-wide survey sponsored by a plumbing and heating trade journal in 1963. "How wrong I was! Once I started using it, it became indispensable. The convenience is out of this world. I'd never give it up, and I can't imagine any woman not wanting one when it's explained to her what it can do." About 22 percent of the women surveyed used garbage disposers, and most of them shared the California woman's enthusiasm. A Denver woman called hers "a little jewel" that "eliminates trips to my back alley in rain, snow and subzero weather." A Florida homemaker supplied the hot-weather view-point: "I think any woman who lives in a warm climate would be out of her mind not to want a disposer," she told the interviewer. "We have so many problems with insects. . . . Anything that will cut down on garbage and discourage the appearance of vermin . . . is a godsend."[1]

The survey responses highlight fundamental issues in the marketing of the electric garbage disposer, a device for grinding food waste that is com-monplace in the kitchen sinks of American houses, although it is virtually unknown in Europe. Invented in 1935, its commercial development awaited recovery from World War II, like that of many other consumer products, and the way of life it represents constituted a major postwar trans-

Thanks to Warren Belasco, Lizabeth Cohen, Carolyn Goldstein, and the students and faculty of the University of Virginia history department for comments on earlier versions of this chapter.

1 "Meet Mrs. America: She's the Key to Your Market Break-Through in Disposers," *Domestic Engineering*, July 1963, 64–7.

formation. The garbage disposer offered "convenience" in everyday life, contributed to a level of kitchen hygiene previously attainable only with considerable labor, and turned food that at one time would have been reused into sewage. It suited a culture of consumption based both on ever-increasing desires for household appliances and on casual attitudes about throwing things away. Like the technology itself, the cultural context of the garbage disposer was explicit to postwar America. For the historian, the device may symbolize the environmental consequences of consumer society, and particularly of the period of the most extreme profligacy in American life, before issues related to garbage erupted into public debate. It suggests also the particular vision of an abundant life represented in the new kitchens of postwar American housing and in the effort to market new appliances and kitchen remodeling to prosperous owners of older homes.

Although typical in these ways, the story of the disposer's marketing cannot be told in the terms generally favored by most historians of American marketing and consumption, including me. This is not a tale of businesses developing products and advertising them to those who might use them; at first, most disposers were sold to the builders of postwar housing, and throughout their history they have been promoted more to builders, plumbers, and remodelers than to consumers. Even those markets were constrained by regulations: Sewer departments had to be convinced to allow disposers, in every American community. The appeals to all of these groups depended more on broad changes in attitudes toward cleanliness, convenience, and modernity than on clever ideas for selling disposers.

The most central attitudinal change was a judgment that food waste was something to get rid of. In embodying this idea, the garbage disposer reinforced relatively new assumptions about all kinds of refuse. Well into the twentieth century, people had practiced the habits of reuse that prevailed in communities based on handcraft and agriculture, on both sides of the Atlantic. Although they may be accused of wanton wastefulness when it came to natural resources, nineteenth-century Americans tended to conserve the products of human labor in homes and factories. Items no longer wanted were passed on to people of other classes or generations, or stored for later service. Objects of no use to adults became playthings for children. Broken or torn things might be mended by somebody handy, taken to tradespeople who specialized in repairs, or brought back to their makers. Most items beyond repair could be recycled or their parts reused, for heating fuel if nothing else. And some household wastes – rags, paper, bones, bottles, grease, and old metals – could be sold to peddlers and ragmen, who marketed them as raw materials, eventually to be recycled in industrial processes. Then as now, class was fundamental to reuse; people's relationships to rubbish both underscored and created social differences. What was garbage to the rich was useful to the poor, who scavenged for materials to use and to sell.[2]

Throughout the nineteenth century, leftovers and food scraps were useful by-products of human cooking and eating, not waste at all. Early nineteenth-century housewives mucked around in the garbage, saving morsels of food for three major purposes. The best leftovers would be served again, "to nourish your own family, or a poorer one," as Lydia Maria Child wrote in *The American Frugal Housewife* (1835). Food unfit for humans went into the slop pail, to be fed to pigs, goats, chickens, dogs, and cats. Grease and fat were reused in cooking or manufactured into candles and soap; these were made at home or, as time went on, manufactured by commercial establishments that themselves purchased surplus fat from households for much of the nineteenth century.[3] In addition to the three major categories of leftovers, slops, and grease, other food waste might be saved for further use. Catharine Beecher's 1841 instructions for clearing the table, for example, proposed putting aside "all bits of butter" and keeping used tea leaves; to "brighten the looks of a carpet, and prevent dust," the leaves could be scattered on floors and rugs and then swept up.[4] Although readers of household manuals published later in the century bought most of their soap, writers continued to suggest saving grease, for cooking, making small batches of soap, or selling to peddlers. Unwanted food could also be dried and burned for fuel or shoveled into the ground.[5]

Even in cities, kitchen wastes provided food for animals. European travelers commented on the animals roaming American streets at midcentury, eating unwanted food from the gutter where it had landed, thrown from doors and windows. "Take care of the pigs," Charles Dickens advised New York pedestrians in *American Notes*, published in 1842, the same year the New York *Daily Tribune* estimated ten thousand hogs on the streets.[6] Despite measures to control them, swine, goats, and stray dogs had the run of the

---

2   These forms of reuse will be discussed in my forthcoming book, *Waste and Want: Household Trash and American Consumer Culture* (New York, 1999).

3   Mrs. [Lydia Maria] Child, *The American Frugal Housewife,* 16th ed., enlarged and corrected (Boston, 1835), 8.

4   Catharine Beecher, *A Treatise on Domestic Economy* (1841; reprint, New York, 1977), 341, 368.

5   See Catharine E. Beecher and Harriet Beecher Stowe, *The American Woman's Home* (1869; reprint, Hartford, Conn., 1975), 372; Wm. Paul Gerhard, *The Disposal of Household Wastes* (New York, 1890), 21, 34–5; Park Benjamin, *Wrinkles and Recipes Compiled from the Scientific American* (New York, 1875), 236; Mrs. Julia McNair Wright, *The Complete Home: An Encyclopaedia of Domestic Life and Affairs* (Philadelphia, 1879), 64.

6   Charles Dickens, *American Notes: A Journey* (1842; reprint, New York, 1985), 85–6; John Duffy, *The Sanitarians: A History of American Public Health* (Urbana, Ill., 1990), 71, 86–7.

cities, along with cows and pigs whose owners let them loose to graze. Efforts to ban the scavengers were politically complicated, because they consumed so much garbage and provided so much food for the poor. In smaller cities such as Memphis, hogs and cattle were not driven from public roads until the late 1880s.[7] Even where scavenger animals were banned, "swill children" toured late nineteenth-century urban neighborhoods, gathering kitchen refuse to sell to farmers for fertilizer or hog food.[8] And in factory towns like Homestead, Pennsylvania, and Manchester, New Hampshire, families continued to feed kitchen wastes to the chickens they kept well into the twentieth century.[9]

As cities grew and urban accumulations of garbage mounted, sanitary reformers both in and out of municipal governments recommended that cities either contract for or take over refuse collection instead of depending on swill children or relying on property owners to hire scavengers. Many in the sanitary reform community further demanded that citizens be required to separate their garbage, a practice now called "source separation," and one intended then as now to facilitate reuse and recycling. In New York, the well-known sanitary reformer Colonel George Waring introduced source separation in 1896, backed by forty policemen whom the mayor had assigned to the Street-Cleaning Department "to explain the separation plan to every householder and businessman and assure compliance."[10] Ashes free of organic garbage could be used for fill and street grading; clean rags and paper could be sold to paper factories.

Separated kitchen refuse might be sold to farmers for swine feed or processed to extract marketable materials. Although some large cities did experiment with sales to farmers, this approach was generally adopted by smaller towns. Farmers went to buy garbage at municipal swill yards, located at the city limits; some yards cooked the garbage to curtail vermin and disease and some towns actually operated piggeries and sold hogs for profit. Selling kitchen refuse was popular during World War I as a municipal contribution toward alleviating wartime food shortages; a few towns continued to require source separation and sell food waste as late as the 1960s.[11]

---

7 Duffy, *Sanitarians,* 146.
8 See Judith Walzer Leavitt, "The Wasteland: Garbage and Sanitary Reform in the Nineteenth-Century American City," *Journal of the History of Medicine and Allied Sciences* 35 (Oct. 1980): 431–52; C. Loring Brace, *The Dangerous Classes of New York, and Twenty Years' Work Among Them* (New York, 1872), 152.
9 See Susan Strasser, *Never Done: A History of American Housework* (New York, 1982), 28.
10 Martin Melosi, *Garbage in the Cities: Refuse, Reform, and the Environment, 1880–1980* (Chicago, 1981), 70.
11 On swine feeding, see Gerhard, *Disposal of Household Wastes,* 158, 161, 194; Melosi, *Garbage in the Cities,* 169–70; Joel Tarr, "From City to Farm: Urban Wastes and the American Farmer," *Agricultural History* 49 (Oct. 1975): 602.

Another alternative that provided for reuse of separated kitchen refuse was a garbage treatment method known as reduction, invented in Europe. Giant pressure cookers extracted fertilizer, grease, and a smaller amount of ammonia and glue.[12] Advocates of the process, including Waring in New York, downplayed the expense of the imported machines and the terrible odors they produced, but opponents elsewhere emphasized them. In Milwaukee, the three hundred "solid representative business men" of the West Side Anti-Stench Committee succeeded in shutting down a costly reduction plant a year after it opened.[13]

Despite the considerable publicity generated by Waring's work, interest in reduction waned after 1910. The process was introduced at a point when the entire ethos of reuse was in decline; the recycling and reuse practices inherent to an economy based on handcraft and household production were giving way to urbanization and industrialization.[14] Fewer people kept livestock or tended gardens. Campbell's and Franco-American sold soup in cans. Sanitary reformers did away with scavenger pigs. The giant modern meat packers produced and sold enough by-products to put an end to house-to-house bone collections. The decline in household reuse contributed to the mounting piles of municipal trash, a phenomenon bolstered also by the substantial population increase during the decades around the turn of the twentieth century and the increasing availability of more goods at prices that the masses of working people could afford. Food refuse, once habitually reused, became the most volatile component of municipal solid waste, the smelly stuff that attracted vermin.

II

By the early 1920s, when engineers in a number of cities began conducting experiments on grinding municipal garbage so it could be put through sewer systems, food waste had become simply something to get rid of, a problem best left to technical experts.[15] The domestic garbage grinder required no additional conceptual leap, and its invention soon engaged engineers in both the public and private sectors. General Electric (GE)

---

12 On reduction, see Melosi, *Garbage in the Cities*, 176–81, 217; Leavitt, "The Wasteland," 436ff; John McGaw Woodbury, "The Wastes of a Great City," *Scribner's*, Oct. 1903, 394–5; George E. Waring Jr., "The Utilization of City Garbage," *Cosmopolitan Magazine*, Feb. 1898, 408–11.

13 Leavitt, "The Wasteland," 437.

14 For a discussion of this decline, see Strasser, *Waste and Want*.

15 On early experiments with municipal grinders, see Suellen Hoy, "The Garbage Disposer, the Public Health, and the Good Life," in Marcel C. LaFollette and Jeffrey K. Stine, eds., *Technology and Choice: Readings from Technology and Culture* (Chicago, 1991), 140.

began selling the "Disposall" in 1935, the same year that John Hammes of Racine, Wisconsin, received a patent for his "In-Sink-Erator."[16]

The GE product, the outcome of a six-year research and development process, soon received attention in the popular press. *Scientific American* immediately took note of the new technology, suggesting that the appliance would send the garbage can to oblivion, like the ash can before it. Three years later, the posh *House and Garden* introduced the disposer along with other recent advances in domestic garbage technology. Products pictured ranged from rubber plate scrapers and waxed bags for lining garbage pails ("they would really be a bargain at any price") to a built-in incinerator with a receiving hopper in the kitchen. The highest kudos went to the "spectacular" disposer. "The engineers have done it again," the article declared, "turning out an appliance that will do what is seemingly impossible, and do it well."[17]

Unlike rubber scrapers or waxed bags, the garbage disposer could not be marketed without the cooperation of individual municipalities and their sewer departments, all over the country. It emptied private trash directly into public sewers, echoing the much earlier water closet, but representing a radical departure for nonbodily wastes. The disposer joined garbage to the public realm as soon as it left the kitchen, bypassing the marginal spaces – the literal, spatial interface between the public and the private – that are generally so important in the storage and sorting of waste. At the curb or in the alley, household refuse retains its identification with the household where it originates. At the same time, it becomes both public matter, available for others to claim or reclaim, and *a* public matter, a topic of public debate, a problem to be solved by public means.[18] Grinding food waste into particles too small for reclamation, the disposer took it straight into the public sewers.

Sanitary engineers, however, were not so sure that the particles were small enough. Morris M. Cohn, an engineer for the city of Schenectady who worked with GE in developing the disposer, set out to convince his

---

16 According to an In-Sink-Erator representative, Hammes invented his disposer in 1927, was issued patent no. 2012686 on August 27, 1935, and began manufacturing during the late 1930s. (Telephone conversation with the author, Jan. 28, 1993.) On GE research and development, see Hoy, "The Garbage Disposer," 141–2.

17 "Home Garbage Grinder," *Scientific American,* Sept. 1935, 145. "Good Riddance," *House and Garden,* Feb. 1938, 56–7, 63.

18 Mary Douglas calls attention to separating the clean from the unclean in *Purity and Danger: An Analysis of Concepts of Pollution and Taboo* (London, 1966); on margins and boundaries – of the body and, by analogy, of the household and the city – as locations for the rituals associated with this sorting process, see 114–28.

colleagues in other cities to support the introduction of ground garbage into their sewers. Cohn had first met engineers from the company's Schenectady works in 1929, when they had gone to him wanting to know "what sewage looked like." In the fall of 1934, before the Disposall was marketed, he published two articles in *Municipal Sanitation* extolling the device. Over the next twenty years, Cohn (eventually the Schenectady city manager) wrote numerous articles supporting the garbage disposer, published in a variety of municipal sewage and plumbing industry journals.[19]

Other public health officials debated with Cohn in those magazines, arguing that ground garbage from disposers would overload sewer systems and treatment plants. Moreover, they moved to forbid the devices in their municipalities. Many cities did ban them, including (as of 1949) New York, New Haven, Philadelphia, Miami, and most municipalities in the state of New Jersey; New York City finally legalized them in 1997.[20] When *Consumer Reports* ran its first disposer article in 1959, it commented that some readers might never have seen one as a result of municipal prohibitions. But other towns, including Denver, Detroit, and Columbus, had passed legislation *requiring* the device. Most such laws involved only new construction, but some municipalities even mandated retrofitting existing structures, in an attempt to establish less frequent trash collection and decrease municipal labor costs.[21]

Naturally, manufacturers feared the effect of prohibitions on sales and welcomed the explicit attempts to make consumption mandatory.[22] Direct lobbying would have been expensive because of the many municipalities to be converted to the disposer idea, but public relations materials could help to win converts and create activists. Women's magazine articles, which relied on such materials, expressed opinions on municipal regulations as well as extolling the benefits of the disposer. In 1949, *House Beautiful* and *Better*

19 On Cohn, see Hoy, "The Garbage Disposer," 140–4.
20 See the list for 1949 in "What You Need to Know About Garbage Disposers," *House Beautiful*, Feb. 1949, 84. In May of 1995, the New York City Council held hearings on a bill to lift the prohibition; in August, a Council committee approved a 21–month pilot program testing the disposer in about 500 homes. See David Firestone, "To Toss or Grind in New York: Disposal Reconsidered," *New York Times*, May 6, 1995, 21, 25; Jonathan P. Hicks, "Council Panel Backs Testing of Disposals," *New York Times*, Aug. 30, 1995, B1, B4; Patricia Leigh Brown, "New York Grind," *New York Times*, Oct. 9, 1997, F1, F15.
21 See Hoy, "The Garbage Disposer," esp. 149–58. See also "Food-Waste Disposers," *Consumer Reports*, Aug. 1959, 418–24; Frances Meyer, "What a Waste Disposer Can Mean to You," *Better Homes & Gardens*, Aug. 1949, 93–5, 117; "What You Need to Know About Garbage Disposers," 84–85, 140–141; Sylvia Wright, "No More Garbage in this Town," *McCall's*, Aug. 1950, 86, 91.
22 The strategy of promoting mandatory consumption was later used for marketing smoke detectors. See Jagdish Sheth, "Winning Again in the Marketplace: Nine Strategies for Revitalizing Mature Products," *Journal of Consumer Marketing* 1 (1984): 21.

Homes & Gardens both stated bluntly that the prohibiting statutes were antiquated; *House Beautiful* mentioned two towns where disposers were encouraged.

The next year, *McCall's* told the story of Jasper, Indiana, a town that had long required residents to separate food waste from trash and sold it for hog feed. After a swine cholera outbreak and a polio epidemic, and after considerable debate, the city in 1950 discontinued garbage collection, prohibited the storage of food waste in outside cans, and awarded a contract to General Electric for supplying Jasper homes with Disposalls. "Jasper is the first town in the world," *McCall's* maintained, "to banish that unsavory, unhealthy relic of the dark ages – the garbage can."[23]

The magazines described public action on disposer regulations in hyperbolic terms. "As word has gone abroad of the new era in Jasper," *McCall's* claimed, "American women everywhere are saying to themselves, to their husbands, to their women's clubs and to their city fathers, 'If Jasper, Indiana, can get rid of garbage cans, why can't we too?'" *American Home* was in accord about the potential for grass-roots action. "Any woman who has ever enjoyed the luxury of flushing food wastes, bones and all, down the sink drain, is never quite willing to be without a garbage disposer again," it declared in 1954. "If she moves into a neighborhood where old-hat building ordinances won't permit garbage disposers to empty into city sewer lines, the chances are you'll find her joining up in local politics to try to get the regulations changed – as they have been in hundreds of communities."[24] There is no evidence that such articles actually inspired women to mount local campaigns in favor of disposers, but they probably motivated support in communities where officials were considering the issue.

These articles in the women's magazines were surrounded by advertisements for food and cleaning products, not garbage disposers. Likewise, handyman magazines, which discussed disposers in slightly more technical terms but did not go so far as to offer instructions for installation, juxtaposed those articles with ads for tools and guns.[25] The magazines thus

23 Sylvia Wright, "No More Garbage in this Town," *McCall's,* Aug. 1950, 86, 91; Meyer, "What a Waste Disposer Can Mean to You," 93–5, 117; "What You Need to Know About Garbage Disposers," *House Beautiful,* Feb. 1949, 84–5, 140–1; see also Helen W. Kendall, "Disposing of Kitchen Waste," *Good Housekeeping,* Mar. 1950, 164–5; on Jasper, see Hoy, "The Garbage Disposer," 149–58.

24 Edith Ramsay and Hubbard H. Cobb, "Disposers and Incinerators," *American Home,* Sept. 1954, 83.

25 See, for example, Herbert O. Johansen, "The Controversial Garbage Disposer," *Popular Science,* June 1959, 146–8, 218; Steven J. Howard, "What You Should Know About Garbage Disposers Before You Buy One," *Popular Mechanics,* May 1970, 156–9. Installation instructions did appear during the 1980s, when disposers were more widespread. See Merle Henkenius, "Replace a Kitchen Disposer," *Workbench,* Nov.-Dec. 1987, 82; Steven Willson, "How to Install a Waste Disposer," *Popular Mechanics,* Apr. 1986, 139–42.

reflected the fact that few consumers made purchase decisions about dis-posers; like the California housewife previously quoted, many people owned them only because they came with the house. Instead, businessmen – builders, plumbers, electrical appliance dealers, and the new kitchen remod-eling specialists – were the targets of disposer marketing campaigns. Manu-facturers purchased advertising space in plumbing, building, and electrical appliance trade journals, especially to accompany major articles about garbage disposers. Besides trade magazine advertising, disposer marketing emphasized personal appeals from sales forces, who provided the plumbing contractors and appliance salesmen with "dealer helps" like demonstration models with transparent chambers.[26]

The occasional consumer ad might itself be advertised to the trade. In July 1963, for example, In-Sink-Erator bought a page in a special issue of *House & Garden* "devoted to the man of the house." But attracting consumers was not the advertisement's major purpose. That same month, it was reproduced on one of the two pages that In-Sink-Erator purchased in *Domestic Engineering*, a plumbing trade journal. The metaad, headlined "Over 5,000,000 Prospects Get the In-Sink-Erator Idea," claimed that the *House & Garden* ad would draw "upper income" customers to plumbers who sold In-Sink-Erators.[27] Thus reprinted, the consumer ad advanced a program to attract and hold distributors that enabled this small company with one product line to compete with General Electric, Westinghouse, and Sears.

From the beginning, In-Sink-Erator had sold only through master plumbers. The company attracted attention in the plumbing trade press with design features that plumbers would particularly appreciate. A system of expandable and interchangeable parts, for example, simplified installation in kitchen sinks with a range of drain openings. In 1960, the company established a formal system of authorized dealerships and more than quadru-pled its sales force; by 1961, thirty-five salesmen serviced thirty-seven hun-dred plumbers around the country. The salesman evaluated the plumber and his business, equipped him with promotional materials, and provided continuing education in disposer salesmanship. Authorized dealers were required to put up a banner and either display the merchandise or conduct a direct mail campaign.[28]

---

26 On the principles of marketing to retailers, see Susan Strasser, *Satisfaction Guaranteed: The Making of the American Mass Market* (New York, 1989), 187–202.

27 In-Sink-Erator advertisement, *Domestic Engineering*, July 1963, 50–1.

28 "Converting Inquiries into Sales," *Sales Management*, Nov. 17, 1961, 53–6. On dealer helps, see, for example, "Getting Down to the Sales Floor . . . With Disposers," *Merchandising Week*, Oct. 2, 1972, 31. On authorized dealerships, see Strasser, *Satisfaction Guaranteed*, 79, 87.

Ambitious plumbers were encouraged to sell the disposer not as a separate appliance, but as an essential component of the modern American
home. Plumbers, second only to the builders of postwar housing as disposer
salesmen,[29] might use the appliance as an element in the expansion of their
services from replacing leaky pipes to remodeling lackluster kitchens. The
sales pitch could be part of an argument for remodeling, a service that both
builders and plumbers might provide. Most middle-class American houses
had basic plumbing and electric and gas appliances before World War II; to
older houses, the economic expansion of the 1950s and 1960s introduced
replacement appliances, often as part of remodeled kitchens. Freestanding
white stoves and refrigerators were to be replaced with color-coordinated
appliances designed to be built into cabinets and counters as part of overall
kitchen designs.[30] A 1954 plumbing trade journal profiled Arthur Weil, a
Chicago plumbing and heating contractor who called the garbage disposer
a "perfect door opener" to a remodeling contract. "I always start with the
disposer," Weil said; "then I sell up from there." People who would not lis-
ten to a sales pitch for a dishwasher or a new stove might consider a disposer, which cost far less. "But here is the hooker," Weil explained. "Once
they have bought the *idea* of a disposer they have bought the *idea* of a whole
new kitchen. The whole idea of a real, complete modern kitchen takes hold
of them and then anything can happen. The disposer really is the key to
unlocking their imagination and their pocketbook."[31] Like other appliances, disposers were even eligible for loans from the Federal Housing
Administration, which set standards for design and installation, another
arena of disposer-related public policy.[32]

Disposers were frequently promoted jointly with dishwashers, the other
kitchen appliance being newly introduced into households that already
used electric and gas ranges and refrigerators. Dishwashers and disposers
were usually connected literally, hooked up so that the dishwasher would
drain through the disposer; or they were paired in "electric sinks," free-

29 In 1959, *Electrical Merchandising* published differing estimates of the distribution channels from industry spokesmen, who estimated that builders sold 40–53 percent of disposers, plumbers 25–50 percent, electrical appliance dealers 7–15 percent, and kitchen specialists up to 15 percent. See "Disposers and Incinerators," *Electrical Merchandising,* Jan. 1959, 88.
30 On kitchen remodeling, see Arthur J. Pulos, *The American Design Adventure, 1940–1975* (Cambridge, 1988), 130–9, and the many articles in *House Beautiful*'s special kitchen issue (June 1957).
31 "The Kitchen Appliance with the 1–2 Punch," *Domestic Engineering,* Oct. 1954.
32 "Food-Waste Disposers," 418–24. See also Virginia T. Habeeb, "What You Want to Know About
   Garbage Disposers," *American Home,* Aug. 1961, 81. On FHA standards, see "The Food Waste Disposer and the Septic Tank: Can They Live in Peace?" *Domestic Engineering,* July 1963, 61. On the
   importance of this kind of government regulation, and the relationship between consumption and
   the state, see George Lipsitz's chapter in this book.

standing appliances on the market during the early 1950s, which combined sink, undersink storage, dishwasher, disposer, and counter space.[33] *Good Housekeeping* published a five-page buying guide for dishwashers and disposers in 1956, declaring that the two were "obviously" partners.[34] But five years later, the magazine was still reassuring its readers that the two appliances could be used together and that with proper installation, the disposer would not back up into the dishwasher.[35]

Trade journals likewise promoted the disposer–dishwasher connection without giving dealers the wherewithal to interpret it to consumers. "For More Profit, Sell Dishwashers and Disposers as a Working Team," *Electrical Merchandising Week* urged in 1962. But the text said nothing about how the appliances functioned as a "team"; instead, it exhorted dealers to promote disposers even though they were less glamorous and less profitable than dishwashers.[36] In 1968, an electric appliance trade journal contended that consumers did not see what was obvious about the connection. Quoting marketing executives from Waste King, it suggested that the tie-in was beneficial to dealers, who saved time by installing the two appliances at the same time and might or might not pass on the monetary savings to their customers.[37] Finally in 1972, when the disposer and the dishwasher were both common enough to have engendered new household habits, an article aimed at the trade articulated the connection from the consumer's standpoint by considering the work process. "Demonstrating to the new dishwasher owner the smooth motion flow of from-table-to-sink/disposer-to-dishwasher can go a long way toward convincing her that the dual package purchase is her best buy," the article advised.[38]

The "smooth motion flow" was one version of "convenience," a term used in advertising and in marketing literature to cover a multitude of positive attributes, especially savings in labor and time, and freedom from attention, care, and responsibility. Like other postwar appliances and consumer goods, disposers fostered new habits that saved some work and time, if not as much as washing machines, dishwashers, or prepared foods. They allowed

---

33 See Habeeb, "About Garbage Disposers," 81; Virginia T. Habeeb, "What You Should Know About the New Electric Sinks," *Parents,* Mar. 1953, 56, 149–50; see also Kendall, "Disposing of Kitchen Waste," 164–5.
34 "Dishwashers and Garbage-Disposal Units," *Good Housekeeping,* Mar. 1956, 104.
35 "The Truth about Garbage Disposers," *Good Housekeeping,* Apr. 1961, 145.
36 "For More Profit, Sell Dishwashers and Disposers as a Working Team," *Electrical Merchandising Week,* Oct. 1, 1962, 31.
37 "Food Waste Disposers: A Manufacturer's Marketing Team Pinpoints Merchandising Potentials and Pitfalls for Appliance Dealers and Department Stores," *Merchandising Week,* July 1, 1968, 23.
38 "Getting Down to the Sales Floor," 31.

food preparation to be done at the sink without attention to keeping drains clear. In 1950, when few of its readers had ever seen a disposer, *Good House-keeping* described "A New Experience":

You'll have no further use for a sink strainer, and your sink will be clean every minute of the day. You'll change your habits in preparing fruit and vegetables, too, for instead of collecting parings and pits on paper, you work right over the sink . . . . Clearing the table is different, too. At first, it may seem strange to scrape chicken bones, gravy, baked-potato shells, etc., into the sink instead of into the garbage can. But what an easy way to get rid of them![39]

The contrast with Lydia Maria Child and Catharine Beecher, exhorting nineteenth-century readers to pick suitable morsels off the plates to serve again, is evident; even the family dog and cat now ate commercial pet food. Yet Beecher, an advocate of both up-to-date technology and "habits of system and order," would surely have appreciated the "smooth motion flow of from-table-to-sink/disposer-to-dishwasher" that the new appliances encouraged.

For women who had never used disposers, probably the most attractive phrase in this description was "your sink will be clean every minute of the day." *Consumer Reports* was explicit about cleanliness in its first disposer article. "There should be no garbage cans to clean out, no paper bags full of wet coffee grounds to break open, no odors to attract flies," the magazine's first disposer article explained. "Since a good disposer cleans itself out automatically, there should be no garbage odors at all in your kitchen."[40] A Jasper resident, quoted in a plumbing trade journal more than a decade after his town had done away with garbage cans, complained about life in the outside world: "Every time you want to add to the garbage you have to lift the lid – and out come those nauseous odors. Ugh!"[41] In the alley, cleanliness went beyond odor. *Consumers' Research Bulletin*, rating disposers in 1949, declared that the appliance's greatest fans were homeowners "living in sections where garbage collections were infrequent, as the appliances greatly reduced the problem of rats feeding on decaying garbage."[42]

Clean, odor-free kitchens were a goal of early twentieth-century home economists, but achieving them without considerable labor or hired help required fixtures and appliances not found in most American households until well after World War II. An electric appliance trade journal explained in 1972 that the disposer was but one element in a panoply of up-to-date

39 Kendall, "Disposing of Kitchen Waste," 165.   40 "Food-Waste Disposers," 418.
41 "Meet Mrs. America," 64–7.
42 "Garbage Disposal Units," *Consumers' Research Bulletin,* Feb. 1949, 7.

appliances that made the ideal of the antiseptic kitchen attainable. "The salesman should capitalize on the 'clean kitchen' theme in selling the disposer," the article asserted. "Self-cleaning ranges, self-defrosting refrigerators and 'sparkling' clean dishwashers have all filled a need while making the consumer ultraconscious of 'clean' as a way of living."[43]

The counterpart to this "ultraconsciousness" was the assignment of food waste to an unconscious realm. A century earlier, Americans were not so squeamish about their garbage. They were accustomed to bad odors: They relieved themselves in chamber pots and outdoor privies, and their streets stank from the carcasses of dead horses and the manure of live ones.[44] The disposer turned kitchen refuse, once valuable, into sewage. Like human excrement, it would go down the drain, eliminated from the tasks of daily life and removed from most people's attention. Water would serve as a purifier, and the municipal sewer would act as a servant, sparing the kitchen worker from contact with smelly garbage.

But the kitchen worker was never necessarily the garbage worker. As *Better Homes & Gardens* put it in 1949, "Husbands, too, have opinions on the subject. The most typical comment: 'I was the one elected to take out the garbage every day. Our disposer saves me lots of trouble.'"[45] Indeed, according to at least one study, the device saved labor for men by shifting garbage tasks to women. In ninety-nine Boston families studied during the late 1960s, wives took substantially more responsibility for garbage in the households that owned disposers.[46] This was not, however, the version of household life being sold with the disposer. The *House & Garden* ad that In-Sink-Erator reprinted for the plumbing trade showed a smiling husband holding a disposer behind his back. "Darling . . . you're much too nice to be a garbage collector," the caption read. "K.P. is O.K. for GI's, but not my loving wife . . ." This adman's vision of a housewife's fantasy bore little relation to negotiations about consumption expenditures, nor to the division of labor in many households.[47] In fact, many women did not take out the garbage, but delegated the task to husbands, who could now demonstrate their love by saving themselves a trip to the trash can.

---

43 "Getting Down to the Sales Floor," 31.
44 On horse pollution, see Joel A. Tarr, "Urban Pollution – Many Long Years Ago," *American Heritage,* Oct. 1971, 65–9, 106.
45 Meyer, "What a Waste Disposer Can Mean to You," 94.
46 Charles A. Thrall, "Conservative Use of Modern Household Technology," *Technology and Culture* 23 (Apr. 1982): 175–94.
47 For a discussion of household negotiation about consumption, see Susan Porter Benson's chapter in this book. Benson discusses a different class context and a different time period, but her findings are more generally suggestive about the negotiation process.

Children, too, had often been enlisted to take out the garbage. *Electrical Merchandising*, declaring disposers to be the enemies of psychiatrists, proposed in 1962 that dealers could "sell family harmony." Children assigned to do the dishes and take out the garbage not only griped and revolted, the magazine suggested, but entered "into prolonged sibling conflict, into planned disobedience 'to get even.'" University studies showed that children with dishwashers and disposers "'took more interest . . . had a great pride of ownership.' As products of the machine age they resented the stone-age methods of dishwashing and garbage disposing assigned to them."[48]

In short, as *House Beautiful* wrote in its first disposer article in 1949, "The garbage can is a symbol of the past."[49] This was surely an exaggeration, but the disposer *was* a symbol of the future and the up-to-date present. Even in 1943, when few women had ever seen a disposer and war production kept them out of sight, 80 percent of more than ten thousand women who participated in a *McCall's* essay contest about their "Kitchen of Tomorrow" expressed interest in the appliance. Farm women constituted the major exception; they were "not enthusiastic about feeding an 'electric pig.'"[50]

Modernity was also a fundamental issue in the controversy over garbage in the sewers. Even *Consumer Reports*, not always a supporter of new technologies, commented that some municipal officials were simply afraid of the new. Why was this device to be found in so few homes after twenty-five years on the market? the magazine asked in 1959. "For one thing, the record shows that the very concept of pulverizing garbage and flushing it down the drain was upsetting at first," the article explained. Some city fathers had overreacted. Especially in the populous Northeast, authorities continued to be "concerned about antiquated plumbing lines, overtaxed sewage systems, and possibly undersized sewage-treatment plants." But elsewhere, the magazine contended, officials were impressed by the results of experiments like the one in Jasper, and in some cities the device was even required.[51]

Modernity carried with it the commitment to stay modern, by replacing aging garbage disposers with the latest models. Although disposers were still considered luxuries in 1961,[52] those who owned them were being urged to

48 "Build Customer Enthusiasm with the Use-Value Story," *Electrical Merchandising,* Oct. 1, 1962, 29. The article maintained that dishwashers had a special role to play in promoting family harmony, because men "reacted with a 'loss-of-manhood' guilt" when asked to do women's work, but could now take "the traditional place of a male operating an automatic machine."
49 "What You Need to Know About Garbage Disposers," 84.
50 *McCall's* Magazine, *What Women Want in Their Kitchens of Tomorrow* (New York, 1944), 11, 129.
51 "Food-Waste Disposers," 418–24.
52 See Habeeb, "About Garbage Disposers," 79.

discard them in favor of new ones. In this sense, the marketing of the garbage disposer, like that of so many other household appliances, embodies the ideals of "progressive obsolescence" formulated by Christine Frederick on the eve of the Great Depression and described by her as the source of America's "triumphs and rapidity of progress." Frederick defined the concept to encompass three characteristics: a suggestible state of mind open to new styles, inventions, and life-styles; a "readiness to 'scrap' or lay aside an article *before its natural life of usefulness is completed,* in order to make way for the newer and better thing"; and a willingness to spend a large part of income on buying things "even if it pinches savings." The growth of markets in new products, in other words, depended on getting rid of old things. "Buying plenty of new goods before the old wears out," Frederick wrote, "increases the general income."[53]

Obsolescence was fostered by improved disposers, faster and quieter than the earlier ones. In 1958, when about 8.5 percent of American houses had disposers,[54] marketing executives at the Waste King Corporation decided that the market could support a superdeluxe garbage disposer. They introduced the "Imperial Hush" model, the only machine to merit *Consumer Reports*'s check rating in its first disposer story the next year and, at $129.95, at least $30.00 more expensive than any other.[55] "There was no longer a need to feature disposers at a low price to create acceptance from a skeptical public," *Electrical Merchandising* reported. "The advantages of disposers are known, even to most people who do not yet have them." Most important, a replacement market had developed. Homeowners who were ready for their second garbage disposer "would be conscious of the limitations of earlier and cheaper units" and "receptive to . . . a disposer that would dispose more, better and quieter."[56]

Replacement disposer sales "for the first time produce[d] meaningful figures" in *Electrical Merchandising*'s Replacement and Trade-In Survey in 1958.[57] Four years later, "How to Sell More Dishwashers and Disposers" proposed that aging housing developments provided enough of a potential market for replacement disposers to make neighborhood canvassing profitable. "Deliver special circulars to post-1946 homes," the article suggested, "with a special trade in offer on old dishwashers and disposers. Offer [a] gift

53 Christine Frederick, *Selling Mrs. Consumer* (New York, 1929), 246, 250–1. On Frederick and progressive obsolescence, see also Roland Marchand, *Advertising the American Dream: Making Way for Modernity* (Berkeley, Calif., 1985), 156–60.
54 "Disposers and Incinerators," 88.   55 "Food-Waste Disposers," 418–24.
56 "Disposers: Selling Up," *Electrical Merchandising,* Sept. 1958, 88.
57 "Disposers and Incinerators," 89.

for coming to [your] store to see modern dishwashers (describe features) and *quiet* disposers."[58] Replacement represented more than 40 percent of sales in 1965, and estimates for 1971 ranged from 40 percent to more than 60 percent.[59]

The trade press did not discuss what should happen to old garbage disposers when they were replaced. Decades before, the question had been debated in *Electrical Merchandising* with respect to major appliances. In 1928, the magazine described a Pittsburgh appliance dealer who completely restored, reconditioned, and sold about half the washing machines he took in trade, dismantling the rest for parts. During several years in the late 1930s, it discussed the formation of markets in used radios, washers, and refrigerators and the issues they raised: what should be junked and what reconditioned, how much to give for a trade-in to prevent losing the sale, the high costs of trade-ins, and the kinds of guarantees that should be offered.[60] But by the time the replacement market developed in garbage disposers, there was little debate. Few appliance dealers took trade-ins even for washers and refrigerators; the market for used appliances was conducted through junk dealers and newspaper advertisements. Disposers themselves had become disposable: Used garbage disposers were to be junked. Costing substantially less than major appliances, they were not considered to be worth reuse; nobody knew or wanted to know how to remodel or fix them.

III

The new ecological consciousness of the late 1960s and early 1970s added another consideration – water pollution – to the critique of the garbage disposer, which before then had emphasized sewer capacity. In September 1970, *Merchandising Week* commented on "the growth of anti-disposer feeling among ecologists and other consumers, who feel that emptying disposer wastes into the sewage systems is a large factor in water pollution." As a result, the number of cities with prohibitions had "grown sharply," the magazine reported, although in fact most of the cities it mentioned had prohib-

58 "How to Sell More Dishwashers and Disposers," *Electrical Merchandising Week,* Oct. 1, 1962, 36.
59 "Retail Sales Lift for Disposers Will Come from New NEMA Section," *Merchandising Week,* Feb. 14, 1966, 8; Cathy Ciccolella, "Replacement Market Boosts Disposer Sales," *Merchandising Week,* Feb. 8, 1971, 1.
60 See the following articles in *Electrical Merchandising*: "We Can't Afford to Junk Trade-Ins," July 1928, 60–61, 84; "Do Trade-Ins Work?" Mar. 1936, 31–2; 'We're in the Junk Business," Oct. 1937, 2–3, 29; "The Rising Tide of Trade-Ins," Dec. 1937; "Trade-Ins Again," Feb. 1938, 100; Sam Farnsworth, "Trade-In-Tragedy," Mar. 1938, 22, 89.

ited the appliance for years. Other municipalities continued to pass laws requiring disposers, it told its readership of electrical appliance dealers.[61]

Two years later, in "Getting Down to the Sales Floor ... with Disposers," the magazine attempted to address consumers' concerns directly. The salesman "will find himself able to tell a story that fits in, most appropriately, with the ecological and environmental stresses that are uppermost in most consumer thoughts today," it stated optimistically. A sidebar entitled "Selling Points" echoed the main article: "As in apropose [*sic*] in the '70s, a good sales pitch for the disposers can be made on ecological grounds. Don't ignore this argument because your customers have been made exceptionally environmentally aware by the news media." But these exhortations were the article's only statements about disposers and the environment; nowhere on the page was the ecological story told or the argument made.[62]

Backyard gardeners further asserted that disposers sent valuable soil nutrients down the drain; in making compost, they reaffirmed the value of pea pods and apple cores.[63] Coinciding with the rebirth of recycling as a municipal-solid waste concept, composting was part of a new recognition that trash had value, not a reinstatement of an older system. Saving waste materials so that they might be reused or their value recovered became a moral act, a virtue – a matter of environmental awareness rather than of utility and common sense. In cultures based on handcraft, the stewardship of materials was a concrete element of daily life, valuing materials for the labor embodied in them and the uses to which they might be put. Now the call was for stewardship of the earth and of natural resources.

The new ethos arose from a culture of consumption, rooted in ideas and objects available decades before World War II, but constituting a major postwar transformation in American life-styles. Environmental consciousness was a response to a version of abundance based on the acquisition of appliances like garbage disposers and on the ever-increasing desire for more of them, the "idea of a real, complete modern kitchen." That way of life emphasized consuming, not producing, and it promoted casual attitudes about throwing things away. Reducing the necessity for handling both food and garbage, saving labor, promoting convenience and cleanliness, and stripping value from waste materials, the garbage disposer represents the values of the postwar American household.

61 Cathy Ciccolella, "Disposer Sales at Retail Going Down the Drain," *Merchandising Week,* Sept. 18, 1970, 22.
62 "Getting Down to the Sales Floor," 31.
63 On compost and the counterculture, see Warren J. Belasco, *Appetite for Change: How the Counterculture Took on the Food Industry, 1966–1988* (New York, 1989), 72–5, 158–61.

13

Consumer Culture in the GDR, or How the Struggle for Antimodernity Was Lost on the Battleground of Consumer Culture

INA MERKEL

Those who know me know that I have drunk lots of water and hardly any wine, not to mention vodka or cognac. I really cannot speak of a feudal life, though I could have afforded one on my salary. Every morning I had one or two rolls with butter and honey, at lunch time we were in the Central Committee building and there I had either a grilled sausage with mashed potatoes or macaroni with bacon or goulash. In the evening I stayed at home, watched a bit of television and went to bed. . . . I have to say that it was my lot in life to live modestly and thereby maintain my performance. That way I never lost contact with the people, though security guards and others often created a situation where I was separated from the masses. But I always had direct contact with the masses in spite of it.[1]

Clearly, this man did not need much to live on. He was not a pleasure seeker. He was an ascetic. But since when have people loved ascetics?

If Erich Honecker felt compelled to describe himself as a modest and unpretentious sovereign in this conversation with Reinhold Andert and Wolfgang Herzberg, he was reacting above all to a call to do away with privileges for party bureaucrats that was raised during the *Wende*.[2] In his most recent analysis of the elite of the former German Democratic Republic (GDR), Michael Bodemann found that they all claimed that they did not enjoy special privileges. But their insistence that they lived just like "normal" citizens of the GDR was more deeply rooted, and not just a current strategy for self-justification. In the cultural value system of social democrats and communists, ascetic life-styles are part of the mental tradi-

---

1 Reinhold Andert and Wolfgang Herzberg, *Der Sturz: Erich Honecker im Kreuzverhör* (Berlin, 1990), 377.
2 In English, "the turnaround," i.e., the period of events leading up to the dissolution of the GDR with the (re)unification of Germany on Oct. 3, 1990.

tion of an upwardly mobile social group within the working class. The extent to which privileged access to consumer goods found a way into everyday life is revealed in an anecdote about Egon Krenz, the former head of the Free German Youth and Honecker's successor as party chief in October 1989. Around 1987 Krenz appeared on East German television in his everyday surroundings. While sitting in his living room and chatting amiably, a remark got away from him: ". . . and then in the evening I always drink a *can* of beer [emphasis added]." This exposed him as a drinker of Western beer, since East German beer was only marketed in bottles.

When first broadcast on East German television in late 1989, the first widely circulated report about the life of Politburo members at their forested retreat near Wandlitz, which had been off-limits to the general public until then, triggered profound indignation. Actually, the petit bourgeois ambiance on display was rather ordinary: chrome-plated bathroom fittings and a Western color TV set. Compared to the life-style of Western elites, this looked ridiculous, and East German outrage over the Politburo's interior decorating was difficult to comprehend. People were upset about trivialities, by the beer can and the video recorder, by things that – and this is what started it all – came from the West. "They preached water and drank wine," people said. This did not match the party leadership's claims of egalitarianism. In a society where consumer goods often were not universally available, but restricted and distributed according to strict guidelines, a sense of moral justice had become deeply ingrained – and now it was being challenged. But something else is revealed by these vignettes: Citizens of the GDR and the leaders of the state were obviously longing for the same things. They were, at least in matters of taste, not really very far apart.

The consumer culture of East Germany cannot be viewed as simply a collection of GDR products, a self-sufficient system cut off from the world market, as the few published analyses of East German design have depicted it. The specificity of this culture was shaped by a continual East–West discourse. An inevitable comparison was the constitutive moment right from the start. Fortunately, the struggle between the systems did not take the form of armed conflict, but was rather shifted to the marketplace. And it was here, in the sphere of consumerism, where the battle was won. Two different systems of cultural values collided, and since they developed in different social contexts, they were actually incomparable. On the one hand, in the East, the idea of socialist equality with its holy trinity of work, bread, and housing was paramount. This could be traced to an older generation's need for security after having been devastated by inflation, unemployment, and World War II. On the other hand, social and cultural differentiation in the West had developed and deepened, deriving from experiences of upward mobility and postwar economic successes. Equality versus individuality? Tradition versus modernity? The vocabulary is prejudiced by the older forms of ideological confrontation.

What should be the subject of an essay that develops the study of a toppled state system's consumer culture as a set of hypotheses? Why consumer culture? What can be explained or shown by it? Consumer culture is understood as the relations of a society's individuals to a historically and geographically specific collection of things, things that appear on the market as consumer goods and that are available to be purchased, used, and consumed. Consumer culture comprises the forms in which things are acquired and used in terms of practical appropriation and symbolic communication. The mental relations that individuals form toward the objects and spaces surrounding them, and the changes these relations undergo in the biographical course of possession and use, are the starting point of this historical investigation.

Consumer culture in East Germany is indeed a wide and unexplored terrain. After the *Wende,* Western observers made their first attempts to tackle this problem. The documentary film *Flotter Osten* (Dashing East) was a compilation of advertising films, and the exhibit "SED – Schönes Einheits Design" (Socialist Unity Party – The Beauty of Design Unity) was organized. Not only do such compilations emphasize all the things about GDR society that strike West Germans as peculiar, they also reflect deeply rooted ideas about it as a "society of shortages." Experiences of scarcity are viewed as the basis for mental characteristics that were supposedly typical in East Germany, like greed, the thirst for pleasure, and a sense of entitlement. Such clichés became more firmly established during unification and symbolically converged in the banana.[3]

The term "scarcity" has been constructed from the perspective of a society shaped by consumerism and abundance. Full shop windows over here, long lines over there. But how does this shape the experiences of the residents on either side? What is perceived as a shortage and when, and what are the alternatives for action used to deal with shortages? In what kinds of daily routines and basic mental patterns is scarcity reflected? It is true that the GDR was not capable of adequately satisfying the needs of its citizens

---

3 In the opening scene of the television series "Trotzki," which was broadcast in 1993, a family in Leipzig sits watching TV. At first, father and son watch soccer, then, under general protest, the mother switches to a program on folk music. The daughter continues to change the channel and accidentally gets a news broadcast reporting on the Leipzig Monday rallies. The family's jaws drop. Cut. All four stuff bananas into their open mouths, so that symbolically their mouths are gagged.

in every case. It was not that certain things were too expensive, but that some were always in short supply or altogether absent – this had been a common experience since the 1960s. But it is incorrect to conclude that because of the limited range of consumer goods, life-styles and living conditions in East Germany were broadly undifferentiated, homogenized, or uniform. Compared with that of the Federal Republic, the apparent shabbiness, onesidedness, and cheapness of GDR consumer culture present enough material for such a theory, but this would only describe superficial phenomena. In dealing with scarcity, citizens of the GDR developed a wealth of inventions, the ability to improvise, mutually supportive behavior, patience, and frugality. One of the primary values of East German society (which is currently being nostalgically transfigured) was that basic needs should be subsidized, such as foodstuffs, housing, energy, and children's clothing.

These brief introductory remarks should indicate that the analysis of GDR consumer culture is a highly problematic and multifaceted field of inquiry that has hardly been investigated, except within the polarized framework previously mentioned. A comprehensive examination would have to involve sharpening the eye and directing attention to historical, social, and generation-specific differences within East Germans' living situations and life-styles.

First, such a study would involve the differentiation of an apparently homogeneous consumer culture. Life-styles reveal social differences in class, social standing, gender, and generation in all their cultural dimensions. Apart from the fact that in the GDR there were thoroughly class-specific social differences that are represented in different kinds of life-styles, it is also interesting to look at how cultural distinctions could have functioned in a supposedly classless and egalitarian society. Undoubtedly, differentiating characteristics such as gender and generation or city and state increase in their distinctive value, but that is also true of all modern industrial societies. We should also find a clear expression of political attitudes, social functions, and educational differences in the practices of consumption.

At this point, it is necessary to explain the importance that the Western world of consumer goods had for East Germany. Were the objects from the West simply put to use or were they deliberately used in such a way that, stripped of their original social context, they served totally different cultural functions? Under East German conditions, for example, West German hair shampoo, regardless of the brand, had such a distinctive value for certain people that empty shampoo bottles were lined up in the bathroom like icons for guests to see. Highly fashionable clothing produced in the West was another example. Some readers may recall the huge quantity of Italian raincoats (the "NATO-skins") smuggled into the GDR in the early 1960s. Wearing such clothing was ideally suited for political provocation. In the 1970s teachers could still become irate over the wearing of blue jeans. The possession of Western goods set the owner apart and helped him or her stand out in the crowd. But the opposite was also possible; one could achieve the same effect by consciously and openly refusing to wear or own consumer goods from the West.

Second, an investigation into the cultural practices of acquiring, using, and consuming goods might provide us with information about the historical transformation of specific basic mental patterns and conditions. In this respect, we should avoid a consumer-positivist approach, and our questions should not be restricted to indicators of an improvement in living standards, or per capita consumption, or the degree to which consumers are supplied with the latest consumer goods. Instead, we should focus on changes in primary attitudes. With respect to the analysis of East German consumer culture, we must give special consideration to the specific admixture of existing mental traditions and new attitudes toward consuming. Such a consumer culture can only be reconstructed as a collage of elements with different historical origins, different concepts of aesthetic composition, and contradictory political programs to satisfy primary needs.

The two analytical directions previously sketched aim to reconstruct the social practice of consumption and therefore take place on the level of experience or everyday life. Before attempting to understand something about mental structures from an analysis of specific sources, I briefly outline the theoretical background of the political strategies and orientations that, ideologically mediated, were also contested in the field of consumer culture.

CONSUMER IDEALS IN THE ABSENCE OF CLASS AND SOCIAL STATUS

The class enemy wants to do us harm by trying to direct the needs of the population toward the so-called American life-style. In reality, this American life-style is nothing but a life of luxury for the few, paid for by the majority, who squander the material values that working people have created.

We want all working people to live in prosperity, and working women especially to be liberated from time-consuming household work as much as possible. That is why we also advocate the opening of many more Laundromats.

Sometimes we also have to deal with customers who already want to live in a way that will only be possible once West German militarism has been subdued, once the seven-year plan has been fulfilled, and once socialism has been victorious.

To them, we say: If you want to buy more, you have to produce more. If you want quality goods, you will have to do quality work.[4]

This short text contains the most important elements of public negotiations over the population's needs: The ideal of a better society is constructed in terms of the comparison with Western consumer society, which has the distinct disadvantage of excluding certain social groups from consumerism. Concepts of equality that regard the distribution of socially produced wealth as being independent of class, social position, education, and achievement are also fundamental ideals of communism: "To each according to his needs." Under the conditions of classlessness, consumerism as symbolic capital would no longer make sense. Only those items that were really needed would be available for consumption. Things are reduced, even in their aesthetic form, to their use value. From this ideal perspective, luxury appears to be doubly negative. It excludes the working masses from enjoyment and creativity; labor and material are wasted in the production of such luxury goods.

Under postwar conditions, however, the communist ideal underwent some changes. As a goal of existence, communism receded into the distance, something Bertolt Brecht spoke of as the "troubles of the plains." A slogan from the 1950s, "[t]he way we work today is the way we will live tomorrow," required the working class to forgo consumerism for a relatively long period, and this while neighboring West Germany was enjoying an economic boom in clear view of all East Germans. A conflict of interests resulted that was so strong and pervasive that it not only endangered social peace but also forced the party leadership to revise constantly its plans for economic reform.[5] The economic reform of the early 1960s, the New Economic System (*Neues Ökonomisches System* or NÖS), failed not merely because of the economic and political demands of the Soviet Union but primarily because of working people's resistance, whereby they more or less successfully demanded higher salaries and more stable prices across the board.

The socialist utopia intended to create an alternative society in direct competition with the West: equality instead of social diversity, and commu-

4 Submitted to the East German politburo on Sept. 16, 1961; source: Stiftung Archiv der Parteien und Massenorganisationen der DDR im Bundesarchiv, Berlin (hereafter SAPMO-BArch), DY 30/IV 2/610/14.
5 See André Steiner's chapter in this book.

nity or collectivity instead of privatism. It was based on the experiences of poverty among the working class and peasants during the economic depression of the 1930s and the war years of the 1940s. But instead of increased poverty and visible exploitation, postwar development gave the capitalist countries enormous (and unexpected) prosperity, with a visible increase in affluence among the population. Yet the political elite in the East did not understand the change in capitalist societies and clung to old-fashioned ideals.

The building of a new society was difficult because industry in what had been the middle part of Germany had been largely destroyed or dismantled; reparations to the Soviets had to be paid, and, as a result of disproportional prewar development, the government was forced to focus on reestablishing mining and heavy industry. For many years, textiles and industries that made consumer goods were neglected. For decades, shortages of household goods – from washing machines to refrigerators to clothing – were in fact preprogrammed. An ambivalent, but for the most part restrictive, middle-class policy took care of the rest. In contrast, the Federal Republic was supported and financially subsidized by the United States. The result was the so-called economic miracle of the 1950s, when almost overnight empty shops were filled with an abundance of consumer goods. Yet workers in the West held political demonstrations as employment rates fluctuated. How one evaluated the situation depended on one's point of view: Either side could point to certain criteria and feel superior. The West pointed to consumer opportunities; the East, to high employment and social welfare programs.

Fixated on creating social security and aided by an ongoing rise in prosperity, party leaders in the GDR could be assured of popular support. Both the leadership and the people shared the same idea of what prosperity meant, for example, the increased consumption of butter and meat, and of what modernization meant, for example, an increase in the per capita number of refrigerators, televisions, and automobiles. Frugality, patience, and orderliness were all traditional virtues that were celebrated equally on all sides. This consensus was reached by a generation that, on the basis of shared experiences of need and scarcity, could agree on modest prosperity and social security despite differences in their postwar careers, that is, upward or downward social mobility. This generation agreed to postpone pleasure seeking and laissez-faire tendencies, and this agreement was often expressed in anti-American terms. Such an initial consensus was extremely stabilizing, even under difficult circumstances (e.g., ongoing supply crises) when the population threatened to strike or to refuse to vote.

Because consumer goods are conveyed to individuals through the market, the relation between public and private is also reflected in consumer culture. One of the distinguishing features of East German history is that supplying the population and satisfying basic requirements were both seen as top political priorities and constantly debated in public. The programs for Politburo meetings and party congress debates referred to the "constant improvement in the satisfaction of material, cultural, and intellectual needs." Catching up to Western societies and overtaking them in the competition to improve living standards would once and for all prove the superiority of socialist democracy and its planned economic order.

Competition between the two systems was directly addressed and visible to everyone in the marketplace. In this way, consumer culture takes on another symbolic dimension. It becomes an important means of rating the differences and cultural aspects of the two systems.

It is possible to distinguish discrete historical phases in the GDR's relationship to the West and in its relationship to the growing needs and sense of entitlement of its own citizens. The original ideal of providing for basic needs in a way that was not only adequate but more rational and progressive gradually gave way. When the first boutiques and specialty shops (*Exquisitläden*) opened, the event reflected a new attitude toward consumption.[6] When Honecker came to power, the *Intershops* were also opened to the general East German population, and new delicatessens (*Delikatläden*), selling Western chocolate for East German currency, were established.[7] These measures not only recognized growing popular discontent; they also meant that the government had abandoned its attempt to create an antimodern project.

Those who believed in communist ideals were not concerned with producing more and better refrigerators and televisions, even if these were precisely the criteria by which the people measured the success or failure of public policy; rather, they sought alternatives to limitless consumption, the throw-away society, and consumerism as compensation for boredom. Despite having contrasting or competing aesthetic ideas, the party leadership and the avant-garde intellectual elite shared the antimodern project as a common point of departure.[8] They each wanted what was "best for the

6 At first these shops sold only one-of-a-kind clothing from trade fairs. They later sold clothes made in Paris or London in limited numbers and for astronomical prices.
7 Intershops sold goods for foreign currency. Originally meant for travelers in transit and Western foreigners, these shops were opened to citizens of the GDR with Western currency after 1973. Western currencies eventually functioned as a second currency within East Germany.
8 Bauhaus competed with a minimalist petit bourgeois standard once the idea of bourgeois luxury for the worker had to be withdrawn for economic reasons.

worker." In the late 1950s, opening remarks by a ministry functionary at a conference on standardization, which would become a key concept of the 1960s reform efforts, characterized precisely contemporary discourse:

Colleague Beier: I have yet to find anyone upset about the fact that Volkswagen has a standardized format, although two-and-a-half million cars are on the road. Why not? Because it is a perfected product. I also do not believe that there is anyone here who would complain about a refrigerator that only came in one model, if it was cheap and good and served its purpose, or a vacuum cleaner or whatever. The important thing is that the product really is perfected and has the advantage of being cheap. Those people who want something special and can afford it, they are welcome to it, they should just have it made for them by a craft production cooperative. I do not think we have any fools here who are going to start offering all women standardized hats ... [laughing agreement] ... or making standardized neckties for the men or anything like that. Nobody is going to start getting ideas like that. . . . A lot of people want a Wartburg and do not have any problem with the fact that there are only two models in production. You can order the Wartburg in different colors, with chrome detailing or without. I have yet to meet anyone who is upset about the fact that we really only produce two kinds of cars. The only problem is producing a lot of them.[9]

In this short text, the main discursive element is addressed: standardization versus individuality. For different reasons, the party leadership and the intellectuals agreed that the needs of the people – and here the reference was always to the needs of others and never to their own – could be developed and steered in certain directions. What was best for the working people, however, were price and function. At this conference, most of the discussion concerned the range of goods. Instead of five different models for refrigerators, in the future only one model would be made by a single producer – although in different sizes. With standardization, the East German government justifiably hoped to make products more affordable by saving on development costs and materials. In a planned economy, these kinds of considerations made sense. But this argument also mentioned a possible reservation that future consumers might have: restriction of individual choice might prove too severe. The possible objection to an excessively uniform life-style was then ironically anticipated and trivialized. Hidden in the argument was an agenda for educating working people, which was pursued in different ways by intellectuals and party personnel.

The masses were expected to storm the gates of (bourgeois) high culture and to be systematically exposed to it, especially that of the eighteenth and

9 Pressekonferenz zur Tagung über Standardisierung am 11.2.1959, SAPMO-Barch, DY 30/IV 2/60/65.

nineteenth centuries. And they were also supposed to develop good taste, which was expressed as the rejection of petit bourgeois ostentation. Intellectuals and party functionaries shared aesthetic criteria: They rejected decoration and embraced simplicity and clarity of form, as well as functionality and durability. There was little agreement, however, on the consequences for design itself. As long as it remained a question of stripping the wood curlicues off the cabinets and banning plush and pomp from the apartments, throwing away the family crystal and taking that bellowing stag off the wall, both sides could fully agree. Together they fought against kitsch. But as soon as someone tried to realize modern, Bauhaus-oriented architecture and functionality on a practical level, the two groups ended up on opposite sides of the barricades. For example, the head architect Hermann Henselmann described how Ulbricht demanded overnight that he add a façade in Stalinist confectionery style to his modern glass and concrete design for the now legendary Stalinallee in East Berlin.

Party leaders were suspicious of objects designed in a consistently functional way. They looked ascetic, frugal, and cheap. They therefore failed to serve one of their most important functions: the suitable representation of prosperity in order to document socialism's superiority. The attempt to create an aesthetic alternative eventually failed in the clash between the desire to help the people accumulate things quickly (with inexpensive apartments and affordable furniture, with modern household technology and a small car for everyone) and the fear that these things, and the architecture especially, looked cheaply made. After Honecker attained power in the early 1970s, this was openly admitted and the socialist state visibly began to advocate Western bourgeois aesthetic standards. Ultimately, it even seemed as though the antibourgeois GDR had preserved traditional bourgeois values better than its neighbor.

THE RELATION OF INDIVIDUALS TO THE OBJECTS
OF CONSUMPTION

In this section I discuss the sources and methods that could be used to ground historically concrete definitions of East German consumer culture. Fortunately, a great deal of source material is available for an experiential–historical approach to everyday life in the GDR. In addition to conducting oral history interviews,[10] which is now becoming an accepted

10 Gert Selle proposes to take a complete inventory of houses and to ask owners about their relationships to this world of objects; Andreas Ludwig takes another approach when he asks contributors to tell the history of their material objects. See Gert Selle, "Produktkultur als Aneignungsereignis zwischen industrieller Matrix, sozialen Normen und individuellem Gebrauch: Überlegungen eines kul-

method in Germany, the petitions and citizens' letters to state and communal institutions provide a less well known, yet authentic and extremely valuable resource. A third group of sources includes feature films, documentaries, and literary works – all of which provide rich descriptions of everyday life.[11]

On December 29, 1981, Franz S. from Frankfurt an der Oder wrote to East German television:

Dear Comrades!
While Christmas shopping at an HO[12] shop for leisure and sports equipment in Frankfurt/Oder, I experienced an incident that had an entirely negative effect on the shopping atmosphere. It is not my intention only to criticize. Perhaps when you are making programs, my shopping experience can be treated satirically.
With socialist greetings,
Franz S.

Report on an incident experienced personally while buying snowshoes on 12/21/81 at HO-Freizeit in Frankfurt/Oder:
With this incident I would like to show how consciousness is negatively influenced by lack of interest in commercial activity.
To be specific:
For the last fourteen days, shop employees at HO-Freizeit have been letting citizens know that on 12/21/81 snowshoes could be purchased. At 2 p.m. on 12/21, 100–120 citizens stood waiting for the store to open. (My comment on this: is it necessary to organize such a concentrated sale for this kind of item, price: DM 12.50?)
After the store opened, citizens stormed inside. Seventy citizens went to the back and formed a dense crowd.
After a long wait, a box was pushed out, onto which the 70 citizens threw themselves. There were screams, pushing, and a good deal of rummaging around, since snowshoes come in different sizes.
The saleswoman's reaction: make room here – do not block the door – each person can only buy one pair. It would have been better if the salesclerks had undertaken to presort the shoes, instead of expressing their unqualified and impolite views to the citizens. The store organization here was an organized chaos! Another incident: There were wooden sleds on sale. Citizens asked if there were any fiberglass sleds and if some could be brought out from the back? The saleswoman's answer: Yes we have some, but the wooden sleds have to be sold first and then we'll bring the others out.

turarchäologischen Amateurs," in Wolfgang Ruppert, ed., *Chiffren des Alltags: Erkundungen zur Geschichte der industriellen Massenkultur* (Marburg, 1993), 23–47, and Andreas Ludwig, "Sensibilität für die Alltagskultur," in Stadt Eisenhüttenstadt, ed., *Alltagskultur der DDR: Begleitbuch zur Ausstellung "Tempolinsen und P2"* (Berlin, 1996).
11 Regarding feature films as source material, see Ina Merkel, "Die Nackten und die Roten: Zum Verhältnis von Nacktheit und Öffentlichkeit in der DDR," *Mitteilungen aus der kulturwissenschaftlichen Forschung* 18 (1995): 36.
12 Retail outlets were organized as "trade organizations" (*Handelsorganisation* or HO) for specific types of goods.

292   *Ina Merkel*

The final blow! At the exit there was a roll of wrapping paper and every citizen was supposed to tear off a piece for himself. On the paper it said:"Merry Christmas and happy shopping."13

In this report, which I take to be an ethnographic description in the best sense of the term, different basic patterns of typical East German forms for acquiring goods are illustrated. They include waiting and hunting and, I would add, gathering – three topoi that imply a deferment of needs satisfaction.

In this text, three kinds of waiting are practiced. First, one waits for the delivery of the snowshoes; second, one waits for the store to open after the lunch break; and third, one waits for the wooden sleds to be sold out so that the fiberglass sleds can be purchased. Waiting for the delivery refers to production capacities that were unsatisfactory in terms of quantity, a fact that GDR citizens had to face when shopping for all kinds of consumer goods. Beginning with a new automobile (which had an average waiting period of eight to fifteen years), the list is endless: refrigerators, washing machines, mopeds, oranges, telephones, and so forth. Added to this were the strategies for distribution, which differed with each consumer item, but basically followed the pattern of first come, first served. The list of orders and the lines that formed were prototypical cultural–historical forms. Both had egalitarian consequences for the consumer: You were served when it was your turn, regardless of your gender, income, or social function. As this basic democratic principle was violated ever more openly over the course of East German history, the socially explosive charge inherent in waiting was exposed. An important part of the cultural–historical figure of waiting were personal relationships to the distributors, which could be established through relatives, acquaintances, corruption, or direct petition. The usual metaphors for that were terms like *Bückware* (*bücken* is the German word for "to bow down") or *Vitamin B* (as in *Beziehung* or connections).

This indicates a dynamic that was even stronger in the other two examples of waiting: namely, the power relations that are often established between the salesclerks and the shoppers resulting from the shortage of goods. Historically, this was not unique to East Germany and is often witnessed in times of war and natural disaster. In this case, however, there was a certain gratification in the power of control. The sales personnel made the

---

13 Regarding letters from TV viewers as a historical source, see Ina Merkel, "'In Hoyerswerda leben jedenfalls keine so kleinen viereckigen Menschen': Briefe an das Fernsehen der DDR," paper presented at the conference "What is the Text of the Text? Reading the Files of East German Bureaucracies" at the German Historical Institute, Washington, D.C., Oct. 1994. Revised versions of these papers will be published in Peter Becker and Alf Lüdtke, eds., *Akten, Eingaben, Schaufenster: Die DDR und ihre Texte: Erkundungen zu Herrschaft und Alltag* (Berlin, 1997).

customers wait as long as they pleased. Countless jokes about unfriendly and slow customer service in the GDR demonstrated that the snowshoes were not a unique or even extreme case.

For the other topoi, hunting and gathering, I have also chosen consciously archaic-sounding terms to emphasize the anachronistic aspects of these consumer practices. In this case, the consumer tracks down an object in the truest sense of the word. It was spotted somewhere, this or that friend has already tracked it down, and now the hunter has been lurking around a specific place for weeks, waiting for the moment to ambush. Together with other hunters, he or she finally pounces on the object, grabs it, and holds tightly onto it. Often objects were hunted even though one could not make immediate use of them. Gathering and hoarding for later use, or for trading, were also part of the game. I know someone who stored three complete Trabant exhaust systems in his cellar. Experience had made him wise after he had been forced to wait weeks to have his car repaired. For this reason, GDR citizens always had a shopping bag with them – you just never knew what you might encounter in the course of any given day. You would first get in line and only then ask what was being sold.

The chain of associations for hunting and gathering can be played out even further. The most closely related figure was that of trade. The widely celebrated social networks were often not much more than private markets for trading in kind; anyone could take part if he or she had something to exchange or was prepared to pay a higher price for something that someone else had tracked down or gathered. Cars were traded for land, a vacation spot on the Baltic Sea was traded for work laying tiles, West German currency was traded at the rate of 1:5, and so forth.

It was then only a small step from exchanging services to the small-scale production of goods. East Germans had always taken care of themselves, especially when it came to fashion and dress. When you bought an article of clothing at the local HO, you altered it that very same evening. A pleat was sewn into pant legs or diapers were dyed, and you made your own pottery in an alcove in your apartment.

To make the opposite point, however, I would like to return to the story of the wooden sleds. I have already reported that all of them had to be sold before the fiberglass sleds would be offered. In other words, there was something in the store for which you did not have to stand in line. I can say with reasonable certainty, based on experience, that the store was full of items. They might have had jump ropes and gymnastic batons, clamp-on ice skates and roller skates, canvas sport shoes and two-piece gymnastics outfits, and all might have been available in huge quantities. Only the snowshoes and fiberglass sleds were in short supply. Perhaps there were also no downhill

skis or bindings. But the typical visit to an East German store ended with a
successful purchase, an experience so normal that it is missing from government files. Everyday routines were not the subject of consumer complaints.
The shortage of some goods was counterbalanced by the abundance of
others. They comprised the standardized range of goods or remained on the
shelves unnoticed. Dead stock was not necessarily ugly or unusable. Intellectuals bought slow-selling items, such as bowls made of unpainted and
unpolished glass or plain white dishes, at rural outlets by the truckload and
took them to Berlin. And villagers hauled unwanted goods languishing in
urban stores back to the countryside.

Although it happened later than in West Germany, by the end of the
1950s stores in the GDR were fully stocked with goods for sale. State television broadcast advertisements each evening, shopping bags were filled,
people were well dressed, apartments were comfortably decorated, and the
dining tables groaned under the weight of plentiful abundance during family celebrations. East Germans, however, remained unsatisfied and continued to search longingly for that extra special something. GDR consumers
were not characterized by proverbial modesty or patience but by dissatisfaction loudly expressed. "Grumbling," which became habitual, illustrated
an important mental characteristic. One grumbled at someone or grumbled
with someone about something. At the dinner table, family celebrations,
collective events, the alliances that formed spontaneously while waiting in
line – everywhere you went there was something to grumble about. Grumbling illustrates one form of psychic compensation that relieved some of
the pressure of everyday hassles and helped people overcome a difficult
daily life. At the same time, it showed a certain sense of community, since
what was articulated in the family or on the street were often interests that
transcended the individual. Grumbling constituted the GDR citizens' internal consensus that in being annoyed they were one. It was a form of collective refusal to agree with the party and government, or just an objection to
new slogans and extra demands of the local authorities or the boss at work.
You grumbled about those above you but also about those below you.
Related to the habit of grumbling was a specific form of humor that revealed
an ability to laugh at one's self, one's situation, and the shortcomings of
GDR daily life.

Inherent in this grumbling were elements that served to stabilize the system, since it often included suggestions for improvement, which indicated
that people were still willing to put up with the system and believe in its
possible reformation. It was only when criticism turned to anger, resigna-
tion, or desperation that the system was really endangered. Grumbling in

the GDR and generally certainly has many more cultural meanings – now constructive, now subversive. East German society developed and became colorful precisely by the very fact of grumbling.

Was East Germany really a country of stymied hunters and gatherers; of traders, craftspeople, and tailors; of snappish salespeople and sloppy waiters; of pontificators, grumblers, and naggers? There is a danger that the practices and strategies described here will be interpreted as personality characteristics, as fixed mental traits. Have they all disappeared with the society that gave rise to them? Or have they proved to be just as useful in the new society? Are Westerners not also always on the prowl? What is the difference between today's bargain and yesterday's convenient opportunity? If you looked for a printed T-shirt then, now you look in vain for a plain one. The monotony of the GDR consumer world has just been replaced with a new monotony of Western consumerism. As a result, to locate the peculiarities of consumer culture in East Germany, we are forced to use a different approach.

The activities that have been heretofore discussed (waiting, hunting, gathering, trading, and subsistence production) not only focus on shortages but also highlight specific kinds of social groups that determined the cultural value of certain goods, that is, which goods were luxury or specialty items and were therefore suitable for distinguishing oneself. To get at the root of the particularities of GDR consumer culture, we must not rely solely on scarcity as a blanket explanation. We should also ask what social, cultural, and generational differences were expressed in the specific forms of the acquisition of consumer goods and what were the consequences for their function as a means of distinction in social discourse.

When they started to produce the Schwalbe, I was seven; by the age of fourteen I had one of my own. I used it to go to school, to the outdoor swimming pool, or to my vacation job. Later it brought me punctually to work in all kinds of weather, even in snow and ice. Almost always anyway. When it failed to start, I tried to push start it; if that did not work, I went at it with screwdrivers and a wrench. In no time the most important parts were taken apart and usually repaired as well. . . . However there were times when I hated the little bike. Schwalbe riders know the feeling. Burned into my memory are the moments when the ignition failed in the pouring rain and I had to work on it while freezing on the side of the road.

I loved my Schwalbe passionately when I raced through the countryside in high summer with my shirt open – my hair, which was long then, flying in the wind. A bit of "Easy Rider," Made in the GDR.[14]

14 Jörg Engelhardt, *Schwalbe, Duo, Kultmobil: Vom Acker auf den Boulevard* (Berlin, 1995), 7ff.

The object described here so emotionally was quite ordinary – a 1960s mass production moped that underwent few changes and is still in use. There were times when one had to wait to buy one, but almost everyone in the village got around on it. Originally conceived as a vehicle for older people with knee problems, it had footrests and side fenders. Yet this owner describes a deeply felt relationship that he had as a young person with this object, a sort of love–hate relationship. It was only after the *Wende*, when it was no longer produced, that the Schwalbe became a cult object and achieved a symbolic meaning far beyond its use and exchange value (and it was from this perspective that the author describes it). Much like the Trabant, the Schwalbe has come to represent the everyday life of a lost world. It has this specific value primarily for young people and for Westerners – in other words, for those who did not have to ride one around in the former GDR. Today, they are letting their Schwalbes slowly rot in their sheds. Aside from the act of cultural revaluation, what is left of the personal relationship between the Schwalbe rider and his or her vehicle?

Remarkably, the highly personal relationship to this commodity remains intact. It is based on long-term use. Individual biography and object biography are welded to one another and help take each other's measure. The object has memory value for that period in life that is the most intensely remembered, namely, youth. In addition, through these specific memories, which are bound up with the strengths and weaknesses of the object, the individual finds himself among an illustrious and extensive society of Schwalbe riders. Because the designs remained unchanged over long periods, East German consumer goods possessed the capacity to create communities of consumers around loyalty to well-known brands.

You can, for example, distinguish associations of kitchen appliance owners by generation. The first generation of couples, married in the 1950s, owned the same refrigerator, the Kristall 140l; used a belt-driven washing machine from Schwarza (the WM 66) into the 1980s; and called the Multimax drill their own. The next cohort formed fifteen years later around the same products, with somewhat newer designs and manufactured by the same companies. Eastern Germans still bond over certain standardized and mass-produced commodities. Catchwords are enough for mutual recognition. "Remember the Multimax?" is enough to start a lively conversation. At a time when GDR-specific experiences are being disqualified and are proving to be dysfunctional in relation to Western consumer society – the private hoarding of commodities makes no sense in a capitalist economy – the discourse about specific brands is enough to reestablish an East German identity. Advertisers have tried repeatedly to exploit the recognition value of these products. Only a few have managed, however, not to miss completely the feeling of life in the GDR.

With extraordinary rapidity, an entire world of objects has disappeared from our material world. The few remaining commodities will likely attract increased attention. Even the old "shelf warmers" – unpopular products – have assumed a kind of cult value. It would be interesting to discover which objects produced in the GDR still exist in eastern German households, are needed and used there, and which objects have found a place as representative pieces in western German cupboards. (Western Germans are especially fond of relics from the former political culture, such as pins and flags.) The results of such an inquiry could tell us a great deal about the symbols and signs being used in the discourse between East and West – and their respective meanings.

ON CONTINUITY AND CHANGE IN CONSUMER MENTALITIES

The history of users of kitchen appliances shows a profound continuity in the East German world of objects. It is inevitable that mental traditions will be imputed to East German consumers. The cultural–historical figures of waiting, hunting, gathering, and trading that have been described are also relevant for the entire history of the former GDR, although we should not lose sight of their historically specific forms. For this reason, I would like to examine the historical transformation of the primary attitudes toward consumerism in yet another way. Continuity and change in consumer culture can be studied in terms of the introduction of new consumer goods and new sales practices, such as self-service. I would like to suggest an approach to periodization that is based on generational change. The different, almost antagonistic, relations that successive generations assume toward consumption essentially depend on consumer experiences each generation had when it was young. For the changes that took place during the period analyzed here, several themes regarding the generationally specific transformation of basic mental attitudes emerge. They are based on observations made within the framework of a life-history research project with a different topic and would therefore have to be further analyzed and worked out separately.

First, we can observe one transformation in the shift from durable consumer goods to those based on fashion trends and fads. Whereas it was common for the prewar generation to spend its whole life with one set of furniture (which it usually acquired when a young couple started a family), the postwar generation can already talk about two or three complete changes of furniture and interior decoration. Whether this is because the objects themselves are no longer designed and produced for long-term use or whether it has to do with increased mobility in terms of space and relationships remains unclear. It is true, however, that these generations differ profoundly in their mental relations to objects. The new generation no longer maintains, repairs, or protects them for long-term use. Generation-specific differences in maintenance and care can be observed even with those objects for which one had to wait for years in the former GDR, such as automobiles, and which therefore required care and maintenance.

The result is an inability to throw something away and, inherent in this attitude, an enduring defense against renewing household technology. Objects that had become obsolete or no longer worked properly were kept in storage for years. The renunciation of such attitudes does not take place within one generation; rather, it is inevitably relinquished piecemeal over the course of generations.

Second, we can also observe a mental shift from long-term planning, long-term deferment, and saving of money for a purchase, to spontaneous purchases that sometimes require credit or loans. This not only implies the cultural devaluation of individual debt to the status of a peccadillo. It also means that one goes into debt for things not necessary for daily living but required for cultural distinction: a high-end amplifier, a new automobile, and so forth. Values of frugality and modesty have been abandoned for a sense of entitlement that represents their exact opposite.

Third, stocking up practices that were customary twenty years ago have disappeared almost entirely: Potatoes are no longer stored in cellars, fruit and vegetables are not conserved, even coal for the winter is bought weekly as needed. The disappearance of storage habits has a lot to do with the industrialization of foodstuffs, but it also implies an increased feeling of security in terms of one's immediate, short-term survival and the easy availability of consumer goods.

This feeling of security has been confirmed and strengthened by a new form of selling, namely, self-service, that was introduced in Germany in the 1940s. The depersonalization of sales transactions has been perceived as a democratization of access to goods, even if that is not actually always the case. Self-service suggests that one can take what one needs and make independent decisions about products.

To understand better the historical transformation in dominant mental attitudes toward consumption (which have only been thematically explored here), it is necessary to analyze historical source material more closely to determine the extent to which the change is generational and class-specific. This is also true of any attempt to say which salient features of East German consumer culture will remain and what this will mean for the collision of the everyday worlds of eastern and western Germans.

Buying and selling are public acts, yet consumption takes place in private. Within consumer culture, the relations between public and private, between individual and society, are reflected in a special way. The discourse about consumerism as outlined in this chapter must be analyzed in terms of its general societal meanings. What changes in consumer mentalities portend for a society's cultural values, and what the consequences will be, continue to be the decisive questions.

14

Changes in Consumption as Social Practice in West Germany During the 1950s

MICHAEL WILDT

At the beginning of the 1950s, West Germany had not yet started to develop into a "consumer society." The preconditions for this development, at least in embryonic form, could nevertheless already be seen. By the end of the decade, even people on very limited household budgets were able to afford some of the new consumer products flowing from the country's prodigious factories. Consumption of these products, however, required people to learn new skills. Accordingly, to examine the development of consumption during the postwar years, it is necessary to look at the multifaceted changes in people's everyday practice.

In this chapter, "consumption" is used in a broad sense and incorporates not only the "production of consumption" but also what Marx, in his *Theses on Feuerbach,* called "sensual" human activity or "practice." The term must connote more than the mere consumption of food or possession of goods. Analyzing the "practice of consumption" does not mean simply chronicling the quantitative consumption patterns of working-class families – what and how much they generally ate – but also examining how food was bought and cooked and how cooking technology changed. Finally, we must also investigate the fabrication of representations and associations connected with food and consumption, that is, the "production" of embedded cultural meanings.[1]

In the first section, I look at consumer experiences in pre-1939 Germany and then focus on the war years through the currency reform of

---

1 For this approach to consumption, see Michel de Certeau, *L'inventon du quotidien: Arts de faire* (Paris, 1980); de Certeau's book has been translated into English by Steven Randall as *The Practice of Everyday Life* (Berkeley, Calif., 1984); see also Grant McCracken, *Culture and Consumption: New Approaches to the Symbolic Character of Consumer Goods and Activities* (Bloomington, Ind., 1988); and John Brewer and Roy Porter, ed., *Consumption and the World of Goods* (London and New York, 1993).

1948 – a watershed for the wider history and the history of consumption in West Germany. In Section II, I provide a quantitative analysis of the development of consumption based on household budgets kept by working-class families between 1949 and 1963. In the third section, I discuss changes in cooking and housework and the arrival of modern technical gadgets and appliances in the kitchen. I concentrate on the fundamental shift in the selling and buying of food, namely, the introduction of self-service, in Section IV. The buying and selling of items would no longer be mediated by personal relations between buyer and seller. Instead, goods now spoke to customers directly from the supermarket shelf, where they struggled with their rivals for space and attention. The new language of consumption is drawn on recipes published by the consumer magazine *Die kluge Hausfrau* (The clever housewife). The rhetoric of food developed in the 1950s evoked and disseminated new possibilities and ideals for the consumer. This fundamental shift in the semiotic dimension of consumption symbolizes the new role that consumers had to learn in West Germany during the 1950s. I argue here that these new practices created, in turn, a new "consumer subject," whose development did not coincide with a democratic society as the contemporaries believed but raised new questions about the relationship between mass consumption and democracy.[2]

I

We cannot fully understand the history of consumption in West Germany after World War II without tracing developments before and during the rationing period from 1939 to 1948. Everyday life during World War I and the following years was dominated by scarcity and hunger. Older people still remembered the *Steckrübenwinter* (turnip winter) of 1916, when turnips were nearly the only available foodstuff. The food supply did not improve when the war ended in 1919; shortages persisted into the early 1920s. During the hyperinflation in 1923, many households, especially those of workers, found that tremendous effort was required to feed everyone. The Great Depression meant unemployment and increased distress. The brief periods of economic stability between 1924 and 1929 and the mid-1930s never lasted long enough for people to lose the feeling of uncertainty and insecurity.[3]

2 This chapter is based on a larger study of consumption in West Germany during the 1950s. See Michael Wildt, *Am Beginn der "Konsumgesellschaft": Mangelerfahrung, Lebenshaltung, Wohlstandshoffnung in Westdeutschland in den fünfziger Jahren* (Hamburg, 1994).
3 Alf Lüdtke, "Hunger in der Grossen Depression," *Archiv für Sozialgeschichte* 27 (1987): 145–76.

When food was rationed in September 1939, that did not strike people as a dramatic measure. During the first years of military successes, moreover, the Nazi regime was able to meet the needs of the domestic "Aryan" population by exploiting occupied countries, but after the German defeat in 1943 at Stalingrad, food supplies deteriorated. The wartime rationing system collapsed in May 1945. Germans were now entirely dependent on wheat imports from Canada and the United States. The official daily ration was small, and on some days, especially in winter, intake fell below one thousand calories per day.[4] People could survive only by tapping into every possible source of food. Alongside the official ration system, a secondary economy emerged – the black market.[5] This illegal market existed everywhere: in the streets and squares, in factories, and in the countryside. Barter was very common. People who lived in cities and towns traveled to rural areas looking for butter, bacon, or potatoes in exchange for cigarettes, jewelry, and household items; or workers would produce extra goods, for example, rubber boots, that would then be taken out to farms and exchanged for food. For many, the inability of the government rationing system to feed people and the capacity of the illegal black-market economy to offer everything to those who could pay constituted a formative experience. Everybody had to rely on his or her own individual effort. The lesson learned was that a controlled economy was unable to supply all of their immediate needs, and that a market economy was a hard but efficient alternative.

The currency reform of June 1948 marked a caesura in postwar history. Because the Nazis had left behind a bloated money supply, this reform was long overdue. The emerging Cold War prevented the Allies of World War II from taking joint action, as agreed on at the Potsdam Conference. As a result, the United States and Great Britain each decided to carry out currency reform in their respective zones of occupation.[6] The rumors about the date when the new notes would be issued prompted many people to hoard goods and foodstuffs – in spite of official appeals and warnings. In early 1948, for example, the rations of meat were curtailed once again, not because of a lack of cattle but because of farmers' unwillingness to deliver

---

4 Günter J. Trittel, *Hunger und Politik: Die Ernährungskrise in der Bizone, 1945–1949* (Frankfurt am Main, 1990); Rainer Gries, *Die Rationen-Gesellschaft: Versorgungskampf und Vergleichsmentalität: Leipzig, München and Köln nach dem Krieg* (Münster, 1991).

5 For a regional study of the black market, see Michael Wildt, *Der Traum von Sattwerden: Hunger und Protest, Schwarzmarkt und Selbsthilfe in Hamburg, 1945–48* (Hamburg, 1986), esp. 101–23.

6 Christoph Buchheim, "The Currency Reform in West Germany in 1948," *German Yearbook on Business History* (1993): 85–120; Frank Zschaler, "Die vergessene Währungsreform: Vorgeschichte, Durchführung und Ergebnisse der Geldumstellung in der SBZ, 1948," *Vierteljahrshefte für Zeitgeschichte* 45 (1997): 191–223; Michael Brackmann, *Vom totalen Krieg zum Wirtschaftswunder: Die Vorgeschichte der westdeutschen Währungsreform 1948* (Essen, 1993).

their product. Laws passed by the bizonal economic council that criminal-ized hoarding were ineffectual, since the director of the economic board, Ludwig Erhard, had publicly suggested that, although officially forbidden, hoarding would be tolerated because a surfeit of salable goods would be urgently needed to back the value of the new deutschmark (DM) when it was introduced.

The economic crisis following the currency reform produced a rapid increase in prices – some goods such as eggs, sugar, or milk still had to be rationed – and unemployment. It also favored those who owned material goods and real estate. The social gap between rich and poor was widened as a result of the currency reform. In November 1948, West German trade unions called a twenty-four-hour general strike in which nearly 10 million workers participated.[7]

Nevertheless, Erhard's gambit paid off handsomely. Almost overnight all kinds of goods that had been unobtainable for years filled the shops. Public opinion surveys organized by the American authorities in their occupied zone found that people's greatest worries concerned food, clothing, and missing relatives. At the moment of the currency reform, however, all their worries focused on money.[8] Now that the value of money was restored after great scarcity and hunger, they expected normality to return to the household economy. After nearly ten years of monotonous rations, people could once more afford delicacies like butter, cream, coffee, or white flour.

The significance of the currency reform cannot thus be measured solely by its role in the forthcoming takeoff of the West German economy. Its decisive importance lies in the fact that it symbolized the end of the war years and times of deprivation. It was the beginning of the long-expected return to "normality," security, and welfare. Significantly, during the 1950s the conservative Christian Democratic Union (Christlich Demokratische Union or CDU) won elections using the slogan "No experiments!" West Germans wanted their government to allow the economy to develop rela-tively unfettered.

II

The following years are known as those of the economic miracle or *Wirtschaftswunder,* with a boom in consumption described in terms of a series of waves: the *Fresswelle,* or food wave, the *Kleidungswelle,* or clothing

---

7 Gerhard Beier, *Der Demonstrations- und Generalstreik vom 12. November 1948* (Frankfurt am Main, 1975).
8 A. J. Merritt and R. J. Merritt, *Public Opinion in Occupied Germany* (Urbana, Ill., 1970), 16ff.

wave, and the *Urlaubswelle,* or travel wave. Reality proved to be much less miraculous that these terms suggest. The average monthly income of a working-class household composed of parents and two children (*Vier-Personen-Arbeitnehmerhaushalt*) rose from DM 343 in 1950 to DM 975 in 1963, with the greatest increase in the early 1950s. After subtracting taxes, the level of average disposable income per household in the sample rose from DM 305 in 1950 to DM 847 in 1963.[9]

Household expenditure on food was still the dominant feature in total living costs. In 1950 German households spent DM 133 each month on food, or 46 percent of the total. By 1963 the figure (in real terms based on 1950 prices) had risen to DM 193, or 36 percent. These families spent an increasing amount, both in absolute and in relative terms, on "luxury" items such as coffee, beer, and cigarettes. In 1950, 6 percent of their expenditure was on luxury items; in 1960, it was 10 percent. Preferences within this luxury category also changed: In the early 1950s, households spent most of their budget for such items on tobacco, but from 1954 onward, beer and other alcohol pulled ahead.

Moreover, it took time for the consumption of high-priced foodstuffs to reach prewar levels. In the early 1950s meat was not served every day. An investigation in 1955 found that 70 percent of West Germans ate meat three times a week, and only 27 percent were accustomed to having it daily. Coffee remained a Sunday treat all through the 1950s; average monthly consumption in the sample households was only 91 grams in 1950, as against 372 grams of coffee substitutes like chicory and grain. Consumption of real coffee had overtaken that of substitutes by 1955, but it reached the monthly level of 500 grams per family only in 1960.

In short, then, these working-class households still lived on tight budgets until the late 1950s. Despite notions of an "economic miracle" and the "affluent society," the majority lived frugally. However, the late 1950s and early 1960s marked a break in postwar developments. The consumption of butter and poultry increased, and cold meats and ham could be found in abundance in working-class households. Independent of season and region, fruit supplies rose dramatically and the variety of fruits available, especially from the tropics, expanded remarkably. Canned food and other prepared items became increasingly a part of everyday meals.

These developments signaled the transition from one phase of consumption to another. In the early 1950s, the satisfaction of basic needs had the

9 Statistisches Bundesamt, ed., *Fachserie Preise, Löhne, Wirtschaftsrechnungen,* series 13: *Wirtschaftsrechnungen* (Wiesbaden, 1949ff).

highest priority in working-class households, who spent the most money on foods and other necessities that had been impossible to obtain during and immediately after the war. By the late 1950s, as incomes rose, people could afford to acquire some of the new consumer goods. Of course, working-class families continued to live on limited budgets, but they no longer exhibited the "taste for necessities" of the immediate postwar years.[10] To paraphrase Ernest Zahn, consumers now wanted to purchase items not because they were in short supply but because they fancied them.[11]

The everyday experiences of the late 1950s show a difference between the years of scarcity and the start of the "affluent society" (Galbraith), when people began to open their eyes to a world of goods of which they previously had never dreamed. And despite a scenario that portrays the continuous and homogeneous development of mass consumption in West Germany shared equally by all social classes, which was supposed to lead to "social leveling," as the sociologist Helmut Schelsky has suggested,[12] the consumption of goods in worker households between 1949 and 1963 exhibited many differences and discontinuities that undermine universal assumptions.

III

Where food is concerned, consumption involves not only quantifiable purchase, but also "production." Food has to be supplied, prepared, cooked, and – last but not least – served. "The investigation of consumption," as Alf Lüdtke points out, "is meaningless if cooking, eating, and going hungry are not included as forms of social practice."[13] For example, the quantity of potatoes consumed, as an item in the household budget, certainly fell during the 1950s (as it had early in the century), but ready-made items using dehydrated potatoes, such as dumplings or pancakes, took their place, and later on the consumption of potato chips increased markedly.

Another example is baking. The Federal Board of Statistics shows a decline in the purchase of flour and an increase in the purchase of biscuits and cakes

---

10 The phrase is used by Pierre Bourdieu in *La Distinction: critique sociale du jugement* (Paris, 1979); translated into English by Richard Nice as *Distinction: A Social Critique of the Judgement of Taste* (London, 1986).

11 Ernest Zahn, *Soziologie der Prosperität* (Cologne, 1960), 22. In German this allows a play on the words *entbehrt* (missed) and *begehrt* (desired).

12 Helmut Schelsky, "Gesellschaftlicher Wandel," in *Auf der Suche nach Wirklichkeit: Gesammelte Aufsätze* (Düsseldorf, 1965), 337–51.

13 Alf Lüdtke, "Hunger, Essens-'Genuss' und Politik bei Fabrikarbeitern und Arbeiterfrauen: Beispiele aus dem rheinisch-westfälischen Industriegebiet, 1910–1940," in his *Eigen-Sinn: Fabrikalltag, Arbeitererfahrungen und Politik vom Kaiserreich bis in den Faschismus* (Hamburg, 1993), 195.

in household budgets. The obvious inference is confirmed in the records of the Oetker Company, the leading producer of baking powder in West Germany. Their product, Backin, experienced declining sales in the 1950s as, according to the sales manager, "the joy of home baking was trickling away."[14] Home baking was indeed in decline: What the managers and the marketing board (presumably male) described as "joy" was hard work, and one can easily imagine why housewives might choose to abandon kneading dough or beating eggs and instead patronize the bakery. But they did not give up home baking altogether. Indeed, the Oetker Company was surprised by the success of their *Tortenguss*, a new glaze for fruit tarts introduced in 1950. Fruit tarts were the hit of the 1950s: Unlike the old-fashioned cakes, which involved much work, they could be prepared quickly and easily, and their fresh fruit taste was valued as healthy and light. They also were a reassurance to the housewife that she was not feeding her family entirely on store-bought food but still had the skill to do her own baking.

This tension, between making work easier, on the one hand, and retaining the housewife's sense of competence, on the other, also affected the use of electric appliances. Such new durable goods appeared first in the kitchen. In the early 1960s, more than 10 percent of all four-member households in West Germany had at least one electric kitchen appliance. The most coveted item during the 1950s was the refrigerator. In a 1955 opinion poll only 10 percent of all households owned one, but nearly 50 percent dreamed of buying one. In 1958 the refrigerator again topped the list of desired goods. Ownership of refrigerators rose from 29 percent in 1958 to 39 percent in 1961, and two years later the percentage rose to more than 51 percent of West German private households.[15]

A tension can again be seen between making use of "modern" industrial products like canned food and maintaining traditional but labor-intensive skills such as preserving food. In 1953, 76 percent of all private households in West Germany bottled or canned their own fruit. Rural households were more likely to do this than urban ones, and households with several members more than those with only one or two; younger housewives were slightly less likely than older ones to do their own preserving. Their main reason for home preserving was unequivocal – they wanted to save money, and in the early 1950s these home products were much cheaper than their purchased equivalents, even when the produce to be preserved was not home grown. (Well over half of housewives preserved food, although they

14 Jahresberichte der Verkaufsabteilung, 1955ff, Firmenarchiv Oetker, Bielefeld, Pl/431.
15 *Ausstattung der privaten Haushalte mit ausgewählten langebigen Gebrauchsgütern 1962/63*, Statistisches Bundesamt, Fachserie M, series no. 18 (Stuttgart, 1964).

did not have their own gardens.) The second reason was the superior taste of home preserves. This superiority justified the continued practice of home preserving, even when rising incomes allowed consumers to buy the more expensive commercial products more frequently.

From the mid-1950s, the sample working-class households bought more and more canned food. The opinion polls taken by the Allensbach Institute suggest why. For more than half the housewives asked, canned food was convenient because they were able to prepare a quick meal every time. A third of them believed canned food tasted better, and a third thought it looked fresh and delicious. Most of them had bought cans when the vegetables they wanted were out of season, so clearly it was a way to overcome seasonal dependency. Those who went out to work and also had domestic responsibilities were especially likely to use cans to save time and effort.

There was another reason for using canned food and preserves in new and different ways: the generation gap. More than the half of those house-wives who were still preserving during the 1950s wanted to carry on a tradition they had experienced while growing up in their parents' home. Forty-four percent of women over sixty years of age disliked canned food, and only 37 percent were familiar with canned food. In contrast, more than 60 percent of the women between eighteen and twenty-nine preferred food in cans.[16] These young housewives wanted to manage a "modern" household on their own, not an old-fashioned one like their mother's. World War II and its aftermath had torn families apart and had made it difficult to transfer household skills from mother to daughter. These young women had to master their household skills independently, often without the helping hands of their mothers. They were open to new ideas, to "modernity," and to rationalizing housework.

Much as women before them, 1950s housewives had to do hard physical work that consumed a great deal of time. According to a contemporary study, the day of working-class housewives began at five o'clock in the morning and ended at half past nine in the evening.[17] A typical housewife in West Germany during the 1950s worked seventy hours a week – not including the "immaterial" work women did for their husbands, their children, and their families.[18]

16 Institut für Demoskopie Allensbach, Gemüse- und Obstkonserven, 1956: Bundesarchiv I, Koblenz, Zsg 132–544 I.
17 Elisabeth Pfeil, *Die Berufstätigkeit von Müttern* (Tübingen, 1961), 301–10.
18 Ursula Schroth-Pritzel, "Der Arbeitszeitaufwand im städtischen Haushalt," *Hauswirtschaft und Wissenschaft* 4 (1958): 7–22; Ernst Zander, "Arbeitszeitaufwand in städtischen Haushalten," *Hauswirtschaft und Wissenschaft* 13 (1967): 71–81.

Understandably, most housewives appreciated any technical innovation that eased their daily work. In several opinion polls taken during the 1950s, women said that their work was easier with kitchen appliances, and that they would save time and energy. Those who acquired the new labor-saving machines had good reason to be proud of them, and owning these gadgets and machines identified them as modern. Yet there could be a difference between owning such equipment and using it. Survey findings in the early 1960s likewise indicate that women made their own decisions about the use of gadgets and machines and did not simply follow the manufacturers' instructions. Tiring work, like mixing dough or beating eggs, was gladly given over to machines, but women preferred to peel potatoes or scrub vegetables by hand.

Kitchen appliances and prepared foods meant that knowledge and skill gained through experience became less essential; appliances formalized understanding of weights, quantities, and timing. Nevertheless, the complex and differentiated practices involved in the daily production of meals could not be reduced to the purely technical. Despite the industrial law of efficiency, it was still necessary to "waste" time or energy to improve the taste of meals or to experiment.

The washing machine was of course one of the most prized goods during the 1950s, because women hoped that the slavery of wash day would come to an end. But did these machines really save time? Surely, the soaking, boiling, and rinsing of clothes were now done by machine, but the clothes still had to be hung out to dry and then ironed. Far more important, after the advent of the washing machine, West German households did not wash less but more often. The new appliance surely facilitated the housework but did not save time. For example, underwear was no longer worn for several days but was changed more frequently; husbands demanded a fresh shirt daily for making a proper impression at the office; housewives themselves no longer protected their clothes with an apron but washed them instead.[19]

Owning a refrigerator meant fewer trips to the grocer, baker, or butcher. Now even fresh food like butter, cheese, or meat could be stored for several days, and one could use special offers in the new self-service stores without fear of buying too much. But the refrigerator did not simply reduce the number of errands, it also changed the way of buying itself.

19 Karin Hausen, "Grosse Wäsche," *Geschichte und Gesellschaft* 13, no. 3 (1987): 273–303; Barbara Orland, *Wäsche waschen: Technik- und Sozialgeschichte der häuslichen Wäschepflege* (Reinbek bei Hamburg, 1991).

IV

The shift in consumption patterns was reinforced by the self-service store, which caused fundamental changes in the way people bought food. In 1951 there were still only 39 self-service stores in West Germany, but they soon began to spread. By 1955 there were 203; and by 1960, only five years later, their number had skyrocketed to 17,132. By 1965, West Germany had more than 53,000 self-service shops.[20]

The rupture with the past could hardly have been greater. From the nineteenth century until the 1950s, it had been an everyday experience to buy supplies at shops where the shopkeeper or an assistant stood behind a counter, asked what you wanted, fetched the articles from behind the counter, weighed or measured them out, wrapped them, added up the prices, and took the cash. Not only did the counter now disappear, the whole shop was reshaped for self-service. Now everything was in reach, ready to grasp at the level of eyes and hands; the arrangement of goods, lighting, decor – everything was organized around the presentation of commodities. In the grocery there had always been a chance to talk with neighbors, to hear local gossip, to "waste" time. The new self-service stores represented instead modern ideas about the efficient use of time. Saving time was the justification housewives gave most often when asked about the advantages of self-service.[21]

When people entered a self-service store for the first time, they were overwhelmed by the wealth of goods for sale. After the initial confusion, their second important impression was that freedom of choice was staged as a glittering world of merchandise. The attraction of self-service was the ability to choose and purchase on your own. Paradoxically, as options widened and the choice of goods became more and more complicated, the customer's desire for advice did not increase. In place of the personal relationship between the shopkeeper (or assistant) and the customer, the goods now spoke directly to the customers and had to compete with their "rivals" on the shelves. The communication previously effected by shop staff (often salesgirls) had now to be achieved by the actual articles and their presentation. This transfer of influence from the personal to the semiotic constituted a decisive change in West German consumption after the 1950s.

---

20 Wolfgang K. A. Disch, *Der Gross- und Einzelhandel in der Bundesrepublik* (Cologne, 1966); Institut für Selbstbedienung, ed., "50 Jahre Selbstbedienung," *Dynamik im Handel: Sonderausgabe* (Cologne, 1988).
21 Gesellschaft für Konsumforschung, "Einkaufsgewohnheiten in Deutschland," Nuremberg 1953, typescript in the Archiv der Gesellschaft für Konsumforschung, Nuremberg, U 183.

This semiotic shift increasingly involved the stimulation of desire through coded references, especially (though not exclusively) in advertising. This language of semiotic reference, which consumers now had to learn, can be examined in the recipes of the consumer magazine *Die kluge Hausfrau,* a free weekly produced by the Edeka company.[22]

Far from being repetitive and standardized, the rhetoric of *Die kluge Hausfrau* was diverse and multifaceted. In the first years after the 1948 currency reform, the recipes it published were rather simple and frugal. They included such dishes as a macaroni pudding made with mincemeat and mushrooms; beef and butter were seldom mentioned. Their limits were geographical and pecuniary, lacking any intentional flair or extravagance and bounded by domestic cuisine within the former limits of the German Reich. Dishes from Hamburg, Silesia, or East Prussia appeared along with recipes such as "cheap pumpkin," recommended for economy in the household budget.

In 1951 *Die kluge Hausfrau* began to broaden its horizons. For a Sunday meal it proposed a pork cutlet prepared "à la Milano." Subsequent dishes "à la Milano" did not share a uniform way of preparing the food, but were all associated in various ways with cheese and tomatoes. From the mid-1950s, the recipes became increasingly international. Cabbage was no longer just cabbage, but "Swiss," "Scottish," and "Norman" cabbage, or even cabbage "à la Strasbourg." In 1958 *Die kluge Hausfrau* invited its readers on a "culinary journey around the world": Italy, "Fish Milanese"; Portugal, "Portuguese spinach roll"; France, "omelette parisienne"; the Netherlands, "soup hollandaise" – even Africa, "banana salad"!

Eurocentrism was firmly internalized. Africa was depicted as a single country and was represented through bananas – the stereotypical white assumption about what black people in Africa would eat. Through this caricature it becomes clear that all the international connotations were simply cultural constructs. Just as the Milanese dishes had little to do with the authentic cuisine of northern Italy, so too did the recipes for the culinary journey around the world not represent authentic local cuisines but German longing for international rapport, for acceptance back into the family of nations. The rhetoric of the recipes was less concerned with practices of preparation than with the conjuring up of dreams.

---

22 *Die kluge Hausfrau* had already begun to appear before World War II. It was revived in 1949 and by the end of the 1950s had a circulation of over a million. It was the most widely read consumer magazine in the food trade and can be compared with famous public affairs magazines like *Stern, Quick,* or *Constanze*; see Wildt, *Konsumgesellschaft,* 214–55.

This phenomenon of internationalization was not unique to Germany, but after the failed attempt at world conquest, it was especially noticeable there. In the famous West German periodical *Magnum,* Klaus Harpprecht described in 1960 this postwar mentality:

> The Germans long to be part of the "family of nations." They are sick of standing apart, being alone, whether in a brilliant or in a miserable state. The yearning to be assimilated to the international standard of taste, desires, and needs has engulfed their architecture as well as their menus. (No architect would dare to build an office block in any but the same style as his colleagues in Louisville, Nagasaki, or Lyon. No urban restaurant would forgo serving "Steak à la Hawaii" or Nasi Goreng.) The Germans desperately want to strike lucky, and the world wants finally to have better luck with the Germans. So we are resolved to be happy and mediocre.[23]

Hence *Die kluge Hausfrau* could recommend that West Germans sample the Mediterranean atmosphere by eating lamb cutlets "à la Murillo" long before they would make their first trips to Southern Europe. Germans could demonstrate their modernity and American life-style by serving light low-calorie meals. After the frugal recipes of the early 1950s with their references to shortages and the need to save money, there were now timid excursions into everyday specialties, then the first attempts to open up the rhetoric to modest luxuries and international dishes. The multitude of little snacks, the miniaturization of meals, and finally the "new conscience" eating – "healthy and light" – were all part of the evolving rhetoric. They show that these recipes did not stand outside social reality in West Germany, but were a text for popular mentality.

Paralleling the discourse in medical magazines, *Die kluge Hausfrau* also took up "healthy nutrition" in an increasingly "scientific" way. In the early 1950s the term "healthy nutrition" was associated with an antimodern perception and a critique that civilization was unhealthy. Along the lines of earlier concepts of *Volksgesundheit,* during these years *Die kluge Hausfrau* recommended whole-grain bread and exercise. In the late 1950s it had to respond to changing living conditions and became increasingly realistic. The discourse on "healthy nutrition" shifted: Now the focus was on either fitness at work, especially for husbands and for children at school, or "the slim line." This linking of nutrition to new socially defined standards (fitness at work or a specific, male-oriented imaging of the female body) signaled an important change in the discourse about eating. The "modern house-

23 Klaus Harpprecht, "Die Lust an der Normalität," *Magnum* 29 (April 1960): 18.

wife" as portrayed by *Die kluge Hausfrau* knew all about calories, vitamins, and other essentials of healthy nutrition; she was busy rationalizing her household and making extensive use of appliances; she thus saved enough time to make herself pretty. The modern woman was not only a good house-wife and mother; she was also clever with machines and knew how to make herself attractive.

V

The qualitative change in consumption at the end of the 1950s was not simply a matter of further economic growth, higher rates of consumption, and buying of better appliances. It was above all a multiplication of options and a diversification of practices. Entering a self-service shop, buying indus-trially produced food, taking home frozen food for the weekend because the refrigerator would keep it fresh, preparing snacks ("TV dinners") in order not to interrupt the television program for a family meal, cooking "light and healthy" so as not to endanger the "slim line" – all these were becoming familiar practices. Consumers, or more specifically, housewives, had to acquire all sorts of new habits. They had to navigate through a com-plex, unstable, and confusing new world of commodities; learn the new language of advertisers; and decipher the various semiotic codes underlying the presentation of goods.

The memory of hunger, ever-present in the minds of the older genera-tion, was disappearing. The stores overflowing with goods and the abundant displays in the butcher-shop windows – all demonstrated not just a tran-sient dream of prosperity, but permanent affluence. Of course, many house-holds still had to stick to budgets, still had to count pennies, but by the end of the 1950s, the need for frugality was receding, along with structural restrictions of the past and the cultural limitations of an older way of life. With the extension of the "universe of goods" and the variety of consumer options, working-class households began to abandon their "proletarian" life-style.

Social disparity continued, but traditional consumer hierarchies gave way to finer distinctions. Social inequality was no longer defined by occupation and role in production. What counted more were working conditions and leisure time, social security, and the potential for individual development. Gender, however, continued (and continues) to play a part in social inequal-ity. In the words of Pierre Bourdieu, everyone had to take care "not to differ from the ordinary, but to differ differently" in order to become part of consumer society.[24]

Consumption patterns in West Germany displayed a great many discontinuities within the process of modernization. West German consumers were burdened with the past experience of scarcity and even hunger. For them, the Nazi and the war years were extraordinary. At the same time, as the Germans were exterminating the European Jews, the war reached their own towns. Thousands died in the bombing of German cities; millions more lost their homes. Several million had to flee the front or were later expelled from their homeland. In this shattered society not only had houses collapsed but so too had the familiar structures of everyday life. Men who had rampaged as *Herrenmenschen* in Eastern Europe and the Soviet Union, women who were forced to devote all their energies to feed their families, and youngsters who learned to survive as thieves and black marketeers – all of them had undergone extreme experiences and were now longing for normalcy and security.

Looking back at the 1950s usually evokes some unease: Some remember the frugal years with a touch of shame because of the subsequent period of plenty; others connect these years with political stagnation. Indeed, on the surface of the 1950s one can recognize an authoritarian and narrow-minded atmosphere. Konrad Adenauer, a man in his seventies, governed the country; the political Left was paralyzed by the Cold War; and the Communist Party was outlawed. The churches and the conservatives supported the patriarchal family structure and traditional gender roles. Discussing sexuality was taboo. In the German *Heimatfilme* (homeland films) made in the 1950s, the philistinism of these years is clearly evident.[25]

Politically, Germany was a democracy without democrats. The Federal Republic was established by the Western Allies in the hope that over time Germans would grow accustomed to new political structures. In reality, antidemocratic opinions dominated the German mentality until the 1960s. In 1946, 37 percent of West Germans denied the statement that the extermination of the Jews was not necessary for the security of Germany; 33 percent did not accept equal rights for Jews, and 30 percent considered black people to be inferior.[26] At the beginning of the 1950s half of those

---

24 Pierre Bourdieu, "Klassenstellung und Klassenlage," in Pierre Bourdieu, *Zur Soziologie der symbolischen Formen* (Frankfurt am Main, 1975), 70.

25 For West Germany during the 1950s, see Axel Schildt and Arnold Sywottek, eds., *Modernisierung im Wiederaufbau: Die westdeutsche Gesellschaft der 50er Jahre* (Bonn, 1993).

26 Felix P. Lutz, "Empirisches Datenmaterial zum historisch-politischen Bewusstsein," *Bundesrepublik Deutschland: Geschichte – Bewusstsein,* published by the Bundeszentrale für politische Bildung (Bonn, 1989), 150–69.

West Germans asked thought Hitler would have been the greatest German statesman ever if he had not started the war. And in public opinion surveys throughout the 1950s nearly half stated that things were going well in the years between 1933 and 1939. The number of those who regarded the present as the best period only gradually increased. It is significant that the curves of both trends – the first declining, the second increasing – crossed in 1956.[27]

The parallel between the beginning of a new phase of consumption and the accommodation to democracy in the late 1950s is striking. Indeed, the loyalty of the West Germans to their new republic was based on the development of an affluent society. The perspective of more welfare, economic growth, and a gradual but steady rise in the standard of living created not only consumers but also democrats. Despite the fears of some conservatives that modern mass consumption would leave people disoriented – like straws in the wind, as one of them had put it – the practices of consumption had fractured society and untied traditional fetters. Beneath a fixed, unchanging, and authoritarian surface, West German society was deeply transformed. There was still a need to economize on household budgets, but it became obvious that the years of scarcity had come to an end. An individual's efficiency now determined whether he or she had enough money to buy the desired goods. The new societal ideal focused on the individual pursuit of happiness, wealth, and full participation in mass consumption.

As the celebrated sociologist Ralf Dahrendorf described it (along with most of the liberal historians in West Germany), the West Germans, after their grave and costly errors, had at last become members of Western civilization.[28] But the connections among welfare, mass consumption, and democratization in West Germany cannot be denied. West Germans became democrats through consumption; they did not fight for democracy but rather struggled for prosperity.

On the one hand, the West Germans became accustomed to democracy over a period of more than forty years, and by 1989 the political culture looked pluralistic and even tolerant. On the other hand, the East Germans, who have been citizens of a unified Germany since then, have never had the opportunity to practice democracy. Even the sated West Germans did not really have to fight for democracy and human rights, and they have not been tested in truly difficult times. The development of consumption and democratization in West Germany after 1945 reminds us that moderniza-

---

27 *Jahrbuch der öffentlichen Meinung 1957*, ed., Elisabeth Noelle und Erich Peter Neumann (Allensbach, 1957).
28 Ralf Dahrendorf, *Gesellschaft und Freiheit* (Munich, 1961), 297.

tion is not an irreversible process and that modernity itself may yet have an unsettling, imponderable undercurrent.

The familiar practice of consumption after the late 1950s was to create new patterns and expectations. Although the process of producing and transporting food and other commodities to the shelves of the self-service store involves many people at all levels, the consumer is unlikely to be aware of the physical labor involved. The cash nexus and semiotic presentation in a world of commodities together obliterate the physical effort and skill by which the shelves are filled. The new "consumer subject," then, is far removed from production and sets a high value on individual freedom of choice. But because consumption and happiness are still supposed to be equivalent, after more than thirty years of the "affluent society" and an abundance of goods that no one dreamed of in the early 1950s, this new consumer, skilled in the reading of semiotic references and codes and in the exercise of individual choice, is still consumed by unsatisfied desires.

15

Reshaping Shopping Environments

The Competition Between the City of Boston and Its Suburbs

MATTHIAS JUDT

INTRODUCTION

The German notion "Stadtluft macht frei" refers, above all, to the rights of citizenship that townspeople in Germany and other European countries enjoyed during the Middle Ages. Once you had resided in a city or town for a year and a day, you were free of any obligation of servitude; in short, the peasant became a burgher. Yet, in a broader sense, this notion also refers to the cultural and economic opportunities that medieval towns offered. It is no wonder that urbanized areas often located near the sea or on important rivers became centers of economic progress. The development of trade and commerce made towns in Europe distinct from rural areas. Eventually, the process of industrialization in the nineteenth and early twentieth centuries allowed urban centers in Europe and North America to become regional economic powerhouses. In addition, the development of suburban areas displaced farmland to regions farther away from the center and absorbed the population surplus from the burgeoning cities.

Today, the role of cities in the industrialized world has changed profoundly. In contrast to those in previous periods of history, contemporary European and American cities show signs of decline, with the decay of spaces previously used for industrial and commercial purposes. Cities and towns seem to have lost their edge – to the benefit of their surrounding areas. The suburbs not only benefit from the out-migration of upwardly mobile people but also offer business opportunities to industrial and commercial enterprises that formerly looked for locations within the cities themselves.

At present, it seems that suburban rather than city or town air makes you free, that is, free of the burdens of structural change, the problems of city

317

life, and the high cost of urban public infrastructure. Thus, suburbanization – besides its demographic and sociological definition – may also be defined as a process of modern economic development.

What the Germans call the *Speckgürtel* (highly developed commercial and manufacturing ring) around older urban centers has eroded the tax base of cities, and small villages and towns on the periphery have become prosperous new centers of commercial activity. In contrast to previous historical periods, now these suburban areas are strong enough to resist incorporation into the central city. The balance of power on the regional level has shifted to the advantage of suburban cities and towns. They are now the places that have the "magnetic" power to attract new residential and commercial development.

If cities have for centuries been magnets for population development and economic growth, what is or was the cause of their declining attraction? One of the obvious answers to the question is the development of transportation or, rather, the development of transportation opportunities.

The town where inhabitants had to travel by foot was small; the city that offered various kinds of efficient and affordable mass transit grew rapidly and permitted the accommodation of hundreds of thousands of people. Indeed, buses and horse-drawn streetcars (both later electrified) and early subway systems improved the already advantageous position of cities in competition with suburbs as places to produce things and to do business. With public transportation systems, suburbs remained the "bedroom communities" of the urban work force. They were not yet valid competitors of the cities in terms of production, administration, and commerce.

Even when a new luxury good – the automobile – arrived on the scene around the turn of the twentieth century, it did not at first harm the leading economic position of the big cities. When it became a consumer good available to an ever greater portion of the population, however, it immediately threatened cities' regional economic position.

In this way, automobiles became the factor that made suburbanization multifunctional.[1] Private automobiles "solved" the technical problem of commuting between home and work. The greater the number of people who owned automobiles, the more inhabitants could consider relocating to the suburbs. Likewise, those automobiles promoted the intentional establishment of industrial and commercial facilities in suburban areas because workplaces no longer had to be in "central" places or had to be reached by "centralized," that is, public, transportation.

1   See, e.g., John R. Borchert, "American Metropolitan Evolution," *Geographical Review* 67 (1967): 301–32. Borchert argues that the triumph of automobiles opened up a new era in urban history.

In this chapter I use the city of Boston as an example of the changing relationship between cities and suburbs.[2] I have chosen Boston because it was one of the first cities in the United States to develop modern systems of transportation: streetcars and subways as well as a dense network of highways for automobiles. I have selected the field of retailing in order to examine demographic growth in connection with economic development. I discuss the interaction of traditional regional attitudes toward the biggest city in Massachusetts, the revolution in retailing after 1945 with the arrival of suburban shopping centers, and the "triumph" of the automobile as the most important means of transportation. I investigate Boston's retailing sector as an example of what happened to older central cities as a result of this interaction. Similar to what happened to the Central Business Districts (CBDs) of other American cities,[3] Boston's CBD also became obsolete, falling behind the emerging suburban retail market with regard to size, accessibility, architecture, and, above all, sales.

Boston's similarities to some European urban centers offer another reason for studying it. Cities and towns in Europe typically lack hinterland as a basic natural resource; high population densities and a great concentration of industrial and commercial facilities are the result. Experiencing the decline of traditional "old" industries, such as steel production, coal mining, or shipbuilding, private investors often use the abandoned properties for new businesses. Local, regional, and, in some cases, even national governments often support these efforts as components of state-run redevelopment and revitalization strategies. Because cities and regions with high population densities are unable simply to abandon areas in economic crisis, as well as what Walter Firey has called the "sentiments" and "symbolic values" that are connected with those areas, residents frequently demand that public officials attempt to revitalize the respective areas after former major industries have departed.[4]

Restricted by geography and situated in a densely populated area, Boston also experienced a restructuring of its economic base. Already during the

---

2 To understand the special conditions of Boston's inability to "reclaim administratively" its share of the regional retailing business by annexing surrounding cities and towns, see Sam Bass Warner Jr., *Streetcar Suburbs: The Process of Growth in Boston, 1870–1900,* 2d ed. (1962; reprint, Cambridge, Mass., 1978).

3 Cf. Pierce F. Lewis, "The Galactic Metropolis," in Rutherford H. Platt and George Macino, eds., *Beyond the Urban Fringe: Land Use Issues of Nonmetropolitan America* (Minneapolis, 1983), 23–49; Edward L. Ullman, "The Nature of Cities, Reconsidered," in Regional Science Association, ed., *Papers and Proceedings* 9 (1962): 7–23.

4 Cf. Walter Firey, "Sentiment and Symbolism as Ecological Variables," *American Sociological Review* 10 (Apr. 1945): 140–8, reprinted in George A. Theorson, ed., *Urban Patterns* (University Park, Pa., 1982), 129–36.

antebellum period shipping lost out to manufacturing as the major pillar of Boston's economy. In the 1920s Boston's textile industry entered into crisis. In contrast, banking, insurance, and investment management achieved and maintained a leading economic position over the last 100 to 150 years of the city's history. Furthermore, retailing can be viewed as an example of regional development and redevelopment.

DEFINITION OF THE BOSTON METROPOLITAN REGION

Although this chapter focuses on twentieth-century developments, to understand the special conditions of Boston's economic and demographic evolution, one has to look further back into the city's history. Like most older cities the world over, Boston has experienced tremendous demographic and economic change. With the rise of industrialization in the nineteenth century, Boston's population rose dramatically. In 1800 the city's population was nearly 25,000; one hundred years later, the population had reached 574,000.

Boston differs from other towns, however, in its relationship to its neighboring communities. Besides topographical conditions (division of land by rivers and lakes), the area's social and functional segregation[5] is also based on long-standing religious and political traditions.[6] The founding of Boston in 1630 was accompanied by the establishment of other towns in eastern Massachusetts. Wherever Puritans founded new parishes, the arrangement of governmental structures for the handling of secular affairs soon followed, eventually cemented by the incorporation of new towns.[7]

This fragmentation continued during the nineteenth century. Religious motives for the incorporation of new towns, however, were replaced by

---

5 According to Joachim Burdack, social segregation means the spatial differentiation between certain social groups, whereas functional segregation indicates the differentiation of areas according to their respective dominant function. Cf. Joachim Burdack, *Entwicklungstendenzen der Raumstruktur in Metropolitan Areas der USA* (Bamberg, 1985), 8.

6 In this chapter, I do not discuss social segregation of Boston in detail, although such a discussion would also include the problem of racial segregation. The latter, certainly a significant problem in metropolitan Boston (and other American cities), became a prominent factor in the discussions about the so-called red-lining of certain neighborhoods, that is, the practice of many banks and insurance companies of refusing to do business in there. This was one of the topics of the hearings held by the "National Commission on Urban Problems," appointed by President Lyndon B. Johnson on Jan. 12, 1967, which interviewed representatives from the Boston area in late May 1967. See National Committee on Urban Problems, *Hearings Before the National Commission on Urban Problems,* vol. 1: *May–June 1967: Baltimore, New Haven, Boston, Pittsburgh* (Washington, D.C., 1968), 187–265.

7 Theodore Bullen, "Summary of *The Political Disintegration and Reintegration of Metropolitan Boston* by George Herbert McCaffrey," Ph.D. diss., Harvard University, 1937, 2; James Anthony Morino, "A Great City and its Suburbs: Attempts to Integrate Metropolitan Boston, 1865–1920," Ph.D. diss., University of Texas, 1968, 5–6.

social and economic ones. Studies indicate that the area's fragmentation was the result of the competing political interests of two social groups: Those living in urbanized portions of the "old" towns desired city status, whereas inhabitants of more rural sections wanted to preserve the traditional town meeting form of government in their respective locations.[8]

Socioeconomic goals of particular groups began to play a major role in the founding of Winchester in 1850 and of Belmont in 1859.[9] Anthony Morino points out that moderately wealthy people tried to escape taxation in the towns of original jurisdiction.[10] Sam Bass Warner Jr. observes that the middle class "escaped the social and fiscal burdens and conflicts that inevitably attend the hierarchical distribution of the nation's wealth and income."[11] The latter process was supported "technically" by the implementation of early building codes in Boston, which hindered rather than promoted the further development of multifamily houses. When Boston required in 1897 that all tenement houses be fireproofed if they had more than three families living above the second story, for example, this really meant an "unofficial zoning" that promoted the construction of smaller houses.[12]

Logically consistent in this sense were regular attempts, most of which failed, to reintegrate the Boston area through annexation. The city, in its 367 year history, managed to absorb only eight surrounding locations – in 1637, 1804, 1868, 1870, 1874, and 1912.[13] As a consequence, Boston was unable to "reclaim administratively" its share of the regional retailing business by annexing surrounding cities and towns after 1912.

However, facing the effects of industrialization and population growth, Boston and its surrounding towns had to look for a makeshift arrangement. The creation of common metropolitan authorities between 1889 and 1919 aimed to ease the management of sanitation, parks, and streets.[14] Around

8 Morino, "Great City," 5–6.

9 Morino, "Great City," 6; Albert N. Gorwood, *Massachusetts Municipal Profiles, 1986–1987* (Wellesley Hills, Mass , 1986), 57, 78.

10 Morino, "Great City," 6.   11 Warner, *Streetcar Suburbs,* xii.

12 For the case of Boston, see Kenneth Baar, "The National Movement to Halt the Spread of Multi-family Housing, 1890–1926," *Journal of the American Planning Association* 58, no. 1 (1992): 42.

13 Annexation of Noodle Island, 1637; annexation of Dorchester Neck, 1804; annexation of Roxbury, 1868; annexation of Dorchester proper, 1870; annexation of Charlestown, Brighton, and West Roxbury, 1874; annexation of Hyde Park, 1912. See George J. Lankevich, *Boston: A Chronological and Documentary History* (Dobbs Ferry, N.Y., 1974), 5–57.

14 Foundation of the Metropolitan Sewerage Board, 1889; Metropolitan Water Board and Metropolitan Parks Commission, 1895; consolidation of sewerage and water boards, 1901; consolidation of Metropolitan Water and Sewerage Boards and Metropolitan Parks Commission into Metropolitan District Commission, 1919. Cf. Boston Chamber of Commerce, *Metropolitan Planning and Development in Boston and Its Environs* (Boston, 1922) 29.

1900, Boston was no longer "the old settlement" founded by Puritan immigrants but had become the "principal zone of work – the industrial, commercial, and communications center of the metropolitan region."[15] A network of streetcar lines linked the inner city, where people worked and consumed, to what was called Boston's "playground and [its] bedroom," namely, the suburbs.[16]

By 1900, the area that later came to be called the "Boston Metropolitan Area" sprawled over a ten-mile radius and contained "only" thirty-one cities[17] and towns.[18] Twenty years later the U.S. Bureau of the Census included fifty-seven cities and towns in the area it considered to be metropolitan Boston.[19] By 1941, a study on retailing in the Boston area in the 1930s encompassed 146 cities and towns.[20] Beginning in the 1950s, the census bureau defined approximately 150 municipalities as part of the Boston Standardized Metropolitan Statistical Area (SMSA).

In 1980 and 1990, the census bureau replaced the SMSA concept with a new definition: the Boston–Worcester–Lawrence Consolidated Metropolitan Statistical Area (Boston CMSA). This area stretches from the southern part of Maine in the north to southeastern Massachusetts, from the Atlantic Ocean in the east to almost the middle of the state in the west.

To facilitate a study that is as comprehensive and as complete as possible, however, I limit my study to the Massachusetts part of the Boston CMSA. In doing so, I apply more or less the "old" Boston SMSA definition, which had also been the basis for other studies of the Boston Metropolitan Area.[21] I call the area for this study the Boston metropolitan region; it consists of 150 cities and towns located in three subareas: the core area, the inner suburbs, and the outer suburbs.[22]

---

15 Warner, *Streetcar Suburbs,* 5.

16 March C. Bennett, "Metropolitan Boston: What It Is and How It Should Be Governed," *New Boston,* July 10, 1910, 107.

17 A town in Massachusetts that has more than 12,000 inhabitants over a reasonable period can apply to become incorporated as a "city" according to Massachusetts law.

18 Warner, *Streetcar Suburbs,* 5.   19 Cf. Boston Chamber of Commerce, *Metropolitan Planning,* 27.

20 Richard P. Doherty, *Trends in Retail Trade and the Consumer Buying Habits in the Metropolitan Boston Retail Area* [Report] (Boston, 1941), 6.

21 See, e.g., Greater Boston Economic Study Committee (ESC), *Land Use in Greater Boston in 1960* (Boston, 1962). I deviate from the ESC's report by including more towns in both the Core Area (26 instead of 15) and the Inner-suburban Area (41 instead of 34). In addition, a fourth category, the "Outer Cities," is not applied; the four locations are included in the "Outer suburban Area."

22 The "core area" stretches ten miles from the State House in Boston to include Arlington, Belmont, Boston, Brookline, Cambridge, Chelsea, Dedham, Everett, Lexington, Lynn, Malden, Medford, Melrose, Milton, Newton, Quincy, Revere, Saugus, Somerville, Stoneham, Wakefield, Waltham, Watertown, Winchester, Winthrop, and Woburn. The Inner Suburbs stretch 10 to 20 miles from Boston's center and include Abington, Avon, Beverly, Braintree, Brockton, Burlington, Canton, Cohasset, Concord, Danvers, Dover, Framingham, Hanover, Hingham, Holbrook, Hull, Lincoln, Lynnfield, Marblehead, Nahant, Natick, Needham, Norwell, Norwood, Peabody, Randolph, Reading, Rockland, Salem, Scituate, Sharon, Stoughton, Sudbury, Swampscott, Walpole, Wellesley, Wenham, Weston,

POPULATION DEVELOPMENT IN THE
METROPOLITAN REGION

The prodigious growth of Boston's population in the nineteenth century continued during the first half of the twentieth century (see Table 15.1).[23] It grew steadily until 1930, and then it grew again in the 1940s. By 1950, the number of Bostonians reached its historic peak of 801,000.[24] Afterward, the population started to decline, dropping to nearly 563,000 in 1980. Since 1980 the city's population has recovered to the level it had in 1900.[25]

The decline in Boston's population since 1950 has been more than offset by the growth of the metropolitan population as a whole. Yet the increases have gone to other subareas of the Boston metropolitan region. In 1990, almost 3.58 million people lived in the region, but Boston's share of the total had dropped from about 35 percent at the turn of the century to around 16 percent in 1990.

This shift in population growth within the Boston metropolitan region also affected other subareas. First, a decline similar to the city of Boston's occurred in the core metropolitan area, albeit delayed by twenty years. This area's population grew until 1950, but its share of the region's population stopped increasing even earlier (1930). Whereas this subarea housed over 70

Westwood, Weymouth, and Wilmington. The "outer suburbs" 20 to 35 miles from Boston's center are composed of Acton, Amesbury, Andover, Ashland, Attleboro, Ayer, Bedford, Bellingham, Berlin, Billrica, Bolton, Boxborough, Boxford, Bridgewater, Carlisle, Chelmsford, Dracut, Dunstable, Duxbury, E. Bridgewater, Easton, Essex, Foxborough, Franklin, Georgetown, Gloucester, Groton, Groveland, Halifax, Hamilton, Hanson, Harvard, Holliston, Hopedale, Hopkinton, Hudson, Ipswich, Kingston, Littleton, Manchester, Mansfield, Marlborough, Marshfield, Maynard, Medfield, Medway, Mendon, Merrimac, Methuen, Middleborough, Middleton, Milford, Millis, Newbury, Newburyport, Norfolk, N. Andover, Northborough, N. Reading, Norton, Pembroke, Plainville, Plympton, Raynham, Rockport, Rowley, Salisbury, Sherborn, Southborough, Stow, Taunton, Tewksbury, Topsfield, Tyngsborough, Upton, Wayland, Westborough, W. Bridgewater, Westforf, W. Newbury, Whitman, and Wrentham.

23 Unless otherwise indicated, the population data is compiled from the following sources: for 1890, U.S. Bureau of the Census, *Bulletin of the Twelfth Census of the United States, no. 13: Population of Massachusetts by Counties and Minor Civil Divisions* (Washington, D.C., Nov. 8, 1900), 3–5; for 1900–1920, U.S. Bureau of the Census, *Fourteenth Census of the United States; States Compendium: Pamphlet no. 20* (Washington, D.C., 1924), 11–13; for 1930, U.S. Bureau of the Census, *Fifteenth Census of the United States: 1930,* vol. 3: *Reports by States,* pt. 1: *Alabama-Missouri* (Washington, D.C., 1932), 1105–9; for 1940: U.S. Bureau of the Census, *Sixteenth Census of the United States: 1940,* vol. 2: *Characteristics of the Population,* pt. 3: *Kansas-Michigan* (Washington, D.C., 1943), 626–34; for 1950: Bureau of the Census, *Census of the United States: 1950,* vol. 2: *Characteristics of the Population,* pt. 21: *Massachusetts* (Washington, D.C., 1951), 21–11; for 1960, Metropolitan Area Planning Council, *The Population of Cities and Towns in Metropolitan Boston Projected to 1990* (Boston, Apr. 1968), A1–A6; Greater Boston Economic Study Committee, *The Population of Cities and Towns in Metropolitan Boston Projected to 1970* (Boston, 1959), 13–20; 1970–1980: John L. Andriot, *Population Abstracts of the United States,* vol. 1: *Tables* (McLean, Va., 1983), 362–7; for 1990, U.S. Bureau of the Census, *1990 Census of the United States,* electronic data on CD-ROM, Library of Congress, Washington, D.C.
24 Cf. *1950 Census,* 21–11.
25 Cf. *1890 Census,* 3; Andriot, *Population Abstracts,* 362–7, *1990 Census.*

Table 15.1 *Population development in the Boston metropolitan area (Massachusetts only), 1890–1990*

| Year | Core area | | | | | | Inner suburbs | | Outer suburbs | | Total study area | |
| | City of Boston | | Outside Boston | | Total core area | | | | | | | |
	Total	%	Total	%	Total	%	Total	%	Total	%	Total	Share
1890	458.7	34.9	405.8	30.9	864.5	65.8	172.2	13.1	276.3	21.0	1313.0	100.0
1900	574.1	35.2	545.1	33.4	1119.2	68.7	200.4	12.3	310.3	19.0	1629.9	100.0
1910	686.1	35.2	679.3	34.8	1365.4	70.0	236.3	12.1	348.3	17.9	1950.0	100.0
1920	748.1	33.6	835.3	37.5	1583.4	71.0	271.4	12.2	374.3	16.8	2229.1	100.0
1930	781.1	30.5	1040.2	40.6	1821.3	71.0	330.3	12.9	412.6	16.1	2564.2	100.0
1940	770.8	29.5	1058.8	40.5	1829.6	69.9	355.0	13.6	432.6	16.5	2617.2	100.0
1950	801.4	27.9	1140.3	39.7	1941.7	67.6	436.4	15.2	495.2	17.2	2873.3	100.0
1960	697.2	21.9	1185.7	37.2	1882.9	59.1	645.3	20.3	657.7	20.6	3185.9	100.0
1970	641.1	18.0	1207.4	33.9	1848.5	52.0	805.4	22.6	903.5	25.4	3557.4	100.0
1980	562.9	16.1	1114.3	31.9	1677.2	48.0	811.3	23.2	1006.0	28.8	3494.5	100.0
1990	574.3	16.1	1078.0	30.1	1652.3	46.2	814.1	22.8	1109.7	31.0	3576.1	100.0

percent of the people in the 1920s and 1930s, this portion declined to well under 50 percent in the 1980s and 1990s.

The clear winners in the shifting of population growth until the 1970s were the inner suburbs. Here, the number of inhabitants more than quadrupled between 1890 and 1970, while the subarea's share of the total population increased by 10 percentage points. Since the 1970s, however, the portion of inner suburbia's population in the region has stagnated.

Boston's outer suburbs, that is, towns and cities located at a greater distance from the Massachusetts capital, benefited the most from the population growth since the 1970s. In addition, the Boston metropolitan region demonstrates the nationwide process of exurbanization, that is, the movement of people to formerly rural areas and the transfer of urban life-styles to the countryside. Examples include the adoption of construction codes developed in the city and the establishment of urban commercial and cultural amenities.

AUTOMOBILES AND ECONOMIC SUBURBANIZATION

The increasing importance of commercial activities outside large urban centers is strongly related to the development of automobile travel in the United States. The growth in the number of automobiles in the country intensified not only the out-migration of people to the suburbs (even those located at a greater distance from the big city) but also had other implications.

The number of registered automobiles in the United States increased elevenfold between 1920 and 1970, expanding by about 50 percent in every decade (except for the 1930s).[26] In the post–World War II period, automobiles became the major mode of transportation.

Various factors promoted the private acquisition of automobiles in the United States. One was the greater availability of disposable income. This stemmed from wage increases during the war and restrictions on spending due to rationing or shortages of consumer goods. In addition, wartime price controls improved the real value of money earned during World War II. In Massachusetts alone, the real value of average annual income in 1945 was 61.1 percent higher than the average between 1935 and 1939.[27]

In this connection, federal and state programs promoted the economic development of the Boston metropolitan region. They aimed to mobilize

26 Cf. Burdack, *Entwicklungstendenzen,* 141.
27 Commonwealth of Massachusetts, Department of Labor and Industries, *Report of the Division of Statistics: 1953,* 9, Massachusetts State Archives, LA 1.03/1318x.

wartime savings while limiting the danger of inflation. The programs also aided the conversion of the American war economy to peacetime production. Among the programs, the following were the most important.

The Servicemen Readjustment Act of 1944, also known as the "GI Bill of Rights," provided for tuition programs that enabled war veterans to attend institutions of higher education (and also kept them out of the labor market temporarily). Higher education led to better professional lives and, in the end, to higher incomes. The GI Bill also made demobilized veterans of World War II (later joined by those from the Korean and Vietnam wars) eligible for subsidies for the construction of houses.

Federal and state road construction projects like Eisenhower's highway program provided for a net of interstate roads as well as for beltways around cities. This program not only eased automobile access to the entire metropolitan area but also contributed to their growing impact as well as improvements in the traffic infrastructure.

In this respect, the Commonwealth of Massachusetts, as one of the first states in the union to establish a highway commission and undertake ambitious street construction projects, could not build on previous experience in other states. Efforts to improve the road system in Massachusetts, already begun in the late 1890s, had an unintended effect on Boston's demographic and commercial development. What was meant to ease traffic to Boston also eased the movement of people away from Boston.

The four-tiered system of road improvements laid out by the Massachusetts Highway Commission in 1897 consisted of a radial network serving Boston, two east–west links between the Atlantic Ocean and Upstate New York, rural-service roads along river valleys, and a recreational link between Boston and Cope Cod.[28]

After 1945, the construction of State Route 128, completed in 1959,[29] and then Interstate 495 supplemented the historic radial network serving Boston. The combination of the street infrastructure and the greater availability of automobiles in the Boston metropolitan region made daily travel for longer distances within the region possible. Already in the late 1950s, the majority of those working in downtown Boston traveled to their workplace by automobile rather than by other means.[30]

---

28 Peter J. Hugill, "Good Roads and the Automobile in the United States, 1880–1929," *The Geographical Review* 72 (July 1982): 3, 332–3.

29 Robert T. Killam, "Boston's Golden Industrial Semicircle," in Greater Boston Chamber of Commerce, ed., *Greater Boston Business: Route 128 Supplement,* (Boston, Mar. 1959), 1–2.

30 Of the 500,000 commuters who traveled to their workplaces in Downtown Boston on a daily basis in the late 1950s, 60 percent used private automobiles, one-third buses, subways, and streetcars, while the rest went by regional commuter trains. Cf. Edward C. Keane: "Problems of Boston, the Central City of a Metropolitan Area," *Journal of the Boston Society of Civil Engineers* 47, no. 2 (1960): 106.

Moreover, the creation of a system of highways, especially Route 128 and Interstate 495, promoted the transfer of workplaces and centers of consumption away from locations within Boston to areas along these major arteries. The effect of the construction of multilane highways on retailing and on the relocation of industrial sites was tremendous. Until the end of 1959, industrial businesses had hired 30,000 people to work in new facilities located along Route 128.[31] The importance of the Route 128 corridor as a workplace continued to grow in the 1960s and 1970s. Between 1970 and 1980 alone, 151,000 jobs were created along that corridor.[32]

RETAIL DEVELOPMENT IN METROPOLITAN BOSTON UNTIL WORLD WAR II

Retailing has undergone basic changes since the beginning of the Industrial Revolution.[33] The growth of industries as well as the expansion of towns promoted the development of new kinds of "retailers."[34] The new retail outlets also used the growing public transportation systems in big cities,

---

31 Killam, "Boston's Semicircle," 1.
32 Governor, Economic Development, Regional Development Files: Dukakis, "Route 128 Analysis," n.d. [?June 1985], Massachusetts State Archives, GO-15/1367.
33 Unless otherwise indicated, the retail data is compiled from the following sources: 1929: Melvin T. Morse, Massachusetts State Planning Board, *Development of Retail Trade in Massachusetts Cities and Towns, 1929–1939* (Boston, Nov. 1941), 1; 1933: Bureau of the Census, *Census of American Business: Retail Distribution: 1933: By Areas, Stores and Sales by Business Groups for States, Counties and Cities* (Washington, D.C., 1935), 77–9; 1935: Bureau of the Census, *Census of Business: 1935 Retail Distribution*, vol. 3: *Kinds of Business by Areas, Stores and Sales for States, Counties and Cities* (Washington, D.C., 1936), 154–6; 1939: Bureau of the Census, *Sixteenth Census of the United States: 1940*, vol. 1: *Retail Trade 1939*, pt. 3: *Kinds of Business by Areas, States, Counties and Cities* (Washington, D.C., 1941), 324–7; 1948: Bureau of the Census, *United States Census of Business 1948*, vol. 2: *Retail Trade: Area Statistics* (Washington, D.C., 1951), 20-12–20-14; 1954: Bureau of the Census, *United States Census of Business 1954*, vol. 2: *Retail Trade: Area Statistics*, pt. 1: *United States Summary and Alabama-Mississippi* (Washington, D.C., 1956), 21-6–21-7; 1958: Bureau of the Census, *United States Census of Business 1958*, vol. 2: *Retail Trade: Area Statistics*, pt. 1: *United States Summary and Alabama-Mississippi* (Washington, D.C., 1961), 21-8–21-11; 1963: Bureau of the Census, *1963 Census of Business*, vol. 2: *Retail Trade Area Statistics*, pt. 2: *Indiana-New York* (Washington, D.C., 1966), 23-10–23-13; 1967: Bureau of the Census, *1967 Census of Business*, vol. 2: *Retail Trade Area Statistics*, pt. 2: *Iowa-N.C.* (Washington, D.C., 1970), 23-8–23-13; 1972: Bureau of the Census, *1972 Census of Retail Trade*, vol. 2: *Area Statistics*, pt. 2: *Iowa-North Carolina* (Washington, D.C., May 1976), 22-70–22-75; 1977: Bureau of the Census, *1977 Census of Retail Trade*, vol. 2: *Geographic Area Statistics*, pt. 2: *Iowa-North Carolina* (Washington, D.C., 1978), 22-68–22-73; 1982: Bureau of the Census, *1982 Census of Retail Trade Geographic Area Series: Massachusetts* (Washington, D.C., Sept. 1984), Mass56–Mass61; 1987: Bureau of the Census, *1987 Census of Retail Trade Geographic Area Series: Massachusetts* (Washington, D.C., July 1989), MA14–MA18; 1992: Bureau of the Census, *1992 Census of Retail Trade* (Electronic Data on CD-ROM at Library of Congress).
34 For more analysis I refer to the chapters by Victoria de Grazia and Susan Benson Porter in this book. In addition, see William Leach, *Land of Desire: Merchants, Power, and the Rise of a New American Culture* (New York, 1993); Susan Strasser, *Satisfaction Guaranteed: The Making of the American Mass Market* (New York, 1989).

easing the "commuting" of customers between the "centralized" retail outlets and residential neighborhoods.

There is a strong connection between the establishment of streetcar or
subway systems and the opening of department stores and other retail outlets in city centers.[35] Along with still existing specialized stores, they began
to concentrate in certain areas of the cities, the CBDs, where stage theaters
(later also cinemas) and other entertainment venues were located. In addition, banks, hotels, and other commercial businesses in search of high-
prestige addresses found appropriate locations in the CBDs.[36]

Textile traders, such as Samuel Lord and George Washington Taylor in
New York (already in 1826), Simon Lazarus in Columbus, Ohio (1851),
John Wanamaker in Philadelphia (1861), and Morris Rich in Atlanta (1867),
were among those who established retailing enterprises in central city areas
that later became known as department stores.[37]

In Boston, Eben Jordan as well as William, Edward, and Lincoln Filene
were the founders of businesses that become the leading local and regional
department store companies. Jordan opened in 1851; William Filene, in
1881. Based on the traditionally developed textile trade, which itself had its
foundation in local textile manufacturing and wholesaling of raw materials,
the establishment of department stores in Boston was a logical step in the
development of retailing.[38]

When the Federal Bureau of the Census in 1929 conducted its first business census, the retail trade data collected confirmed the dominant position
of cities and large towns in retailing. Table 15.2 shows the population and
the retail trade development in the Boston metropolitan region. The comparison of these two factors indicates the conditions of retailing in the
region prior to World War II.

The retail data for the eleven years between 1929 and 1939, at first glance,
indicate Boston's dominance in retail trade. Compared to its share of the
region's population, Boston was able to garner significantly higher shares in
retail trading in both the core area and the whole study area. All other sub-

---

35 Eleanor G. May, "A Retail Odyssey," *Journal of Retailing* 65, no. 3 (1989): 361.
36 Cf. Ernest W. Burgess, "The Growth of the City: A Research Project," in Robert E. Park, Ernest W.
   Burgess, and Roderick D. McKienzie, eds., *The City* (Chicago, 1925), 47–62; see also Burdack,
   Entwicklungsstrukturen, 26–7.
37 Tom Mahorney and Leonard Sloane, *Grosse Kaufleute: Von Tiffany bis Woolworth* (Düsseldorf, 1970),
   19. (American ed.: *The Great Merchants* [New York, 1966]). See also Ronald Savitt, "Looking Back To
   See Ahead: Writing the History of American Retailing," *Journal of Retailing* 65, no. 3 (1989): 333.
38 Cf. *Report of Mr. Sturgis' Committee to Twenty-Eight Manufacturing Companies* (Boston, 1852), quoted
   in Mona Domash, "Shaping the Commercial Districts in Nineteenth-Century New York and
   Boston," *Annals of the Association of American Geographers* 80, no. 2 (1990): 271.

Table 15.2 *Population and retail trade development in the Boston metropolitan area (Massachusetts only), 1929–1940*

	Population development		Retail trade development			
Area	1930	1940	1929	1933	1935	1939
Core area	71.0	69.9	74.3	74.3	73.4	72.4
City of Boston	30.5	29.5	47.9	46.0	44.2	42.3
Outside Boston	40.6	40.5	26.4	28.3	29.2	30.1
Inner suburbs	12.9	13.6	10.8	11.2	11.5	12.2
Outer suburbs	16.1	16.5	14.8	14.5	15.1	15.4

areas show similar rates for retail and for population shares indicating that commuting customers were doing most of their shopping in Boston rather than in their hometown.[39]

The great inner-city retailers, such as Jordan Marsh and Filene's, benefited especially from the dominant position of the city's CBD. In 1929, Boston's department stores had 49.9 percent of the city's whole retail trade.[40] As was the case in other American and European cities, department stores in Boston also remained the "where-to-buy" places.[41] But in the 1930s Boston retail stores were superior in performance; customers preferred them for buying durable goods and apparel.[42]

Table 15.2 also indicates, however, that Boston started to lose business to other towns during the 1930s. Prior to World War II the other core area cities and towns managed to absorb most of the losses Boston suffered. Table 15.3 shows that between 1929 and 1939, Boston's share of the core area's total retailing decreased from over two-thirds to about 58 percent.

More significant was the decline in sales of several important product lines, such as automobiles and other durable goods. In the long run, the decline in durable-goods retailing was detrimental to Boston's retail industry as a whole. In the years to come, it was about to lose its leading position in retailing not only within the core area but also within the total study area (see Table 15.4).[43]

39 One can assume that this was true for the first half of the twentieth century in general. An article in *Boston Business,* published in 1934, refers to the historical importance Boston's CBD had in wholesale and retail trading in 1909. Cf. "Looking Back a Quarter-Century" in Boston Chamber of Commerce, ed., *Boston Business,* May 1934, 13.
40 Richard Doherty and Stuart Cox, *An Analysis of Retail Trade and Consumer Buying in the Boston Retail Market,* manuscript, Boston, n.d. [1931], 22.
41 May, "Retail Odyssey," 360.
42 Doherty, *Trends in Retail Trade,* 14b.
43 Even though the size of the area Doherty studied in 1941 differs slightly from the one I have cho-

Table 15.3 *City of Boston's share of core area
retail sales, 1929 and 1939*

	1929	1939
Total retail sales	64.5	58.4
Food	44.8	43.9
General merchandise	86.6	81.7
Apparel	80.5	75.7
Furniture	72.0	63.6
Automobile	55.8	38.1
Hardware and lumber	39.8	45.9

Contrary to the findings of the U.S. Bureau of the Census, the Massachusetts Department of Commerce in 1940 denied that the ongoing migration of people to the suburbs had an impact on the performance of Boston retail stores.[44] Contemporary advertisements in local newspapers and magazines also give the impression that retailing in the late 1940s and early 1950s took place mainly in Boston proper.[45]

By the early 1940s, however, suburban retail centers had begun to offer genuine competition to Boston's CBD. Several factors contributed to this development. First, as the average population growth in the core area exceeded that of Boston, the importance of suburban towns and cities as retail locations increased. Hard hit by the Great Depression, which cut Boston's retail trade by more than 44 percent,[46] the recovery of Boston's retail sector lasted longer than that of other towns in the core area. Under difficult economic conditions, eleven of twenty-six cities and towns in the core area could surpass their 1929 retail data by 1939, whereas other locations, including Boston, did not experience "relief" until the beginning of World War II.[47]

Second, the increasing population in the suburbs justified the establishment of new stores there that offered at least those product lines typical of food and drug stores. In addition, retail demanded a lot of space outside the

sen, the data compiled in the table indicate how Boston also lost significant shares in the retailing of durable goods to other locations, even to those outside the core area.

44 Commonwealth of Massachusetts, Department of Labor and Industries, "Report of the Division of Statistics: Reprint of the Annual Report of the Department of Labor and Industries for the year ending November 30, 1940," Massachusetts State Archives, LA 1.03/1318x, 29.

45 See the yearly volumes of the *Boston Globe, Boston Herald-Traveller,* and *Boston Business* until the early 1950s.

46 Calculated for 1929 according to Doherty and Cox, "Analysis," 10, and for 1933, "1933 Census," 77–9.

47 Cf. "1939 Census," 324–7; "1948 Census," 20-12–20-14.

Table 15.4 *City of Boston's share of metropolitan area retail sales, 1929, 1935, and 1939*

	1929	1935	1939
Food	33.1	33.4	32.6
General merchandise	76.2	71.7	70.7
Apparel	63.4	64.0	55.8
Automobile	41.5	33.1	28.4
Furniture	56.0	54.9	47.3

city. This affected not only car dealers but also furniture retailers and others who looked for larger and cheaper spaces outside Boston.[48]

Third, traffic problems within the city limits diverted retail sales to suburban areas. Even though public transportation granted excellent access to Boston's department stores on Washington Street, the increasing importance of automobiles as means of individual transportation would, in the future, disadvantage Boston retailers. Besides potential customers, who had difficulties finding parking, merchandisers were also interested in locating principal factories and warehouses on the urban periphery.[49]

Fourth, locally organized department stores often had only a few outlets.[50] With this precondition, department store companies such as Boston's Jordan Marsh Company and Filene's had a clear disadvantage compared to low-price chain stores. Those five-and-dime stores such as S. S. Kresge (which later became Kmart) and F. W. Woolworth, with a limited but still wide selection of goods, became strong competitors for inner-city department stores.

RETAIL DEVELOPMENT IN METROPOLITAN BOSTON
AFTER 1945

The development of retailing in the United States after World War II illustrates important differences from developments in European countries.[51]

48 An ad for the New England supermarket chain First National in the magazine of the Boston Chamber of Commerce asked the male readers to buy bread at its South Station outlet in Boston to give "relief" to their (house)wives waiting at home.
49 The traffic problem was a permanent topic of the magazine of the (Greater) Boston Chamber of Commerce. See, e.g., Harvey D. Dunn, "Solving Boston's Traffic Problems," in Boston Chamber of Commerce, *Boston Business* (Boston, Nov. 1929), 5, 36–40, 48; Daniel J. Ahern, "A City on Wheels," in Greater Boston Chamber of Commerce, *Greater Boston Business* (Boston, Aug. 1956), 12–13, 42–50.
50 Only a minority of department store companies had four or more retail outlets in the years before World War II. Cf. Stanley C. Hollander and Glenn S. Omura, "Chain Store Developments and Their Political, Strategic, and Social Interdependencies," *Journal of Retailing* 65 (1989): 3, 306.
51 For details see Victoria de Grazia's chapter in this book.

The spread of huge shopping centers outside American cities revolutionized the way the retailing industry "stage-managed" consumption. Although
historical forerunners of strip and covered shopping centers can be found
in Europe and in the Middle East (oriental bazaars, arcades in nineteenth-
century Italy and England, colonnaded streets in Bern, Switzerland),[52] the
success of what later were called shopping malls was based on the American
way of consumption.

One step in the development toward the establishment of shopping malls
in the United States was the so-called miracle mile. At the edges of big
cities, they complemented conventional inner-city main streets. Portions of
exit roads and other appropriate streets were dedicated to the sole purpose
of shopping. Here, car dealerships, supermarkets, and five-and-dime stores
found new and bigger homes. The shopping mall pioneer Victor Gruen,[53]
who was born in Vienna, described it as follows: "The greater the 'miracle'
of merchandising success became, the more intense became the 'misery' for
those ... who wished to engage in shopping."[54]

The problem of traffic jams, already familiar to inner-city areas, also
became manifest in suburban cities and towns. In this sense, strip malls and
covered shopping centers solved various problems connected to the conventional monofunctional shopping areas like CBDs and miracle miles.
First, they "perfected" the old main-street concept. The real estate firm
owning a mall was able to create the "perfect" mixture of tenants in its
shopping center, something the genuine main streets could never have
achieved. Second, by providing huge parking lots, shopping centers had a
clear advantage compared to CBDs and even to miracle miles.[55] This fact
also indicates the deliberate dependence on customers arriving by automobile rather than by public transportation. Gruen even assumed that "shopping centers have taken on the character of urban organisms serving a multitude of human needs and activities."[56]

Besides the different architecture and the new dependence on automobiles, the very approach to the customer also changed here. Whereas the

52 Victor Gruen, *Centers for the Urban Environment: Survival for the Cities* (New York, 1973), 14–16.
53 Victor Gruen was born in 1903 in Vienna, Austria, fled the Nazis in 1938, and became one of the
   leading architects for shopping malls in the United States. He died in 1980.
54 Gruen, *Urban Environment,* 19.
55 In the downtown section of Boston in 1956, there were 15 parking garages which could hold 6,784
   vehicles, 87 public parking spaces for 4,498 automobiles, and another 3,814 legal curb spaces. Cf.
   William Arthur Riley, "Only 15,096 Parking Spaces For the 200,000 Cars Entering Downtown
   Boston Each Day," in Greater Boston Chamber of Commerce, *Greater Boston Business* (Boston, Dec.
   1956), 24.
56 Victor Gruen and Larry Smith, *Shopping Towns USA: The Planning of Shopping Centers* (New York,
   1960), 23; quoted in Howard Gilette Jr., "The Evolution of the Planned Shopping Center in Suburb
   and City," *Journal of the American Planning Association* 51, no. 4 (1985): 452.

pre–World War II customer was invited to be a "buyer," the postwar one was induced to become a "shopper." The difference was that the former usually had a predetermined aim for his trip, whereas the latter was enticed to the shopping center without clearly defined goals – ostensibly just to browse.

Special architectural settings in those new shopping centers were – and are – supposed to "catch" potential customers within their walls. The ideal "trap" was the covered shopping center, the mall. Here, even the interior design was guided by the goal of keeping the shopper in the building as long as possible. Whereas department stores provide easy access and good ways to leave the building, covered shopping centers cloak exits and let the customer search for escalators to expose him or her to as many store windows or as much merchandise as possible.

This completely different concept of retailing arrived in New England in 1951. Shopper's World in Framingham, west of Boston, opened as the first mall in the Northeast. It had only a few predecessors in other parts of the country.[57] The aforementioned Route 128 and Interstate 495 provided the infrastructure for the construction of huge retail centers like Shopper's World at a greater distance from the traditional commercial centers in Boston itself. The inner beltway, Route 128, became the new "wonderland" of retailing. Here, covered malls in Framingham, Peabody, and Saugus as well as strip malls in Chestnut Hill, Waltham, and Quincy opened their doors by the end of the 1950s. Almost 1.6 million people lived within an hour's drive of the region's largest mall at that time, the Northshore Shopping Center in Peabody.[58]

By allowing the construction of new shopping centers, cities and towns used their zoning privileges to strengthen the local economies. Therefore, not only industrial facilities, which were constructed along the two beltways near Boston, but also shopping malls promoted the general economic development of suburban towns and cities – at Boston's expense.

Table 15.5 shows the direct impact malls had on the performance of the local retail industry in these cities and towns. Whenever and wherever malls opened, the communities experienced a "jump" in sales at local retailing outlets. The comparison of business census data from the year before the

57 Probably the oldest mall in America is Roland Park Shop in Baltimore, Maryland, which opened its doors in 1907. A few others opened in the years leading up to World War II. However, the actual "malling" of America started just after 1945, beginning on the West Coast and in the Midwest. Shopper's World was one of the first postwar malls on the East Coast. See *Top Shopping Centers: Major Markets, 1–50* (Chicago, 1992).

58 Paul R. Stevens, "Modern Retail Shopping Centers Serve Route 128 Communities," in "Route 128 Supplement," 11.

Table 15.5 *Local retail trade after the opening of new shopping malls*

Shopping center	Town	Subarea	Open since	Previous census = 100
Shopper's World	Framingham	Inner suburbs	1951	186.5
Northshore Shopping Center	Peabody	Inner suburbs	1958	267.0
New England Shopping Center	Saugus	Core area	1959	331.2
Southshore Plaza	Braintree	Inner suburbs	1961	262.5
Westgate Mall	Brockton	Inner suburbs	1963	131.6
Dedham Mall	Dedham	Core area	1964	183.4
Natick Mall	Natick	Inner suburbs	1966	209.9
Burlington Mall	Burlington	Inner suburbs	1968	620.6
Hanover Mall	Hanover	Inner suburbs	1971	NA
Liberty Free Mall	Danvers	Inner suburbs	1972	352.1
Methuen Mall	Methuen	Outer suburbs	1973	251.9
The Mall at Chestnut Hill	Chestnut Hill	Inner suburbs	1974	NA
The Mall at Assembly Square	Somerville	Core area	1981	157.6
Arsenal Mall	Watertown	Core area	1983	206.6
Copley Place	Boston	Boston	1983	138.5
Lafayette Place	Boston	Boston	1984	138.5
Independence	Kingston	Outer suburbs	1989	NA
Cambridge Side Galleria	Cambridge	Core area	1990	124.0

opening of the mall with those of the year after shows the tremendous impact of these shopping centers.

Even if the malls were not the only cause of growth, the cities and towns in which they were located clearly profited economically. In some cases, the very existence of a new shopping mall rendered the localities eligible for inclusion in the publication of local retail trade data by the U.S. Bureau of the Census.

In contrast, Boston's retail trade began to feel the negative effects of the region's malling. Within as little as two years after the opening of Shopper's World, department stores in Boston had lost nearly 10 percent of their business to suburban retail outlets.[59]

In the long run, new suburban shopping centers in the region changed customers' behavior. In 1953 the *Boston Herald-Traveler* financed a survey conducted by Boston University. The report "Downtown and Suburban

59 Calculated for 1948–56 in constant 1947–9 dollars by author according to Federal Reserve Bank of Boston. Research & Statistics Department, "Boston Department Store Sales," quoted in Arthur D. Little, Inc., *Report to Boston City Planning Board: Preliminary Research for the Development of Boston's Retail Development* (Cambridge, Mass., Dec. 3, 1957), 7.

Shopping Habits Study of Greater Boston" showed some early effects of suburban shopping centers. Customers in the 1950s still preferred to buy apparel in Boston's stores, even if they lived outside the city limits. However, those purchases were limited to upscale clothing. Non-Bostonian customers preferred to buy children's wear and shoes in stores outside Boston.[60]

Most significant was the change regarding the purchase of durable goods, such as refrigerators, television sets, radios, and appliances. Retail stores outside Boston's city limits not only captured the major part of the business with non-Bostonians, they even began to attract the business of native Bostonians.[61]

This change in customer behavior contributed to the fact that Boston lost its leading position in the retail trade in its metropolitan area earlier than other American cities.[62] The 1958 Census of Business indicated that the other core-area cities and towns had a higher share of the region's retailing than did Boston itself.[63] In 1967 inner-suburban cities and towns surpassed Boston in their share of retailing,[64] and in 1972 they were joined even by the outer suburban locations (see Table 15.6).[65]

Redevelopment activities in Boston were also intended to renew local retailing. When Mayor John Hynes created the Boston Redevelopment Authority in 1957, one of its major tasks – besides the development of housing – was to find ways to revitalize inner-city areas abandoned by businesses. The Boston Redevelopment Authority also targeted the CBD, with different success and different social effects. In the 1970s, for example, Boston adapted the concept of "pedestrian malls" to its traditional CBD along Washington Street. This was an attempt to copy the atmosphere of suburban covered shopping malls by banning traffic on some streets. It resulted in a slight improvement of retailing in downtown Boston.[66]

Finally, in the 1980s, two downtown shopping malls were built, with mixed results. Copley Place is a successfully run shopping mall that opened

60 John P. Alevezios and Allen E. Beckwith, *Downtown and Suburban Shopping Habits Study of Greater Boston* (Boston, 1954), 49–53; see also Little, *Preliminary Research,* 12–15.
61 Cf. Alevezios and Beckwith, *Shopping Habits,* 49–53.
62 In March 1965, the National Retail Merchants Association presented its report "Financial and Operating Results of Department and Specialty Stores" (for the year ending on Jan. 31, 1965). According to this report, in 1964 the turnover at suburban retail outlets was higher than in inner-city stores. Cf. *New York Times,* Mar. 5, 1965. See also Kent A. Robertson, "Downtown Retail Activity in Large American Cities, 1954–1977," *The Geographical Review* 73, no. 3 (1983): 315.
63 Calculated by author. Cf. "1958 Census," 21-8–21-11. See also Doherty, *Trends in Retail Trade,* appendix, table A.
64 Calculated by author. Cf. "1967 Census," 23-8–23-13.
65 Calculated by author. Cf. "1972 Census," 22-70–22-75.
66 Cf. Glen Weisbrod and Henry O. Pollakowski, "Effects of Downtown Improvement Project on Retail Activity," *Journal of the American Planning Association* 50, no. 2 (1984): 156–7; see also "1982," "1987," and "1992 Censuses."

Table 15.6 *Population and retail trade development in the Boston metropolitan area (Massachusetts only), 1940–1992*

Population	1940	1950	1960	1970	1980	1990
Core Area	69.9	67.6	59.1	52.0	48.0	46.2
City of Boston	29.5	27.9	21.9	18.0	16.1	16.1
Outside Boston	40.5	27.9	37.2	34.0	31.9	30.1
Inner suburbs	13.6	15.2	20.3	22.6	23.2	22.8
Outer suburbs	16.5	17.2	20.6	25.4	28.8	

Retail trade	1948	1954	1958	1963	1967	1972	1977	1982	1987	1992
Core area	70.2	70.1	66.5	60.0	55.9	49.0	45.5	44.6	41.8	43.1
City of Boston	39.0	36.4	32.5	25.4	23.5	18.8	15.5	14.8	13.4	14.1
Outside Boston	31.2	33.7	34.0	34.6	32.4	30.2	30.0	29.8	28.4	29.0
Inner suburbs	13.1	14.8	17.2	21.9	26.2	28.7	30.7	32.5	34.5	32.9
Outer suburbs	16.7	15.1	16.3	18.1	17.9	22.3	23.8	22.9	23.7	24.0

in 1983. However, it also forced hundreds of people who had lived in the area to relocate. In this way, it exemplifies the negative effects of urban redevelopment. In contrast to Copley Place, Lafayette Place on Washington Street opened in 1984 and went bankrupt in 1992.[67] The mall closed after only eight years of operation and continues to stand empty, despite efforts to reopen it.

The opening of a mall in downtown Cambridge just across the Charles River certainly contributed to the failure of Lafayette Place. Cambridge-Side Galleria opened in 1990 and is located near large employers, such as Lotus, and large institutions, such as MIT. Both Copley Place and CambridgeSide Galleria are disadvantaged, however, when it comes to attracting business from people traveling by car. The persistent parking problem in these locations limits the types of business to upscale clothing, jewelry, books, and so forth.

The question remains whether Boston will be able to reverse the decline of its retail trade in the face of general trends in American retailing. There is, for example, the experience of Detroit, which no longer has a department store in its CBD. Moreover, it seems that these problems are also becoming familiar to European cities.

The transformation of the retailing industry in eastern Germany is one example of the type of development taking place in Europe. Since the collapse of socialism and the unification with western Germany that occurred in 1989, eastern German towns and their outskirts are experiencing the "Americanization" of the retail industry. On the one hand, large suburban shopping centers are spreading even faster than in western Germany, also affecting small cities. On the other hand, retailers refuse to build new department stores in cities where shopping centers already exist in the surrounding areas. In addition, traditional shopping areas in such cities are in danger of losing department stores that remain within the city limits.[68]

---

67 Cf. Jerry Ackerman, "Lafayette Place may be sold in the next 60 days, BRA says," *Boston Globe,* Feb. 2, 1993, 41.
68 See, e.g., referring to Frankfurt an der Oder on the German-Polish border: "Frankfurts einziges Kaufhaus in Nöten," *Der Tagesspiegel* [Berlin], Feb. 19, 1996, 12; with reference to Leipzig, see *Der Tagesspiegel,* Feb. 6, 1996, 15.

16

Toys, Socialization, and the Commodification of Play

STEPHEN KLINE

PLAY ASCENDANT

"Culture arises in the form of play," claimed Johan Huizinga, who celebrated play for that transcendent spirit of human creativity "which accom-
plishes itself outside and above the necessities and seriousness of everyday
life."[1] The dynamics of contemporary consumerism are similarly characterized by the rapid opening of leisure activities that accompanies the "shift in
the derivation of social meaning from the public world of production to a
more private world of buying, using and imagining – rather than making – goods."[2] The "postmodern" culture of consumption, argues Baudrillard, therefore marks a radical rupture with the prior modernist val-
orizations of rationality, utility, and hard work because consumerism
overturns the universalized conception of needs and with it the craft,
instrumentalist, and pragmatic relationships to goods that held sway in the
modernist era.[3] Especially in the postwar period, amplified by the explo-
sion of commercial communication media, the "free play" of consumerism
seemed increasingly to define all aspects of social life, dissolving reality in a
swirl of fantastic commodity signs. In the consumer culture "symbolic play"
seems to have become the dominant mode of consumption.

The reference to play, however metaphoric, is not incidental. Few scenes
conjure the symbolic dynamics of postmodern consumer culture as readily
as the image of the contemporary child alone in his or her room fantasizing
with dolls or absorbed in the imaginary world of video games. By 1977 the
typical six-year-old in the United States had accumulated over ninety-six

---

1 Johan Huizinga, *Homo Ludens* (Boston, 1955), 26.
2 Sharon Zukin, "Socio-Spatial Prototypes of a New Organization of Consumption: The Role of Real
   Cultural Capital," *Sociology* 24 (fall 1990): 48.
3 Jean Baudrillard, *The Ecstasy of Communication* (New York, 1988).

toys.[4] The average American family spent close to $400 a year on toys per child (Germany topped the globe at $423). Contemporary consumerism is deeply rooted in new social attitudes that emphasize the playful over the serious, leisure over work, and ultimately the urgency of consumption over production. Likewise, play aids the analysis of contemporary consumerism by revealing the implications of a zone of social life that, like childhood itself, has been freed of the pressures of necessity.

Like the contemporary child playing with toys, the postmodern consumer has a relation to goods that is often construed as primarily symbolic, autonomous, and mediated by fantasy. Yet anthropologists studying play have noted that, however important the creative impulse, play is also social. The content and form of children's play articulate the specific social circumstances, ideologies, and social rituals of the broader social order. Play is a type of social communication that vivifies cultural categories by making cultural knowledge engaging and practical. It is an integral part of the system of socialization that transmits attitudes, precepts, skills, and cultural values through generations.[5] In this sense we might note that toys are also the first possessions to be called "mine," the first things children can learn to influence on their own, and the first objects children begin to purchase and collect. In the consumer society, suggests Brian Sutton-Smith, toys are not just playthings, but prototype consumer goods, because they are also the "possessions with which children can learn the materialistic culture habits of late-twentieth-century, American civilization."[6]

But does this emphasis on playful fantasy in the realm of children's consumption confirm a radical break with the past (as implied by postmodern theorists), or does it suggest that we should better appreciate the forces in market society that have made "the play of commodities" such a force in children's cultural life? Throughout this century, toys, like all other commodities, have been increasingly produced and distributed to consumers through the marketplace. Especially since the 1950s, the leisure boom has induced toy makers to become a leading "consumer-oriented" industry. To survive in this fashion-driven and competitive marketplace, toy and game designers have become more innovative than most manufacturers – not only does the industry introduce five thousand to six thousand new products annually but it must funnel over $1 billion annually into promoting these new toy lines. During the postwar years, the American toy industry

4 Harvey Rheingold and R.V. Cook, "The Content of Boys' and Girls' Rooms as an Index of Parents' Behavior," *Child Development* 46 (1975): 459–63.
5 Helen Schwartzman, *Transformations: The Anthropology of Children's Play* (New York, 1979).
6 Brian Sutton-Smith, *Toys and Culture* (New York, 1986), 6.

changed its marketing practices dramatically, becoming a leading innovator in children's marketing and media promotion techniques.

Today's consumers can choose from among the 150,000 toys that are currently designed, manufactured, and distributed through expanding networks of wholesalers, retailers, and specialty outlets across the globe. Toy superstores on a grander scale than most cathedrals, day care and nursery schools dedicated to playthings, video-game arcades, and theme parks have become common (some might say defining) features of our consumer socialization. Yet the making and selling of playthings barely describe the activities of the complex promotional industry, which includes toy designers, filmmakers, animators, toy manufacturers, distributors, discounters, retailers, wholesalers, character licensing agents, advertisers, and direct marketers. Sutton-Smith sees the toy market as an "enormous institution for the control of play."[7] As the global toy market approaches $50 billion annually, some critics see the imminent realignment of children's leisure activities throughout the world.[8]

In this chapter, I use a historical overview of children's play as a mode of consumption to reflect on some of the general theorization of the culture of consumption discussed elsewhere in this book. The postwar shift in the cultural attitudes and practices of consumerism must be seen in the light of a fundamental restructuring of the economy, in which the legitimation and promotion of leisure have themselves become significant aspects of global economic expansion. In the United States, for example, leisure accounted for $341 billion of disposable spending in 1994, of which playthings were the major component.[9] To analyze the emergence of play as a mode of consumption, I focus on the growing sophistication in postwar toy merchandising and its influence on children's play, arguing that the consumer culture cannot be theorized independently of the expanding domain of marketing and its role in the commodification of play.

I have broken down the progressive commodification of children's play into two phases. The first half of this century was characterized by the modernist attitude to play as the "work of the child," and toys were therefore seen as the child's primary tools for learning the productive use of leisure time. But in the postwar period, with the commercialization of the media and the development of children's marketing, toys have been repositioned within the entertainment industries. Especially with the synergistic market-

7 Sutton-Smith, *Toys and Culture,* 54.
8 Stephen Kline, "The Play of the Market: On the Internationalization of Children's Culture," *Theory, Culture and Society* 12 (1995): 103–29.
9 "The Entertainment Economy," *Business Week,* Mar. 14, 1994, 60–4.

ing strategies of the 1980s, a new sense of play associated with escape and
adventurism has helped make it the essence of children's consumerism.

As children were increasingly barred from industrial work in the last century, modernizing nations underwent significant transformation in public
conceptions of childhood that gave new force and legitimacy to children's
leisure and their learning. Turn-of-the-century conceptions of play were
not intimately bound up with toys, nor were toys considered the preferred
means for children's socialization. Indeed, in the nineteenth century play
became increasingly associated with the benefits of imaginary release from
the pressures of the manufactured world and from the tensions of everyday
life; it was meant to introduce a natural exuberance into children's lives.
Froebel's educational writings popularized this romantic view of play, and
the kindergartens he proposed were intended as *Spielraum* (space for playing) to help nourish children's natural instincts for imaginative play. The
kindergarten was intended to loosen the social and moral control of restrictive pedagogy by imbuing education with the freedom of the garden world
of childhood innocence. Also celebrated in children's literature, this romantic sensibility of childhood innocence expressed an absolute faith in the
playful imagination extolling the freedom of play. Rudolph Steiner recommended only those play activities that explicitly avoided an association
between play and the restrictive world of manufactured toys (exploring,
gardening, tag, hide and seek, drawing, simple manipulation, and crafts):
"Small children can be very pleased with simple things, and they sense the
caring that goes into creating something for themselves. They can bring a
wonderful imaginative world of their own to surround a simple toy."

Turn-of-the-century toy manufacture in the United States was quite
limited, and until World War I, 90 percent of the toys sold were imported
from Germany. Even middle-class children might have only two or three
manufactured toys, whereas other playthings would be made by the children themselves and their families. They might also be made in small local
craft industries, which followed the European traditions of toy design by
using materials like paper, wood, fabric, wrought iron, and tin to make dolls
and doll houses, toy soldiers, carved animals, various balls, puzzles, games,
toy weapons, puppets and puppet theaters, and cutouts. Indeed, many of the
objects that have found their way into toy museums – the wooden animals,
finely dressed dolls, puppets, rocking horses, and model weapons and sol-

diers – might never have been used directly in children's play and were actually made for adults to collect and display.[10]

We cannot assume that nineteenth-century play at school or home required any toys. Given the agrarian roots of American society and the narrow concentration of wealth in urban centers, toys probably did not enter significantly into the thoughts of most American children, except perhaps at Christmas. Their daily social and creative activities either required no toys (singing, rough and tumble, tag) or incorporated a few natural objects (skipping stones, stick swords). In children's books, we also encounter this gilded image of the imaginative child happily occupied in leisure pursuits without toys – except those things they "discovered," made themselves (bows and arrows, skipping ropes, handmade balls, fishing rods), or sometimes received as a special gift. As I remember from my own 1950s childhood, an attitude of bricolage remained essential to play; boxes, pots and pans, and decorative consumer goods (such as the airplane on my grandfather's stand-up ash tray) might happily be used as playthings – although they were never designed or sanctioned as toys for children.

These early conceptions of children's play arose in the paradoxical milieu of early twentieth-century childhood, which, although freed from expectations of work, was being stringently inducted into the new rhythms and attitudes of modernity.[11] Children's play had long been valued as a crucial means of learning and socialization.[12] Yet for fear that "idle hands" might be up to the devil's work, play was also increasingly extolled as an important means of social control and character development integral to socialization in an "enlightened and progressive era."[13] Wellington's dictum that the "Battle of Waterloo was won on the playing fields of Eton" had long provided a social justification that made sports and structured games of action and strategy part of the preparation for the rigors of life. The idea of guiding the character formation of youth through play was enthusiastically taken up by the playground movement as organized sports and playgrounds began to dot the urban landscape. Throughout this century toys, playgrounds, and sports equipment have increasingly become visible within child-oriented spaces and environments.[14] Anywhere that children were

10 Beatrice Lewis, "Antique Toys Vestiges of Childhoods Past," *Children's Environments Quarterly* 1, no. 1 (1984): 3–6.
11 L. DeMause, *The History of Childhood* (New York, 1974).
12 Brian Sutton-Smith, John Gerstmyer, and Alice Meckley, "Playfighting as Folkplay amongst Preschool Children," *Western Folklore* 47, no. 3 (1988): 171–6.
13 Gary Cross, *A Social History of Leisure since 1600* (State College, Pa., 1990).
14 Linda Pollock, *Forgotten Children: Parent-Child Relations from 1500 to 1900* (New York, 1983); Thomas Jordan, *Victorian Childhood: Themes and Variations* (New York, 1987).

socialized or educated – in schools, playgrounds, parks, and bedrooms – play was being linked with the supervision of the vulnerable and innocent child in the confusing and rapidly changing modern world.[15]

As the nineteenth-century interest in children's socialization and maturation grew, so did a broad reconsideration of the role of play in early education. Play was proposed as the primary work of childhood, and toys or playthings the necessary tools of its training and happiness. John Locke was among the first to recommend giving children educational toys – but not too many, he warned, lest they become easily distracted and bored. Educators like Maria Montessori in Italy began to reconsider the potential link between learning (mainly mathematics and reading) and object manipulation, designing a set of toys that could facilitate such learning within the classroom. The acceptance of toys as an educational technology was particularly pronounced among North American educators.[16] The alphabet blocks John Locke devised for his children were among the first educational toys to be experimented with in some nursery schools in the United States. Developmental toys encouraged children's hand-eye coordination, problem solving, language skills, and conceptual development; the ability to learn through performative doing was the central motif in the growing theorization of the maturational benefits. Playskool's hammer-and-peg game, for example, became a common artifact in many American nurseries. In the 1920s and 1930s, the toy makers began working with educators in order to align their claims about the benefits of the perception toys, pull toys, skill toys, and puzzle games with the new theories of the educational value of play.

In the 1930s, domestic role-playing toys were introduced into the British nursery school by Susan Isaacs. More recently, early childhood educators have followed Piaget's notion of enactive and sensory stages of learning that precede cognitive growth and have expanded the play equipment in the nursery designed to support the other developmental sequences and maturational needs of children. Early childhood educators throughout the United States have integrated pull toys, riding toys, construction toys, sandboxes, color blocks, and hundreds of other toys into their basic curriculum to the point where preschools are simply overgrown toy boxes.[17] France introduced its "toy libraries" to make educational toys more broadly available, and trained specialists in "ludotech" to support the use of play in

15 Helen Schwartzman, *Transformations: The Anthropology of Children's Play* (New York, 1979).
16 Sutton-Smith, *Toys and Culture.*
17 Donna Varga, "The Historical Ordering of Children's Play as a Developmental Task," *Play and Culture* 4, no. 4 (1991): 322–33.

schools. Others advocate a global toy curriculum.[18] Toys have become a significant educational medium.

The acceptance of educational toys, playgrounds, and sports as beneficial to children's maturation provided the first impetus to leisure goods manufacturers to organize. The American Toy Manufacturers Association (TMA) was formed in 1916 to help mobilize and lobby on behalf of the toy makers. Because many were small-scale craft industries, the TMA was crucial in leading American toy makers gradually to realize that convincing the public that toys were developmentally useful could contribute to the expansion of their industry. Fisher-Price's corporate "creed" developed during this period reflected perhaps the whole industry's modernist belief that children's interest in play was sustained by the quality of their toys. As their corporate creed stated:

Throughout all these plans and preparations, from the assembling of a group of experienced toy makers to the minutest detail of the production we have been guided by our Five-Fold Creed. Modern toys under present conditions must have: (1) Intrinsic play value; (2) Ingenuity; (3) Strong construction; (4) Good value for the money; (5) Action.[19]

The mass market potential for playthings was dramatically demonstrated to toy makers in the late 1920s by the popularity of the yo-yo, the first toy fad to catch the world's imagination. The yo-yo (a toy found in Egyptian tombs) is a classic toy: It requires practice, patience, and the mastering of basic body motions. Simple, and relatively cheap to produce, it was a perfect mass toy. The yo-yo makers quickly learned to promote these toys with traveling shows, demonstrations, contests, and celebrities, which fueled the growing public fascination with the performance of simple yo-yo tricks. For some toy makers, the yo-yo's widespread popularity confirmed the need to learn about the mass production and marketing of toys: They began to innovate product lines as they developed a new understanding of how children's play motivated a purchase.

With new mass-production techniques, toys could be made more cheaply, with less labor and lower prices. But toy makers realized that if children did not play with their toys, parents and teachers would not buy them. Fisher-Price, a company that started as a maker of wooden pull toys, discovered that developmental toys also had to have "play value." Fisher of

18 Louise Swiniarski, "Toys Universals for Teaching Global Education," *Childhood Education* 67, no. 3 (1991): 161–3.
19 Fisher-Price Canada, ed., *Fisher-Price Corporate History* (Mississauga, Ontario, 1987).

Fisher-Price articulated this changing notion of play: "Children love best the cheerful, friendly toys with amusing action, toys that appeal to their imagination, toys that DO something new and surprising and funny. This idea is so simple it is sometimes overlooked – but if you have forgotten your own younger days, test it out on the nearest children."[20]

They had recognized "play value" as the central concept of mass production and the key to the mass market. So they began to design cuter pull and manipulation toys with unusual movements and surprise actions more for the kids than the adults. Fisher-Price, Coleco, Lego, and Marx were among those traditional wooden toy makers who during the 1950s began expanding their lines significantly by using plastics and metals.

Changes in the materials from which playthings were made can also be seen as contributing to the innovations in toy design during this first expansionary period. Construction toys (Mechano, Lincoln Logs, Brick Works), models, electric trains, and toy vehicles were made possible by new materials and techniques of production. It is this transition from "wood to plastic" cars that Barthes sees as the death of the traditional craft toy industry.[21] Indeed, looking at the new playthings marketed between the wars, we can sense the growing modernist fascination with mechanical objects and new technologies. The electric train set is simply a miniature model of a powerful new technology. But as a plaything, it has the potential to control and interact with these technologies – a theme increasingly integrated into children's play by Mechano and other construction toys, Slinky, radio-controlled cars, and, recently, video games. Roland Barthes fails to note that this change in materials is symptomatic of the mass toy manufacturers' rethinking of play action as well as a major shift of emphasis within their organizational cultures from craft producers to industrial mass marketing organizations. Lionel, an innovator in the mass production of electric trains, is also one of the first toy makers to use mass advertising successfully in their marketing plans.

CONSUMER SOCIALIZATION IN THE AGE
OF MASS MARKETING

In spite of the radical changes in attitudes and practices of child rearing during the 1950s, many early U.S. toy manufacturers still chose not to market directly to children. Much of their reluctance can be explained by their modernist-minded belief that such endeavor was unnecessary (demand was

20 Sutton-Smith, *Toys and Culture*.   21 Roland Barthes, *Mythologies* (London, 1973), 53–4.

there). Industry leaders like Louis Marx of Marx Toys noted that toys simply did not need promotion, whereas others argued it would be a waste of money, since children did not have sufficient disposable income or power to be considered as a viable marketing target. Nor, argued some, did they have the consumer skills to process and store the brand names and attributes necessary for successful mass marketing. Indeed, until the mid-1950s, the promotion of toys and games was limited, directed mostly at parents, and sporadic ($1 million annually).

Yet by the early 1960s most major toy, snack, and cereal marketers were rethinking their marketing plans and conducting research on children – tracking their favorite programs on television, their preferences for toys (by collecting letters to Santa), their requests in shops, their allowances, and the way they played with specific toys (Fisher-Price sponsored nursery school research). It is particularly important to note how and why during the 1950s the American toy industry entered the age of children's market research. "Today, with the help of child-development experts, psychiatrists, educators, engineers, and children themselves, toy development has become a profession involving in-depth research, testing, and retesting."[22]

Indeed, since the 1930s, psychologists had begun to consider the symbolic aspect of play. Following Freud, some looked to the deeper psychic significance of play fantasies in children's maturation and development, focusing on "pretending" as an important aspect of play's benefits. Imagination and fantasy also concerned the playthings industries as they realized that, for children, toys were more than objects to manipulate; children interacted with prevailing social constructs, roles, and values through the representational worlds toys conjured. In games, as the play theorist Lev Vygotsky noted, the rules are defined partially as narrative: In chess, knights and castles are invoked; in kick the can or capture the flag, jails, enemies, and victory; in skipping songs, the complex world of social relations.[23] Piaget began to note that children's play after the age of two involved pretending – a type of play that invoked a symbolic transformation of objects through imagination.[24]

Focusing on play reveals the dual status of the toy commodity: an object to be manipulated and a representational medium for the prevailing mores

22 Richard Chase, *Playthings*, Feb. 1983, 344.
23 Lev S. Vygotsky, "Play and its Role in the Mental Development of the Child," in Jerome S. Bruner, A. Jolly, and K. Sylva, eds., *Play: Its Role in Development and Evolution* (Harmondsworth, England, 1976).
24 Jean Piaget, "Symbolic Play," in Bruner, Jolly and Sylva, eds., *Play: Its Role in Development and Evolution*.

of the culture.[25] Toy makers realized they were selling a unique class of consumer objects. Designed for play, a toy had "use value" that was lodged not only in the ownership, status, and value gained through conspicuous consumption, but in its application as a prop or symbolic marker in the production of children's social fantasies and play worlds. Toy makers, therefore, were among the first to discover that goods are really fetish objects: The mystery of their use lies in the user's ability to transform an experience through imagination. Toy makers had to learn to design objects that engaged children's fantasy life, and they used research extensively to enter the child's imaginary worlds. As they studied children in the postwar period of affluence, toy and game makers realized that children were demonstrating their influence within the postwar family and that many had money for discretionary spending. Toys clearly fascinated children; as objects to manipulate (Slinky and Hula Hoops) they provided entertainment, and as representations they helped children anticipate roles they would soon assume (vehicles, cooking sets).

The development of toy marketing also depended on the penetration of commercial television into the patterns of family life. As television became the preferred leisure activity of children, it also fulfilled the final precondition for the growth of children's markets: The commercial viability of a children's TV audience enabled merchandisers to begin to introduce new products that specifically targeted these preferences by saturating children's culture with product images.[26] Given the rapid increase in children's allowances, their influence within the family, and their loyal television viewing (3.5 hours per day), television advertising campaigns directed at children grew steadily in the United States from a few million dollars in 1954. Toy merchandisers especially began to intensify their marketing effort directed at this segment and in the 1980s became the largest spenders on children's advertising.

THE MEDIATIZED CONTEXT OF CHILDHOOD

Watching TV was not just a relaxing distraction – it was fun. As a medium TV was a functional alternative to play. I have a personal memory of the tensions created by the introduction of television into our childhood play culture. While we were playing street hockey (baseball, kick-the-can) a parental voice would emerge from some house, reminding one of our play-

25 Sutton-Smith, *Toys and Culture*, 6.
26 Saturation usually demands a reach of 80 percent of the target market.

mates that Superman (Disney, Batman, the Honeymooners) was on TV. Inevitably, one of our tribe would succumb to the attractions of the blue screen. Quite often the loss of this one child would upset the carefully balanced teams that had been arranged in the first hour of play. One playmate's abandonment of the street scene for television therefore caused our after-school or after-dinner activities to unwind. Television viewing displaced other leisure activities and undermined, in particular, the traditions of peer play, outdoor sports, and street games.[27] To compete with television as a form of entertainment, toys had to become more exciting and fun. Television in fact forced a significant rethinking of toys as part of the entertainment market:

Toys have traditionally mirrored the adult world in size and in form, which quickly and easily can be mastered by children. Scientific advances, technological changes, social attitudes and customs, personal values and moral convictions can all be found reflected in playthings we offer to our children. But perhaps most important of all, the true purpose of a toy or game is to entertain.[28]

During the 1950s, toy marketers not only reconsidered their place within the entertainment sector but also had to reconceptualize the impact of mass media on play. Television excelled at fantastic drama that children could simulate in their imaginary social play. In 1954 Disney's frontier adventure "Davy Crockett" proved again that television supplied more than a romanticized interpretation of American history – this program had kids everywhere in the United States demanding coonskin hats and plastic Bowie knifes within a month of its premiere. With these merchandising spin-offs and a new sense of TV's potential in mind, Walt Disney launched his first theme park, Disneyland in southern California, and the "Mickey Mouse Club" (1955) television show. This show was the first children's program to enjoy sufficient marketing interest to attract major advertising support ($20 million for the season). Not surprisingly, Mattel, then a very small toy maker, was among the show's first advertisers. Not only did the company promote licensed goods like the mouse guitars, but it undertook innovative saturation advertising campaigns for the Burp Gun, which proved the fad-creating efficacy of children's television marketing by selling 1 million units within a month.[29] The basic logic behind the synergy of television selling is

27 Tannis MacBeth Williams, *Impact of Television: A Natural Experiment in Three Communities* (Orlando, Fla., 1986).
28 The Canadian Toy Manufacturers' Association, ed., *Mixing Business and Pleasure: An Outline of the Canadian Toy and Decoration Industry* (1979), 2
29 Sydney Stern and Ted Schoenhaus, *Toyland: The High-Stakes Game of the Toy Industry* (Chicago, 1990), 56.

simple: "If what they see on TV is what they see on the shelf, they will buy it" to play with.[30]

It was during the 1950s and 1960s that children's peer advertising formats were perfected, as marketers learned that children's desire for a product was influenced by peer processes and their willingness to pressure parents was a function of media exposure.[31] It does not require advertising, promotion, and images of their peers using a toy to make children interested in play. Play is fun, and it is intrinsically attractive to children, but advertising and point-of-purchase display can increase the recognition and popularity of particular toy lines and increase the acceptance of new toy concepts. The children's marketer Susan Small-Weil notes that advertising is used in children's marketing mainly to build relationships "between toy manufacturers and consumers, which create an immediate demand for a specific product."[32]

Yet children, especially the very young, have trouble remembering the attributes of branded products. Therefore, well-known personalities from the world of popular culture are enlisted to help inscribe a brand image onto the surface of the product. Already in the 1930s, Disney made money not only through the sale of tickets to his movies but also from the growing business of licensing his characters to toy, clock, and clothing manufacturers.[33] Children's marketers in the 1950s began to employ well-known children's characters or brand personalities (Tony the Tiger, Mickey Mouse) to maintain the child's interest in their products and to increase brand recognition and demand.[34]

Toy companies especially became interested in advertising's potential to fuel excitement and brand awareness. Television advertising had the power to "script" a brand by enveloping it with an elaborate image – a meaningful social narrative that could refer directly to play activities. Although all goods have meaning, toys and games, like other communication media, are cultural goods whose play value is the entertainment they provide. Toy companies, like film and TV producers with whom they competed, had to learn how to capture children's imagination, engage their sense of fun and humor,

30 *Licensing Trends,* Aug.-Sept. 1995, 3.
31 James McNeal, *Children as Consumers* (Lexington, Ky., 1987); Stephen Kline, *Out of the Garden* (London, 1993).
32 *Playthings,* 1990.
33 Douglas Gomery, "Disney's Business History: A Reinterpretation," and Richard de Cordova, "The Mickey in Macy's Window: Childhood, Consumerism, and Disney Animation," both in Eric Smoodin, ed., *Disney Discourse: Producing the Magic Kingdom* (New York, 1994), 71–86 and 203–13, respectively.
34 Brian Young, *Television Advertising and Children* (Oxford, 1990).

or elicit a momentary fascination. Their new links with the world of film and television production helped toy companies reconceptualize play values in terms of narrative and fantasy. Introduced in 1959 by Mattel with a high profile advertising campaign, Barbie's immediate success showed that this tighter scripting of symbolic toys could be a useful tool in marketing new play concepts. Barbie was not a faddish toy (like Hula Hoops and yo-yos) but a new way of thinking about toys as media and the fantasy processes that motivated girls to play with them. The television ad furnished Barbie's "backstory" as a fashion model in an effort to stimulate little girls' fantasies about teen life, which research had revealed grounded the fashion play activity.[35]

Projected through saturation advertising, this orchestration of recognition and fantasy in Barbie's novel "fashion doll" taught Mattel a lot about the dynamics of saturation and timing in mass-marketing playthings. Because Barbie was a "fashion" doll, Mattel quickly realized that to parlay its initial investment in this concept and maintain its position at the forefront of the market, Barbie required constant fashion makeovers to keep her up-to-date. By a timely fine-tuning of Barbie's "look" to fight off successive rivals, Mattel has realized its original advertising investment by optimizing continuity and through saturating a brand image in the American market. Moreover, Barbie was gradually elaborated from a stand-alone "fashion doll" into a more abstract life-style concept at the vortex of a group of friends and an exploding range of accoutrements and accessories that included couturier clothing, life-style clothes, home furnishings and cars, bedding and curtains. The evolution of Barbie demonstrated a novel way to gain marketing efficiencies. By expanding the product universe or "ensembles" of playthings associated with the Barbie image, Mattel could optimize its promotional expenditure. This marketing efficiency has in fact become the key to all promotional toy marketing, in which multiple toys, vehicles, weapons, accoutrements, and play sets are marketed under the same promotional banner.

LICENSED TO SELL: TOYS, TELEVISION, AND SYNERGISTIC MARKETING

In the 1970s and 1980s, when baby boomers hit their childbearing years, children's marketers once again looked at ways of influencing the prolific

---

35 Cy Schneider, *Children's Television: The Art, The Business, and How it Works* (Chicago, 1987), 90.

spending on children's goods, which rose steadily upward to the current
$160 billion.[36] The demographic baby echo, innovative electronics, and the
Reaganite deregulation of television all demanded innovation in the toy
marketer's practices. In the early 1980s, competitive pricing and the need
for corporate strategies to deal with the impact of video games on
the playthings market became leading concerns of the industry. At an indus-
trywide panel convened in 1981 by *Playthings*, the toy industry trade magazine noted that low profitability, fickle consumers who were price-point-
sensitive, and concentrated sales during Christmas were impediments
limiting growth potential for this industry in a period when optimism generated by demographics and the end of recession should have ruled.[37]

As one toy industry commentator claimed, innovative products were the
key to bigger markets. She predicted that "the phenomenal growth of the
video game segment of the industry may be the catalyst necessary to pro-
voke serious studies into the creative process of management" in the toy
industry.[38] She continued, enthusing that "the American toy industry is a
throwback to an era that worked – to a period when success through innovation counted. In fact, it is a model of American ingenuity. Successful toy
companies are America's idea factories. They also remind us that capitalism
works." The playthings industry, especially since the emergence of video
games in the early 1980s, had discovered that it takes creativity to thrive in
the rapidly changing, culturally inflected global marketplace, she claimed,
but "it is almost impossible to expect traditional corporate management to
be motivated to investigate and or learn from creative departments things
which often appear ambiguous and intangible."[39] Ironically, although video
games are the fastest growing sector, accounting for $16 billion of the $54
billion global toy sales, none of the American toy companies that entered
the video-game market in the 1980s has survived.

Yet Kenner's fantastic merchandising success with George Lucas's *Star
Wars* film series, the weighty sales of TV-inspired action toy lines ("Won-
derwoman," "Dukes of Hazzard," and "The A-Team"), and the Smurfs'
mushrooming presence in children's bedrooms led the toy industry to begin
considering whether the trends in play toy merchandising should be left
entirely to the film and television studios. Those in the industry familiar

36 James McNeal, *Kids as Customers* (Lexington, Ky., 1992).
37 Frank Reysen, "Industry must Overcome Contradictory Practices," *Playthings,* May 1982, and Frank
   Reysen, "Critical Issues for 1982," *Playthings,* Jan. 1982.
38 Ritasue Siegel, "What Corporate America Must Learn from the Toy Industry," *Playthings,* July 1982,
   86.
39 Ibid.

with licensing already knew how much "the merchandise blows out the store after the movie release," reaping benefits for manufacturers and retailers alike.[40] These licensed promotional toys or "spin-offs" traditionally incorporated the image, characteristics, or personalities of a popular media hero (primarily from TV, comic books, and films) into the design and appeal of a toy line or game. Clearly, "companies like Disney and Warner Bros. knew how to do it big time" when it came to designing children's characters. But if "their promotional pull up front ... generates not just ticket sales but ... sales at the store level," could not the toy companies learn to do the same?[41]

But the risks of overlicensing a product line were also demonstrated in the case of the "Dukes of Hazzard" when manufacturers flooded the market with spin-offs as soon as the series "started to take off. Then everybody jumped on the bandwagon and the category expanded. Now there are too many items." The situation could be rectified, the commentator suggested, "by having one or two manufacturers take on a key license and control what happens to it."[42] Control of a license meant negotiating exclusivity deals for all toys: "Even though there might be an excellent item, the company will want to get more of an exclusive arrangement. . . . With a non-exclusive license, you're cutting your own throat."[43] With greater experience, these licensing arrangements became more elaborate and comprehensive, specifying product design, packaging, advertising and store displays, and pricing strategies.

The cost of producing a successful animated film or television series alone could range from $15 to $40 million. To companies who felt that video games were already undermining traditional toy play, the future of basic toy making looked bleak: "Licensing means money, big money. Risks will increase if the industry is not careful."[44] But high-profile licenses (like *Star Wars*) could be costly to the manufacturer, in turn raising the price of the toys. A series of industry-inspired hits with He-Man, Transformers, and GI Joe demonstrated the scale of profits to be garnered by those companies that successfully captured children's interests. Optimistic spokespersons began heralding the licensing boom (at the time, 15–20 percent of toy sales) as the solution to the industry's woes but warned, "some people see licensing as a panacea of all ills – and fall into a trap of taking anything with a license on it."[45] Since then, the percentage of licensed toys has climbed

40 *Licensing Trends*, Aug.–Sept. 1995.   41 *Licensing Trends*, July 1995, 6.
42 *Playthings*, July 1982.   43 Frank Reysen, *Playthings*, Aug. 1982.   44 *Playthings*, July 1992, 1.
45 Ibid.

steadily to 75 percent, while Ninja Turtles, the Lion King, and Mighty Mor-
phin' Power Rangers continue to demonstrate that the product sales stimulated by a successful media push can approach $1 billion.

Indeed, the advantages of licensing toy lines were eminently clear from
the start of this boom: "From the consumer angle licensing provides an easily identifiable concept that requires no guessing as to its meaning. All the
initial exposure has already been done through various media. . . . If a customer wants an Annie doll or a certain Star Wars figure he wants it now."[46]
The effect was particularly noted in the action toy lines: "The major reason
is a constant bombardment of TV exposure. Market awareness is high
because all of the names are out in front of the kids."[47] Because of popular
customer demand it is "hard for the retailer to avoid action figures even if
he's so inclined," explained one merchandiser. Moreover, the demand is
very specific as the customers come into the store knowing what they want:
"A G.I. Joe knockoff didn't work out too well. Our customers want the real
thing, so from now on we'll stick to the big names. Knockoffs aren't for
us."[48]

The economics of licensing also had to be assimilated. Although promotional investment is high, the "royalty for a license is 'nominal' compared
to the expense for advertising which also goes into the cost of the product.
In fact, compared to other fees, it brings more mileage," commented an
industry analyst.[49] For promotional toys, the advertising investment in combination with the exposure in the movies could pay off with saturation and
bulk concentrated sales: "We want sell through. Kenner is spending $10
million to promote the *Star Wars* line. Millions were spent on promoting
Columbia Pictures' *Annie* and the Strawberry Shortcake family."[50] The
industry also learned that timing and coordinated store display, as well as
constant excitement generated through advertising, were crucial factors in
the coordination of marketing plans for licensed products: "[T]o maximize
the recognition factor triggered by a well-known license . . . aggressive
retailers are intensifying their efforts to promote characters merchandise
associated with TV series, cartoons, movies, newspaper comics, fashion, and
other sources."

A turn-around occurred in 1982 as the toy industry began to assimilate
the impact of video games and the deregulated media environment into
their marketing strategies and merchandising practices. First, although the
video-game boom (led by Atari but including Coleco and Mattel) did seem

46 Frank Reysen, *Playthings,* Aug. 1992, 38.   47 Frank Reysen, *Playthings,* June 1983.
48 Ibid.   49 *Playthings,* July 1992.   50 Ibid.

to encroach on several categories of toy sales (games, action toys, hobbies), the rest of the toy industry found it also helped acquaint consumers with higher price points for playthings: "Consumers are willing to pay more for a licensed product. That's the guts of the whole business," stated one merchandiser.[51] Moreover, the use of television programs and advertisements to create recognition and interest in toy lines helped to spread toy sales throughout the year, gradually lowering the percentage of toys and games sold at Christmas to 65 percent. This was excellent news to the manufacturers and retailers, who had long fussed over the seasonal nature of toy demand.

Deregulation was crucial for many toy companies' marketing plans, not only because it removed the limit on the amount of advertising, but because it enabled toy makers to enter directly into the promotional market by supporting new product lines with animated TV shows and promoting them with their own advertising. The pragmatics of tie-ins and distribution deals preoccupied the toy industry's marketing analysts and tacticians as they formed a "determination among the largest players to realize massive volume sales of products with little intrinsic appeal, but with a strong marketing and fashion content," through television promotions.[52] The toy industry often participated directly in creating new products or worked through the new licensing agencies and brokers (Those Characters from Cleveland, who created Care Bears and Strawberry Shortcake) that conceived and negotiated many of the deals.[53] Facing low profitability, low mark-ups, and the high overhead of mass audience advertising, most leading American toy makers participated in the creation of over eighty new animated television serials (the thirty-minute commercials) during the last fifteen years in the processes launching a phalanx of licensed products into the market.

From the merchandisers' point of view "traditional toys" and a steady flow of customers were sometimes preferable to these faddish toys: "If it is a success your customers will expect to see it on the shelf. If it is a flop you cannot give it away. If it is based on a movie or an event, the risk increases but so does the chance for big rewards."[54] Even buying frenzies (like those inspired by the Cabbage Patch line) could be a problem, however, as toy manufacturers sometimes had trouble meeting delivery deadlines for items in sudden demand (a problem video-game makers also experienced in 1983). So the cautionary voices were plentiful too, especially among the distributors who could easily get "burned" (many were in 1984 when pro-

51 Frank Reysen, *Playthings,* Aug. 1982.   52 *Playthings,* 1987.
53 Tom Engelhardt, "The Strawberry Shortcake Strategy," in Todd Gitlin, ed., *Watching Television* (New York, 1986).
54 William Adler, *Playthings,* Feb. 1982.

duction again failed to meet pre-Christmas demand) by overstocking slow-moving lines and because "increasingly heavy R&D outlays and advertising support have also resulted in narrowed margins" and escalated prices for promotional toys.

Because deregulated television existed only in Japan and the United States in the 1980s, the toy makers, marketers, and animators in these countries were able to establish the business relationships necessary for character promotions. Marketing a license demands not only a comprehensive promotional plan but also an organizational environment in which the new affiliations and partnerships among animators, manufacturers, retailers, advertisers, and licensing agencies can create the design, cross-marketing, and distribution deals, and syndicated television networks can establish the audience targeting required for character promotion. Not only did partnerships like Disney-Mattel help make licensing work, but the major stores (Sears, Toys 'Я Us) were increasingly encouraged to participate in exclusive promotional deals: "with ever-increasing support from licensers . . . exploiting the licensing bonanza by putting together end-caps, boutiques, feature groupings, and special events."[55] Merchandising was clearly just another arm of promotion.

However, the proliferation of licensed goods in the market increased the uncertainty associated with predicting which characters would catch on: "It's really hard to know which licenses will do anything or for how long," commented one marketer.[56] Yet with growing promotional costs and narrowing margins, the industry needed to know which concepts and new products would merit the investment.[57] The answer to this dilemma lay in beefing up research and development into children's play preferences, particularly their recognition of and identification with the many characters flooding the market. Moreover, the larger toy makers had to figure which categories of toys could benefit from television. "A licensed toy can only be toyetic if the product and license are compatible. It also must have the appropriate packaging, product, and promotion," said one consultant summarizing two simple yet powerful lessons being learned by those venturing into licensing. The selling of a licensed line was like a mysterious alchemical experiment that combined a toy's play values with the magical appeal of the story lines and characterization of their media and advertising to turn the line to gold.

Although almost every branch in the toy industry experimented with

55 Frank Reysen, *Playthings*, Aug. 1982.   56 Ibid.
57 "TMA Explores Licensing Opportunities: Case Histories of Character Properties Studied in Boca Raton During Annual Meeting," *Playthings*, July 1983, 31.

licensing, not all found the arrangements profitable. Hobby, craft, construction, and game makers did not find it easy to connect their play values with popular TV and movie characters. On the other hand, He-Man, Transformers, Jem, and Care Bears proved that television programs could interest children in the toys. In these four years of rapid expansion following deregulation, the toy companies learned many things, but none so important as the difficulty of winning the hearts and minds of children. These experiments showed that some kinds of playthings could benefit from the new licensing arrangements more than others, even when the marketing effort was well planned. "Inhumanoids" had to be withdrawn from TV while the movie *My Ponies* lost money. However, G.I. Joe was fabulously "toyetic": It cost millions to redesign, manufacture, and promote, but this action toy line earned Hasbro over $350 million in sales in 1986. Indeed, when they saw that G.I. Joe vehicle sales almost equaled those of the action figures, Hasbro learned something rather important about marketing action-play accessories.

The deregulation of American television in 1982 allowed more effective promotion of licensed character toys and, later, interactive and video games, pushing the sale of playthings from $4.6 billion in 1977 to over $20 billion in the United States today. Between 1982 and 1986, American toy sales swelled from $6.4 to $12.3 billion, as a succession of licensed toys (action figures, plush and fashion dolls) increased their share from under 20 percent of total sales in 1977 to about 70 percent in 1992.[58] Currently, we encourage children's playful imaginations with those new symbolic media offered in today's entertainment market – the video games; action, fashion, and plush dolls; and role-play equipment – that have made make-believe the most prevalent play value. Licensed goods account for over three-quarters of toy sales.[59] Yet while the playthings sector has boomed, the American toy makers have transformed themselves from manufacturers of playthings into orchestrators of marketing plans. At 75–80 percent of the market, toy imports into the United States have nearly returned to pre–World War I levels, while multinationals based here are enjoying increased profits from their expanding global toy and game sales.

CONCLUSION

Since the turn of the century, the manufacturing of playthings in the United States has grown from an insignificant hobby and craft industry into a major

58 *Playthings,* 1992.
59 Statistics and data are drawn from my reading of *Playthings* between 1980 and 1995.

node in the "synergies" of the global cultural industries. Perhaps Disney exemplifies the corporate repositioning from filmmaker to promotional entertainment industry better than most. While international sales grew from $142 million in 1984 to $2.4 billion in 1994, Disney came to rely for much of its revenue on theme parks (45 percent) and merchandising (20 percent). *The Lion King*, which is Disney's most successful film so far, cost $50 million to produce and took in $780 million in box office receipts, yet the greatest share was earned through global licensed merchandise sales – $1 billion in 1994. The new Disney retail chain, like Disneyland, is just another step along the path of realizing the merchandising spin-offs in the entertainment marketplace.

The scale of play merchandising does not in itself mean that the toy makers and marketers "created" the increasing demand for playthings. Yet as I have been arguing, during the last forty years toy makers have learned a considerable amount about play and its preferred forms of expression in children's lives. They have cultivated a new relationship with consumers. Although changes in production techniques and materials have had a lasting impact on toy design, toy making, and toy sales, it is during the postwar years that the most dramatic expansion of the American toy industry has taken place – largely because the industry learned how to develop, design, and insert new toys and games within the changing attitudes, social conditions, and practices of daily life including the media-intensive environment of contemporary childhood.

The playthings sector in fact provides an object lesson in consumer-oriented business practices because design and marketing have become the means for enhancing corporate profitability and for mounting global expansion. In the consumer society, play has in fact become a significant mode of consumption and nowhere more so than in the lives of children.

17

The "Syndrome of the 1950s" in Switzerland

Cheap Energy, Mass Consumption, and the Environment

CHRISTIAN PFISTER

THE 1950S: WATERSHED OF GLOBAL SUSTAINABILITY

The human economy is a subsystem of a finite global ecosystem. Population and capital are the driving forces behind exponential growth in the world economy. Its potentials cannot be realized without a constant flow or throughput from the planetary sources of materials and energy, through the economic system, to the planetary sinks where wastes and pollutants end up (see Figure 17.1).[1]

The World Bank economist Herman Daly has pointed out that capital and labor are substitutable for each other to a considerable degree, because their qualitative function in production is the same: They are both agents of the transformation of flows of raw materials into finished products. But the qualitative roles of energy and capital are totally different in the physical process of production, as different as transformer and transformed, as different as stock and flow.[2] Environmental economists consider energy to be an independent third factor of production besides labor and capital.[3] There are close relationships among the volume of manufacturing, the use of fossil fuels, and the accumulation of waste and pollutants in the environment. The more fossil fuel that economic activities use (this holds also for consumption), the more emissions they produce.[4] In the United States, the level of

1 Donella Meadows and Dennis Meadows, *Beyond the Limits: Global Collapse or a Sustainable Future* (London, 1992), 45.
2 Herman A. Daly, "Toward Some Operational Principles of Sustainable Development," *Ecological Economics* 2 (1990): 1–6.
3 Thomas Möller, "Energie im gesamtwirtschaftlichen Produktionsmodell: Ein dritter Produktionsfaktor und sein Einfluss auf die langfristige Entwicklung einer energieabhängigen Wirtschaft," Ph.D. diss., St. Gallen University for Economics, 1986.
4 Reiner Kümmel and Thomas Bruckner, "Energie, Entropie – Ökonomie, Ökologie," in Christian Pfister, ed., *Das 1950er Syndrom: Der Weg in die Konsumgesellschaft* (Bern, 1995), 130.

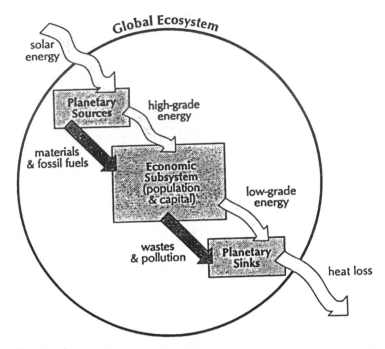

Figure 17.1. Population and capital in the global ecosystem. Population and capital are sustained by flows of fuels and nonrenewable resources, and they produce outflows of heat and waste which contaminate the planet's air, water, and soil. Reprinted by permission of Sterling Lord Literistic, Inc. Copyright © 1991 by Dennis Meadows.

gross national product (GNP) and the use of fossil fuels are correlated at an almost unbelievable level of 0.99 over the period from 1890 to 1980.[5]

The term "sustainable development" was coined in 1988 by a United Nations commission for environment and development headed by Prime Minister Gro Harlem Brundtland of Norway. It points to the fact that the use of a renewable resource – for example, timber or fish – should be equivalent to its natural rate of regeneration in order to maintain its productive potential for future generations. For a nonrenewable resource – fossil fuel, high-grade mineral ore, or fossil groundwater – the sustainable rate of use cannot be greater than the rate at which a renewable resource, used sustainably, can be substituted for it. For example, an oil deposit would be used sustainably if part of the profits from it were systematically invested in solar collectors, so that when the oil was gone an equivalent stream of renewable

5 Charles A. Hall, Cleveland J. Cutler, and Robert Kaufman, *Energy and Resource Quality: The Ecology of the Economic Process* (New York, 1986), 51.

energy would still be available.[6] As a matter of fact, however, global sustainability continues to decline, and the consumption of fossil energy can be taken as a good indicator in this respect, both among nations and over time.

In many textbooks, growth is presented as a kind of natural state of a capitalist economy, as a process that is occasionally interrupted by phases of stagnation and crisis. On the basis of consumption (and real wages), however, the twentieth century clearly falls into two phases of very unequal growth, namely, before and after 1950 (see Figure 17.2).[7]

The increase of global energy consumption since the 1950s can also be seen on the side of the sinks (see Figure 17.3), as greenhouse gases (CO_2, methane, nitrous oxide, and chlorofluorocarbons) in the atmosphere became more rapidly concentrated in the second half of the century.[8]

It is generally admitted that mass consumption in the industrial world, not population growth in the Third World, was the driving force behind this surge in energy use and global pollution. It is true that the take-off of world population also occurred in the 1950s. But we have to bear in mind that the bulk of population increase took place in the Third World, where energy consumption per capita was and is quite low.

It is thought that this transition from a more sustainable form of development to the present situation is closely related to the expansion of "Fordist" consumer societies in the West after World War II. Although this concept is the key to understanding the global environmental situation from a historical perspective, it was not tackled by historians with regard to Western Europe until very recently.[9] The long economic boom in Western Europe after 1945 did not seem to deserve a particular focus because it was seen as just another period of rapid modernization in the paradigm of industrial society.[10] Only recently was it claimed that the postwar years initiated a significant shift that, over the last decades, affected almost every sphere of human activity as well as the relations between society and its natural environment in a fundamental way.[11]

---

6 Daly, "Operational Principles," 6. A more detailed and comprehensive illustration of the term is provided by Meadows and Meadows in *Beyond the Limits*, chap. 7.

7 Source: Meadows and Meadows, *Beyond the Limits*, 67.

8 Source: Meadows and Meadows, *Beyond the Limits*, 94.

9 The most remarkable contributions in the 1980s were made by two sociologists: Burkard Lutz, *Der kurze Traum immerwährender Prosperität* (Frankfurt am Main, 1984), and Volker Bornschier, *Westliche Gesellschaft im Wandel* (Frankfurt am Main, 1988).

10 Gerd Ambrosius and Hartmut Kaelble, "Einleitung," in Gerd Ambrosius and Hartmut Kaelble, eds., *Der Boom 1948–1973: Gesellschaftliche und wirtschaftliche Folgen in der Bundesrepublik Deutschland und in Europa* (Opladen, 1992), 8.

11 Franz Ossing et al., "Innere Widersprüche und äussere Grenzen der Lebensweise: Aspekte der ökologischen Entwicklung," in Klaus Voy, Werner Polster, and Claus Thomasberger, ed., *Gesellschaftliche*

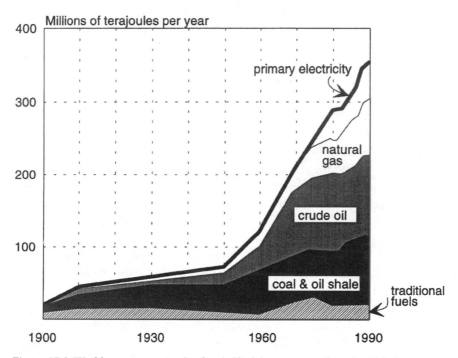

Figure 17.2. World energy use. In the first half of the century, when the global economy was mainly based on coal, the consumption of energy doubled. In the subsequent four decades, when oil and natural gas made up the lion's share, consumption increased fivefold. After Meadows and Meadows 1992. Reprinted by permission of Sterling Lord Literistic, Inc. Copyright © 1991 by Dennis Meadows.

To shed light on the economic and cultural context in which this shift occurred and on its consequences for the situation of the environment, it is advisable to narrow down the focus from the global to the national or to the local level. Such a degree of detail is needed, as long as a set of comprehensive cross-national studies is lacking, to highlight the full set of driving forces and the way in which they interact. This chapter aims to provide some basic arguments from the perspective of environmental history. Most of the examples refer to Switzerland, which is both typical and atypical compared with other Western European societies.[12]

Transformationsprozesse und materielle Lebensweise: Beiträge zur Wirtschafts- und Gesellschaftsgeschichte der Bundesrepublik Deutschland, 1949–1989 (Marburg an der Lahn, 1989), 363.

12 Christian Pfister, "Das '1950er Syndrom' – die umweltgeschichtliche Epochenschwelle zwischen Industriegesellschaft und Konsumgesellschaft," in Pfister, ed., *Das 1950er Syndrom*. For a comprehensive discussion of the German case, see Voy et al., eds., *Gesellschaftliche Transformationsprozesse*.

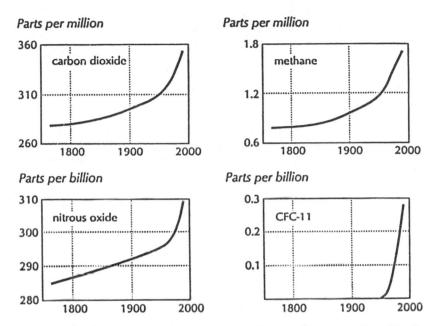

Figure 17.3. Global greenhouse gas concentrations. Reprinted by permission of Sterling Lord Literistic, Inc. Copyright © 1991 by Dennis Meadows.

CONSUMPTION, WORK, AND THE ENVIRONMENT IN 1950

Considering the state of the environment and the level of consumption, in the early 1950s Swiss society still lived quite close to the principles of sustainability. This is summarized as follows:

(1)   Wages covered the basic needs without offering large surpluses for the choice of individual life-styles: Patterns of consumption had not changed much from the midnineteenth century. Most of the household budget was spent on food, clothing, shelter, and the raising of children. The tradition of agricultural societies to curb consumption, to avoid wasting energy, and to recycle resources had been reinforced during the war. Food was rationed and manpower was scarce, as the army had to defend the borders against the potential incursion of foreign armies.

(2)   Residential areas were situated within the range of local public transportation: Workers could not afford commuting by train over a long distance. Thus, they had to live in crowded flats within walking, biking, or tramway distance from their place of work. This residential pattern prevented suburban sprawl and exurban development.

(3)   Food was bought in small retail stores within walking distance: Shopping was part of housework. Meeting the needs of a household was an object of rational planning. The stock in the small "Aunt Emma retail stores" was limited.

Fruit and vegetables originated from the surrounding countryside and changed according to season. The goods were wrapped in paper bags or sold without any packaging.

(4) Agricultural production was close to today's concept of "biodynamic farming": Most of the farmers still worked with horse-drawn machinery. They relied on their own fodder, and most of the manure was produced directly on the farm. Weeds were suppressed mechanically; bugs were picked out by hand.

(5) Industries were agglomerated around railway crossings: Distributing coal was one of the fundamental functions of the railway. After the first phase of industrialization, which in Switzerland was based on the production of textiles in water-powered mills and watch manufacture, the rail network laid the basis for a second phase of industrialization on the basis of coal: food processing, metalworking, production of chemicals, and so forth. Since the transport of coal on highways was very expensive, factories were built close to the rail network. Because Switzerland had no heavy industry and clean hydroelectricity accounted for a large share of energy production, the quality of the environment was somewhat better than in most other countries in Europe. But Rolf Peter Sieferle has made the point that even in Germany, which was among the leading industrial workshops of the world, severe pollution was restricted to those relatively small areas where coal was found, such as the Ruhr basin. The large agricultural areas outside these centers remained almost unaffected by pollution.[13]

Of course, the quasi sustainability of Europe around 1950 had its price. Both men and women, and to some extent even children, had to perform hard physical work for modest wages. The small amount of leisure and vacation time offered little relief, and individual behavior was socially controlled.

THE ABSORPTION OF THE "TRADITIONAL SECTOR"

The relationship between population and basic environmental parameters has changed profoundly over the past forty years (see Figure 17.4).[14] I have labeled the bundle of changes in the economic, social, and ecological spheres, which underlay this profound shift, the "syndrome of the 1950s."[15] The medical term "syndrome" denotes "a set of characteristics indicating the existence of a condition, problem, etc."[16] This term was deliberately chosen to express the fact that our knowledge of the economic and social causes of the syndrome of the 1950s is still at an early stage. It does not just

13 Rolf Peter Sieferle, "Jenseits der Epochenschwelle," *Gaia* 3, no. 2 (1994): 63.
14 Source: Pfister, ed., *Das 1950er Syndrom.*   15 Pfister, "Das '1950er Syndrom,'" 58.
16 *New Collins Concise English Dictionary* (London, 1982), 1186.

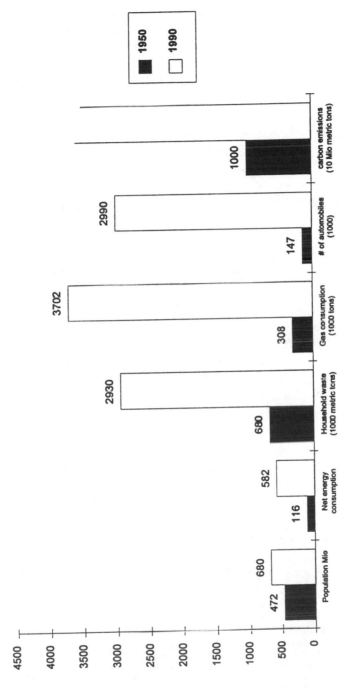

Figure 17.4. Key indicators of environmental change for Switzerland, 1950–90. Over the last forty years the consumption of fossil fuels rose 5-fold, gas consumption 11-fold, production of carbon 4.4-fold, and production of household waste 4.3-fold. The number of cars rose by 1,900 percent. In contrast, population grew by only 44 percent.

describe the situation in the 1950s; rather, it is a blanket term for the entirety of changes that have occurred since the 1950s, that is, over the last four decades. For Switzerland, Arne Andersen has described the changes in the 1950s, that is, the initial shift away from sustainability to mass consumption.[17] This analysis need not be repeated here, but some of the reasons are examined.

Economic growth was the most fundamental (but not the only) driving force behind the changing patterns of consumption after 1950. Considering the per capita growth of GNP, the boom between the late 1940s and the "oil crisis" of the early 1970s was by far the most significant in European history – and this fact does not just take into account real wages, which rose by 400 percent in France, 350 percent in Germany, 260 percent in Switzerland,[18] and 250 percent in Italy between 1950 and 1975. Likewise, it is remarkable that the boom covered most countries of Western Europe regardless of their initial level of development. A third extraordinary feature was the rapid decline of the manpower engaged in agriculture and – to a lesser extent – in industry in favor of activities in the service sector of the economy.[19] Because Switzerland had been spared the destruction of the war, it could assist in rebuilding the economies of neighboring countries from the very beginning.

Generating long-lasting prosperity in Western Europe and protecting it from the communist bacillus had been among the primary goals of American foreign policy in the aftermath of World War II. Indeed, the Roosevelt and Truman administrations created an international economic regime that, to a large extent, met this aim: Under the Bretton Woods Agreement (1944) currencies in Western Europe gradually became convertible and exchange rates were made both stable and favorable for European exports overseas. All members of the General Agreement on Tariffs and Trade or GATT (1947) received equal and ever easier access to the markets of their partners. The European Recovery Program or Marshall Plan (1948) provided the initial injection of dollars needed to restart the economies of the individual countries.[20]

The domestic strategies of the American government to stimulate consumption, such as the pacification of business–labor relations and govern-

17 See Arne Andersen, "From 'The Taste of Necessity' to the Mentality of Wasting: Ecological Consequences of Consumer Society," paper presented at the conference, The Development of Twentieth-Century Consumer Society, German Historical Institute, Washington, D.C., Oct. 1995.
18 Swiss Federal Institute of Statistics.   19 Ambrosius and Kaelble, "Einleitung," 8.
20 Imanuel Wexler, *The Marshall Plan Revisited: The European Recovery Program in Economic Perspective* (Westport, Conn., 1983).

ment spending on highways and home loans, served as a model for most Western European countries, because the United States economy was flourishing in the late 1940s and early 1950s and because these kinds of measures reflected the influential doctrine of John Maynard Keynes.[21] In most cases this doctrine was not strictly applied but helped to create a powerful public mood that encouraged a Keynesian reorientation of national economic policies.

In Switzerland the new economic regime crystallized around three elements: First and most important, a basic consensus between business and metalworkers was reached in 1937 as a result of the already growing threat from neighboring Nazi Germany. Trade unions and employers agreed to regulate wages and working conditions in a comprehensive settlement (*Gesamtarbeitsvertrag*) that was binding on both sides. After the war, this settlement served as a model for other branches of the economy. Its significance may be compared to that of the 1948 contract between the United Automobile Workers (UAW) and General Motors in the United States. In both countries the result of these settlements was a sustained rise in real wages within the entire economy, which created the basis for the transition to mass consumption. But in Switzerland the boom began about ten years later than in the United States. The competition for workers on the job market stiffened in the late 1950s and continued throughout the 1960s until the recession of 1975.

The second element was the creation of a system of social security in 1947. Earlier attempts to create such a system in the interwar period had failed to pass a public referendum.[22] The new system provided a small but regular source of income for the elderly and the handicapped.

The third element concerns the emergence of a political consensus across the entire societal spectrum during and after World War II. In 1943 the Social Democrats, who had been excluded from the federal government before that time, were now entitled to one of the seven cabinet seats. In 1959 they gained an additional one. Since then the so-called magic formula of the government coalition (two Liberals, two Christian Democrats, two Social Democrats, one member of the traditional People's Party) has not been altered.

Undoubtedly, rising real wages as well as social and political stability are important ingredients in the transition from industrial to consumer society. But they do not account for the modifications made within society itself, of

21 See the chapters by George Lipsitz and Lizabeth Cohen in this book.
22 In Switzerland all amendments to the constitution (as a basis for legislation) have to be approved by referendum.

which the changing patterns of consumption are obvious indicators. The German sociologist Burkart Lutz worked out a historical model based on the theory of economic dualism[23] to highlight the multiple aspects of this fundamental transition.[24] In what follows, I briefly summarize this theory.

From the beginning of industrialization through the aftermath of World War II, European economies developed into two main sectors: a modern one and a traditional one. Modern manufacturing and service were part of the international market economy and organized according to the characteristics of competitive capitalist enterprise (production of commodities for wages, profit maximization, and rationalization). In contrast, the traditional sector (agriculture and the trades) was still structured according to the agrarian model of society: Work was organized socially to maintain the subsistence of households under the dominance of a patriarch. Traditional households depended on the ownership of a farm, on a small trade, or on a retail store. Where this basis was not sufficient for the survival of the household, it was complemented with wage labor in the modern sector. Members of traditional households worked for the survival of their family rather than for individual profit. Housewives and children did not receive cash payments, and the wages of servants and apprentices were paid as a yearly lump sum that was unrelated to the number of hours worked.

In times of expanding exports, a part of the labor force in the traditional sector, mostly socially mobile individuals, flowed into the modern sector.[25] This inflow of labor inhibited a substantial rise of wages in this sector, at least at the lower end of the wage scale. Within the traditional sector, the drain of manpower created incentives for mechanized rationalization in some areas. This was paid for by selling a larger amount of traditional goods and services. Yet in periods of export crisis many workers lost their jobs in the modern sector. Those who still had parents or relatives in the traditional sector tried to survive in the family household. Thus, this sector assumed the function of a social buffer, without any compensation from the state.

In the 1950s and 1960s the traditional sector of the economy virtually disappeared. This was the result of interacting push and pull processes that are tightly intertwined.[26] First, through mass production of consumer goods,

---

23 This theory was first advanced by J. H. Boeke, *Economics and Economic Policy in Dual Societies* (New York, 1953).

24 Lutz, *Der kurze Traum*.   25 This concerns chiefly the period from 1890 to 1914.

26 Bukart Lutz, "Die Singularität der europäischen Prosperität nach dem Zweiten Weltkrieg," in Ambrosius and Kaelble, eds., *Der Boom 1948–1973*, 50–1.

the modern sector offered functionally adequate services and goods at lower cost because it could profit by economies of scale. Under these circumstances the traditional ways of producing goods and services were no longer competitive. For instance, the small retail stores were virtually brushed aside by self-service stores and, later on, by shopping malls. As a consequence, the number of food stores in Switzerland shrank by 54 percent from 1948 to 1977, and the number of clients per store tripled over the same period. The 1960s and 1970s witnessed most of this concentration in retailing.[27] Moreover, as Arne Andersen has shown, the modern sector offered durable consumer goods, such as automobiles, refrigerators, or washing machines, at ever lower prices.[28] For those who made their money from selling automobiles, household appliances, or houses in the suburbs, tapping this large new market created the possibility for limitless growth, at least for the foreseeable future. It should be mentioned, however, that most families in the 1950s lived in apartments, housework was done without technical appliances, and men went to work by bicycle or by train.

Second, the remaining core activities of the traditional sector, such as agriculture and some trades, were absorbed by the modern sector. They had to be reorganized along the lines of industrial rationalization and profit maximization. Farming, for example, became in many respects an industrial activity.

Besides the cost-push factors three forces of demand-pull are important: (1) The boom led to an almost incredible search for skilled labor. When qualified workers could no longer be found in sufficient numbers, real wages were raised annually, or even monthly in some branches of the economy. Moreover, workers from Mediterranean countries were recruited in growing numbers. Since a system of settlements had been established between trade unions and employers, pay raises in one branch spread to all the other branches of the sector. In addition, the number of weekly working hours was gradually lowered and the amount of annual vacation was increased. It is not surprising that the attractive working conditions in the modern sector became almost irresistible to people in the traditional sector. (2) At the same time, this sector lost its function and its image as a social buffer. The new system of social security was thought to provide better protection and it was believed that times of economic hardship were gone for good. (3) The impact of American industrial culture on Western Europe in

---

27 Matthias Nast, "Lebensmittelverpackungen im Zeitalter der Konsumgesellschaft: 1950er Jahre bis heute," Ph.D. diss., Bern University, 1996.
28 Andersen, "Taste of Necessity."

the late 1940s and the 1950s should not be underestimated. In these years, the United States was experiencing one of the most pronounced booms in its history, whereas most parts of Europe had not yet recovered physically from the war. Understandably, the Fordist way of life was effectively publicized by American propaganda in contrast to the perceived scarcity of "real" socialism.[29] Indeed, the United States was taken as a model and an unassailable guide to the future. Agreement was so close among the Swiss political parties in this respect that the topic was not even discussed.

Robert Haddow has shown that American administrations, both Democratic and Republican, took an active interest in exposing foreign publics to tangible examples of a prosperous, responsible capitalism, such as a planned city with superhighways, in the belief that popular support would follow visionary planning.[30] To mask their activities, they cooperated with business leaders. This can also be shown in the case of Switzerland, where the planning of expressways was initially sponsored in part by officials of the American oil industry.[31] Nelson Rockefeller, who was president of the powerful Standard Oil Company and special assistant to the president (Eisenhower) for foreign affairs,[32] was probably behind this drive. The industrialists invited the members of the Swiss Planning Commission to the United States for two weeks to familiarize them with the concepts and the technical realization of American expressway planning.[33] The highway network that was eventually built was little more than an ill-advised transfer of American schemes to the small landscape of Switzerland. The most controversial of them aimed at building expressways into the heart of cities.[34] The American oil industrialists were right in their expectation that constructing a dense network of expressways in Switzerland would foster the diffusion of Fordist patterns of consumption. Indeed, over the last forty years, the growing *Autobahn* network promoted a road-oriented reallocation of economic activities and residential patterns that doubled the built-up surface area.[35] Moreover,

29 For Austria, see Reinhold Wagnleitner, *Coca-Colonization and the Cold War: The Cultural Mission of the United States in Austria After the Second World War* (Chapel Hill, N.C., 1994). A similar study is not available for Switzerland. In her chapter in this book, Ina Merkel provides an insider description of East German society at that time.

30 Robert Haddow, "U.S. Policy, Trade Fairs, and Consumer Goods in Europe During the Cold War," paper presented at the conference, The Development of Twentieth-Century Consumer Society, German Historical Institute, Washington, D.C., Oct. 1995.

31 Michael Ackermann, *Konzepte und Entscheidungen in der Planung der schweizerischen Nationalstrassen von 1927 bis 1961* (Bern, 1992).

32 See Haddow, "U.S. Policy, Trade Fairs, and Consumer Goods."

33 Ackermann, *Konzepte und Entscheidungen*, 151–6.

34 Jean-Daniel Blanc, *Die Stadt – ein Verkehrshindernis? Leitbilder städtischer Verkehrsplanung und Verkehrspolitik in Zürich, 1945–1975* (Zurich, 1993), 94.

35 Hans Flückiger, "Raumplanung im Spannungsfeld zwischen Trend und Steuerung," in Pfister, ed., *Das 1950er Syndrom,* 333.

it initiated the construction of large shopping malls on the urban periphery and supported an infrastructure that allowed long-distance mass leisure mobility. All in all, these profound changes in the patterns of urbanization promoted the geographic scattering of where one lived, worked, shopped, or relaxed. This in turn led to structural constraints in a self-perpetuating cycle.[36]

People raised in the traditional sector had been accustomed to a set of popular customs, values, and skills that were related to the careful management of resources. Housewives, for example, had the skills to store food and repair clothes, and they were familiar with a wide variety of recycling strategies.[37] These activities were not motivated by concerns for the environment as we understand that term today. But they resulted in social qualities such as modesty, frugality, solidarity, readiness to work hard, and capacity to improvise solutions for temporary bottlenecks in the supply of vital goods and services. These qualities had played a pivotal role in economic survival under the prevailing conditions of industrial and agrarian society. During the "short dream of everlasting prosperity," they were no longer needed.[38] With the arrival of successor generations, these qualities were gradually supplanted by the hedonistic values of the throwaway society.

THE ROLE OF CHEAP ENERGY IN THE
LOSS OF SUSTAINABILITY

From the late 1950s to the present, the price of (fossil) fuel has declined in relation to the price of labor, services, and most other commodities (see Figure 17.5).[39]

In Switzerland 1 liter of gasoline in 1950 was 62 rappen.[40] This was more than the cost of 1 kilogram of brown bread. A skilled worker's hourly wage was not more than the equivalent of 4.5 liters of gasoline. Forty years later a loaf of bread was four times more expensive than it was in 1950, but a worker's salary was equivalent to more than 20 liters of gasoline. In relation to purchasing power, gasoline has become five times cheaper. If the price of gasoline had risen in proportion to wages since 1950, 1 liter would have cost approximately 5 Swiss francs in 1990. As in many European countries, the price of gasoline in Switzerland is a policy decision. It has always

36 Urs Fuhrer, ed., *Wohnen mit dem Auto: Ursachen und Gestaltung automobiler Freizeit* (Zurich, 1993).
37 Lutz, *Der kurze Traum*.
38 This is an English translation of the title of Lutz's book mentioned previously.
39 Source: Pfister, ed., *Das 1950er Syndrom*.   40 A Swiss franc is equivalent to 100 rappen.

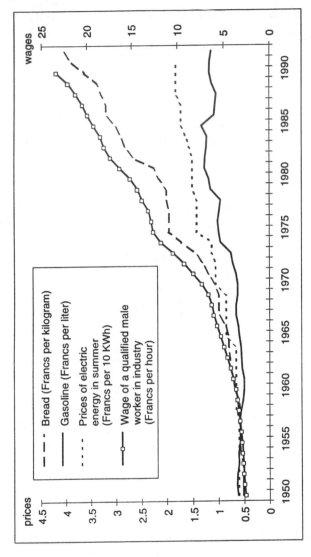

Figure 17.5. Hourly wages of qualified workers in industry compared to prices of brown bread, electric energy, and gasoline in Switzerland, 1950–90. Between 1950 and 1990 the price of gasoline scarcely doubled, whereas nominal hourly wages rose ninefold.

included a tax that since 1950 has fluctuated between 40 and 60 percent of the actual price of gasoline and has to be spent on the construction and maintenance of the *Autobahn* network.[41]

The decline of the real world-market prices for crude oil after the late 1950s is connected to the large number of new producers that entered the market at that time, among which the Soviet Union was the most important. Simultaneously, the de facto cartel of the Seven Sisters became ineffective as a great number of new oil companies got a share of the market.[42] The "oil shock" of 1973 resulted from OPEC's decision to adapt the posted prices to the higher level of market prices that had resulted from a temporary slump in supply. The subsequent price increases in 1979 and 1980 were the backlash of three interrelated events: the Iranian revolution, the Soviet invasion of Afghanistan, and the Iraqi–Iranian war. The setback in 1986 was related to the collapse of the OPEC cartel after the withdrawal of Saudi Arabia.[43]

It has been argued that the considerable cheapening of fossil fuels after the 1950s is one of the main reasons for the exorbitant per capita growth in energy consumption in the Western world since the 1950s.[44] The abstract physical term "energy" must be related to human needs. It is often overlooked that energy as such is not "consumed." Rather, it provides the means to produce services, such as heating, light, transportation, and mechanical work, and to operate networks of communication. "Production" involves converting natural forms of energy (e.g., crude oil) into a specific form of "energy services" (e.g., driving). In this conversion (which in our case involves distilling the crude in a refinery to obtain gasoline and burning gasoline in the engine of a car) a certain part of the primary energy is always lost.[45] What matters from the point of view of environmental quality is the consumption of primary energy. What matters from the point of view of human needs is the availability of energy services. The magnitude of the losses depends on both the kind of energy and the technology that is used for the conversion. Saving energy, therefore, does not necessarily mean cutting down the consumption of "energy services." The same effect can be produced by implementing new kinds of technologies that reduce the losses of conversion from primary energy to energy services.

41 Christoph Maria Merki, "Der Treibstoffzoll aus historischer Sicht: Von der Finanzquelle des Bundes zum Motor des Strassenbaus," in Pfister, ed., *Das 1950er Syndrom*, 311–32.
42 Daniel Yergin, *The Prize: The Epic Quest for Oil, Money and Power* (New York, 1991), 642.
43 Ibid., 851–65.   44 Pfister, "Das '1950er Syndrom,'" 84–5.
45 Daniel Spreng, *Energiebedarf der Informationsgesellschaft* (Baden-Baden, 1988), 14; Georg Erdmann, *Energieökonomik* (Zurich, 1992), 26; Kümmel and Bruckner, "Energie, Entropie – Ökonomie, Ökologie," in Pfister, ed., *Das 1950er Syndrom*, 130.

Measures of this kind are likely to improve the sustainability of an economic system.

Considering the consequences of the long-term decline of energy prices for businesses, mass consumption, and the environment, we need to distinguish two issues that are often conflated. What was the role of cheap energy in the level of business activity and mass consumption? How did the declining price of energy affect the diffusion of energy-saving technologies and, therefore, the quality of the global environment?

The decline in the price of fossil energy is not mentioned in the textbooks as one of the driving forces behind the long economic boom after World War II.[46] In assessing the thesis of the syndrome of the 1950s the influential Swiss economic historian Hansjörg Siegenthaler has argued that cheap energy was not the cause of the boom but rather one of its secondary preconditions.[47] Indeed, the boom put a heavy focus on energy demand, and this demand could be met by an abundant supply at low prices. Moreover, the economic significance of rising oil prices in 1973 should not be overestimated. The term "oil shock" suggests that the impact was psychological; it was not related to a true shortage. In the Swiss case (and probably in that of the Federal Republic of Germany as well) the end of the Bretton Woods era and the transition to freely floating currencies in 1973 were far more decisive. They led to a strong appreciation of the Swiss franc and higher prices for Swiss exports on the world market.[48]

The study of the relation between the price of coal and the level of economic activity supports this argument. In periods of economic expansion – for example, during the two decades prior to World War I (see Figure 17.6) or in the first decade of the *Wirtschaftswunder* (economic miracle in 1948–57) – the price of coal was raised. In periods of crisis, it was lowered. This is linked to the high labor intensity of underground coal mining. For a long time, mechanization of production was limited to the installation of conveyor belts and electric trains and elevators. The hard work of digging the coal was still done mostly by hand. Hence, wages made up the lion's share of the costs of production. In periods of economic boom, additional miners were recruited to meet the demand. When the demand

46 See, e.g., the influential work of Walt Whitman Rostow, ed., *The World Economy: History and Prospects* (Austin, Tex., 1978); on Europe, see Ambrosius and Kaelble, eds., *Der Boom 1948–1973*.
47 Hansjörg Siegenthaler, "Zur These des '1950er Syndroms,'" in Pfister, ed., *Das 1950er Syndrom*, 99.
48 Heidi Schelbert, "Schweizerische Wirtschaftsentwicklung seit 1950," in Pfister, ed., *Das 1950er Syndrom*, 204. Source: Walther G. Hoffmann, *Das Wachstum der deutschen Wirtschaft seit der Mitte des 19. Jahrhunderts* (Berlin, 1965).

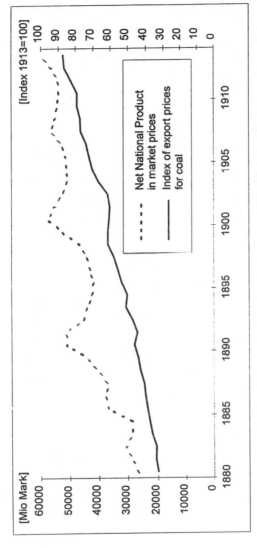

Figure 17.6. Prices of coal and net national product in Germany, 1880–1914. During the long boom prior to World War I, the coal cartel of the Ruhr Valley gradually raised the price of a ton of coal by 100 percent. The rise in coal prices was almost parallel to that of the GNP.

declined, workers were dismissed. In both cases, prices responded to the level of demand.[49]

The impact of the price of energy on the development of technology can be assessed both theoretically and empirically. The assumption that prices of energy and their relative changes affect the evolution of economic systems arises from the principle of substitution. A decline in the relative price of a good increases demand for this good at the expense of others. Efforts to lower the cost of production in a capitalist economy always focus on the factor that is the most expensive in relation to the others. Therefore, a relative decline in the cost of energy in relation to the cost of labor promotes a substitution of energy for labor in the production function.[50] This kind of substitution not only underlay most of the measures of rationalization undertaken in the Western economies over the last forty years. It also profoundly affected everyday life because it allowed for the substitution of energy for time to an ever greater extent. This tendency became so deeply rooted in our way of thinking and acting that it is no longer the object of deliberate decisions. It is not yet clear when this tendency began, how closely it is related to the long-term decline of energy prices, and how far cultural factors need to be taken into account. The preferences in the relative allocation of time and energy in different kinds of work in the traditional and the modern sectors of industrial society might be assessed by means of oral history interviews or by an analysis of autobiographical literature. In any case, it is obvious that the diffusion of energy-intensive forms of production, distribution, and consumption from the late 1950s was almost synchronous to the long-term changes in the relative prices of energy and labor.

The theory of substitution also has a bearing on the adoption of new technologies. The success of new energy-saving technology on the market depends on, among others things, the relative cost of capital and energy as well as the cost of labor. In the midnineteenth century, for example, the relative abundance of cheap labor in Europe was the principal cause of the slower adoption of agricultural machinery when compared to that in the United States. It may be argued that it was profitable to invent and implement new technologies that reduced the losses of conversion from primary

49 Klaus Tenfelde, *Sozialgeschichte der Bergarbeiterschaft an der Ruhr im 19. Jahrhundert* (Bonn, 1981), 292–3; Werner Berg, *Wirtschaft und Gesellschaft in Deutschland und Grossbritannien im Übergang zum "organisierten Kapitalismus"* (Berlin, 1984), 828; Wolfgang Zollitsch, *Arbeiter zwischen Weltwirtschaftskrise und Nationalsozialismus* (Göttingen, 1990), 33.
50 Gunter Stephan, "Das '1950er Syndrom' und Handlungsspielräume: Eine wirtschaftswissenschaftliche Betrachtung," in Pfister, ed., *Das 1950er Syndrom,* 219–32.

energy to energy services as long as the relative price of energy was high. These conditions existed from the beginning of organized human activity to the middle of the twentieth century; many of the technical innovations described as "progress" and "development" contributed to advances in the intensity and efficiency of energy use.[51] As a fringe benefit, they improved the sustainability of the economy. However, with the decline in the relative price of fossil fuels, the incentives to adopt energy-saving technologies slackened – the interlude of the two "energy crises" notwithstanding. We may hypothesize that a continual and gradual rise in energy prices beyond the late 1950s would furthermore have promoted the diffusion of energy-saving technologies without affecting economic activity. This might have promoted the emergence of another type of consumer society that would be more sustainable in the long run.

51 Ervin Laszlo, *Evolution: The Grand Synthesis* (Boston, 1987), 96–8.

18

Reflecting on Ethnic Imagery in the Landscape of Commerce, 1945–1975

FATH DAVIS RUFFINS

I

Between 1945 and 1975, Americans turned their nation into a global powerhouse of production and consumption, and their government bound together foreign policy success, consumerism, and domestic tranquillity in new and explicit ways. During World War II, the Office of War Information – in posters, billboards, pamphlets, and radio programs – had clearly linked the wartime sacrifices to the coming prosperity of the postwar years. The long-term effects of the G.I. Bills supporting veteran's education, home ownership, and business aspirations trickled down even to Afro-Americans and Mexican Americans.[1] By the early 1960s, many working-class Americans could own television sets, washing machines, and perhaps a Chevy or

---

1 Over time, people of African descent within the United States have changed how they wished to be referred to. In the 1700s and earlier, *sons and daughters of Africa* was a common appellation. Consequently, independent churches formed during that era often have names such as the African Methodist Episcopal Church. By the 1830s, another designation became common: *Colored Americans* and *People of Color.* For example, Frederick Douglass often referred to "peoples of color" in his speeches. However, during these same years, *Afro-American* was often used in newspapers and other published work. By the late 1800s, *Colored* was the most frequent name used, in both oral and written language. In the early 1900s, a younger generation of people felt that *Negro* was a term that connoted a new sense of dignity and pride. For years, African-American activists campaigned for white publishers to capitalize the word *Negro.* This was symbolically achieved in the 1940s, when the *New York Times* officially changed its style sheet. During the 1960s, another younger generation felt that *Black* or *Black Americans* were terms that connoted greater racial pride and identification. In the 1990s, *African American* has become more popular, coming almost full circle to the 1700s. Because these name changes reflect significant shifts in the cultural discourse among African Americans, in this chapter I have used the appropriate ethnic self-designations, all capitalized, in their respective historical periods.

For work on the importance of veterans to Afro-American and Mexican-American communities, see David Gutierrez, *Walls and Mirrors: Mexican Americans, Mexican Immigrants, and the Politics of Ethnicity* (Berkeley, Calif., 1995); Aldon Morris, *The Origins of the Civil Rights Movement: Black Communities Organizing for Change* (New York, 1983); Bernard Nalty, *Strength for the Fight: A History of Black Americans in the Military* (New York, 1986); George Sanchez, *Becoming Mexican American: Ethnicity, Culture, and Identity in Chicano Los Angeles, 1900–1945* (New York, 1993).

a Ford. During the Eisenhower presidency, growing consumerism at home was explicitly tied to the fight against communism abroad. At a joint trade fair in Moscow in 1959, Vice President Richard M. Nixon predicted to Soviet Premier Nikita Khrushchev that America would win the fight against communism with its refrigerators, toasters, and cars.[2] Prosperity and world hegemony were integrally connected in the postwar world.

Yet the same nation that was shown proceeding toward consumerist heaven in countless television commercials, Hollywood movies, and print advertisements was also riven by profound internal conflict, especially over questions of race and ethnicity. It was only the threat of a massive march on Washington that forced President Franklin D. Roosevelt to issue Executive Order 8802, which established the Fair Employment Practices Commission (FEPC) to investigate charges of discrimination in hiring by government and business. In 1948 the threat of a close presidential election forced President Harry S. Truman to issue Executive Order 9981 to desegregate the armed forces. The National Association for the Advancement of Colored People (NAACP) had agitated for just such actions for over a generation, and after World War II, its work began to pay off. From the late 1940s through the late 1950s, under Chief Justice Earl Warren, the Supreme Court issued a series of decisions that decreed desegregation in party primaries, public transportation, accommodations, and eventually education, most famously in the 1954 landmark decision *Brown v. The Board of Education of Topeka, Kansas,* which mandated desegregation in American public schools "with all deliberate speed." In 1955 the Afro-American community of Montgomery, Alabama, began its justly famous and successful bus boycott, which catapulted both Rosa Parks and the Reverend Dr. Martin Luther King Jr., then a young man, to national attention. This bus boycott is widely seen today as the symbolic beginning of the modern civil rights movement that was to change American society dramatically over the next ten years.

With a wave of demonstrations, boycotts, and other forms of "direct action," issues of race and equality hit the top of the domestic national agenda. In 1957, a conservative president, Dwight D. Eisenhower, was forced to send federal troops to Little Rock, Arkansas, to protect nine Afro-American children entering a previously whites-only high school. In 1963, the symbolic high water mark of the civil rights movement occurred during the March on Washington: a peaceful demonstration by 250,000 people on the Mall in support of the civil rights bill before Congress. As a result of this demonstration and Martin Luther King Jr.'s famous "I Have a

---

2 For more on the kitchen debate, see Karal Ann Marling, *As Seen on TV: Visual Culture of Everyday Life in the 1950s* (Cambridge, Mass., 1994).

Dream" speech, the Congress in 1964 passed the Civil Rights Act, which outlawed discrimination. In 1965 the Congress passed the Voting Rights Act, which guaranteed all Americans the right to vote. These bills were signed into law by President Lyndon B. Johnson. Such concerns about the civil rights of Afro-Americans had not taken such a progressive tone on the national stage since the era of Reconstruction (1865–77). Indeed, many people during the early and mid-1960s labeled these years "The Second Reconstruction."[3] One recent history of the period is Taylor Branch's *Parting the Waters: America in the King Years* (1988), reflecting the profound significance of these accomplishments for American society in the early Cold War era.

Yet there has been little investigation of the relationship between these serious domestic concerns regarding race and the simultaneous development of the United States as the preeminent consumerist society. One way to begin such an analysis is to ask: What difference did it make in the development of American consumerist practices and products that the United States was a heterogeneous society? How did American racial and ethnic beliefs and practices figure in producing, selling, and consuming goods after World War II? In what ways did the profound social dislocations around race and ethnicity during these years appear in the visualizations of American life embodied in advertising, public relations, and other forms of selling? This chapter is no more than an outline – a series of reflections – about the crucial intersections of growing consumerism and the emerging, conflicted consciousness of race and ethnicity that distinguished the first thirty years of the Cold War era.

II

Commercial imagery depicting distinctively American ideas about race and ethnicity has a very long history. When colonial Virginians labeled their hogsheads of tobacco with pictures of Indian chieftains or enslaved Africans working the fields, they were indicating the authenticity of their product as one from the "New World" – then producing the finest tobacco available. When antebellum printers published runaway ads and slave-sale announcements by the thousands, they depicted some of the key aspects of slavery as a system of buying and selling people as property. Thus, commercial imagery illustrating the complexities of race in America has a history virtually coextensive with the notion of "America" itself.

---

3 For more on the Reconstruction era, see Eric Foner, *Reconstruction: America's Unfinished Revolution, 1863–1877* (New York, 1988).

On first mention of the words "ethnic imagery," many people think immediately of stereotypes. Certainly, commercial imagery before 1930 was rife with many images that would today be labeled stereotypical. Beginning in the 1830s, blackface minstrelsy imbued song, story, and the stage with a panoply of black characters: Jim Crow – the chicken-stealing country bumpkin; Zip Coon – the ridiculous citified dandy; De Judge – a pompous ass given to malapropisms. These characters became staples of American humor itself, eventually appearing in silent films and the talkies.

Aunt Jemima is one of the best known and enduring trademarked images in the United States. Aunt Jemima was a fictitious character devised for selling a new kind of four-flour pancake mix in the 1890s. Introduced to a national market at the Columbian Exposition in 1893, Aunt Jemima and her superlight, easy-to-make pancake mix were an immediate hit. The woman hired to portray Aunt Jemima in person at the fair, Nancy Green, was reputed to have served more than 2 million pancakes to visitors. The company renamed itself after the character and the product itself bore her name. Over the years, this very successful company was purchased by ever larger corporations and today is part of Quaker Oats. The exact visualization of Aunt Jemima has changed drastically over the last hundred years. She began as an enormously fat, dark black woman with huge cheeks, nose, and superwhite eyes whose face took up nearly the entire box. Today the same red and white box exists, but Aunt Jemima is in an oval cameo set in a corner of the top. She no longer wears a kerchief and looks like a medium brown-skinned woman with glossy hair who could be a suburban grandmother.

The history of Aunt Jemima as a character is far too complex to detail here. Scores of scholarly articles and thousands of newspaper pieces have been written about her.[4] Aunt Jemima is quite simply an icon in American culture, although her meaning is deeply contested. As a visual type, Aunt Jemima was the best known of a whole genre of "Mammy" figures. Appearing widely in advertising during the 1880s, the Mammy character became a staple of song, legend, stage, and screen. Eventually, to evoke the "Old South" of "moonlight and magnolias" required a Mammy figure. In the archetypal film of this subject, *Gone with the Wind* (1939), Hattie McDaniels portrayed such a powerful Mammy figure that she became the first (and for many years the only) Afro-American woman to win an Academy Award.

---

4 For more on Aunt Jemima, see Donald Bogle, *Toms, Coons, Mulattoes, Mammies, and Bucks: An Interpretive History of Blacks in American Films*, rev. ed. (New York, 1989); see also Marilyn Kern-Foxworth, *Aunt Jemima, Uncle Ben, and Rastus: Blacks in Advertising: Yesterday, Today, and Tomorrow* (Westport, Conn., 1994).

Scholars are just beginning to plumb the meaning of these Mammy characters in white American society, but already we can ascertain that the Mammy figure, appearing on greeting cards and in numerous sentimental forms, was one version of "the good mother" – uncritical, nurturing, warm, and embracing.

By the 1910s, some southerners began to call for a memorial to honor the Mammy figure. These efforts appeared all across the South and are collectively known as the Black Mammy Memorial movement, which resulted in the formation of an institute chartered for twenty years in Athens, Georgia. In 1923, the Daughters of the Confederacy proposed that a bronze memorial to honor the Mammy of the Old South be placed somewhere on the grounds of the Capitol building in Washington, D.C. Numerous Afro-Americans protested and effectively quashed the petition in the House of Representatives, although several congressional committees seriously considered the idea. Such sentiments underscored the deep vein of positive white sentiment that images of "the Mammy" tapped. The marketers of Aunt Jemima drew on prevailing notions about Afro-American women to craft a brand identity that conveyed authenticity and comfort to their intended market of white consumers.

Because these images visually fixed Afro-American identity at a distinct low social, cultural, and economic level, many Afro-Americans had considerably more negative feelings about Aunt Jemima. In the late 1910s, the NAACP began to protest the use of this image. Before 1910, the fictitious Aunt Jemima was given a full-scale personal history by the Quaker Oats Company that showed her as a loyal slave, happy to serve her heroic Confederate masters, even after freedom came. Early Afro-American criticism of the image concentrated not only on the visual portrayal but also on this demeaning history. Yet this fictitious story remained powerful to many non-Afro-Americans and was retold in many screen versions starting in the 1930s. By the 1950s, many Afro-Americans were calling Aunt Jemima an out-and-out stereotype. Black visual artists lampooned the character; feminist playwrights and poets satirized the image. By the 1970s, Aunt Jemima all by herself served as a handy symbol for the racial stereotyping of all Black Americans by racist white media.

Yet Aunt Jemima remains a brand name with recognition ratings consistently above 95 percent on many American marketing surveys. Such numbers suggest just why Quaker Oats has kept her on the box, despite many protests over the years. Even though most Americans today may feel degrees of discomfort with Aunt Jemima, enough positive regard exists that the company continues to update her image, but never to eliminate it. In 1995, television viewers were treated to a totally modernized advertisement in the form of the famous soul singer Gladys Knight, who was shown enjoying pancakes with her grandchildren in a model American kitchen. Quaker Oats had consulted Dr. Dorothy Height, longtime head of the esteemed National Council of Negro Women, before this marketing campaign. The company strategically placed significant stories in key Afro-American publications such as *Essence* magazine as part of a well-orchestrated public relations effort. What is remarkable is the durability of this image. Aunt Jemima symbolized good eating and great pancakes to nineteenth-century Americans, and, though visually different, her image continues to function similarly for Americans today, even as many Afro-Americans have come to be included among and directly recognized as consumers. Such visually subtle shifts have occurred in only a small number of "stereotypical" images inherited from the last century. They make Aunt Jemima an especially enduring cultural symbol.

Not every broad ethnic image had the visual recognition and power of an Aunt Jemima. American trade cards, advertising posters, print ads, sheet music, and even greeting cards were filled with broad jokes about drunken Paddy the Irishman who was always looking for a fight and a pint, thieving Spaniards as pirates, cheating Jews selling less for more, and savage Indians killing settlers. Some of these stereotypes were more benign, such as Scotsmen who were always pinching a penny ever tighter, or Dutch children who were hyperclean, or Germans who were rotund and red-faced and holding beer steins. Many distinctive American ethnic groups were represented in specific and pejorative commercial images, especially before 1920. Yet stereotyping – though pervasive – was not the entire story of ethnic visualization.

Over the last century, in creating plausible scenarios for the use of particular products, many American companies depicted ethnic, racial, and class distinctions as a matter of course. For example, in Figure 18.1, two women and two children are seen standing in a kitchen – a typical late nineteenth-century trade card advertising a cleanser. The wide-faced blowzy "Bridget the Irish maid" is clearly the servant, and an Anglo-American woman is unquestionably the mistress of the household. The maid is demonstrating the effectiveness of the cleanser by showing the reflection of her round face in the bottom of the frying pan. Images such as these gave visual life to contemporary intersections of class, ethnicity, and gender, even in the selling of low-cost domestic consumables. Although these representations depicted ethnicity, it was not the subject of the image. Rather, the overt text involved "expert" testimony as to the effectiveness of

SCOUR POTS, KETTLES, PANS
& ALL BRASS & COPPER UTENSILS *WITH SAPOLIO.*

Figure 18.1. Trade card, circa 1870–80. Warshaw Collection of Business Americana, Archives Center, National Museum of American History, Smithsonian Institution, Washington. D.C. Used with permission.

a particular product – a housemaid who had used many cleansers must know which one was the best! Rather, ethnicity appeared only because the category "Bridget the Irish maid" was a distinctive classification of the time. Far more American representations of ethnicity presented this kind of subtle story than the overt, more stereotypical elements, especially in the case of European immigrants who evolved into American ethnic groups.

American commercial imagery also depicted how to live in a heterogeneous society. Especially during the 1890s, American producers began to picture the "races of the world" united in their consumption of American products. Thousands of images were created for world fairs, particularly the Columbian Exposition of 1893–4 in Chicago, Illinois. Figure 18.2 shows one version of the "nations of the world" around Uncle Sam, the premier emblem of America, who is shown demonstrating the Enterprise meat grinder. All the world could be united in their expression of consumer choice. In fact, a number of "races" in this image could not at that time become literal citizens of the United States. Neither the "Chinaman" with his long queue nor the "Indian" in his savage garb could be an American citizen in the 1890s, but these political realities were elided in the depiction of their virtual equality as consumers.

More problematic were American visualizations of the blending and borrowing that naturally occur in a multiethnic society. "Interracial" relationships began symbolically with figures such as Pocahontas in Jamestown in the 1610s. For complex reasons that are beyond the scope of this essay to detail, the United States developed a segregated society in which racial groups were seen as rigid, either/or monoliths. One drop of "Negro blood" was believed to make a person black through and through. Unlike in the rest of the Americas, United States laws and practices denied the varied skin colors, facial features, hair textures, and other elements that revealed the sexual realities of interethnic contact. Blackface minstrelsy was literally a denial of the physiological differences among Afro-Americans. Black entertainers struggled for many years to tear away this mask of sameness. However, the depiction of some other American blended peoples was more subtle, both visually and conceptually.

In British North America, the original version of this archetypal story was that of Pocahontas. A child when the English first arrived in what became Jamestown, Virginia, Pocahontas eventually married an Englishman, John Rolfe, and went to England, where she bore several children and then died young (as did many women of that time). The fact of her marriage (and by implication the arrival of their children) was often shown symbolically to be the birth of "America." Ironically, Pocahontas's story

Figure 18.2. Trade Card, the World's Fair of 1893. Warshaw Collection of Business Americana, Archives Center, National Museum of American History, Smithsonian Institution, Washington, D.C. Used with permission.

had become the myth of a new American face since by the late eighteenth century, in this narrative, English pioneers had absorbed – literally – the royalty of the original peoples and had produced the American race whose manifest destiny it was to conquer the continent. Such themes had and continue to have tremendous power as a key patriotic fixture in the visual representation of the American mythos. Numerous posters for world's fairs, especially those in the West, celebrated this notion of the joining of Europeans and Indians. In the United States, the sexual implications of this metaphor were underplayed in comparison to those in imagery from Mexican or Brazilian sources of the same era. "Interracial" romantic and sexual bonding was deeply troubling as a narrative and yet embedded in American practice.[5]

Like Aunt Jemima, Pocahontas became an American narrative with tremendous staying power. In 1995, the Disney company released its most recent version of the Pocahontas story with a full-scale production, including a hit song preformed by the first Black Miss America, Vanessa Williams, and a full range of toys, clothes, games, and collectibles for children from McDonald's. Now available in video, this animated film shows a luscious womanly Pocahontas falling in love with a brawny, blond, blue-eyed Englishman named Captain John Smith, the essential "founder" of this first British colony in the Americas.

Over the course of the twentieth century, other symbols have been advanced that metaphorized positive, liberal notions of a multiethnic America. By the turn of the century, "melting pot" had emerged as the most widely used metaphor. Werner Sollers has now documented that the term "melting pot" first became widely used as a result of a 1908 play by Israel Zangwill depicting the complications involved in a Jewish–Catholic marriage.[6] The children of immigrant parents, a young Jewish man and a young Irish Catholic woman, fall in love and marry. Their fathers are horrified, but a partial rapprochement occurs in a touching Christmas moment. This image reflects a new version of a narrative about "blending." In *The Melting Pot,* Zangwill showed the marriage of two children of a much more recent immigration – not the founding fathers and Indian maidens of the Pocahontas story. Sollers has argued that the myth of immigration has replaced the original colonial myth as the metanarrative of contemporary American

---

5 For more on Pocahontas, see Rayna Green, "The Tribe Called Wannabe: Playing Indian in America and Europe," *Folklore* 99, no. 1 (1988); see also Green, "The Pocahontas Perplex: the Image of Indian Women in American Culture," *Massachusetts Review* 16, no. 4 (autumn 1975): 678–714; see also Philip DeLoria, "Playing Indian: Otherness and Authenticity in the Assumption of American Indian Identity," Ph.D. diss., Yale University, 1995.
6 Werner Sollers, *Beyond Ethnicity: Consent and Descent in American Culture* (New York, 1986).

nationalism. The shift from the blended metaphors of Pocahontas and the blond John in Jamestown to the children of Ellis Island has happened largely since World War II.

III

Perhaps the greatest shift in the metanarrative of the United States reflects the transformation that immigration made in American life with the emergence of a network of immigrant suppliers for many new sets of American consumers. Immigration introduced new products, new consumers, and international marketing networks for the importers of foodstuffs, beverages, candies, liquors, clothes, religious objects, and music of all kinds. All of these products were dispersed by distinct purveyors. By the turn of the century, Jewish and Arab peddlers crisscrossed not only cities but also the American countryside; Italian wine makers found markets in Minnesota; and Italian olive-oil importers were in every major American city. Not only were kosher Jewish bakers selling bagels, gefilte fish, and other foods to Orthodox communities, but nonreligious Jewish delicatessen owners were marketing all kinds of new cheeses, cured meats and fish to both individual consumers and restaurants. The terms "Jewish deli" and "Jewish rye bread" appeared as names of businesses or types of foods in many parts of the United States. Making foods from the "Old Country" that could be consumed by native-born Americans made those immigrants seem more acceptable, more consumable, more assimilable, even as overt discrimination continued against immigrant groups.

Many Chinese families and single men were engaged in restaurant and other food related businesses, such as noodle factories and sauce making companies. But such activities were deeply shaped by the Chinese Exclusion Acts of the 1880s, which created "bachelor societies." Certain types of food, such as "chow mein" and "chop suey," were alleged to have been created solely for the white market in Chinatowns, an early destination for urban tourism in large cities. Some images were created to sell products that had originated in specific ethnic experiences, defined by religious practices, national origins, and language – such as kosher merchants selling to Eastern European Orthodox Jews. Other images were created to develop a wide market outside the immediate communities, as with the Chinese restaurant business.

The tremendous growth of distinctive ethnic communities in cities and suburbs across America greatly widened the array of commercial imagery by opening up new markets for small- and then large-scale entrepreneurs.

Much historical attention has been focused on understanding the advertising and marketing strategies of large-scale American businesses and discerning the ways in which their corporate agendas have shaped the development of new markets, new cultural practices, and new national images. But on a local and regional scale, American businesses (often with an explicitly ethnic character) also produced images and products for new markets. These new businesses arrayed themselves along a cultural spectrum from "keeping all the old ways" to purveying the newest, shiniest, most "assimilated" American object, but to an ethnically defined neighborhood clientele. The visions they created of their consumers and for their new products help construct the now archetypal "old neighborhoods" in many American cities and imaginations.[7]

In this process of building ethnic businesses – defined either through the product, the ownership of the business, and/or the clientele served – ethnic imagery began to be constructed as the "authentic" imagery of America. During the 1930s, many ethnic businesses marketed themselves as different from and in contrast to the homogenized, "white bread" imagery of large-scale food manufacturers like Kraft or Campbell Soups. Small-scale businesses such as Chef Boyardee canned soups and stews (started by the Boiardi family) or Unanue and Sons (which later became Goya Foods, Inc.) sold their customers a taste of the "Old Country."

By the 1950s, many of the smaller, family-owned businesses had been sold by their original owners to such major American corporations as General Foods, General Mills, Pepsi-Cola, and Kraft. In many cases, however, these corporate producers still emphasized aspects of the ethnic origins of the products. For example, a 1964 television ad for Betty Crocker Rice Milanese shows a woman walking home from the market through old-time cobbled streets, listening to a man play a cello.[8] Children are playing with a soccer ball; at this time soccer was coded as an immigrant game. We see a thin, model-like brunette walking up the ivy-covered, stone stairs to her home, which is clearly somewhere in Europe. The voice-over says: "In Italy women still shop and cook in the old-fashioned way." You see a close-up of the woman wearing a blue-black dress with white pearls and a pearl bracelet. She takes all of the ingredients needed for the dish out of her shopping basket – tomatoes, rice, onions, green peppers, spices, and cheese. The voice-over says, "Betty Crocker – it's all in the box! Even the Parmesan! And it is

7 For more on this concept of "imagined communities," see Benedict Anderson, *Imagined Communities: Reflections on the Origin and Spread of Nationalism,* 2d ed. (New York, 1991).
8 Art Directors Club of New York. Tape name: Best of 1964. The ad was produced by the agency Doyle, Dane, Bernbach, reel B632, Museum of Television and Radio, New York City.

as good as if you made it the old Italian way!" Here ethnicity is used to authenticate the product being sold. The Old World setting and ways of cooking produced great results, but the modern American homemaker needed a quicker method. The Betty Crocker product was sold as a solution to that dilemma, while maintaining authenticity of taste.[9]

Warren Belasco and Harvey Levenstein have written of the shifts in American food patterns over the course of the twentieth century. From the Edwardian era to the Kennedy presidency (1961–3), elaborate formal dinners were based on either or both English common customs and French haute cuisine. But in 1996, the quintessential American cuisine is now principally made up of foods that originated in particular ethnic communities.[10] Bagels, pizza, doughnuts, fried chicken, gumbo, and egg rolls – now staples even of fast food restaurants – all have a distinctive ethnic origin. In the 1980s, numerous theme-oriented franchised restaurants opened, such as Bennigans or T.G.I. Fridays, which offered enormous menus made up of various ethnic foods, sold within the visual context of a late nineteenth-century Irish saloon. The advertising for these food products, no matter how commercially processed, purveyed some sense of that ethnic origin. The irony of the setting, food choices, and franchised environment is probably lost on many contemporary Americans, who may not be old enough to remember the "Old Neighborhood" anyway. Especially in food products, but in other consumer categories as well, ethnicity began to be a metaphor for authenticity in the 1930s and remains a powerful subtext even sixty years later.

IV

The visual rhetoric created for World War II and the peace that followed produced a sea change in American commercial imagery in many ways and on many subjects, but especially in relation to ethnicity. The Office of War Information and a number of corporations portrayed the war effort through posters, bond rallies, sheet music, and postcards. The war created unusual

---

9 There is an extensive literature in cultural anthropology on the various constructions of and searches for "authenticity." A key article in this debate is by Richard Handler. "Authenticity," *Anthropology Today,* 2, no. 1 (1986); see also Marta Weigle. "From Desert to Disney World: The Santa Fe Railway and the Fred Harvey Company Display the Indian Southwest," *Journal of Anthropological Research* 45 (1989): 115–37.

10 Warren Belasco, *Appetite for Change: How the Counterculture Took on the Food Industry, 1966–1988* (New York, 1989); Harvey A. Levenstein, *Paradox of Plenty: A Social History of Eating in Modern America* (New York, 1993); see also Harvey A. Levenstein, *Revolution at the Table: The Transformation of the American Diet* (New York, 1988).

alliances, as attested to by a piece of sheet music, "Favorite Songs of the Red Army and Navy," all done up in red, white, and blue, with a foreword by Paul Robeson (1898–1976).[11]

During World War II, Robeson may well have been the most famous living African American in the world. He was an actor, a concert artist, and an activist for human rights on the world stage. Robeson was famous for appearing in many countries and performing in concerts in which he sang Negro spirituals, European "classical" concert songs, and usually some folk songs in the language of the country in which he was appearing. He was a true internationalist and unquestionably associated with Communist circles. For the first time, during World War II, multiethnic groups of American "fighting men" appeared on American posters and even in the movies. Even radical integrationists such as Paul Robeson could speak on Buy Bond platforms for the American war effort as well as support the working people of the world, even in the Soviet Union. All this was in stark contrast to the official images of World War I, which featured tall, straight, blond-haired, blue-eyed mothers and sons in Christian pietistic positions of sacrifice and noble images of martial fortitude. Fighting a propaganda war against the Third Reich forced the American government and some major corporations to represent an America that looked different from the Nazi imagery. This 1930s imagery bore a remarkable and uncomfortable similarity to American images from World War I.

The numerous paperback covers of Norman Mailer's classic World War II novel *The Naked and the Dead* featured a multiethnic platoon, much like those in the postwar films in which Frank Sinatra starred. During World War II, Bill Mauldin's famous G.I. cartoons, stateside comic strips, and even postwar films showed men who looked awfully ethnic by comparison to World War I images of Yankees. In themselves, these official visualizations of identifiably ethnic individuals as Americans were completely new. Yet the changes in images of Afro-Americans were even more striking.

World War II was the first time that an African American was portrayed as an American hero by the United States government. The heavyweight boxing champion Joe Louis was featured in a number of generic government-sponsored war-effort and "buy bond" posters. Known as "the Brown Bomber" and shown in a variety of poses, including one with a rifle and bayonet, Joe Louis embodied the proud Afro-American veteran, whose real experience in the segregated armed forces was quite different from that

---

11 Robeson lived in the Soviet Union for several years and spent most of the 1930s and 1940s outside the United States. During the 1950s, he was hounded viciously by the American government for his earlier activism, labeled "premature antifascism."

of the posters. Having first lost to the German boxer Max Schmeling, Louis triumphed in a comeback victory in 1938. Louis's win underscored the social significance and symbolic meaning of boxing as a sport in the 1930s and 1940s, as it made him a perfect symbol of a rejuvenated America. In this modern age of consumerism, not only were businesses marketing products but the government also needed to sell images, ideologies, and the vision of a renewal of American life.

Eventually, Dorie Miller, an Afro-American navy mess-man, who was one of the few Americans to fire any shots at Pearl Harbor, was also used in government propaganda. Such images were token steps, but they were especially significant to Afro-American men and women of this era. The Office of War Information produced two war films in order to gain Afro-American support for the war. On its release, initially only to the armed forces, *Negro Soldiers* became an instant hit. Recut after the war and released stateside, this film exposed hundreds of thousands of Americans to the stories of Afro-American men who had fought in every American war. (The Civil War was tactfully left out.)[12] After 1945, and especially after 1960, the "mainstream" advertising world looked very different and the highly segmented, but national, "minority" markets had exploded in ways unimaginable earlier.

In short, commercial representations of ethnicity changed after World War II in three significant ways: First, "middle-class" minority market segments emerged, often through new advertising venues like nationally available ethnic magazines. Second, old stereotypes were protested by newly energized political activity on the part of previously unnoticed "minority" communities. Third, expressions of ethnic diversity surfaced in print and on television to help America visualize a desegregated society.

During the 1940s, integration was a dangerous, rebellious, marginalized activity, seen as part of a Bohemian or "Beat" life-style. In the 1950s, when the Highlander Folk School in North Carolina began to sponsor interracial seminars and Gandhian discussion groups, they received death threats and harassment from local authorities. But by 1969, companies such as Coca-Cola began to depict a desegregated America as an expression of social cohesion and wholeness in the face of the disorders of the Vietnam era. By the late 1960s, even the government of the United States started to rely on such imagery to sell an increasingly unpopular war to prospective American soldiers and their families. All of these changes occurred within the first

---

12 For more on these films, see Thomas Cripps, *Making Movies Black: The Hollywood Movie from World War II to the Civil Rights Era* (New York, 1993); see also Thomas Cripps, *Slow Fade to Black: The Negro in American Film 1900–1942* (New York, 1977).

thirty years after World War II ended. Although there was not another world war during this time, the United States was engaged in small "hot wars" all over the globe in its effort to fight communism on every front. Imagery emerged from governmental and business sources that would have been unthinkable only a decade earlier.

The first thirty years of the Cold War were also the "golden era" of Black magazines. Whereas Afro-American newspapers had existed since the 1820s, national newsmagazines were quite new, as Afro-American entrepreneurs in the decade after World War II invested in glossy publications patterned on *Life* and *Look*. Ironically, these mainstream magazines were faltering and losing their markets to television throughout the 1950s and 1960s. The most successful of the Black publishing entrepreneurs was John Johnson, who in 1945 established Johnson Publications in Chicago. Since its founding, Johnson Publications has printed dozens of magazines and books and has even supported some television and film productions, such as "Tony Brown's Journal." Johnson himself has become the patriarch of Afro-American media. But Afro-American life had yet to be portrayed in any significant way on television. The gossip about Afro-American Hollywood celebrities, politicians, and ministers could not be found in the pages of most local, historically white newspapers. The homes of the ever-widening groups of Afro-American professionals and their children were not yet featured in mainstream publications.

Two key publications were the core of Johnson's publishing success: *Ebony* and *Jet*. These are two distinct yet related magazines. Although each has changed its format over the last few decades, *Ebony* was meant to be (and continues to be) a full-service news, information, and entertainment periodical. Feature stories every year included articles about the campuses of historically black colleges and universities: their homecomings, their sororities and fraternities, their presidents, and their building programs. Major articles focused on Afro-American film, television, and music personalities. Virtually everyone was portrayed in as positive a light as possible, and extensive photo treatments featured the commodities and accoutrements of celebrity life-styles. The Johnsons themselves became featured and prominent Afro-American guests in the Kennedy and Johnson White Houses. Johnson Publishing became such an empire that some employees developed their own followings, such as the gossip columnist Gerri Majors and the famed photographer of the civil rights movement Moneeta Sleet Jr. Johnson's wife founded the *Ebony Fashion Fair* in the early 1960s to provide a luxurious setting for Afro-American designers and models to showcase their talents, which were often overlooked by the profoundly racist fashion world of the time. For the last thirty years, the *Ebony Fashion Fair* has also identified a network of black women around the country willing to pay for haute cuisine, designer jewelry, and expensive cosmetics.

Johnson was brilliant at pointing to a market major advertisers had not yet seen: the black middle class. By identifying Afro-Americans with disposable incomes nationwide, Johnson shrewdly perceived that he could fund his publication by going to major advertisers such as Pepsi-Cola, Xerox, General Motors, and American Telephone and Telegraph to suggest that they spend millions of dollars in advertising. Millions of dollars were needed to keep a four-color glossy magazine in print, and Johnson succeeded with *Ebony* by effectively courting a black audience with his subject matter and reliably delivering a new key group of consumers to his advertisers. By comparison, *Jet* was (and is) a small-scale gossip publication. Apparently, subscriptions and over-the-counter sales support the magazine, as *Jet* contains very little advertising.[13] In this publication, Johnson effectively appealed to his ethnic core clientele. An important marketing tool for *Jet* was the presence in every issue of a centerfold of a shapely Afro-American woman wearing a bathing suit. Johnson has often said that this device increased the sale of *Jet* eightfold. Consequently, he has never removed this element, despite criticism at times from various quarters of the black community. For a magazine the size of a large note card, but slick with black-and-white photos and a color cover, *Jet* packed a big punch. This was the place to read about the dirt on black celebrities that would not appear in *Ebony* until it had first appeared in court. According to a 1996 Yankelovich survey, *Ebony* and *Jet* remain the two primary sources of news information for Afro-Americans, followed in close order by other, younger Afro-American publications such as *Essence* and *Emerge,* a testament to the staying power of these niche publications.[14]

Ebony, Jet, and other publications pointed to new avenues for advertising and marketing. In the 1950s, for the first time, Afro-American-oriented and -owned advertising agencies appeared, such as those founded by Ed McBain and Barbara Proctor in Chicago. In the late 1960s, Byron Lewis founded Uniworld and Frank Mingo and Carolyn Jones founded Mingo-Jones in

13 Johnson Publishing is still family owned and there are no available published figures except an annual audited circulation.
14 Published in the *New Yorker,* "Black in America" is the title of this double issue, Apr. 29 and May 6, 1996.

NewYork.[15] These publications and advertising agencies aided in the growing segmentation of American marketing by directly identifying and selling to a national clientele with a key level of disposable income. Johnson paved the way for a large number of Afro-American publications and identified a means of reaching a key market segment for major American advertisers. Just as teenagers and working women were newly discovered markets in the 1950s, the Afro-American middle class began to be explored as a market niche.

Following the pathway paved by Johnson, a number of successful magazines that emerged in the 1970s were directed to even more specific segments of the Black market. Ed Lewis founded *Essence*, a magazine for young Black women, in 1970 with the financial help of Playboy, Inc. Earl Graves Sr., a former FBI agent, established *Black Enterprise,* a magazine devoted to Black people in business and to Black entrepreneurs in 1974 with significant support from the Kennedy clan. Both magazines were launched as (and remain) glossy, four-color publications with national car, major appliance, travel, credit card, and other advertising – especially for cigarettes and liquor, for which they have been sharply criticized. They are available at most stores in or near predominantly Afro-American neighborhoods. All are available by subscription as well, and their circulation figures indicate subscriber loyalty.

The images in the advertising and illustrations in these publications have long been the subject of controversy within Afro-American communities. In later decades, the magazines founded in the 1940s and 1950s were criticized for promoting a kind of class hierarchy based on skin color. Some people believed these magazines gave more attention to entertainers and professionals with lighter skin and more aquiline or European features. Others believed that darker-skinned people were photographed so as to appear lighter, or that their skin tone was deliberately lightened by photographic techniques. Such criticisms reached an intellectual peak with the publication of *Black Bourgeoisie* (1957) by the noted Howard University sociologist E. Franklin Frazier. An entire literature in journalism and communications schools has grown up around the analysis of such images. Although Black magazines served their communities by making Black news front page, they portrayed a narrow vision of ideal attractiveness with class implications. The continuing controversy about skin color highlights how

15 There are no published monographs on advertising agencies owned by or orientated toward Afro-Americans. One important dissertation exists by Marian J. Moore, "The Portrayal of Blacks in Advertising, 1880–1920 and 1968–1980: A Comparative Analysis," Ph.D. diss., Bowling Green State University, 1986.

difficult it can be to interpret the meaning of images ethnic communities generate about themselves.

In addition to the discovery of new markets (for example, Pepsi–Cola advertised in the pages of *Ebony*), major corporations were forced to realize that new political and economic constituencies had emerged. As with Afro-American veterans' families, Hispanic veterans and their families in Texas and along the borders of the American Southwest benefited to some degree from the G.I. programs of World War II and the Korean War. Immigration from Mexico and other parts of Latin America had surged after the closing of eastern and southern European immigration in the 1920s. Although usually encouraged to become migrant workers rather than settled immigrants, Mexican in-migrants and Mexican Americans became far more economically visible in the years after 1955.

The growing consumerist political power of Mexican Americans was first demonstrated on a national scale by the boycott surrounding the Frito Bandito campaign in 1968-71. By the late 1960s, Fritos had existed for a generation. Elmer Dolin bought the recipe for Fritos in 1933 from an unnamed Mexican American in San Antonio, Texas, a center of Mexican business at the time. In the apocryphal story Elmer Dolin visited a small Mexican restaurant in San Antonio, where presumably he first tasted corn tortillas, perhaps in strips on a soup. He had an "ah-hah!" experience and began to think about how to produce a corn chip commercially. (Perhaps he grew up in Texas and had the "eureka" moment when he decided to start a business.) After several attempts, "Fritos" were born.

Similar to pizza, hot dogs, and other fast food staples, Fritos were based on some interpretation of an ethnicized food product. However, by reshaping the corn tortilla to make it a chip and by giving it a distinctive name and packaging, the Frito Company wholly owned this product and could trademark and license it. Fritos, like Velveeta and other processed food products, characterized the largest segment of the branded post–World War II years. In 1961, two years after Dolin's death, the Frito Company merged with H. W. Lay & Company. Herman Lay ran a larger salted snack foods company, one that marketed and sold potato chips and similar products. Within business circles, Lay was famous for his "store-door" distribution system and the care with which he trained his men to arrange displays in supermarkets and other shops. His marketing genius, combined with this fully trademarkable product, had great success in the 1950s. "Munch a Bunch of Fritos" was one of the company's slogans for much of this time. The company also ran memorable television ad campaigns featuring the old vaudeville actor Bert Lahr, famous as the Cowardly Lion in the film

Wizard of Oz (1939). In 1965, Pepsi-Cola purchased Frito-Lay to form PepsiCo.

PepsiCo decided to reintroduce Fritos with a jazzy new campaign. Fritos had an interesting marketing history in that ads for it would clearly increase sales of that product alone and not generally rise and fall with the sale of other salted snack foods. Fritos' very clear product niche was attractive to Pepsi-Cola, which was growing and diversifying into a megacorporation.

In 1968, Frito-Lay began to use the "Frito Bandito" in television and print advertising. Initially, Mexican banditos had appeared in Anglo-American literature, beginning with dime novels in the 1850s that elevated the border war in Texas (1846–8) to heroic status. "Remember the Alamo!" is only the most famous slogan to appear from the patriotic sacralizations of the Mexican-American War. Mexican banditos reemerged in both silent and talking Hollywood films, especially after the Mexican Revolution of 1910. By the early 1960s, banditos were a small staple of cartoons, children's programs, and occasional television ads. For example, in 1964, General Motors produced a television ad to promote its new sports car, the Buick Wildcat. We see a lone cowboy with sideburns in denim jeans and jacket driving the Wildcat through the open desert. The voice-over begins: "What does it take to be a Buick? It takes a car as wild and wonderful as Buick Wildcat 1964." Along with the cowboy we see three Mexican banditos, equipped with huge hats, pistolleros wrapped around their chests, and long rifles appearing to the side of the car. They point their guns. Speaking in an intentionally unintelligible Spanish, they force the car to stop and motion for the cowboy to get out. They brandish their rifles but then are completedly distracted by the gizmos, the sliding windows, the adjustable mirror, and other accoutrements, so that the unarmed cowboy is able to climb back into the car. He drives off with flair, rolling up his convertible hood as he goes. The voice-over states: "When you go the way of the Wildcat – It's the wildest! And above all, It's a Buick!"[16] General Motors ran that advertisement for at least a year without any noticeable resistance.

Presumably, Frito-Lay thought that they had a safe mascot when they introduced the Frito Bandito in 1968. The commercials were animated, an important distancing mechanism that was commonly used in television commercials in the early and mid-1960s. The Bandito stole people's corn chips and caused everyone who tasted Fritos to grow a long pencil-thin mustache, like his own. Wearing a sombrero and shooting his six-guns, the

16 Art Directors Club of New York. Tape name: Best of 1964. The ad was produced by McCann-Erickson, reel B632, Museum of Television and Radio.

Frito Bandito spoke with a heavy accent and robbed to get Fritos. Produced by Foote, Cone, and Belding, the concept was expanded into print in 1969. Perhaps the high point of this campaign was reached around the time of the successful moon landing of 1969. In a new commercial, the astronauts landed on the moon only to discover the Frito Bandito there as a parking attendant. Of course, to park their moon vehicle, the astronauts needed to give him Fritos, which they happened to have handy.

Initially, this image met with little protest. But by 1969, a group of Hollywood figures, including Ricardo Montalban, had formed the Mexican-American Anti-Defamation Committee, the organization of which was patterned on the Jewish Anti-Defamation League, the NAACP, and other integrationist organizations. Spearheaded by DJs at Los Angeles radio station KNBC, protests began and a nationwide boycott was threatened.[17]

However, as with Aunt Jemima, the Frito Bandito had extraordinarily high name recognition and PepsiCo released information stating its polls proved most Mexican Americans were not offended by the ads. Yet by 1971, PepsiCo's subsidiary Frito-Lay backed down. It retired the Frito Bandito despite dramatically increased sales. The Frito Bandito controversy proved the growing ability of previously ignored ethnic communities to flex their economic muscle, following the example of the boycotts of segregated stores and businesses during the civil rights movement. Such successful protest campaigns made more and more major companies sensitive to the problem of ethnic stereotyping in ways that had been unthinkable only a few years before.

Food was not the only big product category to have a strong ethnic component. In the years following World War II, many different kinds of American music leapt onto the record charts. Rock and roll, rhythm and blues (later called soul music), and gospel music surged out of Afro-American communities. Mambo, rumba, and salsa music poured from Cuban-American, Mexican-American, and other Latino neighborhoods. In the mid-1960s, a craze for "bubble gum music" from Brazil swept the nation, epitomized by the Latin jazz group Sergio Mendez and Brasil '66 and the

17 For more on the Frito Bandito fiasco, see "Frito Bandito is First to Moon," *Advertising Age,* Mar. 31, 1969, 102; "KNBC Rules Frito Bandito off Air Waves," *Advertising Age,* Dec. 1, 1969, 1; "Mexican-American Group to Ask Equal Time vs. Bandito" *Advertising Age,* Dec. 15, 1969. 2; "Time to Answer Frito Bandito?" *Broadcasting,* Dec. 15, 1969, 40–1; see also Anne Dingus, "Adios, Bandito," *The Mexican Presence,* Jan. 1986, 186–9; Jane H. Hill, "Hasta La Vista, Baby: Anglo Spanish in the American Southwest." *Critique of Anthropology* 13, no. 2 (1986): 145–76; Enrique Fernandez, "Ay Bandito!" in his El Norte column, *Village Voice,* Oct. 13, 1992, 24; Marty Westerman, "Death of the Frito Bandito," *American Demographics,* Mar. 1989, 28–32.

Antonio Carlos Jobim song "The Girl from Ipanema" (1963). This song alone continues to evoke an absolutely specific moment in the popular musical experience of older members of the Vietnam generation.

Perhaps the richest, most complex source of illustrations of ethnicity were jazz album covers, which changed dramatically after World War II. In the 1930s, most album covers were rather simple designs, influenced by various "modernist," internationalist design aesthetics. A jazz album cover was often purely typological, with the name of the artist or group highlighted and contrasting bands of color placed in a pattern of geometric shapes. After the war, in part because of changes in printing technologies, black and white photographs (and eventually color) could be reproduced effectively at lower cost. Record albums and sheet music covers began to sport photographic images, and designers were no longer limited to drawn or stenciled formats.

These jazz record covers showed a complex and radically integrated world in a still widely segregated American society. Black men and white women, black women and white men were curled together on the covers of these albums. More overt expressions of adult sexuality – such as sensuous evening clothes or the suggestive positioning of a fur wrap on an empty chair – could be pictured. Even more radically, white women could be shown on these covers enraptured by the jazz music they heard. Photographs of unsmiling black jazz musicians began to grace the covers of albums by labels such as Blue Note and Verve, in conscious contrast to the eye-popping, widely smiling publicity pictures of the kings of the swing era, such as Louis Armstrong, Count Basie, and even Duke Ellington. Charlie Parker, Miles Davis, John Coltrane, Dexter Gordon, Sonny Rollins, and others wanted to deemphasize entertainment and elevate seriousness of purpose. Jazz was serious music and only the strong of heart need apply for membership in the clubhouse of jazz. These notions perhaps reached their height when Lester Bowie, noted trumpet player for the Art Ensemble of Chicago, began to appear on stage in the 1970s wearing a white lab coat. What could be more serious in America than science?

As an entertainment format, jazz changed dramatically during the 1940s and 1950s. The kings of the swing era were still playing. However, younger musicians were revolutionizing the sounds of certain instruments such as the saxophone and widening the parameters of composition and interpretation. But these same musicians were also associated with a bluesy netherworld of drugs, drink, interracial sex, and "unstable" opinions. This world of the "hipster" was celebrated by the Beat writers, such as Jack Kerouac and Allen Ginsberg, and epitomized by the tragic–comic talent Lenny

Bruce. In a book that can now be called a classic of American ethnic literature, Norman Mailer published "The White Negro" in *Dissent* in 1957,
elaborating on his and other white men's efforts to become even a little bit
as cool as the hippest black cats. The dustcovers for this work and for those
of Leroi Jones (later Amiri Baraka), James Baldwin, Lorraine Hansberry,
and other black writers reflected changing sensibilities about the images of
black Americans.

These new images were used to promote records and books that gave
vision to an alternative, even countercultural America. Not all jazz images
were related to black people. For example, this was also the era of Frank
Sinatra's greatest fame. He was clearly promoted as an Italian American and
a "tough guy," whose alleged Mafia connections added to his "dangerous"
quality as a superstar of American music. The Blue Note record company
routinely used the blue motif on virtually all its album covers. Although the
specific tone of blue changes with the artist and the setting, the album covers literally visualized the pensive, melancholy, contemplative, and erotic
aspects of "the blues" and blues-influenced jazz. Jazz album covers showed
white jazz listeners and ranged from elaborate, sophisticated "high-class
settings" with men in tuxedos and women in furs, to black and blue
silhouettes of sylphlike models in leotards and tights embodying the
Bohemian/Beat women who listened to a different, more radical kind of
jazz. The marketing and blended cultural performances associated with rock
and roll have been analyzed at great length. Yet these subtle portraits of jazz
composers and musicians are also known the world over, especially in Eastern Europe, the former Soviet Union, and Asia. Many jazz musicians spent
much of the early Cold War as expatriates in Western Europe, especially
Paris, and conducted their disquisitions on life at a great remove from the
profound problems of being black in America. Their edgy portraits of
desegregated jazz clubs were at odds with much of American life in the
years in which they were produced. The album covers remain unusually
vigorous, yet market-driven testaments to the intricacies of image production in postmodern consumerist America.

From the end of World War II and throughout the Vietnam War years,
visual narratives about race and ethnicity became ever more visible in the
mainstream commercial landscape. In some cases, such as the Frito Bandito
fiasco, these issues broke to the surface as protest from heretofore ignored
consumers over a long disliked stereotype. Certain marginalized, yet exotic
segments of American cultural practice, such as the international jazz
underground of the 1940s through the 1960s, could be sold to larger audiences than ever before.

By about 1969, a number of mainstream American corporations realized that in order to appeal to the widest segment of American society, their products should be associated with nonracist imagery.[18] After starring in the hit prime time program, "I Spy," Bill Cosby became the primary television spokesperson for Jell-O. Having first achieved fame as a stand-up comedian in the early 1960s with a hilarious series of comedy albums about childhood, Bill Cosby was featured in dozens of commercials with multiethnic groups of children. Dazzling in his improvisation, Cosby joked with multiethnic groups of kids in outrageous child-oriented scenarios that later became part of the "Sesame Street" routine. Eventually, Cosby went on to become a spokesperson for Ford, Merrill Lynch, cigars, and a whole host of other products, all the while sustaining a prime time television career as a lead actor, director, and producer of the 1980s hit about the Huxtable family "The Bill Cosby Show."

By the early 1970s, American television was awash with images of togetherness. Perhaps the most memorable commercial of this era dates from 1969. Coca-Cola introduced its new musical slogan "I'd like to teach the world to sing in perfect harmony." The ads showed a lovely group of middle-American white kids singing, "I'd like to buy the world a home and furnish it with love." The second image shows a multiethnic group of people singing, "I'd like to teach the world to sing." For the first time, the viewers see a group in which some people appear to be Indochinese. Again the orchestra swells and a larger group sings, "I'd like to teach the world to sing in perfect harmony." The camera zooms over an impossibly green grassy mountain somewhere in Western Europe. The viewer sees several hundred people in different kinds of ethnic or national dress singing the main theme. The Coca-Cola emblem flashes. Then a male voice says, "On a hilltop in Italy, Coca-Cola assembled people from all over the world to bring this message to you."[19] Throughout the 1970s, major food giants, such as McDonald's, Coca-Cola, and PepsiCo, featured these sorts of scenes. For the first time in American broadcast history, America was visualized as a place made up of people of different colors and facial features whose ancestors originated from all across the globe. Such warm and sentimental images of togetherness and family spirit became icons in and of themselves. In the 1970s, a new slang phrase, "a Kodak moment," entered

18 The term "nonracist" comes from the imagery and language of the freedom struggle in South Africa and is not a term commonly used in the United States even today, except by activist organizations such as TransAfrica in Washington, D.C.
19 McCann Erickson Historic tape, "A Paean to the Brand: Coca-Cola, 1955–1991," Museum of Television and Radio.

the American vernacular to describe in real life these moments of manu-factured inclusion.

During the 1970s, images of an America composed of all the peoples of the world may well have functioned to draw attention away from the vicious racial conflicts breaking out all along the American landscape. From the black-out riots in New York in 1964 and the Watts riot in Los Angeles in 1965, to the even larger "urban rebellions" of 1968 in the aftermath of the assassination of Martin Luther King Jr., to the white riots against busing in northern cities in the 1970s, America was aflame with the fires of racial agi-tation, police brutality, and anticolonialist rhetoric. All the Coca-Cola, McDonald's, and Kodak commercials about togetherness attempted to rep-resent an ethnically integrated American society precisely at the time many people began to lose hope in such a prospect. All of these unwittingly ironic narratives about ethnicity came together problematically in the advertising imagery and commercial ephemera of the Vietnam era. The newest dra-matic visual type in Madison Avenue's vocabulary was "the Asian child."

The long history of images of Asian Americans is much too detailed to investigate here. Suffice it to say that in the United States these "orientalist" patterns of representation had focused on nineteenth-century Chinese immigrants, especially men; on exotic, erotic Japanese women, as in Gia-como Puccini's opera *Madame Butterfly* (1904); and on various Hawaiian and Filipino populations, especially after the Spanish-American War of 1896–8. For much of this time, the mainstream and more stereotypical images reflected a conflation of Asian immigrants and native-born Asian Americans, which assumed tragic social proportions with the internment of Japanese immigrants and Japanese Americans from the West Coast during World War II. An extensive literature documents this episode, as does a major exhibition at the Smithsonian's Museum of American History, "A More Perfect Union: Japanese Americans and the Constitution."

The constantly shifting interests and politics of the United States during the Cold War required frequent changes in the propaganda of the national government and other conservative business forces. For example, during World War II China, under General Chiang Kai-shek, was the American ally and Japan, under Air Admiral Hirohito, was the American enemy. Even such banal ephemera as bubble-gum cards depicted horrific battles like "The Rape of Nanking," condemning the evil Japanese and ennobling the heroic Chinese in their martyrdom. But the Communist Revolution in China (1949) changed all that. Aside from touching off a set of major witch hunts in Hollywood, in the State Department, and around the country, these changes complicated the ethnic portrayals of Asians. Suddenly the

Japanese people became America's "little brother" and the Chinese were the evil empire. Armed-forces posters showed American flyers giving Asian (presumably Japanese) boys candy and tours of the plane.[20] This dichotomy between good and evil became even more tortuous during the Korean War, during which the North Koreans were the "bad guys" and the Americans went in to save the South Koreans. Even these distinctions ultimately imploded under the weight of the Vietnam War and the resistance to it. At first, it seemed possible to distinguish between the "good" South Vietnamese and the "bad" North Vietnamese, but as the war engulfed the entire country and inflamed the United States, these neat distinctions collapsed.

Meanwhile, the record of national televised advertising in the 1960s reveals an increasing fascination with Asian and Asian-American faces, particularly those of children. The famous 1960s print and television campaign in New York City "You don't have to be Jewish to love Levy's [bread]" usually featured a multiethnic group of Americans. However, the television commercials often began by showing a child with Asian features or sometimes an old man in a Japanese kimono. These Asians (the old man) or Asian Americans (the young boy) could stand as an icon for the "newest" and therefore the least-expected example of a satisfied non-Jewish customer for this sliced bread (not bagel). By the early 1970s, Jell-O, Coca-Cola, and McDonald's television commercials routinely began to include children with Asian-looking hair and features as part of multiethnic groups. Visions of an integrated America tended to feature Asian, black, and Anglo children, reflecting, if unconsciously, the classic racial typologies agreed on by many anthropologists and biologists in the 1890s.[21]

As the need for troops increased along with resistance to the draft, the American armed forces were forced to keep changing their pitches. In World War II, Joe Louis and others were used to boost the wartime work and spirits of Afro-American troops. However, they were not used on recruiting posters nationwide, perhaps because Negroes could not yet stand as icons for the sacred armed services, dominated as they were by unrecon-

---

20 See the work of Su-Chang Chan, Gary Okihiro, and Ronald Takaki, *Strangers from a Different Shore: A History of Asian Americans* (New York, 1986). A key collector of Asian-American images in film and advertising is Yoshio Kishii, whose collections are located at the San Francisco Chinese Historical Society. See also Su-Chang Chan, *Asian Americans: An Interpretive History* (Boston, 1991), and Gary Okihiro, *Cane Fires: The Anti-Japanese Movement in Hawaii, 1865–1945* (Philadelphia, 1991). The most significant work on the European construction of "The Orient" is Edward Said, *Orientalism* (New York, 1978).

21 See George Stocking, *Race, Culture, and Evolution: Essays in the History of Anthropology* (New York, 1968). For more on the concept of good/evil dichotomizing, see Alain LeRoy Locke, *Race Contacts and Interracial Relations: Lectures on the Theory and Practice of Race,* ed. and introd. Jeffrey C. Stewart (Washington, D.C., 1992).

structed white southerners. Rather, these images testified to the changes that some Americans anticipated in the postwar world. The multicultural recruiting poster of the Vietnam era performed a different function. In the late 1960s and early 1970s, the government had to emphasize the positive aspects of military service in order to encourage working-class American men without hope of deferment to find some dignity in the (nearly inevitable) draft. During the Vietnam War, black men were portrayed for the first time in recruitment posters and in television ads nationwide. The quality of these advertisements shifted significantly over the long decade of the Vietnam War (1964–75).

In 1964, the army, navy, marines, and air force were all running competing commercials on national television encouraging men to join up. These commercials were quite long (some more than two minutes) and emphasized acquiring technical know-how, making money for your family, seeing the world, and expressing your patriotism. Such commercials often resolved into a display of the flag and other red, white, and blue symbols while flashing GO NAVY or some such clear-cut directive. From the mid-1960s into the mid-1980s, the U.S. Army had a single advertising agency, N. W. Ayer, whose client proof sheets from the 1890s to the 1970s are in the National Museum of American History.

Through a series of long-running commercials, Ayer portrayed the army variously as a place to become a man and a place to have adventures. At the height of the Vietnam War, the most common television recruiting images showed American men of all colors helping to build new houses in Southeast Asia, aiding a wounded child, or perhaps erecting a dike to hold back a flooding river. These representations depicted a military career as an opportunity to help people around the world. Images of the brutal war of attrition then being waged across Indochina were excluded from this advertising, although highly visible on the evening news programs of the very same TV stations.

A careful and systematic investigation of how the American government advertised its armed forces to multiethnic Americans riven by racial conflict remains to be written. Fortunately, the resources required for such an investigation are now beginning to become available as television and advertising materials from the 1960s and 1970s enter university libraries and museum collections. By examining how the federal government visualized an integrated America while it waged a "hot war" in Southeast Asia, it is possible to see all the threads of ethnicity – as authenticity, as danger, and as nationhood – combined to form the complicated web that continues to entangle America.

PART THREE

History and Theory

The final part of the book presents three chapters that address more abstract issues, all arguing – in very different ways – that consumer society both is predicated upon and affects changes in fundamental ideas about self and community. Consumption has served as a lightning rod for new ideas of self and subject, of gender and class, of nationality and community, of race and place. Such concepts, while widely shared, are rarely articulated. And although the daily experience of consumption is nearly ubiquitous in the West, its concepts generally take shape only as part of discussions of other topics, a curious paradox of twentieth-century consumer society. So much at the core of the material world, consumption serves as a mirror for deep and abiding issues of the social world. To the extent that those two realms are divorced, consumption remains a useful historical tool; to the extent that they are the same, consumption is inextricable from the deepest issues of modern social and cultural history.

James Livingston argues against the critique of consumption embedded in much recent historical work, the contention that the rise of consumer culture has robbed once-independent producing individuals of their power in the modern economy and has exploited them in a dehumanizing and shallow culture that traffics in goods instead of authentic feelings and social relations. Livingston believes instead that modern consumer society has promoted individual agency by cultivating a new subjectivity, grounded in the pragmatic encounter between the self and the world. This means that consumers cultivate themselves through their goods. Their status as subjects, as self-constituting and self-reflective beings, is bound up in their abilities to consume, to make use of, and to transform their surroundings according to their perceptions of the world. For Livingston, an argument that consumer society demeans and limits consumers by offering false choices and degrading images of themselves misses the conditions in which consumers make choices. His chapter, at odds with the predominant strain in consumption history, promotes a vision of modern subjectivity as grounded in the conditions of modern consumption.

The history of the concepts of consumption and consumer, explored earlier by Kathryn Kish Sklar and Roland Marchand, has received little attention in English since Raymond Williams's pioneering short essay in *Keywords* (1976).[1] As a contribution to the German movement to historicize concepts (*Begriffsgeschichte*), Ulrich Wyrwa discusses the use of the term in German-language writing from the eighteenth century onward, arguing that consumption had generally negative connotations before the 1930s.[2] In contrast to Daniel Horowitz, who emphasizes the attractions that American-style consumption had for Katona and Dichter, Wyrwa contends that few of the German émigré intellectuals who so greatly influenced American ideas about consumption could reconcile their critique with the positive connotations of the concept in the United States. At the core of that critique was a belief that the individual self was too fragile to withstand the depersonalization and trivialization of the mass market. Wyrwa thus locates the critique of consumption squarely within the Enlightenment tradition, which understood humans as fundamentally rational beings whose material world was a projection of their ideas. Citing and contextualizing the work of the historians who have studied consumption in the early modern period, Wyrwa acknowledges that recent writing has done much to discredit spurious and false criticisms of consumption. Still, like many other authors in this volume, he insists on the critical function of historical work.

Jackson Lears focuses on the restrictions imposed on the human psyche by a growth-oriented, corporate-sponsored version of the good life. He points to a number of related images of American abundance: iconography depicting factories and massive quantities of goods, quantitative notions of the "standard of living," and David Potter's history of a "people of plenty." Lears juxtaposes these with a number of alternative visions stemming from older traditions but persisting today in intellectual work. These honor the psychic dimension as well as the physical, and perceive abundance in the individual's pursuit of play, unstructured time, and noneconomic activity.

---

1 Raymond Williams, *Keywords: A Vocabulary of Culture and Society* (New York, 1976). See also Colin Campbell, *The Romantic Ethic and the Spirit of Consumerism* (Cambridge, 1988); and Susan Strasser, "Consumption," in Stanley Kutler, ed., *Encyclopedia of the United States in the Twentieth Century* (New York, 1995).

2 On *Begriffsgeschichte*, see Hartmut Lehmann and Melvin Richter, eds. *The Meaning of Historical Terms and Concepts: New Studies on Begriffsgeschichte*, German Historical Institute, Occasional Paper no. 15 (Washington, D.C., 1996).

He analyzes a variety of early-1970s critiques of postwar consumer afflu-ence as based too strictly upon an accumulation of goods; theorists of the counterculture, environmental critics, and intellectuals and academics in a number of fields argued that Americans confronted continual anxiety in the midst of unprecedented material affluence. Lears ends on a frankly utopian note. Only by detaching ideas of abundance from material goods and by looking to satisfy demand through play and self-cultivation as much as through accumulation, will human beings alter long-standing frustrations with a consumer society that eternally promises but never fulfills.

19

Modern Subjectivity and Consumer Culture

JAMES LIVINGSTON

My purpose in what follows is to explore the relation between modern subjectivity and consumer culture. But I want to emphasize the historiographical dimensions of this relation – I want to demonstrate that the recent critique of consumer culture is an attempt to retrieve the modern subject from the wreckage of nineteenth-century proprietary capitalism, and that the attempt itself continues to command intellectual respect because it reenacts a "primal scene" of American historiography. The point of emphasizing these historiographical dimensions of the relation between modern subjectivity and consumer culture is of course polemical. Ultimately my claim will be that the critique of consumer culture blocks the search for alternatives to the "man of reason" who served as the paradigm of self-determination in the modern epoch and thus blinds us to the political, intellectual, and cultural possibilities of our own postmodern moment.

Let me begin, then, by defining the terms of my inquiry. By "modern subjectivity" I mean the historically specific compound of assumptions, ideas, and sensibilities that convenes each self as a set of radical discontinuities (e.g., mind versus body), which are in turn projected, as deferred desires – as work and language – into an "external" world of inanimate objects denominated as elements of nature and/or pieces of property. The sovereignty of this modern self is experienced and expressed as the ontological priority of the unbound individual, that is, the individual whose freedom resides in the release from obligations determined by political communities, or, what amounts to the same thing, in the exercise of "natural rights" that such communities can neither confer nor abrogate.[1] One virtue

---

1 I am drawing on Alasdair MacIntyre, *After Virtue: A Study in Moral Theory* (Notre Dame, Ind., 1981), chaps. 4–6; Stephen Toulmin, *Cosmopolis: The Hidden Agenda of Modernity* (Chicago, 1990), chap. 3; Charles Taylor, "Legitimation Crisis?" in *Philosophy and the Human Sciences: Philosophical Papers*, 2 vols. (New York, 1985), 2:248–88; and Hiram Caton, *The Origin of Subjectivity: An Essay on Descartes* (New Haven, Conn., 1973), chaps. 2–3, 5. In "Hamlet, *Little Dorritt,* and the History of Character," in Michael Hays, ed., *Critical Conditions* (Minneapolis, 1992), 82–96, Jonathan Arac points out that

of this definition is that it permits the connotation of possessive individualism but does not reduce modern subjectivity to ownership of the property in one's capacity to produce value; the emphasis is instead on those discontinuities that finally hardened into dualisms under the sign of Enlightenment. Another is that it is consistent with Nietzsche's claim that the "most distinctive property of this modern man [is] the remarkable opposition of an inside to which no outside and an outside to which no inside corresponds, an opposition unknown to ancient peoples." If we follow his lead a bit further, we can begin to see that the genuine selfhood of the modern subject simply is the oscillation between epistemological extremes in which Emerson specialized. For all his genius, this modern man was representative because he lived the opposition between *romanticism,* which typically glorifies the "organic" or "subjective" inner self as against the "mechanical" or "objective" circumstances that constitute outward existence, and *positivism,* which typically celebrates the increasing density of that external, thinglike realm of objects as the evidence of progress toward human mastery of nature. By all accounts, the "era of the ego" in which Emersonian self-reliance, that is, modern subjectivity, comes of age is the historical moment, circa 1600–1900, in which the market becomes the organizing principle of European and North American societies, as commodity production comes to reshape and finally to regulate social relations as such.[2]

So conceived, the modern subject has no discernible gender. It discloses an "empty subjectivity" in every sense: Its autonomy is formal and its anatomy is irrelevant because the ends or content of its freedom cannot be specified, let alone embodied. But the new history of subjectivity on which various disciplines have recently collaborated clearly shows that the modern subject was the decidedly male proprietor, the *man* of reason – indeed that the "social contract" animating modern bourgeois narratives of citizenship was also a sexual contract allowing men to supervise women's bodies in private, in the household, and to silence women's voices in public, political discourse.[3] The decline of patriarchal (more or less feudal) states based on kinship and the concurrent return of repressed republican ideology invariably coincided with the emergence of a bourgeois society in which house-

---

"individualism" as such is practically impossible to date; but I would insist that the belief in the ontological priority of the unbound individual is a strictly modern phenomenon, and that this belief radically reshapes inherited notions − the political forms and the cultural context − of individualism.

2 See James Livingston, *Pragmatism and the Political Economy of Cultural Revolution, 1850–1940* (Chapel Hill, N.C., 1994), 201–7, 215–24, 247–50, 365–6 n. 42.

3 See, e.g., Genevieve Lloyd, *The Man of Reason: "Male" and "Female" in Western Philosophy* (Minneapolis, 1984); and Carole Pateman, *The Sexual Contract* (Palo Alto, Calif., 1988).

holds became the typical site of commodity production, and the paterfamilias – the male head of the household – became the paradigm of the citizen. This citizen's public identity presupposed his patriarchal standing within the newly private sphere of the conjugal family; in other words, the political capacities of the modern subject presupposed the integrity of the household. Since that integrity was both a material and a moral question, involving the disposition of property and the display of sobriety if not virtue, its maintenance required the sublimation of female sexuality. If we can then say that the confinement of females to the household (e.g., in the valorization of republican motherhood) becomes the enabling condition of modern subjectivity, we can also say that the extrusion of females from the household signals a crisis of the modern subject. Any devaluation of motherhood or "maternal authority" resulting from a profusion of extrafamilial social roles for women would threaten this subject, simply because it would announce the desublimation of female sexuality, and so would force on male citizens the realization that feminine desire is not synonymous with maternal affection.[4]

By "consumer culture" I mean pretty much what its critics mean, although I see comedy where they see tragedy. I would define it as the culture specific to corporate capitalism, which emerges circa 1890–1930 in the United States (in Europe, it may be more accurate to speak of "cartelization" rather than corporate consolidation until the 1940s and 1950s), and would suggest that it consists of at least four elements: First, consumer demand becomes the fulcrum of economic growth, in the sense that growth no longer requires net additions either to the capital stock or to the labor force that cannot be producing consumer goods because it is producing and operating capital goods. Second, social relations of production can no longer be said to contain or regulate social relations as such, because the quantity of labor time required to enlarge the volume or the capacity of goods production ceases to grow and then actually begins to decline; a class-based division of labor is accordingly complicated by the emergence of alternative principles of social organization. Third, value as such comes increasingly to be determined not by the quantities of labor time required to produce commodities but by the varieties of subject positions from which goods can be appreciated (marginalist economics is one way of acknowl-

4 See Linda J. Nicholson, *Gender and History: The Limits of Social Theory in the Age of Family* (New York, 1986), chap. 4; Hanna Fenichel Pitkin, *Fortune is a Woman: Gender and Politics in the Thought of Niccolo Machiavelli* (Berkeley, Calif., 1984), chaps. 4–5; Susan Moller Okin, *Women in Western Political Thought* (Princeton, N.J., 1979), chaps. 6–8; and Jean Bethke Elshtain, *Public Man, Private Woman: Women in Social and Political Thought* (Princeton, N.J., 1981), chap. 3.

edging this new fact). Fourth, with the completion of proletarianization
under the auspices of corporate management, the commodity form pene-
trates and reshapes dimensions of social life hitherto exempt from its logic,
to the point where subjectivity itself seemingly becomes a commodity to
be bought and sold in the market as beauty, cleanliness, sincerity, even autonomy. In short, consumer culture – the "age of surplus" determined by corporate capitalism – is the solvent of modern subjectivity. I am suggesting by
this definition that consumer culture is a twentieth-century phenomenon
and that the so-called birth of consumer society in late eighteenth-century
England (or in mid-nineteenth-century North America) should be understood instead as the beginning of the transition from a simple to a complex
market society – that is, when a market in labor was institutionalized, when
artisans became operatives, when resources hitherto appropriated through
extraeconomic transactions became commodities with monetary equivalents and designations.[5]

Now, what exactly is wrong with consumer culture so conceived? Its
critics tend to emphasize the fourth of these elements, although, as we shall
see, the third element figures importantly in their worries about the epistemology of excess. They tend, in other words, to see the "bureaucratic rationality" of corporate capitalism or "managerial culture" from the Weberian
standpoint first established by Georg Lukacs in an influential essay of 1923
on "reification." Just as Weber understood bureaucracy as the creature of
the large corporations, so Lukacs understood it as the apogee of proletarianization:

Bureaucracy implies the adjustment of one's way of life, model of work and hence
of consciousness, to the general socioeconomic premises of the capitalist economy,
similar to that which we have observed in the case of the worker in particular business concerns. . . . The split between the worker's labor-power and his personality,
its metamorphosis into a thing, an object that he sells on the market is repeated here
too.

But under the aegis of bureaucracy, "the division of labour which in the
case of Taylorism invaded the psyche, here invades the realm of ethics."[6]

Lukacs took journalism as the perfect example of that invasion: "This
phenomenon can be seen at its most grotesque in journalism. Here it is
precisely subjectivity itself, knowledge, temperament and powers of expres-

5 See Livingston, *Pragmatism and Political Economy,* pt. 1: "The Political Economy of Consumer Culture," 3–118.
6 Georg Lukacs, "Reification and the Consciousness of the Proletariat," in *History and Class Consciousness,* trans. Rodney Livingstone (Cambridge, Mass., 1971), 98–9; see the pertinent citations of Weber
   on 95–6. Page references to Lukacs in text hereafter.

sion that are reduced to an abstract mechanism functioning autonomously and divorced both from the personality of their 'owner' and from the material and concrete nature of the subject matter in hand." At this point of the argument, when it is clear that "bureaucracy" signifies the subjection of mental labor to corporate capital and thus a loss of identity for the man of letters, Lukacs summarizes what he means by "reification":

> The transformation of the commodity relation into a thing of "ghostly objectivity" cannot therefore content itself with the reduction of all objects for the gratification of human needs to commodities. It stamps its imprint upon the whole consciousness of man; his qualities and abilities are no longer an organic part of his personality, they are things which he can "own" and "dispose of" like the various objects of the external world. And there is no natural form in which human relations can be cast, no way in which man can bring his physical and psychic "qualities" into play without their being subjected to this reifying process. (98–100)

So the proletarianization of the intellectuals completes the incessant redivision of labor that is the hallmark of capitalism. Even the well-educated man is subject to "the one-sided specialisation which represents such a violation of man's humanity," and, like an uneducated working-class male, he can expect the "prostitution of his experience and beliefs" by the abstract mechanisms of modern industrial society (99–100). For it is no longer merely manual dexterity that can be bought and sold in the market; now the inner self can be hollowed out as "subjectivity itself" becomes a commodity, as thoughts become things to be owned, as knowledge, temperament, and powers of expression begin to look "like the various objects of the external world."

The critics of consumer culture sound very much like Lukacs because they assume what he did – that the generalization of the commodity form (or "relation"), to the point where every personal attribute can circulate as a consumer good, must be the proximate cause of the cultural disease they propose to diagnose. All agree that this "maturation of the marketplace" was invented around the turn of the century by the "bureaucratic organizations" – presumably the large industrial corporations – in which a "new stratum" of more or less scientific managers came of age. They also agree that reified consciousness, a consumer culture, accompanied and enforced these economic and social changes. Richard Fox and Jackson Lears note, for example, that the "late-nineteenth century link between individual hedonism and bureaucratic organizations – a link that has been strengthened in the twentieth century – marks the point of departure for modern American consumer culture." Finally, Lukacs and his heirs agree that an "older entrepreneurial economy, formed around a shared sense of contractual obligation and of common premises," was displaced, or at any rate muti-lated, by the new corporate economy in which a consumer culture thrived. I am quoting William Leach's *Land of Desire* (1993) here, but I might just as well quote Lears – who defines the "commercial vernacular" of the nine-teenth century as a usable past, as an appealing alternative to the "manager-ial culture" and "bureaucratic rationality" introduced by the corporations – or again call on Lukacs, who could be describing his intellectual heirs among the critics of consumer culture when he suggests that "traditional craft pro-duction preserves in the minds of its individual practitioners the appear-ance of something flexible, something constantly renewing itself, some-thing produced by the producers" (97).[7]

But if I am right to suggest that the critique of consumer culture simply recapitulates the Weberian logic first proposed by Lukacs, I can claim that it is merely a protest against proletarianization *from the standpoint of modern subjectivity,* in the name of possessive individualism. As such, it will typically represent the loss of subjectivity not as the price of entanglement in com-merce, but as the loss of control over the property in one's capacity to pro-duce value through work – in short, as the extremity of proletarianization initiated and managed by modern corporate bureaucracies. From this stand-point, the site of self-discovery is the work of the artisan or small producer who sells the products of his labor, not his labor power; genuine selfhood can no more be derived from the abstract, unskilled social labor of the fully mechanized workplace than it can from the sluggish daily routine of the private household.[8]

I want now to go on to claim that the extant critique of consumer cul-ture reenacts a "primal scene" of American history and does so in a way that permits only one point of entry into, or solution of, the Oedipus com-plex. I want to claim, in other words, that this critique ignores or represses

7 Richard W. Fox and T. J. Jackson Lears, "Introduction," to their *Culture of Consumption* (New York, 1983), xii; William Leach, *Land of Desire: Merchants, Power, and the Rise of a New American Culture* (New York, 1993), 302; T. J. Jackson Lears, *Fables of Abundance: A Cultural History of Advertising in America* (New York, 1994), 142–77.

8 See the discussion of *poesis* and politics in Livingston, *Pragmatism and Political Economy,* 247–55, and more recently in Livingston, "The Politics of Pragmatism," *Social Text* 49 (1996): 149–72. At the same conference where I presented an earlier version of this essay, George Lipsitz and others argued that consumer culture is by definition the solvent of politics as such. I would suggest that they may be unconsciously equating politics as such with the "public sphere" once inhabited by the modern (bourgeois) subject, and thus may be inadvertently ignoring the new domain of *cultural* politics afforded by the rise of corporate capitalism. In any event, it is worth noting that, in Lipsitz's argu-ment, the moment of political opposition to globalized corporate capitalism arrives when consumers become producers – that is, when hip-hop artists become artisans by treating their musical sources as the raw materials of new compositions.

the sexual ambiguities and anxieties produced by proletarianization under corporate auspices and unconsciously reinstates the paterfamilias as the paradigm of subjectivity; this is significant cultural work because it reanimates and validates a certain kind or range of (male) subjectivity.

In psychoanalytical terms, a "primal scene" is more construction than recollection, for it is not so much an event experienced by the patient as a story told by the analyst, a story that gives meaning to irretrievable memory traces, mere fragments from the past. The retelling of the story allows the arrangement of past events in an intelligible sequence and accordingly the insertion of the narrative's subjects (these now include the narrator) into a temporal and moral order: It is a "deferred action" that situates, or rather constitutes, its dramatis personae in the present by orienting them toward a past and the future, but also by providing a provisional subject position from which the identifications impending in the Oedipus complex can be tested. The strong resemblance between the work of the analyst and the work of the historian, which is registered by their mutual commitment to narrative as all-purpose cure for what ails us – notice that the stories told by both are neither "objective" nor "subjective," neither altogether "factual" nor strictly "fictional" – makes me think that we can profitably export the notion of a "primal scene" from its original domain in psychoanalysis.[9]

Until the twentieth century, the primal scene of American historiography was typically a confrontation between cultures construed broadly as incommensurable "races." For example, the European invasion of America, the "removal" of the Indians, and the tragedies of Reconstruction were staged in historical writing as inevitable consequences of competition between civilized white men and primitive races – that is, as the result of the Other's savagery or backwardness. "Progressive" historiography of the early twentieth century constructed a new primal scene by introducing the figure of industrial or financial capital and making it the predator of the small producer and the freeholder. Since then, the hegemonic narratives of American history have habitually been built around this primal

---

9 In transposing the notion of primal scene from psychoanalysis to historiography, I am taking my cue from Jean Laplanche, *Life and Death in Psychoanalysis,* trans. Jeffrey Mehlman (Baltimore, 1976), 38–47; Kaja Silverman, *Male Subjectivity at the Margins* (New York, 1993), 162–6; and Ned Lukacher, *Primal Scenes: Literature, Philosophy, Psychoanalysis* (Ithaca, N.Y., 1986), 19–44, 51–8, 136–56, 237–47, as well as Freud's own ambivalence, as expressed in "From the History of an Infantile Neurosis" (1918) in the *Standard Edition,* trans. James Strachey, 24 vols. (London, 1955), 19:7–122, e.g., at 57 ("There remains the possibility of taking yet another view of the primal scene underlying the dream – a view, moreover, which obviates to a large extent the conclusion that has been arrived at above") and at 120 n. ("It is also a matter of indifference in this connection whether we choose to regard it as a primal *scene* or as a primal *phantasy*").

scene of proletarianization. I am not suggesting that the demise of the
small producer and the decline of proprietary capitalism are the fantasies of
twentieth-century historians. But it is instructive, I believe, that social, labor,
and cultural historians – the cutting edges of American historiography –
cannot agree on the timing or even the cause of the event in question, and
yet can insist on its synchronic significance. That such a consensus exists in
spite of the obvious chronological confusion indicates that the "moment"
of proletarianization is more historiographical convention than historical
event, more construction than recollection.[10]

To see how this primal scene works – how it opens onto the Oedipus
complex, how it inserts us into a temporal and moral order – we must first
consider its "origins." In the Anglo-American world, it began as the para-
noid fantasies of the Commonwealthmen, who saw encroaching effemi-
nacy everywhere they looked, but especially in the growth of public credit
and the machinations of the Bank of England. By the late eighteenth century, it became even more pointed as the parable of corruption, as the story
of how the "hardy virtuous set of men" called Americans might succumb
to "that luxury which effeminates the mind and body": Unless they protected their natural rights of property with the vigilance of the Gothic
freeholder, they would be subject to the whims of Fortune, the goddess of
fantasy, passion, and capricious change. In the nineteenth century this narrative was complicated by trade unionists who claimed that the property in
one's labor-power could be sold without alienating one's manhood and by
suffragists who suggested that women could not be forever confined to the
household. But it persisted in the rhetoric of political antislavery, and in the
languages of most late nineteenth-century subaltern social movements.
The "populist moment" of the 1890s was probably its most poignant expression – or would be, had not the "progressive" historians constructed a new
primal scene out of populist paranoia.[11]

This construction would not matter very much, I admit, if later historians had become skeptical of the "democratic promise" offered by populism.
To my knowledge, however, the brief reign of so-called consensus history,

---

10 On race and nineteenth-century American historiography, see David Levin, *History as Romantic Act: Bancroft, Prescott, Motley, and Parkman* (Palo Alto, Calif., 1959), chap. 6.

11 See Pitkin, *Fortune is a Woman,* chaps. 4–6; J. G. A. Pocock, "Modes of Political and Historical Time in Early Eighteenth-Century England," *Virtue, Commerce, and History* (New York, 1985), 91–102; Ruth H. Bloch, "The Gendered Meanings of Virtue in Revolutionary America," *Signs* 13 (1987): 37–58. If we are to understand Populism as the social movement convened by the idea of modern subjectiv-ity – I mean in the late-twentieth as well as the late-nineteenth century – we need to pay close attention to Steven Hahn's adroit analysis in *The Roots of Southern Populism* (New York, 1983), e.g., at 248–53; and Lawrence Goodwyn's ferocious polemic against "counter-progressive" historiography in *Democratic Promise: The Populist Moment in America* (New York, 1976).

from about 1955 to about 1975, marks the only departure from the hegemony of populism in twentieth-century American historiography. In this interregnum, Richard Hofstadter and William Appleman Williams, among others, offered "counterprogressive" interpretations of modern American history that treated populism as something less than the last best hope for democracy in the United States and that accordingly treated the twentieth century as something other than the nonheroic residue of the tragedy staged in the 1890s. But by the mid-1970s, with the publication of Lawrence Goodwyn's extravagant advertisement for populism and the concurrent ascendance of the new labor historians, "consensus" was effectively discredited, and the primal scene of proletarianization was reinstated as the pivot on which the plot of American history must turn. The critique of consumer culture that emerged in the 1980s as yet another protest against proletarianization might then be understood as a significant contribution to the recuperation of populism that began in the 1970s.[12]

In any event, we can now consider the cultural work of this critique – that is, how it constructs a primal scene that permits only one point of entry into the Oedipus complex, how it ignores or represses the sexual ambiguities and anxieties attending proletarianization under corporate auspices. At the turn of the century these ambiguities and anxieties were clearly expressed in all kinds of publications, from labor journals and popular magazines to scholarly monographs and highbrow novels. That is why Andreas Huyssen, Klaus Theweleit, and Carroll Smith-Rosenberg are so convincing in claiming that the "fear of woman" is a metonymical compression of many other fears, all of which pertained to the dissolution and reconstruction of ego boundaries in an era of profound sexual crisis as well as social conflict. As Huyssen puts it, "Fear of the masses in this age of declining liberalism is always also a fear of woman, a fear of nature out of control, fear of the unconscious, of sexuality, of the loss of identity and stable ego boundaries in the mass."[13]

12 See Richard Hofstadter, *The Age of Reform: From Bryan to F.D.R.* (New York, 1955), and William Appleman Williams, *The Contours of American History* (Cleveland, Ohio, 1961). These and other examples of "counter-progressive" historiography are placed in context by Gene Wise, *American Historical Explanations,* 2d rev. ed. (Minneapolis, 1980), chap. 4; but see also James Livingston, "Radicals All!" *Reviews in American History* 16 (1988): 306–12; and James Livingston, "Why Is There Still Socialism in the United States?" *Reviews in American History* 22 (1994): 577–83. In this last essay, I argue in passing that we can treat Thurman Arnold's books of the late 1930s as the source of "consensus" historiography because Hofstadter treats them as the intellectual antecedent of his own distinction between the Progressive impulse and the New Deal sensibility. I would now broaden the argument in light of discussion and correspondence with Daniel Horowitz, who suggests that Irving Howe and others were outlining the elements of "consensus" in extra-historiographical venues of the late-1930s and 1940s.
13 See Klaus Theweleit, *Male Fantasies,* trans. Stephen Conway, Erica Carter, and Chris Turner, 2 vols. (Minneapolis, 1987–89), 2:3–61; Carroll Smith-Rosenberg, "The New Woman as Androgyne: Social

Not even the masses themselves were immune to such fears. For example, here is how machinists at the New England Bolt Company of Providence, Rhode Island, described their encounter with scientific management in 1913:

"Cameras to the front of them. Cameras to the rear of them. Cameras to the right of them. Cameras to the left of them." Pictures taken of every move so as to eliminate "false moves" and drive the worker into a stride that would be as mechanical as the machine he tends. If the "Taylorisers" only had an apparatus that could tell what the mind of the worker was thinking, they would probably develop a greater "efficiency" by making them "cut out" all thoughts of being men.[14]

Now what troubles the machinists is quite obviously their reduction to items of managerial surveillance. Their trained eye no longer situates them as active subjects in relation to the raw materials and mechanical conditions of their skilled labor; instead they have become specular objects to be monitored by white-collared "Taylorisers." Their "manly bearing" on the job is in question as a result of this visual(ized) inversion. Indeed they use an image that carries the connotation of castration – " 'cut out' all thoughts of being men" – to convey their concerns about their identities. From their standpoint, the passage from the formal to the real subjection of labor that is supervised by scientific management looks like the loss of manhood; by their account, proletarianization implies castration, or the "feminization" of identity, because it makes men visible, and thus penetrable.

If this account sounds simply fantastic, we should recall that in the modern epoch, the male subject typically defined himself by dissociation from the visible, by equating woman with what is seen, what is supervised, by man. The logic of the gaze that constituted modern subjectivity was the property of the "man of reason," who could "rise above" the private matters of the household in order to take the long view in political deliberations and who could get a similarly supervisory distance on the objects of knowledge in order to see them clearly and "objectively."[15] We should also recall

Disorder and Gender Crisis, 1870–1936," in *Disorderly Conduct* (New York, 1985), 245–96; and Andreas Huyssen, "Mass Culture as Woman: Modernism's Other," in *After the Great Divide* (Bloomington, Ind., 1986), 52.

14 The machinists are quoted and discussed in David Montgomery, *The Fall of the House of Labor* (New York, 1987), 220–1. The recent work of Joan Scott, among others, demonstrates that gender is always already implicated in class consciousness as a kind of enabling condition; see her *Gender and the Politics of History* (New York, 1988), and Wai Chee Dimock and Michael T. Gilmore, eds., *Rethinking Class: Social Formations and Literary Studies* (New York, 1994), especially the essays by the editors themselves, 57–104, 215–38.

15 See Kaja Silverman, *The Acoustic Mirror: The Female Voice in Psychoanalysis and Cinema* (Bloomington, Ind., 1988), chap. 1; and Norman Bryson, *Vision and Painting: The Logic of the Gaze* (New Haven, Conn., 1983), chaps. 3–6.

that Henry James, who was hardly a working stiff, proposed the same correlation between the "man without means" and a kind of "feminine" identity. Lambert Strether, the narrative compass of *The Ambassadors* (1903), is perhaps the most obvious example of this correlation – he is wholly dependent on Mrs. Newsome for his income as well as his function, he is the object of her close supervision, he is constantly scrutinized by the female characters with speaking roles in the novel, and he is in the "odd position for a man" of being at home in the "society of women." Like his creator, Strether does not so much observe women as identify with female characters.[16]

According to Henry's brother, William James, who thought of pragmatism as a woman ("she 'unstiffens' our theories," he claimed), no one was immune to the identity crisis of the early twentieth century except the "luxurious classes." He correlated the impending demise of the "manly virtues" with "pacific cosmopolitan industrialism," a stage of development in which an older "pain economy" was giving way to a "pleasure economy" – that is, to a world without producers, "a world of clerks and teachers, of coeducation and zoophily, of 'consumer's leagues' and 'associated charities,' of industrialism unlimited and feminism unabashed." From the standpoint provided by that correlation, the decline of productive labor and the consequent confusion of male and female spheres became the elements of an identity crisis, for they threatened to dissolve ego boundaries normally determined by the sanctions of scarcity: "The transition to a 'pleasure economy' may be fatal to a being wielding no power of defence against its disintegrative influences. If we speak of the *fear of emancipation from the fear-regime,* we put the whole situation into a single phrase; fear regarding ourselves now taking the place of the ancient fear of the enemy." James worried that this "fear of emancipation" from the older "pain economy" would take a regressively masculine and militaristic form; the "manly virtues" could be reinstated by the violent means of war, he believed, and so he designed his moral equivalent with that possibility in mind. He clearly understood that "in the more or less socialistic future toward which mankind seems drifting," a central cultural problem would be how to "continue the manliness" hitherto bred in war and work.[17]

As James paraphrased the social theorist Simon Patten in pondering the

---

16 See Silverman, *Male Subjectivity,* 151–87 n. 36; see also Eve Kosofsky Sedgwick's reading of James in "The Beast in the Closet: James and the Writing of Homosexual Panic," in *The Epistemology of the Closet* (Berkeley, Calif., 1990), 182–212.

17 William James, "The Moral Equivalent of War" (1910), in Henry James Jr., ed., *Memories and Studies* (New York, 1911), 281–7; see Livingston, *Pragmatism and Political Economy,* 211–14, 364–5 n. 41, for a different discussion of this text that addresses the role of Simon Patten in James's periodization of necessity.

effects of a "pleasure economy" on male identity, so Walter Lippmann para-phrased both James and Patten in charting the growth of "consumers' con-sciousness" and the new importance of "woman's position." In *Drift and Mastery* (1914) Lippmann spoke of a future in which "mankind will have emerged from a fear economy," and, like James, he saw that this was a future over which women would presumably preside as the sanctions of scarcity continued to erode. "The mass of women do not look at the world as work-ers," he noted; "in America, at least their prime interest is as consumers. . . . We hear a great deal about the class consciousness of labor; my own obser-vation is that in America to-day consumers' consciousness is growing very much faster." Here, too, the declining salience of productive labor, of the working man's inherited social roles, threatened, or rather promised, to open up identities once fixed by externally imposed imperatives, by the dictates of necessity. And here, too, the identities opened up by political-economic change were male identities.[18]

So the emergence of an "imaginary femininity" was common to very different kinds and levels of discourse at the turn of the century. The insight on which the machinists and the intellectuals converge, for example, is that a male identity or "manly bearing" predicated on a certain political-economic posture was in question as a result of the changes we now sum-marize under the heading of consumer culture. They suggest that the issue thereby raised was not the eclipse of subjectivity as such but the "feminiza-tion" of identity – that is, the real issue was not the erasure but the recon-struction of modern subjectivity in accordance with a confusion of sexual spheres. And this is precisely the issue that the critique of consumer culture elegantly elides. On the assumption that subjectivity itself is dissolved by proletarianization under corporate auspices, the critics of consumer culture can and do ignore the ambiguous sexual identities that turn-of-the-century workers and intellectuals alike recognized as impending realities, as *possibil-ities* residing in the transformation of the labor process and emerging from the "age of surplus" sponsored by "pacific cosmopolitan industrialism." These critics can therefore construct a "primal scene" around the "event" of proletarianization that permits only one point of entry into the Oedipus complex – in other words, they can produce a narrative that promotes an exclusive identification with the figure of the father, and thus proscribes an "imaginary femininity" that would allow for identification with the figure of the mother, or with an intermediate figure that blurs the binary opposi-tion of male and female. The unintended consequences or cultural effects of

18 Cf. the more detailed discussion of Lippmann in Livingston, *Pragmatism and Political Economy,* 69–75.

their critique would seem, then, to be not only the rehabilitation of the paterfamilias as the paradigm of subjectivity, but the validation of essential sexual difference as the condition of genuine selfhood.

In sum, this critique reinstates modern subjectivity as the ethical principle by which the historical circumstances of the twentieth century are to be evaluated, although it treats the consumer culture specific to that century as the solvent of subjectivity as such. But these are understandable and even persuasive positions to take in a corporate-industrial market society, for in such a society, those who control income-producing assets typically have more opportunities and greater social standing than those who do not. Other things being equal, proletarians have fewer life chances in a corporate-industrial market society than their employers, so that protest against proletarianization becomes a protest against an unequal distribution of opportunities – that is, against a class-divided society. In this sense, the critique of consumer culture extends an honorable tradition of Anglo-American radicalism.[19]

And yet it ultimately blinds us to the comic potential, the redeeming value, of proletarianization and reification. I do *not* mean that the twentieth century has been a barrel of laughs. I mean that it was precisely proletarianization and its corollaries that reversed the simple, rigid, transparent relation between active subject and passive object that characterized artisanal forms of work and the household economies they presupposed. By the late nineteenth century, this reversal had gone far enough to allow all manner of intellectuals to treat the reconstruction of the subject-object relation as a pressing practical problem rather than a metaphysical question; we call the result pragmatism. It was also proletarianization and its corollaries that finally extruded females from the confines of the household, so that, as Ellen DuBois points out, they began to "participate directly in society as individuals, not indirectly through their subordinate positions as wives and mothers"; we call the result feminism. Either way we look at it, a protest against proletarianization is probably the worst way to appreciate the political, intellectual, and cultural possibilities – including pragmatism and feminism – that reside in the decomposition of simple market society, circa 1850–1940.[20]

19 See ibid., 273–9. I would add that, in an era that seems determined to forget modern subjectivity (except of course when Newt Gingrich and William Bennett start reminiscing), the critique of consumer culture represents a return of the repressed – that is, a healthy antidote to the radicalism of both left and right.

20 On comic versus tragic forms of narrative, see Hayden White's treatment of Hegel in *Metahistory: The European Historical Imagination in the Nineteenth Century* (Baltimore, 1973), 93–131, and my appropriation of Kenneth Burke's "frames of acceptance" in "The Politics of Pragmatism." On the

Let me take the two most recent contributions to the critique of consumer culture as illustrations of this claim: I mean Leach's *Land of Desire* and Lears's *Fables of Abundance*. We have already seen that Leach celebrates the "older entrepreneurial economy" in which "shared contractual obligations and common moral premises" prevailed. From the standpoint provided by that moral universe, he denounces twentieth-century consumer capitalism as a grotesque "system preoccupied with 'making profits' rather than with 'making goods'" (18), as a "vast system of abstraction" (150: here he is quoting Edmund Wilson approvingly). Indeed it seems that reality itself receded under the new regime of reification. For example, Leach claims that once glass separated shoppers from goods on display, the relation between subjects and objects was obviously attenuated – glass walls "closed off smell and touch, diminishing the consumer's relationship with the goods" (62–3). From here it is a very short step to the conclusion that by the second decade of the twentieth century, "the difference between the real and the unreal" was thoroughly confused if not altogether effaced (189). "The circumstance of material comfort and even of prosperity for most people throughout most of the nineteenth century was being superseded by the idea of possession," according to Leach, "by being through having, by pageantry and show rather than by open confrontation with reality, by desire rather than fulfillment" (190).

So Leach must believe either that a distinction between "the real and the unreal" is self-evident, or that twentieth-century challenges to this version of metaphysical realism – from pragmatists and feminists, among others – can be safely ignored because they are products of postmodernity.[21] He also must believe that once upon a time, presumably in the nineteenth century, desire did not exceed its normal limits or proper receptacles; meanwhile, I would infer, insubstantial symbols, thoughts, and words corresponded to substantial objects, things, and events "out there" in the "real world." When a "corporate money economy" animated by the "drive for profits" emerged around the turn of the century (190), this equilibrium was broken, and the epistemology of excess was born. An "open confrontation with reality"

implications of proletarianizaiton, see ibid. and Livingston, *Pragmatism and Political Economy,* chaps. 8–10; DuBois is quoted from her "Radicalism of the Woman's Suffrage Movement," in Anne Phillips, ed., *Feminism and Equality* (New York, 1987), 131.

21 See, e.g., Richard Rorty, *Objectivity, Relativism, and Truth* (New York, 1991); Donna Haraway, *Simians, Cyborgs, and Women: The Reinvention of Nature* (New York, 1991); Jane Flax, *Thinking Fragments: Psychoanalysis, Feminism, and Postmodernism in the Contemporary West* (Berkeley, Calif., 1990); Mary Hesse, *Revolutions and Reconstructions in the Philosophy of Science* (Bloomington, Ind., 1980); Lynda Birke, *Women, Feminism, and Biology: The Feminist Challenge* (New York, 1986); and Judith Butler, *Gender Trouble: Feminism and the Subversion of Identity* (New York, 1990).

then became impossible because the difference between (monetary) representations of real things and the things themselves no longer seemed to matter. Now these beliefs make perfect sense on the assumption that we can apprehend reality without artifice, without *changing* it as well as designating it in and as symbols, thoughts, and words – on the assumption that we can somehow peek over the edges of our own existence as if we are not there. But can we adopt that assumption without evading or ignoring most of the intellectual innovation of the twentieth century? Can we do so, in other words, without reverting to the discontinuities of desire and reason, or value and fact, or body and mind, each of which underwrote the idea of modern subjectivity and the ideal of scientific objectivity? I confess that I don't see how we can.

Lears expresses similar concerns in *Fables of Abundance.* He shows us that the nineteenth-century market was a more mysterious mechanism than Leach acknowledges and wants us to learn from the carnivalesque qualities of an older "commercial vernacular" because he understands that neither markets nor commodities can or should be abolished in the name of democracy. In short, he understand that nostalgia is more symptom of than cure for what alienates us in – and from – the present. Yet Lears is also determined to reclaim the "things themselves" from the weird abstractions of the commodity form as it has been redefined by corporate power and "managerial culture" – that is, from the "bureaucratic rationality" that enforces reification.[22] So he must posit some moment in the past when desire was somehow fixed to its natural or obvious correspondent, when subjects and objects were properly aligned if not perfectly united in what he calls "symbolic consciousness" (19–21). Otherwise his remarks on the "dematerialization of desire" (20, 127, 215) and the related results of a consumer culture animated by advertising lose their critical edge; at any rate they make me want to ask when desire was materialized or grounded, and whether we can think about human desire except in terms of its immaterial excesses.

Lears locates the normative moment he needs in a preoedipal state of bliss that somehow exudes "matriarchal values" (129–33). But, like Teresa Brennan, he understands how difficult it is to find our way back to this moment *before* the acquisition of language and the loss of the Other; for he lets the "carnivalesque commercial vernacular" of the nineteenth century – that is, the vernacular of simple market society – serve the same normative purpose (127–9, 144–9, 152–3, 159, 161–3, 192, 215).[23] And so that

---

22 See *Fables of Abundance,* chaps. 2–3, 12; page reference hereafter in text.
23 See Teresa Brennan, *History after Lacan* (New York, 1993), 102–17.

vernacular becomes a kind of substitute for the "symbolic consciousness" specific to a preoedipal moment of transcendent insight. In other words, it is itself a "deferred action," a way of returning us to, or at least reminding us of, the excruciating wonders of that originating moment. It is not so much an event experienced by nineteenth-century Americans as a story told by a historian, a story that gives meaning to irretrievable memory traces, mere fragments of the past. How, then, does it situate or constitute its dramatis personae in the present? Does it reinstate the primal scene of proletarianization or construct another? My answers derive from a reading of those passages in *Fables of Abundance* that assess the status and the symbolism of the female.[24]

In the pivotal chapter 4, "The Disembodiment of Abundance," Lears claims that the icons of abundance, from "mythic emblems" to modern lithographs, have always been female, but that by the turn of the century, these images had been "denatured" and disembodied in accordance with the "broad cultural tendencies that accompanied the rise of an urban market economy." As the "source of material wealth became more abstract," and as corporations replaced entrepreneurs, it became easier for Americans "to forget the biological sources of material abundance and to attribute generative powers to male dominated institutions." When corporations finally "claimed a major share of the mass circulation of images" in the 1890s, "the symbolism of abundance began to be more systematically rationalized"; for the new admen were not only Protestants, they were also "corporate employees rather than artisan-entrepreneurs." As a result, "the images they designed reflected the marginalizing of female generativity in the managerial worldview" (109–11). Meanwhile, "popular notions of abundance were moving away from their origins in the rhythms of agrarian life and bodily existence," because under the regime of reification perfected by corporate managers, "factory and office employees were increasingly cut off from the vernacular artisanal traditions that linked brain and hand in 'local knowledge'" (117).

Lears concludes, in view of these claims, that the "disembodiment of abundance" involved not only the "containment of Carnival" – of the playful and grotesque confusions specific to the "commercial vernacular" and its antecedents – but the "devaluation of female authority" (118). A few pages later, he restates this conclusion in slightly but significantly different language. Now the issue becomes "the devaluation of maternal authority," which flowed, it seems, from two sources – on the one hand, "changes in

---

24 In addition to the pages cited hereafter in the text, see *Fables of Abundance*, 183–92.

gender mythology," through which the makers of mass-produced images abandoned "the ancient idea of the maternal origins of abundance," and, on the other, "the strain of masculine protest" in modernist aesthetics, through which artists like Kandinsky hoped to "free art from its bonds to material reality" (122).

So there can be little doubt that Lears sees the conversion of artisan-entrepreneurs into corporate employees as the turning point in the "disembodiment of abundance," or that the primal scene of proletarianization still regulates his narrative. But what are we to make of the apparent confusion of female and maternal authority? This confusion is allowed, I think, by Lears's equation of the female as such with the material, the bodily, and the biological "sources" of abundance – that is, with the "generativity" that is typically associated with the "nature" of the female body, with the *maternal* functions of women. That essentializing equation blinds him to the possibility that the *devaluation* of maternal authority was the necessary condition of the *revaluation* of female authority that reshaped American culture as well as politics after the turn of the century and led directly to modern feminism in all its diversity. But what if we can claim that the extrusion of females from the household in the late nineteenth century opened up a new, discursive space between the "maternal" and the "female" – and for that matter between men and women – where desublimated female desire, free at last of its bonds to maternal reality, could circulate and so create new sources of subjectivity for men and women alike? Don't we then need some way of appreciating the comic potential and redeeming value of the postartisanal market society that entails proletarianization, corporate bureaucracies, scientific management, and consumer culture? Don't we then need some way of telling the story of nineteenth-century artisan-entrepreneurs that does not treat the decomposition of the simple market society they created as a tragedy – in other words, don't we need a way of criticizing the corporate, postindustrial capitalism of the twentieth century that is not merely a protest against proletarianization? We do, of course, but it is not to be found in the extant critique of consumer culture, for that critique merely reenacts the primal scene of modern American historiography and functions accordingly as a kind of defense against the "imaginary femininity" produced in, and by, an "age of surplus."

20

Consumption and Consumer Society

A Contribution to the History of Ideas

ULRICH WYRWA

I

In a little essay from the year 1772, Denis Diderot complained bitterly about his new jacket.[1] With melancholy, he remembered his old housecoat and how well he felt in it, how he and it were one. "Why didn't I hold onto it? It fit me, I fit it." Not only was he extremely uncomfortable in his new coat, it had also succeeded in turning his whole life topsy-turvy, even laying waste to his household. His old coat had been in conformity with the things of everyday life: Coat, table, and chair formed a harmonious ensemble. "Now everything has gone to pieces" was Diderot's angry remark. "The harmony is a thing of the past; and with it, the proper proportion." The cause of this senseless destruction is so-called good, discriminating taste, the unhappy urge to prettify and renew everything. Instead of "practicing thrift and economy," Diderot had ruined his household. All that remains is a small painting, and it is this that gives him consolation in face of the current devastation. The painting takes up the motif of destruction, not that of the drive for new items, but rather that called forth by time, that which "corrodes even the hardest things of this world," a natural mutability that sets itself against the destruction wrought by new fashions.

With this little essay, Diderot showed himself to be an early critic of consumption.[2] He anticipated essential motifs and central arguments of twentieth-century critics of consumption, even though he never employed the

---

I would like to thank Kevin McAleer for the translation from the German.

1 Denis Diderot, *Gründe, meinem alten Hausrock nachzutrauern (1772); Über die Frauen: Zwei Essays*, trans. Hans Magnus Enzensberger (Berlin, 1993).

2 See also Grant McCracken, "Diderot Unities and the Diderot Effect: Neglected Cultural Aspects of Consumption," in Grant McCracken, ed., *Culture and Consumption: New Approaches to the Symbolic Character of Consumer Goods and Activities* (Bloomington, Ind., 1988), 118–29.

term. In current academic exchange, the meaning of the term "consumption" is undergoing a metamorphosis. Whereas in the 1970s it was used as either a purely quantitative economic indicator or, negatively, as a measure of alienation and manipulation, in the recent academic literature it has begun to lose its pejorative undertones. Consumption is no longer understood only as passive suffering, but rather as a communicative act, as a moment of social and political exchange.[3] Nevertheless, in this chapter I argue that if the concept of consumption loses its critical character then its analytic power for historical research will also be lost. Accordingly, I first give a historical outline of the concept of consumption and take up several motifs of the critique of consumer society. I then illuminate the transvaluation of the concept of consumer society and its historical spread in order to introduce several considerations for using the concept in historical research.

II

In antiquity the Latin word *consumere* designated not only the use of things but also any type of removal and various forms of disposal.[4] The rural, self-sufficient, corporative-familial world of the Middle Ages had no special term for the provision of the basic needs of food, clothing, and shelter, and even in the language of the medieval traders no term for consumption appears. Only with the advent of mercantilism, devoted to the fiscal interests of the sovereign, does the Latin derivative "consumption" begin to take on real meaning. In 1663 the theologian and writer Johann Balthasar Schupp used the word *consumieren* in the sense of usage and taxing, and likewise in Christian Ludwig's *Teutsch-Englischem Lexicon* of 1716, the word "consumption, from the Latin, for tax" also appears.[5] Zedler's *Universallexikon* of 1773 starts by defining the word as "that which is taxed." The next sentence expands this definition: "Even a certain type of princely tax can be called *Consumtions Accise*," in which "food, drink, and everything that is necessary for the daily upkeep of life, is obliged to be taxed."[6] In Krünitz's *Oeconomischer Encyklopädie* of 1776, the aspect of taxation is placed

---

3 See the important essay by David Sabean, "Die Produktion von Sinn beim Konsum der Dinge," in Wolfgang Ruppert, ed., *Fahrrad, Auto, Kühlschrank: Zur Kulturgeschichte der Alltagsdinge* (Frankfurt am Main, 1993). For a brief overview of the uses of the term "consumer," see also Raymond Williams, *Keywords: A Vocabulary of Culture and Society* (London, 1976), 68–70.
4 Georg Wissowa, ed., *Paulys Realencyklopädie der classischen Altertumswissenschaft,* 8 vols. (Stuttgart, 1900), 7:1145.
5 Cited in F. L. K. Weigand, *Deutsches Wörterbuch,* 5th ed., 2 vols. (Giessen, 1909), 1:1114.
6 Johann Heinrich Zedler, *Grosses Vollständiges Universallexicon,* 64 vols. (Halle and Leipzig, 1732–54), 6:1108.

clearly in the foreground: "Therefore, excise-duties, *Consumption-Accise,* is a levy by the sovereign on all necessities of life that are used up, such as food, drink, and clothing."[7] The *Deutsche Encyclopädie* of 1782 does not even list "consumption" but merely "excise tax." As was duly noted in its introductory article, there were many types of these, and "many more are being invented of which we are not completely aware."[8] Also Johann Hübner's *Konversationslexicon* of 1795 says that "a certain type of princely levy" is called *Consumtionsaccise,* "because all *Consumtibilia* such as food, drink, and that which is necessary to the daily upkeep of life, must be taxed."[9] Significantly, the sole word *Consumtionssteuern* (excise tax) appears even in the fifth and sixth editions of the Brockhaus *Enzyklopädie* of 1820 and 1824, respectively.[10]

Although with his essay Diderot can be judged an early critic of consumption, his *Encyclopedie* mentions it only briefly in the sense of "using up," first and foremost in reference to the distribution of goods through traders. According to the *Encyclopedie,* the second usage of the term was in the maritime trade for those things necessary for sailing – ropes, canvas, and so forth. The article devotes yet more room to the legal meaning of the term "the consummation of a marriage."[11]

Physiocratic economic theory did not limit itself to the tax revenue of the state but attempted to get to the very bottom of all trade and commerce. The *Allgemeine Encyclopädie der Wissenschaften und Künste* by Johann Samuel Ersch and Johann Gottfried Gruber states, "Consumption is the state-economic term for the antithesis of production. . . . The use of such words in their state-economic meaning comes from the physiocrats, who conceived masterfully the interaction between production and consumption."[12] While describing the patterns of economic circulation, the enlightened economists made observations on consumption. The chemist and physician Johann Joachim Becher dubbed consumption the soul of "civil society," forming as it did the connecting tissue among craftsmen and farmers and merchants, and through *consumtio* the various levels of society were

---

7 Johann Georg Krünitz, *Oeconomische Encyclopädie, oder Allgemeines System der Land-, Haus-, Staats-Wirthschaft,* 242 vol. (Berlin, 1773–1858), 8:330.
8 *Deutsche Encyclopädie, oder Allgemeines Real-Wörterbuch aller Künste und Wissenschaften,* 17 vols. (Frankfurt am Main, 1778–1804), 6:297.
9 Johann Hübner, *Reales Staats-Zeitung- und Conversations-Lexicon* (Leipzig, 1795), 530.
10 See *Allgemeine Deutsche Real-Encyklopädie für die gebildeten Stände,* 5th ed., 10 vols. (Leipzig, 1822–6), vol. 2, and ibid., 6th ed., 11 vols. (Leipzig, 1827–9), vol. 2.
11 Denis Diderot and Jean Lerond d'Alembert, eds., *Encyclopedie ou dictionnaire Maisonné des Sciences des Arts et de Métiers par une societé de gens de lettres,* 17 vols. (Paris, 1751–72), 14:49.
12 Johann Samuel Ersch and Johann Gottfried Gruber, eds., *Allgemeine Encyclopädie der Wissenschaften und Künste,* 167 vols. (Leipzig, 1818–89), 19:193.

made mutually dependent.[13] And the enlightened Hamburg writer and political scientist Johann Georg Büsch contended that farmers, previously regarded only as producers, also needed to be seen as consumers so as to afford them inducements to increase production.[14]

Life in England during the Industrial Revolution had influenced Adam Smith in the conviction that it would be most advantageous for future economic development if each individual followed his own economic self-interest. Even if in his classic study *The Wealth of Nations* (1776) "consumption" is defined as the actual purpose and goal of production,[15] it is given little attention as an economic factor in classic political economy. In the same tradition, Jean Baptiste Say divided political economy into three areas – production, distribution, and consumption – but the relationships among these were barely addressed and the concept of consumption was not further elaborated.[16] In English political economy, the inherent barter value of articles was far more important than their worth as consumables. For example, in the chapter on supply and demand in his *Principles of Political Economy*, John Stuart Mill focused exclusively on the barter value of wares.[17] Even the corresponding article in Pierer's *Universal Conversation Lexikon* of 1876 concentrated on barter value: "Consumption is . . . in contrast to production, the whole or partial usage of certain goods, that is, the reduction of their barter value."[18]

The emphasis on value in the literature of political economy led to considerable confusion and problems of definition with regard to "consumption," as in 1832 when Friedrich Benedikt von Hermann in his state-economic study defined "consumption" exclusively as the opposite of production, as the destruction of barter value, whether through tax, decay, fire, or natural catastrophe.[19] Likewise, Brockhaus's *Real-Encyklopädie* added its own entry under the heading "Consumtion": "The consumption of goods is the result of nature – which often destroys to no human

13 See the following two works by Johann Joachim Becher: *Politischer Discurs von den eigentlichen Ursachen des Auff- und Abnehmens der Städte, Länder und Republicken* (Frankfurt am Main, 1668) and *Moral Discurs von Beschaffenheit, Cultivierung und Bewohnung, Privilegien und Benefizen* (Frankfurt am Main, 1669).

14 Johann Georg Büsch, *Abhandlungen von dem Geldumlauf,* 2 vols. (Hamburg, 1780).

15 Adam Smith, *Der Wohlstand der Nationen: Eine Untersuchung seiner Natur und seiner Ursachen* (Munich, 1974), 558.

16 Jean Baptiste Say, *Vollständiges Handbuch der praktischen Nationalökonomie,* 6 vols. (Stuttgart, 1829–30).

17 John Stuart Mill, *Grundsätze der politischen Ökonomie,* 2 vols. (Hamburg, 1852), 1: chap. 2.

18 H. A. Pierer, *Universal-Conversations-Lexikon: Neuestes encyklopädisches Wörterbuch aller Wissenschaften, Künste und Gewerbe,* 6th ed., 14 vols. (Leipzig, 1876–8), 5:344.

19 Friedrich Benedikt W. von Hermann, *Staatswirtschaftliche Untersuchungen,* 2d ed. (Munich, 1870), 599.

advantage – and through usage and fashion."[20] A corresponding article in Hermann Wagener's conservative *Gesellschaftslexikon* also had difficulties with the term "consumption," which attempted to distinguish "unproductive and productive or reproductive consumption" from one another.[21] In the liberal *Deutschen Staatswörterbuch*, it is defined as depreciation, "which can be called forth through usage, destruction, a change in taste, or loss."[22] Even toward the end of the nineteenth century, *Meyers Konversations-Lexikon* distinguished among three forms of consumption: first, productive consumption, "the transformation from raw materials into manufactured items, including the accompanying wear and tear on machines"; second, the consumption of luxuries, or consumption in the narrower sense; and third, "consumption through public opinion," the depreciation of goods, for example, through "obsolete labels, démodé items, and calendars at the end of the year."[23] The third edition of the *Konversations-Lexikon* defined consumption as an "alteration in form . . . that removes its usability,"[24] and also appearing in this article was a concept that would prove essential to future definitions: A consumption that "fails to satisfy a need is destruction." As here elaborated, the concept of need was not used to define consumption in a positive sense. As late as 1918, in his collection of essays on the origins of political economy, Karl Bücher wrote that the destruction of wares was more important for political economy doctrines than the satisfaction of needs.[25] The author of Pierer's *Universalexikon* entry on "Consumtion" attempted conceptually to link barter value with need: "Consumption therefore, is an exchange, in which goods are surrendered against the satisfaction of a personal need, or against receipt of another type of product."[26]

When the younger school of historical national economists took up the idea of needs in their concept, a new, more human understanding of consumption became possible. An 1857 essay by Franz Vorländer on "the ethical principle of consumption in political economy" emphasized needs as the ultimate and decisive motive in consumption and showed that "consumption has been treated by political economy as something of a

---

20 *Allgemeine Deutsche Real-Encyklopädie für die gebildeten Stände: Conversations Lexikon,* 10th ed., 15 vols. (Leipzig, 1851–5), 4:384.
21 Hermann Wagener, *Staats- und Gesellschaftslexikon,* 23 vols. (Berlin, 1858–61), 5:562.
22 Johann Caspar Bluntschli and Karl Brater, *Deutsches Staatswörterbuch,* 11 vols. (Stuttgart, 1857–60), 5:749ff.
23 *Meyers Konversations-Lexikon: Eine Encyklopädie des allgemeinen Wissens,* 5th ed., 17 vols. (Leipzig, 1897), 10:505–6.
24 *Meyers Konversations-Lexikon: Eine Encyklopädie des allgemeinen Wissens,* 3d ed., 16 vols. (Leipzig, 1877), 10:237.
25 Karl Bücher, *Die Entstehung der Volkswirtschaft,* 6th ed. (Tübingen, 1908).
26 Pierer, *Universal-Conversations-Lexikon,* 5:344.

stepchild."[27] The academic literature of the time, however, did not take up this notion. In an outline of political economy doctrines, Gustav Schmoller devoted a chapter to needs while neglecting to develop the concept of consumption.[28] Werner Sombart was the only one to indicate the significance of luxury consumption as a source for detecting historical change,[29] and in his historical portrayal of the development of capitalism, he introduced need – or "care-maintenance" – as the fundamental fact of economic life, emphasizing how production, distribution, and consumption form an endless cycle.[30] But even with Sombart the question of production remained in the foreground. It was only after Lujo Brentano issued his "Attempt at a Theory of Needs"[31] that Alexander Wirminghaus was able to work out the meaning of consumption for political economy in a comprehensive volume on the occasion of Schmoller's seventieth birthday.[32] Likewise, the *Handwörterbuch der Staatswissenschaften* from 1923 notes that there is no uniform usage of the word "consumption," neither "in the language of commerce" nor in the economic sciences.[33] In that same year, Karl Oldenberg, a political scientist at the University of Göttingen and assistant editor of Schmoller's *Yearbook for Legislation, Administration, and Political Economy in the German Empire,* contributed a piece to the handbook *Outline of Social Economy,* thus signaling the decisive breakthrough in the formulation of a socioeconomic concept of consumption.[34] Oldenberg defined consumption as the satisfaction of human needs through economic means.[35] In judging the historical development of consumption and production, Oldenberg warned against the "jubilee scale," the idea that rising productivity would result in "a parallel rise in consumer welfare."[36] With the dissolution of this traditional interdependence, the principle of distinction replaces that of recognition. This stimulates social ambition and the

27 Franz Vorländer, "Über das ethische Princip der volkswirtschaftlichen Consumtion," *Zeitschrift für die gesamte Staatswissenschaft* 13 (1857): 535.
28 Gustav Schmoller, *Grundriss der allgemeinen Volkswirtschaftslehre,* 2 vols. (Leipzig, 1900–1904).
29 See Werner Sombart, *Luxus und Kapitalismus* (Munich, 1922); and Werner Sombert, *Der moderne Kapitalismus,* vol. 1: *Die vorkapitalistische Wirtschaft,* 2d ed. (Munich and Leipzig, 1916), 717–49.
30 Sombart, *Der moderne Kapitalismus,* 3–4.
31 Lujo Brentano, "Versuch einer Theorie der Bedürfnisse," in *Sitzungsberichte der Königlichen Bayrischen Akademie der Wissenschaften: Philosophisch-philologische Klasse* (Munich, 1908).
32 Alexander Wirminghaus, "Die Lehre von der Konsumption und ihrem Verhältnis zur Produktion," in *Die Entwicklung der deutschen Volkswirtschaftslehre im 19. Jahrhundert: Gustav Schmoller zur 70. Wiederkehr seines Geburtstages* (Leipzig, 1908).
33 Hans Mayer, "Konsumtion," in Ludwig Elster and Adolf Weher, eds., *Handwörterbuch der Staatswissenschaften,* 4th ed., 8 vols. (Jena, 1921–5), 5:867.
34 Karl Oldenberg, "Die Konsumtion," in Sally Altmann and Karl Bücher, eds., *Grundriss der Sozialökonomik,* 2d sec., pt. 1: "Wirtschaft und Natur" (Tübingen, 1923), 188–263.
35 Ibid., 190. 36 Ibid., 198.

striving to impress, as consumer interests replace overarching life goals. This is coupled with "demonstrative display," an assertion of life-style that is constantly stimulated by changes in fashion. By growing accustomed to each new level of need satisfaction, the consumer abandons himself to the "soft pressure" that entangles him in ever-changing needs.

With this piece, Oldenberg worked out not only the socioeconomic but also the sociocultural aspects of consumption, similarly to the American sociologist Thorstein Veblen's analysis of the initial phase of mass consumption in North America at the beginning of the twentieth century. Seizing on an older, hitherto unheeded book about the "snob effect,"[37] Veblen described the significance of luxury – of "conspicuous consumption" – in the process of social stratification.[38]

The introduction of rationalization, new methods of production, and a more effective division of labor in the United States in the early 1900s was achieved by greater production; by reducing the price of the product, more social classes were now to be won over to the cause of consumerism. With the organization of production along Taylorist principles – an aspect that the German-language literature on Taylorism has neglected – the entire social and cultural life of the nation was transformed.[39] In contrast to comparable European reference works, however, the *Deutsch-ameri-kanische Conversations-Lexikon* of 1870 clearly had less difficulty in defining "consumption": "In political economy, consumption designates the usage of produced goods. It is the ultimate purpose . . . of all production, because if the item does not find a consumer, its production must cease."[40] The increasing respect that consumption as a factor in economic growth has gained in America since the end of the nineteenth century and especially in the twentieth century corresponds with the increased attention that the various disciplines have dedicated to this theme.[41] Hazel Kyrk's *A Theory of Consumption* was strongly influenced by the optimistic ideas of

37 John Rae, *Statement of Some Principles on the Subject of Political Economy* (Boston, 1834).
38 Thorstein Veblen, *Theorie der feine Leute: Eine Untersuchung der Institutionen* (1899; reprint, Frankfurt am Main, 1986)
39 Martyn J. Lee, *Consumer Culture Reborn: The Cultural Politics of Consumption* (London, 1993), 733ff.
40 *Deutsch-amerikanisches Conversations-Lexikon: mit Specieller Rücksicht auf das Bedürfniss der in Amerika lebenden Deutschen,* 11 vols. (New York, 1869–1974), 3:401.
41 This is expressed, e.g., in the series Getting and Spending: The Consumer's Dilemma, which reissued numerous studies of consumption from the interwar years. See, among others, William A. Berridge et al., *Purchasing Power of the Consumer* (Boston and New York, 1925); J. Grist Brainerd, *The Ultimate Consumer* (Boston and New York, 1933); Evans Clark, *Financing the Consumer* (Boston and New York, 1933); Elizabeth Ellis Hoyt, *The Consumption of Wealth* (Boston, 1928); Paul Henry Nystrom, *Economic Principles of Consumption* (Boston, 1929); Carle Clark Zimmerman, *Consumption and Standards of Living* (Boston, 1936).

the time.[42] According to Kyrk, our very culture and civilization are expressed through consumption, and an analysis of this phenomenon is equivalent to an anthropological investigation of human behavior. The goal of her study is to explain how certain standards of living originate, change, and develop. The objective side of such questions entails the description of and statistics for nutrition, clothing, shelter, and recreation, but behind all this stands the individual with his interests and desires. According to Kyrk's main thesis, the consumer always has freedom of choice, and it is he or she who decides what will be produced. But the consumer's freedom is limited by the unequal distribution of prosperity and depends on the current technical standards and the financial interests of the producers. Through the expression of his or her individual taste, the consumer gives new impulses to economic development. Kyrk concludes her investigation with the hope that further developments in the standard of living will lead to a higher level of human existence.

Hazel Kyrk's theory of consumption was in harmony with the progress-minded Henry Ford, who hoped to produce not only more and cheaper autos but also new forms of consumption – indeed, to create a surplus of products.[43]

Toward the end of the nineteenth century, the focus of consumption in German usage was in consumer cooperatives and consumer leagues. Symptomatic of this shift in the word's meaning is that the entry "consumer league" in the *Brockhaus Konversationslexikon* is more than double the length of its entry covering "consumption,"[44] and the sixth edition of *Pierers Lexikon* is also much more comprehensive on the subject of consumer leagues than it is on the topic of consumption itself.[45] This shift in interest to the consumer cooperatives is made yet clearer in the third edition of *Herders Konversationslexikon* of 1902. Whereas the entry on "consumption" makes only a brief reference to the article on *Verbrauch* (consumption), the entry for "consumer cooperative" is a comprehensive two-page supplement with detailed information on the historical development and organization of consumer cooperatives. It also discusses their legal status, including statistical data on the number of cooperatives and the social standing of their members.[46] The shift in meaning went so far that the *Duden* from 1923 asserted that, in the general vernacular, "consumption" had become a syn-

42 Hazel Kyrk, *A Theory of Consumption* (Boston and New York, 1923).
43 See the self-portrayal by Henry Ford, *Das grosse Heute – das grössere Morgen* (Leipzig, 1926), esp. chap. 1: "Unser aller Überfluss."
44 *Brockhaus Konversations-Lexikon*, 14th ed., 17 vols. (Leipzig, 1898), 10:595–6.
45 A. Pierer, *Universal-Conversations-Lexikon: Neuestes encyklopädisches Wörterbuch aller Wissenschaften, Künste und Gewerbe*, 6th ed., 14 vols. (Leipzig, 1876–8), 5:344.
46 *Herders Konversations-Lexikon*, 3d ed., 8 vols. (Freiburg/Breisgau, 1902), 5:85ff.

onym for "consumer cooperative" – "the popular term for consumer league."[47]

The destruction of these consumer cooperatives during the Nazi period was scrupulously documented in the reference works of the time. In the encyclopedia issued by Propyläen entitled *The Clever Alphabet,* we read, "In 1933 both central unions of the German consumer cooperatives were separated from the political party with which they had been associated."[48]

National Socialist policy toward consumption was quite contradictory. On the one hand, it promised, at least on paper, a meteoric rise in consumption and its extension to a broader mass public. The reality, however, was that expanding war production caused consumption to remain far below expected levels. For the most part, only products that had some importance for propaganda purposes, such as the *Volksempfänger,* a cheap radio, were allowed to become generally available. Other schemes apparently derived to encourage consumption, such as the saving program directed to consumer goods like the *KdF Wagen* (the *Volkswagen* or people's car), remained entirely illusory.[49] Despite these poor results, Nazi policy was not hostile to consumption as such. In sharp contrast to the declared aim of promoting mass consumption (regardless of the reality), Nazi ideologists criticized the consumer culture of America as symptomatic of the materialistic mentality. Among National Socialists the word "consumption" retained a distinctly negative connotation. This is clearly the case, for example, in the frequently used term "consumer margarine," a "margarine for the especially needy."[50] Significantly, the word "consumption" no longer appears in connection with Nazi successor organizations to consumer leagues, which were thrown together with the commercial sector and craftsmen to form the Reichsverband der Verbrauchergenossenschaften (Reich union of consumer cooperatives).[51]

Yet positive attitudes toward consumption and consumer theories from the United States were also present. The future chancellor of the Federal Republic, Ludwig Erhard, for example, who had worked on his doctorate under the Jewish sociologist and national economist Franz Oppenheimer

---

47 *Duden: Rechtschreibung der deutschen Sprache und der Fremdwörter,* 9th ed. (Leipzig, 1923), 256.

48 *Das kluge Alphabet: Konversationslexikon,* 10 vols. (Berlin, 1935), 6:13.

49 Bernd Weisbrod, "Der Schein der Modernität: Zur Historisierung der 'Volksgemeinschaft,'" in Karsten Rudolph and Christl Wickert, eds., *Geschichte als Möglichkeit: Festschrift für Helga Grebing* (Essen, 1995), 229. See also Kurt Möser's chapter in this book for information on the anticipated, yet never realized, mass production of the people's car or *Volkswagen.*

50 Karl-Heinz Brackmann and Renate Birkenhauser, *NS-Deutsch: Selbstverständliche Begriffe und Schlagwörter aus der Zeit des Nationalsozialismus* (Straelen, 1988), 113; see also Heinz Paechter, *Nazi-Deutsche: A Glossary of Contemporary German Usage* (New York, 1944).

51 *Das kluge Alphabet,* 6:13.

and who had been an assistant at the Institute for Economic Surveillance (Institut für Wirtschaftsbeobachtung) in Nuremberg since 1928, held a positive view of consumption.[52] In 1932, Erhard wrote that only by an expansion of consumption would it be possible to stimulate the economy.[53] The following year, he criticized the economic policy of the German empire, arguing that the problem of deficiency could only be solved if consumption were stimulated by increasing people's incomes.[54] Indeed, in 1935 he was one of the founders of the Society for Consumer Research (Gesellschaft für Konsumforschung e.V.), the aim of which was to give expression to the interests of consumers and carry out surveys of consumer behavior, as was made clear in the editorial of the first number of the journal.[55]

In general, however, a positive conception of consumption could not emerge until the collapse of National Socialism, and it was only toward the end of the 1950s that, at least in West Germany, the Volkswagen was finally able to keep the promises made during the Nazi period.[56] In East Germany, however, there was a return to the language of the working-class movement, and the term "consumption" became prominent in the name of the distribution chain Konsum. Significantly, the accent in this word falls on the first syllable, with a short *u* in the second.[57]

III

In North America at midtwentieth century, numerous sociological studies documented the increasing orientation of a broad middle class toward consumption. These basic historical changes in mentality helped lead to the development of the throwaway consumer society.[58] Most influential were the studies of George Katona[59] on the status of the consumer in society,[60]

---

52 See the biography by Volker Hentschel, *Ludwig Erhard: Ein Politikerleben* (Munich, 1996).
53 Ludwig Erhard, "Wirtschaftsbelebung von der Verbrauchereite," *Der deutsche Ökonimist,* Oct. 7, 1932, 1323–5.
54 Ludwig Erhard, "Der Reichskommissar für Arbeitsbeschaffung und der Gehrke-Plan," *Wirtschaftsdienst,* no. 2 (1933): 44–5.
55 *Mitteilungsblatt der Gesellschaft für Konsumforschung e.V. (Nürnberg),* no. 1 (1936).
56 Weisbrod, *Der Schein der Modernität,* 229. For the development of West German consumption in the 1950s, see Michael Wildt, *Am Beginn der "Konsumgesellschaft": Mangelerfahrung, Lebenshaltung und Wohlstandshoffnung in Westdeutschland in den fünfziger Jahren* (Hamburg, 1994). See also Arnold Sywottek, "Zwei Wege in die 'Konsumgesellschaft,'" in Axel Schildt and Arnold Sywottek, eds., *Modernisierung im Wiederaufbau: Die westdeutsche Gesellschaft der 50er Jahre* (Bonn, 1993).
57 For consumption in the GDR, see the chapters by Ina Merkel and André Steiner in this book.
58 See the entry "Konsumgesellschaft," in Joachim Ritter, ed., *Historisches Wörterbuch der Philosophie,* 8 vols. (Darmstadt, 1971–92), 4:1021.
59 See Daniel Horowitz's chapter in this book.
60 George Katona, *Die Mächte der Verbraucher* (Düsseldorf, 1962); the original title was *The Powerful Consumer.*

especially his *The Mass Consumption Society,* which gave a conceptual boost to the idea of a consumer society.[61] A critical examination of industrial society's development in America, which is forever creating new needs and thereby promoting consumption, was *The Affluent Society* by the American economist John Kenneth Galbraith.[62] One of the first German contributions that used the term "consumer society" was the short essay "Unsere Konsumgesellschaft"[63] by Heinz-Dietrich Ortlieb about the German "economic miracle." By the beginning of the 1960s the word had already found its way into journalistic language.[64]

The Marxist intellectuals who fled Nazi Germany for the United States were astonished by the extent of capitalist development in America and by the scale of its mass consumption. But they were unable to share in the optimistic attitudes toward consumption that Americans expressed. Their criticism of American consumer society stemmed from their experience of the collapse of European bourgeois civilization.[65] "Capitalistic production," according to Max Horkheimer and Theodor W. Adorno in their *Dialectic of the Enlightenment,* imprisons the consumer, "the worker and the employee, the farmer and petit bourgeois," heart and soul, so that he "falls irresistibly under the spell" of the various wares.[66] Capitalism promises to operate according to the needs of human beings, but it is really a "circle of manipulation and retrospective need" in which the economically strongest always exercise their power over society. The principle is that, on the one hand, industry can imagine all needs as "fulfillable, whereas, on the other hand, these needs are so furnished that through them the human being only experiences himself as an eternal consumer, as an object" of industry.[67] The more solid an industry's position, the more "summarily can it process the needs of consumers, produce them, steer them, and discipline them."[68] As an example of the mechanism of consumer society, Horkheimer and Adorno cite "[t]he cultural industry[, which] is perpetually deceiving its consumers with the very thing that it is perpetually promising."[69]

---

61 George Katona, *Der Massenkonsum* (Düsseldorf, 1965).

62 John Kenneth Galbraith, *Gesellschaft im Überfluss* (Munich, 1959).

63 Heinz-Dietrich Ortlieb, "Unsere Konsumgesellschaft: Glanz und Elend des deutschen Wirtschaftswunders," *Hamburger Jahrbuch für Wirtschafts- und Gesellschaftspolitik* 4 (1959): 224–46.

64 See, e.g., "Das Forum der Welt," *Die Welt,* Jan. 6, 1962; "Die geistige Welt," *Die Welt,* May 26, 1962; "Die geistige Welt," *Die Welt,* Oct. 27, 1962.

65 On Georg Lukacs – one critic of the capitalist world who had not yet used the word "consumption" – see James Livingston's chapter in this book.

66 Max Horkheimer and Theodor W. Adorno, *Dialektik der Aufklärung* (Amsterdam, 1947; reprint, Frankfurt am Main, 1971), 120.

67 Ibid., 127.   68 Ibid., 129.

69 Ibid., 125. Consumption can also represent a protest against asceticism, as Theodor W. Adorno shows in his essay, "Veblens Angriff auf die Kultur," in Prismen: Kulturkritik und Gesellschaft (Frank-

Herbert Marcuse took up this critique of advanced industrial society with his thesis of the one-dimensional man. According to his argument, industry destroys the unfolding and realization of human needs, and the production apparatus increasingly defines individual wishes and forces humans to consume useless things. The individual is subordinated to an oppressive compulsion to consume. False needs replace true ones, as the consumer goods of food, clothing, and shelter go along with prescribed attitudes that the consumer accepts and that bind him ever closer to the producer.[70] According to Marcuse's critique of hedonism, the moral posture of consumer society – the overcoming of the divorce between production and consumption – is one of the prerequisites of freedom, for the unfolding of material needs must go along with the unfolding of spiritual ones.[71]

This critique of consumer society belongs to the basic convictions of Western Marxism.[72] It is found in the works of Marxists André Gorz[73] and Henri Lefebvre, in the pamphlets of the New Left and in the writings of the Italian sociologist Francesco Alberoni,[74] as well as in the works of the writer and film director Pier Paulo Pasolini. Pasolini had criticized hedonism as a destructive and leveling ideology of consumer society,[75] and Gorz writes that the proffered compensations in consumer society and in leisure time are "alibis for the justification of an authoritarian and repressive society."[76] In his *Critique of Everyday Life,* Lefebvre asserts that the producers of consumer items are at the same time given to production of the consumer himself. "The consumer 'wishes' nothing for himself. He submits himself."

furt am Main, 1955); see also Martin Jay, Dialektische Phantasie: die Geschichte der Frankfurter Schule und des Instituts für Sozialforschung (Frankfurt am Main, 1981), 217.

70 Herbert Marcuse, *Der eindimensionale Mensch: Studien zur Ideologie in der fortgeschrittenen Industriegesellschaft* (Neuwied, 1967), 11–39.

71 Herbert Marcuse, "Zur Kritik des Hedonismus," *Kultur und Gesellschaft,* 2 vols. (Frankfurt am Main, 1965), 1:167. Here I can discuss neither the philosophical substance of the argument nor whether various emphases within critical theory exist, i.e., whether Walter Benjamin's fascination with the Parisian arcades is a more pertinent entrée into the world of goods than either Horkheimer and Marcuse. See Walter Benjamin, *Das Passagen-Werk* (Frankfurt am Main, 1982); see also the excerpts on fashion and advertising, and whether Adorno's turning away from the masses had skewed his understanding of modern society. E.g., see Adorno's disparaging remarks concerning jazz and popular music, "Über Jazz," in *Moments musicaux: Neu gedruckte Aufsätze, 1928–1962* (Frankfurt am Main, 1964).

72 The concept of need also is one of the central categories of Marxism-Leninism. See Martin Döbler, *Triebkraft Bedürfnis: Die Entwicklung der Bedürfnisse der sozialistischen Persönlichkeit* (Berlin, 1969).

73 André Gorz, "Work and Consumption," in Perry Anderson and Robin Blackburn, eds., *Towards Socialism* (London, 1966).

74 Francesco Alberoni, *Consumi e società* (Bologna, 1964).

75 Pier Paolo Pasolini, *Freibeuterschriften: Die Zerstörung des Einzelnen durch die Konsumgesellschaft* (Berlin, 1978).

76 André Gorz, *Der schwierige Sozialismus* (Frankfurt am Main, 1968), 132; see also Gorz, "Work and Consumption," 317–53.

He obeys the suggestions and the orders that are ceaselessly hammered into him by advertising, organized merchandising, and the demands of his own social prestige. "The desires no longer correspond to actual needs, but rather are artificially induced."[77] In the organ of the Situational International – that Parisian student group of the 1960s that through its comportment and actions exercised a considerable influence on the protest movement of those years – Guy Debord characterized consumption as "a quotidian, capitalist-produced and capitalist-controlled passivity." Consumer needs are "created and constantly stimulated" by modern industry, and society aims "to atomize human beings into isolated consumers."[78]

The critique of an increasing consumer orientation, of a leveling and depersonalization of human beings in an industrial society defined as "surplus," "affluent," or "throwaway," is also to be found among the conservative sociologists. In his critique of Western industrial society Herbert Marcuse could refer to his former teacher Martin Heidegger, who through the example of the phenomenology of the jug illustrated his views on ownership and the materiality of things, and the ways modern technology distorts, packages, and finally destroys them.[79] According to Heidegger's cultural critique of the technical age, things have been drained of substance and reduced to mere shadows and outlines.[80] In very similar language, the conservative-Right sociologist Hans Freyer elaborated his theory of the contemporary age, stating that "secondary systems" standardize human beings as consumers. The assignment of certain consumer habits to certain social circles was now shattered: Everything is offered everyone. What had started out as a luxury item had become an article of mass consumption. "The standard of living is the god of our age, and production is his prophet."[81] In Hannah Arendt's diagnosis of consumer society, she asserts that the dilemma in which modern developments have placed human beings is that of a "deeply disturbed balance between work and consumption."[82]

Marxist and conservative intellectuals were united in the cultural pessimism of their critique of the technical age, their conviction of the seductive and manipulative power of advertising, and their concern with the ability of fashionable currents to categorize and label human beings. But despite

77 Henri Lefebvre, *Kritik des Alltagslebens,* vol. 2 of *Grundrisse einer Soziologie der Alltäglichkeit* (1947; reprint, Munich, 1975), 17.
78 Guy Debord, "Perspektiven einer bewussten Änderung des alltäglichen Lebens," in *Situationistische Internationale 1958–1969: Gesammelte Ausgaben des Organs der Situationistischen Internationale,* 2 vols. (Hamburg, 1976), 1:226–34.
79 Martin Heidegger, *Vorträge und Aufsätze,* 4th ed. (Pfullingen, 1978).
80 Günter Seubold, *Heideggers Analyse der neuzeitlichen Technik* (Freiburg, 1986).
81 Hans Freyer, *Theorie des gegenwärtigen Zeitalters* (Stuttgart, 1955), 91.
82 Hannah Arendt, *Vita activa oder vom tätigen Leben* (Munich, 1981), 121.

these apparently similar diagnoses of the modern world, in their respective etiologies Marxists and conservatives followed separate paths. Whereas Marxists pinpointed the main problem in a smothering of human nature and its true needs through the overwhelming power of capitalist production, moral conservatives and/or Christian critics located the ailment in a loss of social interdependence and the dissolution of the traditional order.

IV

These negative conceptions of consumption, although they still help to define current usage in Western industrial society,[83] have slowly begun to give way to a more positive understanding of consumption. This transvaluation of the term "consumption" is due in no small part to the work of the historians Neil McKendrick, John Brewer, and John H. Plumb in their cooperative effort, *The Birth of a Consumer Society: The Commercialisation of Eighteenth-Century England*.[84] According to the book's central thesis, what took place in eighteenth-century England was not only a revolution in production but the birth of consumer society. More people could afford material goods than ever before. Within a few generations, products that once only the privileged few could afford were now accessible to the broad masses; the daily necessities of life began following the dictates of fashion in their incessant changing of style and form. The basis of the Industrial Revolution was not so much heavy industry as the production of a large number of relatively cheap disposable goods.

Since its first appearance, *The Birth of a Consumer Society* has stimulated a great number of studies on the origins and development of consumer society and the ways consumption habits have changed in modern industrial society. Indeed, the very idea of the eighteenth-century origins of consumer society has led to a recapitulation of the discussion of the origins of capitalism itself, this time including the concept of consumer society. In these discussions, the objection is frequently raised that consumer society did not originate in the eighteenth century, but rather in the sixteenth and seventeenth centuries.[85] Other historians, however, view the late nineteenth century as the decisive phase, with its large increase in consumer

---

83 See "Kritik des Konsumismus," in Jürgen Habermas, ed., *Stichworte zur "Geistigen Situation der Zeit,"* 2 vols. (Frankfurt am Main, 1979), vol. 2.

84 Neil McKendrick, John Brewer, and John H. Plumb, *The Birth of a Consumer Society: The Commercialisation of Eighteenth-Century England* (London, 1982).

85 See Margret Spufford, *The Great Reclothing of Rural England: Petty Chapmen and Their Wares in the Seventeenth Century* (London, 1984); Lorna Weatherhill, *Consumer Behaviour and Material Culture in Britain, 1660–1760* (London, 1988); Carol Shammas, *The Preindustrial Consumer in England and America* (Oxford, 1990); Beverly Lemire, *Fashion's Favourite: The Cotton Trade and the Consumer in Britain, 1660–1800* (Oxford, 1992).

items, the rise of department stores, and the emergence of new forms of presentation and advertising, especially electrical lighting.[86] American investigations, in particular, see the mass production and motorization of America in the 1920s as the beginning of consumer society.[87] From the German perspective, the 1950s is regarded as the decisive breakthrough, a period of mass motorization, television, refrigerators, and washing machines.[88]

Even if the "consumer society" in the context of the eighteenth and nineteenth centuries is simply a matter of postdating a clearly discernible twentieth-century phenomenon – thus running the danger of historical obfuscation – McKendrick, Brewer, and Plumb's book gives new and innovative impulses for future investigations of the change from an agrarian to an industrial society. The transvaluation of consumer society as a concept also provides the basis for the new conceptual definitions of consumption as a sociocultural transaction. Particularly fruitful are the new questions being raised by women's history. As demonstrated by Gunilla-Friedericke Budde in her paper delivered at a Berlin conference on consumption,[89] historically speaking, women have been the consumption experts. After families had fulfilled the daily needs of their household - chiefly in the market place – the returning producers would become consumers, whose inner life and social relations were bound together by consumption and the role played by the housewife.[90] As formulated by John Brewer and Roy Porter in their ambitious research agenda for a history of consumption in the early modern era, the aim of new interrogations into consumption is not to introduce the concept of consumption as the key to an all-encompassing explanation of modern history.[91] Rather, it is to suggest an unusual perspective and a novel interpretation that may expose the historical development of several relatively unexplored aspects of modern life.

Although the concept of consumption in academic usage has lately been

86 Michael B. Miller, *The Bon Marché: Bourgeois Culture and the Department Store, 1869–1920* (Oxford, 1992).

87 See, e.g., Ronald W. Edsforth, *Class Conflict and Cultural Consensus: The Making of a Mass Consumer Society in Flint, Michigan* (New Brunswick, N.J., 1987).

88 See Arnold Sywottek, "Zwei Wege in die 'Konsumgesellschaft,'" and Wildt, *Am Beginn der "Konsumgesellschaft."*

89 This conference was organized by Hartmut Kaelble, Jürgen Kocka, and Hannes Siegrist at the Center for Comparative Social History in January and June 1994 in Berlin. The proceedings have been published as Hartmut Kaelble, Jürgen Kocka, and Hannes Siegrist, eds., *Europäische Konsumgeschichte: Eine Gesellschafts- und Kulturgeschichte des Konsums (18. bis 20. Jahrhundert)* (Frankfurt am Main, 1997).

90 Gunilla-Friedericke Budde, "Die Hausfrau als Konsumexpertin des deutschen und englischen Bürgertums im 19. und frühen 20. Jahrhundert," in Kaelble, Kocka, and Siegrist, eds., *Europäische Konsumgeschichte.*

91 John Brewer and Roy Porter, eds., *Consumption and the World of Goods* (London, 1993), 7.

characterized by a change in meaning, it retains negative associations in general German usage. Granted, the nineteenth edition of *Brockhaus* pays much greater attention to consumption by affording it a nicely detailed entry; however, the indicated changes in the meaning of the concept are absent.[92] Even in the relevant dictionaries there are absolutely no indications of a shift in meaning. On the contrary, in the new eight-volume edition of *Duden: Das grosse Wörterbuch der deutschen Sprache,* published in 1994, the old, negative catchphrase is taken over from the edition of 1978, "to be dominated by a consumer view of life." Moreover, also revived is the adjective "consumerist" as well as "consumer idiot" and "consumer temple," a denigrative term for department store.[93] Additionally, during Christmas 1993 the lead article in *Der Spiegel* was entitled "Children as Consumer Terrorists." Children and youth, according to the article, increasingly draw their self-esteem from consumption; the result is a total commercialization of childhood. The author found "the little consumer terrorists" especially suspicious because of their fascination with advertising and their detailed knowledge of brand names and trademarks.[94] But even if this *Spiegel* article renewed all the standard critiques of consumerism, a change does indeed seem to have taken place in how consumption is interpreted in colloquial German. Of no small importance to this transvaluation is a new attitude toward the question of life-style and of the construction of one's everyday life. Moreover, the collapse of communism in eastern Germany in the early 1990s made clear the social and political dynamite of suppressed consumer desires. Consumption is no longer deemed merely a symptom of manipulation and alienation but is also understood as a natural craving. The idea of "false needs" and the thesis of the manipulative character of consumption are no longer convincing.[95] Whereas the concept of consumption was previously wholly negative, used as a criticism of mass society in the twentieth century and of affluent society in the postwar years, it now possesses a positive meaning denoting social exchange and the act of communication.[96]

Nevertheless, I argue that historical research cannot afford to sacrifice its critical impulse and its reservations vis-à-vis the concept of consumption. These encompass the problems of contemporary industrial society, while going beyond such concerns.[97] Questions yet to be asked are whether the

---

92 *Brockhaus Enzyklopädie,* 19th ed., 24 vols. (Mannheim, 1990), 12:299–302.
93 *Duden: Das grosse Wörterbuch der deutschen Sprache in sechs Bänden,* 6 vols. (Mannheim, 1978), 4:1542.
94 *Der Spiegel,* no. 50, Dec. 13, 1993.
95 For the antinomy of true vs. false needs, see Jackson Lears's chapter in this book.
96 See Sabean, "Die Produktion von Sinn beim Konsum der Dinge," 38, 50, and Lears's chapter in this book.
97 See the concluding thoughts of Wildt, *Am Beginn der "Konsumgesellschaft,"* 269.

transvaluation of the concept of consumption is not merely a semantic trick to help magically cast aside the negative aspects – the buying of senseless things, the deception surrounding bad products, and so forth – without indicating which conceptual instruments are being used to analyze this particular aspect of consumption. Historical scholarship must address the problem of the conquest by consumption of everyday lives, for if the concept of consumption loses its critical content and becomes too affirmative, the history of consumption will threaten to gloss over the negative features of this world of goods. It is important to retain the ambivalence of a concept such as consumer culture,[98] a concept that is enjoying a boom in historical research, and one that Jürgen Habermas in the 1950s specified as a contradiction in terms: "Consumer culture designates the unity of two incompatible elements; incompatible, among other reasons, because culture is critical and consumption is not."[99] If we insist on approaching consumption from its positive side, then historians have a duty to pose certain questions. Just how do commercial mechanisms displace forms of social integration and cultural exchange? How do material goods assume an increasing and inescapable power over human beings? To borrow an idea from Max Weber: How is it that the need to consume – which should be a "light coat" about the shoulders – has become a "steel-hard housing," that is, a compulsion to consume? How has the orientation toward consumption created "heartless bon viveurs" or *Genussmenschen ohne Herz*?[100] These are the critical questions. In this chapter I have argued that "consumer society" can be a useful analytical concept only if it preserves its original critical impulse and takes consumption's destructive aspects into account, that is, if historical scholarship – recalling Diderot's mourning for his old jacket – also considers the losses and casualties.

98 See Gary Cross, *Time and Money: The Making of Consumer Culture* (London, 1993).
99 Jürgen Habermas, "Konsumkritik: eigens zum Konsumieren," *Frankfurter Hefte* 12 (1957): 641.
100 Max Weber, "Die protestantische Ethik und der Geist des Kapitalismus," in Max Weber, *Gesammelte Aufsätze zur Religionssoziologie,* 3 vols. (Tübingen, 1920), 1:203.

21

Reconsidering Abundance

A Plea for Ambiguity

JACKSON LEARS

Attitudes toward ambiguity have a revealing history. Certain people, under certain conditions, tolerate uncertainty better than others. To American intellectuals of the post–World War II era, respect for ambiguity was a sign of emancipation from the sentimental dualisms of the liberal-progressive tradition. For Lionel Trilling and Richard Hofstadter (to mention just two prominent examples), ambiguity was almost always "rich."

Amid this widespread trend toward ambiguity worship, one intellectual product of the era remains a puzzling anomaly: David Potter's *People of Plenty* (1954), the book that has virtually defined economic abundance for Americanists. Potter was a contemporary of Hofstadter – indeed they formed a mutual admiration society – and the author of some extraordinarily nuanced interpretations of the Civil War and (white) southern culture. One might imagine him a plausible devotée of ambiguity.

Yet Potter's description of American abundance was anything but ambiguous. It was absolutely straightforward. Potter noted the extraordinary availability of natural resources, as well as the advanced technology, fluid society, and enterprising spirit that allowed Americans to transform those resources into the raw materials of economic development; the result of that development, in his view, was a huge and growing pile of mass-produced things. That was American abundance. Americans were a people of plenty because they had lots of stuff. Their relation to things was unproblematic: They liked things and wanted more. The flatness of this interpretation reflected the influence of mainstream midcentury American social science. Unlike Potter's other work, *People of Plenty* was positivist in epistemology, behaviorist in psychology, and functionalist in sociology.

For decades, *People of Plenty* has been honored (and assigned) by historians. But only rarely have they critically interrogated Potter's concept of abundance. Robert Collins has made a useful start, observing that Americans have often disagreed or even fought over the distribution of abundance, that many have remained ambivalent about its moral or cultural effects, and that its significance has changed with the spread of mass consumption.[1] I want to go further, to question the definition of abundance assumed by Potter, to complicate it historically and conceptually.

It is no secret that Potter's definition of abundance was rooted in a particular historical moment – the high tide of the American century, the pinnacle of postwar prosperity. What is less widely recognized is that, despite his distaste for advertising, Potter's definition closely resembled the one embedded in the corporate-sponsored iconography of mass production. Both assumed abundance was best signified by a surfeit of mass-produced, disposable commodities.

Yet this vision of abundance was only one thread in a tapestry of older traditions. Long before the modern corporation called its version of advertising into being (and long before *People of Plenty* appeared), Americans imagined abundance in complex and various ways. They continued their imaginings during the decades after Potter published his book. In the 1960s and 1970s, as the American century came to an early end, commentators on abundance struggled to reconcile their familiar feelings of entitlement with a heightened awareness of ecological and economic limits. In the 1980s and 1990s, entrepreneurial ideologues and some on the postmodern Left sought to revive the belief in boundless possibility by asking whether the new sense of limits was rooted in inescapable conditions or merely constructed by elites. Whatever their answer to that question, recent contributors to the discourse of abundance have joined a long-standing conversation that, over several centuries, has produced a variety of alternatives to advertising's one-dimensional vision of mass-produced plenty. One aim of this essay is to recover the major themes of that conversation.

My other purpose here is related to the first: It is to cultivate a more capacious definition of abundance by recognizing the importance of subjective states of mind. The concept of abundance has a crucial psychic dimension, as anyone can see who cares to notice the link between the traditional lyric of plenty and Jewish or Catholic visions of paradise, not to mention Protestant notions of "abundant life" after conversion. Religious insights into psychic abundance parallel and overlap a long tradition of

---

1 Robert M. Collins, "David Potter's *People of Plenty* and the Recycling of Consensus History," *Reviews in American History* 16 (June 1988): 321–35. For a promising departure along the lines suggested by Collins, see Andrew Heinze, *Adapting to Abundance: Jewish Immigrants, Mass Consumption, and the Search for American Identity* (New York, 1990).

philosophical speculation about what might be anachronistically called "consumer psychology" – the structure of human needs and desires. From Plato and the Stoics to Norman O. Brown and Ivan Illich, serious thinkers have posed the question, Why do people feel a nagging sense of want even amid a superabundance of things?

It is time for an updated vision of abundance, one that reflects our concerns at this historical moment. We need to move beyond a quantitative "standard of living" based on batch processing of washing machines, word processors, and pasteurized processed cheese food. We need to cultivate ecological sensitivity without slipping into didactic asceticism. We need to recognize, as many theologians and philosophers have before us, that abundance is psychic as well as physical. We need, in short, a vision of abundance that is characterized not by the seductive simplifications of social science but by a recognition of human character in all its rich ambiguity.

Traditional imagery of abundance mingled matter and spirit in an animated universe. Animistic tendencies in religious belief shaped the ancient lyric of plenty. The doctrines of the incarnation and the resurrection of the body linked divinity and humanity, here and hereafter. Early Christian apologists borrowed from Jewish and classical traditions as well as from popular millenarian fantasies as they imagined a paradise of effortless nurturance. For the second-century church father Irenaeus (to mention only one of many examples), the whole point of emphasizing the sensuous delights of paradise was to stress "the salvation of the flesh" – the eventual resurrection of bodies as well as souls, the obliteration of the distinction between earthly and heavenly enjoyments in the life of the world to come.[2]

The European voyages to the New World gave traditional visions of paradise a local habitation and a name. The literature of colonization reaffirmed the tendency to meld spiritual with sensual abundance – and to imagine the source of both as the maternal breast. Columbus, at the mouth of the Orinoco River, assumed he was in the vicinity of the Earthly Paradise, the highest point on earth; he concluded that the earth was "the form of a pear, which is very round except where the stalk grows, at which part it is most prominent; or like a round ball, upon one part of which is a prominence like a woman's nipple, this protrusion being the highest and nearest the sky." Metaphorically at least, the Earthly Paradise was also the nipple of the world.[3]

2 This and the following paragraphs summarize the argument in Jackson Lears, *Fables of Abundance: A Cultural History of Advertising in America* (New York, 1994), chap. 1.
3 Quoted in ibid., 27.

The tendency to merge abundance with femininity reflected men's longings for maternal nurturance and erotic pleasure as well their fears of devouring, insatiable women. Unbounded plenitude promised suffocation as well as sensuality. In Western intellectual tradition, *mater* and matter have been indissolubly linked, and the meanings of matter have been revealingly ambiguous. Matter has been the thing that matters, the essential, original thing – but also the excrementitious, the too, too solid, the gross and weighty as opposed to the spiritual. Western thought and economic advance have been based on the containment and disembodiment of natural abundance.

The rise of a market economy in early modern Europe transformed material goods into purchasable commodities and the representation of their value into the abstraction called money. Yet alongside these rationalizing tendencies, market exchange also arose from and in some ways reinforced carnival traditions – festivals of abundance that were anything but disembodied, weeks when people ate like pigs and copulated like rabbits. Carnival was celebrated in the marketplace and its timing often coincided with the market fair; vendors from foreign parts added a profusion of exotic artifacts and entertainments to the traditional celebrations of gluttony and lust. Overflowing excess acquired a sharper profile against the backdrop of frequent famine and the specter of starvation. Lent made a virtue of necessity – but also a spiritual and erotic point – by ritualizing a dialectic of deprivation and desire. Gratification could be the greater for being postponed and was temporarily relegated to the realm of fantasy.

Fantasy played a key role in cultural developments on the North American side of the Atlantic, where a romantic Protestant cult of feeling combined with evangelical moralism to create an American version of carnivalesque experience. Although the American carnivalesque celebrated sensuality, it did so at a remove, vicariously, through furtive glimpses rather than public rituals, with loud insistence on didactic intent. Protestant patterns of conversion, fostering oscillation between anxiety and elation, paralleled the manic-depressive movements of the business cycle; together they refigured the dialectic of deprivation and desire into an endless, restless longing. Peddlers and shopkeepers addressed that longing as they sought to create an erotic relationship between consuming subject and desired object. To sustain excitement, fulfillment had to remain fleeting at best. Consumption became as much a matter of looking and longing as of filling one's belly. Religion and commerce combined to redefine abundance in psychic as well as physical terms.

Through the end of the nineteenth century, in the United States, the carnivalesque commercial vernacular continued to represent material abundance with the traditional imagery of female fecundity and nurturance. In seed and farm implement catalogs, buxom mother goddesses befriended tumescent vegetables. Psychic abundance often took similar feminine form, on the labels of patent medicines promising magical regeneration of vital force.

But during the early 1900s, with the emergence of a managerial economy dominated by large corporations, the iconography of abundance changed dramatically. Formidable females disappeared. In corporate advertising, the new icon of abundance was the factory – emblem of the male genius of mass production. Behind it lay a reified vision of science – a deus ex machina that generated everything from free-flowing intestines to smooth shaves.[4]

The theorist of this disembodied, managerial version of abundance was Simon N. Patten, an economist, whose *The New Basis of Civilization* (1907) celebrated the passage from an "era of scarcity" to an "era of abundance" characterized by a never-ending stream of mass-produced goods and amusements. Patten assumed that technological control over nature was complete: "Serious crop failures will occur no more," he announced. In his writing, as in advertising rhetoric, technological determinism masked the relationship between consumption and empire. Americans' developing taste for products like bananas and sugar could be met, Patten wrote, by the plentiful supplies "latent in Porto Rico and Cuba, and beyond them by the teeming lands of South America, and beyond them by the virgin tropics of another hemisphere. . . . Rapid distribution of food carries civilization with it, and the prosperity that gives us a Panama canal with which to reach untouched tropic riches is a distinctive resource, ranking with refrigerated express and quick freight carriage." Patten sanitized the spoils of empire by endowing "prosperity" and technology with autonomous force.[5]

Assuming that industrial work was inevitably dull and that workers would seek satisfaction off the job, Patten urged that they be taught how to be consistent consumers of entertainment and goods. Perhaps most important, unlike earlier moralists, Patten understood that good consumers made good workers. "The worker steadily and cheerfully chooses the deprivations of this week in order to secure the gratifications of a coming holiday." Increased consumption reinforced the acceptance of industrial routine and the persistence of puritanical norms.[6]

By the time Patten published *New Basis*, both popular and elite notions

---

4 The preceding five paragraphs summarize Lears, *Fables of Abundance*, chaps. 2–4.
5 Simon Nelson Patten, *The New Basis of Civilization* (1907; reprint, Cambridge, Mass., 1968), 15–22.
6 Ibid., 141.

of abundance were moving away from their origins in the rhythms of agrarian life and bodily existence. It was not simply that farmers were displaced from the land but that, in the scientifically managed workplace, factory and office employees were increasingly cut off from the vernacular artisanal traditions that linked brain and hand in "local knowledge."[7] What was obscured was any sense that abundance could be the result of patient cooperation between the human mind and the material world. In a disembodied discourse of abundance, enjoyment of the fruits of one's labors became less important than the pursuit of disposable goods.

The most powerful and pervasive portrayal of those goods was in the image empire manufactured by modern advertising. By the 1920s, advertising had created a symbolic universe that would remain unchanged in many of its main features until the 1960s. Its representation of the things themselves was often less important than its picture of the people who bought them. Victorian patriarchs and matriarchs gave way to bustling boy-men and their giggling girl-brides, grateful recipients of mass-produced corporate largesse. The juvenilization of the consumer reflected the contempt for the mass audience shared by advertisers and their critics throughout much of this period. During the age of totalitarian dictatorship, the vision of whole populations as manipulable herds haunted *Advertising Age* as well as *Partisan Review*. Whether they liked the prospect or not, market researchers and social critics viewed much of the industrialized world as an emerging "mass society."[8]

This was the worldview behind *People of Plenty*. Potter presented human beings as the passive respondents to stimuli from outside "forces." Early on he announced his determination to understand "the influence of an environmental factor upon the character of a group of people" by considering both "the operation of the factor" (abundance) and "the human receptor upon which the factor impinges" (Americans).[9] Yet Potter's Americans were not only all alike, their motives were all equally rudimentary. They were the mass audience constructed by market research and Veblenesque critiques of consumer culture – shiny happy people, driven by cravings for comfort, status, and mountains of things.

This vision of the American population pervaded the social thought of

---

7 The phrase and the concept are deceptively simple. For explorations of their complexities, see Clifford Geertz, "Local Knowledge: Fact and Law in Comparative Perspective," in his *Local Knowledge: Further Essays in Interpretive Anthropology* (New York, 1983), 167–234; David Harper, *Working Knowledge: Skill and Community in a Small Shop* (Chicago and London, 1987); John Forrest, *Lord I'm Coming Home: Everyday Aesthetics in Tidewater North Carolina* (Ithaca and London, 1988).
8 Lears, *Fables of Abundance,* chaps. 7–8.
9 David M. Potter, *People of Plenty: Economic Abundance and the American Character* (Chicago, 1954), 24.

the postwar era, encouraging intellectuals to transform issues of power into matters of taste. Even thinkers like David Riesman, who were comparatively sympathetic to mass consumption, wondered "abundance for what?" when they surveyed the developing landscape of split-levels and shopping malls. Among the most pressing problems Americans faced, social critics agreed, was "the problem of leisure" – the puzzle of how to fill workers' idle hours with something more fruitful than sitcoms and soap operas. Given the aesthetic preoccupations of Potter's milieu, it should come as no surprise that among his main complaints about advertising were its standardization and debasement of popular taste – precisely the sort of criticism favored by mass society theorists – or that his dismissive view of the "radio consumer" depended on a long excerpt from Paul Lazarsfeld, the Columbia University sociologist who pioneered putting survey research at the service of media marketing.[10]

Economic abundance, meanwhile, remained a reified "factor" hovering over Potter's argument, an uncaused cause. "As abundance raised the standard of living," Potter wrote, "*it* did more than multiply the existing kinds of goods. *It* caused us to use new goods, new services, and by doing so, *it* transformed our way of life more than once every generation." Abundance played the same rhetorical role for Potter that "society" played for Talcott Parsons and other functionalists: as "an immense tutelary deity" (Tocqueville's phrase) that orchestrated the "responses" of "human receptors."[11]

Potter's account of American society was effectively challenged by the scholarship of the 1960s and 1970s. The rise of social history was rooted in fears of "elitism" and yearnings to reconstitute ordinary people as subjects. Behaviorist and functionalist assumptions gradually fell away – though shreds and patches of positivism clung to the myriad mobility studies, community studies, and other counting exercises that proliferated during the mercifully brief hegemony of quantitative history.

More fruitfully, studies of alternative or oppositional cultures revealed the variety and complexity of American attitudes toward abundance. By the late 1970s, few historians would risk the sweeping assertions that Potter had produced in plenty, and the concept of "national character" became about as popular as "the American mind."

Yet the historiographical fashions of the 1960s and 1970s were less

10 Ibid., 185. See also David Riesman, *Abundance for What? and Other Essays* (New York, 1964), esp. 300–10; William Whyte, *The Organization Man* (New York, 1956); Jackson Lears, "A Matter of Taste: Corporate Cultural Hegemony in a Mass Consumption Society," in Lary May, ed. *Recasting America* (New York, 1988).
11 Potter, *People of Plenty*, 68, emphasis mine; Alexis de Tocqueville, *Democracy in America,* trans. Henry Reeve (London, 1835–40), 2:131–2.

important in discrediting *People of Plenty* than were the broader intellectual and political changes of that era. The most significant intellectual development was the resurgence of a countercultural critique of the corporate model of abundance. Beat poets and assorted other visionaries (such as the editors of *Mad* magazine) signaled some of the earliest signs of unrest, but Norman O. Brown's *Life Against Death* (1959) was the first sustained effort to explore philosophical alternatives to the relentless pursuit of postwar prosperity.

Looking about him and seeing driven anxiety at every turn, Brown wondered, Why are Americans – why are human beings generally – prone to be troubled in mind, even amid material abundance? For Brown, this unquiet heart (*cor irrequietum* in Augustine) was not simply the result of a ruling class imposing "the drive to produce a surplus" on the rest of the population; the disquiet was more deeply embedded. "There is something in the human psyche which commits man to nonenjoyment, to work (*negotium*, nonleisure)," he announced.[12] To discover what that something was, the reader had to fight through thickets of psychoanalytic prose and accept many Freudian categories uncritically.

Yet, however skeptical one remained about the details of Brown's argument, *Life Against Death* posed a powerful indictment of the "death instinct" at the heart of much "economic development." The impulse to transform living matter into the "impersonal, inhuman, abstract world" of the money economy was rooted, Brown believed, in the desire to deny death through the frenetic pursuit of monumental achievement, which in its haste and urgency embodied the very beating of the unquiet heart.[13] For all its Freudian baggage, *Life Against Death* was essentially a work of the religious imagination.

Brown drank deeply at the springs of romantic, primitivist, and mystical traditions. He dismissed the linear sense of time as a product of the flight from bodily finitude. "The war against death takes the form of a preoccupation with the past and the future, and the present tense, the tense of life, is lost," he wrote.[14] If we ignore the religious dimension of Brown's argument, his critique of sexual repression becomes just another manifesto in the sexual "revolution" of the 1960s. But his plea for "polymorphous perversity" against the oral, anal, or genital organization of sex was really an attempt to imagine the possibilities of erotic play in the largest sense, to conceive a "resurrection of the body" in an eternal present where bound-

12 Norman O. Brown, *Life Against Death: the Psychoanalytical Meaning of History* (Middletown, Conn., 1959), 256.
13 Ibid., esp. chaps. 15–16, quotation, 303.   14 Ibid., 284.

aries are blurred between matter and spirit, inner and outer worlds – where people, having learned how to die, can finally live.

This utopian vision had explicit economic implications. "There is something in the structure of the human animal which compels him to produce superfluously, but obviously the compulsion will apply only so long as the human animal draws no distinction between the necessary and the superfluous," Brown wrote. In his scheme, the abolition of repression would allow people to make that distinction. Unburdened by debts to the past and the future, they could live in the moment. Abandoning the effort to keep death at bay by surrounding themselves with commodities, they could finally heed "Thoreau's desperate insistence on the distinction between the necessary and the superfluous." To be a true hedonist, one had to escape from the squirrel cage of endless production and consumption – the very basis of hedonism (and abundance) in most conventional accounts. "The time has come to ask liberal humanists – who, to their honor, entertain 'freedom from want' as a goal – how they will deal with Plato's point that poverty consists not so much in small property as in large desires," Brown said. The definition of abundance became more problematic after his exploration of its psychic – and spiritual – dimensions.[15]

In the two decades following its publication, *Life Against Death* acquired an almost mythic stature as a "bible" of the counterculture – although it is doubtful that most hippies' interpretation of polymorphous perversity went much beyond the young Morris Dickstein's "Fucking – lots of it." Brown was largely misunderstood by a popular audience, and he himself succumbed to the temptations of orphic pronouncement and unwitting self-parody ("The loins are the place of judgment," he once announced).[16] Still, Brown's major themes reinforced an emerging critical outlook. This perspective included suspicion of mass-produced abundance and impatience with a work ethic that seemed to mean little more than adjustment to office or factory routine.

The new skepticism was part of a broader change in the economic, ecological, and intellectual weather. Historians and economists now routinely use 1973, the year of the OPEC oil boycott and the "energy crisis," as a convenient marker for the end of the Good Life. The postwar interlude of a Porterhouse steak on every table and a Chevrolet in every garage (the period Potter took to be characteristic of American history as a whole) turned out to be briefer than most Americans anticipated. As American

15 Ibid., 255–6.
16 Morris Dickstein, *Gates of Eden: American Culture in the 60s* (New York, 1975), 113; Brown quoted in Andrew Ross, *The Chicago Gangster Theory of Life* (New York, 1994), 214.

economic hegemony came under increasingly effective challenge from abroad, and as American corporations went multinational and began to export jobs overseas, the institutional base of the postwar consumer culture – a well-paid working population – began to crumble.

Feelings of scarcity, sharpened by soaring oil prices and lengthening gas lines, finally forced many Americans to take seriously the warnings of Rachel Carson, Paul Ehrlich, Barry Commoner, and others who argued that heedless economic growth might eventually eliminate or poison the natural bases of prosperity. Issues of international equity also arose; a Harris poll of 1975 revealed that a majority of respondents believed it "'morally wrong' for Americans – 6 percent of the world's population – to consume an estimated 40 percent of the world's output of energy and raw materials."[17] For people with egalitarian ideals, imperial relationships were coming home to roost; more equitable patterns of consumption would almost certainly require the fattest nation on earth to reduce its steady intake of stereos, steaks, and scuba gear.

Yet as Brown and others had long recognized, slowing the pace of consumption did not necessarily mean abandoning hedonism. It could mean a liberating redefinition of abundance. The phrase "quality of life" began to buzz about public discourse, as even politicians questioned quantitative standards of well-being. Aesthetic issues were swept up in the debate as well. The monumental scale of the Fordist moment in American modernist design came under assault from postmodern architects and urban planners, not to mention utopians like E. F. Shumacher, whose *Small Is Beautiful* (1973) gave antigrowth skepticism a slogan. Despite the formulaic quality of some contributions to the conversation, the concept of abundance was becoming fruitfully ambiguous.

The ferment in public discourse even stirred the normally placid waters of academic social science. In *The Harried Leisure Class* (1970), the economist Staffan Linder observed what Veblen had not anticipated: The leaders of the American ruling elites refused to become a leisure class at all; instead they embraced a busy managerial ethos. They were too driven by inner compulsions to enjoy the abundance of things they could afford to accumulate; amid a surfeit of goods, they suffered from time famine. As Brown and other critics had observed, feelings of deprivation could survive the experience of unprecedented plenty. The idea that abundance could be psychic as well as physical was implicit in the anthropologist Marshall Sahlins's *Stone Age Economics* (1972), which argued that Paleolithic hunter-

17 Quoted in Julian Simon, *The Ultimate Resource* (Princeton, N.J., 1981), 148.

gatherers constituted "the original affluent society" in their capacity to meet and often exceed what their culture defined as human needs. In disciplines still carrying the baggage of quantitative methods and modernization theory, Linder and Sahlins posed subversive questions.[18]

By the mid-1970s, a developing strain in social thought reflected the sense of contracting possibilities that had entered parts of the political culture; it also expressed a sense of frustration, an insistence that the existing economic system failed to meet fundamental human needs. According to the economist Tibor Scitovsky, writing in 1976, the dominance of large corporations created a "joyless economy" that thrived on standardization and mass marketing; this blocked possibilities for novelty, which was (Scitovsky believed) "among the most fundamental of human needs." Assertions about fundamental human needs popped up everywhere in the 1970s. New Left ideologues, influenced by Herbert Marcuse, among others, sought to distinguish "true needs" from the "false needs" promoted by the propaganda of commodities. Even the most idiosyncratic Left conservatives stayed at least implicitly within this framework (which was common to Thoreau, Marx, and Norman O. Brown): the necessary versus the superfluous, use value versus exchange value, objective needs versus subjective wants.[19]

The first significant exception was William Leiss's *The Limits to Satisfaction* (1976). Leiss rejected the true versus false needs antinomy, observing that it assumed a natural core of true needs untainted by cultural values and prejudices, whereas nearly all human needs were in fact constituted in a collaboration between nature and culture. Despite this departure, Leiss's main critique echoed that of his predecessors. Even if the high-consumption culture were ecologically sustainable (which, Leiss noted, it was not), it still could not deliver the satisfaction it promised.

There is no apparent end to the escalation of demand and no assurance that a sense of contentment or well-being will be found in the higher reaches of material abundance. The society which promotes the ideal of the high-consumption lifestyle seems to lack any reliable measure of the improvement of the quality of life that we should expect to result from its expanding productive capacity. The personal objectives sought in the frenetic activity of the market are more and more obscure.

Leiss attributed this increasing obscurity to the institution of advertising. By promoting the assumption that a self could be constructed through assembling the right commodities, advertising "fragmented" human needs,

18 Staffan Linder, *The Harried Leisure Class* (New York, 1970); Marshall Sahlins, *Stone Age Economics* (Chicago, 1972), chap. 1.

19 Tibor Scitovsky, *The Joyless Economy* (New York, 1976), 282; Patricia Springborg, *The Problem of Human Needs and the Critique of Civilization* (London, 1981), chap. 9.

sowing a sense of diffuse anxiety and ultimately incompleteness among the consumer audience. The limits to satisfaction were enacted in the drama of deprivation and desire.[20]

Toward the end of the decade, similar arguments were articulated by Ivan Illich in *Toward a History of Needs* (1978) and Christopher Lasch in *The Culture of Narcissism* (1979). Like Veblen, Vance Packard, John Kenneth Galbraith, and other "producerist" critics of consumption, both Illich and Lasch assumed a basic human need for a coherent, independent identity, to be secured through satisfying, useful work. Both assumed that mass-produced abundance was being purchased at a fearful ecological price; both saw advanced industrial society (capitalist or socialist) as a huge apparatus that not only wasted natural resources and degraded work but also fostered undue dependence on the spurious expertise of technocratic or therapeutic elites. Accurate as these critiques were, they tended to confuse high consumption with hedonism; to overlook the suspicion of play at the core of the managerial ethos; and to omit any discussion of the aesthetic and sensuous pleasures that might have existed in a genuine "culture of abundance."

Producerist critics like Illich and Lasch left themselves open to the charges of "pessimism" and "asceticism." Lasch consorted openly with Jimmy Carter during the weeks before the president's Camp David address of August 1979. That speech called for ecologically grounded sacrifice and injudiciously dropped the fatal word "malaise" into political debate. Within a year, Carter (and Lasch) had been linked to an un-American respect for limits. Reagan rode to victory on strategies of systematic denial. "America is back," he announced after his election. Reagan's America was, above all else, the land of endless growth and high-level consumption.

Soon it was again chic to deny limits. With astounding suddenness, the winds of "responsible opinion" shifted sharply to the Right. Ecological concerns were driven to the margins of debate. A disparate combination of Reaganite boosters, social-cultural historians, and postmodern critics reasserted Potter's (and corporate advertisers') definition of abundance. Among the most fervent boosters was the economist Julian Simon, whose *The Ultimate Resource* (1981) attacked the Malthusian assumptions and apocalyptic scenarios at the heart of much ecological thinking. This latter-day Dr. Pangloss wrote:

There is no physical or economic reason why human resourcefulness and enterprise cannot forever continue to respond to impending shortages and existing problems

---

20 William Leiss, *The Limits to Satisfaction: An Essay on the Problem of Needs and Commodities* (Toronto, 1976), 6–7. For an intelligent critique see Springborg, chap. 12.

with new expedients that, after an adjustment period, leave us better off than before the problem arose. Adding more people will cause us more such problems, but at the same time there will be more people to solve these problems and leave us with the bonus of lower costs and less scarcity in the long run.[21]

The ultimate resource, he concluded, was the human population itself. Human ingenuity would render energy sources and other natural resources literally inexhaustible. Don't worry; be happy.

Simon's invocation of the "long run" was a familiar strategy of free-market ideologues, one that provoked Keynes's famous riposte "In the long run we are all dead." Nevertheless, environmentalists' predictions of imminent doom had left them vulnerable to some of Simon's charges. In 1980, Simon even bet Ehrlich a thousand dollars that the price of five key metals – copper, nickel, tungsten, tin, and chrome would not rise sharply during the next ten years. Both men assumed (perhaps falsely) that the price of each metal directly reflected the existing supply; higher prices would mean increasing scarcity. Simon won the bet. Ehrlich could be faulted for falling into a relatively simpleminded formulation of the problem and playing Cassandra to Simon's Pangloss.[22]

Simpleminded formulations cropped up everywhere in discussions of abundance during the 1980s, even in the work of otherwise thoughtful historians. Potter's example proved symptomatic. There was something about the subject of abundance that seemed to cripple the analytic capacities of even the most imaginative historical thinkers. Consider Warren Susman, whose *Culture as History* collected some of the subtlest essays in the business; yet Susman prefaced the collection with a morality play pitting the Protestant-republican-producerist culture of scarcity against the secular-corporatist-consumerist "culture of abundance." The transition from the first to the second occurred during the early twentieth century, Susman claimed, but the two value systems remained locked in dubious battle; indeed, in Susman's view all critiques of mass consumption were rooted in repressive republican producerism. This was Simon Nelson Patten with a vengeance.[23]

Susman transferred the social historian's search for the-people-as-subjects to the realm of consumption: According to him, mass-produced abundance was democratic and liberating; critics were snobbish killjoys. What was curious about this screed was how perfectly it embodied a century of corporate advertising apologetics – in its refusal to consider the elite

21 Simon, *Ultimate Resource*, 345–6.
22 John Tierney, "Betting the Planet," *New York Times Magazine,* Dec. 2, 1990, 52–3, 74ff.
23 Warren Susman, "Introduction," to his *Culture as History* (New York, 1984).

origins of consumer culture; its dualistic antitheses between past and present, repression and liberation; its uncritical faith in linear progress; its penchant for demonizing all criticism of advertising as "puritanical"; and its
complete inattention to ecological issues. What was even more curious was
the influence of Susman's cartoonish views on subsequent debate over the
meaning of consumer culture.

Yet by the mid-1980s, the schematic progress-or-repression framework
was not the only one available for discussing issues of abundance and
scarcity. Two European theorists, the Russian literary critic Mikhail Bakhtin
and the French surrealist Georges Bataille, helped to instigate fresh thinking
about the intersection between cultural values and economic life. Neither
was well known to American readers until his work was translated and reissued during the 1980s; both located emancipatory energies in traditional
festivals of abundance – Bakhtin in the fleshly exuberance of the carnival
tradition, Bataille in the ecstatic expenditure of the potlatch. It was easy to
see how these two celebrants of the gross, the impure, and the marginal
could appeal to the identity politics of the postmodern Left, with its *nostal-
gie de la boue* and fond memories of 1968-style anarchism.[24]

But there was more than intellectual fashion involved in their appeal.
Bakhtin and Bataille allowed a relaxation of the didactic tendency in
producerist tradition; they reinforced an emphasis on the utopian possibilities embedded in consumption, the promise of magical self-transformation,
of effortless ease in a land of plenty. Those possibilities arose from the "base,"
"regressive" populations on the margins of society, not from the modernizers at the center of industrial civilization. On the contrary the modernizers
sought to contain carnival at every turn. According to Bataille, the bourgeoisie filled the void left by the death of God with a series of "antireligious
and ethereal values" including the secular religion of progress.[25] Rejecting
this disenchanted progressive ideology might be the first step toward recov-
ering bodily existence as a fit subject for public discourse. Bakhtin and
Bataille provided useful ammunition for attacking the linear models of
progress that continue to imprison American historical thought.

Still, there was enough ambiguity in both thinkers to create new theoretical justifications for celebrating late twentieth-century consumer cul-

---

24 Three key translations are M. M. Bakhtin, *Rabelais and His World,* trans. H. Iswolsky (Cambridge,
   Mass., 1968); M.M. Bakhtin, *The Dialogic Imagination: Four Essays,* trans. C. Emerson and M. Holquist
   (Austin, Tex., 1981); Georges Bataille, *Visions of Excess: selected Writings, 1927–1939,* trans. Allan
   Stoekl, Carl Lovitt, and Donald M. Leslie Jr. (Minneapolis, 1985). Bataille's writing has been popu-
   larized on the postmodern Left by Jean Baudrillard, and in such journals as *Semiotext(e)* 5 (1976) and
   October 36 (spring 1986). On Baudrillard and Bataille, see Douglas Kellner, *Jean Baudrillard: From
   Marxism to Postmodernism and Beyond* (Stanford, 1989), esp. 42–5.
25 Bataille, "The 'Old Mole' and the Prefix *Sur,*" in *Visions,* 38–9.

ture. Both tended to sentimentalize and exaggerate the "revolutionary" potential embodied in carnivalesque gestures and in-your-face refusals; neither fully recognized the enduring tension between coercion and release at the heart of market culture. Bataille further implied that elite conspicuous consumption was merely a parody of social practices that could (and should) be available to all. The problem with this idea was not that it was false – consumption and display really did play a creative cultural role, one unfairly denied by producerist tradition – the problem was that it was too easily appropriated to ahistorical and apolitical purposes.[26]

The celebration of modern consumption as carnival or potlatch overlooked the driven managerial ethos (not to mention the managerial institutions) that contained the contemporary festival of abundance and made it little more than a necessary component in the relentless process of economic growth. The ahistorical appropriation of Bakhtin's praise of excess or Bataille's of expenditure required a willful indifference to the ecological discourse of limits. The zeitgeist of the 1980s worked its impish way even into the obscure reaches of cultural theory.

But not all theorists ignored the question of limits. Andrew Ross, for example, addressed it directly. In many ways, Ross's work embodied the postmodern politics of the academic Left. But it also transcended that genre and pointed toward more fruitful ways of reimagining scarcity and abundance in an era of reactionary politics and ecological emergency.

Ross's main aim was to "warn against the tendency, surfacing again, and often in the name of environmentalism, to wield biological authority as a model for social well-being." His critique of biologism stemmed from a tradition of social ecology. He assumed (rightly) that ecological problems arose from reversible human choices rather than inexorable biological laws. But his slash-and-burn rhetoric sometimes obscured his ecological sympathies. Postmodern cultural critics had been deconstructing the category of "the natural" for well over a decade, showing how resort to imagined biological imperatives had been used to keep minorities and women in their place. Ross now brought the same strategies to bear on diverse bearers of ecological thought ranging from middle-class conservationists to bioregionalists, ecofeminists, and devotees of Gaia. All, in his view, resorted to a rhetoric of scarcity stemming from the allegedly immutable laws of nature.[27]

26 See the cogent critiques offered by Allan Stoekl in the "Introduction" to *Visions*, xvii–xviii, and by Peter Stallybrass and Allon White, *The Politics and Poetics of Transgression* (Ithaca, N.Y., and London, 1986), esp. 1–59, 171–202. My own effort to incorporate Bakhtinian insights without populist sentimentality is in *Fables of Abundance*, pt. 1.
27 Ross, *Chicago Gangster Theory*, 5. Emphasis mine. Among the subtlest and most thoughtful deconstructions of nature is Neil Smith, *Uneven Developments* (New York, 1984). Recent attempts to move beyond this theoretical posture and reinstate a dialectic between nature and culture include Daniel

In Ross's view, the Malthusian rhetoric of scarcity linked environmentalists with the forces of right-wing repression: on the one hand with the representatives of multinational capital who argued that the need to reduce the
United States budget deficit required a massive popular exercise in belt
tightening, on the other with Nazis, fascists, and other sentimental sons of
the soil. (For Leftists and liberals, there has always been a slippery slope from
pastoral tastes to goose-stepping authoritarianism.) Bioregionalists, for
example, sentimentalized "a low-density rural-tribal past when communities 'coincided' geographically with bioregions defined by watersheds, or
microclimates, or biomes," Ross wrote. They could not convince him "that
they will improve on the repressive history of most autonomous communities, often characterized by the persecution of minorities . . . and by parochial
hostility to outsiders," or that they could overcome the "fundamentalist
strains of biological determinism" in environmentalist thought. Like the
right-wing moralists whose views they unwittingly reinforced, Ross
charged, environmentalists threatened to roll back "liberties of the sort that
were created on the back of the postwar boom, and that generated a crisis
in the authority of the state at the end of the 1960s." Scarcity was little
more than a category to contain emancipatory energies.[28]

Against biologism, Ross insisted that "the roots of today's global ecological crisis are as much social as they are 'natural.'" The point was crucial
(though familiar), but the telltale inverted commas betrayed the imbalance
of Ross's polemical agenda. He aimed to deconstruct "the natural" but not
the social. He insisted that "conditions of scarcity and deprivation recommended in the name of limits are *always* the result of social decisions not
natural imperatives." This kind of absolutist assertion confused the recognition of limits with the recommendation of limits. However debatable the
concern over declining biodiversity, there is no doubt that the debate is
about actual, irreversible scarcity.[29]

A more serious problem was the shortage of empirical evidence. Apart
from one excerpt quoted from the neoconservative intellectual Shelby
Steele, Ross's link between natural-law economics and natural-law environmentalism was composed of rhetorical resemblances rather than substantive ideas or policies. The connection neglected complex differences in

Botkin, *Discordant Harmonies: a New Ecology for the Twenty-first Century* (New York, 1990), and William
   Cronon, *Nature's Metropolis: Chicago and the Great West* (New York, 1991).
28 Ibid., 11–12.
29 Andrew Ross, *Strange Weather: Culture, Science, and Technology in the Age of Limits* (London, 1991), 5;
   "The Biodiversity Debate," *Wilson Quarterly* 30 (spring 1993): 141–3. For a good journalistic summary of one dimension of the problem, the limits to agribusiness development, see Robert West
   Howard, *The Vanishing Land* (New York, 1985).

the competing definitions of scarcity and abundance. Deficit cutters do not want to throttle economic growth; they want to liberate "the economy" from "burdensome government regulations" – above all, environmental regulations – and rekindle the faith in limitless prosperity that characterized the postwar boom.

Unlike Ross, many free-market ideologues look to the postwar era as a period when Judeo-Christian morality and economic growth worked hand in glove. Economic abundance, from this view, is the product of stable, productive workers embracing an ethos of self-control and disciplined achievement. The key to renewed prosperity is the revival of Old Testament values: the patriarchal family, a vengeful system of justice, and above all the reassertion of human dominion over the earth and its creatures.

Many environmentalists, on the other hand, tend toward libertarian experimentation in personal morality, often under the aegis of New Age harmonics or vestigial romantic primitivism – the "cult beliefs" that fundamentalist Christians insist are straight from the Antichrist. Other more respectable environmentalists still tend to be liberal on issues of sexual preference, drug use, and abortion rights. Although there are occasions when environmentalist exhortations can sound prissy or puritanical, there is simply no clear or demonstrable link between ecological calls for limits on economic growth and New Right demands for restrictive personal morality. The opposition is far greater than the connection. Ross was right to call for a politics of sensuous pleasure and aesthetic variety, but he was mistaken to target ecology movements as a major obstacle to that goal – or to suggest (however obliquely) that a politics of pleasure could be created by harking back to the postwar vision of mass-produced abundance.

Yet Ross was finally too smart to be trapped in the dead end of consumerist nostalgia. Even if our most cherished institutions, liberties, and rights are rooted in an expansionist liberal economy, he wrote, "it does not follow . . . that those institutions, liberties, and rights are directly tied to the fortunes of an economic system based on unlimited growth. Indeed, it is precisely *because* of the existence of public freedoms that limits on growth can be democratically chosen and agreed upon." True to the postmodern tradition, Ross concluded with a fruitful deconstruction of binaries: nature and nurture, necessity and freedom, scarcity and abundance. Urging that we abolish the concept of scarcity, he asked: "But doesn't that mean doing away with abundance as well? If scarcity is an invention of modernity, then surely the concept of plenty is equally a myth of modernity's ideas about the future, not to mention the lost golden age?"[30]

30 Ross, *Chicago Gangster Theory*, 264, 269–70. Emphasis in original.

Yes and no. Rather than abolishing the notion of abundance, we might redefine it to capture the complexities explored by Brown, Leiss, and other critics in the countercultural and ecological traditions. Why not cultivate the possibilities of psychic abundance? Why not seek to abolish time famine and to create genuine leisure by abandoning obsessions with productivity? (This, incidentally, was the task left uncompleted by the American labor movement in the 1930s. After decades of demanding shorter workdays, union leaders struck an implicit bargain with their corporate counterparts: labor discipline in exchange for job security. Now that business has reneged on its side of the bargain, it may be time to reopen the question of a more satisfying, shorter workday.)

These questions are utopian but worth pondering. They resonate with ancient visions of paradise; they lead away from the ceaseless consumption of commodities and toward a more playful, more nurturant connection with the material world. To ask them is not to genuflect before a static, timeless Nature. But it is to acknowledge the ambiguities of abundance, and the impossibility of discussing a politics of pleasure with reference to economic formulas or quantitative standards. Of happiness and despair, we have no measure.

Index

Italicized page numbers indicate illustrations.

AAA, *see* Agricultural Adjustment
  Administration
ABC, *see* American Broadcasting Company
abundance, 5, 54, 191, 223; defining, 449–51;
  466; disembodied view of, 453–4; and
  femininity, 451–3; psychic dimension to,
  410–11, 458–9; and satisfaction, 459–60
Adenauer, Konrad, 314
Addams, Jane, 20
Adorno, Theodor, 1; *Dialectic of the Enlightenment*,
  441
advertising: ethnicity in, 48–9, 193, 381–405; of
  food in interwar Germany, 250; of garbage
  disposers, 271, 275; and human needs,
  459–60; as invoking ideals, 12; label
  campaigns as, 33; language of, 4, 42–50;
  market practices of commercials, 145; as
  moral consumer's enemy, 31; nationalism in,
  48–50; position of, 39; professionalization of,
  38–50, 67; and semiotic references, 311;
  stereotypes in, 193, 382; of toys on television,
  349–57; as untruthful, 52–3; and women,
  45–6; *see also* customers; public relations
affluence, *see* abundance
AFL, *see* American Federation of Labor
African Americans: civil rights of, 380–1;
  commercial imagery of, 381–4; and
  consumer activism, 125; garment industry,
  22; identity of, 383; magazines for, 394–7
Agricultural Adjustment Administration (AAA),
  55, 119, 122
Alberoni, Francesco, 442
Allgemeine Automobil Zeitung, 197
Altgeld, John Peter, 21
American Broadcasting Company (ABC), 137,
  144
American Federation of Labor (AFL), 33
American Toy Manufacturers Association
  (TMA), 345
Americanism, 49, 212
Americanization, 12, 60–1, 73
Andersen, Arne, 366

animals, and food waste, 265–6
Annales school, 1
Annals of the American Academy, 25
antimodernism, in GDR, 288
appliances, electric, 182, 190, 224, 246, 263–80,
  287, 296–8
Arendt, Hannah, 443
armed services: advertising for, 405;
  desegregation of, 380; *see also* military
  transport
artisans, and housewives, 242, 258–60
asceticism, in GDR, 281
Asia, industrialization in, 6
Asian Americans, imagery of, 403–4
Atkins v. Children's Hospital, 33
Aunt Jemima, 193, 382–4
automobiles: advertisements for, 214; as luxury
  goods, 195–6, 318; popularity of, 207–9,
  214–15; in postwar Germany, 195–222;
  restrictions on ownership, 196; and social
  values, 214; and suburbanization, 318, 325–7;
  symbolic meanings of, 199–201; *see also*
  General Motors; motor vehicles
Automotive Industries, 196–7
Ayer, N. W., advertising agency, 405

Baker, Jacob, 120
Baker, Newton, 21
Bakhtin, Mikhail, 462–3
bananas, as symbol in GDR, 283
Barbie dolls, 351
Barthes, Roland, 346
Barton, Bruce, 43, 56–7
Barton, Ralph Starr, 49
Bataille, Georges, 462–3
Bauhaus movement: architecture in GDR, 290;
  furniture, 245
Beat generation: life-style, 393; writers, 400–1
Beecher, Catharine, 265, 274
Belasco, Warren, 391
Bello, Walden, 128
Bender, Thomas, on public culture, 21

Benjamin, Walter, 1
Benson, Susan Porter, 189–90
Berle, Adolph, 116
Berlin Wall, 171–2
Bernays, Edward, 85, 89, 91–2
Birth of a Consumer Society, The, 444, 445
Black Enterprise, 396
Black Mammy Memorial movement, 383
black market, and food rationing in postwar West
    Germany, 303
Blaisdell, Thomas, 120
Bodemann, Michael, 281
Boorstin, Daniel J., *The Americans*, 2
Boston, Mass.: economic suburbanization of,
    325–7, 330–1; metropolitan area defined,
    320–2; population development in, 323–5,
    329, 336; segregation in, 320; shopping
    environments in, 327–37
bourgeois consumption, 67–74, 414–15, 462; of
    German housewives, 241–6, 260
boycotts, 19–20, 22, 380, 457
Bradley, W. F., 196–7
Branch, Taylor, *Parting the Waters*, 381
Brandeis Brief, 32
Brecht, Bertolt, 221, 286
Brennan, Teresa, 427
Brentano, Lujo, 436
Breton Woods Agreement (1944), 366
Brewer, John, 2, 444, 445
British Labour Party, 117
broadcasting, *see* radio; television
Brooks, John, 21
Brown, JoAnne, 41
Brown, Norman O., *Life Against Death*, 456–8
Brown v. The Board of Education of Topeka, Kansas,
    380
Bruce, Lenny, 400–1
Brundtland, Gro Harlem, 360
Bücher, Karl, 435
Budde, Gunilla-Fredericke, 445
Bühler, Charlotte, 157
Bureau of Home Economics, 39
Bureau of Standards, 39
Burnett, Mattie, 234
Burns, Gary, 145
bus boycott, in Montgomery, Ala., 380
Business Week, 140
butter consumption, politics of, 250–1
buyers, vs. consumers, 25

CAB, *see* Consumer Advisory Board
candy industry, 33
capitalism: compared to socialism, 286–7; and
    consumption, 1–2, 13, 441; corporate, 2;
    inequalities of, 58; "Jewish," 66
Carson, Rachel, 458
Carter, Jimmy, 460
Catholic Housewives' Union, 243, 250, 254

Catholic Women's League, 254–5
Cavan, Ruth Shonle, 227–30, 237
CBS, *see* Columbia Broadcasting System
CDU, *see* Christian Democratic Union
chain stores: and consumer sovereignty, 74–8;
    influence on shopkeepers, 12
Chase, Stuart: *The Tragedy of Waste*, 51, 115; *Your
    Money's Worth*, 51, 52, 54, 115–16
Child, Irvin, 227
Child, Lydia Maria, 274; *The American Frugal
    Housewife*, 265
child labor, 27, 30, 226–7, 239
Child Labor Law, 29, 226
children: impact of consumer culture on, 192; *see
    also* toys
Chinese Exclusion Act, 22
Christian Democratic Union (CDU), 304
CIO, *see* Congress of Industrial Organizations
citizen consumers, 111–25; *see also* democracy
citizenship: and consumption, 11–13, 15, 37–58,
    61; *see also* democracy; social citizenship
Civil Rights Act, 381
civil rights movement, 380–1, 394
class, 34–5; and distribution, 67–9, 73; and GDR
    consumer culture, 285–90; *see also* middle
    class; social equality; working class
Clayton Anti-Trust Act (1914), 121
clothing, ready-made, 21, 223; and spending on,
    232–8, 240
Coca-Cola, 393, 402–4
Cohen, Lizabeth, 13, 55, 131
Cohn, Morris M., 268–9
Cold War: civil rights during, 380–1; and
    consumption, 1–2, 133–4, 380; effect on
    currency reform, 303; industrialization
    following, 7
Coleco, 346
Collins, James, 45
Collins, Robert, 450
Columbia Broadcasting System (CBS), 143
Columbian Exposition (1893), 382
commerce: demands of, 141; vs. distribution, 63
commercial imagery, *see* advertising; ethnicity
commercials, *see* advertising
Commoner, Barry, 458
communism, and consumption, 1–2, 6, 286
Community Employment Training Act, 142
Compulsory Education Law, 29, 226
Congress of Industrial Organizations (CIO),
    223
Consumer Advisory Board (CAB), 118–19, 121
consumer culture, 6–7; acquisition practices in
    GDR, 290–7; ascetic, 281; and change from
    agrarian to industrial society, 445; and
    classlessness, 285–90; consumer subject,
    creation of, 302, 316; continuity and change
    in, 297–9; critique of, 409, 413, 417–29,
    441–4; defined, 415; elite origin of, 461–2;

global, 6–7; in GDR, 281–99; heterogeneity of, 193; and individuals, 409, 425; and modern subjectivity, 413–29; and political culture, 12, 17; relation of public and private in, 288, 299; of working class, 190; *see also* cultural values

consumer goods: cult value of, 296–7; durable vs. trendy, 297; exhibitions on, 245–7; as material culture, 1, 190–1; national, 48, 190; as psychological instruments, 14; quality of, 76; as symbolic, 190; and values in interwar Germany, 242, 244–6; as weapons in Cold War, 1–2; Western, in GDR, 284–5; *see also* foods; product testing

consumer republicanism, 50–5; and antimarket sentiment, 53; as Jeffersonian independence, 12, 51; and self-sufficiency, 52, 54–5

consumer spending, *see* spending

consumers: vs. buyers, 25; centrality of, 25–7, 115; consumer advocacy, 50–5; consumer citizenship, 61; consumer subject, creation of, 302, 316; and customers, 87; and economic reform, 25–7; and market relations, 12; vs. workers, 5; *see also* citizen consumers; housewives; middle class; women; working class

Consumers Guide, 119

Consumers' Leagues (local), 23–4, Cincinnati, 232, 234, 238; Illinois, 23; Kentucky, 28–9; Massachusetts, 24, 28; Michigan, 30; New Jersey, 30; New York, 21–2, 25, 28; Oregon, 32; South Carolina, 30; Utah, 30; Washington, 30; Wisconsin, 30; *see also* National Consumers' League

Consumers' Research, 39–40, 50–1, 54, 56, 116

Consumers' Research Bulletin, 53, 116

Consumers' White Label Campaign, *see* White Label Campaign

consumption: critiques of, 431–2, 433, 441–7; definition and usage, 301, 410, 432–40; ethical, 113–14; as female, 226; and hedonism, 458; history of, 1–7; positive view of, 444; in public and private life, 4, 191; as social practice in West Germany, 301–16; sociological studies of, 440–1; *see also* bourgeois consumption; mass consumption

Converse, Jean, 95

Corley, Mary Lou, 232

corporations, consumption as central to, 3–4

Cosby, Bill, 402

cultural values: and advertisements, 214; of consumer economy, 6, 189; and consumer goods, 190–1, 242, 244–6, 298–9; and foods, 249–53; *see also* consumer culture

currency reform, 303–4

Curtis Publishing Company, 86

customer research, 85–110

customers: and consumers, 87; marketing

research as public relations, 13, 45, 85–109; vs. markets, 87; postwar changes in, 333

Dahrendorf, Ralf, 315

Daly, Herman, 359

Daughters of the Confederacy, 383

Debord, Guy, 443

de Grazia, Victoria, 12

democracy: and consumption, 5, 6, 11, 14, 15, 37, 45, 124, 192; and customer marketing research, 13, 45; of goods, 47; and social equality, 46–7; in West Germany, 314–15; *see also* citizen consumers; citizenship

Department of Commerce (United States), 65

department stores, effect of public transport on, 328

depression, *see* Great Depression

desegregation, 380–1; of armed services, 380

Deutsche Hausfrau, Die, 250, 252, 253

Deutsche Hauswirtschaft, 257, 258

Dewey, John, 116–17

Dichter, Ernest, 14, 149–50, 157 66

Dickens, Charles, *American Notes,* 265

Dickstein, Morris, 457

Diderot, Denis, 431

Dirty Dancing (film), 144

dishwashers, marketing with garbage disposers, 272–3

Disney, Walt, 136–7, 349, 350

Disney corporation, 353, 356, 358

Disneyland, 135, 136–42, 349

Disposall, 267–8, 270

disposers, *see* garbage disposers

distribution: and bourgeois consumption, 67–74; changes in, 3; and class, 67–9, 73; vs. commerce, 63; comparative perspectives on, 59–83; as consumer ally, 72; defining problem of, 59–60, 61–4; and economic growth, 72; in Europe, 59–83; evolution of modern systems of, 59–60, 61–4; middle market, absence of, 68–9; as social power structure, 60; as social question, 73

Dolin, Elmer, 397

Dorn, Vera, 231

Douglas, Paul, 116–17; and CAB, 119; *The Coming of a New Party,* 117

DuBois, Ellen, 425

East Germany, *see* German Democratic Republic

Ebony, 394–5

Ebony Fashion Fair, 394–5

Eccles, Marriner, 55

ecology: and garbage disposers, 278–9; and sacrifice, 460; *see also* environment

economic dualism theory, 368–70

economic growth, 458; and death instinct, 456

economics: of locality, 73; pleasure, 424; postwar,

in West Germany, 191–2; reform in GDR, 167–85, 286

Edelman, Murray, 42

Ehrlich, Paul, 458

Eisenhower, Dwight D., 380

electric appliances, *see* appliances; garbage disposers

Emerson, Ralph Waldo, 414

émigrés, and American consumer culture, 149–66

energy use, 359–62; crisis in 1973, 457–8; and sustainability, 371–7

Engels, Frederick, 20; *The Condition of the Working Class in England in 1844*, 20

environment: and consequences of consumption, 5, 6, 192–3, 363–4; and economics, 463–5; and global sustainability, 6, 359–62, 374; and population, 364–6; *see also* ecology

Erber, Ernest, 123

Erhard, Ludwig, 80, 304

ERP, *see* European Recovery Program

Essence magazine, 384, 396

ethnicity: in advertising, 48–9, 193, 381–405; in businesses, 389–91; and consumer activism, 125; and consumption, 49; growth of communities, 389–90; and propaganda, 391–3; *see also* race

European Productivity Agency, 64

European Recovery Program (ERP), 64, 79, 366

Ewen, Stuart, *Captains of Consciousness*, 2

factory inspections, in garment industry, 18–19, 24, 30

Fair Employment Practices Commission (FEPC), 380

Fair Labor Standards Act, 32

fascism, 134

FDA, *see* Food and Drug Administration

FDIC, *see* Federal Deposit Insurance Corporation

Federal Deposit Insurance Corporation (FDIC), 120

Federal Housing Administration (FHA), 120, 131–2

Federal Republic of Germany: consumption as social practice in, 301–16; food consumption, postwar, 304–9

Federal Trade Commission (FTC), *see* Federal Trade Commission Act

Federal Trade Commission Act, 112–13, 121–2

Fehér, Ferenc, 167

feminism, and consumer culture, 426

FEPC, *see* Fair Employment Practices Commission

FHA, *see* Federal Housing Administration

Filene, Edward, 44, 328

Filene, Lincoln, 328

Filene, William, 328

Firey, Walter, 319

Fisher-Price, 345–6

fishing industry, German, 251–2

Flotter Osten (documentary film), 283

Food, Drug, and Cosmetic Act, 121

Food and Drug Administration (FDA), 112–13, 121

foods: consumption patterns, in postwar Germany, 304–9; and ethnicity, 382–4, 389, 391; rhetoric of, 302; values of in interwar Germany, 241, 242, 248–53, 256, 260; wartime distribution, 242, 303; waste, use of, 264–7

Ford, Henry, 44, 106, 437

Ford Motor Company, 85–6, 89, 212–13, 380, 402

Fordism, 12, 65–9, 73, 212–13, 458; *see also* post-Fordism

Fortune magazine, 88, 100, 109, 140

Four Freedoms, 134

Fox, Richard, 417

Frankfurt School, 1, 6, 166

Frazier, E. Franklin, 396

Frederick, Christine, 43–4, 243

Frederick, J. George, 43

Freud, Sigmund, 157–8

Freyer, Hans, 443

Friedan, Betty, *The Feminine Mystique*, 162–3

Frito Bandito, 193, 397–9

FTC, *see* Federal Trade Commission Act

Galbraith, John Kenneth, 154, 160; *The Affluent Society*, 441; *American Capitalism*, 114; on Keynesianism, 123–4; on New Deal, 114

garbage collection, *see* sanitation

garbage disposers, 190–1, 263–79; articles on, 268, 269–70; and cleanliness, 274; as convenient, 263, 264, 273–4; development of, 267–8; and dishwashers, marketing of, 272–3; and ecology, 278–9; effect on sewer systems, 268–9, 276; marketing of, 263–4, 268–78; municipal prohibitions/requirements on, 269, 278–9; public action on, 270; replacement of, 276–8; as symbol of consumerism, 190, 264, 279

garment industry: factory inspections, 18–19, 24, 30; health issues in, 18–19

Garrett, Paul, 88, 91, 92

GATT, *see* General Agreement on Tariffs and Trade

GDR, *see* German Democratic Republic

GE, *see* General Electric

Geertz, Clifford, 22–3

gender: and consumption, 189, 190, 223–40; and modern subjectivity, 414; roles in West Germany, 314; *see also* housewives; women

General Agreement on Tariffs and Trade, 366
General Electric (GE), Disposall developed by, 267–8
General Federation of Women's Clubs (GFWC), 28–9, 30, 56
General Motors Corporation (GM): advertising of, *98, 101, 104, 108,* 398; as anti-New Deal, 97–9, 107; customer research as public relations, 13, 45, 85–109, *89, 90, 94, 97;* and United Auto Workers, 367; *see also* automobiles; motor vehicles
generations, and consumption, 223–40
germ theory, of disease transmission, 18–19
German Dairy Board, 251
German Democratic Republic (GDR): antimodernism in, 288; consumer culture in, 5, 14, 191, 167–85, 281–99; discontent within, 183–4; dissolution of, 281; economic reform in, 8–9, 167–85, 286; mass consumption in, 14, 191; prosperity in, 287; Western goods in, 284–5
German Economist, The, 150, 151
German Standards Committee, 245
Germany: consumer experiences, pre-1939, 301–4; *see also* German Democratic Republic; Federal Republic of Germany
GFWC, *see* General Federation of Women's Clubs
GI Bill of Rights, *see* Servicemen Readjustment Act
Giddens, Anthony, *Constitution of Society,* 22–3
Gide, Charles, 77
Ginsberg, Allen, 400
global economy, 5, 6–7; and complexity, 189
GM, *see* General Motors Corporation
GNP, *see* gross national product
Goldmark, Josephine, 32
goods, *see* consumer goods
Gorz, André, 442
government agencies, consumption as central to, 3–4
Graebner, William, 107
Grease (film), 144
Great Depression, 37, 55–8, 71, 114–15; vs. capitalism, 131
greeting cards, as social links, 164
Griger, Helen, 237
gross national product (GNP), 127–8, 360
Gruen, Victor, 332
Guderian, Heinz, 215–16
Gunton, George, 26

Habermas, Jürgen, 447
Haddow, Robert, 370
Hadley, Arthur, 25
Hall, Stuart, 147
Hammes, John, 268

Harpprecht, Klaus, 312
Harvard Business Review, 86
Harvard Business School, 98
Harvard Journal of Economics, 25
Hawley, Ellis: on New Deal, 114–15; *The New Deal and the Problem of Monopoly,* 114
hedonism: and consumption, 458; critique of, 442; vs. puritanism, 164
Heidegger, Martin, 443
Height, Dorothy, 384
Hench, John, 139
Henderson, Leon, 55, 120
Hennings, Alice, 234
Henselmann, Hermann, 290
Hesse, Hermann, *Steppenwolf,* 211
highway systems: *Autobahn,* 219, 370, 373; in Massachusetts, 326–7
Hindenburg, Paul von, 249–50
hip hop musicians, 145
Hitler, Adolf, 219
Hofstadter, Richard, 421, 449
HOLC, *see* Home Loan Corporation
Home Economics Division (National Socialist Party), 255–60
home economists, 38–9
Home Loan Corporation (HOLC), 120
homemakers, *see* housewives
Honecker, Erich, 184, 281, 290
Hopkins, Claude, 47
Horkheimer, Max, 1; *Dialectic of the Enlightenment,* 441
Horowitz, Daniel, 14, 26, 410
households: commodity production in, 414–15; cultural values of consumer goods in, 4, 27, 46–7, 90, 191, 244; and rationalization, 244–8, 253
housewives: balance of power with retailers, 242, 258–60; consumer education of, 243–4, 248, 250; consumer fairs for, 245–7; and consumption in interwar Germany, 241–61; and consumption in postwar Germany, 309; effect on national economy, 252–7; German vs. American consumption by, 245–6, 253; kitchen as workplace, 244; Nazi model, 254, 258; and rationalization, 244–8, 253
housewives' organizations, German, 242–4; consumer education by, 243–4, 248, 250; on mass production, 247; promotion of foods by, 249–52; protests by, 242; on purchasing habits and national economy, 252–7; and rationalization, 245, 253
Housewives' Union of the Catholic Women's League, *see* Catholic Women's League
Houser, J. David, 88–9
Howe, Frederick C., 119
Hühnlein, Adolf, 218
Hula Hoops, 351

Hull House, 20–1
human needs, 459–60
Huyssen, Andreas, 421
Hynes, John, 335

ICC, *see* International Chamber of Commerce
Illich, Ivan, *Toward a History of Needs*, 460
immigration, and importation of consumer
    goods, 389
Imperial Automobile Corps Volunteers, 202–3
individualism: and consumer culture, 409, 425;
    and liberalism, 13; of men vs. women, 240
industrialization: in Asia, 6; and Cold War, 7; and
    politics, 56–7; in South America, 6; of third
    world, 7; vs. welfare state, 6
In-Sink-Erator, 268, 271
installment credit, 238–9
Institute for Social Research, 1
International Bureau of Distribution, 63
International Car Exhibition (1933), 219
International Chamber of Commerce (ICC),
    62–3, 64, 65, 80
International Monetary Fund, 127
Isaacs, Susan, 344

Jackson, J. B., 141
Jacoby, Sanford, 107
James, Henry, *The Ambassadors*, 423
James, William, 423
jazz album covers, 400
Jell-O, 47, 402, 404
Jena glass cookware, 245
Jet magazine, 394–5
Jewish Anti-Defamation League, 399
"Jewish" capitalism, 66
Jewish retailing, international influence, 72
Jewish rights, 314
Jews, status in West Germany, 314
Jobim, Antonio Carlos, 400
Johnson, Hugh, 118
Johnson, John, 394–6
Johnson, Lyndon B., 381
Jones, Carolyn, 395–6
Jordan, Eben, 328
Judt, Matthias, 192
Jünger, Ernst, 215, 217

Kallet, Arthur, *100,000,000 Guinea Pigs*, 115
Kampf dem Verderb, 256, 259
Katona, George, 14, 149–57, 165–6; *The Mass
    Consumption Society*, 440–1
Kelley, Florence, 12, 18–35; and grass-roots
    movement, 23; at Hull House, 20–1;
    informed morality campaign, 27–8, 31;
    Quaker-Unitarian background, 19, 20; on
    scientific materialism, 20
Kelley, William Darrah, 19
Kerouac, Jack, 400

Keynes, John Maynard, 367, 461; *The General
    Theory of Employment, Interest, and Money*, 122
Keynesianism, 38, 55, 122–3
Khrushchev, Nikita, 380
King, Martin Luther, 380–1, 403
Klenke, Dietmar, 221–2
Kline, Steven, 192
Kluge Hausfrau, Die, 302, 311, 312–13
Knight, Gladys, 384
Kodak, 402–3
Komarovsky, Mirra, 230
Kracauer, Siegfried, 1
Krenz, Egon, 282
Kyrk, Hazel, *A Theory of Consumption*, 437–8

labor, wasting labor vs. wasting resources, 242,
    253–9, 261
Lahr, Bert, 397–8
laissez-faire, 69
language: of consumption, 5, 13, 42–50; *see also*
    advertising
Lasch, Christopher, *The Culture of Narcissism*, 460
Lazarus, Simon, 328
Leach, William, *Land of Desire*, 418, 426
League for Independent Political Action, 116–17
Lears, Jackson, 98n34, 410–11, 417, 418; *Fables of
    Abundance*, 427–9
Leclerc, Edouard, 82
Lefebvre, Henri, *Critique of Everyday Life*, 442–3
Lego, 346
Leiss, William, *The Limits to Satisfaction*, 459
Lemlish, Clara, 19
Levenstein, Harvey, 391
Levy, Hermann, 73n26
Lewis, Ed, 396
liberalism, 12; and individualism, 13; and
    militarism, 222; and public culture, 35
Linder, Staffan, *The Harried Leisure Class*, 458–9
Lippmann, Walter, 38; *Drift and Mastery*, 424
Lipsitz, George, 13–14, 38–9
Livingston, James, 57, 409–10
Lloyd George, David, 201
locality, economies of, 73
Locke, John, 344
Long, Huey, 131
Lord, Samuel, 328
Louis, Joe, 392–3, 404
Lowell, Josephine Shaw, 21
Lukacs, Georg, 416–18
Lutz, Burkart, 368
Lynd, Robert S., 51, 119

McBain, Ed, 395
McDaniels, Hattie, 382
McDonald's restaurants, 388, 402–4
McGovern, Charles, 12, 13, 92, 131
McKendrick, Neil, 2, 444, 445
Magnum, 312

Mailer, Norman, *The Naked and the Dead*, 392
Majors, Gerri, 394
Mammy character, 382–3
management, scientific, 243, 422
Marchand, Roland, 13, 45, 47, 410
Marcuse, Herbert, 442, 443, 459
margarine, and butter consumption, 251
Marinetti, Filippo Tommaso, 211
market research, *see* customer research; product testing
marketing, 66–7; and commercials, 145; consumer relations, 12, 346–8; consumer republicanism on, 53; and corporate decision making, 4; of garbage disposers, 263–4, 268–78; of toys, 341, 347–8, 349–57; *see also* customers; public relations
marketplace: and individual identity, 53–4; *see also* black market
markets: as integral, 11; segmented, 13, 143–6; types of, 64
Marshall, T. H., 25, 61n4
Marshall Plan, 64, 366
Marx, Karl, 20; on commodity fetishism, 6
Marx, Louis, *see* Marx Toys
Marx Toys, 346–7
Marxism, on mass consumption, 441–4
Mason, Tim, 255
mass consumption, 3, 4, 26, 123–4; and automobiles, 212–13; and daily life, 4, 38; in East Germany, 14, 191; vs. individual consumers, 124; Marxism on, 441–4; and nationality, 14; and social experience, 4, 38
mass production, 3, 52
mass society, 454
materialism, 20
Mattel, 349, 351, 356
Means, Gardiner, 116, 121
Meat Inspection Act (1906), 112
melting pot metaphor, 388–9
Mendras, Henri, 81
Merkel, Ina, 191
Mexican-American Anti-Defamation Committee, 399
Mexican Americans, in advertising, 397–9
Meyer, Erna, *The New Household*, 243, 252
middle class: consumption by, 17–35, 190; vs. working-class, 26
Mighty Ducks, The (film), 145
migrants, and structural adjustments, 128
military, *see* armed services
military transport, in postwar Germany, 199–209, *201, 202, 216,* 221
Mill, John Stuart, *Principles of Political Economy*, 434
millennialism, 27
Miller, Dorie, 393
Mingo, Frank, 395–6
minorities, *see* ethnicity; race; *specific groups*

Mittelstand, 64, 71
modernity, and garbage disposers, 276–7
Modleski, Tania, 144
Mohl, Raymond, 116
"Monday Night Football" (television program), 144
Montalban, Ricardo, 399
Montessori, Maria, 344
Montgomery, Donald E., 119
Möser, Kurt, 189
Mossell, Sadie Tanner, 237–8
motivational research (MR), 159, 161
motor vehicles: elitist vs. utility, 210–15; relevance of, 199–200; symbolic value of, 189, 206 *see also* automobiles; General Motors; military transport
MR, *see* motivational research
Municipal Sanitation, 269
music, ethnic, 399–400

National American Woman Suffrage Association, 30
National Association for the Advancement of Colored People (NAACP), 380, 383, 399
National Association of Manufacturers, 56
National Bituminous Coal Commission, 120
National Bureau of Economic Research, 65
National Congress of Mothers, 30
National Consumers' League (NCL), 11–12, 17–35, 51n40; and ethical consumption, 113–14; function of, 28; and grass-roots movement, 23; labor campaigns as advertising, 33; and market relationships, 26; and protections for wage earners, 32; as women's organization, 21, 25; *see also* Consumers' Leagues (local); White Label Campaign
National Council of Negro Women, 384
National Department Store Association, 65
National Housing Act, 131
National Industrial Conference Board, 65
National Labor Relations Act, 125
National Labor Relations Board, 131
National League of German Housewives' Associations, 243m 247
National Productivity Board, 244, 245
National Recovery Administration (NRA), 55–6, 117–19, 122, 125
National Socialism: consumer boycotts of Jewish businesses, 255; effect on women's organizations, 254–6, 260; policy on consumption, 439; policy on food supply, 303
National Socialist Automobile Club, 219
National Socialist Women's Bureau, *see* Women's Bureau (Nazi Party)
National Women's Service, 242–3
nationalism: in advertising, 48–50; and consumption, 48–50, 77–8; and menu planning in households, 190

nationality, and consumption, 14
Nazism, *see* National Socialism
NCL, *see* National Consumers' League
needs, 459–60
neoconservatives, and control of state policy 127, 130–1
neomercantilism, 12; vs. reform coalitions, 71–4
Neues Deutschland (newspaper), 178
New Age, 465
New Deal, 37–8, 55–8; and consumers, 117, 120–2, 125; and consumption as political interest, 13; lasting impact of, 114–15; and making of citizen consumers, 111–25; postwar break from, 13–14; and public interest, 115, 125
New Economic System, 167–8, 172–4, 181, 185, 286
New England Bolt Company, 422
New Left, 2, 459
New Republic, 117
Newcomb, Horace, 144–5
Niekisch, Ernst, 219–20
Nietzsche, Friedrich, on property, 414
Nineteenth Amendment, 33–4
Nixon, Richard M., on Cold War consumerism, 380
NRA, *see* National Recovery Administration

O'Connor, Martin, 235
Office of War Information, 379, 391
Oldenberg, Karl, 436–7
Oppenheimer, Franz, 439–40
Organization for European Economic Cooperation, 64
Ortlieb, Heinz-Dietrich, 441
Orwell, George, on war as agent of change, 195

Packard, Vance, 160, 162
Pankau, Winnie, 229
Parks, Rosa, 380
Parlin, Charles Coolidge, 86
Parsons, Talcott, 455
Pasolini, Pier Paulo, 442
Patten, Simon N., 26, 38, 78, 453–4; *The New Basis of Civilization*, 26, 453
Peiss, Kathy, 232
Pestock, Rose, 232–3
Pfister, Christian, 192–3
play: and consumption, 341; and culture, 339–40; role of toys in, 342–6
Playskool, 344
Playthings, 352
pleasure economy, 424
Plumb, John H., 2, 444–5
plumbers, sales of garbage disposers by, 272
Pocahontas, 386–8
Politburo, special privileges of, 282

politics: of consumption, 12, 13, 14–15, 17, 42–50, 242–4; and industry, 56–7
pollution, *see* environment
population, development in Boston, 323–5, 329, 336
populism, 420–1
Porsche, Ferdinand, 219
Porter, Ray, 445
positivism, vs. romanticism, 414
post-Fordism, 59–60, 82–3
postmodernism, and consumption, 5
Potter, David: definition of abundance, 450, 454, 455, 460; *People of Plenty*, 2, 410, 449–50, 454, 456
Presbrey, Frank, 49
private enterprise: vs. consumerists, 55; state support of, 12
Proctor, Barbara, 395
product testing, 115–16; and housewives' associations, 247; profession of, 38–40, 50–5
production: as male, 226; *see also* mass production
products, *see* consumer goods
Progressive reform, 21, 33, 113, 117
proletarianization, 416–17, 418, 420, 424–25
propaganda, and ethnicity, 391–3
property, and subjectivity, 414
Prosanis label, 32n37
prosperity, in GDR, 287
public culture: defined, 21; and liberalism, 35
public relations: customer research as, 13, 45, 85–109; *see also* marketing
Puccini, Giacomo, *Madame Butterfly*, 403
Pugh, Sarah, 19–20
purchasing: as choice, 43; as moral act, 28; compared to voting, 43–5; *see also* spending
Pure Food and Drug Act, 112
puritanism, vs. hedonism, 164

Quaker Oats, 382, 383, 384
quality of life, 458
Quark (German dairy product), 251–2, 256, 259–60
questionnaires, *see* customer research

race: in advertising, 48–9, 193, 381–4; and consumption, 49; discrimination, 380–1; and equality, 380–1; interracial relationships, 386–9; and the National Consumers' League, 22; *see also* ethnicity
radio: advertising, 40, 56; boycotts, use in, 399; and consumer information, dissemination of, 119, 256; and Nazi propaganda, 439; sets in GDR, 171; sets in U.S., 113; and U.S. popular culture, 58, 145; Western, in GDR, 191; and World War II in U.S., 379
Radway, Janice, 144
Ranck, Katherine Howland, 227–30, 237
rationing of food, 303

rationalization, household, 244–8, 253
REA, *see* Rural Electrification Administration
Reagan, Ronald, 142, 144, 147
Reagin, Nancy, 190–1
recycling of waste, 264–5, 279
reduction garbage treatment, 267
refrigerators: in GDR, 169, 180, 182, 287–9, 292, 296; in U.S., 272, 275, 278; in postwar Germany, 307, 309, 313
refugees, *see* migrants
reification, 416–17, 425–6
republicanism, 12; *see also* consumer republicanism
research, *see* customer research; motivational research; product testing
resources, wasting resources vs. wasting labor, 242, 253–9, 261
retailers/retailing: balance of power with housewives, 242, 258–60; centrality of, 69–71; and consumers, 191; development in Boston, 327–37; after Industrial Revolution, 327; small retailers, centrality of, 69–71; *see also* chain stores; department stores; self-service stores
Rich, Morris, 328
Ridgway, Charles, 139
Riesman, David, 455
Robeson, Paul, 392
Rockefeller, Nelson, 370
Rolfe, John, 386
romanticism, vs. positivism, 414
Roosevelt, Franklin Delano: on discrimination, 380; election of, 37; on importance of consumers, 38n5, 55, 115, 116, 120–1, 124, 125, 131; *see also* New Deal
Ross, Andrew, 463–5
Rouse, James W., 140–1
Rouse Corporation, 140–2
Ruffins, Fath Davis, 48–9, 193
Rural Electrification Administration (REA), 120

Sachs, Wolfgang, 210
Sahlins, Marshall, *Stone Age Economics*, 458–9
sanitation: effect of garbage disposers on, 268–9, 276; reform in, 266–7
Saturday Evening Post, 86–7; General Motors ads, 98, 101, 104, 108
Sawbol, Katherine, 231
scarcity, 5, 464; in GDR, 283–4, 287; oil, 458; in West Germany, 314
Schlink, F. J.: *100,000,000 Guinea Pigs*, 115; *Your Money's Worth*, 51, 52, 54, 115–16
Schmeling, Max, 393
Schmoller, Gustav, 436
schools: desegregation in, 380
Schumacher, E. F., *Small Is Beautiful*, 458
Schwarte, Max, *Die Technik im Weltkriege*, 215
scientific management, 243, 422

scientific materialism, 20
Scitovsky, Tibor, 459
Securities and Exchange Commission (SEC), 120
SED, *see* Socialist Unity Party
segregation, in Boston, 320
self, and consumer culture, 409, 425
self-denial, and budget limitations vs. consumption, 190
self-determination, 57–8
self-esteem, 14
self-indulgence, 233–4
self-service stores, 310
self-sufficiency, 52, 54–5, and dependence on market, 2–3; and foods in interwar Germany, 249; *see also* sovereignty
semiotics, 191, 311
Servicemen Readjustment Act (1944), 326, 379
sewer systems, *see* sanitation
sexuality: repression of, 456–7; taboos on 314
Shop Closing Act (1956), 80
shopkeepers, *see* retailers
shopping environments, changes in, 327–37
shopping malls, 332–7, 371
shortages, *see* scarcity
Simon, Julian, *The Ultimate Resource*, 460–1
Sinatra, Frank, 401
Situational International, 443
"Sixty Minutes" (television program), 143
Sklar, Kathryn Kish, 12, 13, 410
slave labor, boycott against, 19–20
Sleet, Moneeta, 394
Sloan, Alfred, 89–90, 92, 106
Small-Weil, Susan, 350
Smith, Adam, *The Wealth of Nations*, 434
Smith-Rosenberg, Carroll, 421
social citizenship, 61; of women consumers, 12, 34
social classes, *see* class
social equality: and consumption, 46–7; and democracy, 46–7
Social Security Act (1935), 132
social security system, in Switzerland, 367
social utility, 73
socialism: compared to capitalism, 286–7; equality in, 282–3, 286; failure of, 1–2; replaced by market capitalism, 127
Socialist Labor Party, 20
Socialist Unity Party (SED), 167–85; consumption controlled by, 168–70; and distribution, 180; and economic reform, 172–3; egalitarianism typical of, 185; power struggles within, 184; price sanctions by, 172; and standards of living, 174
Sollers, Werner, 388
Sombart, Werner, 70, 436
South America, industrialization in, 6
sovereignty: consumer, 12, 74–8; and economic

activity, 44; political, 44; *see also* self-
  sufficiency
Sozialistische Einheitspartei Deutschlands (SED),
  see Socialist Unity Party
spatial dimensions, of postwar consumption,
  192
spending: as state project, 127–47; *see also*
  purchasing
Spigel, Lynn, 135–6
state: consumption as critical to policy, 11,
  13–14, 127–47; role of, 5, 14–15, 189
Steckrübenwinter, 302
Steele, Shelby, 464
Steiner, André, 14
stereotypes, in advertising, 193, 382
stores, *see* chain stores; department stores; self-
  service stores; shopping malls
Strasser, Susan, 190–1
strip malls, *see* shopping malls
subjectivity, modern: and consumer culture,
  413–29; defined, 413–14; and gender, 414;
  and proletarianization, 418, 424
substitution theory, 376–7
suburbanization, 135–6, 192; and economic
  development, 317–18, 330–1; effect of
  automobile on, 318, 325–7; and shopping
  malls, 332–7
suffrage: consumer, 45; school, 33–4
surveys, *see* customer research
Susman, Warren, *Culture as History*, 461–2
sustainability, 360, 366, 371–7
sweatshops, in United States, 17, 18–19
Switzerland, economic and environmental
  analysis of, 192–3, 366–77

Taft-Hartley law, 134
Taylor, Washington, 328
Taylorism, 243, 416, 422, 437
technology, 129–30
television, 131, 135–40, 142–5: advertising of
  toys, 349–57; and African Americans, 394,
  402, 405; commercials on, in U.S., 380, 384,
  390, 393, 397–8, 402; and consumption, 445;
  effect on play, 348–9; ethnic diversity on,
  402, 404; importance of, in U.S., 394;
  marketing research in U.S., 347; marketing to
  children, 192; role of, in GDR, 291, 294; sets
  in GDR, 169, 176, 182, 281–2, 287–8; sets in
  U.S., 379; in U.S., 335; in West Germany, 313;
  Western, in GDR, 191
Tennessee Valley Authority (TVA), 120
Theweleit, Klaus, 421
Third World, industrialization of, 7
Thomas, Bob, 137
Thompson, J. Walter, 41
time-and-motion studies, and rationalization, 244
Time magazine, 100

TMA, *see* American Toy Manufacturers
  Association
totalitarianism, 155
toys: and global economic expansion, 192;
  licensing of, 350, 351–7; marketing of, 341,
  347–8, 349–57; role of in play, 192, 342–6
trade cards, *385, 387*
transnational corporations, 129
transportation: changes in, 3; *see also* motor
  vehicles
Treaty of Versailles, reparations required in, 252
Trilling, Lionel, 449
Truman, Harry S., on desegregation of armed
  services, 380
Tugwell, Rexford, 55, 116, 121
TVA, *see* Tennessee Valley Authority

UAW, *see* United Auto Workers
Ulbricht, Walter, 176, 184
United Auto Workers (UAW), 132, 367
United Garment Workers' Union, 33
United States: citizenship and consumption in,
  37–58; working-class families in interwar
  period, 223–40
United States Chamber of Commerce, 65
urbanization, 81

values, *see* cultural values
Veblen, Thorstein, 50–1, 437
Vietnam War, propaganda for, 405
Volkswagen, 219–20
Vorländer, Franz, 435
Vorwerck, Else, 241
voting, purchasing and consumption compared
  to, 43–5
Voting Rights Act, 381
Vygotsky, Lev S., 347

wage earning: and consumption, 26, 189–90;
  protection of, 32; by women, 189–90
Walker, Amasa, 25
Wanamaker, John, 31–2, 328
war: as agent of change, 195; *see also* armed
  services; military transport
Waring, George, 266, 267
Warner, Sam Bass, 321
Warren, Earl, 380
washing machines: in GDR, 171, 175–6, 287,
  292, 296, 182; in postwar West Germany, 309;
  in U.S., 224, 273, 278
Weaver, Henry (Buck) G., 85–109
Weber, Max, 416
welfare state, vs. industrialization, 6
Wende (turnaround), special privileges during,
  281
Wertheimer, Max, 150, 151
West Germany, *see* Federal Republic of Germany

Weyl, Walter, 38
Wheeler-Lea Amendment, 121
Whitaker, Craig, 141
White Label Campaign, 11–12, 17–35; and
American standard of living, 22; and candy
industry, 33; conclusions about, 34–5; end of,
32–3; economic power of, 31; factory
inspections, 24, 30; and health issues, 18–19;
and millennialism, 27; reinforcement of racial
distinctions, 22; as symbolic, 22–3; as white
middle-class device, 22–3; *see also* National
Consumers' League
Wildt, Michael, 135, 191–2
Williams, Raymond, *Keywords*, 25, 410
Williams, William Appelman, 421
Wirminghaus, Alexander, 436
Wirtschaftswunder (economic miracle), 304
Wischnetetzky, Lazare, 20
women: and activism, 33–4, 125; bourgeois
women's organizations, 241–6; as consumers,
18, 29, 45, 190; dependency on family, 240;
fear of, 421; female symbolism in consumer
culture, 422–4, 427–9; femininity and
abundance, 451–3; and power in public life,
18, 21, 25, 29, 34; as social citizens, 12, 34;
wage earning and consumption, 189–90

Women's Bureau (Nazi Party), 254–5
Women's Bureau (U.S. Dept. of Labor), 189–90,
225–39
Women's Clubs, 28–9
"Wonder Years, The" (television program), 144
working class: consumer culture of, 190, 379–80;
vs. consumers, 5; defined, 223n1; gendered
family economies of, 235–40; in interwar
U.S., 223–40; vs. middle-class, 26
Working Women's Society, 22
Works Progress Administration, 131
World Bank, 127
World War I: and creation of desire for
automobiles in Germany, 189, 195 222;
prosperity following, 38; and road transport,
201–7
World War II: defense spending and economic
growth, 132; housing increases following,
133; propaganda and ethnicity, 391–3; and
television technology, 135–7; transformations
following, 5, 6, 12, 78–82
Wright, Carroll, *Outline of Practical Sociology*, 25
Wyrwa, Ulrich, 410

yo-yos, 351

Zangwill, Israel, *The Melting Pot*, 388